Romania since 1989

Romania since 1989

Politics, Economics, and Society

Edited by
Henry F. Carey

LEXINGTON BOOKS
Lanham • Boulder • New York • Toronto • Oxford

LEXINGTON BOOKS

Published in the United States of America
by Lexington Books
An imprint of The Rowman & Littlefield Publishing Group, Inc.
4501 Forbes Boulevard, Suite 200, Lanham, Maryland 20706

PO Box 317
Oxford
OX2 9RU, UK

British Library Cataloguing in Publication Information Available

Library of Congress Cataloging-in-Publication Data

Romania since 1989 : politics, economics, and society / edited by Henry F. Carey.
p. cm.
Includes bibliographical references and index.

ISBN: 978-0-7391-0592-4

1. Romania—Politics and government—1989– 2. Post-communism—Romania.
3. Romania—Economic conditions—1989– I. Carey, Henry F., 1953–

JN9630.R665 2003
320.9498—dc21 2003014082

Printed in the United States of America

∞™ The paper used in this publication meets the minimum requirements of American National Standard for Information Sciences—Permanence of Paper for Printed Library Materials, ANSI/NISO Z39.48–1992.

Contents

Tables

Foreword

The sudden downfall of Communism in Eastern Europe did not lead, as many had hoped, to an equally sudden transition to a democratic and prosperous society. In both the East and the West, the disappointment is obvious. Freedom has once again proven to be more complex and delicate than force, as Thomas Mann once observed.

It suffices, however, to recall similar historic events in order to realize that our perplexity at the perceived lack of progress in Romania is just a form of naiveté, if not arrogance. France in the aftermath of the French Revolution, and even Germany and France in the transitional period after World War II are the first examples that come to mind. The rough transition from a Communist police state to the civil society of the current capitalist system naturally involves drastic dislocations and difficulties. After the failed bloody experiment to abolish the "exploitation of man by fellow man," a traumatic new experience challenges the survivors: the transition from state ownership of evil to private ownership of good and evil.

In the first decade of the post-Communist era, Eastern Europe went forward and backward, simultaneously. The "forward" movement reflected the contract with the future, the adaptation to the economic and social requirements of the capitalist world, and the pursuit of international recognition. The "backward" movement reflected the pressing burden of having to reevaluate the country's history both before and during Communism—a history that was manipulated and falsified by the ideology and interests of a single party that dominated the totalitarian state. This transitional tension within Romania, between the movement forward and the movement backward, is further complicated by the international context in which it is taking place—in a "global," computerized, postmodern era, with all its overwhelming influences and implications for Romanian society.

As if these factors were not enough, Romania adds a picturesque set of paradoxes and profound disjunctures, which make it a fascinating anthropological case for study and research. It is a country with Latin roots and a Latin language, and yet with a predominantly Christian Orthodox religion. Not only is it a Latin island with Western aspirations in the middle of a vast Slav territory, it is also the religious frontier toward the "East" of Eastern Europe, sitting at a crossroad of ethnicities and influences which are in perpetual transit. Modernization has kept on traveling through these places without ever truly reaching its destination. Frustration and fanfare, fatalism and humor, hedonism and melancholy, corruption and lyricism have all gradually cooperated to create a strategy of survival through prevarication, rather than through efficiency.

The peculiar way Romanians define their predicament could elucidate, in fact, some of the contradictions that have defined this Carpathian–Danube territory. The Romanian is said to be a "born poet." Romania is said to be a "sad country full of laughter" and a "Dada country," poised "between good and evil" where "nothing is incompatible." Yet, the musician Georges Enesco once remarked, "If only our administration and politics were on the same level as the arts, we would be one of the happiest countries on earth."

Communism has enhanced the paradox of unfinished transition. From a small political faction of around a thousand members in 1944, the Romanian Communist Party had grown by 1989 to almost 4 million members, among whom one could hardly find 1,000 true Communists. After the execution of the dictator, most of the opportunists who had carried the Red Party ID became fervent anti-Communists (one might say "Bolshevik anti-Communists"), which did not help the reconciliation and reconstruction of the country. The unexpected, anti-Soviet dissidence of Communist Romania, initiated by the Party in the 1960s, did not lead to a lasting approach to the West, but gradually evolved toward a disastrous, Byzantine nationalist-socialist system. Similarly, the violent overthrow of the "sultan-like" style of Romanian Communism in 1989 has not yet led to a revolutionary social restructuring. Despite some obvious signs of evolution, corruption cooperates with apathy and demagogy (dominated by the rhetoric of "self-sufficient greatness," which some of the studies in this volume introduce) to retard the progress of the country.

Paradoxes are also not few among the intellectual elite, who have always claimed an important role in the social and political arena. The constant dissociation of the elite from the masses has remained, however, a "phenomenon of the third world," as Mariana Celac, a distinguished intellectual and architect, stated in one of her articles in *22*, "An elite which didn't assume this country as it is." Those who study the current Romanian situation may find it even more interesting to scrutinize such notions as authority and hierarchy, which Romanians rank in public opinion polls as their country's most important values. Surprisingly or not, such concepts reappear, in disguise, in the country's cultural life. Not rarely, leading members of the cultural elite also claim authority and hierarchy for their own legitimization. The differences and similarities between the preferences of the popular culture and those of intellectuals who claim to be separate from, and superior to, the "vulgar" taste of the majority may prove significant for the social-political landscape of transitional Romania. This theme is discussed in several chapters of this volume.

Contradictions between the public and private realm, between rhetoric and real belief, and between old habits and new aspirations (as well as those paradoxes and contradictions already mentioned) lead to moral dilemmas that define the general state of the nation, and its potential for social-political conflict and/or social-political change. Self-criticism, honest scrutiny of facts, acknowledgment of past and present errors, as well as lucidity, compassion, and solidarity are not to be found very often, unfortunately, in the current national debates. This has been evident in recent years in the public debates concerning the rehabilitation of General Antonescu (the military dictator of Romania during the alliance with Hitler), the convoluted controversies concerning some of the right-wing intellectuals before and during World War II (Nae Ionescu, Mircea Eliade, Emil Cioran, etc.), the "Holocaust versus Gulag" polemic, the debates about the disclosure of secret police files, the legitimacy of NATO's intervention in Kosovo, and Romania's ongoing attempts to integrate itself with NATO and the EU.

These controversial "hot subjects" have brought to the surface some disturbing memories of the past, and have revealed much more about the current state of Romanian culture and society than the well-known xenophobic and anti-Western slogans of vulgar political tabloids like *România Mare* (Great Romania). Intellectuals espousing democratic rhetoric have proven confused by the complications of a controversial democratic reality, and often even nostalgic about their own evanesced prestige and authority. It is hard to believe, but what has sometimes resurfaced in the post-Communist era are the old clichés, masked by a superficial democratic language and legitimized by a pretentious, intangible elitism. This inherited, dogmatic way of thinking can be found even in cultural publications. One literary monthly compared the Stalinists of the 1950s, who facilitated Romania's subordination to the Soviet Union, to present-day "modernists" who struggle to assimilate Romania with the rest of Europe. Another prestigious literary weekly denounced a French court's decision to ban a Roger Garaudy book, which diminished the scope and proportion of the Holocaust, as evidence of a plot by a certain "lobby" that did not want to lose its "monopoly of suffering."

Last but not least, we cannot ignore, in this often confusing and sad social-political landscape, the great potential that lay in the intellectual and moral commitment of a brave minority of eminent believers in a civil society. Their iconoclastic, difficult, and courageous struggle with the prejudices and habits of the present social environment and, occasionally, with their own errors and misunderstandings, deserves respect and support.

These are only some of the many premises that justify interest in Romania's *Sonderweg*, as F. Peter Wagner refers to it in this volume, and which make it a difficult and challenging case for social-political research. A number of authors, both Romanian and foreign, bring, in this anthology, various and valuable contributions to the evaluation of the post-Communist transition in Romania. However, the complex problem of the relation between the armed forces, civil administration, and the secret police seems to me oversimplified in the chapter entitled "Civil–Military Relations: Continuity or Exceptionalism?" The author, Larry L. Watts, has also authored a controversial and disturbing book about Hitler's Romanian ally during World War II, General Ion Antonescu, titled *Romanian Cassandra*. In his contribution to this volume, Watts emphasizes the always "positive" role of the Romanian military and the mostly "negative" role of the current civilian leaders.

Complicated and provocative situations sometimes call for the redefining of criteria and evaluative strategies: in this case, the topic of "transition" needs to be redefined—the transition not only from Communism to capitalism, but also from the actual state of modernization toward the uncertainties of future metamorphoses.

It would be appropriate probably to emphasize, in the end, the words of F. Peter Wagner in this anthology:

> Modernity and modernization are not anymore, if they ever truly were, self-understood, nonproblematic notions, they themselves have become highly problematic, the center of concern and investigation. . . . Western scholarship has found in Romania an exemplary test-case for the analysis of the development of underdevelopment, or the development of a periphery.

The paradoxes that have stimulated the investigations of the authors are, in fact, the very ones that so often have ill-fated effects in the daily life of Romanians. As it may lead to a better understanding of these paradoxes—and possible solutions to them—this intellectual enterprise remains useful and praiseworthy. If enough attention is paid to the social-political reality of Romania, from inside and out, we may finally see a promise of hope, however slow and painful the transition discussed in this volume proves to be. Romania's integration into a common Europe represents its best chance to fully develop its potential and to find, finally, its stable place in the modern, civilized world. This long postponed goal deserves, certainly, support. The exacting critical analysis of this anthology seems one of the preliminary, right steps in this direction.

Norman Manea
New York
April 2000

P.S. Since this brief introduction was written, the "lack of progress" and the "great potential" were evolving, of course, toward new tensions and a new balance. Closer now to European and global integration, Romania was pushed and is pushing herself toward more visible progress, still struggling with the old and new difficulties mentioned in my text.

Norman Manea
December 2003

Preface

During the Communist period, scholars of Eastern Europe often studied several countries at once, perhaps because there were few crucial differences between the different states, which, particularly in the late 1940s and 1950s, closely resembled the standard Stalinist model. Now that they are experiencing the dynamic process of the transition to democracy and the free market, the simple study of Stalinism, oligarchy, or personal autocracy will no longer suffice to explain the varying political situations in all the countries of Eastern Europe. In this often-chaotic process, the influence of international factors has been confusing and contradictory, and they have contributed to the increasing variation one finds among the countries of the former "East Bloc." The variations among these countries have also been magnified by the vagaries of electoral, parliamentary, judicial, and bureaucratic politics, as well as the ongoing institutionalization of democratic processes and values. For comparativists, there remains the scholarly need to generalize, synthesize, and theorize about the countries and the region, a project that requires study of the new complexities of both internal and international variables.

This book represents an effort to collect data and to conduct the concomitant analysis and synthesis of the complex problems of Romania's transition, one that will hopefully be useful for singular and comparative efforts at understanding this phenomena. Following the format of the two country studies edited by Daniel Nelson, *Romania in the 1980s* (1981) and *Romania after Tyranny* (1992), this book attempts to elucidate the key aspects of a country undergoing a profound transformation from a repressive totalitarianism to an as yet unreached and undefined democratic future. If Sorin Antohi's chapter is correct in arguing that few Romania-based Romanians publish in the "global academic press," then this book, with six such authors included, is a major new contribution. More generally and immodestly, it is possibly the most comprehensive study of Romanian politics ever published abroad.

But why study Romania? Romanians often say, "Because we are unique." And unique they are—though no more or less than any other country's *Gestalt*. The different contributors to this volume offer different reasons for studying Romania. Manea, Tismăneanu, and Wagner, for example, all refer to the specificity of Romania's transition, its special path, or *Sonderweg*. Hall and Sellin emphasize the importance of the cultural–institutional nexus and the continuity in patterns developed under Communism. Daniel Nelson focuses on the security policies of transitional Romania. Others focus on the institutional aspects of transitional Romania—Bush on unions, Roper on parliament, Birnir on the party system, and Ramet on the Church.

In its post-Communist era, Romania has traveled the proverbial miles, with miles still to go to eliminate the danger of polarization and breakdown. Clearly, the signs are ominous, even though human rights protection has been an outstanding, if not the outstanding, achievement of the Revolution. What makes human rights still precarious is the perpetuation of political class as the new political society, utterly lacking in former anti-Communists under the age of sixty. Such individuals lack the moral credibility to condemn fascistic elements whose collaboration under Communism was no worse than the country's typical politicians—leaders and followers alike. So, when the Greater Romania Party becomes the leading opposition party in the 2000 elections, and Holocaust deniers, hagiographers of the Iron Guard and Marshal Ion Antonescu, and anti-Semitic, anti-Hungarian agitators become not atypical national legislators, democratic stability is threatened. Open debate becomes an occasion for hateful dissemination of lies, rather than exchange and compromise based on common liberal principles, as anti-Western and illiberal discourse, justified in terms of Romanian relativism, legitimates antidemocratic elements. We also have seen two assaults, however preliminary, on the lynchpins of liberty during the Constantinescu presidency: the Justice Minister's assumption of direct supervision of judges and the legalized arrest of journalists. That these actions were two of the main pieces of legislation during the Constantinescu presidency only illustrates that bipartisan agreement is deeper for authoritarianism than democracy. With no more guarantees of an independent press and judiciary, the vigilance needed to stop tyranny is ebbing. Romania's elites lack a consensus of where they want the country to head and a track record or sense of how to pact agreements to avoid going where they might agree that the country needs to avoid. Romania's leaders have had choices to make. Too often, they have made the wrong ones or failed to make any.

Thus, students of Romania face a number of puzzles, both in the nature of its development and about the democratization process. Some of these puzzles are merely curious and not important. Others, however, comprise the crux of both crucial problems: the large distance Romania has come from sultanistic, national Communism and the fierce dangers of steady erosion that lie ahead. I leave to the reader to decide which of the questions that follow are crucial, and which merely get headlines:

- Why do such topics as Brigitte Bardot and the Mayor of Bucharest clashing over the latter's attempts to slaughter stray dogs, or the very high rates of pediatric AIDS cases, the equally high numbers of homeless, street children, high rates of abortion, and, of course, Dracula seem to get most or all of the foreign press coverage of Romania?
- Do the authoritarian prerogatives enjoyed by the former Communists, particularly over the economy, most explain why Romania has enjoyed more political stability than most post-Communist, East European countries, even if those prerogatives are the main cause of its stagnating economy?
- Why, for the most part, were there no dissidents and nongovernmental organizations (NGOs) in Romania before 1989? And now, why does Romania have the most NGOs in Eastern Europe, even if most of them are for-profit companies or collaborationist NGOs with the government, neither of which really constitute NGOs by standard definitions?
- Why are two of the worst problems harming Romania's democratization and its chances of entering the EU by 2007, racial discrimination against Roma and especially judicial interference, rarely mentioned in the Romanian press, with the public discourse identifying the problem as with the Roma and not with the larger society as well? Why are Roma refugees from Romania automatically deemed to be fleeing for economic motives rather than from persecution?
- Notwithstanding its inherent insecurity, what identity is being constructed for the Romanian state, liberal/Western, Eastern corporatist, kleptocratic, ethnocentric, eclectic, *sui generis*, or incoherent and amorphous?
- Why has Romanian aversion, even to limited ethnic autonomy, prevented a choice for Roma parents for parallel, Roma-managed schools with bilingual education (as opposed to Romanian-managed, but Roma segregated schools or Romanian majority schools lacking bilingual language)? Why is there such a large gap between official Roma access to health and education, but no effective access?
- Can the unequal bargaining power in the founding moments be compensated with additional negotiations from NGO or opposition party representatives?
- Did the Romanian government's support for NATO's humanitarian intervention in 1999, to reverse the ethnic cleansing in Kosovo, help the election of Ion Iliescu to the presidency and the PDSR as the plurality party in parliament, as well as the second place finishes of Vadim Tudor for president and his Great Romania Party as opposition?

- Why do public discourses impose treasonous guilt by association for anyone, such as then-SRI Director Radu Timofte, for alleged links to Gorbachev's KGB or for having been a *Securitate* activist, while someone having joined the Communist Party led by Nicolae Ceaușescu, is tantamount to a "union card" for eligibility in post-Communist political society, bearing no stigma or imposing no costs?
- Why have the battles among ex-*Securitate* personnel and their allies in and out of the intelligence services not been covered in the press?
- Why is the council reviewing *Securitate* records (CNSAS) controlled by or at the mercy of the SRI intelligence agency, the opposite of what Senator Ticu Dumitrescu, the author of the law that created the Council, had originally intended?
- Why Bulgaria's Western-oriented, democratic opposition did a much better job in office during the same period as Constantinescu's presidency, which resulted in Bulgaria having a clear policy direction and Romania unsure of its future, as well as the EU ending visa restrictions for Bulgarians, but not for Romanians?
- Why the symbolic appeal of the NATO and EU membership is so enormous compared with their intrinsic value. What consequences would ensue if Romania's candidacy is rejected by the EU by 2007 if states like Slovakia and Slovenia, or even the Baltic states or Bulgaria, are admitted?
- Has Romania really accepted NATO and EU conditionality, or does it merely implicitly accept the stipulations for entry in public statements and permit others to undermine those commitments?
- Was the historic rapprochement between Hungary and Romania motivated by insincere promises and understandings on minority rights, and does that make any difference?
- Why ethnic Hungarians and ethnic Romanians consider the issue of a state-supported, ethnic Hungarian university to be so important, and why can the two sides not agree to set up such a university without first debating the history of who settled Transylvania first?
- Has President Iliescu's dance between East and West reflected genuine confusion, a complicated political game, or Machiavellian brilliance?
- Why does blatant official corruption, leaving precious few, if any, honest politicians in the country, not scandalize or induce prosecutions?
- Why does sultanism continue under democratization, as Romania's class structure remains related to state power and the "new" oligarchy reflects direct personal connections to that power?
- Why does the restoration of several large Brancuși monuments and statues in Romania occur with massive charges of corruption?
- Why has Romania more genocide denial than any East European country other than the former Yugoslavia?

- Why do so few analysts see the direct relationship between Romania's electoral and official corruption?
- Since democracy supposedly changes how people relate to authority, why has Romanian civil society remained largely deferential to the ruling oligarchy?
- Why do analysts presume that the illiberal aspects of Romanian democratization do not result from the "mere trappings of procedural democracy," which are assumed erroneously to exist?
- Why did Iliescu join *Vatră Românească*, as he revealed in 1999?
- Do voters support Iliescu more for his quasi-Western political liberalism or for his antieconomic neoliberalism?
- Why does Romania glorify criminals who did wrong, like Marshal Ion Antonescu or a traitor like General Gheorghe Avramescu, who let various *Legionari* escape to Nazi Germany after 23 August 1944, while imprisoned heroes like Iuliu Maniu and Corneliu Coposu, do not receive equivalent support (except by a few intellectuals led by Ana Blandiana in Sighet)?
- Why Romania permitted the dominant, SRI intelligence agency, to operate businesses, in addition to intimidation through surveillance and vote rigging, rather than just concentrate on information gathering? And why the first SRI leader, Virgil Măgureanu, subsequently retired from intelligence activities with great wealth and access to intelligence files of other politicians, while operating with impunity?
- Why is there no scandal about official intelligence gathering whose chief purpose is for conducting businesses linked to the former *Securitate*, and why this does not produce friction with legitimate intelligence and defense agency officials who do not mix business with intelligence gathering?
- Why do analysts of Romania accuse Romanian officials and organized crime of corruption, but also of being organized well enough to achieve these conspiracy feats?
- Why there were no scandals when politicians like Petre Roman declared their personal property, required under new laws, but without revealing their enormous holdings?
- Why the army, which supported a largely non-*Securitate* coalition in the December 1989 overthrow of Iliescu, acceded to a weak position in the new regime, compared with the SRI and other intelligence agencies that emerged from the organizational map of the former *Securitate*?
- Whether the army's increased role in politics will lead to articulated military contestation and vetoes, or whether the army will gradually yield its new authoritarian prerogatives and democratize to Western models of civilian supremacy?
- How Iliescu has been able to keep his disparate coalition more or less united over the past dozen years?

- Why neopatrimonialism/sultanism remains so entrenched behind individual leaders (e.g., Of the Trocadero Group, Severin went "with Roman"; Paşcu "went with Iliescu," etc.)?
- Why did the U.S. accept the 1992 parliamentary electoral fraud (or was in denial about it)?
- Why did the IRI representative not get his contract renewed after writing a report on the stolen 1992 elections, a report that IRI circulated?
- Why do elections, charisma, traditional deference to authority, and collective memory of Communism, and the interwar and postwar democratic breakdowns have greater impact on legitimation than elections and the rule of law?
- Is the Greater Romania Party a loyal, semiloyal, or disloyal party, and will its proclamations of legitimacy follow the pattern of the former Legionnaire and Socialist parties that had made similar declarations, only to become antidemocratic?
- Given the need to please the United States, why do genocide denial and Nazi revival in the cult of Antonescu, who declared war on the U.S., have any resonance in mainstream Romania?
- Do large sectors in the Romanian peasantry and urbanized, rural proletariat really have some misgivings about joining the West, which it may fear after its experience under Hungarian domination?
- Why was Romania, as of the publication of this book, admirably the only state to ratify COP-III of the Kyoto Protocol to reduce Greenhouse Gases?

My family has had connections with Romania for three generations. My paternal grandparents lived in Bucharest when my grandfather was the Third Secretary of the U.S. Embassy. My parents visited in 1980 when my father was one of two public members of a U.S. Delegation to discuss whether the Romanian Government should receive Most Favored Nation status on tariffs during some future period. He met Dumitru Mazilu, who eight years later was a colleague on the UN Human Rights Subcommission. My father attempted to help Mazilu after he was placed under house arrest after reporting on the abuse of Romanian youth to the Subcommission. Mazilu's report was an early sign of efforts to undermine Ceauşescu. My scholarly interest in Romania is almost entirely attributable to the encouragement from, and two-decade-plus friendships with, John Florescu and his wife Gina, his brother Radu Jr. and his wife Helène, and their father Radu Sr., along with the rest of the family. They have immeasurably enriched my life and my understanding of Romanian history and culture, which included John and Gina's 1993 marriage at the Sinaia *peleş*. In gratitude, this book is dedicated to all the Florescu's. Because of their influence, I was one of the few applicants to the Civic Education Project to state a preference for Romania, which was realized from 1992 to 1994, as part of my doctoral fieldwork. Five other families made my pleasant stay in Bucharest, where I met so many wonderful people, including the especially kind friends, the Ştefanescu's, Muntean's, Szabo's, Radeş's, and Dimitriu's—thanks for all the warm *ciorbeas* and hugs. I have been very fortunate to have been guided and inspired by many students of Romania in small and large ways. While I am grateful to all whom I do not name, I would like to thank particularly Dinu Giurescu, the late Pavel Câmpeanu, Michal Shafir, Dragoş Munteanu, Sandra Pralong, Sorin Antohi, Radu Munteanu, Kris Kristof, Gabor Vermes, Steven Sampson, Dorel Abraham, Ilie Bădescu, Dumitru Sandu, David Kideckel, Larry Watts, Aurelian Craiuţu, Coen Hilbrink, Steve Roper, Mark Temple, Frank Sellin, Liliana Pop, Daniel Nelson, Vladimir Tismăneanu, and especially Richard Hall, as well as posthumously to the late Alexandru Duţu. Vladimir Tismăneanu's initial commitment to the project helped to make recruiting contributors easier. Though we have never actually met in person, Gail Kligman has kindly advised me as if we had. None of them are responsible for the infelicities, errors, or opinions expressed in this book. And I have been guided throughout the course of this project—deeply, persistently, and indefatigably—by Sabrina Ramet. To this day, I still cannot believe she is not really a marathon runner. Her incredible experience and wisdom has helped me to hopefully produce a volume that meets her standards. I have had the benefit of one of the strongest sets of collaborators I have ever worked with, and have endeavored to produce as thorough and as helpful a volume as possible. I also greatly appreciate the help of several Georgia State graduate students. In the early stages, Mihnea Năstase provided exemplary research assistance, tireless copyediting, and expert diacritics checking. Christopher Eisterhold picked up the ball in 2000 and contributed painstaking editing and constant effort, volunteering enormous hours to the project after the budget expired. I can never properly and fully acknowledge his contribution. Both Mihnea and Kit have contributed articles to this volume as well. As always, I am immeasurably grateful to my parents and my three siblings for their lifelong love, guidance, and patience, and to Faye, John-Henry, and Miho for the inestimable joy and patience they bring to my life, as well as their patience with my work habits.

Henry F. Carey
Atlanta, Georgia
March 2003

Introduction

Henry F. Carey and Christopher Eisterhold

Of all the revolutions of the *annus mirabilis* 1989, the Romanian revolution was arguably the most dramatic. From the spontaneous uprising in Timişoara, and the chanting of the crowds *"Ceauşescu dictatorul!"* in the Palace Square, to the gun battles in the streets of Bucharest, it most closely resembled an uncontrollable, passionate, and violent revolution. At the time, many Romanians regarded it as such; and in those heady days of December 1989, it released a profound sense of euphoria, a feeling that the hour of liberation from national Communism to capitalism, freedom, and democracy had come. That the direct descendants of the elites installed by the Soviets remained in power was a matter of great disappointment to many intellectuals and middle-class urbanites. This "velvet restoration," to use Michnik's phrase, was not as distressing to the struggling masses, as the perpetuation of economic exigencies, rooted in uncertainty as well as Ceauşescu's austerity.

Today, more than fourteen years after the revolution, most of the euphoria has evaporated, along with the dreams and aspirations that it had temporarily let loose in the Romanian people. Some faith was restored in November 2002 with Romania's invitation into NATO, only to be shocked by French President Chirac three months later, when he asserted that Romania (and Bulgaria) had harmed their chances of entering into the European Union (EU) by publicly siding with the U.S. over whether to go to war in Iraq. Such symbolic, foreign issues of huge import, however, have not overshadowed the issues of everyday struggle. Many of the hoped for, and long promised, democratic reforms have yet to be completed, or even initiated. While there is a constitution, its provisions have often been ignored, and the courts have not enforced them. A democratic civil society has yet to take root, and while the public has voted in meaningful numbers, all four legislative elections and two constitutional plebiscites since 1990 have been delegitimated by inordinate rates of spoiled ballots and other irregularities. The parliament remains a relatively weak institution, and the party structure remains fragmented, driven by clientelism and patrimonialism, and obligated to an oligarchy of elites drawn primarily from the former *nomenklatura*, with control over of ownership of the state—from the factories, banks, and utilities, to the personal fortune of the Ceauşescus—remaining close to where it was before December 1989. By the criteria of Skocpol and Moore,[1] this was not a social revolution, though it was a regime change from totalitarianism to authoritarianism. The Byzantine assortment of intelligence services have been spawned from the institutional remains of the *Securitate*, staffed with an alarming percentage of ex-*Securitate* personnel, who continue many of the functions of that dreaded institution.

Much debate has transpired, but not much light has been shed on the events of 1989. Whether or not it was a revolution or a coup is an important question in order to understand the motives and consequences. Whether the impetus came from civil society, from within the Communist regime, or from abroad is not only worth documenting, but has implications politically. The word "coup" in Romania, as Richard Hall has argued, connotes the staging of combat by forces loyal to Iliescu, presumably from the army and not the *Securitate*,[2] either or both of which were behind the attacks on civilians after 22 December. Yet, clearly, the causes came from the international system, Gorbachev's desire for reforms and noninterventionist tactics except to signal approval for reformers to assume power, preferably by consensus in the political bureaus. This does not mean any orders or even plans emerged from the Kremlin. Second, regime elements were crucial. The sultanistic totalitarian regime, what others call national Stalinism, was not amenable even to intraparty pluralism, let alone to a parallel intellectual culture. When the events began as a protest in Timişoara and then a rebellion from society, the signal from Gorbachev for a Bulgarian succession could be inferred, but without any Soviet intervention. When the Praetorian Guard split, violence resulted to decide whom, among those with guns, would gain the upper hand. The *nomenklatura's* contempt for civil society in Romania meant there was little chance for a revolution as in East Central Europe, where the Communist state was conquered by civil society on the basis of prestige and alternative leadership. Iliescu was one of the few conceivable alternatives to Ceauşescu because he had advocated something other than Stalinism. The Romanian civil–military revolt could ignore the claims of the people that had initiated the process. Legitimacy in Romania has not inspired protest of stolen elections but in protest to Ceauşescu's version of socialism. Were it not for the country's patent cultural desire to integrate with the West and for economic normality, Iliescu's new regime, from sultanistic totalitarianism to post-totalitarianism, could have survived. While many would have asserted that the velvet restoration was a fraud, many more would have continued to give him credit for effecting the revolution. For many peasants and marginal workers, the regime change on 22 December 1989 was a dramatic political revolution since it initially introduced *perestroika* and *glasnost*.

With the perspective of almost fifteen years, we can refer to the events of December 1989 as an unintended revolution in effects, which began as a palace coup in response to a civil uprising, which resulted in violence around the country for a few more days. The losers in this battle among the Communist *aparat* denigrated the events as a coup because the alternative term—revolution—connoted December 1989 in Romania as a positive change, something dialectically determined. Romania's revolution was just as iffy as the Bolshevik one. There is little doubt that Iliescu did not intend a revolution either. The "truth" of the revolution has not been told, but neither have all the details of the revolutions of 1776, 1789, 1918, and 1949. The Russian surrender in World War I and the Japanese invasion of China in World War II permitted two of those revolutions. Romania's revolution, as well, would not have succeeded without Gorbachev and the prior events in East Central Europe of the previous five months. Many have complained that Iliescu "stole" the revolution, just as the Philippine and Haitian armies "stole" their 1986 revolutions. However, the reason that the Philippines had an alternative to Marcos, but the reason why Haiti and Romania did not have a democratic alternative to Ceauşescu, is that their civil societies had been flattened by sultanism and low economic development. Iliescu exploited the vacuum of political leadership in civil society, which Romanian intellectuals, lacking an ongoing *samizdat* press, could not fill. Most of intellectual society had made its peace with Communism and lacked the moral authority and civil society following to "speak truth to power." Nor have the anti-Communist parties been drawn from longstanding anti-Communists. In fact, the former political prisoners and the surviving interwar political leaders were threatening to many, maybe even a majority of civil society, rather than a source of pride. As they passed from the scene, most of political society drew from former Communist aspirants or activists. Socialized in the compromising norms of the UTC, or Communist Youth, politicians have easily ignored the claims to moral authority of writers and journalists who also had sold out to the system of connections, cabals, conspiracies, crime, and corruption.

Public cynicism about "democracy" has grown. It is not the "only game in town," in Linz's formulation. On the other hand, the government is not so ineffective, corrupt, and/or perceived as so illegitimate that a blatantly unconstitutional and supposedly temporary seizure of power, where no peaceful alternative is perceived, is likely to be staged and generally accepted. However, if decisions are not taken in the next few years to reduce official corruption, establish judicial independence and professionalism, and to reform the economy, such a scenario could become plausible. The legitimation of a large, antisystem party and leader as the second leading forces in the 2000 elections only reinforces evidence of public gullibility for demagoguery in the self-serving name of public virtue. The specter of *conducător* Vadim Tudor leading an authoritarian regime, whose rules would be enforced by a brown-shirted, miner militia, is quite conceivable after more economic decline during the third term of Ion Iliescu. The latter president had let the Tudor genie out of the autocratic bottle to make peace with him after the September 1991 miners' attacks and as a coconspirator in the 1992 electoral fraud, rather than accommodating the forces behind his first prime minister, Petre Roman.

So far, democratic political learning has consisted largely of elites learning that to get ahead, one still has to sell to the highest bidder, regardless of the price, so long as the forms of democracy mimic the caricature that can only emerge in a state without courts giving democratic meaning to the rules. As in Russia, a "new class" of oligarchs, consisting of different factions of the same class of Communist activists, has risen from the ashes of the Communist regime, a "directocracy" set above the formal institutions of democracy. Many have begun to express skepticism about the "Western" model of development. Astonishingly, polls have revealed that a majority of Romanians now believe that they were better off under Ceauşescu. Clearly, Romania's transition to democracy is in trouble. Some have even argued that Romania has become a "special case," a worst-case scenario even, "exemplary and indicative of the problems, rather than the promise, of the transition to democracy and the free market."[3]

Romania's current predicaments should not have been surprising, given that its conditions in 1990 were less propitious for democratic stability than those of any other state in southeast Europe, excepting Albania. Romania has shared in the region's propensity for incomplete state-building (the lack of territorial control) and nation-building (the lack of a unified national identity), as well as its low levels of political participation and economic productivity. Aggravating these circumstance for decades prior to 1989, the country had been ruled by a regime that combined the attributes of the two worst nondemocratic regime types of the four originally formulated by Linz and Stephan: *totalitarianism*, with state domination of civil society, and *sultanism*, with unrestrained personal rulership. This led to the flattening of almost all autonomy and structural differentiation within civil society to a far greater degree than what had occurred in other countries of Eastern Europe. As a result, Romania is now faced with what we would characterize as a *quintuple* transition, as it must build from scratch political, civil, and economic societies, develop an autonomous—yet accountable—state bureaucracy, and all the while constraining these aforementioned areas through the development of the rule of law and an independent judicial system to enforce the equal rights of Romania's citizenry. Like so many other transitional democracies, Romania faces the universal dilemma of having to confront more than one of these five challenges concurrently. It risks, as they all do, the "future shock," to borrow the phrase of Alvin Toffler, of attempting too much, too soon, and doing all of it badly. Furthermore, the politics of postponing some of these tasks is wrought with perverse incentives for corruption, given the absence of any consensus among the polarized elites who lack any tradition or knowledge about the methods, or even the benefits, of cooperation.

This book attempts to provide the reader with an understanding of the problems facing contemporary Romania in its painful transition to democracy. It is divided into five sections, each covering a different aspect of contemporary Romania. The first is an introductory section, intended to provide the reader with a sense of Romanian political history and culture, as well as of the circumstances that led to the revolution of 1989 and the legacy it has left the Romanian people. The second section not only concerns state institutions, such as the parliament and the political parties, but also how they interact with the larger political culture as well. Part 3 analyzes civil society and its components like women's, gay, and minority rights, and church–state relations. Part 4 analyzes economic issues, including labor relations, fiscal and monetary policy, and issues of political economy. The fifth and final section deals with security issues, including internal security, foreign relations, and military alliances. Inevitably, the authors vary widely in methodology, theoretical approaches, and assessment of the relative progress Romania has made toward democracy. Yet, in toto, they provide the reader with a comprehensive picture of the state of Romania since 1989. The contributors provide empirical contributions to theoretical debates on democratic transitions, political culture, and economic development. Ample predictions and normative conclusions are also generated about public policies and future directions. The following is a brief summary of the chapters.

PART 1: INTRODUCTION

The first chapter, by Vladimir Tismăneanu, provides a cultural-theoretical background to the arcane, Byzantine world of Romanian politics. While he largely analyzes the politics of the Ceauşescu era, it is not a mere historical primer, but an interpretive framework of "Ceauşescuism" in contemporary Romanian politics. Tismăneanu emphasizes the informal aspects of decision-making, "secretive, cliquish, and programmatically deceptive," the "exact opposite of the presumably transparent, consensual, and impersonal procedural systems of democratic polities." As orality and informality were the modus operandi of the Ceauşescu regime, little formal institutional memory exists, and orality and informality continue as the politico-cultural expectation of elites under "democracy." In the absence of formal information—meaningful statistics, transcripts of conversations among government officials, and descriptions of policies—Tismăneanu argues that personalities arbitrarily determine decision processes and outcomes.

Ceauşescuism represented the attempt by a beleaguered and barely legitimate sultanistic elite, loyal only to the ruling family, to gain domestic authority and international recognition based on a contrived nationalist heritage and Stalinist controls. This explains why interpretations of the events of December 1989 also result from orality, informality, and contrivance, as under Communism, from the show trial of the Ceauşescu's to the alleged terrorists, to the salvation role of the army and the Front (as detailed later in the Ely and Stoica chapter), and the ongoing legitimacy crises of successive post-Communist governments. Romania has been liberated from Communism, but not from its Communist elites and the indigence of the masses, who have accepted their salvation on these terms. The party that ruled until the November 1996 elections, Ion Iliescu's PDSR, was dominated by personalities belonging to the "second and third echelon" of the deposed regime. Thus, while the Ceauşescu regime collapsed, Ceauşescuism has survived in "widespread network of vested interests, connections, protections, and more often than not, fear of change."

In "*Sonderweg* Romania?" F. Peter Wagner directly questions the modernization perspective that has animated much contemporary discussion on Romania and Eastern Europe. Specifically, he questions the developmental model, which posited a relatively linear transition from Communism to the Western model of a liberal democratic state and a capitalist market economy. Wagner contends that the failure of Romania's transition to follow this developmental model "challenges some fundamental assumptions in the field of transition studies" and renders problematic the categories by which Romania has been constructed and analyzed. Wagner argues that the case of Romania "challenges the basic idea behind transition studies," which is the very "*idea* of a transition"—the linear movement from one fixed point (a stage *A*) to another (a stage *B*). Noting that "stage B" (the Western model to which the former Eastern European states are supposed to be making the transition) is itself undergoing a profound transformation, he asks us to move beyond the conceptualizations that animate current debates. In their place, Wagner presents an alternative transitional framework based on the concept of a *"double syncronicity"*—denoting attempted integration of these states into a "Western" order which is itself undergoing a profound transformation.

The problem of Romania's uniqueness is applied to the issue of collective historical memory in Michael Shafir's, "Memory, Memorials, and Membership: Romanian Utilitarian Anti-Semitism and Marshal Antonescu." He argues that Romanian socialization has reinforced extremist attitudes, especially anti-Semitism among marginalized social groups with a proclivity to scapegoat. They should instead be taught the truth. The manipulation of collective memory, he argues, breeds false resentments and induces recidivism against the innocent, including, but not only Jews. Rather than a reasonable degree of shame and commitment toward future improvement, those groups susceptible to extremism induce "clashes of collective memories." The post-Communist cult of Romania's wartime leader Marshal Ion Antonescu exploits what Shafir terms "utilitarian anti-Semitism," which describes the use and misuse of anti-Semitic discourse and its historical memory-loaded values by politicians and intellectual elites who are not, in fact, anti-Semites. Of course, there are also the ideologically committed, blatant exponents of the Antonescu cult, who also seek political benefits from support for radical nationalism and anti-Semitism.

Romania's quest for NATO membership resulted in a "clash of historic memories." The apparent official renunciation of the Antonescu cult, in submission to NATO edicts, has constrained the continued socialization and the teaching of historical lies. The outcome has not, Shafir argues, obliterated deeply entrenched, hyper-nationalist values and anti-Semitism. Rather, he sees a public display of cognitive dissonance or dissimulation to buy time until the scrutiny of NATO cosmopolitan forces are looking elsewhere. Then, the symbols of xenophobia can be cherished again. Of course, Romania is not unique in this regard, with the United States maintaining its own welter of streets, flags, monuments, and other earmarks of Confederacy heritage throughout the U.S. South,[4] as well as a blissful ignorance of its genocide of Native Americans. Shafir's chapter reminds the reader of the dangers that hero models of intolerance pose to historical memory in various national contexts.

In "Re-Membering Romania," John F. Ely and Cătălin Augustin Stoica remind us that "history" can be manipulated to affect the present, as society's understanding of history helps form its collective identity and memory, thereby influencing the potential for and the direction of collective action in a democratic or authoritarian direction. "As the euphoria of those cathartic days died away, the old pathologies (e.g., distrust of the public sphere, lack of a legitimate 'legitimate' narrative, proliferation of alternative 'legitimate' narratives) reemerged, superseding any hope that a shared 'revolution' myth would offer a common identity and a clear break with the 'old.'"

They examine a specific historical event and ask whether the "revolution" of 1989 could provide a sense of solidarity and identity to the Romanian people. Their analysis, drawn from a survey carried out by the Center for Urban and Regional Sociology (CURS) in October 1999, reveals the lack of a minimal consensus as to what really occurred in December 1989. Some believe it was a revolution, while many others believe it was a coup. In the end, they conclude that, ten years after the fall of the Ceauşescu regime, there is still no "collective memory" on which to build Romania's identity as a truly democratic nation, nor any motivation for collective action to realize it. In this manner, the lack of a shared past retards the progress of Romanian society in its transition to a democratic future.

In his chapter "Democratization in the Shadows," Frank Sellin discusses the legacy of how the patrimonial political culture of the Ceauşescu era complicates and obstructs political and economic reform, as parties purse their interests through patronage and favoritism in public policy. The patrimonial style of party politics resurrected former Communist networks, which directed state resources to the still powerful vested interests of the old party-state. As a result, their hold on power since the turbulent aftermath of the "revolution" of 1989 "contributed heavily to the fusion of political and economic power" and condemned the subordinated and nominally democratic institutions to "extra-constitutional dominance of a personal and partisan nature."

Because of this, Sellin contends, anticorruption and other reform measures have become difficult to carry out. In fact, patrimonial politics have made Romania ungovernable since the opposition coalition took power in 1996, due to the complicated "algorithms" for the dispensation of patronage necessary to hold together the fractious "coalition of coalitions," to use Michael Shafir's phrase. In the end, he concludes, short of a significant exogenous shock, political fragmentation and stagnation will continue for the foreseeable future.

PART 2: THE STATE AND POLITICS

In her chapter, Jóhanna Kristín Birnir discusses the electoral and party laws, which structure the party system in Romania, particularly those that have been passed to reduce its fragmentation and volatility and to institutionalize a stable party system. She finds some progress in both. The irregularities in the legislative elections of 1990, 1992, and 1996, however, do make the analysis more difficult, as they may contribute to either consolidation or volatility of the party system. Success in reducing both fragmentation and volatility over the first decade and a half of democratization results partly from recent changes in electoral legislation—particularly increasing entry thresholds to enter parliament, thus eliminating small parties, and increasingly restrictive party registration requirements, thereby eliminating weak or disorganized ones. This solidifies existing parties at the expense of smaller but potentially strong ones. "Romanian institutions have established a system of around six parties and coalitions," she writes, which is a rather large number. This suggests some difficulty transcending clientelism, personalism, and corruption as a basis for party competition, rather than the primacy of party ideology and policies, leadership qualities, and retrospective and prospective governing records. While still developing, the institutionalization of the party system is progressing about as rapidly as can be expected, given the persistent voting irregularities and political disequilibrium generated by the spasmodic process of democratization and reform.

Steven D. Roper examines the interwar and Communist legacies which have influenced contemporary parliamentary development, analyzes the impact of post-Communist institutional choices on policy debates, and explores the development of the parliament and its relationship with the presidency. Roper notes that, almost since its conception in 1990, the post-Communist parliament has been the least trusted and most ridiculed institution in Romania. "Charges of corruption and inactivity plagued the first parliament; coalitional instability stymied legislative efforts during the second. The third parliament was supposed to overcome these problems and focus on economic reform and privatization, but the governing coalition proved fragile." Instead of legislating, the stifling patrimonialism and ideological polarization have led both Iliescu and Constantinescu to rely on executive decrees and to hope that the legislature would not allow the government to fall. Romania's legislative power vacuum is one of the main obstacles to reform. As a result, the parliament today is held in the same disrepute as it was during the mid-1990s. Western governments and organizations have been largely unsuccessful in professionalizing the parliament. Until the parliament begins to exert its authority over the government, he warns, Romania will continue to fall further behind other East European countries in marketization and democratization.

With the establishment of at least formal democratic institutions in Romania, it was hoped that the public would be able, for the first time, to participate in the political process in a meaningful way. In their chapter, Paul E. Sum and Gabriel Bădescu answer the question of whether the Romanian public has actually been able, or willing, to take advantage of that opportunity. Specifically, they evaluate six forms of political participation including voting, political campaign activity, and joining legal protests to determine the extent to which the contemporary Romanian public actually participates in the political process. Unfortunately, they find that, with the exception of voting, relatively few Romanians actually involve themselves in politics. "With the exception of voting, aggregate levels of Romanian political participation are low, and participation rates reflect discrepancies across corresponding social categories." They attribute this, in part, to the limited extent of "organized group activity" in Romania, but write, hopefully, that "strengthening civil society will overcome these discrepancies, especially in rural areas."

If strengthening civil society could induce more Romanians to participate politically, it would hold out the hope that a mobilized public might counter the patrimonial, patronage-driven politics, which have heretofore governed the state and help establish a truly functioning democracy. They do not evaluate how to strengthen civil society. This question is left to other authors in this book, some of whom (viz., Frank Sellin or Richard Hall) suggest that the traditional, patrimonial aspects of Romanian political culture continue to thwart attempts to build a viable civil society.

Peter Gross directly addresses the extent to which an independent media is necessary to establish democracy in transitional states. He notes that, in the case of Romania, a truly professional and independent media has yet to establish itself. It remains, for the most part, politically and economically subordinate to various interests. Its coverage of contemporary political events continues to be highly partisan and ideologically driven. Yet, Romanian media inform their audiences without fact-based journalism because of politicization and partisanship. The mobilization of media resources from elitist and ethnic political configurations to express their political opinions has brought to the fore new issues, parties, leaders, and ideas, but it is often biased. Their owners see to it that they serve functions of manipulation, propaganda, and mobilization because various partisan and outside interests politicize reporting. In addition, the Constantinescu presidency was marked by the selective arrests of journalists, after Justice Minister Valeriu Stoica, supposedly a liberal, issued "an ordinance which would have made it even easier to drag the media into court under the existing definitions of damage to 'honor and dignity,' and which gave the impression that high monetary penalties would be mandatory." Were it not for the subsequent uproar, the ordinance would not have been rescinded. Yet, prosecutors obtained convictions of journalists, an ominous development on top of the media's already convoluted posturing and intelligence agency interference.

Yet, Gross concludes that the media are sufficiently pluralist and that the open-minded reader can obtain a general sense of Romania's politics by reading several newspapers—something that few readers can or will do. Instead, readers can obtain some important information, which does function (more or less) consistently with contemporary theories of democratization, which are not too stringent in their prerequisites. "For the present," Gross writes, "media are expressions of extant political culture, and reinforces of this culture; but they are also, concurrently, mechanisms of change by virtue of the new ideas, debates, and opportunities they present to the public."

Richard Andrew Hall analyzes cultural constraints on democratization. He argues that many of the broader features of political culture in the Communist era—the passive attitudes of a "mass society," the use of patronage in politics, the rent-seeking behavior of bureaucrats, and the continuing preference of the Romanian citizenry for informal networks of *pile, cunoştiinţe, şi relaţii* in their everyday personal and political matters—have persisted and have undermined democratic political development in the entire post-Communist era.

The retention of Communist political culture is also reflected in the apparent unwillingness of the Romanian citizenry to participate directly in politics and in civil society and to form long-term partisan commitments. These cultural traits have contributed to the volatility of post-Communist elections and the failure to form and maintain stable democratic governing coalitions. Hall concludes that Romania's amoral familialism is a distorting, though not deterministic cultural influence. He concludes, "While the legacy of Communist political culture will not inevitably foreclose on the process of democratization, it remains a substantial impediment. Older facets of political culture often prove stronger, more flexible, and more adaptable than the prophets of change have predicted. Moreover, they have the capacity to shape the operation and outcomes of these new formal institutions."

PART 3: CIVIL SOCIETY AND SOCIAL ISSUES

Whereas Sum and Bădescu assume that strengthening civil society would contribute to the process of democratization, Sandra Pralong directly addresses the quality and traits needed to develop civil society in Romania. Some have pointed to the growing number of nongovernmental organizations (NGOs), some 17,000 in one count, as indicative of a vigorous and growing civil society. She warns us against automatically equating quantity with quality, especially of a healthy civil society as most people would conceptualize it. Most of these NGOs counted are quasi-companies or for-profit concerns, not grassroots organizations, which are self-funded and bottom-up in motive. The NGOs that do exist to articulate the interests of their members, whether of business interests, political causes, or simple common concerns, are often utterly dependent on foreign funding and direction. Since Communism, Romania has lacked the resources and the traditions of philanthropy. Yet, Pralong finds positive signs in this large NGO growth. What does it represent?

Instead of localized cooperation among free and equal, civic-minded persons and groups working together to discuss and possibly resolve public issues, as envisioned by Alexis de Tocqueville, market-oriented associations have emerged among the nonforeign dependent NGOs, as envisioned by Hegel. Pralong argues, "Tocqueville's view is not (yet) an appropriate framework for post-Communist Romania. Romania's voluntary associations belong, in fact, to a subsegment of the market rather than to the sphere of civil society proper." Unlike in Poland, the Czech Republic, or Hungary, virtually no organized civil society existed in Romania prior to 1989. NGOs initially sprang up more or less in response to available Western funding, as transnational flows, international assistance, and generous tax loopholes for for-profit companies have helped create a "market," which has facilitated the emergence of an NGO sector. Its workers have received higher wages, which bolsters the private sector, but leaves the bureaucratic "dead wood" or worse, the corrupt officials, in place. Formal NGOs staffed by salaried workers remain the backbone of Romania's "civil society." Less than 16 percent of Romanian NGOs actually work with volunteers, she notes, while some 62 percent employ salaried workers. In fact, the NGO sector has relatively more salaried employees than many traditional sectors of the economy, including radio and telecommunications as well as oil and gas processing. Furthermore, many NGOs are mere fronts for thriving black-market businesses, profiting from tax deductions granted to for-profit NGOs. Still others constitute what Pralong calls "political frauds."

The most positive role of the NGO sector has been as social "leapfrogging" agents. Some of the most progressive social causes would not have been put on the political agenda without NGO dissemination of information on issues like women's and children's rights, consumer protection, and environmental safety. She hopes that, as ownership spreads and enlightened self-interest becomes legitimate and pervasive in civil society, the market-oriented, associative sector idealized by Hegel may evolve into the democratic civil society of Tocqueville.

In "Multiculturalism and Ethnic Relations in Transylvania," Claude Karnoouh examines Hungarian–Romanian interethnic relations in the context of the controversial proposal to create an independent, mono-lingual Hungarian University at Cluj. Noting that the concept of "multiculturalism" is derived from countries where immigration has founded the society (such as the United States), Karnoouh questions its appropriateness in Eastern Europe, where various ethnic groups are more insular, historically rooted, and nationalistic. East European interethnic relations are better characterized by "inter" culturalism, not "multi" culturalism, with the Latin prefix *inter* denoting the symbiotic interaction between cultures which remain, at the same time, separate and distinct. Karnoouh warns, "To try to treat [ethnic identity] through multiculturalism is, at a minimum, to condemn it to its disappearance."

He endorses the group rights of ethnic groups as communities, rather than the "multicultural" system of the United States, with its emphasis on individual rights and a common culture based on conformity to a market-based identity. Karnoouh argues that the blind obeisance of Romanian intellectual toward Western cultural mores and norms reflects their unquestioned faith that pluralism can adapt to the uncertain transitions in intercultural societies where ethnicity is close to an unalterable identity, only reinforced by a postmodernity without much in the way of competing dogmas or religious inspiration. That is, Romanian and Hungarian ethnic groups need their separate spheres guaranteed by rights protected by the state. Otherwise, they will be assimilated by Western or Romanian culture, or produce a violent backlash against assimilation.

The chapter by Zoltan Barany, "Romani Marginality and Politics," analyzes the mixed socioeconomic and political progress which the Romanian Roma—the most marginalized ethnic minority in Romania—have made since the fall of Communism. He examines contemporary interethnic relations in postsocialist Romania, the process of Romani political mobilization, and policies toward the Roma. "There is hardly any media discussion of Romani culture, history, and accomplishments, and nearly every media portrayal of them is a negative one." Considerable interethnic tensions between Roma on the one hand and Hungarians and Romanians on the other remain in persistent patterns of social and residential segregation, discrimination, and random violence. Educational levels remain low and poverty high. While Romanian law currently provides for one guaranteed seat in parliament for the Roma, its political participation is very low. Institutions like the Department of Protection National Minorities and the National Office for Roma remain understaffed and without the resources to significantly aid the Roma in overcoming their marginalization within Romanian society. He notes, "The government has clearly become more aware of the Roma's intensifying problems, although the lack of financial resources has meant that only minimal substantive changes could occur in the Roma's condition." Romanian politicians have not recognized that successful European integration requires resources for improved state–minority relations.

Sabrina P. Ramet evaluates church–state relations, especially regarding the dominant, Romanian Orthodox Church, which was thoroughly co-opted by the state during the Ceauşescu era and has gained a relatively privileged position in the politics of post-Communist Romania. This lack of separation of church and state has inhibited the autonomy, differentiation, and secularization of democratic political development.

During the Ceauşescu era, the Romanian Orthodox Church, in exchange for supporting the regime and collaborating with the *Securitate*, benefited from the suppression of rival faiths and the transfer of 2,500 church buildings owned by the Greek-Rite Catholic Church to the Romanian Orthodox Church. Some current religious problems stem from the legacy of this collaboration, including ignoring demands of Eastern-Rite Catholics for the return of properties confiscated from them by Communist authorities and other tensions between the Greek-Rite Catholic Church and the Orthodox Church, religious intolerance within Romanian society, and in the refusal to enact a law protecting freedom of religious association, a universal human right that Romania is legally bound to honor under both European and United Nations human rights conventions.

During post-Communism, the church has embraced the coalition and president in power—first with Iliescu and his appointed government and then with Constantinescu and his—and has used its considerable new political clout, based in part on public opinion's high confidence in the Church, second only to the army as highest of all, to impede efforts by less privileged denominations to obtain compensation for confiscated properties or guarantees of rights of proselytization. As the self-professed bearer of Romanian national identity, culture, and tradition, the Romanian Orthodox Church inhibits liberalization and has fanned religious, sexual, and ethnic intolerance. As one of the five pillars of liberalism, according to Ramet, tolerance needs to be promoted instead of being suppressed because it is antithetical to the social thought of the Orthodox Church. Nevertheless, the Orthodox Church extended an invitation to Pope John Paul II in 1998, resulting in the first visit of a Roman Catholic leader to an Orthodox country for fifteen centuries. However, the Church has weighed in on social concerns like opposing decriminalizing homosexuality, suppressing Protestant evangelism, and other "tools of Satan." Thus, Ramet concludes, "The hierarchy of the Romanian Orthodox Church [is] acting in a way injurious to the development of a stable and functioning liberal democracy in Romania."

Next, Mihaela Miroiu and Liliana Popescu's "Post-Totalitarian Pre-Feminism" argues that the primary obstacle to women's equality in Romania is the revival of traditional, rural patriarchical values in the aftermath of Communism. The most important feminist demands—the rights to vote, to equal pay for equal work, to an abortion—were achieved under Communism, and thus were, along with the larger feminist project, largely discredited with Communism. Because they were preached from the top-down, rather than stemming from a grassroots feminist movement proceeding from and supported by civil society, feminist values have never really been acknowledged and internalized by citizens.

Women make up a disproportionate number of "unpaid family workers" in the largely low-wage, agricultural sector, and are driven by a "survivor mentality" without much political participation and gender equality. "For these women," Miroiu and Popescu note, "the problem of human rights is just a city business they hear of on television." Even women-oriented NGOs have internalized these traditional values. Instead of gender awareness, they focus on family charity and support for women in traditional roles, rather than emancipating them.

They argue that a feminist movement along Western lines is unlikely to develop because women share the bias of Romanian society toward accepting paternalist protection of authoritarian institutions, rather than asserting their rights and liberties in democratic ones. The larger liberal dimension, as they put it, remains the "great absent" from the landscape. Any feminist movement that might tentatively take root will ultimately share the same fate of the larger liberal project, which has thus far stalled in Romania.

Mihnea Ion Năstase, in "Gay and Lesbian Rights," explores the legal issues of homosexuality, focusing on the disparity between current Romanian laws and policies, which had criminalized homosexual behavior, and the international laws monitored by human rights NGOs and the Council of Europe, which forbid gender preference discrimination. The political push and pull within the Romanian parliament reflects the conflicting agendas of the Romanian Orthodox Church and some other churches and other traditional, anti-homosexual constituents, including many Christian Democrats and other parties on the one hand, and the advocacy of more progressive elements such as liberal politicians, human rights groups abroad and in Romania, and the West European states, on the other.

Năstase specifically evaluates how Article 200 of the criminal code, which used to criminalize homosexual behavior, posed a problem for Romania's candidacy for entry to the EU, as well as its current good standing within the Council of Europe. Romania was the only state seeking entry into the EU with a law that criminalized consensual gay activity. The Constantinescu presidency recommended legislative reform, but the legislature did not enact it. In recent years, there has been less persecution in practice than before, when dozens of gays were imprisoned. However, with the new Iliescu presidency and a small liberal opposition, the repeal of Article 200 finally occurred, though threats of gay persecution continue. This ongoing controversy, where the new law is not accepted in practice, has illuminated the fault line between the liberal culture of Western Europe and the more traditional Orthodox culture, and the large distance to "join Europe" institutionally, culturally, and socially. Năstase concludes, "By stating that the law, while remaining 'formally' on the books, is not actually *enforced*, the government straddled the metaphorical fence."

Finally, Sorin Antohi, in "Higher Education and the Post-Communist Generation of Students," analyzes contemporary Romanian academia, which atrophied under forty-five years of Communist purges and politicization of research, which was largely segregated in nonuniversity institutes. He notes that, in the 1990s, Romania-based authors were then still nearly absent from global academic debates, other than Ovidiu Trăsnea, former vice president of the International Political Science Association, and Pavel Câmpeanu of Bucharest University. When an author does publish in influential media abroad, then deep criticism of his work may be mobilized when he is unread or unnoticed at home. Romania is almost exclusively represented, analyzed, and interpreted abroad by their Western counterparts. Internally, Romania-based authors are usually preferred in the more nationalistic, academic circles, which maintain that Romania is misunderstood by foreigners who perpetuate Romania's poor image—as if Romanians did not often harbor that same negative view of themselves.

Antohi notes the recent progress that has been made in revitalizing the academic scene. Résumés are replacing party or cadre files, with letters of recommendation and job interviews increasingly resembling Western models. For academic institutions and processes, however, funding and investment is insufficient, except for the lucky few with TEMPUS and USIA grants. Academics must get by on less than $100 per month in wages, though the more enterprising individuals can moonlight by teaching extra courses in private universities and by working as commentators, political consultants, and pollsters, among various entrepreneurial distractions from research and collegial activities. The group cohesion and quality of higher education suffer. One consequence is that primitive, ethnocratic discourses in Romanian letters and social sciences persist. As many talented Romanian academics cannot be bothered to debate those espousing ethnic intolerance, the ideas and research of the latter often go unchallenged. This could change, given Antohi's experience with Romania's talented young students. Unfortunately, most do not see a future for themselves, not only in academia, but even in any Romanian field. As he laments, "Today's Romanian citizen sees her or himself as the victim of ethnic minority threats. He fails to realize that he is the victim of an ingrained nationalist pride which has obliterated all ethnic influences."

PART 4: ECONOMICS AND ENVIRONMENT

In "The New Business Elite: From *Nomenklatura* to Oligarchy," Anneli Ute Gabanyi refutes the illusion fostered at the time that the "revolution" of 1989 replaced the Communist hierarchy in Romania. Most members of this elite have used their insider knowledge, political power, and control over state resources, especially *Securitate* businesses and overseas bank accounts, to *privatize* their personal control over the economy and, increasingly, over the polity by bankrolling a variety of political parties of all ideologies. They have transformed the political domination of the old *nomenklatura* into the economic domination of an oligarchy vis-à-vis society. Because the new oligarchy is entrepreneurial, as well as heterogeneous and fragmented, the gap between the dominant class and society is larger today than it was under Communism. If ever there were a ruling class and a proletariat, it has been under the vanguard of the proletariat. Though not quite a dictatorship, the oligarchy has mastered state domination for personal advantage without respect to law, first under Communism and continuing today.

Oligarchic domination, she contends, is the primary impediment to reform. Despite changes in government personnel, passive but effective resistance to the anticorruption measures inside the bureaucracy and within the governing coalitions has been pervasive. Networks of interlocking political and economic interests support state enterprises and newly privatized industries (usually small and medium sized). A few of the large state enterprises have state-of-the-art technology, though sometimes also benefiting from import controls. Some new high-technology firms utilize Romania's highly skilled electrical and software engineers. On the downside, privatization has been occurring like the proverbial fire sales, for prices that render public assets as private patrimony. Reform stalls in the Romanian mix of corrupt privatization sales; state firms managed for the benefit of the parties placed on its boards and officers, many paying Western salaries (along with insider companies like Gelsor, Inc., run by Sorin Vântul and other ex-*Securitate* capitalists cum political insiders from all parties and interests); or swindles involving "investment" Ponzi schemes, which the government pretends to back, while funds have been embezzled, with Justice Ministers like Valeriu Soica refusing to process extradition requests for fugitives overseas. The stranglehold through misdirected, subsidized credits and extortion and protection schemes creates a crony capitalism without a sultan to oversee the careful distribution of insider access. The transparency and the public accountability which the EU will demand for Romania's entry in 2007 is nowhere evident. Gabanyi predicts that the oligarchy will steadily impoverish the masses while enriching itself, a formula for political extremism. She ends by quoting Stelian Tănase: "The liquidation of this mafia is not only a judicial or moral issue, or an issue for the economy in the narrow sense; it is especially a political issue—and therefore of vital importance for the process of democratization of the Romanian society." Aside from the oligarchy's rule by law, rather than under law, Stalinist economic policies have left Romania in a worse position than most Eastern European countries. This makes the oligarchy even more advantaged, but desperate for privileged positions, rather than competing in the private sector.

Wally Bacon's study, "Economic Reform," evaluates the relative progress made in micro-privatization and the delays in macro. The seeming inability of all post-Communist governments to make any substantial headway in large-scale privatization, except in the most venal way, has not been accompanied by stricter control of uneconomic subsidies to white elephant state enterprises, to say nothing of credits that show no signs of productive investment and no repayment from the cash flow generated. Monetization of Romania's *leu* results directly from such nonrecurring loans and banks without any oversight. Inter-enterprise arrears, at best, accumulate or, at worst, disappear without a trace.

Saddled with enormous, centralized, and insolvent large-state enterprises, and the concomitant large number of employees and vested interests threatened by their closures, the financially and politically weak post-Communist governments have rarely been willing or able to privatize state firms. Bacon describes a "vicious circle" whereby the privatization of banking is problematic due to high ratios of nonperforming loans, which result from failed privatizations and growing inter-enterprise arrears in larger state-owned or formerly state-owned businesses. They, in turn, cannot be liquidated due to the political considerations of the ruling class, and the dire needs of many employees who would be laid off. This gridlock is broken only by the occasional intervention of the World Bank and the International Monetary Fund, which periodically withhold loan and credit *tranches* on which the Romanian economy is dependent. Bacon concludes by noting that public opinion is showing the strain. A CURS poll found that "Eighty-two percent of those polled thought the privatization process was dishonest. Significantly, majorities also endorsed state control of prices and wages, in addition to state ownership of public utilities."

Daniel Dăianu's chapter on "Fiscal and Monetary Policies" argues that the strain which current liberalization efforts have had on unprivatized or underdeveloped institutions explains the stop–go policies, boom and bust cycles, and setbacks and inconsistencies in the painful transition to free market economics. Political pressures have generated massive fiscal and monetary deficits, leading to inflation and delayed economic liberalization. Dăianu suggests that this "shell game" cannot go on forever. The recurring credit crises over which successive governments have presided will elicit more pressure from international creditors. He calls for greater and transparent privatization and rational fiscal and monetary policies, which will hopefully attract foreign capital, alleviate illiquidity, and halt monetization. He admonishes, "Unless financial discipline is imposed on the budget process, the pressure on the central bank, and on the banking sector in general, will become a constant feature of the way the system functions. This will also proliferate into wide-ranging rent-seeking and demand for cheap credit. Here one sees the combination of the pressure exerted by those who cannot pay at the new relative prices with that of those who do not wish to pay for 'it pays not to pay' (the moral hazard issue)."

Larry S. Bush's chapter on "Trade Unions and Labor Relations" reviews the progress made since 1989 toward establishing a viable labor movement and the nascent structures for tripartite negotiations on the Central European, corporatist model. The first trade confederations broke completely from the Communist stooge unions of the Ceauşescu era and have emerged as the most militant social movement in the country. The first collective bargaining contracts were effected nationally in 1992, and trade unions like *Cartel Alfa*, *Frăţia*, and *Confederaţia Naţionala a Sindicatelor Libere din România* (CNSLR) have been robust ever since on behalf of their members. The mainstream unions are in stark contrast—Bush predicts one that will be finished, by the coal miners, who have used massive violence and never seem to renounce its use explicitly. The formal unions have been models of nonviolent, economic struggle for higher wages, job security, and open organizing. With the assistance and monitoring of union internationals, the Iliescu presidency has been remarkably tolerant of their rapid growth and demands.

Bush recapitulates the cleavages among trade unions, their political interaction with successive governments, and their effect on policy, particularly relating to privatization and wage liberalization. While they have been, up to now, advocates of privatization, the leaderships of these confederations will now have to respond increasingly to the concerns of their members who face job losses as the huge state enterprises are liquidated or sold in the ongoing privation efforts. A key element of future union negotiations and a possible brake on its past support for privatization are union fears that concessions in the short run will not lead to better management leading to higher wages in the long run.

The Romanian form of "corporatism," which was endorsed by Iliescu and which emerged under the Constantinescu presidency in 1997 and the Economic and Social Council, was one of Constantinescu's best achievements. However, the formal mechanisms for tripartite decision making have not yet been transformed into stable, cooperative relationships among union, employer, and government representatives. Completion of the project will be one of the various requirements for EU admission. Plans for a labor code, a pension scheme, and labor administrative tribunals were developed in the last two years of the Constantinescu presidency. He concludes by noting, "Only time will tell whether Romania's trade unions will follow the pattern of many of their Western [European] counterparts and remain strong only in the public sector, or whether they will develop the capacity to unionize workplaces in the private sector" as historically in the U.S.

The final chapter in Part 4, "The Environment in Transition" by Clifford F. Zinnes, evaluates the limited environmental protection during post-Communism. He examines the sources of pollution, its effects on people, livestock, and the environment, as well as the legislation passed and the institutional changes made to ameliorate these problems. Like much of Eastern Europe, the gigantic Stalinist enterprises, which formed the backbone of the Romanian economy, were constructed with little regard for the environment. After the fall of Communism, the government under international donor pressure took steps to try to rectify these problems. Romania established a network of environmental protection agencies in 1990 and the Ministry of Water, Forests, and Environmental Protection in 1992. In the first of two subsequent phases of environmental policy making following Communism, marketization incentives were designed to permit local input into environmental investments and projects with environmental impacts, at the risk that local input might undermine national standards. This effort, Zinnes reports, was not successful, but neither were analogous efforts in the U.S. Since 1998, a third phase of potentially radical shifts in environmental protection included "a reduction in the number of river basin units, the start of a departmental reorganization based on function rather than media, and the development of a sustainable financing mechanism for the environmental protection agencies."

Because of the diffuse sources of air, water, and toxic pollutants, decentralized regulation may be desirable, if minimum national standards of pollution reduction are not threatened. So far, legislation and follow-up regulation have occurred without sufficient public and NGO participation. Underfunding of regulatory enforcement has encouraged noncompliance by firms, which are already under financial strain from some transitional restructuring and which shirk environmental standards to minimize costs. On a more optimistic note, Zinnes finds that "though privatized firms, in seeking profits, could have abused the weak regulatory environment, new evidence suggests that cost minimization and waste reduction incentives have had a dominating effect, and that these firms have proven themselves to be more environmentally friendly than the state enterprises which preceded them." If privatization proceeds with enforcement of environmental standards, Romania's air, water, and toxic problems are more likely to be alleviated because firms best able to control pollution will be the most competitive.

PART 5: SECURITY AND CONCLUSION

Leading the final section, Daniel N. Nelson's chapter on "Romanian Security" analyzes Romania's struggle to formulate a new security policy since Communism. Part of the chapter is devoted Romania's initial failure to gain first-round entry into NATO—the strategies employed, the new policies engendered, and the implications for future policy formulation. Nelson suggests that Romanian foreign policy has been historically based on avoiding isolation, domination by Russia/USSR, and ensuring its internal and external territorial integrity. NATO membership would deter Russian power in the region, as well as alleviate Romania's isolation and foster territorial control from external threats, as well as encourage domestic democratization that could reduce internal instability. Thus, Romania's foreign (and much of domestic) policy during the first decade of the post-Communist era focused primarily on NATO admission.

Because of factors like Romania's improved participation in the economic embargo of the countries in the former Yugoslavia, its offering NATO the use of its airspace in spring 1999, its treaty with Hungary, the manifest desire of all Romanians to join NATO, and its geopolitical advantages, Nelson argues, Romania deserved its invitation in November 2002 to join NATO within two years. Aside from the euphoria and stabilization of Romania's strategic and democratic developments, the entry into NATO has reduced the chance that rightist politicians could advocate autarchy and anti-Western positions, rather than Euro-Atlantic integration. Still, partial renationalization of Romanian foreign and defense policy may be a troublesome scenario with which to contend over the next decade. As Nelson warns, democratization is imperiled if the country finds itself looking for internal and external threats, which would distract from institution-building and foster more centralized decisions. Now is the time for Romanians to reduce such threats, with or without NATO. "Absent robust, collective security organizations with which to abate threats, reliance on the capacities of states and their alliances remains the primary method of ensuring security. Enlargement of both invariably will be sought by states in an insecure world."

Robert Weiner, in "Romanian Bilateral Relations with Russia and Hungary: 1989–2002," reviews Romania's foreign relations with two erstwhile enemies: Russia and Hungary. Romania's failure to conclude a new basic treaty with Russia in the aftermath of the 1991 treaty with the USSR and its subsequent collapse resulted in part from issues like reparations demanded for the alleged Romanian treasure stolen by the Russians during World War II, the secessionist conflict in Transnistria, the unresolved demands for revision of the Molotov–Ribbentrop Pact of 1939, and the return of some of the territories taken during World War II in Bessarabia and Northern Bukovina. Nationalist opposition in the Romanian parliament stokes these issues, even though Romanian public opinion has no stomach for a war to resolve these matters.

Though Russia opposes NATO expansion and still considers the Balkans as part of its sphere of influence, Moscow has not opposed Romania's entry into NATO or the EU at present. By the same token, Romania has deferred to Russian security and economic interests in Transcaucasia, implicitly tolerating the suppression of rebels in Dagestan and Chechnya, so that Russia can maintain its boundaries and secure a route for oil and gas pipelines from the Caspian basin. Weiner warns that, with its myriad outstanding (and potential) conflicts of interest with Russia, Romania's lack of a basic treaty could have contributed to the delay of Romania's admission to NATO, which required that potential members resolve any outstanding differences they may have with their neighbors by treaty prior to admission.

Unlike those with Russia, Romania's relations with Hungary have improved somewhat over the past decade, propelled by the desire on the part of both countries to join NATO, which led them to conclude a basic treaty in 1996. Weiner discusses the somewhat thorny issue of ethnic relations in the context of the treaty, such as Romanian fears of legitimation of the collective rights of its Hungarian minority, which could be used to justify demands for territorial autonomy in Transylvania. This issue was put in abeyance after West European countries themselves were frightened by demands for autonomy in their own countries. Weiner also details Romanian–Hungarian progress in security, such as the "Open Skies" agreement concluded in 1991, the creation of a joint peacekeeping battalion in 1998, and the unprecedented decision by the Romanian government to allow Hungarian troops to cross its territory to reach Kosovo during the eleven-week war in the spring of 1999. Weiner notes that many of Romania's cooperative efforts with Hungary were the result of its desire to join NATO and pressure from the West. However, the NATO intervention offered an unsettling precedent for resolution of a potential conflict in Transylvania for Romanians worried that the ethnic Hungarian minority in the Serb province of Vojvodina might also seek secession to join Hungary. Most disturbing, of course, was that Romania's initial candidacy for NATO membership was rejected, while Hungary's was accepted. This did not renew the rift between the two powers, because

Romania did not stray from its NATO-oriented foreign policy. Functional relations with Hungary made cooperation the preferred course. By 1998, "commercial trade between Romania and Hungary was about $704.5 million, actually larger than its trade with Russia."

Next, Dennis Deletant, in "The Security Services since 1989: Turning over a New Leaf," evaluates the extent to which democratic accountability has been introduced to the Romanian security services, the true litmus test of Romania's commitment to break with its Communist past. He presents the array of security services which have succeeded the *Securitate* and other agencies, and briefly surveys the degree of accountability introduced to their heirs, such as SRI, UM 0215, and SPP. Many of these services, Deletant finds, were formed around the nucleus of a former *Securitate* directorate or unit, or an analogous Communist-era intelligence agency, like presidential protection and foreign intelligence. As under Communism, many have become "intelligence industries," engaging in commerce, as well as spying, as opposed to focusing on the analysis of real security threats at home and abroad. The *Securitate*, far from having been eliminated by the Revolution of 1989, was partly purged, but mostly integrated into the new, evolving system of government and effectively legitimized. He discusses the lack of prosecution of former *Securitate* officers, their membership in the new agencies, some of the abuses of power they have committed, the lack of a credible system of judicial supervision, and the attempts by parliament to bring them under its control. Particularly interesting is his description of the use of the security services for politically partisan purposes, as occurred between Roman and Iliescu in the early 1990s and has continued under current Prime Minister Adrian Năstase.

Deletant notes that the files and dossiers left over from the former *Securitate* leave a constant threat of political blackmail hanging over the politicians in the parliament, who are expected to enforce democratic accountability under a new security regime. Deletant observes, "It is now up to the Romanian parliament to use the legislation at its disposal to enforce that accountability." He then rhetorically asks, "Will it have the political will to do this effectively? Or will the skeletons in the closet of many of its members make them wary of monitoring these new state security bodies?" Unfortunately his answer is "no" to the first and "yes" to the second.

In the final chapter on security, "Civil-Military Relations: Continuity or Exceptionalism?" Larry L. Watts argues that Romanian government relations with the army during Iliescu's first two terms ought to be emulated by most post-Communist states. The reason is that the army was trained to be independent of foreign powers under Communism after Soviet troops withdrew in the 1960s. The Romanian military is exceptional in the degree to which it has managed to steer clear of politics during the democratic transition. He attributes this to characteristics embedded in the military from the Communist era, the most important of which has been its legacy of nonintervention against the domestic population, which created a situation in which the military was not viewed as a threat by the general population, the newly elected governments, or the various opposition parties. This became evident when the army, after the December 1989 killings in Timişoara, refrained from shooting civilians.

During the first six years of post-Communism under President Iliescu, the army hierarchy was always consulted so that the assumption of civilian supremacy was not rushed until civilians had developed the capability to develop strategy. He attributes this success in part to the establishment of a military science academy, where dozens of important officials and legislators have learned how militaries operate. Unfortunately, according to Watts, this pattern was partly reversed under the Constantinescu presidency, when Defense Minister Victor Babiuc managed the army as part of his political intrigues, where promotions were made for lower-ranking officers on political criteria, and where the army was mobilized to stop an economic crisis involving the miners in January 1999. Watts argues that Constantinesu did not understand that the norms of a "civil army" do not include its use against domestic political factions, a misunderstanding which creates the potential for future conflict between the civilian leadership and the military in coming years. He also introduced strains in civil-military relations through the trial of former Defense Minister Victor Stănculescu for killing civilians in December 1989, a charge that the military and many civilians regarded as blatantly political, even though Stănculescu ordered the killings, violated human rights norms against shooting civilians. Ironically, this was the very crime which the army later found so threatening, after the miners had attacked police in January 1999. The army, in our view, wants it both ways.

Watts also criticizes the Western "cookie-cutter" model of military reform in the region, which he insists does not take into account the exceptionalism of Romania's case. He attacks Western demands that Romania impose its version of military reform, which would deny the military a transitional role in security policy making. He observes that, whereas countries like Poland and the Czech Republic, which have insisted on civilian supremacy, have suffered civil-military tensions, Romania, by contrast, had experienced, prior to the Constantinescu administration, relatively smooth civil-military relations and the gradual reduction of authoritarian military prerogatives. Watts argues that the effort of the Constantinescu administration to eliminate all military involvement in policy making (in line with Western advice) was premature. However, Watts concludes, "The military has proven remarkably sophisticated in knowing when to hold back, and when to push, in establishing itself as a reliable partner in Romania's new democracy."

In the "Conclusion," Carey argues that Romania has reached the beginning of the completion of its democratic transition, but still has a long way to go before democracy is consolidated. He outlines the areas that will require improvement before the liberal project is to be completed and a truly democratic society will establish itself. He notes that the country has yet to establish a consensus among elites about what the goals of the democratic transition are and how to proceed, even though EU entry requirements are clear. There has been less democratic learning than that needed for compromise for the sake of the liberal project and the country. Romania lacks accountable and integrated political parties, and legal as well as electoral institutions to ensure accountability and due process. The patrimonial culture has hardly been altered as politics continue to represent, for many, not the art of the possible, but rather the way to wealth.

Carey's assessment suggests that it will take many decades to consolidate democracy in Romania. The most likely scenario is that the country will remain a semidemocracy for many years to come. Moreover, its international "limbo" status may be expected to continue in the near future though the West, because of geopolitical concerns, may embrace a country without the political will to assure the minority rights of Roma and Hungarians. Romania will not be totally irrelevant to the West either. This means that outside pressure for democratic, economic, and military reforms will continue; it will not, however, suffice to bring about the implementation of what only Romanians can do for themselves, no matter what is required of them for NATO and the EU membership.

NOTES

1. Barrington Moore Jr., *Social Origins of Dictatorship and Democracy: Lord and Peasant in the Making of the Modern World* (Boston: Beacon Press, 1996); and Theda Skocpol, *States and Social Revolutions: A Comparative Analysis of France, Russia and China* (Cambridge: Cambridge University Press, 1988).

2. Richard Andrew Hall, "The Uses of Absurdity: The Staged War Theory and the Romanian Revolution of December 1989," in *East European Politics and Societies* 13, no. 3 (Fall 1999), pp. 501–42.

3. Trond Gilberg, *Nationalism and Communism in Romania: The Rise and Fall of Ceauşescu's Personal Dictatorship* (Boulder, CO: Westview Press, 1990); Tom Gallagher, *Romania after Ceauşescu: The Politics of Intolerance* (Edinburgh, UK: Edinburgh University Press, 1995); and Anneli Ute Gabanyi, *Systemwechsel in Rumänien: Von der Revolution zur Transformation* (München: Oldenbourg, 1998).

4. See for example, James H. Madison, *A Lynching in the Heartland: Race and Memory in America* (New York: Palgrave/St. Martin's Press, 2002).

I

ROMANIAN EXCEPTIONALISM?

1

Understanding National Stalinism: Legacies of Ceauşescu's Socialism

Vladimir Tismăneanu

> There is no fortress we Bolsheviks cannot storm.
>
> —Joseph Stalin

> My personal hobby is the building of socialism in Romania.
>
> —Nicolae Ceauşescu, August 1989

Of all the revolutions that took place during the *annus mirabilis* 1989, only the Romanian one was violent. Furthermore, despite its ostensible radicalism and the strong-worded, overblown, antitotalitarian rhetoric of its paragons, the Leninist heritage in Romania has turned out to be more persistent and resilient than in the other countries in Eastern Europe. While the self-described, post-Communists are still peripheral in Romania, the party that ruled until the November 1996 elections, Ion Iliescu's *Partidul Democraţiei Sociale* [*The Party of Social Democracy*], remains dominated by personalities belonging to the "second and third echelon" of the deposed regime. The ideological fervor is, of course, long since exhausted; what remains is a widespread network of vested interests, connections, protections, and, more often than not, fear of change.

This chapter explores the sources of Romania's different path, the extraordinary vitality of the authoritarian mentalities and practices in that country, and the co-mingling of Leninist and Byzantine traditions in a uniquely cynical and manipulative political formation. We will refer to the birth of the Romanian Communist Party (RCP) from the previous socialist movement; its failure to develop and expand a powerful mass base during the interwar period; the political profiles of successive elites; the enduring patterns of conspiracy, sectarianism, intrigue, and vindictiveness that left their imprint on the mindset of various bureaucratic generations; the personalization of power within an increasingly corrupt oligarchy; and the transformation of the party elite into a mafia-style clique dominated by a paranoid despot and his immediate family. That this latter statement is far from hyperbole is born out by Ion Iliescu's analysis of the degeneration of the RCP under Ceauşescu. In his memoirs, Romania's former president, and for many years a member of the top party elite under Nicolae Ceauşescu, admits that by the end of the dictatorship, the RCP had ceased to perform any of the traditional roles of a Leninist regime: mobilization, orientation, and promotion. Instead, Iliescu admits, the gargantuan, oversized party was nothing but a propaganda fiction, a tool for satisfying Ceauşescu's endless hubris:

> Political obtuseness, ignorance and even stupidity, overgrown vanity, arbitrariness, and despotism that for a period of time coexisted with an aggressive and arrogant Narcissism, together with the dogmas and the practices of a system that had already shown its limits, transformed the monopersonal leadership into an immense parody and the source of monumental errors.[1]

Needless to say, Iliescu's self-serving critique of his predecessor sounds more like a neo-Khrushchevite (or better said, Gorbachevite) attempt to attribute the main errors of the Communist regime to the vagaries of an individual like Stalin rather than to the very system that permitted Ceauşescu's erratic policies. But then, how could Iliescu engage in an overall demystification of the political ideology and system, the very existence of which guaranteed his whole political career? In other words, Iliescu's claims to a dissident past notwithstanding, there was no liberal, reform-oriented faction within the RCP. There was no group of individuals whose belief-system and aspirations were informed by the logic of Marxist revisionism.[2] At best, there were private conversations in which individuals were deploring certain "exaggerations" and "distortions" of the regime. This is not to say that every member of the party elite, especially in the 1970s, was fully supporting Ceauşescu's obsessions. We know for sure that, in the late 1970s, certain important figures were considering different options (including political murder) to get rid of the increasingly obnoxious tyrant. The most significant among them was Vasile Patilineţ, a former Central Committee secretary in charge of the *Securitate* and the army (between 1965 and 1970), and later, the ambassador to Turkey (where he died in a suspicious car accident in the early 1980s).[3] Neither Patilineţ nor the later authors of the "Letter of the Six" (March 1989) ever considered a fundamental overthrow of the existing system as their preferred path of action. They despaired over Ceauşescu's follies of grandeur, but not over the system's inherent and insurmountable irrationality. While they were bitter critics of the personal dictatorship, they never questioned the legitimacy of the party's monopoly on power.

Be that as it may, the RCP—which was, with its almost 4 million members, perhaps the largest party, in proportional terms, in the world—disappeared almost overnight on 22 December 1989. The chants of "*ole, ole, Ceauşescu nu mai e*" marked not only the end of the bicephalous dictatorship, but also the irresistible and irrevocable demise of the seventy-eight-year-old RCP. When Nicolae and Elena Ceauşescu fled the Central Committee building by helicopter and the enraged masses stormed the party headquarters, it seemed that a whole chapter of history was over and that Romanians would eventually get out of the asphyxiating totalitarian order in which they had been living for more than four decades.

This chapter tries to capture the saga of Romanian Communism: its metamorphoses and whereabouts; its vicious, factious struggles; and the never-consummated hatred, envies, and vendettas between shifting coalitions that explain the continuation of Stalinist patterns of domination for so many years, including since 1989. Herein, we visit certain telltale biographies and examine the political careers of certain individuals whose role in the establishment of the Communist regime, as well as its perpetuation, was paramount. My thesis is that the focus of a political history of any Leninist regime should be on the interaction between biographies, institutions, factions, and the endless struggle for power. Secretive, cliquish, and programmatically deceptive, the decision-making process in this type of organization is the exact opposite of the presumably transparent, consensual, and impersonal procedural systems of democratic polities. For instance, if one does not grasp the role of political thugs and Soviet spies like Pintilie Bodnarenko (Pantiuşa) and Alexandru Nikolsk, their personal connections with Gheorghe Gheorghiu-Dej and members of Dej's entourage, and their contribution to the exercise of political terror in Romania, too little will be understood of the origins of the *Securitate*.[4] Without comprehending of the *Securitate's* role, what would be the meaning of any political analysis of Romanian Communism? Furthermore, as a general rule, orality and informality (i.e., nonrecordability) characterized this power system. There was very little accessible, institutional memory and far too many conflicting personal views of what the past had been about. The leaders brought to the top during Ceauşescu's last decade in power knew almost nothing about Dej, Ana Pauker, and Iosif Chişinevschi. Even somebody like Dumitru Popescu, the chief ideologue of the RCP during the 1970s, is extremely vague in his memoirs in trying to define the nature of interpersonal relations in Dej's Politburo.[5] Likewise, as A. James McAdams poignantly noted about the interviews with former German Democratic Republic (GDR) potentates:

> . . . one of the most interesting findings is how little most policy-makers, including many members of the SED's (Socialist Unity Party) highest circles, actually knew about the most important events and controversies of the East German past. Politically significant information was restricted to very few people. At Politburo meetings, leaders discussed very little of substance. Important decisions were frequently made by two or three individuals walking in the woods on a weekend, and expertise rarely played a major role.[6]

MESSIANIC PRETENSE AND PARIAH COMMUNISM

The sudden and violent collapse of the Ceauşescu regime, and with it the whole Communist institutional infrastructure, could have been anticipated. Some authors detected the increased chasm between the ruling clique and the party rank-and-file. There were also signs of discontent within the elite, which indicated anxiety and panic within its ranks rather than the coalescence of potential successor groups. A Bulgarian-style, intraparty coup resulting in the nonviolent ouster of the *lider maximo* was thus unthinkable in Romania. The reasons for this situation were threefold. First, there was the uniqueness of Ceauşescu's monopolization of political authority and power. Second, there was an absence of even minimally credible, reform-oriented groups and/or individuals among the top elite, which included Prime Minister Constantin Dăscălescu, his predecessor Ilie Verdeţ, and even former Foreign Minister Ştefan Andrei—men who were hardly the equivalent of a Petar Mladenov, Todor Zhivkov's successor as Bulgarian Communist Party leader. They had all participated in the cultic pageants, praised Ceauşescu to the sky, and endorsed his vagaries. As a matter of fact, even applying the term elite would be too generous a compliment to bestow upon a group of scared, humiliated, and slavishly obsequious individuals who were unable to envision, let alone to undertake, any action against the ruling clan.[7] Third, the impact of the Soviet changes during the *pereistroika* period were experienced less powerfully in increasingly isolated Romania than in traditionally Soviet-echoing Bulgaria. In other words, whereas Bulgarian Communist elites had always derived their legitimacy from their unflinching solidarity with Moscow, the Romanians (especially after the 1964 "divorce" from the Kremlin) founded their domestic and international prestige on being different from, and even challenging, the Russians.

The economic and social conditions were, of course, catastrophic in Romania at the end of the Ceauşescu regime. A widespread atmosphere of *fin-de-règne* was imbued with a sense of hopelessness, corruption, and universal fear. However, while discontent was rampant, it seemed that Ceauşescu managed to keep strict control over the country in general, nipping in the bud any form of dissent and resistance. His cult was unique in its absurdity and shallowness. Dedicated to an experiment in dynastic socialism, Ceauşescu surrounded himself with sycophants, many of whom were recruited from his own extended family. This "familialization of socialism" (a term coined by Ken Jowitt in his pathbreaking analyses of "neo-traditionalism") speeded up during the 1980s.[8] We need to explain how and why this unique experiment in dynastic Communism was possible. What characteristics of political values, style, and mentalities within the Romanian Communist elite made possible Ceauşescu's absolutism and his pharaoh-like cult of personality, and the ultimately grotesque outgrowths of what Belu Zilber, an extremely controversial survivor of the Pătrășcanu show trial, called "the monarchy of dialectical right."[9] To understand these dynamics, one has to look beyond visible sociological structures, and ponder the less manifest psychological components of a given political culture. In this case, we will have to search for the interplay of Leninist and Byzantine symbols, values, and styles in the making of Romania's Communist power elite. We should, thus, focus on certain emblematic biographies that highlight the main tensions in the political history of the RCP: the clash between home-Communists and Muscovites, the enduring persecution of the intellectuals, the elimination of any Marxist revisionism, and the combination of crypto-fascist and Stalinist beliefs, especially during the last stage of Ceaușescuism. The model in this case is, of course, Robert C. Tucker's masterful studies on Stalin and on Leninist political culture.[10]

At a time when other Soviet-style regimes had embarked on more or less radical reforms, and when the politics of *glasnost* proclaimed by Mikhail Gorbachev had threatened to contaminate and destabilize the long slumbering East European elites, the Romanian regime behaved in an eccentric way, asserting its willingness to abide by a strange vision of socialism that blended Stalinist tenets and romantic-nativist, ethnocentric nostalgias in a uniquely Baroque construct. On the one hand, Ceaușescu emphasized the party's monopoly on power, the need to preserve collective property over the means of production, and the historical competition with the capitalist West. On the other, his rhetoric was unabashedly chauvinistic, anti-Hungarian, and obsessed with the need to establish a perfectly "homogenous" ethnic community. Programmatically self-enclosed and suspicious of domestic liberalization, Ceaușescu's system had displayed an unprecedented contempt for its own subjects. The *conducător* and his underlings had succeeded in erecting a self-styled version of socialism, with repressive features that allowed many Romania-watchers to reach the most pessimistic conclusions about her future. It seemed that, in the heart of Europe, an attempt was undertaken to establish a *sui generis* form of Asiatic despotism, where the political state, as Karl Marx noted, was "nothing but the personal caprice of a single individual."[11]

The plight of the Romanians under Ceaușescu's dictatorship was acknowledged and deplored in both East and West. For instance, on 1 February 1988, independent activists from Czechoslovakia, Hungary, Poland, and the GDR demonstrated in solidarity with the victims of Ceaușescu's tyranny. Their action was a response to an appeal issued one month earlier by the Czechoslovak human rights group, Charter 77. According to the Chartists:

> Just as peace and freedom in Europe are the common and indivisible cause of all Europeans, so is what goes on in Romania the common concern of us all. Just as he who is indifferent to the lack of freedom of his neighbor and fellow citizen can only enjoy doubtful freedom himself, so must his feeling of warmth and his sense of light remain doubtful if he combines them with indifference to the cold and darkness in which his less fortunate neighbors are consigned to live.[12]

Several months later, the often restrained *Economist* published an editorial urging the West to treat Ceauşescu as a pariah of the international community:

> . . . Romania's dictator does have one exploitable weakness: huge vanity. He longs for flattery in the big wide world. Insult this vanity—by vocal condemnation and ridicule at the United Nations and other international gatherings—and Western countries might just prevent a lot of senseless destruction in Romania. Noisy protests could slow down systematization (the razing of half of Romania's 15,000 villages—VT) until, with a bit of luck, the death of Romania's seventy-year-old sick despot made the whole idea a dismal and surreal memory.[13]

In a similar vein, commenting on Ceauşescu's mania for grandiose buildings, Daniel Chirot predicted that the huge edifices erected to please the *conducator's* Mussolini-like, architectural taste would remain as "a monument to the catastrophe that one unconstrained mad-man can inflict on society, a living reminder of the 'Epoch of Gold, the Epoch of Ceauşescu.'"[14]

There is a growing tendency nowadays to dismiss the Romanian experiment in autocracy as an historical anomaly, irrelevant to the general development of Soviet-style regimes. However, the truth is that Ceauşescu did nothing but exacerbate and carry to the utmost extremes certain characteristics of the Stalinist political culture within the peculiar conditions of Romania. It is important, therefore, to go beyond the mere blaming of the late leader and try to fathom the inner logic of Romanian Communist history. After all, Nicolae Ceauşescu was part and parcel of a political family, not only with its own memories, settling of accounts, and frustrations, but also with romantic dreams, hopes, and expectations.[15] Before being selected as general secretary in March 1965, he had made a successful-enough career within the Communist bureaucracy to succeed one of Eastern Europe's most skillful Communist maneuverers, Gheorghe Gheorghiu-Dej. A number of books have come out in Romania in which Ceauşescu's former Politburo colleagues and rivals admit his unique capacity for dissembling, pseudo-modesty, and initially unthreatening behavior.[16] It is important to note, however, that these interviews and memoirs are impregnated with nostalgia for Dej's times, and rarely reveal any repentance or remorse (including for Silviu Brucan's memoirs, as well). When he succeeded Dej in 1965, Ceauşescu was not a greenhorn in the world of Communist stabs-in-the-back and merciless intrigues: In the late 1940s, he had studied in Moscow, later he witnessed Khrushchev's virulent anti-Stalin speeches at the 22nd CPSU Congress (1961), and he frequently visited China, North Korea, and Yugoslavia. It is true that Dej did not expect his demise to come so soon and so fast, but it is also true that among all his Politburo colleagues, Ceauşescu had the most palpably Leninist credentials to aspire to inherit Dej's mantle. He was disciplined, obedient, cautious, and self-effacing. His prospects were presciently observed by Ghiţă

Ionescu, the secretary in charge of cadres in 1964 (one year before Dej's death), who identified Ceauşescu as the most likely successor to Dej. Like Stalin during 1923–1924, he was the symbol of the apparatus and the guarantor of the group's chances to enjoy accelerated social mobility by getting rid of party old-timers.[17]

My thesis is that Ceauşescu and his cult were less of an aberration than they appeared to external observers. The phenomenon has to be analyzed in the light of such concepts as power, authority, and legitimacy. As Jowitt has shown, the Romanian Communist political culture could never fully overcome its pariah genealogy: during the clandestine times, prior to World War II, the party elite had little understanding of the predominant, Romanian national values and aspirations. The party championed ideas and slogans with minimal impact on the class it claimed to represent, portrayed Romania as a "multinational imperialist country," and advocated the dismemberment of the Romanian nation-state as it had been formed after the Versailles and Trianon treaties of 1919–20. The RCP endorsed Russian territorial claims on Bessarabia and Northern Bukovina and failed, therefore, to stir responsive chords within Romania's urban proletariat or radical intelligentsia (who were overwhelmingly attracted by the extreme right).[18] Without a mass base, dominated by foreign cadres, fractured and pathetically impotent, the RCP was treated in a most humiliating way by the COMINTERN. This patronizing behavior on the part of Moscow further enhanced its pariah psychology and the excruciating inferiority complex of the cadres. Thus, anti-Soviet outbursts associated with Dej's last years and Ceauşescu's twenty-four-year rule have to be analyzed against the history of the Soviet domination of Romanian Communism. In any other East Central European Communist Party, it would have been much more difficult for Ceauşescu to amass the same amount of absolute power.

ANTI-SOVIET STALINISTS

Ceauşescu's success within the Romanian Communist elite, and his victory in the political struggles with his rivals that followed Gheorghiu-Dej's death in March 1965, was foreshadowed, predetermined, and facilitated by the party's history of unmitigated commitment to the exclusive logic of Stalinism. Generations of Romanian Communists had treated their nation as a maneuvering mass. With the exception of Enver Hoxha's Albania, Romania was the only country in Eastern Europe to have shunned the shockwaves of Khrushchev's denunciation of Stalin's cult[19] at the 20th Congress of the Communist Party of the Soviet Union. This is particularly symptomatic if we consider that between 1948 and 1956, the Romanians had been the host country for the COMINFORM and its weekly journal, *For a Lasting Peace, For People's Democracy.*

Khrushchev had presumably tested the trustworthiness of the Romanians in the turbulent fall of 1956, when, unlike Hungary or Poland, Romania was spared any significant mass movement for liberalization (this is not to deny or gloss over the significance of student unrest in Bucharest, Cluj, and Timişoara). Moreover, Dej had persuaded the Soviet leaders that Romania was immune to any "bourgeois" or "revisionist virus." In June 1958, based on complex arrangements between the Romanians, the Soviets, and the Yugoslavs, the Soviet army units left Romania.[20] In Khrushchev's mind this was a gesture of goodwill sent to the West, meant to appease those outraged by the news coming from Budapest about the execution of Imre Nagy and other leaders of Hungary's revolutionary government.

But Khrushchev's calculations went wrong. Far from emulating the Soviets in their limited relaxation, the leaders of the Romanian Communists further tightened their grip over society. The Romanian Communists were 100 percent on the Soviet side only on those occasions when Moscow was restoring Stalinist practices. For instance, not only did Dej and his Politburo warmly endorse, and in fact offered logistic support for, the Soviet crushing of the Budapest uprising in 1956, but they used the specter of the "revisionist" danger in order to wage a massive witch-hunt within their own party during 1957–1958, and to initiate new purges of the intelligentsia.[21]

The reprehensible features of the last stage of Ceauşescu's rule should not obscure the cultural and institutional underpinnings of that regime and its structural relationship to the totalitarian traditions of a political formation beset by an overwhelming inferiority complex. This pariah syndrome is perhaps the main key for grasping the hidden meaning of the otherwise wayward conduct of Ceauşescu during the last decade of his reign. Yes, there a paranoid style in Romanian Leninist politics, but its foundations lay in the underdog mentality of the party elite, its problematic national credentials, its long-held subservience to the Kremlin, and its deep distrust of anything smacking of democratization or liberalization. First in Dej's and then in Ceauşescu's personalities (different as they certainly were), one could discover all the characteristics of a political culture obsessed with its questionable heredity. This statement is valid not only in regard to the inordinate concern with Romanian authenticity within the RCP culture, but also, at a more general scale, to the endless fixation on national identity and historical predestination among the non- and often anti-Communist intelligentsia.[22]

Unlike the Bulgarian, Hungarian, Polish, and Yugoslav Leninist parties, the underground RCP was a dramatically peripheral formation, entirely dominated by the COMINTERN apparatus. It managed to achieve national prominence, and to impose its hegemony, only with the direct support of the Soviet Army after the country's occupation in August 1944. This subservience to Moscow, and the worshipping of the Kremlin as the ultimate Mecca of proletarian internationalism, resulted in a complete annihilation of the critical faculties of both top elites and rank-and-file party members. There were exceptions, but they were swiftly marginalized and silenced.[23] The party's claim to legitimacy, therefore, has always been questionable, even after General Secretary Gheorghiu-Dej decided to simulate born-again Romanianism during 1963–64. Of the many Western observers interested in Romania's *Sonderweg*, the emigré historian Georges Haupt suggested that the best interpretation of the break with Khrushchev was that of an inventive, and generally successful, exercise in authority-building by an elite bereft of any political legitimacy.[24] Combined with limited domestic liberalization from above, this distancing from Moscow constituted the ideological mainstay of an increasingly self-confident new wave of party bureaucrats. Ceauşescu's supporters and protégés during the late 1960s were middle-aged apparatchiks who took themselves seriously as exponents of a national managerial class *in statu nascendi*. The elimination of the Stalinist Old Guard offered them long-expected opportunities for upward political mobility. Many of these party and government bureaucrats such as Maxim Berghianu, Janos Fazekaş, Ion Iliescu, Ion Ioniţă, Paul Niculescu-Mizil, Cornel Onescu, Gheorghe Pană, Vasile Patilineţ, Ion Stănescu, and Ilie Verdeţ, identified themselves with the autonomist promises of the first stage of Ceauşescuism, and participated eagerly in the consolidation of the general secretary's personal power. Many of them had worked in the 1950s and early 1960s under his guidance, and few thought that his pledge to enhance collective leadership was more than a temporary device used to get rid of the veteran Stalinists. Later, as Ceauşescu realized that they were aiming to initiate semi-reformist and potentially destabilizing policies, he did an about-face and restored a superannuated, extremely rigid, ideologically dominated leadership pattern. Whatever resembled competence, modernity, rational analysis, or intellectual dignity had to be attacked and humiliated. Provocations were organized to manufacture ideological heresies, sometimes under the most bizarre pretexts, as in the case of the notorious scandal in 1982 against members of an alleged "Transcendental Meditation Sect."

Hence, both in theory and in practice, Ceauşescuism was a desperate attempt by a beleaguered elite to gain domestic authority and international recognition by emphasizing precisely the quality it had most conspicuously lacked for most of its history: national prestige and influence.[25] This is not to say that Ceauşescu had always been unanimously hated or despised. Far from it: During the 1960s and early 1970s, large social segments found themselves stirred and exhilarated by what they saw as Romania's prospects for grandeur, the *conducător's* defiance of the Soviet controls, and the rapprochement with Yugoslavia and the West. How this capital was squandered, and how their commander-in-chief politically emasculated the elite remains a fascinating topic to be further explored. Suffice it to compare the RCP's international status in July 1965 at the Ninth Congress (the first to confirm Ceauşescu's supremacy at the top), and the abysmal international isolation of both party and leader when the Fourteenth Congress convened in November 1989. Boycotted by the Warsaw Pact "brotherly" countries, and an embarrassment to the Western Marxist parties, the RCP Congress could count only on the solidarity of North Korea and certain third world radical movements.[26]

DECREPIT TYRANNY

The xenophobic outbursts of the *conducător*, his romanticization of Romania's archaic past, his passionate identification with mythological Thracian-Dacian chieftains and power-thirsty feudal princes, the fascination with organic corporatism, and the rehabilitation of both militaristic and *volkisch* symbols, all had deeper sources than Ceauşescu's personal psychology: they originated in the RCP's problematic relationship with Romanian cultural traditions and patterns. To understand this, it is enough to look through party documents dating from its clandestine period as well as those from the period when it remained a bulwark of Stalinism: they were marked by a complete rejection of Romanian national values, a deep distrust of the intelligentsia, and even an ignorance of the basic notions of Romanian history. A vulgar materialist interpretation of history was used to demonstrate that Romanians were eager to espouse the cause of the world proletarian revolution. For the Communist doctrinaires, such problems as the country's coming to terms with modernization, and the adoption of Western institutional models, mattered little. They had their universal recipes borrowed from the COMINTERN's arsenal and did not hesitate to impose them on Romania. Later, when the RCP rewrote its own history, and its leaders postured as champions of national values, this patriotic travesty would ensure a gigantic manipulation. The same people who had unswervingly served Soviet interests were the very ones who deplored the loss of national identity. Together with Dej, then even stronger with Ceauşescu, the Romanian Communist political class would dress itself in nationalist clothes, would swear by the tricolor flag, and would sing patriotic anthems to show its commitment to the values of "sovereignty and independence."[27]

With his spasmodic gestures and flaming harangues, Ceauşescu became the embodiment of this impossible change of persona. He tried to combine a residual attachment to Leninist faith with a newly discovered sense of the usefulness of nationalist symbols and demagoguery. Whether he became a true Romanian nationalist or was merely a pragmatic opportunist is still to be assessed. As in the case of Serbia's Slobodan Milošević, there are persuasive arguments for both explanations. The true value for him, however, was personal power. He was ready to sacrifice principles and loyalties, without any reticence, in order to preserve it. By the end of his life, Ceauşescu had nothing to deliver but his hollow rhetoric and hysterical calls for more repression. *A strînge rîndurile*, closing the ranks around the *conducător* became the *leitmotif* of the propaganda warfare against the Romanian population. For all practical purposes, by the end of the 1980s, the RCP was already extinct. What remained was a series of ill-concocted legends and huge gatherings of robot-like individuals mechanically applauding an entranced dictator. Think of the 14th RCP Congress in November 1989: the Berlin Wall had been broken down, Zhivkov had been eliminated by the Mladenov-Dzhurov conspiracy, and Milos Jakes and his team of Soviet-backed puppets had been ousted by the "Velvet Revolution." Yet, Ceaușescu single-mindedly believed in the pageants skillfully engineered by his devoted cheerleaders; or at least they seemed loyal, because among the delegates to the Congress and among the elected members of the last Central Committee figured a man who one month later would be one of the main architects of Ceaușescu's execution: General Victor Atanasie Stănculescu, First Deputy Minister of Armed Forces, and one of Elena Ceaușescu's dear protégés. Indeed, by this time, the writing was on the wall for the Romanian leader and his party. One can only speculate about Stănculescu's real thoughts during the long minutes of thunderous applauds and rhythmic chants: "*Ceaușescu și poporul*" ("Ceaușescu and the people"). But one may think that it was during those moments that he, together with other party and government bureaucrats (including perhaps *Securitate* chief Lt. General Iulian Vlad), realized that Ceaușescu and his clan had no future. They may have understood that, unless something radical was done, a popular uprising would annihilate the much-acclaimed "multilaterally developed socialist society." But nothing was undertaken, and the spontaneous revolt came like a bolt of lightning in Timișoara in mid-December 1989. The RCP, the organization that made possible Ceaușescu's ascent to absolute power, was challenged by a plebeian, nonviolent rebellion that eventually became contagious and spread to other cities, including Bucharest. As the propaganda had proclaimed, the RCP and Ceaușescu were identical. It was perhaps the only true thing in the ocean of mendacity that had flooded the everyday life of the Romanians. Therefore, once Ceaușescu was executed, his party, already a political ghost, disappeared. Later, some died-in-the-wool ex-cadres and sycophants tried to resurrect it and promote the legend of Ceaușescu's heroism, but these were pathetic attempts to revive a political corpse.[28] The RCP was finished, both as an ideological movement and as a mobilizational bureaucracy. This was understood by unrepentant but lucid Leninists like Ion Iliescu and Silviu Brucan, who would form a successor party which pretended to break with all totalitarian traditions: the National Salvation Front. In this they enjoyed the help and know-how of a group of younger Marxist political scientists and sociologists, most of whom had been active in the "Ștefan Gheorghiu" Party Academy and the Center for Military History, under the Ministry of Defense (for many years headed by Lt. General Ilie Ceaușescu, the *conducător's* brother). The most influential among them was Virgil Măgureanu (an old acquaintance of Iliescu's according to the latter's memoir), who became a powerful figure as head of the Romanian Service of Information (SRI). It was only after the Democratic Convention's electoral victory in 1996 that Măgureanu was finally dismissed (in the spring of 1997). Others served in significant executive advisory positions at various stages of the post-Ceaușescu era, such as Vasile Secăreș, Ioan Talpeș, Cornel Codiță, Paul Dobrescu, and Ioan Mircea Pașcu. This demonstrates that, underneath the apparent cleavage and the ostentatious hiatus that separated the demise of the RCP and the rise of the NSF, there was a relative continuity in terms of political elites. The most compromised figures of the *ancien regime* (Emil Bobu, Manea Mănescu, Ion Dincă, and Constantin Dăscălescu) had been sent to prison. The *conducător* and his execrated wife were conveniently executed. But the new power elite did not emerge out of nowhere. It carried with it the memories and loyalties that allowed it to stick together in the ensuing confrontations. Certain relative newcomers, like Petre Roman, were to discover the dangers of political *caudillismo* in the absence of an institutional base.[29] But it is not my objective here to explore the current Romanian situation. It is more important that we look into the behavioral and intellectual patterns of various generations of Communist and post-Communist elites, and discover the continuities, clashes, and affinities, as well as irreducible divergences, which existed among them.

My interpretive paradigm for the extremely personalistic and clientelist dictatorial model embodied by Nicolae Ceaușescu is rooted in political culture: a set of mentalities, attitudes, beliefs, symbols, values, and aspirations that define the political profile of a given group or subgroup at a certain historical moment. I use this term in the sense proposed in Sidney Verba's classical 1965 definition and developed by Robert C. Tucker in his enlightening contributions on the Bolshevik political culture.[30] Within this cultural framework, the causal structure of the insecure Romanian Communist regime, and its inferiority complex, can be depicted. I eschew a rigid, fatalistic determinism that obscures the impact of personalities on events. Rather, I underscore the interplay of the often obscure and subliminal motives of the actors with the motivational networks that stabilized political constellations. Hence, we need to perceive the unsaid and unavowable strata underneath the self-serving discourse of various Romanian Communist personalities in order to explain their commitment to an extremely dogmatic, Stalinist vision of socialism. In other words, both Dej's and Ceaușescu's rules are regarded here as persistent efforts to circumvent the evolution of the Romanian Communist political culture into a post-totalitarian, more permissive configuration in which the party's monopolistic hold on power (the constitutionally enshrined "leading role") would be significantly limited by the orchestrated rise of semi-official and unofficial groups and associations; where the principles of expertise would supplant the increasingly obsolete, "heroic-militant," mobilizational ethos.

I agree with those authors, such as Linz and Stepan, who portray "Ceauşescuism" as more than an excessive variant of personal dictatorship in the mold of Idi Amin Dada or Jean Bedel Bokassa. There were, of course, imperial pageants, hunting parties, collections of jewels, and other elements of megalomania hardly reconcilable with the Stalinist ascetic tenets. But they did not exhaust the nature of the Ceauşescu regime. The truth is that, following Dej's obstinate anti-Khrushchevism, Ceauşescu pursued a policy of constant rejection of any genuine reforms, a line of neo-Stalinist, autarchic retrenchment that included elements of nepotism, kleptocracy, and corruption characteristic of Brezhnevite "neo-traditionalism":

> [Ceauşescuism] was, rather, an expression of a complex of political, social, and economic policies which, taken together, comprised a coherent alternative to the development strategies pursued by other state-socialist regimes in Eastern Europe.[31]

Starting in the late 1950s and evolving in a convoluted and sometimes perplexing way, increasingly self-centered and self-enclosed, Romanian domesticism turned out to be a "conservative" (almost "reactionary") political strategy devised to preserve and enhance precisely those values, symbols, and institutions questioned by the proponents of "socialism with a human face"—from Imre Nagy and Alexander Dubček to Mikhail Gorbachev. Paradoxically, for about fifteen years, between 1964 and 1980, Romania enjoyed the sympathy of both Western governments and democratic socialists.

As one of the most vocal critics of Gorbachevism, Nicolae Ceauşescu emerged in the second half of the 1980s as the champion of an updated version of militant Stalinism. In a bizarre fashion, he seemed intent on reneging on his own advocacy of "creative Marxism" and single-mindedly returning to Stalin's catechistic definitions from *Questions of Leninism*. As we shall see, during 1968–69, Ceauşescu condemned the Soviet intervention in Czechoslovakia and seemed to encourage innovative Marxist approaches. It was in that period that translations into Romanian of Antonio Gramsci, Roger Garaudy, Mikel Dufrenne, Georg Lukacs, Herbert Marcuse, and Louis Althusser were authorized. After 1971, however, Ceauşescu renounced this orientation to embark on a path of radical re-Stalinization.[32] In the late 1980s, as the Soviet Union launched dramatic reforms, he excoriated Gorbachevism as a dangerous "right-wing deviation" within world Communism and proclaimed the vital need to reassert uniformity. He could question the supremacy of Moscow, but he was viscerally opposed to any doubt regarding the ultimate infallibility of the Marxist-Leninist dogma. To an even greater extent than Erich Honecker, Miloš Jakeš, or Todor Zhivkov, Ceauşescu lamented the very impulse to rethink the Marxist-Leninist experience. The same individual who, in 1974, had admitted the obsolescence of the notion of the dictatorship of the proletariat, and who had seemed inclined to favor the Euro-Communist search for an alternative Marxism, was now calling for the reinforcement of repressive institutions and denouncing the transition to pluralism as the restoration of capitalism.[33]

Indeed, in his opposition to Gorbachev's semi-Menshevik, revisionist offensive, Ceauşescu carried to an extreme the logic of national Stalinism.

Among Warsaw Pact leaders, Ceauşescu engaged in the most virulent attack on Gorbachev's reformist program. Speaking in April 1988, he emphasized Romania's alleged priority to the U.S.S.R. in terms of "developing socialist democracy." At the same time, he lambasted the attempts to revise the Marxist-Leninist tenets of what Czeslaw Milosz once called "the New Faith."[34] That his Marxism was a primitive and amazingly anachronistic one is beyond any doubt; but it was precisely this rudimentary and archaic, almost mythical structure of his belief system that made him basically immune to self-doubt or opening to other views. Interestingly enough, Ceauşescu urged other like-minded leaders within international Communism to close ranks and withstand the dangerous attempts at de-Stalinization and democratization:

> We must bear in mind that there are a number of theoretical and practical deviations, both on the right and on the left. Of course, both of them are equally dangerous. . . . However, it is my opinion that the main danger today comes from the rightist deviations, which can seriously harm the socialist construction and the struggle for disarmament, peace and mankind's overall progress.[35]

NATIONAL COMMUNISM AND NATIONAL STALINISM

There is a significant distinction that has to be made between national Communism and national Stalinism. The former appeared as a critical reaction to Soviet imperialism, hegemonic designs, and rigid ideological orthodoxy. It was relatively innovative, flexible, and tolerant of political relaxation. National Communism encouraged intellectual creativity and theoretical heresies. Rejecting the Soviet tutelage, national Communists generally favored revisionist (both moderate and radical) alternatives to the enshrined Stalinist model. The most important exponents of national Communism were Josip Broz Tito and his closest associate Edvard Kardelj, Imre Nagy, Alexander Dubček, Palmiro Togliatti, Enrico Berlinguer, and Santiago Carrillo. For some time after his return to power in 1956, Polish Communist leader Wladyslaw Gomulka appeared as a proponent of this direction. By repudiating universal recipes and theoretical ossification by maintaining the right of each party to pursue its own strategy regardless of the Soviet interests, national Communism included a relatively open-minded and progressive component. It questioned the dogma of the dictatorship of the proletariat and stated that reform, including party reform, was inevitable. In its most advanced forms, it broke with the monotheistic vision of the party's predestined historical role and accepted the principles of political pluralism, including the idea of a genuine multiparty system. For instance, national Communism was the starting point for the Hungarian Revolution of 1956, which completely tore down the Stalinist institutional system.[36]

In contrast, national Stalinism systematically opposed any form of liberalization, let alone democratization. Reactionary and self-centered, it valued autarky and exclusiveness. It adhered to a militaristic vision of both domestic and international settings. National Stalinism clung to a number of presumably universal laws concerning socialist revolution and treated any "deviation" from these as a betrayal of class principles. It voiced political anguishes and played on sentiments of national isolation, humiliation, and panic. It frequently tempted Leninist elites in countries where the pre-Stalinist radical left had been weak or totally nonexistent and/or where the regime's legitimacy had been derived from an external source: Romania, Albania, North Korea, Czechoslovakia after 1968, and the GDR.

In brief, *national Communism was the opposite of national Stalinism.* While national Communism promised regeneration, national Stalinism was a symptom of degeneration. National Communism valued diversity and was potentially pluralistic. National Stalinism was narcissistic and anachronistic; it valued uniformity and exploited tribalistic resentment and allegiances. If we take the case of the former Yugoslavia, we see that Slobodan Milošević, the Serbian strongman, embarked on an unequivocally national Stalinist platform. In more than one respect, it was reminiscent of Ceauşescu's nationalist frenzy: militaristic, tribalistic, collectivistic, and intolerant. Like Ceauşescu, Milošević is more than a gray apparatchik (of course, he knew how to simulate one as long as he was in a subordinate position). He is indeed possessed by the myth of his own predestined mission as a national redeemer. To attain his goals, he needs a totally dedicated following made up of people unreservedly loyal to him. In the words of Aleksa Djilas:

> . . . (w)hile undoubtedly a product of the Yugoslav communist political machine, he lacks the docility and devotion to routine that a true man of the *apparat* should possess. He resembles, rather, a leader of some revolutionary conspiracy who works in secret, surrounded by mystery, and is permanently busy appointing and dismissing members of the central committee.[37]

This contrasts sharply with the Slovene national Communists, who were able to lead their country toward a pluralist polity.

Here, we are dealing with theoretical archetypes: national Communism and national Stalinism can thus "dialectically" coexist, and one leader can be at some times a national Communist while at another time he can move toward national Stalinism (for reasons linked to his personal preferences, but also to international and domestic constraints and challenges). The denouement of national Communism could be a post-Communist order. The goal of national Stalinism was the achievement of the Leninist utopia, even if the price was generalized poverty. As I said, these are descriptions of two ideal types, and mixed situations have occurred more often than not, with Castroism and Maoism being the most significant cases.

In introducing this dichotomy, I am aware of the risks of idealizing national Communism as a "benign" alternative to the Stalinist model. And yet, historically, the transition to pluralism was stimulated by reformist initiatives from within the ruling elites under national Communism. Think of the role of factious struggles between the Natolinian and the Pulawska groups within the fragmentation of the Polish orthodoxy in 1956. Or, in a similar vein, the role played by Imre Nagy and his associates in catalyzing the revolt of the mind in Hungary. National Communist options, although half-hearted and often inconsistent, can be considered "progressive" within the framework of one-party regimes. Within the same political paradigm, national Stalinism appears as "reactionary." Once this paradigm is abolished and the free competition of political forces gathers momentum, the distinction between "socialism with a human face" and national Stalinism presents more than historical interest: the path to democracy from national Stalinism is much more tortuous, if not unbridgeable in the short run. This explains the pathetic irrelevance of Alexander Dubček's originally heretic political views once the Czechs and Slovaks had the chance to exit from the straitjacket of self-limited reforms.

I want to make clear a very important point: This chapter does not offer a conventional historical perspective, but rather a theoretical-cultural one. I am less interested in chronologies and description of policies than in the role of values, beliefs, and interests (individual and social) in shaping political strategies. My goal is to offer a rational interpretation of Ceauşescu's political doctrine and praxis as part and parcel of the Romanian Communist tradition. Nicolae Ceauşescu, a man of immense will and ambition, did indeed imprint his *differentia specifica* on this tradition, modifying it at some critical points. However, what is most important is that the principal features of Romania's Stalinist political culture were not decisively changed by Ceauşescu. The apparent uniqueness and outrageous eccentricity of the Romanian experiment, together with its striking contrast to other Communist regimes, should not obfuscate the preservation of values, attitudes, and options adopted at the party's founding congress in May 1921 and maintained ever since: political voluntarism, sectarianism, radicalism, cult of hierarchy and authority, and scorn for parliamentary democracy and constitutionalism. To be sure, numerous additional attributes were developed and expanded over the years: cleavages within the party's identity and self-definition, fractures, and turning points.

The leading assumption of my approach that in Romania, whether under Gheorghiu-Dej or Ceauşescu, the legacy of radical Stalinism was never thoroughly questioned—and could therefore not be abandoned.[38] It is symptomatic that, although Romania's intelligentsia was one of the most sophisticated in Eastern Europe, and definitely one of the most intimately influenced by French literary and academic standards, it was never contaminated with the French passion for leftist values. In the absence of a social group espousing an egalitarian creed, and without a powerful tradition of working class activism, there was little source of autonomous revisionist initiatives.

Even the student movement that developed in 1956 was primarily committed to the slogans of national awakening rather than to the ones of a free and democratic polity. The student and intellectual unrest in Romania in the summer and fall of 1956 was of a different nature than the humanistic-socialist onslaught on Stalinism in Hungary and Poland. In many respects, its goals coincided with certain points of the emerging nationalist line: the elimination of mandatory Russian language in schools, the withdrawal of Soviet troops from Romania, the renunciation of some of the most egregious industrial investments by the regime, the rehabilitation of major figures of the national culture, the reconsideration of the status of the Hungarian minority, and the launching of a strong "homogenizing" strategy. But the Romanian leaders were not just nationalists. They were first foremost Stalinists, which was demonstrated by their peculiarly Stalinist hostility to any form of private property and their decision to complete the collectivization of agriculture against all odds. In this latter action, Ceaușescu distinguished himself through cruelty, intransigence, and an almost total lack of scruples.

CAN THE HISTORY OF COMMUNISM BE WRITTEN?

Hegel once wrote that the problem of history is the history of the problem. Intellectual history cannot be separated from sociological and psychological approaches. Especially in the field of Communist studies, biographies, interviews, and memoirs matter as much as the official documents. However, as we know so well, no memory is infallible, and this is especially true when we listen to people whose whole life had been plagued by a denial of their most humane sentiments. Survival and success within the Communist elite was not the result of dedication to truth and honesty. Even those who may now repent are still interested in presenting their past as one less sadistic and despicable than that of their erstwhile accomplices. A political history of Romanian Communism has therefore to go beyond the mere description of the stages in the rise and fall of this party movement: We have to grasp the why's. We have to grasp the deep causalities that explain such occurrences as Lucrețiu Pătrășcanu's trial and execution in 1954; the power-sharing arrangements between Pauker and Luca (the Muscovites) and Dej's domestic center (Center of the Prisons); Stalin's role in both Dej's ascent, and, no less significant, in de-legitimizing Ana Pauker's grip on the party elite; and Ceaușescu's rise to power, his first attempts at de-Stalinization, and the later, erratic, and ultimately suicidal choices that led to his fatal experiment in dynastic socialism.

The whereabouts, tribulations, and consequences of Romanian Communism are no less emblematic for twentieth century radicalism than Yugoslav, Czech, or Hungarian ones. In other words, it is important to grant Romanian Communism the thorough and unbiased treatment it deserves. Contemporary developments in that country would look irretrievably nonsensical without such an effort at historical comprehension. In order to understand Ion Iliescu's attachment to his Communist youth ideals, we have to know what those ideals consisted of and why so many people found them so appealing. On the other hand, such a political history cannot be oblivious of the price paid by the Romanians for their Communist utopian experiment. One has to insist on the Romanian Gulag, the Danube–Black Sea canal initiated by Dej and eventually completed as one of Ceauşescu's megalomaniacal projects, the extermination of the whole political class, the destruction of national values, and the persecution of the intelligentsia. One has to mention that, in order to fulfill their Leninist blueprints, Romanian Communists acted ruthlessly. The names of such prisons as Sighet, Jilava, Gherla, Aiud, and Poarta Albă are so many testimonials to the extent of the terror in that country. What I propose here is a less traditional version of political history, one which refuses the anecdotal and event-oriented schemes and which insists on the psycho-biography of the principal actors involved in this murderous drama that came to an end in the carnage of Timişoara and Bucharest in December 1989.

There were enough blameworthy features in Ceauşescu's absurd attempt to build a "multilaterally developed socialist society." Saying this, we have not attained a heuristic vision and fatally condemn our discourse to the level of moral outrage. Hence, the most daunting task is not to deplore the path of Romanian Communism, but rather to seek its political and intellectual roots, to reveal the interplay of national and international variables, and to disclose the unavowed continuities that made it a unique political construct, from the moment of its inception in May 1921 to its inglorious demise in December 1989.

NOTES

1. An earlier version of this essay was originally published in volume 32 of *Communist and Post-Communist Studies* and is reprinted with permission. On this point, see Ion Iliescu, *Reformă şi revoluţie* (Bucharest: *Redacţia publicaţiilor pentru străinatate*, 1993), p. 9. These points had long since been made by Western analysts, primarily Ken Jowitt, Daniel Chirot, and this author. See for instance my article, "Ceauşescu's Socialism," *Problems of Communism* (January–March 1985); for analyses of the turbulent Romanian exit from Communism, see the chapter "The Effects of Totalitarianism-cum-Sultanism on Democratic Transition: Romania," in Juan J. Linz and Alfred Stepan, *Problems of Democratic Transition and Consolidation: Southern Europe, South America, and Post-Communist Europe* (Baltimore and London: Johns

Hopkins University Press, 1996), pp. 344–65; and Vladimir Tismăneanu, "Romanian Exceptionalism? Democracy, Ethnocracy and Uncertain Pluralism in Post-Ceaușescu Romania," in Karen Dawisha and Bruce Parrott, eds., *Politics, Power and the Struggle for Democracy in South-East Europe* (Cambridge and New York: Cambridge University Press, 1997), pp. 403–51.

2. A point admitted by former Ceaușescu opponent, Silviu Brucan. See his book *De la capitalism la socialism și retur. O biografie între două revoluții* (Bucharest: *Editura Nemira*, 1998).

3. Information about the Patilinet conspiracy is from my interview with Mircea Răceanu, (Washington, DC, 19 May 1994). A high-ranking Romanian diplomat, Răceanu was arrested and sentenced to death in 1989. Western pressure forced Ceaușescu to change the sentence to life in prison. After the December 1989 events, Răceanu was released, became active in the democratic opposition to the Iliescu regime, and was forced to leave Romania in 1990. For a lucid analysis of the events of December 1989 and their aftermath, see Nestor Ratesh, *Romania: The Entangled Revolution* (New York: Praeger, 1991).

4. Vladimir Tismăneanu, *Arheologia terorii* (Bucharest: *Editura All*, 1998).

5. Dumitru Popescu, *Am fost și eu cioplitor de cuvinte: Un fost lider comunist se destăinuie* (Bucharest: *Editura Expres*, n.d., probably 1992).

6. A. James McAdams, "GDR Oral History Project," (American Association for the Advancement of Slavic Studies, Newsletter, March 1994), p. 5.

7. Personal interview with former Foreign Minister Ștefan Andrei, (Bucharest, June 1994.) According to Andrei, arguably one of the most intelligent members of Ceaușescu's entourage, the best hope for the *nomenklatura* was to promote Nicu, Ceaușescu's youngest son, as a way of preventing Elena from succeeding her husband at the top of both party and state. Neither Andrei, nor other members of the Political Executive Committee, realized how explosive the situation was in 1989.

8. Ken Jowitt, *New World Disorder: The Leninist Extinction* (Berkeley and Los Angeles: University of California Press, 1992), especially pp. 121–219.

9. Andrei Șerbulescu (Belu Zilber), *Monarhia de drept dialectic* (Bucharest: *Editura Humanitas*, 1991).

10. Robert C. Tucker, *Stalin in Power: The Revolution from Above, 1928–1941* (New York: Norton, 1990).

11. Marx, "Contributions to Hegel's Philosophy of Right," in Robert C. Tucker, (ed.), *The Marx-Engels Reader* (New York and London: Norton, 1978), p. 23.

12. See "Charter 77 Appeals for Solidarity with Romania," *Radio Free Europe Research* (Czechoslovak SR, 21 January 1988), pp. 39–40.

13. "Pogrom in Romania," *The Economist* (London, 3 September 1988), p. 15.

14. Daniel Chirot, "Romania: Ceaușescu's Last Folly," *Dissent* (Summer 1988), p. 275.

15. Pavel Câmpeanu, "*Ceaușescu: Anii numărătorii inverse*," *Revista 22* (Bucharest, 2–8 February 1999).

16. Lavinia Bețea, *Maurer și lumea de ieri: Mărturii despre stalinizarea României* (Arad: *Fundația Culturală "Ion Slavici*," 1995). This book is a striking example of the enduring pro-Dej sentiment among many members of the RCP "Old Guard."

17. Ghiță Ionescu, *Communism in Romānia: 1944–1962* (London and New York: Oxford University Press, 1964), p. 351; Vladimir Tismăneanu, *Fantoma lui Gheorghiu-Dej* (Bucharest: *Editura Univers*, 1995).

18. Z. Ornea, *Anii treizeci: Extrema dreaptă românească* (Bucharest: *Editura Fundaţiei Culturale Române*, 1995).

19. Stelian Tănase, *Elite şi societate: Guvernarea Gheorghiu-Dej* (Bucharest: *Editura Humanitas*, 1998).

20. Sergiu Verona, *Military Occupation and Diplomacy: Soviet Troops in Romania, 1944–1958* (Durham and London: Duke University Press, 1992).

21. For the post-1958 anti-intellectual campaigns, see Stelian Tănase, *Anatomia mistificării, 1944–1989* (Bucharest: Editura Humanitas, 1997).

22. Alexandra Laignel-Lavastine, *Filosofie şi naţionalism: Paradoxul Noica* (Bucharest: *Editura Humanitas*, 1998); Norman Manea, *On Clowns: The Dictator and the Artist* (New York: Grove Weidenfeld, 1992); Katherine Verdey, *National Ideology under Socialism* (Berkeley and Los Angeles: University of California Press, 1991).

23. For instance, the cases of Alexandru Iliescu (Ion's father who died in 1945), Grigore Răceanu, apparently Grigore Preoteasa who, at different moments and with different intensity, questioned the wisdom of the leadership's slavishly toeing the COMINTERN's line. But, as a rule, the party elite valued orthodoxy and discipline as the most precious virtues of a militant. This explains Lucreţiu Pătrăşcanu's failure to break with the party in spite of his intimate knowldge of the criminal methods used by Stalin's secret police to exterminate the RCP's Old Guard during the Soviet Great Purge.

24. Georges Haupt, "*La genese du conflit sovieto-roumain*," *Revue francaise de science politique*, no. 4 (1967).

25. For a comprehensive analysis of the ideological and political underpinnings of the Ceauşescu regime, see Michael Shafir, *Romania: Politics, Economics and Society. Political Stagnation and Simulated Change* (Boulder: Lynne Rienner, 1985).

26. In 1965, the Soviet delegation to the RCP's Ninth Congress was headed by Leonid Brezhnev and the Chinese one by Deng Xiaoping. See *Congresul al IX-lea al Partidului Comunist Român* (Bucharest: *Editura Politică*, 1966).

27. One should thus mention the myth of the "patriotic faction" (*gruparea naţională*) used by former Communist leaders (Alexandru Bârlădeanu, Paul Niculescu-Mizil) to foster the image of radical discontinuity between the early Stalinist stage and the post-1960 developments. See Lucian Boia, "Un mit Gheorghiu-Dej?" in Lucian Boia, ed., *Miturile comunismului românesc* (Bucharest: *Editura Humanitas*, 1998), pp. 359–69. For former Politburo member Bârlădeanu's effort to offer a benign image of Gheorghiu-Dej, opposed to Ceauşescu's dictatorship, see Lavinia Beţea, *Alexandru Bârlădeanu despre Dej, Ceauşescu si Iliescu* (Bucharest: *Editura Evenimentul Românesc*, 1997). For one of the most lucid and devastating critiques of Romanian Stalinism, coming from a disillusioned former top Communist intellectual, see Titus Popovici, *Disciplina dezordinii: Roman memorialistic* (Bucharest: *Editura Maşina de scris*, 1998).

28. Dan Ionescu, "The Posthumous Cult of Ceauşescu and Its High Priests," *Report on Eastern Europe*, Vol. 2, no. 22 (31 May 1991), pp. 23–27.

29. Although not a former member of the party apparatus, Petre Roman had deep connections with it. His father, the late Valter Roman, a former Spanish Civil war veteran, had been a member of the Central Committee and director of the party publishing house (*Editura Politică*) until his death in 1983.

30. Verba writes, "The political culture of a society consists of the system of empirical beliefs, expressive symbols, and values which defines the situation in which political action takes place. It provides the subjective orientation to politics. The political culture is of course but one aspect of politics." Sidney Verba, "Comparative Political Culture," in Lucian Pye and Sidney Verba, eds., *Political Culture and Political Development* (Princeton: Princeton University Press, 1965), p. 513. See also Robert C. Tucker, *Political Culture and Leadership in Soviet Russia* (New York: Norton, 1987), especially the chapter "The Breakdown of a Revolutionary Culture," pp. 51–71.

31. William E. Crowther, *The Political Economy of Romanian Socialism* (New York: Praeger, 1988).

32. Vladimir Tismăneanu, "From Arrogance to Irrelevance: Avatars of Marxism in Romania," in Ray Taras, ed., *The Road to Disillusion: From Critical Marxism to Postcommunism in Eastern Europe* (Armonk, NY: M. E. Sharpe, 1992), pp. 135–50.

33. For Ceaușescu's denunciations of reformism in the 1980s, see Michael Shafir, "'Ceaușescuism' against 'Gorbachevism'," *Radio Free Europe Research*, RAD Background Report/95 (30 May 1988); and Vladimir Tismăneanu, "*Ceaușescu gegen Glasnost*," *Kontinent*, no. 3 (Munich, 1988), pp. 48–53.

34. Czeslaw Milosz, *The Captive Mind* (New York: Vintage International, 1990).

35. *Scînteia*, (4 May 1988), p. 1.

36. Ferenc Feher and Agnes Heller, *Hungary 1956 Revisited: The Message of a Revolution—A Quarter of a Century After* (London: George Allen & Unwin, 1983).

37. Aleksa Djilas, "A Profile of Slobodan Milosevic," *Foreign Affairs*, (Summer 1993), pp. 81–96; for insightful interpretations of the Yugoslav debacle, see Laura Silber and Allan Little, *Yugoslavia: Death of a Nation* (New York: Penguin Books, 1997) and Sabrina P. Ramet, *Balkan Babel: The Disintegration of Yugoslavia from the Death of Tito to the War for Kosovo*, 3rd ed. (Boulder: Westview Press, 1999).

38. Vladimir Tismăneanu, "*Moștenirea Republicii Populare Române*," *Revista 22* (Bucharest, 30 December 1997–5 January 1998), p. 6.

2

Sonderweg Romania?

F. Peter Wagner

The title of this chapter pays homage to the title of a book by the Banat-German writer Richard Wagner on Romania's political and social conditions, and their historical sources and possible trajectories, after the fall of the Ceauşescu regime.[1] Yet, I have recast as a question what in Wagner's account is presented as a statement of fact. As will become clear in the following, *the question* of a Romanian *Sonderweg* (special path of development) puts into sharp relief some fundamental problems in the present discussion about the transition of/in "Eastern Europe," and thus asks us to move beyond the conceptualizations that animate the present discussion. In response, I will present an alternative framework based on the general thesis of a *double syncronicity*. I argue that the task confronting the former socialist countries of Eastern Europe is to integrate themselves into an international (global) and regional (European) order which is undergoing a profound transformation. But before going at this point any further, let me return to the key question at hand: the question of a Romanian *Sonderweg*.

ROMANIA AS A CHALLENGE IN TRANSITION STUDIES

Romania is one of the least known and least studied cases of the new democratic European Southeast. Although Romania is the second largest and second most populated country of the former "Eastern Europe," it actually lacks in extensive scholarly coverage.[2] At the same time, however, Romania has always attracted considerable scholarly and public attention. This seeming paradox between the lack of general coverage and the attention that the case of Romania has attracted points to the peculiarities that define the historical, political, and societal space in question.[3]

With the fall of the Communist regimes across Eastern Europe in 1989, the case of Romania has acquired heightened scholarly importance and even considerable public notoriety. Especially in the field of transition studies, broadly understood, the case of Romania has attracted considerable attention due to the problematic transition that ensued following the bloody collapse of the Ceauşescu dictatorship; it was a transition that has been characterized by the reconstitution of old elites, more or less violent ethnic conflict, and the rise of nationalist political parties and intellectual currents.

Romania's position within transition studies is best articulated in Linz and Stepan's synthesizing study on democratic transitions and consolidations.[4] Linz and Stepan make use of a special regime subcategory, "Sultanism," to deal with Romania's version of state socialism (i.e., totalitarianism) and its particularly detrimental effects on the country's democratic transition. Sultanism, a term borrowed from Max Weber, is used in this context to describe a totalitarian regime which relies solely on the personality and the discretionary power of one ruler, and which exhibits "a strong tendency toward familial power and dynastic succession without any rationalized impersonal ideological foundation."[5] Although Linz and Stepan occasionally hint at a possibly larger historical context and deeper-seated political-cultural roots of Romanian "Sultanism," their focus is on the transformation that Romanian totalitarianism underwent during Ceauşescu's almost twenty-five-year reign. Romania, in comparison to all other East European countries, "never became less totalitarian, but it did become increasingly sultanistic."[6] The bloody downfall of the dictatorship and the problematic transition are therefore but the consequences of this particular regime subtype. The total absence of even the vestiges of a civil society (a dissident culture, such as in the East Central European cases), brought about by the closing tendencies and severity of sultanism, especially haunts the current Romanian transition. Also, the lack of reform skills and knowledge in both the economic and the political spheres appears to be an ongoing consequence of sultanism's utter refusal, indeed, incapacity, to have engaged in any reform. Linz and Stepan's conclusions for the case of Romania are therefore rather cautious, if not pessimistic: as long as the past continues to rule the present, Romania's transition will remain stunted and incomplete.[7]

The contemporary literature on Romania after the fall of the Ceauşescu regime only substantiates Linz and Stepan's critical analysis. Romania has become a "special case," a kind of worst case even—exemplary and indicative of the *problems* of the transition.[8] The "numerous distinctions" of the case of Romania that have been noted in the literature can be systematized by using the three main points of discussion in the field of transition studies:

- State Socialism: In transition studies, the heritage of the prior regime type is considered vital for the kind and course of the transition and the process of consolidation. The case of Romania doubly supports this point. In the first place, the Ceauşescu regime is considered to have been one of Eastern Europe's most brutal state socialist regimes, determined by an extreme form of the cult of personality. Second, Ceauşescu's regime presented an anomaly even in the context of Eastern Europe because it developed during a period in which, in other countries of the region, reforms were either already being undertaken or there existed significant pressure from below for reform.
- Revolution: Characteristic but surprising was the peaceful implosion of the Communist regimes across Eastern Europe. In Romania, the events unfolded in a manner that was actually closer to what might have been expected—the collapse was violent and bloody, yet presented the exception to the norm of the "velvet revolutions."
- Institutionalization/Consolidation: Romanian post-Communism illustrates fundamentally that a change in regime (*Regimewechsel*) as such does not guarantee a specific trajectory of reform (i.e., it does not necessarily lead to liberal-democratic, market-capitalist development). The importance of civil society, reform-oriented political parties, and reform-willing and capable political leaders are therefore central and exemplary points of discussion in this case.

Thus, it comes as no surprise that the Banat-German writer Richard Wagner chose the term *Sonderweg* (special path) for the title of his book about Romania. Barring a kind of hyperbole, the term certainly captures Romania's special position within the field of transition studies by synthesizing the structural and the historical properties of the case into one eye-catching and highly evocative formulation. Yet is Romania's special position truly warranted? Or are the categories by which the case of Romania has been constructed and analyzed thus far themselves problematic?

Romania's "numerous distinctions," I think, are a sign that the course of Romania's post-Communist development challenges some fundamental assumptions in the field of transition studies. First and foremost, the "Romanian way of post-Communism" (pardon the pun) challenges the basic idea behind transition studies: the *idea* of a transition. As opposed to "transformation" or "change," the term transition explicitly refers to a stage *A* that turns or is turned into a stage *B*. Both beginning and endpoint are known and clearly defined, which makes evaluations as to path and progress of a particular transition possible. These epistemological-methodological features have in fact provided transition studies with considerable strength in argumentative and scientific status. The neatness of the conceptualization is also, however, the field's Achilles heal. *What* was supposed to happen in the countries of the former Eastern Europe was, and continues to be, not in doubt—*only the how* has proven to be somewhat more complicated, even intractable. Thus, within transition studies, there has developed a neat division of labor, so to speak, between countries that are considered reformers and countries that are considered problem cases. But as is the case in the field of comparative politics in general, "problem cases" may be indicative of problems in theory building, asking us, in fact, to integrate the *what* into our analysis.[9]

Before any misunderstandings might arise, I wish to emphasize that the "numerous distinctions" that the field of transition studies has identified in the case of Romania are not simply matters of a discursive construction of "otherness."[10] On the contrary: *the problems are real.* Time and again, the standard indicators of economic and social development have demonstrated the precarious nature of Romania's development after the fall of the Ceauşescu regime.[11] And if the problematic economic and social development is not a figment of some (Western) scholar's imagination, neither is the problematic political development that has characterized Romania in the past years. The point I wish to make is threefold and concerns the adequacy and efficacy of the transition framework for the study of post-Communist societies in general, and problem cases such as Romania in particular: (1) as a normative framework, the perspective of a "transition" can not adequately grasp the process of development as a process of the creation of inequalities; that is, it cannot actually grasp the differentiated development of underdevelopment in the countries of the former Eastern Europe; (2) furthermore, the entire indigenous, internal dynamic (*Eigendynamik*) of the political process, including the role of indigenous conceptualizations and leitmotifs, can not be grasped, especially if that process does not fully reproduce the expected; (3) last but not least, in sustaining "the West" as a model of development, the transition framework refuses to reflect upon its own categories, upholds an East/West divide, and is therefore unable to integrate the former East into the new, post-Communist European, international, and global context(s). I will concentrate on the second, ideational-political point and connect it in my discussion to the third point, thereby sketching, however briefly, what I suggest to call the "double syncronicity" of the Eastern process of transformation. The reader should keep the first, socioeconomic point in mind as an integral part of the general argument.

TRANSFORMATION OF SOCIETY AND THE QUESTION OF SOCIETAL IDENTITY

The common explanations for the peculiarities of Romanian post-Communist politics have revolved around the marshalling of the legacy of the past. Emphasis has been placed on a continuity of nationalism from Romanian national state–building to the national Communism of the Ceauşescu regime, and especially on the impact that the latter has had on Romanian society.[12] Yet while history may provide a *guide* to the "peculiarities" of Romanian politics—its leitmotifs and cognitive determinants—it cannot offer an *explanation* for their persistence and efficacy. Neglected in such historical explanations are the conditions and the dynamics of the present context itself. To grasp and analyze *why* certain leitmotifs and cognitive determinants guide political development, it is necessary to engage the present context of what has been termed a "transition."[13] As a first step, I suggest that one needs to clarify the situational horizon of the political actors. What do they know? And how do they know it? In the case of Romania, two determinants can be identified. At first, the political development stood under the impression of those fateful days in December 1989 when the Ceauşescu regime fell. A second determinant, however, quickly entered and surpassed the first in importance: the question of Romania's identity and future, both in Europe and in the international and global system(s).

How the events of December 1989 came to be interpreted is already an integral part of *post-Communist* Romania's history in the making. From the beginning, with the consolidation of the National Salvation Front into a "Communist successor" organization (later the Party of Social Democracy of Romania [PDSR], now PSD) around Ion Iliescu and Petre Roman,[14] a divide developed between those who claimed to be, and legitimized themselves as, inheritors of a revolution, and those who saw that revolution betrayed by exactly those people who came to power (or even usurped power), and who subsequently used that power to reign in and stop the revolution. Since that time, those who thought the Romanian people had, in fact, lost by January 1990 what they had gained in those December days, recognized and analyzed Romanian politics as a struggle between the "opposition" (*opoziţia*) and the "power" (*puterea*).[15] The latter, that is, the PDSR, implicitly accepted the political-moral claim mounted by the forces inside and sympathetic to the Democratic Convention and battled for its own version of the division between "power" and "opposition." They contended that, not only was the revolution successful—leading to an elected, legitimate government—but the success of the revolution was actually endangered by radical forces who, in the name of battling neo- and crypto-Communism, attempted to reign in the democratic process, and thereby even risked the stability of the entire country.[16] Standing quite apart from both those paradigmatic interpretations is the argument that the nationalistic groups have put forth. For them, even the FSN/PDSR, not to mention the Democratic Convention and its supporters, have actually acted against Romania's national interest, beginning with the "assassination" of the Ceauşescus.[17]

The change in government as a result of the Parliamentary and Presidential elections of 1996 brought the division between "power" and "opposition" to a close. After four years of the former opposition in government, "power" and "opposition" were not meaningful categories anymore—not in the least because the former opposition failed to produce its long promised developmental miracle. Thus, the Parliamentary and Presidential elections of the year 2000, which proved to be a political disaster for the 1996 government coalition and resulted in the return of the PDSR (now PSD) and Iliescu at the helm of government, can be interpreted as a "triumph of reality." Although the former opposition around the Democratic Convention had attempted in the electoral campaign to revive the moral-political division of "power" and "opposition" again, the Romanian voters were simply disappointed with the former "opposition's" governmental record.[18]

Yet, since December 1989, more fundamental considerations about the course of Romanian development, Romania's position within Europe, and its position compared to the other countries of the former Eastern Europe have also come to the fore. With the persistent economic and social problems of Romania, and the issue of integration into the developing structures of the European Union, the turn in Romanian political discourse toward issues of development is hardly surprising. What is important to realize about this turn, however, is that it draws on the motifs and arguments of the debate about modernization that took place in Romania from the nineteenth to the early twentieth century. In this classic debate, development was defined by allegiance, or opposition to, the model of the perceived forerunners—mainly France and Germany (or "the West" as this model came to be referred to). The debate pitted those who wanted to pursue a course of development modeled after those forerunners (state-induced and state-led industrialization) against those who saw in the wholesale acceptance of that model at best a kind of mirage unfit for the conditions of their own country, or at worst, a careless destruction of all that was genuine and worthy in Romania. In the language of the times, "Westerners" struggled against "Easterners," integrationists against autochthonists, the champions of the bourgeoisie and industrial society against those of the peasantry and the village community, and the imitationists against their critics.[19]

The return of the classic debate as a reference point in Romanian post-Communist politics alerts us to the openness and contingency that defines the condition of post-Communism. With the fall of the Ceauşescu regime, the entire problematic of modernization and development has opened up again; and Romanian politicians, intellectuals, and experts have quickly resorted to known ideational, rhetorical, and discoursive devices to stake out the reopened terrain and craft their own positions. Obviously the terms of reference have somewhat changed, but the lines of the classic debate are still present. Europe has become a key reference point in Romanian political discourse, and the "West" has once again become a fixture of political-strategic identification. While the "East" has been discredited as a viable point of political-strategic reference for development, "autochthonism" (the vision of a Romanian self-sufficient greatness) has been revived as an anti-Western stance.

It would certainly be tempting at this point to divide Romanian post-Communist politics along the lines of "Western/Anti-Western," or "reform/anti-reform," or even "new system/old system," just as the above explained bifurcation of "opposition" and "power" wishes to suggest. For the radical margins of Romanian politics such a bifurcation does have explanatory merits. The nationalist political parties (the Greater Romania Party, the Party of Romanian National Unity, and the Socialist Party of Labor, to name the most important ones) are fighting rapid and wholesale privatization on the grounds that it is tantamount to selling the country to foreign interests. Western values are perceived, at best, as rather problematic because they apparently imply rights for all kinds of minorities and special interests (not only ethnic, but also sexual).[20] On the other side of the spectrum, radical liberal parties such as the Civic Alliance Party (dissolved and absorbed by the National Liberal Party in March 1998) are for absolute and rapid privatization, and would like to see as much foreign direct investment as possible. They champion minority rights and, in general, see the future of Romania only in Western integration.[21]

The trouble with such a neat bifurcation of Romanian post-Communist politics sets in when one has to consider the "middle" of the political spectrum (i.e., everything between the two extremes of an outright, uncompromising nationalism and an outright, uncompromising liberalism). In this middle ground, organizationally represented by the National Liberal Party, the National Peasant Party, the Democratic Party, the Alliance for Romania, and PDSR (now PSD), to name only some of the most important ones, one finds both liberal and national elements, and both Romanian "right" and Romanian "left" politics and policies. Organizational delineations such as political party identifications, and even policy orientations, are not enough to come to terms with this "middle" ground. Rather, one finds a common concern about the reconstruction of "Romania" as a *national project*. Whatever the programmatic differences, the national presents a common ground and provides a common language for Romanian politicians, intellectuals, and experts, as well as a common ground and language for their communication with the (ethnic) Romanian populace.

While a shared cultural-historical horizon makes this criss-crossing of political-discoursive lines possible in the first place, the actual criss-crossing itself is brought about by an equally shared context in the present. It is the condition of post-Communist development that has prompted the reliance on the above-delineated classic debate. In the context of post-Communism, the classic debate presents an intellectual and cultural resource that charts a future by making the uncertain present of the post-Communist condition intelligible to the political actors involved. For Romanian politicians, intellectuals, and experts, the national has become, willy-nilly, the processing unit (*Durchlauferhitzer*) of post-Communist politics and policies.[22]

For minority representatives, in turn, it is the absence of such a common ground and language that presents the central problem. Whether such a common ground and a common language beyond the national might not be created, for example, by reevaluating the past from the standpoint of a multicultural vision, still remains to be seen. The vision of a united "Europe" and the demands of the European Union (EU) and the Council of Europe appear to be working in this regard.[23] Yet the point remains: neither the European, nor, for that matter, the international and global context(s) work in a vacuum; they are dependent on the indigenous, domestic reception they receive.

Of course, it is more complicated to assess the reality of choices, and the room for maneuvering, that Romanian political leaders have faced since December 1989. Even under the best of circumstances, a developmental miracle would hardly have been likely. The Ceauşescu regime had left Romania in a severe state of economic and social stagnation, and the country's geographical middle position in Southeastern Europe is not very enticing to foreign investors. Aggravating the situation is the fact that the old *entrepratchiks* and the new *Lumpen* businessmen that are governing the economy are not concerned about Romania's political standing, let alone some vision of the "common good."[24] Again, the objective problems of development are not in question.

What the reconstruction tried to achieve was to trace the indigenous conceptions of politics, of the problems and perspectives of Romanian post-Communist development. The mist that surrounds the political divisions in the case of Romania begins to clear when one realizes that the political divisions have a common center, that they share a common problematic and a common language. At the center of Romanian post-Communist politics and political discourse stands the problematic of Romania's *societal identity*, defined at the crossroads of several developmental spaces and visions: that of a self-sufficient greatness compromised in the past by Eastern, and in the present by Western, ideals; and that of an outpost and defender of the West compromised in the past by Eastern realities, and in the present by Eastern ideals.

The above considerations lead us to an integrative approach toward the problems of Romanian development based on a reevaluation of the notion of "transition"—replacing it, in effect, with the notion of transformation or, perhaps, the even more general and open "change." Vladimir Tismăneanu once pointed out that the notions of "left, right, center" have "strange and elusive meanings under post-Communism." Yet does this mean that "using interpretive Western paradigms would simply create false analogies and would explain little, if anything?"[25] As I have tried to show, Romanian politics and political discourse do support Tismăneanu's claim. However, at the same time, they cannot be understood without reference to the "Western paradigm" of "development." In the next section, I will make the argument that it is quite necessary *in a definite sense* to use Western political notions in the explication of Eastern political realities—*because today Western notions cannot help but reflect the struggle with "the West" and with the idea of development itself.*

INTEGRATING THE PROBLEMATIC OF DEVELOPMENT

With the demise of state socialism, Europe has again opened up *as a space of development.* Yet therein also lies the crux of the matter: it is a prestructured space, prestructured by the already existing—formerly "Western"—institutions (most prominently the EU) and by a reinvigoration of the historical "East/West" borderline of development. Przeworski's famous dictum, "the East has become the South," in fact, only articulates the irony of the collapse of what had once been considered the organizational alternative to the Western model of development. The countries of the former Eastern Europe have returned to their status before the advent of state socialism: they are once again Western Europe's original periphery.[26]

Romania's special position within transition studies also reflects this general situation of development after the fall of Communism. At issue in this particular Romanian case is not only the division of Europe as a space of development into a "Western" and an "Eastern" half, but also the further regional differentiation of the latter into a "Southeastern," "East Central" and strictly "Eastern" part. This fundamental historical differentiation had, in fact, been cast aside by the division into "East" and "West" inaugurated by the Bolshevik Revolution. What had been a question of development cast in terms of modernity and modernization came to stand for a fundamental difference in "systems." "North" and "South" became the spatial representations of the question of development, while the "East" came to be known as the "Second World," and the significant difference between "East" and "West" came to be considered as a *political* one.[27]

Romanian politics reflects this context of development in its indigenous, domestic form. The persistence and ubiquity of the national question in Romanian politics and the contemporary relevance of the terms of the classic debate on development are expressions of the attempt to come to terms with the condition of post-Communism. Yet the Romanian political debate relies on the developmental split between East and West as its fundamental point of reference. Here, the Romanian debate and the scholarly debate in the West find themselves on common ground. As the German sociologist Klaus Müller has noted in reaction to the demise of state socialism, modernization theory has experienced a virtual "renaissance."[28] Already, J. Habermas and R. Dahrendorf saw the historical events of 1989 as something of a "recuperation" or a "catching-up." Adam Przeworski, and especially Claus Offe, have developed the vision of a "revolution of recuperation" into a powerful framework for the analysis of the problems and perspectives of the Eastern transition. In their footsteps, the vision of the synchronicity of political and economic reforms, predicated on the integration of the countries of the former Eastern Europe into the existing western political and economic structures, has become quite accepted by political and social scientists, no matter what their respective political allegiances. It is from this modernization perspective that the transition in Eastern Europe has come to be understood: as a transition from state socialism (or Communism) to the Western model of a liberal-democratic polity and a capitalist market economy.

However, this renaissance of modernization theory is actually oblivious to the history and development of the theory itself. Since the late 1960s, political and social science research in the (former) West has successively come to abandon a universalistic and unilinear conception of modernity and modernization.[29] The seeming failure of the Western model of development, the persistence of underdevelopment in the Third World, and the special case of Japan and the rise of the Southeast Asian "little tigers" cast doubt on the standard developmental model. These "anomalies" demonstrated that development could not be conceived of in terms of a linear, ready-made catching-up with the Western model by way of a standardized and unified process of "diffusion" and "acceptance." The relationship between capitalist development, prosperity, and democracy has proven to be especially problematic. Thus, the idea of a golden path of development and of a "grand theory" to account for its failure and/or success has been virtually abandoned in the literature. Instead, a differentiated view of development has been called for that, although still aware of the global North–South divide, emphasizes the internal, indigenous conditions for development. To this one needs to add yet another—global—dimension brought about by the realization that the Western path of development, predicated as it is on economic growth, creates severe ecological problems.

At the same time, the modernization of modern (i.e., "Western") societies has become a central theme in political and social science research.[30] The process of transformation that is being debated, in this case, ranges from changes in the industrial-economic organization of these societies, to changes in the political system and the large social structure as well. Regardless of whether these changes are summed up as "reflexive modernization," as "consequences of modernity" or a "second modernity," as post-modernization, or even as a new phase in the process of "globalization," the issue is a process that changes the foundational structures of the Western societies themselves, and thereby tears open the teleological self-understanding (*Endzeitverständnis*) of modernity, pace Fukuyama,[31] from within its very center. Modernity and modernization are no longer, if they ever truly were, self-understood, nonproblematic notions; they themselves have become highly problematic, the center of concern and investigation.[32]

The lessons to be drawn for our present purposes from the contours of a new modernization theory based on "multiple modernities" (S. N. Eisenstadt) are twofold. First, the integration of the former "Eastern Europe" into the former "West" is not a one-way process—meaning the alignment of one system "East" to the other system "West"—but rather concerns both sides. The countries of the former East have to integrate themselves into an international and regional context that is undergoing a profound change itself. Thus, the very model that they are being asked to emulate in their reform course is something of an anachronism and cannot help but remain a rather elusive goal. To put it bluntly, there simply is no catching-up with an imaginary nineteenth century, however hard one is willing to try. Second, what the countries of the former Eastern Europe are facing internally is best described as another "great transformation" (K. Polanyi), a process akin to the transformation from an agrarian to an industrial society, and one that affects all aspects and elements associated with the organizational patterns and capacities of the society itself. Therein lies what one can call the *double synchronicity* of the eastern transformation.

The process commonly referred to as a "transition" characterizes nothing less than a total overhaul at the level of society itself.[33] Thus, the politics of reform, the very complex of policy making, amounts to a societal project. To formulate this differently: reform in the East European context is a matter of *Ordnungs-* and *Gesellschaftspolitik*.[34] This, of course, also distinguishes policy making in the East European transformation process from policy making in the West, where "political steering" has come to be considered only "a particular social process (*Teilprozeß*) that interacts with many other social processes and thus contributes to social change without being able to steer it."[35] In the case of the East European process of transformation, the "political steering of society" (the politically initiated and controlled makeover of society) animates the entire process.[36] Politics, thus, do come first. Yet by the same token, politics cannot be reduced to the creation of institutions in the narrow sense of the term,[37] or to the implementation of a particular set of economic measures, exclusively labeled "reform," and set to make up "the transition."[38]

The consequences of the historical-structural, international, and regional context of "post-state socialism" therefore present, in each case, an *Eigendynamik* grounded in the challenge to conceive and construct a *new societal identity*. In the case of Romania, as noted, this *Eigendynamik* is commonly held to be rather "special." What makes the Romanian development "special," however, lies in the expectations of a normal course of development: the vision of a transition to "liberal democracy" and "market capitalism" posited by the assumptions of a classical modernization theory which lies at the heart of contemporary transition studies. It is against the expectations of such a normality that the Romanian development is set apart and thus considered "special." Well into the second decade of post-Communist development, however, "differentiation" and "variation" have already been acknowledged by some as new key terms in the study of the former Eastern Europe. The transition framework, one might say, has become part of history itself and thus, by extension, anachronistic in the present context of analysis.

One way of coming to terms with the problem of being confronted with too many problems in development has been to assert the uniqueness of each case—every case a "special case," so to speak. At the most radical, namely the previous quote by Tismăneanu, the Western paradigm has been questioned in its explicatory value. The idea of an *Eigendynamik* grounded in the process, or rather the challenge, of societal transformation, helps us not only to come to terms with the specificities of a case, but also to put those specificities into a larger context, thereby normalizing, even demystifying them. While this in no way implies the absolution of political foolishness and/or political-moral bankruptcy, it does lead us to understand the political process of a problem case like Romania better; perhaps thereby aiding us at last in accepting "development" as a common question after the demise of state socialism.

CONCLUDING REMARKS

I have tried to show that the conclusions reached about the process of transformation in Eastern Europe in general, and the Romanian case in particular, depend heavily, all too heavily, on the expectations that the Western path of development has engendered. The alternative framework elaborated in response rests on two foundations: accepting that the fall of state socialism as a political geographic borderline means that "East" and "West" are not self-evident categories anymore and, at the same time, accepting the consequences of the "Western" debates about modernity and modernization for the Eastern transformation. The *Ordnungspolitik* and *Gesellschaftspolitik* in the new Eastern great transformation are determined by two contexts. On the one hand, there is the indigenous context of an "imagined community," which is having to reimagine itself, in part by appropriating its "history" in the light of the demise of state socialism. On the other hand, there is also the creation of something like a new national strategy of development that cannot be seen as divorced from a particular model of socioeconomic and political order. This strategy, namely the pursuit of a liberal-democratic polity and a capitalist market economy, is part of the internal longing *and* is also the basis of the international and regional demands placed upon the Eastern transformation. Yet, at the same time, the model of a liberal-democratic polity and a capitalist market economy is itself undergoing a profound transformation at the international (global) and regional (European) level. And therein lies what I suggest to call the *double synchronicity* of the Eastern transformation: the countries of the former Eastern Europe have no choice but to integrate themselves into a regional (European) and international (global) order which are themselves undergoing a profound transformation. Thus, the domestic, indigenous transformation, itself a national-societal challenge and project, is also part of another "great transformation" (Polanyi).

At the time of this writing, the suggested framework of a "double syncronicity" has been powerfully supported by the unfolding events. On the one hand, Romania continues to struggle with "Europe" as a rather ambiguous term of sociocultural identification and political strategy. The 1999 meeting of the European Council in Helsinki appeared to signal a radical breakthrough in this regard because Romania was admitted as one of the candidates for future membership in the EU. Almost two years later, in November 2001, the European Commission concluded that Romania, together with Bulgaria, will not be among the countries for the upcoming round of EU enlargement, a decision that was only confirmed by the European Commission and accepted by the European Council (Copenhagen Summit) in the fall/winter of 2002. Thus, as a result, nothing fundamental has really changed in Romania–EU relations. The ball continues to lie in Romania's court as the European Commission maintains that Romania is not yet ready for integration. That there is some, arguably a lot of, hypocrisy at work in the EU's standard setting and pressure for compliance,is true, but also beside the point. For all of Romania's claims to belong to Europe, the EU is not "Europe." The EU presents an institutionalized cooperation between its member-states and those who are already in set the standards for all those who wish to join, like in all associations and private clubs around the world. If the existing EU programs and the "stabilization pact" that has been initiated in the aftermath of the Kosovo war will constitute a real impetus to the reconstruction of the entire Southeast European region, including the *other* Balkans—Romania and Bulgaria—still remains to be seen.

In the meantime, on the other hand, Romania's bid for NATO membership has finally been successful. NATO's Prague Summit in November 2002 included Romania as one of the former East European countries to join no later than in May 2004. Undoubtedly, Romania's military reforms have contributed significantly to the decision to include Romania in this, NATO's second and largest round of enlargement. But the decisive factor has been political, indeed geopolitical. The context of the post–September 11 war on terrorism and the U.S. government's continuing pressure in this context for allied action made NATO's final Eastern enlargement all but inevitable. The present Romanian government in fact read this context quite well. After September 11, Romania has given its unconditional support to the war on terrorism and has even signed a separate agreement with the United States on the exemption of U.S. citizens from possible charges brought against them in the new International Criminal Court. This has certainly pleased the U.S. government, as the official visit of President Bush to Bucharest immediately after NATO's Prague Summit amply demonstrated. The risk to alienate EU-Europe in the process, even if perhaps not planned, was well worth taking, one might say, given the rather negative news that was to be expected from the European Commission anyway.

The drifting apart of the European (EU) process of integration and the Euro-Atlantic (NATO) process of integration and the fate of Romania in both processes only underlines the fact that the process of post-Communist transformation cannot be seen as divorced from regional (European) and international (global) developments. The reconstruction of a new European identity and the reconstruction of a new transatlantic (security) identity after the fall of Communism determine, to a large extent, the problems and opportunities that Romania and all other countries of the former Eastern Europe see themselves confronted with. To be sure, given already existing closing tendencies and a new differentiation into center-periphery relations, both the new Europe and the new international, global order may not hold much hope for Romania, in particular, and the southeastern part of Europe, in general. I should therefore stress again that the indigenous, domestic context matters: how Romania—better yet, all Romanian citizens—come to terms with those problems and opportunities, including the role that material and ideational sources and resources play in this process, presents the "transformer" in the process of transformation. In this double (dialectical) sense, the case of Romania only reflects the question of "development" after the demise of Communism.

NOTES

1. Richard Wagner, *Sonderweg Rumänien: Bericht aus einem Entwicklungsland* (Berlin: Rotbuch, 1991). Wagner (no relation to the present author) was one of the founders of the *Aktionsgruppe Banat*, a circle of writers (William Totok, Herta Müller, and others) in the 1970s who came into conflict with the Ceauşescu regime. Wagner left (as ethnic Germans were "allowed" to leave by the authorities) in the early 1980s and now lives in Berlin. His short book is still the only general assessment of Romanian politics and society in light of the fall of the Ceauşescu regime available in the German language, hence the importance that the present author attributes to the book.

2. As in other areas and disciplines of the political and social sciences, as well as in the political and social sciences in general, there are significant national differences. In the United States, political and social science scholarship on Romania and on Southeastern Europe, in general, has fared somewhat better than in Germany, due for the most part to the existence of an "area studies" tradition. In Germany, by con-

trast, Romania and Southeastern Europe have traditionally been covered by historians, and German *Ostforschung* has had a strong (and problematic) tradition in the field of history. In the pages of *Osteuropa*, the journal of the German Association for East European Studies, a highly interesting, soul-searching debate about the future of East European Studies after "1989" has and continues to take place. On German *Ostforschung* and as an introduction to the debate, see: Thomas Bremer, Wim van Meurs, and Klaus Müller, "*Vorwärts in die Vergangenheit? Zur Zukunft der Osteuropaforschung*," *Osteuropa*, vol. 48, 4 (April 1998), pp. 408–16.

3. Western scholarship has found in Romania an exemplary test case for the analysis of the development of underdevelopment, or the development of a periphery in Europe in general and the articulation of that development in Southeastern Europe in particular. Especially the influences of Habsburg and Ottoman domination, Romania's specific national state formation, and the struggle between agrarian and industrial forces and interests have attracted attention. For anthropologists, ethnologists, and agrarian sociologists, Romania became a field-laboratory of the relationship between the traditional and the modern. The Communist takeover and the bolshevist modernization of Romanian society have attracted considerable attention as well. See for example: Henry L. Roberts, *Rumania: Political Problems of an Agrarian State* (New Haven, CT: Yale University Press, 1951); Daniel Chirot, *Social Change in a Peripheral Society: The Creation of a Balkan Colony* (New York: Academic Press, 1976); Kenneth Jowitt, *Revolutionary Breakthroughs and National Development: The Case of Romania, 1944–1965.* (Berkeley, CA: University of California Press); Katherine Verdery, *Transylvanian Villagers: Three Centuries of Political, Economic, and Ethnic Change* (Berkeley, CA: University of California Press, 1983); Claude Karnoouh, *L'Invention du Peuple: Chroniques de Roumanie* (Paris: Arcantère, 1990).

4. Juan J. Linz and Alfred Stepan, *Problems of Democratic Transition and Consolidation: Southern Europe, South America, and Post-Communist Europe* (Baltimore, MD: Johns Hopkins University Press, 1996).

5. Linz and Stepan, *Problems of Democratic Transition and Consolidation*, p. 52.

6. Linz and Stepan, *Problems*, p. 349.

7. Linz and Stepan, *Problems*, pp. 362–65.

8 Trond Gilberg, *Nationalism and Communism in Romania: The Rise and Fall of Ceauşescu's Personal Dictatorship* (Boulder, CO: Westview Press, 1990); Tom Gallagher, *Romania after Ceauşescu: The Politics of Intolerance* (Edinburgh, UK: Edinburgh University Press, 1995); Anneli Ute Gabanyi, *Systemwechsel in Rumänien: Von der Revolution zur Transformation* (München: Oldenbourg, 1998).

9. For comparative politics in general, see Ali Kazancigil, "The Deviant Case in Comparative Analysis: High Stateness in a Muslim Society: The Case of Turkey," in Mattei Dogan and Ali Kazancigil, eds., *Comparing Nations: Concepts, Strategies, Substance* (Oxford, UK and Cambridge, MA: Blackwell, 1994), pp. 213–38, also pp. 11–12.

10. Maria Todorova, *Imagining the Balkans* (New York: Oxford, University Press 1997); Larry Wolff, *Inventing Eastern Europe: The Map of Civilization on the Mind of the Enlightenment* (Stanford, CA: Stanford University Press, 1994).

11. After a period of positive GDP growth rates from 1993 to 1996, negative growth resumed in 1997 with a slump of –6.7 per cent compared to the previous year; for the entire period of 1990–99, the annual growth rate of GDP was –0.5 percent. Although since 1999 (–3.2), some recovery has set in, it is still a precarious development

with GDP per capita in purchasing power parity at 5,533 USD in the year 2000—still down compared to 1996 (6,595 USD, highest after 1989), and nowhere near pre-1989 levels (problematic, but in 1986: 8,822 USD). Unemployment continues to be a major problem: the national registration for most years is above 10 percent (2000: 10.5) with rates according to International Labor Organization methodology (in Romania: the Labor Force Survey in Households, AMIGO) above 6 percent for most years (1994–2000, in 2000: 6.8). Furthermore, poverty and income inequality continue to be major problems and have hampered the development of a middle class: according to a national study, in 1998, 6.8 percent of the Romanian population lived at or below the poverty threshold of 2 USD per day and 44.5 percent lived at or below the poverty threshold of 4 USD per day. Data taken from United Nations Development Programme (UNDP), *National Human Development Report Romania 2001–2002: A Decade Later—Understanding the Transition Process in Romania* (Bucharest: UNDP, 2002); Cornelia Mihaela Teşliuc, Lucian Pop, and Emil Daniel Teşliuc, *Sărăcia şi Sistemul de Protecţie Socială* (Iaşi: Editura Polirom, 2001), pp. 23–24.

12. Compare Irina Livezeanu, *Cultural Politics in Greater Romania: Regionalism, Nation Building, and Ethnic Struggle, 1918–1930* (Ithaca, NY: Cornell University Press, 1995) and Katherine Verdery, *National Ideology under Socialism: Identity and Cultural Politics in Ceauşescu's Romania* (Berkeley, CA: University of California Press, 1991) with the explanation provided by Linz and Stepan, *Problems* (see note 4).

13. For my general position: A (historical) context cannot be *explained* historically.

14. The term "successor-party" for a political party that developed out of the Communist party of a country is here used in a neutral sense; Dieter Segert, "*Geschichte des Spätsozialismus als Schlüssel zum Verständnis 'postkommunistischer' Parteiensysteme*," in Dieter Segert, ed., *Spätsozialismus und Parteienbildung in Osteuropa nach 1989* (Berlin: Berliner Debatte Wissenschaftsverlag, 1996), pp. 11–30.

15. Vladimir Pasti, Mihaela Miroiu, Cornel Codiţa, *România—Starea de Fapt, Vol. 1: Societatea* (Bucharest: Editura Nemira, 1997), p. 134—yet this is something that actually needs no "authoritative backup."

16. The argument is best presented in Ion Iliescu, *Revoluţie si Reformâ* (Bucharest: Editura Enciclopedică, 1994), esp. pp. 122–34.

17. Again and again, the leader of the Great Romania Party, Corneliu Vadim Tudor, has raised such charges and also presented charges of corruption against the Romanian political leadership: one such incident can be found reported in Domniţa Ştefănescu, *Doi Anii din Istoria României: o cronologie a evenimentelor ianuarie 1995–ianuarie 1997* (Bucharest: Editura Maşina de scris, 1998), pp. 134–35. This, needless to say, has not prevented the Great Romania Party to be a member of the governing coalition in 1995.

18. Almost needless to say, the election results, including the extremely strong showing of the nationalist Great Romania Party and its leader, Corneliu Vadim Tudor, in the first round of the Presidential elections, have elicited some strong reactions among Romanian and foreign analysts: Alina Mungiu-Pippidi, "The Return of Populism: The 2000 Romanian Elections," *Government and Opposition*, vol. 36, no. 2 (2001), pp. 230–52; Dorothée de Nève, "Wahlen in Rumänien: Eine ganz normale Katastrophe?," *Osteuropa*, vol. 51, no. 3 (2001), pp. 281–98. Compare: F. Peter Wagner, *Die rumänischen Parlaments- und Präsidentschaftswahlen im Jahre 2000: Zurück in die Zukunft?* Politikinformationen Osteuropa 88 (Bonn: Friedrich-Ebert-Stiftung, 2001).

19. See on this the contributions in Kenneth Jowitt (ed.), *Social Change in Romania, 1860–1940: A Debate on Development in a European Nation* (Berkeley, CA: Institute of International Studies, 1978) and Lucian Boia, *Istorie şi Mit în Conştiinţa Româneasca* (Bucharest: Humanitas, 1997), pp. 27–64.

20. Interview with Ioan Tănase, Great Romania Party, representative from Cluj in the Chamber of Deputies (1992–1996), December 1993.

21. Partidul Alianţei Civice, *De la Communism spre Libertate: Istoric, Declaraţie de Principii, Programul, Statutul* (Mimeo, no date).

22. This explains why the influence of the nationalistic political parties goes well beyond their institutional participation in the political system proper.

23. György Frunda (Hungarian Democratic Federation of Romania and member of the Parliamentary Assembly of the Council of Europe) is stressing the European component in his speeches and activities: *Drept Minoritar, Spaime Naţionale: György Frunda în dialog cu Elena Ştefoi* (Bucharest: Editura Kriterion, 1997); clearly, the conflict between Romania and Hungary over the status and treatment of the Hungarian minority in Romania (and by implication the status of Transylvania) has not taken place—we remember, it was one of the conflicts high on the list immediately after the events of 1989, see F. Stephen Larrabee, "Long Memories and Short Fuses: Change and Instability in the Balkans," *International Security*, vol. 15, no. 3 (Winter 1990/91).

24. Katherine Verdery, *What Was Socialism, and What Comes Next?* (Princeton, NJ: Princeton University Press, 1996), p. 33. As a reminder: one also needs to consider the material aspect—development does not necessarily mean development for all or that a country in its entirety flourishes. Some in Romania have profited and continue to profit from the conditions *as they are*.

25. Vladimir Tismăneanu, "The Leninist Debris or Waiting for Perón," *East European Politics and Societies*, vol. 10, no. 3, Fall 1996, pp. 504–35, quote p. 504.

26. Iván T. Berend, *Central and Eastern Europe, 1944–1993: Detour from the Periphery to the Periphery* (Cambridge, UK: Cambridge University Press, 1996).

27. F. Peter Wagner, "Beyond 'East' and 'West': On the European and Global Dimensions of the Fall of Communism" in Gerhard Preyer and Mathias Bös, eds., *Borderlines in a Globalized World: New Perspectives in a Sociology of the World System* (Dordrecht: Kluwer Academic Publishers, 2002), pp. 189–215.

28. Klaus Müller, "*Nachholende Modernisierung? Die Konjunkturen der Modernisierungstheorie und ihre Anwendung auf die Transformation der osteuropäischen Gesellschaften*," *Leviathan*, vol. 19, no. 2 (1991), pp. 261–91, Klaus Müller, "'Modernising' Eastern Europe: Theoretical Problems and Political Dilemmas," *European Journal of Sociology*, vol. 33 (1992), pp. 109–50.

29. Compare for this: Cyril E. Black, *The Dynamics of Modernization* (New York: Harper and Row, 1966) and S. N. Eisenstadt, *Tradition, Wandel und Modernität*. Übers. von Suzanne Heintz (Frankfurt/M.: Suhrkamp, 1979).

30. Wolfgang Zapf, "*Modernisierung und Modernisierungstheorien*," in Wolfgang Zapf, ed., *Die Modernisierung moderner Gesellschaften. Verhandlungen des 25. Deutschen Soziologentages in Frankfurt am Main* (Frankfurt/M. and New York: Campus Verlag, 1990), pp. 23–39.

31. Francis Fukuyama, "The End of History?" *The National Interest*, vol. 16 (Summer 1989), pp. 3–18.

32. The above paragraph draws on discussions best exemplified in: Ulrich Beck, *Die Erfindung des Politischen: Zu einer Theorie reflexiver Modernisierung* (Frankfurt/M.: Suhrkamp, 1993); Anthony Giddens, *The Consequences of Modernity* (Stanford, CA: Stanford University Press, 1990); Mike Featherstone, Scott Lash, and Roland Robertson (eds.), *Global Modernities* (London, UK: Sage Publications, 1995); Roland Robertson, *Globalization. Social Theory and Global Culture* (London, UK: Sage Publications, 1992).

33. Jadwiga Staniszkis, "*Dilemmata der Demokratie in Osteuropa*," in Rainer Deppe, Helmut Dubiel, and Ulrich Rödel, eds., *Demokratischer Umbruch in Osteuropa* (Frankfurt/M.: Suhrkamp, 1991), pp. 326–47.

34. As with so many German terms, these two are also virtually untranslatable. "Ordering politics" and "Social politics" are rather awkward. What both terms encompass is the general "ordering" function that politics also needs to fulfill: having an "industrial policy," for example, based on general ideas and ideals about development in its relation to an existent or desired public order; see Marian Döhler, "*Ordnungspolitische Ideen und sozialpolitische Institutionen*," in Roland Czada und Manfred G. Schmidt, eds., *Verhandlungsdemokratie, Interessenvermittlung, Regierbarkeit: Festschrift für Gerhard Lehmbruch* (Opladen: Westdeutscher Verlag, 1993), pp. 123–41.

35. Renate Mayntz, "*Politische Steuerung: Aufstieg, Niedergang und Transformation einer Theorie*," in Klaus von Beyme and Claus Offe, eds., *Politische Theorien in der Ära der Transformation: PVS Sonderheft 26* (Opladen: Westdeutscher Verlag, 1995), p. 165.

36. And this even where the mix of state intervention and market forces is at issue.

37. Wolfgang Merkel, "*Institutionalisierung und Konsolidierung der Demokratie in Ostmitteleuropa*," in Wolfgang Merkel, Eberhard Sandschneider, and Dieter Segert (eds.), *Systemwechsel 2. Die Institutionalisierung der Demokratie* (Opladen: Leske und Budrich, 1996), p. 74.

38. Compare the contributions in Olivier Blanchard, Kenneth A. Froot, and Jeffrey D. Sachs, eds., *The Transition in Eastern Europe, Vol. 2: Restructuring* (Chicago and London: University of Chicago Press, 1994).

3

Memory, Memorials, and Membership: Romanian Utilitarian Anti-Semitism and Marshal Antonescu*

Michael Shafir

There can be little doubt that memory and memorials are interconnected. "Memorials" are etymologically linked to "memory," that is to say to that function defined by the *Concise Oxford Dictionary* as a "faculty by which things are recalled to or kept in the mind." The link between either of the two notions and "membership" is less apparent at first sight. Yet from the same dictionary one learns that memorials, that is to say man-created objects or events "serving to commemorate," are implicitly fulfilling a social function. The dictionary mentions as exemplification memorials statues, festivals, buildings, and religious services. It is hard to imagine either of these being inaugurated or held in the presence of a single individual. Those who unveil statues, launch festivals, build memorials, or conduct a religious service have in mind other human beings. Whether "memory" is *singularly* social, as Maurice Halbwachs argued,[1] is, of course, debatable. There can be no doubt, however, that at least *one* of memory's functions is both socially induced and *socializing*—in other words linked to group-membership.[2]

MEMORY, MEMORIALS, AND MEMBERSHIP IN A POST-COMMUNIST SETTING

People belong to multiple social groups and associations. Compatibility among them is not always smooth. What is more, people *aspire* to belong to groups or associations other than those in which they were born, raised or professionalized. Collectively, each of these groups may have not only *different* "memories," but those memories may clash with one another and even more so with the collective memory of the associations of which one aspires to become a member. In a world about to become one large village, aspirations to membership necessarily translate into a multiplication of those clashes. How many different "memories" are involved in, say, the Liberal International? What sort of common "memory" can a Socialist International made up by both traditional social democratic parties and Communist successor parties have? Which is to "impose" its memory on the other, for what reasons, and how? Finally, can a NATO enlarged to include both former World War II allies and former Axis powers have a joint "memory?" It is quite obvious it can, since Germany and Italy have long been part of the Atlantic Alliance. But the forging of the collective NATO memory only became possible after one side "imposed" its memory on the other. At the end of World War II it was clear who the losers and who the winners were. It is less blatantly clear who the losers are at the end of the Cold War, though the winners may be indisputable. The "losing" side at the turn of the twenty-first century can—and does—claim victory as well. The argument of "return to one's own self" may not be very convincing to foreign audiences, but is very persuasive for domestic ones. Where, then, is the new collective memory to start from? Whatever the "Global Village" is or will become we might be uncertain of, but one thing is inevitable: it is (and will remain) one huge festival of Festingerian "cognitive dissonance."[3]

The literature on "memory" is by now so vast that one would need a huge, well, memory and a correspondingly enormous footnote to just mention the most prominent names associated with it in the last decades. Suffice it to mention that Paul Ricoeur traces preoccupation with what "memory" is all about to the ancient Greek philosophers, Augustin, John Locke, Freud, Halbwachs, Yersushalmi, and Pierre Nora (to mention but a few) before he produces his own theory.[4] Nora's name, of course, is above all linked to that aspect of memory that is focused on memorials. The immense success of Nora's seven-volume *Les Lieux de mémoire*, the first of which was published in 1997,[5] is, as Jean-Charles Szurek would eventually observe, both emblematic and paradoxical. What started as an enterprise aimed at "saving national memory" ended up in concluding that there was nothing to save; on the contrary, we are living in the age of a "*tyranny* of memory."[6]

Whence the obsession? Numerous explanations have been provided. Despite their multiple differences, historians, sociologists, anthropologists and political scientists converge on one point: memory is about *the present*. If the "tyranny of memory" cannot be escaped, this is because no one has yet devised the time machine for escaping from the present. In other words, there is no way to deal with the "then" without telescoping it from the "here and now." As Martin Malia wrote after citing Benedetto Croce's famous remark that "all history is contemporary history," we "invariably read the past through the prism of the present with all its political, cultural, and ethical passions."[7] Memory, memorials and commemorations are all about legitimation processes, be this the personal legitimation of politicians and the politics they are supposed to represent, or the collective legitimation of a society's perceptions of itself. Anthropologists, such as Katherine Verdery, may strive to "think of legitimation in less rationalistic and more suitable "cosmic" terms, showing it as rich, complex and disputatious processes of political meaning-creation," indeed even to formulate theories on the space–time axis proceeding from introspecting what happens with the movement of anonymous, reinterred dead bodies in the former Yugoslavia. But there is nothing "cosmic" about legitimation processes. Politicians and historical figures can be legitimized (or delegitimized, or relegitimized) only for the purpose of the present. Legitimacy will not thereby descend on the past, nor is there any guarantee that it would survive as such in the future. But Verdery, I believe, is quite correct in appreciating legitimation as "a process that employs symbols."[8] Much as they diverge in their approach, Verdery converges on this point with Romanian historian Andrei Pippidi. For better or worse, Pippidi's views are also closer to mine than those of Verdery.

Pippidi speaks of the need to develop a "theory of symbolic history" for the purpose of comprehending the handling (or mishandling) of memory as a social phenomenon.[9] Symbols for what? For configuring or reconfiguring the present, of course. One can, as George Schöpflin does when he analyzes "commemoration," see in it a "ritualized" recalling of what societies stand for. "A society without memory is blind to its own present and future, because it lacks a moral framework into which to place its experiences."[10] There is, on face, little to argue against that perception. No polity can function without—to use Benedict Anderson's terminology—a positive, "imagined community" to which reference can be made.[11] For, as Romanian historian Lucian Boia put it, "The past means legitimation and justification. Without having a past, we can be certain of nothing."[12] The symbolic aspect of memorials and commemorations is even more pronounced in societies where the national identity is fragile and whose future is uncertain. The distortion (but not obliteration!) of national symbols in East Central Europe under the Communist regimes and the search for either new or renewed "symbols" in the wake of regime change made Jacques Rupnik observe in the early 1990s that "demolition of [communist] statues, restoration of former denomination to streets, are but the exterior aspects of the search for a "usable past," whose force is proportional to the fragility of national identity and uncertainty in face of the future."[13]

But one cannot ignore the other side of the coin, and that side is particularly strong in societies that left behind one past but are uncertain of what they should replace it with and who should be chosen to symbolize it. Which past is deemed as worthy to be "used" or "re-used?" What Pippidi calls the "macabre comedy of posthumous rehabilitations all over Eastern Europe after 1989" demonstrated that the past was undergoing a process of being reshaped "by partisan passions, with each political family introducing in the national pantheon those historic figures in whom it can recognize itself or whom it abusively claims [as its own]." One must ask, we are told by Pippidi, "Who Is On the Way Out? Who Is on the Way In?" all while bearing in mind that "[At] a time when all Central East European Countries reject the Soviet model, searching for an own (old or new) national identity, historians and politicians compete for the reinterpretation of the past."[14]

One of the main reasons for the emergence of this situation rests in what elsewhere I called the double dilemma of *Vergangenheitsbewältigung:* Is it possible to overcome the Communist past without leaning on what preceded it and is it possible to overcome the authoritarian past that antedated Communism without idealizing that past beyond recognition?[15]

Memory can be, and memory is, used for the purpose of manipulation, precisely *because* it has little in common with the past and is all about the present and future. Choosing between different "memories," Pippidi writes, is also a choice on different options for the future.[16] This is exactly what Ricoeur has in mind when he writes that "the same events may mean glory for some, humiliation for others. One side's celebration is the other side's hatred."[17] Schöpflin seems to choose an apparently irreproachably democratic, but reproachably impractical way out of the dilemma. "It is very difficult," he writes, "for one community to look with nothing worse than indifference at the commemoration pursued by another. Yet if we are all to survive in the European tradition that I believe is our heritage, living in diversity is a *sine qua non.*" This, he adds, is difficult at moments, but "If we have the confidence in ourselves, in our values, then the commemorations of the others need not be seen as offensive." His advice is particularly directed at minorities, which are told that "Majorities have the same rights to cultural reproduction as minorities and those rights should be respected." That Schöpflin is aware of the "clash of memories" mentioned above there can be no doubt. What is, however, debatable is whether his rejection of a "multiculturalism that seeks to impose particular restrictions on majorities" is taking into account that *cultural* reproduction entrenched on the commemoration of those who denied *reproduction* from others may be off the line of "European tradition."[18] It may rather be related to what Ricoeur terms as "manipulated memory," and may have little in common with democratic attitudes. On the contrary, that manipulation may reflect what Ricoeur describes as the "ideological" aspect of manipulated memory, and it is not by chance that he cites at this stage Tzvetan Todorov's *Abuses of Memory*, taking distance from the "contemporary frenzy of commemorations, with their convoys of rites and meetings." Furthermore, it is not by chance that Ricoeur cites the Bulgarian-French historian's warning that the monopolization of memory is by no means singularly restricted to totalitarian regimes. It is, we are told, shared by all those who seek glory.[19] In other words, when we speak of the symbolic aspects of "memory," the question of "symbols for what?" must never leave aside the no less relevant accompanying questions of "which symbols?" and of "symbols for whom?"

It was precisely these questions that I posed in a previous article on Marshal Ion Antonescu's process of rehabilitation in post-Communist Romania, as the "*Cui bono*" part of the article's title illustrates.[20] This study is a sequel to that article, tracing developments since its publication in 1997. There were three main points that the previous article made. First, that the rehabilitation process was mainly aimed at undermining the nascent Romanian democracy, being inspired and (up to a certain point) instrumentalized by personalities with strong links with Nicolae Ceauşescu's Communist secret police; second, that the Greater Romania Party (PRM) led by Corneliu Vadim Tudor was the main venue through which the process was pursued, but at the same time its partial success was imbedded in the strong roots of Romanian national Communism; and, finally, that the "utilitarian anti-Semitism" of the country's "successor party" (first called the Front of National Salvation, then Democratic Front of National Salvation, then Party of Social Democracy in Romania, or PDSR, and, as of 16 June 2000 Social Democratic Party, or PSD) leadership had also played an important, if somewhat self-defeating, role in that process. "Utilitarian anti-Semitism" refers to the occasional exploitation of anti-Semitic prejudice for the needs of the hour by politicians who, by and large, are probably not anti-Semitic. As described in that article, the drive to rehabilitate the wartime Hitler ally had included:

> those in whose eyes the rehabilitation is mainly perceived in utilitarian terms: if it serves the political needs of the hour, these forces are ready to "close an eye" to it, expecting to deal with its unwelcome implications at a later stage. Evidence shows that this is precisely the case of the PDSR. For a second group, however, Antonescu's figure is not merely an instrument (though it is that too) but a "legitimation model." In other words, the Marshal is not only a means but also a purpose. And the purpose is simply the liquidation of Romania's incipient democracy. The members of this group have one thing in common: some direct or mediated link to what . . . I am inclined to label as "the Forces of Old." I mean that Romanian version of the "extended family" that is the "extended Securitate."[21]

I was pointing out in that article that the Communist mishandling of history is partly explaining the facility with which Antonescu had been transformed into a "hero-model." Yet the study also insisted on the attraction Antonescu could exert as an anti-Communist symbol. At that point in time, I was not sufficiently aware of parallels elsewhere in the region, which I eventually came to "dissect" in my subsequent research.[22] As Tony Judt would put it in 2000, the:

> mismemory of communism is . . . contributing . . . to a mismemory of anticommunism. Marshal Antonescu, the wartime Romanian leader who was executed in June 1945 [*sic*], defended himself at his trial with the claim that he had sought to protect his country from the Soviet Union. He is now being rewritten into Romanian popular history as a hero, his part in the massacre of Jews and others in wartime Romania weighing little in the balance against his anti-Russian credentials. Anticommunist clerics throughout the region; nationalists who fought alongside the Nazis in Estonia, Lithuania, and Hungary; right-wing partisans

> who indiscriminately murdered Jews, communists, and liberals in the vicious score settling of the immediate postwar years before the communists took effective control are all candidates for rehabilitation as men of laudable convictions; their strongest suit, of course, is the obloquy heaped upon them by the former regime.[23]

Unlike the earlier article, this sequel will not concentrate its attention on the PRM, whose activity "in the service of the marshal" (the title of an apologetic book on Antonescu that does not deserve citation) and its own deriving self-serving political purposes hardly underwent any change in the years that elapsed since the completion of *Cui bono*. Instead, the present study first surveys developments in the four-year time span that Romania was governed by a coalition of center-right parties and by President Emil Constantinescu, seeking to inquire whether official or officially related attitudes displayed toward the legacy of the *Conducător* underwent any significant change in that period. It then returns to scrutinize utilitarian anti-Semitic attitudes in the old-new regime, returned to power by the electorate in the year 2000. The study concentrates its attention, in the third part, on the reasons that prompted the issuance of Emergency Ordinance 31, which forbade the cult of Antonescu and introduced penalties for Holocaust denial, as well as on an analysis of that ordinance's saga. It concludes by posing a few questions pertaining to "constrained memory."

BETWEEN ONE GOVERNANCE AND THE NEXT

When President Emil Constantinescu replaced his predecessor, Ion Iliescu, in 1996, there was hope that the age of utilitarian anti-Semitism had come to an end. The new governing coalition was no longer leaning on extremist parties. It encompassed a broad spectrum of center-right parties and the ethnic Hungarian Democratic Federation of Romania—in other words, what for the last seven years had been described by the generic term of "the democratic opposition." As if to illustrate that the hope was well-founded, the country's new head of state, in a message addressed to the Federation of Jewish Communities in Romania on 4 May 1997, for the first time acknowledged Romania's collective responsibility for the perpetration of the Holocaust. In the message that marked Holocaust Day, the head of state told his Jewish co-nationals that while the Holocaust was not "planned by Romanians" and while some Romanians risked their life to save Jews,

> We are also aware that other Romanians, blinded by criminal furor, participated in this horrible crime, in implementing the Nazi project of the "final solution." Romania's wartime authorities more than once attempted to oppose the Nazi demand for the full liquidation of the Jewish population, organized the immi-

gration of groups of Jews to Palestine, even openly protected some personalities of the Jewish community in Romania. But the same authorities organized deportations and promoted a racial legislation. Today *we accept responsibility for this dramatic inconsistency*. The sacrifice of hundreds of thousands of Jews from all over Romania is a burden on our heart, on all Romanians. The death of innocents can neither be forgiven, nor undone, nor forgotten. It is our duty to offer the victims of the Holocaust time and time again our memory, the assurance that nothing will be forgotten—no deed and no name. It is my duty as president of Romania, as president of all Romanian citizens, to be the guarantor of that memory, no matter how painful it may be; it is my duty to keep alive the memory of Jews who fell victim of the genocide. You are therefore not alone at this commemoration; through me, all Romanians remember every single Jewish fellow-citizen who perished without any guilt more than five decades ago. Our common memory is their posthumous victory. It is the weapon that helps us over decades and generations, to struggle against the temptation of not feeling guilty for our own past.[24]

The president was certainly taking a position his predecessor had never taken, for Iliescu had condemned the atrocities committed by the Iron Guard and the anti-Semitic policies of the Antonescu regime, but never spoke of any Romanian contribution to the implementation of the "final solution." Even if Constantinescu was intentionally getting his chronology upside-down (whatever steps were taken by the Antonescu regime to remedy the plight of Jews followed Stalingrad and were aimed at sending a signal to the Allied powers, not the other way around as presented in the message), the president was for the first admitting that the *individual guilt* of leaders and their followers can translate into the *collective responsibility* of future generations. This is precisely what *Vergangenheitsbewältigung* is all about. Only individual guilt can be subject to criminal prosecution, but only admittance of collective responsibility can attest to a will to overcome the burdens of the past. Unfortunately, Constantinescu's statement was largely ignored in Romania.[25] It was, in fact, ignored to such extent that at the end of 2000, writer Nicolae Balotă was making public a letter he had written to Constantinescu in 1997 in which he urged the president to do precisely what Constantinescu did when he addressed the Jewish community; to no avail, Balotă was wrongly persuaded three years on, when he claimed Constantinescu had not even bothered to reflect on his suggestions "with any [sense of] profundity."[26] During a visit of the U.S. Holocaust Memorial Museum in Washington on 18 July 1998, Constantinescu once more employed an inverse chronology in his speech, speaking first about the saving of Jews rather than start with the persecution that preceded it, but at the same time the president remarked that

Despite these [commendable acts] no one has the right to ignore that the Holocaust tragedy did not shun Romania; no one has the right to deny the tragic fate of Jews who lost their life and their beloved ones in Bessarabia and Bukovina,

> in Transnistria, in Iaşi, Bucharest or Dorohoi . . . the persecutions and the humiliation to which they were subjected during the Legionary governance and the [Antonescu] governance that followed it. Even if Nazi Germany's direct or indirect involvement was not negligible either, responsibility for those Romanian citizens who were persecuted rather than being protected by the Romanian state cannot be and must not be eluded.[27]

Between the two declarations, however, facts were not quite matching words. On 22 October 1997, Prosecutor General Sorin Moisescu launched procedure for the official rehabilitation of eight members of the Antonescu government. The procedure, called *recurs în anulare* or "extraordinary appeal," would have clearly opened the path toward Antonescu's own posthumous judicial rehabilitation, long demanded by the PRM and other ultranationalists in Romania.[28] Moisescu explained that the Romanian Penal Code does not provide for "collective responsibility" and that by suspending the constitution, dissolving the parliament, and assuming full personal power, Antonescu had by implication also abolished the principle of collective ministerial responsibility.[29] While on a visit to Berlin on 7 November, Constantinescu told Radio Free Europe/Radio Liberty correspondent William Totok that he was aware of the "delicate international implications" the rehabilitation might raise but that the officials involved had been "outstanding Romanian cultural figures" who were not associated with any of the "negative aspects" of Antonescu's rule.[30] The claim was quite thin. Most ministers involved had indeed been "cultural figures," but their alleged noninvolvement was more than questionable. In a decree signed on 7 March 1941, for instance, General Radu Rosetti, Antonescu's first Minister of Culture, Cults and the Arts (January–December 1941), stated, "The ethnicity of our nation must be shielded from mixing with Jewish blood."[31] As Minister of Culture in Romania's first short-lived (December 1937–February 1938) anti-Semitic government of Octavian Goga and Alexandru C. Cuza, philosopher Ion Petrovici was personally responsible for the introduction of a *numerus clausus* in schools and collectively responsible for the government's decision to deprive some 200,000 Romanian Jews of their citizenship. Petrovici was again Minister of Culture and Cults in the Antonescu government between December 1941 and 1944, organizing, among other things, an intergovernmental agency that coordinated the deportation of Jewish converts.[32]

Moisescu's decision to launch the rehabilitations triggered the protests of US Helsinki Committee co-chairmen Senator Alfonse D'Amato and Representative Christopher Smith. It was neither the first nor the last such protest from the two prominent congressmen.[33] In a letter to President Constantinescu, they said the officials whose rehabilitation was sought had been "cabinet members in a government that was responsible for the persecution of the entire Romanian Jewish community and the deportation and murder of at least 250,000 Romanian and Ukrainian Jews." Their rehabilitation "would call into question the sincerity of Romania's commitment to the West's most fundamental shared values and is likely to trigger a reassessment of support for Romania's candidacy for membership in our economic and security institutions" (i.e., NATO and, presumably, the EU as well).[34] "Memory" was thus for the first time being unambiguously linked to "membership."

Only one day earlier, Moisescu had attempted to explain why he deemed it proper to rehabilitate the eight officials. On 22 November, compliance followed. Closer examination, it was now said, has established that "collective ministerial responsibility" did, after all, apply to in all but one of the eight cases. The other seven ministers, according to the same statement, could not be absolved of the "political responsibility" they carried for "military, economic and social decisions" taken by the cabinet they had been members of, such as "socially discriminatory measures taken against some Jews on 30 June 1941" (a euphemism for the Iaşi pogrom) and the waging of war on the Soviet Union in November 1941.[35] Following the Nuremberg trials model, these had been considered to be "crimes against peace" by the tribunal that had sentenced the eight in 1949. The only exception was to be made for Toma Petre Ghiţulescu, who had only briefly (5 April–26 May 1941) served as Undersecretary of State in the National Economy Minister and resigned prior to 30 June 1941. Ghiţulescu was rehabilitated by the Supreme Court on 26 October 1998, and the occasion proved that apprehensions that the "extraordinary appeal" launched by Moisescu could be but the first step toward Antonescu's own rehabilitation had not been exaggerated: Ghiţulescu's family asked the court to rehabilitate the entire Antonescu cabinet, including the *Conducător*. The plea, however, was dismissed.[36] On 17 January 2000 the same court also rehabilitated Netta Gheron (not included on the list submitted by Moisescu), who served as Finance Minister at the twilight of the Antonescu cabinet between 1 April and 23 August 1944.[37]

In "Marshal Antonescu's Post-Communist Rehabilitation: *Cui Bono?*" I examined closely the rehabilitation process used and abused by the Communist-successor parties and the extremist ultranationalist formations. It is not insignificant to scrutinize reactions to the rehabilitation attempts among the former "democratic opposition," now that it had taken over power.

The National Liberal Party (PNL) has a particularly long post-1989 record on support of Antonescu's rehabilitation drive. The most emphatic spokesman for this cause among parliamentarians representing the party was Dan Amadeo Lăzărescu, who also claims to be a historian. In the first (1990–1992) legislature he spoke in parliament several times in praise of Antonescu and seemed to have never changed his mind. By 1997, in an article published in *Aldine*—an ultranationalist, fundamentalist Orthodoxist and anti-Semitic supplement of the "democratic" daily *România liberă*—Lăzărescu was defending Moisescu's rehabilitation initiative and was writing that the Romanian people "cannot comprehend the absurd pretensions of some [Jewish or Jewish-supporting] circles over the ocean to except [Antonescu and his cabinet ministers] from the noble principle of rehabilitation and restitution of property confiscated by a regime eager to liquidate by all means Romania's political, military and social elites."[38] Lăzărescu eventually turned out to have been a *Securitate* informer.[39] His opinions on Antonescu were certainly reflecting those of the "Forces of Old."

As William Totok showed, even PNL's first post-Communist party chairman, Radu Câmpeanu, was a staunch defender of Antonescu and a "Holocaust negationist."[40] Câmpeanu had also been suspected in some circles of having collaborated with the *Securitate* during his Parisian exile, from which he had returned in 1989. In his case, however, the suspicion has never been confirmed. But PNL Senator Alexandru Paleologu, one of the few to have openly admitted to have been recruited by the *Securitate* as an informer while in prison but to have never actually informed,[41] should not be suspected of "serving the Cause" when he rushed to Antonescu's defense. Largely considered to be a liberal spirit—though somewhat of a maverick—he belongs to that category of Romanian intellectuals who are simply unable to take a critical look at the country's contemporary history. Not an extreme nationalist, he nonetheless insists on ignoring historic evidence and on considering Romania's nationalism as a "benign" and "necessary" form of identity-searching,[42] hence often finding himself on the same barricades with Romania's ultranationalists whom he otherwise opposes—perhaps to his own surprise.[43]

It was consequently hardly unusual to find Paleologu denouncing Marshal Antonescu's perception as a fascist. Antonescu's rule, he wrote, was "at most" one that can be qualified as "a national regime with authoritarian features."[44] As for some of his cabinet members whose rehabilitation Moisescu had just initiated, Paleologu wrote that he had personally known them and could vouch for their being "people of integrity and a strong character." Some of them might have been anti-Semites, the Senator added, but opinions "cannot be put on trial." Even the Nuremberg trials should never have taken place, since they were nothing but the "trial of the vanquished by the victors." He would not deny that "the massacre, killing or starving to death of some Jews through mishandling is a horrible, monstrous thing." The question remained open, however, whether Antonescu's cabinet members knew about those massacres and approved of them. And even if they did, "Could they possibly have resigned from the cabinet?" Paleologu added, apparently unaware that he was contradicting his own statement on the regime being merely an "authoritarian" one.[45] Never missing an occasion whenever he writes on Antonescu to point out that he had been a staunch opponent of the marshal after Antonescu decided to continue the war beyond its scope of retaking the Soviet-annexed territories, Paleologu is apparently unaware how oblivious he is to Jewish suffering (which he never claims to have opposed) under the marshal.

In a nutshell, Paleologu was arguing that Antonescu should never have been tried because victors must not administer justice onto the vanquished, and that his ministers should not have been put on trial because Antonescu's views may not have been their own; and even if they were, they could not be held responsible for overseeing that these views were translated into deeds.

Another prominent PNL defender of Antonescu was the party's then National Council Chairman (and thus practically the second man in the PNL hierarchy), literary critic Nicolae Manolescu, who as early as December 1995 was writing in an editorial in the weekly *România literară* that Jewish historians should finally comprehend that Antonescu cannot be judged solely from the perspectives of the crimes he had committed against their brethren.[46] I have extensively dealt with his case elsewhere, and it will not benefit anyone (least of all Manolescu) to tell his saga all over again.[47] But his undoubtedly is a sad case. A brilliant literary critic and an opponent of the Ceauşescu national-Communist policies, after the change of regime Manolescu became involved in politics but applied to it the same "impressionistic" approach that guides his literary output. Just as he sees nothing wrong with contradicting himself when he writes about literature,[48] he would contradict himself—including on Antonescu—time and time again.[49] Indeed, Manolescu would go as far as to come out in defense of the 2002 governmental ordinance (see below) forbidding the cult of the same man about whom he wrote only a few years earlier that he must be evaluated less unilaterally than Jewish historians are in the habit of doing.[50] His most inspired political step appears to have been his 2001 decision to leave politics behind and return to what he does best.[51]

The largest party in the now-ruling coalition was the National Peasant Party Christian Democratic (PNŢCD)—the PNL's main partner in the umbrella organization of the Democratic Convention of Romania (CDR). Although less present in the media, PNŢCD politicians were in fact more active than their PNL peers in pursing Antonescu's judicial rehabilitation. On 14 June 1999, PNŢCD Senator Ion Moisin demanded that the house pass a resolution rehabilitating Antonescu, describing the marshal as "a great Romanian patriot, who fought for his country till his death."[52]

There were also drives to rehabilitate Antonescu emerging "from below," in civic society. In 1999, six Timişoara-based NGOs initiated a "rehabilitation trial," which, expectedly ended in Antonescu's exoneration by a "moral jury."[53] Earlier, the town's local council, on which the ruling CDR had a majority, named a street in the marshal's honor. With Pippidi's remarkable exception, historians asked to react to Moisescu's initiative tended to be explicitly or implicitly supportive. What is more, among those expressing such indirect or direct support there were some who by no means belonged to the category of Holocaust deniers—for example, Dinu C. Giurescu and Alexandru Zub.[54] The most emphatic, however, was Florin Constantiniu, who in what would become with him a recurrent favorite theme, compared U.S. pressures to annul the rehabilitation drive with the Sovietization of Romania. In an article suggestively entitled "Yesterday Moscow, Today Washington," Constantiniu presented the d'Amato–Smith protest letter as an attempt to censor healthy historical debate in Romania. According to the historian, the letter was tantamount to an act of censorship, and was the more unacceptable as this censorship attempt stemmed from those who had abandoned Eastern Europe to the U.S.S.R. after World War II. The same people, he wrote, prove time and again to be very sensitive to the crimes of fascism, but are oblivious to those of communism.[55] Many allegedly democratic media outlets echoed the same line. For journalist Ion Cristoiu, the two U.S. congressmen were "Two Bolsheviks from the American Congress," as the title of his editorial in the daily *Național* had them depicted on 25 November 1997.

The four years of CDR in power, in sum, had demonstrated that with a few notable exceptions, the "choice of memory" had remained problematic. The refusal of *Vergangenheitsbewältigung,* as Alexandra Laignel-Lavastine showed in 1999, was not limited to the opportunists and the ultranationalists.[56] Even if their motivations were different, opinion leaders in Romanian society were contemplating the past from a perspective that was obviously different from that of the group they all wished to become members of the Western democracies and, more specifically, NATO.

UTILITARIAN ANTI-SEMITISM REVISITED

The outcome of the 2000 parliamentary and presidential elections in Romania should have taught the PDSR (or its successor, the PSD) a hard lesson in the dangers inherent in the ambivalence of courting the extreme nationalist electorate and its representatives. The PRM garnered nearly 20 percent of the vote for the Chamber of Deputies and more than one voter in five (21.01 percent) cast a ballot for Romania's extreme nationalist party. Moreover, Corneliu Vadim Tudor, the party's leader, forced Iliescu into a runoff in which he obtained 33.17 percent of the vote. It would be inaccurate to claim that anti-Semitism, or extreme-nationalism in general, was the main factor behind the PRM's electoral performance, one that had transformed the party into Romania's second-largest parliamentary formation.[57] The vote was above all a protest vote triggered by the dismal governance performance of the center-right government that was voted out of power. Even so, for many Romanians the anti-Semitic and xenophobic attitudes of the PRM were not reason enough to refrain from supporting that party, which increased its parliamentary representation nearly fourfold from the previous elections. The question with which I ended an article on extremism in Romania up to the 1996 elections ("But what about the year 2000, when the next elections are due? Or 2004, or 2008, for that matter?") had been prophetically more accurate than I wished it would be.[58]

Much of Ion Iliescu's campaign between the runoffs was geared toward emphasizing his rival's extremist postures and the dangers involved in them for Romania's international image. Yet as he kicked off his campaign to regain the office he had lost to Emil Constantinescu in 1996, quite different notes were being played on the electoral score. In October 2000, in an interview with the daily *Adevărul*, Iliescu was keen to tell the electorate that he had always valiantly defended Romania's historical record. His detractors—among whom Tudor had been orchestra conductor, one should add—were insisting on unimportant gestures (Iliescu had covered his head during visits paid to the Choral Temple in Bucharest and to the United States Holocaust Memorial Museum in Washington in 1993) but were overlooking significant content, Iliescu said. For instance, he added, no one had remarked the difference between himself and Polish President Lech Wałęsa. Unlike the latter, when visiting the Israeli Knesset Iliescu had refrained from apologizing for his countrymen's participation in the Holocaust. The issue, Iliescu emphasized, was one that still required elucidation by historians.[59]

Instead of telling his critics that time has come to assume collective responsibility (which is by no means tantamount to collective culpability), Iliescu was thus striking one more note of utilitarian anti-Semitism. While stopping short of exonerating Antonescu, he was "leaving judgment" to historians. On the eve of his renewed mandate, he told an audience at a Radio Free Europe/Radio Liberty briefing in Washington that Marshal Ion Antonescu "had some merits" too. It was Antonescu, he said, who had quashed the Iron Guard rebellion in early 1941, and "Antonescu had proved more tolerance" toward the Jews than did Admiral Miklós Horthy's Hungary, not to mention the fact that he "had the merit of liberating the territory occupied by the Soviets." And why, he asked, are double standards applied: Why is Romania being singled out for attempts by some people to rehabilitate Antonescu, while the fact that Marshal Philippe Pétain in France is being venerated by some followers is overlooked, as indeed is the fact that Marshal Carl Gustaf Mannerheim is considered a national hero in Finland? Unfortunately, no one in the audience had either the knowledge or the audacity to point out that (despite his personal responsibility for anti-Jewish legislation and the death of enforced labor Jews in 1941 or those massacred as "alien Jews" in and around Novi Sad in 1942) Horthy was a strange anti-Semite who, up to the country's invasion by Germany in March 1944, had in many ways protected Hungarian Jews from a worse fate.[60] And there was no one in the audience to tell Iliescu that Mannerheim, while a Hitler ally because of the Soviet's invasion of Finland, had kept Finnish democracy in place, was not guilty of any war crimes, and that a total of seven Finnish Jews had perished in the Holocaust—indeed that at least 300 members of the tiny (2,000-strong) Jewish community in that country had fought in Finish uniform alongside the German army for their country's liberation.[61] Estimates for Jews exterminated during the war in the territories under Romanian rule, on the other hand, range between 102,000 and 410,000.[62]

Having regained the presidency, Iliescu had lost the electoral "excuse" for employing utilitarian anti-Semitism. Yet he was showing no sign of renouncing it. In a speech at the Choral Temple in Bucharest marking the sixtieth anniversary of the Iron Guard pogrom in Bucharest on 21 January 2001, he said the Iron Guardist "aberration" had been a "delirium of intolerance and anti-Semitism." However, the president added, that brief "delirium" excepted, there has been no Romanian contribution to "the long European history" of persecution of the Jews, and it was "significant" that there was "no Romanian word for pogrom." In other words, there had been no "Antonescu episode" in the history of Romanian Jews. Furthermore, he hastened to add, it was "unjustified to attribute to Romania an artificially inflated number of Jewish victims for the sake of media impact." Romania's distorted image, according to Iliescu, was likely to be corrected when "Romanian (i.e., rather than Jewish) historians will tackle the subject."[63]

Hardly six months had passed, however, and Iliescu's "unique aberration" of 1941 grew slightly larger. With Romania banging on NATO's doors and against the protests in the U.S. and Israel triggered by the Antonescu cult in Romania, Iliescu attended a ceremony marking the Iași pogrom where he felt compelled to declare that "*no matter what we may think*, international public opinion considers Antonescu to have been a war criminal."[64] But what he called "international public opinion" had spoken out before, and had then been largely ignored; or rather, attempts were made to misinform those protesting the Antonescu cult, including by Iliescu himself.[65] Suddenly, Iliescu was discovering it. Still, he was not telling his countrymen that they must change their *minds* about Antonescu (no matter what we *think*)—only that they must change their *discourses* about him—an option with which Romanians were certainly not unfamiliar with after nearly half a century of Communism.[66]

At the beginning of the same month, a scandal of major proportion had shattered the Romanian military, and with it the public at large. General Mircea Chelaru, former chief of staff of the Romanian Army, attended in Bucharest on 1 June the ceremony of the unveiling of a bust of Antonescu. The event took place on the fifty-fifth anniversary of the marshal's execution, with the bust being displayed in the courtyard of the Saints Constantin and Elena church, which Antonescu had founded in 1943. Alongside Chelaru, present at the ceremony were also PRM leader Corneliu Vadim Tudor, his deputy and Senate Deputy Chairman, historian Gheorghe Buzatu, and Marshal Antonescu League honorary chairman Iosif Constantin Drăgan.[67] Known for his extreme nationalist postures, Chelaru had the briefest term a post-Communist chief of staff ever had: from 15 February 2000 to 31 October. In that period, he presided over an attempt to unveil an Antonescu statue in Iași, on what was planned to be a "Marshals' Alley." The alley was to host the busts of Romania's two other marshals—Marshal Constantin Prezan and Marshal Alexandru Averescu. Following protests of the town's Jewish community, the planned Antonescu bust was replaced by one of King Ferdinand, and the bust representing Antonescu was removed to the nearby Leţcani cemetery, which was named on the occasion in Antonescu's honor. According to media reports, there had been pressure to renounce the project from abroad as well, in other words, from the U.S.[68]

Chelaru was forced to resign as chief of staff after having displayed what appeared to be Bonapartist postures: he warned publicly against alleged dangers to the country's territorial integrity by "enclaves" being formed not only in Transylvania—under Hungarian inspiration—but also in the southern parts of the country, allegedly under Bulgarian inspiration. The suspicion arose that Chelaru might be contemplating some form of military takeover, and that suspicion was perhaps confirmed by his joining a group calling itself the National Association of Military Personnel upon his dismissal. The group comprised active and retired soldiers who purported to represent an effort to "prevent corruption, anti-social and anti-national acts, and the struggle against crime." Since the group infringed on military statutes, it was not recognized by the Defense Ministry and was forced to disband. According to a U.S. intelligence report, President Constantinescu had argued against Chelaru's resignation, but the Supreme Defense Council decided to impose it "to avoid any misinterpretation [on] . . . the exercise of democratic control over the armed forces" by NATO.[69] The general became chief of the army's Institute of Strategic Studies upon his resignation as chief of staff.

His participation in the bust-unveiling ceremony was to lead to his departure from the Army itself. Under obvious pressure from NATO circles—as could be read between the lines of a press release of the Defense Ministry—the general was charged with having infringed on military regulations forbidding participation in manifestations of political character. "It is regrettable," the press release said, that "individual gestures that are connected to a person who has been condemned by the international community [risk to] overshadow the collective efforts of the Army . . . to join NATO and the European Union."[70] Prime Minister Adrian Năstase intervened personally in the affair, telling a forum of his party that "at least two countries," the U.S. and Israel are "disturbed" by the continued Antonescu cult in Romania. As a "representative of the Army," the premier added, Chelaru should have "taken into account these sensibilities, particularly at a time when politics are vital for Romania in its relations with NATO and its members" ahead of the planned November 2002 summit in Prague, where the organization's enlargement figured on its agenda.[71] President Iliescu, in turn, said that each time Chelaru had visited the U.S. as chief of staff, he had been confronted with the "bad impression" the pro-Antonescu cult created there and has been questioned on the matter by his counterparts. A man in Chelaru's position, Iliescu added, should have been aware of the "bad marks" detrimental for the country's present efforts to improve its image abroad.[72] Rather than face being court-martialed, Chelaru retired from the army.

Before submitting his resignation, Chelaru stated on Romanian television that he was "wondering why we should take into account the sensibilities of others, while everybody can scoff at and mock our own sensibilities." Earlier, he told Mediafax, "We are being ordered to spit [on everything that is dear to Romanian collective memory], so spit, brothers, spit."[73] In an interview with the Romanian Radio about one month after his departure from the ranks, Chelaru emphasized that his decision to leave the Army had been determined by the inner conflict (Festinger would have called it "dissonance") he was confronting as a result of an "arbitrary cosmopolitan act" toward a "high-ranking officer" committed by that very organization that should be the "guardian of the nation's symbolic values." As a result, he said, he took the decision to go into retirement and "regenerate" himself.[74] On the other side of the Atlantic, Christopher Smith was professing to be "encouraged by the swift and unequivocal response by the Romanian government to the inexcusable participation of General Mircea Chelaru" in the bust-unveiling ceremony of "Romania's wartime dictator."[75] The "clash of memories" could not be more blatant. As for "regeneration," Chelaru reemerged in 2002 as the newly elected chairman of the extraparliamentary extreme nationalist Party of Romanian National Unity.

Utilitarian anti-Semitism had thus reached a crossroads. On one hand, what was once a bastion of the marshal's rehabilitation—the Army itself—was beginning to get rid of some of the cult's most ardent supporters. On the other hand, there could be no doubt that there was both resistance and rejection of the drive within the ranks of the military. Perhaps nothing illustrates this better than a volume produced by military historians from the Institute for Defense Political and Military History Studies in 2000. The body of the volume, whose "co-ordinator," that is to say editor, was Antonescu-apologist Colonel Dr. Alexandru Duţu, was a continuation of what Romanian military historians had produced ever since the institute was still called the Center for Military History and Theory and headed by presidential brother Ilie Ceauşescu. The introduction, however, took the opposite position. It carried the telling title "A Futile Saga" and was authored by General Mihail Ionescu, who became the new head of the institute in August 2000.[76] Which of the two sides would now get the ear of Romania's hitherto utilitarian anti-Semites?

AN ORDINANCE IMPOSED FROM AFAR

On 13 March 2002, the Romanian government issued an emergency ordinance banning the cult of Marshal Ion Antonescu. The ordinance came into force on 28 March, with its publication in the official gazette, the *Monitorul oficial*. For unclear reasons, the issuance of the document was kept a secret for five days, its contents emerging only on 18 March. The most likely explanation for the briefly kept secrecy should probably be sought in a concerted public relations campaign targeting foreign, rather than domestic audiences. For it was also on 18 March that, at the National Defense College in Bucharest, the first syllabus for high-ranking officials on the Holocaust in Romania was launched. Teaching the first course was Dr. Radu Ioanid of the United States Holocaust Memorial Museum in Washington, a Romanian-born historian and author of several books on anti-Semitism and the Holocaust in Romania.[77] Not without reason (see below), Ioanid was viewed by many in Romania as some sort of "chief monitor" of the thriving Antonescu cult, the man who was behind alerting U.S. congressmen and Jewish American organizations that time and again protested against the transformation of the country's wartime leader into an object of semiofficially sanctioned cult. It was apparently hoped that the impact of the announcement on the ordinance would be enhanced by Ioanid's presence at the inauguration of the syllabus—and its echoes on the Hill would not be missed.[78]

By issuing the ordinance, Premier Năstase was fulfilling a pledge made during an October 2001 visit to the Holocaust Memorial Museum and at a meeting with U.S. Jewish leaders in New York. That the Romanian premier was also received on the occasion of that visit by U.S. President George W. Bush for a previously unscheduled meeting had probably little to do with the way the Holocaust was treated in his country;[79] rather, it was a "friendly signal" for the premier of a country that had rallied behind Washington more than others in East Central Europe did after the terrorist attack on New York and Washington on 11 September 2001. But the signal was being beamed at a time when Romania was intensifying its efforts to be accepted as a member of NATO at the alliance's November summit in Prague; and perceptions in Bucharest about who can influence a positive decision had been unmistakably displayed during a visit paid by Năstase to Israel in July that year, when he sought to enlist the support of the country's two chief rabbis for Romania's membership of NATO.[80]

In interviews granted on the occasion, Ioanid bluntly told his hosts that Romania "cannot enter NATO with Antonescu on its banners." To become a member of the alliance, he said, Romania must also become a member in the family that shares its values.[81] To make that statement at the heart of one of the Antonescu cult cradles—the Army—showed no little measure of self-confidence (as well as some *chutzpa*). As mentioned, the Romanian military and the college that was launching the syllabus had been long among the main promoters of the cult. But Ioanid was drawing attention to recent statements by U.S. NATO Committee Chairman Bruce Jackson. Indeed, on a visit to Bucharest some three weeks earlier, and despite praising the progress made by Romania in military reforms toward NATO accession, Jackson did not mince words: "Give me a bulldozer and I shall immediately destroy all Antonescu statues," he said, adding that adherence to democratic values includes facing one's historical past and is "not negotiable" in the accession process.[82]

The ordinance prohibited the display of "racist or fascist symbols," the erection of statues or commemorative plaques for those condemned in Romania or abroad for "crimes against peace" and for "crimes against humanity," as well as the naming of streets and other places after those personalities. Exceptions were to be made only for museums, where such statues could be displayed for the purpose of "scientific activity" carried out outside "public space." It also outlawed organizations of "fascist, racist, and xenophobic character" that promote ideas "on ethnic, racist, or religious grounds" and extended this prohibition to both registered and unregistered foundations or any other form of organization consisting of three persons or more. Finally, it provided penalties ranging from fines to fifteen years in prison for those infringing its regulations or denying the Holocaust.[83] In other words, the ordinance reflected the response to a situation in which the country's ruling political elite had been told it can no longer procrastinate. For what Jackson had told his hosts in February was that an option has to be made between two clashing "memories." On the one hand, there was the "memory" of those promoting the Antonescu cult and of those who acquiesced to that promotion out of utilitarian motivations; on the other hand, there was the "memory" of Antonescu as chief perpetrator of the Romanian Holocaust reflected in Jewish and (more rarely) Romany commemorations of his victims. And Jackson had made it crystal clear that the latter "memory" coincided with the collective "memory" of the organization Romania was striving to join.

For the purpose of domestic consumption and in what may have been an attempt to sweeten the pill of the foreign-prescribed medicine, the country's leadership seemed to employ an idiom different from that employed for outside usage even after the ordinance's issuance. On 22 March, Năstase was emphasizing that he was opposed to attempts to "indict the Romanian people for the Holocaust,"[84] and that responsibility for its perpetration "squarely falls on the leaders and the government of the times, and on them alone." Năstase was thereby legitimizing the jargon of Romanian Holocaust deniers, who always protest against what they claim are attempts to "indict the Romanian people" for the purpose of squeezing out from the country fabulous amounts of compensation. Last but by no means least, the premier was also indulging in the "comparative trivialization" of the Holocaust[85] when he claimed that "history has encountered situations that were a lot more grievous, any yet nobody tried to indict the German, Russian, or the American peoples."

In turn, President Iliescu was reiterating—though in a slightly modified formulation—his deflection of negative perceptions of Antonescu onto foreigners. Addressing a seminar organized in Bucharest under the auspices of U.S. Jewish organizations, Iliescu said that Antonescu is considered "*by the states who fought in World War II for democracy and against Hitler*" to be a war criminal and that consequently "any manifestation of an Antonescu cult" in Romania, "*no matter how one tries to justify it,*" is perceived there as being "in defiance of the international community attached to democratic ideals and values."[86] The encoded messages of the country's two highest officials thus read: You can rest assured that we shall not force you into facing collective responsibility and you must understand that we do not necessarily identify with what is being imposed on us.

An additional signal for internal consumption came when the government, in an obvious contradiction to its own ordinance, decided to display at its official seat the portraits of all Romanian premiers. The gallery, of course, included the marshal's portrait, which triggered a letter of protest by the U.S. Helsinki Commission, objecting to both that step and to procrastination in removing the Antonescu statues.[87] Culture Minister Răzvan Theodorescu, however, had claimed on 27 May that all Antonescu statues—except a bust displayed in Bucharest in the courtyard of the church built by him—had been dismantled.[88] As for the governmental portrait gallery, Theodorescu explained that the exhibit was outside "public space," and thus within the restrictions of the ordinance.[89] One could just as well have argued that the official seat of the government was the very center of "public space."

According to the Federation of Jewish Communities in Romania, since 1993 six statues had been erected in the memory of the marshal—in Bucharest, Iaşi, Jilava, Slobozia, Piatra-Neamţ and Târgovişte.[90] The pro-Antonescu forces, on the other hand, counted only four statues.[91] Two more statues—in Sărmaş and Călăraşi—were mentioned in the U.S. Helsinki Committee protest letter. Which of these belonged to the category of "public space" and would thus have to be dismantled according to the ordinance's stipulation was not quite clear. At Jilava, a cross (not a statue) had been erected on the spot of Antonescu's execution sometime in the early 1990s, without any public announcement having been made on it. Being administered by the Justice Ministry, the Jilava prison grounds are arguably "public space," but it seems that the cross is still on its place. Two busts—in Bucharest and in Sărmaş (Mureş County) were on church grounds, the one in the capital being in the courtyard of the church built by the dictator, whose unveiling had been attended by Chelaru. Were these monuments on "public space?" The Bucharest statue was not dismantled, but was ordered to be "covered."[92] The mayor of Călăraşi denied that the statue in his town was displayed on "public space," saying that the bust was on the grounds of the Marshal Ion Antonescu League and thus untouchable.[93] That left in fact three statues undoubtedly erected on "public space": the one in Leţcani, near Iaşi, in a military cemetery—"Heroes' Cemetery Ion Antonescu!" in Slobozia; and in Piatra-Neamţ (the statue in Târgovişte apparently does not exist). These were all dismantled.[94] Finally, procedures were launched in early August against PRM Cluj Mayor Gheorghe Funar, who had displayed several blueprints for a planned statue in the town's city hall and had refused to dismantle them.[95]

The cheapest statue, Pippidi writes, is the renaming of a street. "Street signs can be replaced as one political regime chases out its predecessor."[96] According to Premier Năstase, by 31 July, fourteen out of the twenty-five streets named after Antonescu had been renamed and the rest were to soon follow.[97] But there was also clearly local resistance. Oradea Mayor Petru Filip announced that the municipal council (located on Ion Antonescu street, one of the town's largest avenues) has rejected the government's ordinance because "it is unclear whether the marshal was a war criminal or not." He eventually gave in. Botoşani municipal council followed in its footsteps, with several councilors representing the ruling party joining those of the PRM in opposing the ordinance, but had to change the decision after receiving a stern dissolution threat from Bucharest.[98] Other local councils simply ignored the ordinance without bothering to react at all.

Far more important, the fate of the ordinance itself was becoming unclear. Emergency ordinances become effective upon their issuance, but must eventually be approved by the parliament in order to become laws. Debates in commissions had shown that this was by no means to be taken for granted.

While the Senate's Human Rights Commission approved the ordinance's text without amendments on 9 April, in the Defense Commission representatives of the PNL (among them former party chairman Mircea Ionescu-Quintus) joined those of the PRM in demanding that the text be amended. It was claimed that the Holocaust was a diffuse concept that needed clarification; and it was also claimed that the article in the ordinance prohibiting Holocaust denial infringes on the human rights in general and on the right of freedom of expression in particular.[99] Although the PNL leadership distanced itself from its representatives on the commission,[100] their position was partly embraced by the same chamber's Judicial Commission. After twice postponing approval, this commission agreed on 5 June to an amended text, based on the proposal made by Senator Gheorghe Buzatu, a PRM deputy chairman and a historian specializing in Holocaust denial. Buzatu had proposed that the Holocaust be defined as "*the systematic massive extermination of the Jewish population in Europe, organized by the Nazi authorities during the Second World War.*" In other words, *by definition* there has been no Holocaust in Romania, since the extermination of Jews there had not been "organized by the Nazi authorities." The commission also reduced the maximum penalty for setting up organizations of a "fascist, racist, or xenophobe" character from fifteen to five years in prison.[101]

The definition is perfectly in line with Buzatu and his associates' peculiar "selective negationism," which does not deny the Holocaust as having taken place *elsewhere* but excludes *any* participation of members of one's own nation in its perpetration.[102] Should the plenum of the Senate approve the amendments proposed by the two commissions—and should the Chamber of Deputies, whose commissions have not yet debated the ordinance—also heed them, the government's emergency ordinance would be emptied of relevance.

The efforts by Theodorescu to preempt this situation, while apparently prompted by an attempt to overcome resistance, rendered a sense of the tragicomic. He proposed—as he would do at a special session of the Academy called to debate the issue of the Holocaust and Romania's role in it—that it be specified that while no Holocaust had taken place in Romania, "Holocaust-like" policies were implemented by the Antonescu regime on territories under "temporary Romanian occupation."[103] The Nazis could almost make the same claim, in fact. Most Holocaust atrocities, they could contend, had been perpetrated on non-German territory. Besides, to consider Bessarabia and northern Bukovina "occupied territories" called in to question the legitimacy of Antonescu's joining of the war launched by Hitler against the Soviet Union—in other words, that very legitimacy on whose grounds many Romanians rejected any parallel between the two countries' wartime acts.

IN LIEU OF CONCLUSION: CONSTRAINED MEMORY AND ITS DISCONTENTS

The "clash of memories" has expectedly resulted in the victory of the stronger. How secure that victory can be considered to be is, however, a different matter. Historical experience advocates caution. The 1923 extension of full citizenship rights to Romanian Jews was also achieved under considerable Western pressure over a long period of time, dating as far back as the 1866 constitution. Like then, the pressures extended by the *Alliance Israélite Universelle* via the Western powers was much resented, and in the end the 1923 "achievement" proved short-lived.[104]

Reactions to the ordinance confirm that a word of caution is in order. First, the acceptance of the Buzatu version of the "definition" of the Holocaust speaks miles of the Romanian attempt to "have the cake and eat it too." Second, the Romanian leadership's ambivalence in presenting the necessity of having the ordinance approved was telling a different story to domestic ears than the tune played for international listenership. In defending the ordinance, Defense Minister Ioan Mircea Paşcu went as far as urging young PSD members to be "rational, rather than emotional." Medieval prince Vlad the Impaler—for many, a national hero—would have been condemned for "crimes against humanity," had he been put on trial at Nuremberg, Paşcu said,[105] thus hinting that he agrees that Antonescu's condemnation was quite unfair, but also that history's *final* judgment may produce a different verdict. Moreover, and third, there was obvious reluctance within the ranks of the ruling party itself to the government-initiated measures. This was hardly surprising, as the PSD has always willingly included in its own ranks nationalists and extreme nationalists. Former Iliescu critic regarding Antonescu and his positions on the Holocaust, Adrian Păunescu was now a PSD Senator and he did not hesitate to wage war on his own party's position. In fact, the debate at the Romanian Academy was prompted by Păunescu's insistence that "history must be left to historians"—which was also one of the main anti-ordinance postures displayed by the PRM—and not only by it.[106] Nor was Păunescu alone within the PSD ranks in his resistance. He was joined, for example, by PSD Cultural Commission Deputy Chairman Grigore Zanc.[107]

Positions displayed by Romania's historians in the ensuing debate were not a surprise either. The most militant on the rejectionist side was, of course, Buzatu. The only ethnic Romanian historian to come out clearly in favor of the ordinance was, again unsurprisingly, Andrei Pippidi. His spouse, political scientist Alina Mungiu-Pippidi, pointed out that the ordinance was in itself insufficient. Public perceptions of Antonescu, she said, will change only if the legislation is followed by a more critical debate of what the marshal actually did. "From now on, it is the duty of liberal intellectuals to say that they have another opinion of Romania's past."[108] Indeed, a public opinion poll carried by the daily *Ziua* among its readers in 2001 showed that less than one in four (24.59 percent) were of the opinion that Antonescu had been a war criminal, and a large majority of over 75 percent held the opposite opinion.[109] This is, by and large, precisely what historians *failed* to do, however, and as Mungiu-Pippidi hinted in the same interview, there were good reasons to suspect this would be so. "Ceaușescu," she said, had needed these intellectuals to "show that his policy, independent from the West and from the East, was a national policy," and for this purpose he had used them; "but Ceaușescu is now dead and the groups are still here."

In the ensuing debates, former party-subservient but nationalist-minded historians would seize the occasion to make clear their opposition. This, for example, was the case of university professor Mihail Retegan, who (as if he had ever raised his voice against the party under the previous regime), said that he thought the days when the Communist regime was interfering with historical research had been left behind. This was similarly the case of the head of the Academy's Historical Section, Dan Berindei, who stated that Romania needed no legislation against Holocaust denial, because "there has been no Holocaust in Romania. There have been some deportation to Transnistria, [Romania] was a anteroom of the Holocaust, but not [the place of the] Holocaust."[110] Or, as Berindei would put it at the debate of the Romanian Academy, the country had only been "a wing of the phenomenon, that touched Romania as well."[111] Florin Constantiniu, a correspondent member of the Academy, on the other hand, put on his habitual performance of "objectivity:" on one hand, he praised Antonescu for being "the only politician in Romania's history" who attempted to restore the country's territorial integrity, while on the other hand deeming his policies toward the Jews as "more than a crime—a mistake!" At a symposium at the Bucharest Institute for Defense Political and Military History Studies on 1 July, which I had the honor to attend, the historian complained, on the other hand, about attempts to impose "political correctness" and dictates from abroad, and wondered why do historians, political scientists, and politicians in general display such "haste" toward Romania's "Antonescu problem," which, he claimed, would find its clarification and solution in due time. Constantiniu's criticism was common to several anti-ordinance postures. Though obviously driven by radically different motivations, the PRM or Şerban Suru, leader of the neo-Iron Guard in Romania, found themselves sharing the same boat with the Romanian Association for the Defense of Human Rights-Helsinki Committee, which issued a position paper on the ordinance. Gabriel Andreescu, a prominent defender of human rights in his country, emphasized in that position paper that the Emergency Ordinance 31 lacked any "emergency" except for bowing to pressure from the West.[112] I must admit that at the symposium I was unable to refrain from asking Constantiniu whether having waited for twelve years—the time that has passed since the fall of the Communist regime—was actually "hasty."

But historians habitually perceived to have been on the other side of the national-Communist Ceauşescu fence did not display any eagerness to support the ordinance either. Interviewed on Romanian Radio on 19 April, Dinu C. Giurescu said that "because of geostrategic, *not because of historical* reasons," Antonescu's statues should be displayed in the private, rather than in the public space. However, he added, the time will come when "that statue's merits and responsibilities will be reconsidered."[113] Membership considerations, in other words, may prevail over monuments, but whether they can prevail over memory is another matter. Without knowing it, Giurescu was thus vindicating his peer Andrei Pippidi, who in the interview with Reuters observed that "those defending Antonescu feel . . . the admission of his role in the Holocaust would be humiliating for Romania."

The reader should note that the PRM has been left out of this study's focus. There were good grounds to do so. Nothing the PRM said or did in connection with ordinance was in any way surprising or unexpected. That Tudor declared that he was ready to place in the "private space" of his courtyard an Antonescu bust was part of his habitual provocative postures, as indeed was his unveiling in Cluj of a bust of U.S. President Woodrow Wilson, into which ceremony he unsuccessfully tried to lure U.S. Ambassador Michael Guest, or his announced intention to unveil a bust in Braşov of assassinated Israeli Prime Minister Yizthak Rabin.[114] At most, the Wilson and

Rabin busts could be viewed as an extension of the negationist counteroffensive hitherto limited to making use of Holocaust terminology to refute the "enemy's argument." The linguistic war had thus been extended over the war waged over public space. Remarkably, the PRM also drew attention to the absence of similar legislation directed against Communist symbols and the denial of the Communist genocide.[115] Not only Andreescu, but also Pippidi, in the interview with Reuters, had also done so. The author of these lines has already expressed his position over this contentious issue[116] and cannot but reiterate it in the briefest possible form: the PRM is right, even if for the wrong reasons! I only urge the reader to remember that *non est idem, si duo dicunt idem*! [It is not necessarily the same thing if two say the same thing.] But I also urge him or her to remember that repeated adoption of identical or similar positions cannot be mere accidents—and that is precisely the case of Andreescu whenever the "Jewish problem" is brought up.

But what about utilitarian anti-Semitism's prospects? I fear that this study's conclusion must be that precious little has changed in elite political culture in Romania in the twelve years that have passed since the overthrow of the former regime. What I had termed as "simulated change" remains just as prominent a feature of that political culture as was under the previous regime.[117] Nothing perhaps demonstrates better this simulative aspect than an event registered almost parallel with the saga of Ordinance 31/2002. In an attempt to demonstrate to the Western world that extremism is on the wane, in early 2002 the ruling PSD accepted among its members two defectors from the ranks of the PRM parliamentarians. One of them was a former member of the Communist secret police; the other, Ilie Neacşu, was the former editor-in-chief of Romania's post-Communist most anti-Semitic weekly (typically called no less than *Europa*!) and a deputy chairman of the Marshal Antonescu League.[118]

Memory, it seems, can be constrained. But a constrained memory might, at best, display either cognitive dissonance or indulge into simulation. At worst, it will resist, biding its time—an asset that collective memories are never lacking. And that can hardly be said of memberships.

NOTES

*The Scientific Research Center of the Slovenian Academy of Sciences and Arts, Ljubljana, Slovenia, has granted permission to publish this article.

1. See Maurice Halbwachs, *On Collective Memory* (Edited, Translated and with an Introduction by Lewis A. Coser) (Chicago: University of Chicago Press, 1992), particularly pp. 167–89.

2. I am not qualified to elucidate the link between individual, historic and collective memory. For what they are worth, my thoughts were recently (1 July 2002) presented at a seminar in Bucharest: Memory, I said on that occasion, "is not only about

remembering. To remember is to recall the past. But memory is not only about the past. It is also about the present and about the future. Memory is instinctive. A child who does not remember that fire burns, would put its hand in the flame again and again. We instinctively remember the past in order to be able to function at present and in order to be able to cope with the future. . . . But just as memory is instinctive, so is forgetting. If we could not function without learning from experience, it is no less true that we cannot function if experience becomes obsessive. If we were to spend our lives in bemoaning personal, and above all collective traumas, we would become just as dysfunctional as human beings as we would be as walking *tabulae rasae*. It is hard to establish with certainty where the line between remembering and forgetting must be drawn. We know that we mourn in order to remember, but also in order to be able to forget. Mourning, including collective mourning, thus has a double healing function. It is, on one hand, directed at understanding what happened to ourselves or our kin, but at the same time it is directed toward enabling ourselves to survive. The trouble is that memory in general, and collective memory in particular, is also selective. We 'forget' what we do not like to remember, we eliminate from our *psyche*, including the collective *psyche*, what we wish it did not happen. Even when we are forced by evidence to recognize our guilt, we tend to deflect responsibility unto others." Michael Shafir, "The Holocaust-Gulag Post-Communist 'Competition:'An Insurmountable Obstacle to Mutual Reconciliation?" published in *Revista de istorie militară*, nos. 5–6 (2002). See Paul Ricoeur, *Memoria, istoria, uitarea* (Timişoara: Editura Amarcord, 2001), translated from the original *La mémoire, l'histoire, l'oubli* (Paris: Éditions du Seuil, 2000), pp. 500–611.

3. See Leon Festinger, *A Theory of Cognitive Dissonance* (White Plains, NY: Row Peterson, 1957).

4. Ricoeur, *Memoria, istoria, uitarea*.

5. Pierre Nora, *Les lieux de mémoire* (Paris: Gallimard, 1997).

6. Jean-Charles Szurek, "Pentru o memorie democratică a trecuturilor traumatizante" [For a Democratic Memory of Traumatizing Pasts], in Colegiul Noua Europă, *Istoria recentă în Europa: Obiecte de studiu, surse, metode* (Bucureşti: Lucrările simpozionului internaţional organizat de Colegiul Noua Europă, 7–8 aprilie 2000), pp. 53–54. Emphasis in original.

7. Martin Malia, "Judging Nazism and Communism," *The National Interest* (Fall 2002), p. 69.

8. Katherine Verdery, *The Political Lives of Dead Bodies: Reburial and Postsocialist Change* (New York: Columbia University Press, 1999), p. 52 and pp. 98–127, respectively.

9. See Andrei Pippidi, *Despre statui şi morminte: Pentru o teorie a istoriei simbolice* [On Statues and Tombs: Toward a Theory of Historic Symbols] (Iaşi: Polirom, 2000), particularly pp. 5–10.

10. George Schöpflin, *Nations, Identity, Power* (London: Hurst and Company, 2000), p. 74.

11. Benedict Anderson, *Imagined Communities: Reflections on the Origins and Spread of Nationalism* (London: Verso, 1991).

12. Lucian Boia, *Jocul cu trecutul: Istoria între adevăr şi ficţiune* [The Game with the Past: History between Truth and Fiction] (Bucharest: Humanitas, 1998), p. 7.

13. Jacques Rupnik, "Revoluţie-restauraţie" [Revolution-Restoration], in *Lettre internationale* (Romanian edition), no. 4 (Winter 1992/1993), p. 4.

14. Pippidi, *Depre statui şi morminte,* pp. 8 and 22, respectively.

15. Michael Shafir, "Antisemitism in Post-Communist East Central Europe: Its Whys and Hows," paper presented at the international symposium "Die nationale Wende und das kollektive Gedächtnis in Osteuropa nach 1990," organized by the Austrian Academy of Sciences and the Brno Masaryk University, Brno (14–17 March 2002).

16. Pippidi, *Despre statui şi morminte*, p. 78.

17. Ricoeur, *Memoria, istoria, uitarea*, p. 104.

18. Schöpflin, *Nations, Identity, Power*, p. 77–78.

19. Ricoeur, *Memoria, istoria, uitarea*, p. 108.

20. Michael Shafir, "Marshal Antonescu's Post-Communist Rehabilitation: *Cui Bono?*" in Randolph L. Braham (ed.), *The Destruction of Romanian and Ukrainian Jews During the Antonescu Era* (New York: Columbia University Press, 1997), pp. 349–410.

21. *Ibid*, p. 364. My analysis in that article was extensively confirmed (also in 1997) by Romanian historian Lucian Boia, in a book not yet marketed when I wrote the study. See his *Istorie şi mit în conştiinţa românească* [History and Myth in Romanian Consciousness] (Bucharest: Humanitas, 1997), pp. 75–76, 273, 277–78. For a subsequent analysis by Boia, see his *România: Ţară de frontieră a Europei* [Romania: European Borderland] (Bucharest: Humanitas, 2002), pp. 193–95, 214.

22. In particular, Michael Shafir, "Between Denial and 'Comparative Trivialization': Holocaust Negationism in Post-Communist East Central Europe," *ACTA,* no. 19 (2002).

23. Tony Judt, "The Past Is Another Country: Myth and Memory in Postwar Europe," in István Deák, Jan T. Gross, and Tony Judt, eds., *The Politics of Retribution in Europe: World War II and Its Aftermath* (Princeton, NJ: Princeton University Press, 2000), pp. 309–10. The year of Antonescu's execution is, in fact, 1946.

24. *Realitatea evreiască,* no. 49–50 (16 April–15 May 1997). Emphasis is mine.

25. See Radu Ioanid, "Revisionism in the Post-Communist Romanian Political Culture—Attempts to Rehabilitate the Perpetrators of the Holocaust," in Margot Levy (ed.), *Remembering for the Future: The Holocaust in the Age of Genocide* (London: Macmillan), vol. 1, pp. 813–32.

26. See the interview with Balotă in *Apostrof,* no. 11–12 (Cluj, 2000), which also published his letter to Constantinescu (17 February 1997).

27. *Realitatea evreiască,* no. 76 (July 1998).

28. For details, see Shafir, "Marshal Antonescu's Post-Communist Rehabilitation" pp. 358–61.

29. *Adevărul* (21 November 1997).

30. *RFE/RL Newsline* (10 November 1997).

31. Cited in Ioanid, "Revisionism in the Post-Communist Romanian Political Culture."

32. See Lya Benjamin, "Dreptul la convertire şi statutul evreilor convertiţi în perioada antonesciană [The Right to Conversion and the Status of Converted Jews in the Antonescu Period], in *Studia et acta historiae iudeaorum Romaniae*, vol. 3 (Bucureşti: Editura Hasefer, 1998), pp. 245–62 and Michael Shafir, "Paradigme, parademonstraţii, paratrăsnete" (III) [Paradigmae, Pseudo-Demonstrations, Lighting Rods], *Sfera politicii* no. 86 (Bucharest, 2000), pp. 29–39.

33. See Shafir, "Antonescu's Rehabilitation," p. 357.

34. *RFE/RL Newsline* (17 November 1997).

35. ARPress (23 November 1997).

36. *RFE/RL Newsline* (27 October 1998).

37. *Ibid* (18 January 2000).

38. *România liberă* (6 March 1997).

39. See *RFE/RL Newsline* (25 April 2001).

40. William Totok, "Discursul revizionist" [The Revisionist Discourse], *Sfera* (supplement of the Bucharest monthly *Sfera politicii*, September 1998), no. 1, pp. 26–32.

41. Alexandru Paleologu and Stelian Tănase, *Sfidarea memoriei* [Defying Memory] (Bucureşti: Editura Du Style, 1996), pp. 186–96.

42. See Gabriel Andreescu, *Naţionalişti, antinaţionalişti: O polemică în publicistica românească* [Nationalists, Anti-nationalists: A Polemical Debate in the Romanian Media] (Iaşi: Polirom, 1996), pp. 25–69.

43. In 1998, for example, in an interview with a daily published in Iaşi, he called for a "short-term dictatorship" to overcome the "foolish and selfish" ambitions of political parties, which, he said, are corrupted or encourage corruption and fail to place the "national interest" at the head of their priority list. See *România liberă* (6 April 1998).

44. Cited in Totok, "Discursul revizionist," p. 32.

45. Cited in *Ibid*, p. 29.

46. *România literară* (27 December 1995 and 9 January 1996).

47. See Michael Shafir, "The Man They Love to Hate: Norman Manea's 'Snail House' between Holocaust and *Gulag*," in *East European Jewish Affairs*, vol. 30, no. 1 (2000), pp. 60–81.

48. See the interview with Manolescu in *Adevărul literar şi artistic*, no. 629 (13 August 2002).

49. The reader should try comparing Manolescu's articles cited in Shafir, "The Man They Love to Hate" or the similarly spirited "G. M. Támas faţă cu reacţiunea" [G. M. Támas Confronts the Reactionaries] in *România literară*, no. 8 (28 February–6 March 2001), with the following articles which adopt precisely the opposite position: "Cine l-a inventat pe Vadim?" [Who Invented Vadim?], *Ibid*, no. 50 (20–26 December 2000); "Despre revizuiri" [On Revisions], *Ibid*, no. 48 (6–12 December 2000); "Cînd ne despart ideile" [When Ideas Divide Us], *Ibid*, no. 34 (29 August–4 September 2001); and "Apel către Europa" [An Appeal to Europe], *Ibid*, no. 44 (7–13 November 2001).

50. See Manolescu, "Sfîrşitul unei ambiguităţi" [The End of an Ambiguity], *Ibid*, no. 46 (21–27 November 2001).

51. See *RFE/RL Newsline* (17 July 2001). On Manolescu's less appealing positions see also George Voicu, "Reacţia de prestigiu" [A Reaction of Prestige], *Sfera politicii*, vol. 6, no. 63 (1998), pp. 57–62. For a French-language translation of this excellent essay, see "L'honneur national roumain en question," *Les Temps Modernes*, vol. 54, no. 606 (November–December 1999), pp. 142–52.

52. *RFE/RL's Newsline* (15 June 1999).

53. *Ziua* (22 October 1999).

54. See the interviews with them in the weekly *22*, no. 48 (2–8 December 1997).

55. *Ziua* (29 November 1997).

56. See Alexandra Laignel-Lavastine, "Fascisme et Communisme en Roumanie: enjeux et usages d'une comparaison," in Henry Rousso (ed.), *Stalinisme et nazisme: Histoire et mémoire comparées* (Bruxelles: Editions Complexe, 1999), pp. 201–46.

57. For a discussion of the 2000 electoral outcome see Michael Shafir, "The Greater Romania Party and the 2000 Elections in Romania: How Obvious Is the Obvious?" in *The Romanian Journal of Society and Politics,* vol. 1, no. 2 (2001), pp. 91–126. See also Alina Mungiu-Pippidi, *Politica după comunism* [Politics after Communism] (Bucharest: Humanitas, 2002), pp. 126–31.

58. Michael Shafir, "Marginalization or Mainstream? The Extreme Right in Post-Communist Romania," in Paul Hainsworth, ed., *The Politics of the Extreme Right: From the Margins to the Mainstream* (London: Pinter, 2000), p. 265.

59. *Adevărul* (12 October 2000).

60. Horthy no doubt shares many traits with Antonescu, but there are certainly also important differences, not the least important resting in the fact that there has never been a Hungarian "Transnistria." This may or may not explain the fact that in his Portugese exile, Horthy and his wife "survived thanks mostly to the generosity of some Jewish friends," as we learn from István Deák. One should also mention that Horthy briefly halted deportations to Auschwitz in July 1944. While none of these clears Horthy of responsibility, he was a complex figure perhaps best described by Deák: "He was neither a fascist nor a liberal; he was not a monster, but he was not a humanitarian either. He claimed to have been a lifelong anti-Semite; still, under his reign and despite the deportations, more Jews survived the Nazi terror, in sheer numbers, than in any other country within Hitler's Europe, except perhaps Romania." István Deák, "A Fatal Compromise? The Debate over Collaboration and Resistance in Hungary," in Deák, Gross, and Judt, eds., *The Politics of Retribution,* pp. 55–56.

61. See Pippidi, *Despre statui şi morminte,* pp. 241–42; Deák, "A Fatal Compromise?" p. 73n.

62. Shafir, "Between Denial and 'Comparative Trivialization'," pp. 35–36.

63. *RFE/RL Newsline* (22 January 2001).

64. *Ibid* (26 June 2001). Emphasis added.

65. See Shafir, "Antonescu's Rehabilitation," p. 357.

66. There is a good discussion of "duplicity" in Gail Kligman, *The Politics of Duplicity: Controlling Reproduction in Ceausescu's Romania* (Berkeley: University of California Press, 1998), pp. 13–18, 37–41 and *passim.* Unfortunately, it is also one that largely ignores my own pioneering work on this important aspect of Romanian political culture, antedating all other works mentioned in Kligman's impressive study. See Michael Shafir, "Political Culture, Intellectual Dissent and Intellectual Consent: The Case of Romania," *Orbis,* vol. 27, no. 2 (Summer 1983), pp. 393–421.

67. Mediafax and AP (1 June 2001).

68. See the article in the daily *Azi* (3 April 2000), which was highly critical of the Army's having allegedly failed to "defend its dignity and honor."

69. See *RFE/RL Newsline* (1 and 2 November 2001).

70. AP (3 June 2001) and Mediafax (4 June 2001).

71. Romanian Radio and Mediafax (4 June 2001).

72. Romanian Television, Channel 1 (5 June 2001).

73. Romanian Television, Channel 1 (4 June 2001) and Mediafax (4 June 2001).

74. Romanian Radio (6 July 2001).

75. Smith declaration in the House of Representatives (27 July 2002).

76. See Mihail Ionescu, "O epopee inutilă," in *Golgota Estului (iulie 1942–martie 1944)* [The Golgota of the East (July 1942–March 1944)], Coordinator, Colonel Dr.

Alexandru Duţu (Bucharest: Editura Fundaţiei Culturale Române, 2000), pp. 5–12. For an expanded version see Mihail Ionescu, "Ion Antonescu în faţa războiului asimetric: Greşeli de neiertat" [Ion Antonescu Faced with the Asymmetric War: Unforgivable Mistakes], *Magazin istoric*, vol. 36, no. 6 (423) (June 2002), pp. 14–20.

77. See Radu Ioanid, *The Sword of the Archangel* (Boulder, CO: East European Monographs, 1990), and *The Holocaust in Romania: The Destruction of Jews and Gypsies under the Antonescu Regime, 1940–1944* (Chicago: Ivan R. Dee, 2000).

78. For the "combined announcement" see Mediafax (18 March 2002). Although the ordinance had been approved five days earlier, Prime Minister Adrian Năstase announced an "intention" to approve the ordinance, as did Culture and Cults Minister Răzvan Theodorescu.

79. See *RFE/RL Newsline* (31 October, 2 November 2001); *Cotidianul* and *Curentul* (5 November 2001).

80. Romanian Television (17 July 2001).

81. Mediafax (18 March 2002).

82. *România liberă* (27 February 2002).

83. *RFE/RL Newsline* (19 March 2002); *Cotidianul* (19 March 2002); *Monitorul oficial al României* (28 March 2002).

84. Romanian Radio (22 and 23 March 2002).

85. For a discussion of the "Comparative Trivialization" notion, see Shafir, "Between Denial and 'Comparative Trivialization'," pp. 60–75.

86. *Adevărul* (26 March 2002). Emphasis added.

87. *Ibid* (29–30 June 2002).

88. *Cotidianul* (28 May 2002).

89. Mediafax (29 June 2002).

90. *Ibid* (18 March 2002).

91. *România mare*, no. 612 (5 April 2002).

92. Mediafax (29 June 2002). For a photo of the covered Antonescu bust, see *România mare*, no. 628 (26 July 2002).

93. *Jurnalul naţional* (2 July 2002).

94. Mediafax (29 March and 15 April, 2002); William Totok, "Cazul Antonescu" [The Antonescu Case], *Focus Vest*, no. 27 (Timişoara, 5–11 July 2002).

95. Mediafax (1 August 2002); *România mare*, no. 632 (23 August 2002) (transcript of interview with PRM leader Tudor and Funar on the extreme nationalist television channel OTV). The Antonescu statue saga in Cluj is in itself remarkable. After several failed attempts to have the town council (on which he does not have a majority) approve the statue, in 1999 Funar managed to do so by "bribing" municipal councilors belonging to the opposition CDR to let his pet project come through in exchange of erecting statues to Iuliu Maniu and Ion C. Brătianu as well. The two were leaders of the National Peasant Party and the PNL, respectively, and their successor formations were the two main parties of the CDR. Their leaderships were silent on the "bargain" and only Péter Eckstein Kovács, who represented the Hungarian Democratic Federation of Romania in the then-ruling coalition government, protested the council's decision (see *RFE/RL Newsline* [1 and 8 November 1999]). The decision was appealed by the local prefect and after many subsequent developments, the hearings on prefect's complaint were transferred to a Iaşi tribunal, where they were still pending when the ordinance was issued (*Ibid*, 3 April 2000).

96. Pippidi, *Despre statui şi morminte*, p. 8.

97. Mediafax (31 July 2002).

98. *Jurnalul naţional* (2 July and 1 August 2002). For the PRM protests after the Oradea municipal council changed its initial decision, see *România mare*, no. 634 (6 September 2002).

99. For the debates in the Human Rights Commission, see Mediafax (9 April 2002); for the debates in the Defense Commission, *Cotidianul* (15 April 2002).

100. Mediafax (17 April 2002).

101. Mediafax (5 June 2002).

102. For a discussion see Shafir, "Between Denial and 'Comparative Trivialization,'" p. 52.

103. Theodorescu's argument appeared on Romanian Television's (RTV) First Channel and in Mediafax (8 May 2002); Mediafax (27 May 2002); Rompres (28 June 2002).

104. See Carol Iancu, *Evreii din România de la excludere la emancipare (1866–1919)* [The Jews in Romania from Exclusion to Emancipation (1866–1919)] (Bucureşti: Hasefer, 1996) and Irina Livezeanu, *Cultural Politics in Greater Romania: Regionalism, Nation Building & Ethnic Struggle, 1918–1930* (Ithaca, NY: Cornell University Press, 1995).

105. Mediafax (26 July 2002).

106. See *Cotidianul* (26 March 2002) and *Curierul naţional* (3 April 2002).

107. See Gabriel Andreescu, "Necesitatea amendării Ordonanţei de urgenţă nr. 31 privind organizaţiile şi simbolurile cu caracter fascist, rasist sau xenofob" [The Necessity of Amending Ordinance 31 on Organizations and Symbols of a Fascist, Racist or Xenophobic Character], in *Revista română de drepturile omului*, no. 23 (2002), pp. 8–19.

108. See his interview with Reuters (6 May 2002).

109. *RFE/ RL Newsline* (26 June 2001).

110. *Jurnalul naţional* (8 May 2002).

110. Rompres (28 June 2002).

112. For the PRM, see the declarations of Mihai Lupoi and Mihai Ungheanu, Romanian Radio (26 March and 16 April 2002) and Buzatu's speech at the Romanian Academy session in *România mare*, nos. 625–30 (5 July–9 August 2002); for Suru, see *România mare*, no. 618 (17 May 2002); for the Association for the Defense of Human Rights-Helsinki Committee, see Andreescu, "Necesitatea amendării Ordonanţei de urgenţă nr. 31 privind organizaţiile şi simbolurile cu caracter fascist, rasist sau xenofob" [The Necessity of Amending Ordinance 31 on Organizations and Symbols of a Fascist, Racist, or Xenophobic Character] in *Revista română de drepturile omului*, no. 23 (2002), pp. 8–19.

113. Romanian Radio (14 April 2002). Emphasis added.

114. Mediafax (24 May 2002) and *România mare*, nos. 610, 611, 627 (22 March, 29 March and 12 July 2002, respectively).

115. See, among others, Buzatu's speech at the Romanian Academy Session, in *România mare* nos. 625–630, 5 July through 9 August 2002.

116. See Shafir, "Between Denial and 'Comparative Trivialization,'" pp. 72–75.

117. Shafir, *Romania. Politics, Economics and Society: Political Stagnation and Simulated Change* (London: Frances Pinter, 1985).

118. See Andrei Corbea, "Gustul social-democraţiei originale" [The Taste of Original Social-Democracy], in *Observator cultural*, no. 106 (5 March–11 March 2002).

4

Re-Membering Romania

John F. Ely and Cătălin Augustin Stoica

> Empty pedestals represent the unfinished Eastern European drama. For us, history is no longer "terra firma," as the Venetian Italians say. It seems we don't feel secure until we cry doubt about everything—having for a half century only false certainties, and statues we silently detested
>
> Octavian Paler[1]

The Romanian writer Octavian Paler uses the pedestals, left empty after the statues of the "great" Communists were torn down during the tumult of 1989, as a metaphor for the importance of understanding history. After the euphoria of the events of 1989 died down, Romanians not only had to confront how they would deal with their uncertain future, they also had to confront how they would deal with their contested past. "History" is an important factor in the cohesion of any society, for it can provide both a collective identity ("We, the people . . .") and a motivation for collective action ("Remember the Alamo!!!"). After having been manipulated by the Communist regime for over fifty years, could "history" foster identity and bring solidarity to Romanians? This can be a difficult thing to measure, but one place to start would be an analysis of an event that would seem to be particularly suited to providing Romanians with solidarity through shared experience: the "Revolution" of December 1989. In this chapter, we will address the making of this historical event by looking at the tenuous relationship between collective memories and the public sphere in Romania. As we will discuss, rather than causing cohesion, the events of 1989 (i.e., the popular uprisings, the Ceauşescus' trial and execution, and the transition of power) have led to the creation of fragmented narratives. We will also employ survey data from 1999 to show that the "Revolution" of December 1989 is still a divisive issue.

COLLECTIVE MEMORY IN ROMANIA

Collective Memory and the Public Sphere

We will draw on Mark Osiel for a working definition of *collective memory*. He writes that collective memory:

> consists of the stories a society tells about the momentous events in its history, the events that most profoundly affect the lives of its members and most arouse their passions for long periods. This category includes wars, revolutions, economic depressions, large-scale riots, and genocides.[2]

According to Osiel, collective memories can cultivate a shared identity. They can be used as a tool by, and provide legitimacy for, the state in that they can be "later invoked to help define what such people have in common to guide them in collective action."[3] Collective memory is found in what Jürgen Habermas defines as *the public sphere*.[4] He argues that with the rise of the modern bourgeois state and civil society comes the rise of a cultural manifestation of the state, one that is shared by all (i.e., the public), and which exists in a social space that is independent of the self interests and private lives of the citizenry. It is in this public sphere that collective memories are fostered, negotiated, and activated.

"History" and the "Public Sphere" before Ceauşescu

Historically, Romania has been the victim of many incursions by many empires. According to Ken Jowitt, this has led to a "ghetto" political culture in Romania in which there is an antagonistic relationship between public and private spheres.[5] This distrust of the public sphere by Romanians was only exacerbated by the imposition of Stalinist practices, which came with the rise to power of the Communists in 1948. In Romania, the first ten years of Communism were marked by a deep, coercive institutional isomorphic change.[6] Along with nationalizing policies, the abolition of the multiparty system, the imprisonment of a large number of the pre–World War II intellectual and political elites, and the beginning of a rapid industrialization, the "history" of Romania was also revised to show, for instance, the allegedly positive role that Russia had played in Romania's past. Aside from pro-Soviet propaganda, words themselves were changed to play down Romania's Latin roots and emphasize its Slavic influences. Even the country's name was changed from the Latin *Romănia* to the more Slavic *Romînia*.[7] Romanian Communists under Gheorghiu-Dej were so successful in cloning the Soviet model that in 1958 the Soviet troops pulled out of the country, deeming it "safe."[8]

This era of copycat Stalinism would partially come to an end with Stalin's death. Fearful that he would be replaced with one of Khrushchev's favorites,

Gheorghiu-Dej refused to follow the de-Stalinization path preached by Moscow and started to mobilize resources within the field of cultural production to impose a Romanian (i.e., national) road to socialism. Writings of Marx which had been previously banned because they talked of Russia's imperialistic tendencies toward Romania were published. Also, some intellectual figures who had been barred from the public sphere for their perceived nationalism were rehabilitated.[9] This policy of impregnating an externally imposed Communist model with nationalism was not only continued by the person who succeeded Dej after his death in 1965, but also expanded.

Ceauşescu's Manipulation of History

Ceauşescu moved away from the more purely coercive, "iron fist" of Stalinism, to a subtler mode of domination through the manipulation of national symbols, "collective memories," and sentiments. For instance, although he criticized Dej in a de-Stalinizing manner, he continued Dej's moves toward independence from Moscow. This independent stance, and the internal support it brought, culminated in the summer of 1968 with Ceauşescu's refusal to join, and his criticism of, the Warsaw pact's invasion of Czechoslovakia. This initial phase, often referred to as the "Golden Years," was also marked by a lessening of the top-down control of cultural production that had marked his predecessor's reign. Censorship was loosened and intellectuals were able to gain access to information and ideas that had been forbidden due to their "subversive" Western origins. This positive collective memory of the Golden Years was also influenced by general improvements in living standards and by short-term (and timid) economic reforms (i.e., allowance of small private firms, economic decentralization, and increased power to middle level professionals in decision making).[10]

Unfortunately, the Golden Years came to an end in 1971 when, while visiting China and North Korea, Ceauşescu became enamored of Mao's and Kim Il Sung's models of Communism and their near-total control over every institution, especially those in the field of cultural production. Once again, under his strict supervision, the official history was rewritten. Yet this time, rather than limiting himself to anti-Soviet manipulations, he presented himself as the savior of Romania. In addition to having himself referred to as "Genius of the Carpathians," "Romania's Most Beloved Son," a "Luminous Beacon," "the Helmsman Who Guides," "The Thinking Polar Star," and "The First Thinker of This Earth," mass rallies were held and televised that showed thousands of people "genuinely" and "spontaneously" expressing their "boundless love and gratitude" for "the *Conducător*" (i.e., the Leader).

As time went on, manipulation of discourse within the public sphere became more and more defined by ideological ends and increasingly, as Gail Kligman writes, the "enemy of empirical reality."[11] An interesting example of this was "protochronism," wherein academics could gain favor and support from the government if they produced works that showed that touted Western discoveries (from Communism to the airplane) were actually Romanian in origin.[12]

Considering Romanians' traditional aversion toward the public sphere, such practices, along with the state's increasing intrusions into the private sphere, were doomed to fail and could not bring legitimacy to the official sphere. Jowitt explains how the Romanian state was perceived as threatening, inducing societal alienation:

> As in the past and as in a ghetto, under the dictatorship of the proletariat, the regime or official sphere represented "trouble," being identified as the locus of demands and sanctions rather than of political support or recognition.[13]

In addition to the practices of propaganda and the personality cult, this perception of the public sphere as "trouble" was heightened by the threat, real or perceived, that if one talked counter to the party line, it would be detected and lead to grave repercussions. This prevented the rise of such shared alternative meaning systems as those found with the dissident movements of Czechoslovakia (the Charter 1977) and Poland (Solidarity).

All these things taken together led to a delegitimized "legitimate" narrative and a fragmented system of rumors that people used to make sense of their day-to-day lives. Following Tamotsu Shibutani's analogy, Romanian citizens were "like a driver who cannot see through his rain-obscured windshield [but] must still find his way."[14] This "way" often took the form of "improvised news" or rumors. As the daily lives of Romanians became more and more problematic in the 1980s—another cause of rumor proliferation, according to Shibutani—rumors became even more widespread.

With an illegitimate collective narrative, rising economic hardship, and the events going on throughout Eastern Europe, by the end of 1989, Ceauşescu's regime had no ability to bend, but only to break.

TURBULENCE AND TRIAL

The "December Events": Fact versus Fiction

Romanians' use of rumor and fragmented narratives to make sense of their day-to-day lives is nowhere more evident than in their interpretation of the "revolution" of December 1989. With a political culture that was already ghettoized, the momentous events of that period only lead to further balkanization of meaning. Shibutani writes that there is a direct relationship between the formation of rumors and the "intensity of collective excitement."[15] It is difficult to imagine a society more marked by collective excitement than

Romania in December 1989. Even though there is a great deal of confusion over what actually happened, we offer a brief description of some of the few undisputed facts. On 15 December, people in Timişoara rallied around an outspoken Hungarian priest who was about to be exiled by the *Securitate*. The Army was called in and forty people were killed in the following melee. On 21 December, Ceauşescu organized a televised rally in the Palace Square to show the Romanian people that he still held power. There is much disagreement on what happened at this rally and why, but what the camera showed, before quickly cutting away, was Ceauşescu paralyzed by fear and confusion as people yelled, "Timişoara! Timişoara!" Despite the violent efforts to repress them, the demonstrators continued to protest throughout the night. In the morning, Ceauşescu stated in a news bulletin that General Vasile Milea, the head of the Romanian army, had betrayed the country and committed suicide. After this, the army switched sides and joined the antigovernment forces. As protesters forced their way into the television station, Ceauşescu and his wife fled from Bucharest by helicopter. The helicopter pilot feigned technical problems and told them that they would be forced to land. The Ceauşescus, the "Father and Mother of Romania," were left by the side of the road to try to hitchhike to safety. They were soon arrested and taken to an army base. They were kept there until their trial and execution on 25 December. During all this, fighting between revolutionaries and alleged Ceauşescu's loyalists continued in Bucharest, and a coalition known as the National Salvation Front (NSF) began governing the country.

The above account addresses only a few of the undisputed facts about the events of December 1989. These were greatly outnumbered by the various representations or myths about what "really happened."[16] In the first days after the Romanian uprisings, the most widely shared understanding for Romanians was that of a "revolution." Some of the most exaggerated representations of this "revolution" were offered by the foreign media, such as those of the Yugoslav news agency Tanjug, which estimated the fatalities at 60,000 (where the actual number ended up being less than 1,200). Despite such distorted accounts, foreign media did play a significant role in informing Romanians about the events in Timişoara, and their coverage helped to mobilize the people in Bucharest on the morning of 22 December. Yet, once the Ceauşescus had fled, the major mediums of myth-making were the Romanian state radio and television. On their television screens, Romanians all over the country witnessed various groups vie to fill the political void. One of these groups, which eventually became known as the NSF, won the support of the revolutionaries who had taken over the television station. This group was led by Ion Iliescu, a former high-ranking member of the Romanian Communist Party who, in the 1970s, had criticized Ceauşescu for his growing extremism. On 22 December, the NSF began broadcasting that they had taken over as the new governing body, and for the citizens to be aware of dangerous factions of *Securitate*—"fanatical terrorists" as they called them—who still supported Ceauşescu. The twenty-four-hour-a-day broadcasts that followed showed images of street fighting in the Palace Square, television headquarters, and other places in the city. Breaking "news" was continuously reported, and its content often had an Orwellian tone. For instance, Ceauşescu's supporters were presented as children taken from orphanages to be raised and trained to be loyal to him and his close family. There were also "news" reports about the poisoning of water systems, planned terrorist bombings of water reservoirs, and the imminent march upon Bucharest by *Securitate* troops still loyal to Ceauşescu. At this time, most Romanians did believe that they were witnesses of a genuine, glorious revolution of "us" (the people) versus "them" (the Ceauşescus and their few but fanatical supporters).

The first challenges to this version came from the international media after the trial, which was perceived as a "show trial," and the execution of the Ceauşescu had been broadcast across the globe. In the initial days following the "revolution" and "trial," many Romanians (who were unaccustomed to Western standards of meting out justice) were surprised by the West's criticism of the trial and the doubts that were expressed about the credibility of the revolution. However, some of these doubts were also being echoed by Romania's few former dissidents, who were upset at seeing too many former Communists among the ranks of the NSF. Still, the new authorities stuck with the initial version of a genuine revolution, and Ion Iliescu holds to it to this day.

Despite their official story, some members of the National Salvation Front fed into Romanians' "plot" mind-set by refusing to share their new power with the reestablished political parties, and by their decision to change their role from care takers of a transitional government to candidates in the coming elections. Also feeding the conspiracy-minded people were the declarations of some of the new top officials. In a video made during the constitution of the new government, General Nicolae Militaru insisted on naming the new authority the NSF, saying that this Front—of which he claimed to be a member—was allegedly formed months before the overthrow of Ceauşescu. Tales of such a plot, led by Ion Iliescu, were also alluded to by others, including Silviu Brucan, an NSF top official, and Nicolae Radu, Iliescu's former friend.[17]

Soon, the story of the "revolution" began to compete with other narratives, such as a "stolen revolution" or "coup d'état." According to these new narratives, what happened in December 1989 was, at best, a popular revolt that was later "stolen" by members of the former regime. At worst, the revolution was a purely scripted affair produced by second-tier *nomenklatura* who, seeing the events unfolding throughout Eastern Europe, wanted to make sure they did not fall with "the great *Conducător*."

The major proponents of these interpretations were the small opposition parties that had formed in early 1990, former dissidents who left the NSF, and independent intellectuals. However, such challenges to the official story of the "revolution" were not limited to the opposition. Richard Hall points out that versions of the coup story have also been vigorously supported by former *Securitate* officers.[18] The central theme of their story is that the *Securitate* did not stay loyal to Ceauşescu and were not among the "terrorists" shooting in the streets. Rather, the *Securitate* was a victim of a "staged war" which hid the backstage power struggles between the Army and other forces by turning the *Securitate* into a scapegoat. Although these interpretations were mostly published in extremist, nationalistic, neo-Communist newspapers, Hall emphasizes that the opposition press and independent media also gave these advocates the opportunity to popularize their views. It should be mentioned that in the extremist publications, such revisionist accounts of December 1989 are more varied and more seasoned with flavors of an international plot against Romania than the bifurcated, "revolution" versus "coup" description offered by Hall and others. For example, there were many interpretations that saw the December 1989 events as the result of various covert, external forces, which were masterminded by, but not limited to, the Hungarians, the CIA, the KGB, and the Free Masons.

Why is there no minimal consensus as to what happened in 1989? The Communist legacy can partially explain this. However, we argue that post-socialist Romania had opportunities to create a shared understanding, or "collective memory," of its recent past, but has failed to do so. In the following section, we look at the Ceauşescus' trial as a failed attempt to accomplish this.

The "Trial" as Failed Myth-Making

Historically, trials are put forth as ways of repairing tears in the public fabric and organizing the emotions of the community. As David Garland writes,

> Ritual—including rituals of criminal justice—are ceremonies which, through manipulation of emotion, prompt particular value commitments on the part of the participants and the audience and thus act as a kind of sentimental education.[19]

Through this "didactic theater the onlooker is taught what to feel, how to react, which sentiments are called for."[20] Beyond prompting value commitments for the community through criminal justice, trials are also employed for consolidating public sentiments for much broader trans-historical cases. Mark Osiel writes,

> A traumatized society that is deeply divided about its recent past can greatly benefit from the collective representations of that past, created and cultivated by a process of prosecution and judgment, accompanied by public discussion about the trial and its result.[21]

Considering the historical distrust of the public sphere among Romanians and the confusion and trauma that accompanied the "December Events," a public trial could have offered an opportunity to formulate a "collective representation," by which Romania could confront, categorize, and move beyond its past by constructing a "collective memory." Unfortunately, this did not come to pass.

As already discussed, it is almost impossible to find out what actually happened during this tumultuous time. The myriad of narratives that occupied the newly enlarged public sphere ran the gamut from an authentic, spontaneous "revolution" to a cynical, Machiavellian production. A similar gamut of explanations arose for interpreting the trial of Nicolae and Elena Ceauşescu, ranging from an authentic expression of public justice to a staged production that was meant to offer both a distraction from the coup and an excuse to kill the Ceauşescus before they could name the plotters. Furthering this fragmentation of narratives regarding the trial is the lack of any evidence that can be trusted to not be the product of disinformation. One of the few hard pieces of available data to survive the "December Events" is the videotape of the Ceauşescus' trial and execution that was broadcast to the country the morning of 26 December. It is this videotape that we will briefly analyze in the context of "revolution" myth-making. Even with the "hard" evidence of the videotape, it must be recognized that it is only "front stage" behavior and thus, like much of the "December Events," it is impossible to know what was actually going on backstage.[22] This being said, we feel that textual analysis of the trial allows us to hypothesize that a third interpretation (besides "authentic versus Machiavellian") can be put forth: the trial can be seen as a clumsy attempt at myth-making by people caught between two mutually exclusive narratives. These mutually exclusive narratives to which we refer in the following analysis are "Rule of Law" and "Wooden Language."

The New: Rule of Law. When viewed by Westerners, the trial can appear absurd. For example, the following is a statement by Ceauşescu's own *defense attorney*: "I will not add anything to the indictment that has already been made . . . *for the crimes committed, everyone must receive punishment.*" An important reason for this perceived absurdity is based on different understandings of *rule of law*.

By definition, totalitarian governments such as Ceauşescu's carry total power over the practices of the state. Linz and Stepan, inspired by Weber, use his ideal-type of sultanism to describe the political and legal practices in such a regime:

> In sultanism the private and the public are fused, there is a strong tendency toward familial power and dynastic succession, there is no distinction between a state career and personal service to the ruler, there is lack of rational, impersonal ideology the ruler acts only according to his on unchecked discretion, with no larger impersonal goals.[23]

Under Ceauşescu there was little distinction between statutory criminals and political criminals. The means of the legal system were always secondary to the ends of the state.

Anyone from a "rule-bound" nation is familiar with such clichés as "No one is above the law" and "A government of laws, not of men." As Max Weber sees it, the rule of law is characteristic of a broader, historical form of authority called legal-rational authority. It represents a deeply ingrained institutional system that is self-referential and understood without question. This is why the invoking of the rule of law by the court actors in this trial can seem so absurd to Westerners: the actors in the trial only incorporate fragmented symbols of "rule of law," without the institutional foundation to understand them.

All the major players in the trial (prosecutor, judge, and defense attorneys) repeatedly made statements that would seem to denote that a rule-bound trial was in process (e.g., "This court is legally constituted," "We are offering you a legal defense as stipulated by law," etc.). Beyond the Ceauşescus being degraded by their own attorneys and the general catharsis that marked the proceedings, the greatest evidence that this was not a real "trial" by Western standards is the fact the prosecutor was given only one hour for the proceedings.[24] This illustrates that "rule of law," with its understanding of "means over ends," was not being employed. Rather, it was feigned by drawing on positive but fragmented symbols from the West in an attempt to weave a "revolution" myth favorable to the new power.

The Old: Wooden Language. Beyond drawing on new models that were desired but not understood, we argue that old symbols were also employed in "revolution" myth-making in the form of *wooden language*. As previously discussed, under the Ceauşescu regime, official propaganda became increasingly severed from empirical reality. In place of this, the political discourse moved further and further toward what Romanians refer to as *limba de lemn* or wooden language. Wooden language is flowery and grandiose, yet, in the end, consists of empty words that are used to "lift the human spirit" and, at the same time, mask the reality of the situation. Anybody familiar with political discourse is familiar with wooden language to some degree. Still it is hard to convey the extent to which Ceauşescu politically lived by wooden language. Phrases such as "Romania's Brightest and Luminous Future!" still ring in the ears of many Romanians today.

When viewing the trial, the prevalence of wooden language is self-evident. Imagine the following statement being made by a defense attorney in a Western court of law: "But [Ceauşescu's] most horrid crime was to shackle the Romanian spirit, the soul of his people!" There are numerous examples of such empty discourse. The most striking example of the use of wooden language, by both the court and the defendants, is their use and abuse of the term "the people."

The symbolic use of "the people" is not unique to Ceaușescu's discourse. Hannah Arendt, in referring to the line "We, the people . . ." in the Declaration of Independence, writes that these words are a performative act.[25] It is only by invoking "the people" that we create their identity. Yet the extent to which "the people" were abused by, and then against, Ceaușescu is extreme. In his speeches, declarations, writings, and slogans "the people" were referred to *ad nauseam*. Throughout the trial, the court actors invoked "the people" thirty-seven times. Here is an example of the Judge's attempts to bring legitimacy to the newly formed government by using Ceaușescu's own phraseology (in italics):

> Judge: The Grand National Assembly [the Communist parliament] has been dissolved by *the unshaken will of the people!* We have another body of power: the Council of the Front of National Salvation . . . legally constituted!

The following is an example of the court invoking the "the people" to mock Ceaușescu's use of "the people":

> Judge: He refuses to have a dialogue with *the people*, even though he has spoken in the name of *the people* as the most beloved son of *the people* . . . in derision he mocked these *people*!

It is hard to imagine that, in trying to gain legitimacy for a new authority, one would want to repeat the same abusive practices of the old. Yet, in weaving a myth of legitimacy, the performers had to reach for whatever was available. Being consumers of Ceaușescu's stilted rhetoric for many years, they respond to a normative discourse of power. For Romanians, this was how power acted.

When caught between the fall of an old order and the uncertainty of the new, those in power use whatever symbolic tools are at hand to construct a myth of legitimacy. This leads to a contradictory situation in which the tools that are employed are both those that the people have grown to know, yet hate (wooden language), and those that they idealize, yet do not have the experience to understand (rule of law). As the actual events faded, rather than the trial effectively shaping a collective memory of "revolution," these contradictions only reflected, revealed, and represented a failed break between "old" and "new." Challenges to the "trial" and the "revolution" arose in the years that followed. These came initially from the West and then, increasingly, from within Romania. Even though in the early 1990s Iliescu won two presidential elections (1990 and 1992), these challenges became increasingly vocal and, in time, more numerous. Eventually, Emil Constantinescu, head of the opposition coalition, won the presidential election of 1996. One of his campaign promises was to investigate what "really happened" in December 1989. He failed to follow through on this promise and Iliescu was reelected in 2000.

"TRANS(M)ITION"

Up to this point, most of our discussion has relied upon scholarly and nonscholarly accounts of these events, on sources within the Romanian and international media, on the videotape of the trial, and on our own Romanian experiences. Some readers might feel a certain dissatisfaction with such speculations built upon speculations and rightfully ask: "But what of Romanians themselves? What do *they* think about these events?"

We are fortunate enough to be able to offer at least a partial answer to these questions by drawing on survey data from Romania. In this section, we present the results of a causal-type analysis, which throws some light on what people believe "really happened" in December 1989, and on some of the sociodemographic factors that influence these beliefs. Before this, we must offer a few caveats. First, both our analysis and its results are only of an exploratory character. This is why we have avoided formulating a series of formal hypotheses. Second, the causal structure of beliefs about the Romanian revolution is more complex than the one we can depict here. Also, the list of our independent variables is by no means exhaustive.

The data we use comes from a survey that was conducted by the Center for Urban and Regional Sociology (CURS) in October 1999, at the request of the Open Society Foundation-Romania. The section of the questionnaire upon which our analysis relies included questions that address the "1989 Events." Our sample of 2,019 people is representative of Romania's adult population, ages eighteen years and over. Table 4.1 shows the percentage point distribution for the answers to "What happened in December 1989?"

The lack of an agreed upon collective memory regarding what happened in 1989 is self-evident. Although the "revolution" version was the dominant interpretation of those interviewed (40 percent), 36 percent of the sample still believed it was a "coup d'état." Only 5 percent saw the events of 1989 as "something else."[26] It should be noted that almost one-fifth of the total sample

Table 4.1. Percentage Point Distribution of the Answers Regarding December 1989 (Romania, 1999)

In your opinion, what happened in December 1989 was . . .	
A revolution	40 percent
A coup d'état	36 percent
Something else	5 percent
Don't know/no answer	19 percent

Source: "Human and Social Resources of the Romanian Transition," October, 1999 (N=2,019).

(i.e., 19 percent) either did not answer or did not know what to answer to this question. One might think that this group would be made up of those interviewees who were too young to have strong opinions about the "December Events." Yet, results of bivariate analysis show that, in general, those who did not answer or did not know what to answer come not from the youngest, but from the oldest people in the sample, ages sixty-six and higher.

The passage of time can also alter perceptions about the 1989 events. For instance, we can speculate that as time goes by, the understandings of 1989 would become more diverse, blurred, and subject to modification in the light of disparate new "facts" that have emerged in the Romanian public sphere. Furthermore, the temporal context in which a survey is conducted can influence its results. The data we rely on were collected in late October 1999, against the background of a perceived economic and social crisis that had been attributed by many to the inability of the Democratic Convention (which had taken power in 1996) to live up to the hopes it generated in the electoral campaign of 1996. These economic and social hardships culminated with a governmental crisis in December 1999. Thus, one can speculate that, as dissatisfaction with the current economic, social, and political situation increases, the chances of believing that it was a radical rupture with the past (i.e., a revolution) decrease. This hypothesis tends to be supported by the findings reported by Pavel Câmpeanu.[27] His national survey in December 1994 found that 51 percent of Romanians saw December 1989 as a "revolution." Another 30 percent of those interviewed in 1994 thought that it was an "internal plot," while 16 percent deemed it as "an external plot." Even though the formulation of the question was different in the survey from 1999, it can be argued that, in 1994, against the background of a somewhat better (or, at least, more stable) economic situation, the proportion of those who viewed December 1989 as a radical rupture with the past (i.e., a revolution) is significantly higher than in the 1999 survey (i.e., 51 percent versus 40 percent).

Those who believe it was a revolution were asked a supplementary question regarding the success or failure of the revolution. Almost two thirds of those who believe it was a revolution also think it succeeded (62 percent), while 27 percent believe that it failed; 3 percent did not answer or could not make a choice, and 8 percent chose "other situation" (e.g., the revolution succeeded in some aspects and failed in others). More evidence for the lack of a shared understanding within Romania's collective memory of the December Events comes from the answers to the question: "In your opinion, who or what force(s) contributed the most to the downfall of Ceaușescu?" This was an open-ended question and the array of answers is impressive, varying from "members of the [present day] parliament," "Elena Ceaușescu," "Jacques Chirac,"[!][28] to the "Mafia," "American Imperialism," and "The Russians and the Hungarians." Noting that one-third of the respondents in the sample did not answer this question, the most common answers were "the People" (19 percent), "Ion Iliescu" (7 percent), and the "Army" (4 percent).

Measures. In this analysis, the dependent variable is "Beliefs about December 1989" and is coded as follows: 1=revolution; 2=coup d'état; 3=something else. The survey asked respondents what they believe happened in December 1989. The respondents who did not answer this question (NA) or who could not make a choice (DK) were recorded in a separate category, and are excluded from this analysis. (See table 4.2.)

Independent variables. Most of the independent variables we employ in this analysis are self-explanatory, but some need further clarification. In terms of spatial location, we consider two dummy variables: resident of Bucharest (1=yes), and resident of Moldova (1=yes). Through these variables, we attempt to partially account for the effects of spatial proximity on beliefs about the 1989 December events. There are different possible hypotheses for understanding how one's residence would influence her interpretation of December 1989. For instance, actual street fighting occurred in only a few large urban centers of Romania, such as Bucharest, Timişoara, Cluj, Sibiu, or Braşov, leaving the more rural areas (such as the historical region of Moldova, in Northeast Romania) relatively unaffected. For most residents in these rural areas, the experience of a revolution had only a mediated character (i.e., television and radio). One could hypothesize that the closer one was to a site of violent confrontation (i.e., urban areas), the higher the chances that she will believe that it was a revolution versus something else. But this hypothesis ignores the fact that alternative or independent media sources (which questioned the "revolution" and conveyed many of the counter narratives) are more readily available in large urban centers. A more complex hypothesis would state that, all other factors being equal, where there are fewer sources for alternative information, residents of these areas are more likely to believe the official story of a "revolution." Unfortunately, our data does not allow us to test this hypothesis. Our measures of "spatial proximity" are only approximations as our survey recorded only a respondent's residence in 1999.

We included in the list of the independent variables the respondent's voting preference for presidential candidates. The source-item asked: "Should presidential elections be held next Sunday, what candidate would you vote for?" We selected the preferences for the two most important candidates, "voting for Ion Iliescu (1=yes)" and "voting for Emil Constantinescu (1=yes)." Being the head of the neo-Communist government, Iliescu has been one of the major advocates of a genuine revolution story. During his 1996 electoral campaign, Emil Constantinescu, the candidate for the oppositional Democratic Convention, often challenged Iliescu's "revolution" narrative. In his view, even if a revolution did take place in December 1989, it would remain only a partial, incomplete revolution as long as Iliescu remained in power. This version was also sustained by Constantinescu's supporters.

Table 4.2. Descriptive Statistics for the Variables Included in the Analysis of Beliefs about December 1989 Events

Variables	*Median*	*Mean*	*S.D.*	*Valid N*
Dependent				
Revolution[a]		.50		1,626
Coup d'état		.45		1,626
Something else		.05		1,626
Independent				
Age (in years)	47.00	46.75	17.04	2,019
Female[b]		.51		2,019
Education				
University graduate[b]		.11		2,019
Secondary school[b]		.32		2,019
Vocational education[b]		.20		2,019
General education[a]		.37		2,019
Spatial Location				
Resident in Bucharest[b]		.09		2,019
Resident in Moldova[b]		.21		2,019
Life satisfaction (1–4)	2.00	1.78	.72	1,986
Voting preference				
Vote for:				
Emil Constantinescu[b]		.17		1,176
Ion Iliescu[b]		.44		1,176

Notes: [a]Reference category; [b]Dummy variables. N=2,019.
Source: "Human and Social Resources of the Romanian Transition," October 1999.

As we have previously suggested, the features of the socioeconomic context can influence a respondent's beliefs and opinions about December 1989. We attempt to account for these influences by employing "life satisfaction," an ordinal variable on a four-point scale, ranging from extremely satisfied (4) to extremely dissatisfied (1). We maintain that the lower an individual's life satisfaction, the lower the chances that she will believe in a radical rupture with the past (a revolution). Before turning to the results of our analysis, we would like to reiterate that it has only an exploratory character. The causal structure of the opinions about December 1989 is far more complex than the one we propose here, and the list of the so-called independent variables is by no means exhaustive.

Estimation model. We account for the determinants of the various interpretations of the December 1989 events by a multinomial logistic regression. The dependent variable, "Beliefs about December 1989," is nominal with the following categories: "revolution," "coup d'état," "something else." "(belief in) revolution" is the reference category in our analysis. That is, we estimate the chances of believing that it was a "Coup d'état" or "something else" versus (believing that it was a) "revolution." In comparison with binary logit models, a multinomial logistic regression simultaneously estimates all the logits.[29] Table 4.3 presents the coefficients from our multinomial logistic regression analysis.

Coup d'état. With respect to sociodemographic variables, a respondent's age has a significant, negative effect on the likelihood of believing that it was a coup d'état rather than revolution. As age increases, the chances of believing that it was a coup d'état decrease. Women are less likely to believe that it was a coup d'état rather than a revolution; education has no statistically significant effects on the chances of embracing the "coup d'état" story (versus the "revolution" story). None of the "spatial location" variables has any significant effect on viewing the December events as a coup d'état. An individual's life satisfaction has negative, significant effects on the chances of viewing the December events as a "coup d'état." That is, as life

Table 4.3. Coefficients from the Multinomial Logistic Regression Analysis of Believing That It Was a Coup d'état or That Something Else Happened in December 1989 versus Believing That It Was a Revolution

Independent Variables Variables	*Belief in a Coup d'état (vs. a Revolution)*[a]	*Belief that Something Else Happened (vs. a Revolution)*[a]
Age (in years)	−.021***	.015
Female[b]	−349**	−.654†
Education		
University graduate[b]	−.367	1.617***
Secondary school[b]	.092	1.063*
Vocational education[b]	.026	.614
Spatial Location		
Resident in Bucharest[b]	.186	.320
Resident in Moldova[b]	.108	.736*
Life satisfaction (1–4)	−.184*	.119
Voting preference		
Vote for Emil Constantinescu[b]	.153	.872
Vote for Ion Iliescu[b]	−.340*	−.612
INTERCEPT	1.585	−3.766
Likelihood Ratio Chi-Square (20 d.f.)		79.71***

Notes: [a]The reference category is "Belief in Revolution," [b]Dummy variables. †=p < .10; * = p < .05; ** = p < .01; *** = p < .001. (N=2,019)
Source: "Human and Social Resources of the Romanian Transition," October 1999.

satisfaction increases, the chances of believing that it was a "coup d'état" decrease. This finding supports our initial expectations: the more satisfied one is with her current situation, the higher the chances of perceiving the present as a radical rupture ("revolution") with the past. Also, consonant with our initial expectations, the supporters of the former president Ion Iliescu are less likely to believe in the coup d'état thesis versus the revolution thesis.

Something else happened. Controlling for other factors, residents of Moldova are more likely to believe that what happened was neither a "revolution" nor a "coup d'état" but, rather, "something else." This finding runs counter to our initial expectations: ten years after, residents of Moldova—a former stronghold of Iliescu's party and the place where the revolution was mainly a mediated event—seem to be less prone to believe in either the revolution or the coup d'état versions. University graduates are three times as likely as individuals with ten (or less) years of schooling to view the December Events as "something else" rather than as a revolution. As we expected, highly educated individuals tend to be less willing to embrace the official story of a pure revolution. Secondary school graduates join university graduates in their suspicion of a definite answer. Voting preferences and life satisfaction do not make any statistical difference on the chances of believing that "something else happened in 1989."

Various interpretations of the events of December 1989 are influenced by factors such as age, education, place of residence, voting preferences, and life satisfaction. This variance in beliefs is important: Ten years after the fall of the Ceauşescu regime, a regime that caused so much trauma to Romanians, there is still no collective memory or a shared understanding regarding what "really happened" in 1989.

CONCLUSIONS

Even though distrust of the public sphere and the Machiavellian manipulation of collective memory preceded Ceauşescu, he took it to new heights. Throughout the 1980s, these machinations became only more absurd when seen against the background of growing economic hardship. Given this, it should come as no surprise that Romanians were ecstatic about the "revolution" of 1989. Yet, as the euphoria of those cathartic days died away, the old pathologies (e.g., distrust of the public sphere, lack of a legitimate, legitimating narrative, and proliferation of alternative "legitimate" narratives) reemerged, superseding any hope that a shared "revolution" myth would offer a common identity and a clear break with the "old." The inability of the trial, a traditional forum for creating shared memories, to reaffirm the "revolution" myth can also be understood through this failed break with the "old." Between this "old" and "new," a hole still remains in Romania's collective memory of the December Events.

Fourteen years after the events of 1989, one can walk through Heroes' Cemetery, where Bucharest's martyred demonstrators are buried, and see parents visiting their children. C. V. is a sixty-eight-year-old pensioner who has visited his son's grave every Sunday since the "Events." When asked what happened during those turbulent days, he responds, "Don't believe what others say about a coup, it was a true revolution that my son gave his life to!" While walking away from the grave a middle-age woman comes up and says, with a sense of annoyance, "Don't believe him. It was a coup d'état!" Declining to give any details about herself, all she will say is that she is visiting her nephew's grave and that "He gave his life and for what? For nothing!" Further on is E. C., a seventy-eight-year-old pensioner who had lost his only son to the revolution and, in 1990, formed "The Association for Honoring the Martyred Heroes of the Revolution of 1989." He said that the survivors of those killed in the December Events have wanted answers since 1989, and that one of the main goals of Association is "to learn the truth. We have heard many stories, many beautiful words, but no truth." He talked about an honest state prosecutor who, in the in mid 1990s, had told him "We have the facts but we can't publish them." When asked why, he said, "there are too many people in high positions who were involved in what went on in 1989 and they don't want the truth to come out."

Somewhere between those who have benefited from the events of December 1989, who prefer that a true picture of "the events" never emerge, and those, like the parents of the martyrs, who struggle for clarity, lies the majority of Romania. These are people who are trying to ignore a wound that never healed, but recoil whenever something bumps into it. In contemporary Romania, one confronts a common scenario: When asked about the revolution, people will usually say, "Oh, that was so long ago!" or "Questions about the revolution? What questions are left?" But as the discussion deepens, strong emotions come to the surface. Dana is an articulate twenty-nine-year-old sociologist who is trying to get funding to study in the West. After initially dismissing questions about the revolution, she was soon in tears while recalling a family friend who, bloodied and maimed by bullets, had to drag himself to the train station to flee the city. Then there's the man on the train who was on the streets of Bucharest during those chaotic days. He also initially dismissed questions about his experience as merely "history," but by the end of the conversation he is angrily shaking his clenched fist and yelling: "We put our lives on the line and for what? So the same people who screwed us before, can screw us again?!?!"

In John Reed's travelogue *War in Eastern Europe: Travels through the Balkans in 1915*, the journalist wrote about the Romanian peasants' belief that if a person did not die properly (with a candle in his hand), he would not reach heaven, and he could potentially become a vampire. Reed concluded that the church used the myth as a way to collect money from peasants to perform death rites: "To lay this murdering ghost, the body must be exhumed in the dead of night and the heart torn out by an ordained priest, who drives a wooden peg through it. For this he charges a hundred francs." For contemporary Romania, there may be a cautionary tale in these superstitions: If a nation does not bury its dead properly, be they the martyrs of the revolution or the machinations of Communism, their restless spirits may cost much more to exorcize later.

NOTES

1. Octavian Paler, "The East's New Malady," in *Christian Science Monitor* (30 March 1992), p. 18.

2. Mark Osiel, *Mass Atrocity: Atrocity, Collective Memory, and the Law* (New Brunswick, NJ: Transaction Publishers, 1997), pp. 18–19.

3. *Ibid*, footnote on p. 18.

4. Jürgen Habermas, *The Structural Transformation of the Public Sphere*, trans. by Thomas Burger (Cambridge: MIT Press, 1994), pp. 1–4.

5. Ken Jowitt, *New World Disorder: The Leninist Extinction* (Berkeley: University of California Press, 1992), p. 70.

6. For a definition of this type of institutional change, see Paul J. DiMaggion and William W. Powell, "The Iron Cage Revisited: Institutional Isomorphism and Collective Rationality in Organizational Fields" in *American Sociological Review*, vol. 48, no. 2 (April 1983), p. 150.

7. Vlad Georgescu, *Istoria românilor: de la origini pînă în zilele noastre* (București: *Editura Humanitas*, 1992), p. 264.

8. Georgescu, *Istoria* românilor, p. 268.

9. Georgescu, *Istoria românilor*, p. 271.

10. *Ibid.*

11. Gail Kligman, *The Politics of Duplicity: Controlling Reproduction in Ceaușescu's Romania* (Berkeley: University of California Press, 1998), p. 117.

12. For an excellent, in-depth analysis of protochronism, see Katherine Verdery, *National Ideology under Socialism: Identity and Cultural Politics in Ceaușescu's Romania* (Berkeley: University of California Press, 1991), ch. 5.

13. Jowitt, *New World Disorder*, pp. 70–71.

14. Tamotsu Shibutani, *Improvised News: A Sociological Study of Rumor* (New York: The Bobbs-Merrill Company, 1966), p. 57.

15. Shibutani, *Improvised News*, p. 164.

16. For more in-depth coverage of rumors surrounding the December events, see Gail Kligman and Katherine Verdery, "Romania after Ceaușescu: Post-Communist Communism," in Ivo Banac, ed., *Eastern Europe in Revolution* (Ithaca, NY: Cornell University Press, 1992); and Richard Andrew Hall, "The Uses of Absurdity: The Staged War Theory and the Romanian Revolution of December 1989," in *East European Politics and Societies*, vol. 13, no. 3 (Fall 1999), pp. 501–42.

17. Hall, "Uses of Absurdity," footnote on p. 540.

18. Hall, "Uses of Absurdity," p. 502.

19. David Garland, *Punishment and Modern Society* (Chicago: University of Chicago Press, 1990) p. 67.

20. *Ibid.*

21. Osiel, *Mass Atrocity*, p. 39.

22. For a more detailed analysis of the trial see Cătălin Augustin Stoica's "Romania's Failed Attempt at a Revolutionary Myth," in *Polish Sociological Review*, no. 4 (1999).

23. Juan Linz and Alfred Stepan, *Problems of Democratic Transition and Consolidation* (Baltimore: Johns Hopkins University Press, 1996), p. 52.

24. *Expresul de Marţi* (1995), p. 9.

25. Hannah Arendt, *On Revolution* (New York: Viking Press, 1963).

26. From our discussions with those who did the fieldwork, this category often comprises different combinations of "revolution" and "coup d'état."

27. Pavel Câmpeanu, "*Simboluri ale Revoluţiei Române*" in *Polis*, no. 4 (1994).

28. Jacques Chirac was president of France at the time of the survey, though Francois Mitterand was president in 1989.

29. J. Scott Long, *Regression Models for Categorical and Limited Dependent Variables* (London: Sage Publications, 1997), p. 15.

5

Democratization in the Shadows: Post-Communist Patrimonialism

Frank Sellin[1]

Patrimonialism has long been a hallmark of largely agrarian societies grappling with increasingly powerful and intrusive modern states.[2] Viewed from the top down, observers of patrimonial systems see heavily personalized, often authoritarian or semi-authoritarian regimes, which penetrate society less through the means of formal representative institutions—if any exist—than through patron–client relationships. Viewed from the bottom up, patron-client networks are frequently the vehicle by which seemingly powerless, atomized individuals attempt to neutralize or minimize the costs associated with coercive, interventionist states, and/or to cut through immense bureaucratic obstacles to obtain access to state resources. Not surprisingly, contemporary patrimonialism has a strong heritage in the Balkans, where most countries have only recently approached or crossed the divide from rural to urban under Communism, and where many people still retain links to, and the habits of, a rural social environment. Such is the case with Romania.

"*Patrimonialism*," wrote Weber, "and, in the extreme case, *sultanism* tend to arise whenever traditional domination develops an administration and a military force which are purely personal instruments of the master."[3] Weber also recognized that the ruler's staff could themselves develop bases of support, and eventually substantial, even hereditary, claims to their position and perquisites in what he termed *estate-type domination*. This, in Weber's view, would contribute to a process of growing competition, and thus decentralization, within the framework of a patrimonial system.[4]

Recent works on patrimonialism have explored its extreme form, "sultanism" (following the Weberian nomenclature), wherein a dictator, often aided and abetted by his extended familial relations, masters an entire state and society with near-total control—a form of control which is of an extremely personalized, but otherwise ideologically weak, nature.[5] Sultanistic regimes, in the Weberian sense, have been rare, and as the concept itself seems to demand, historically limited to the reign of the family dictatorship in question: such as Kim Il Sung and Kim Jong Il's North Korea, Papa Doc and Baby Doc's Haiti, Tacho and Tachito Somoza's Nicaragua, and Nicolae Ceauşescu's Romania. Alfred Stepan and Juan Linz seem to construe sultanism more broadly than Weber, classifying it as one of five major regime types (along with totalitarianism, authoritarianism, democracy, and post-totalitarianism). Here, I prefer to avoid any narrowness or other ambiguity about the term, and instead apply the term "patrimonial" to a broader cross section of regimes.[6]

While there has been a fair amount of literature on the subject, scholarly analysis has rarely addressed the question of what happens to *post*-sultanistic societies likely to join the larger class of patrimonial regimes. The question becomes all the more urgent now that we have a decade of post-Communist experience, which both illuminates the troubles afflicting democratization and identifies a need to train the spotlight on the relationship of patrimonialism to democratization. This chapter is intended to fill part of that lacuna, by addressing the case of Romania. The analysis will survey, in very broad and brief terms, the political effects of what I call post-Communist patrimonialism in Romania since 1989.[7] I will argue that ten years of post-Communist patrimonialism, though it started out as very centralized, is largely responsible for slowly producing, and to some extent perpetuating, an increasingly fractured and semidecentralized political system at the level of state institutions and especially political parties. I further contend that post-Communist patrimonialism complicates, and even obstructs, political and economic reform through a symbiotic relationship that protects powerful elite interests in the status quo. Change in this system would probably require a significant exogenous shock (e.g., the sustained progressive movements that brought civil service reform to the U.S. and Western Europe).

Post-Communist patrimonialism consists of (a) a leader unequivocally acknowledged (though not necessarily unchallenged) as the top political authority; (b) a leader who retains and funds a staff beholden to him alone (appointed on the basis of personal loyalty from among relatives, friends, and clients) as well as a coercive apparatus beholden to him personally (and not controlled by civilian authorities in a rational-legal bureaucracy); (c) creating a regime where the line between public and private property, and between private and state action, is blurred in favor of the ruler and his clients, such that (d) much of society responds by organizing itself, in large part, along similar patron-client lines in the competition for state resources, power, and prestige.

The modern, contingent elements of post-Communist patrimonialism extend the ideal type with: (e) the need to administer a huge state bureaucracy, often collectively inefficient and divided among competing patron-client chains and (f) the promotion of charismatic elements from Communist days (e.g., control of the media, cults of personality, both in opposition as well as within the regime). Post-Communist patrimonial politics is thus manifested in the battle for control of cadres with personalized loyalties across multiple institutional and policy channels. I also reorient the concept away from Weber's notions of "legitimacy" and "authority," as I prefer to think of patrimonalism as one approach to state-building and the (re)organization of a political system after the fall of Communism—one that does not depend on popular confirmation in its initial stages, if ever. Here I focus on the effects of post-Communist patrimonialism on democratic development. I especially focus on the role of parties and the state as agents of patronage disbursement, rather than as agents engaged in the aggregation of public preferences and rational public policy formulation.

THE COMMUNIST PATRIMONIAL INHERITANCE

Close observers of Romanian politics would note the many continuities with the practices of Communist-era regimes, particularly the emphasis given to identifying, promoting, and rotating cadres loyal to key patrons at the top, under the famous *nomenklatura* system. Both Gheorghe Gheorghiu-Dej and his protégé and successor Nicolae Ceauşescu (who served the former as party secretary in charge of organization and cadres) displayed considerable worries about factions or potential rivals in the party, and both leaders consequently spent considerable effort cultivating loyal supporters in the party.[8] One illustrative example of how the game was played was Ceauşescu's politicking among colleagues on the post-Dej politburo, ultimately aimed at sacking and replacing his main rival and fellow Dej protégé, Alexandru Drăghici, as Minister of Internal Affairs (where he was head of most of the state security apparatus) on 24 July 1965. Drăghici's replacement, not surprisingly, was a Ceauşescu loyalist, Cornel Onescu.[9] Moreover, Ceauşescu was even more intent than Gheorghiu-Dej on "clearing the decks" of potential rivals, as he implemented the so-called rotation principle[10] (a strategy frequently seen in other sultanistic regimes). The idea was to isolate potential rivals from their power bases, as well as spread the wealth among prospective clients, all with the understanding that everyone save the *conducător* was vulnerable to arbitrary dismissal at any time. Romania's first post-Communist president, Ion Iliescu, benefited from Ceauşescu's favoritism, and even reached the political executive committee, until his demotion in 1971. Some of the central figures in the initial National Salvation Front (FSN) leadership, and in the events of 22–28 December 1989, had either been long-time close associates of Iliescu, such as Marţian Dan, or targets of persistent cultivation by Iliescu, such as General Nicolae Militaru.[11]

If Romania's patrimonial pedigree is a logical, even genetic, outcome of Ceauşescu's sultanism, the sudden, violent collapse of sultanism explains why Iliescu's FSN rebuilt a neo-patrimonial state. Iliescu and the FSN had to reconstruct the essential attributes of a badly weakened state in a very short time. At the same time, they had to co-opt vested and still powerful interests within the ruins of the old party-state. Primarily, this meant convincing multiple splinter groups from the former *Securitate* and the army to accede to the FSN leadership in the rough-and-tumble bargaining that followed the collapse of the Ceauşescu regime in 1989.[12] The bitter departures of leaders like Dumitru Mazilu and Silviu Brucan in early 1990, followed shortly thereafter by General Mihai Chiţac and Gelu Voican Voiculescu in the aftermath of the miners' June 1990 rampage, exemplified the casualties of the turbulent struggle of prospective patrons.

Still, such turbulence did not prevent the FSN from quickly asserting its hold, aided by control of the state media and state patronage. In rebuilding the state, the FSN could not deploy direct coercion on a large scale against a long-victimized population—though it could apply "selective" violence against anti-regime demonstrators, opposition political parties, and ethnic Hungarians. Instead, the FSN resurrected old Communist networks, visible in the numerous local FSN councils that sprang up almost overnight in workplaces and villages throughout Romania in January 1990. Such patrimonial co-optation was followed by the distribution of mayoral positions and agricultural resources "down to the village level."[13] During 1990–91, the FSN used patrimonial incentives (e.g., ministerial portfolios) to cultivate opposition leaders and contribute to their disunity, particularly among liberal splinters.

PATRIMONIALISM UNDER ILIESCU

The wedge that split the FSN hierarchy during 1991–92 took unmistakably patrimonial form. From early on, both Iliescu and Prime Minister Petre Roman had developed their own separate entourages.[14] While the initial split was, to some degree, over the pace of reform, it was also fundamentally a battle for power and patronage that quickly dragged in the "bosses," and politicized institutions ranging from the Roman cabinet to the new Romanian Information Service (SRI), which backed Iliescu.[15] Roman's support lay with many of his former ministers and part of the central party apparatus. Iliescu's came primarily from the FSN parliamentary delegation, particularly senators, with personal connections and loyalties to Iliescu traceable to promotion in the early days of the FSN and the Provisional National Council of Unity (CPUN). The intense struggle (prior to the formal split in the spring of 1992) targeted not only the central apparatus, but also spread to local party branches as well, whose support had to be bought, even screened, before the scheduled FSN congress.[16] Iliescu's new party, the Democratic National Salvation Front (FDSN), metamorphosed into the Party of Social Democracy (PDSR) a year later, and Roman's FSN was eventually renamed the Democratic Party (PD). The split's coda highlighted the symbiosis between the personalized party and the state: Iliescu's FDSN inherited its new headquarters from the SRI (the most significant heir to the *Securitate*) and mobilized other state resources, including its own media, in order to establish itself in the few scant months prior to the September 1992 elections, where it won a plurality.[17]

With the ouster of Roman in September 1991 (after the fourth miners' intervention) and the installation of a new government under Nicolae Văcăroiu following the September 1992 elections, the lines of patrimonial authority to Iliescu were simplified, despite some continuing chaos. Iliescu was unquestionably the dominant political patron, able to command (or veto) appointments, ranging from the PDSR leadership to all levels of the government (including the prime-minister and his cabinet), state television, and certainly to his own staff at Cotroceni. This is not to say that Iliescu regularly exercised his political supremacy: Romanian political observers have routinely commented on his trademark hesitation, and his willingness to let subordinates engage in their own prolonged schemes and conflicts. Thus, while the PDSR leadership and the government itself would frequently consult the president—barred by the Constitution from partisan affiliation—and would keep one eye over their shoulders in case of Iliescu's veto or intervention, many political "barons" competed to establish their own clientelist fiefdoms. These included figures such as Adrian Năstase (PDSR first vice-president and president of the Chamber of Deputies), Miron Mitrea (a former trade union leader co-opted as a PDSR vice-president), and Viorel Hrebenciuc (secretary general of the government). There was a sense that while the government handled day-to-day state management and dispensation of resources, the most important issues (e.g., price hikes) were decided by the PDSR leadership and Iliescu, and then passed down to the government itself.

This is not to argue that Iliescu and the PDSR enjoyed absolute hegemony. Starting in 1992, the minority Văcăroiu government depended for support on allies, namely radical nationalist parties such as the Greater Romania Party (PRM), and the Party of Romanian National Unity (PUNR), and a hard left/"Ceauşist" party, the Socialist Labor Party (PSM). All put increasing pressure on PDSR for state offices and other perquisites in return. By 1994, PRM, PUNR and PSM—all abetted at their inception during 1990–91 by the then FSN regime—leveraged their formal entry into a pseudo-coalition government, despite PDSR reluctance, obtaining more access to state posts and resources in the bargain. However, these posts were usually outside the "power" ministries and/or at the sub-ministerial level, and largely did not supplant the control of Iliescu and the PDSR over key areas, such as defense, internal affairs, finance, the leadership of SRI and other semi-secret services, or state television. The real levers of state power thus remained comfortably with PDSR.

Starting in late 1995, the junior partners (PRM, PSM, and PUNR) were successively kicked out of the governing coalition for increasingly criticizing the government in which they participated. Yet despite the thundering of PRM, PSM, and PUNR about corruption, the disastrous standard of living, and the betrayal of Romania to foreign interests, the latter two parties clung tenaciously to their central and provincial offices, delaying the final break with PDSR for months, until 1996. Patrimonial rewards could thus triumph at least temporarily over electoral incentives (namely, declining poll ratings) to leave the coalition and reestablish party identities; at least this was the case until the PDSR itself began to move toward expulsion of its former partners.

There were other limitations on patrimonial power, mostly involving competition within the regime itself. Though SRI director Virgil Măgureanu was reputed to be the second most powerful man in the regime (after Iliescu, and some even argued the reverse), he did not have total control over that institution, and appeared to be waging war with some of his own nominal subordinates.[18] He did, however, outlast even Iliescu as the only two surviving members of the original FSN Council.[19] Similarly, Iliescu and the PDSR found their assets in state media to be weakened by the granting of national access to semi-independent TV stations such as PRO TV and *Antena 1*, and on the local level by independent media in districts controlled by the opposition since 1992.

Still, patrimonialism under Iliescu and the PDSR predictably resulted in a system that blurred the separation of powers; and it produced *de facto* executive rule, subordinating the legislative and judicial branches of government to an extra-constitutional dominance of a personal and partisan nature. The "Iliescu constitution" approved by referendum on 9 December 1991 (mostly over the objections of the opposition) did much to enhance presidential rule in a quasi-French-type system.[20] The judiciary, while nominally independent, is largely subject to executive and partisan preferences. While they are appointed for life, judges are still subject to disciplinary action, as well as promotion and transfer by the Supreme Council of Magistrates, the same body (chosen by the legislature) that proposes candidates to the president for appointment. Certainly the post-Communist Romanian judiciary has never had a reputation for independence from the executive, despite the efforts of individual judges and prosecutors,[21] and this pattern of judicial vulnerability continues under the second Iliescu regime (2000–present).

Parliament, which Article 58 of the constitution declares to be "the supreme representative of the people," can and does vote to give the government the power to emit ordinances. Rule by governmental decree has increasingly become a more prolific way to govern the country, before, and especially after, 1996. This is not surprising, considering that the Romanian parliament has 484 seats, divided into two chambers which exercise nearly identical powers, and which have very murky procedures in proposing, reconciling, and passing legislation.[22] Despite intermittent calls for reform, Romania's disproportionate supply of parliamentary seats (with their attendant access to legislative resources—posts in the chamber leaderships, offices, foreign travel, etc.) is a welcome mainstay in the pool of state-sponsored assets available for patrimonial distribution.[23] Moreover, we should keep in mind that Romania's parliamentary elections operate by proportional representation, with lists of names controlled, by and large, by the central apparatus of most parties (where parliamentarians frequently sit on ruling bodies). In short, the institutional system, as it currently exists, reflects the interests of a lot of people—parties and party leaders above all—such that the status quo would be heavily defended against those who might insist on reforming big government.

Patrimonialism has contributed heavily to the fusion of political and economic power. The ruling PDSR was renowned for its intense efforts at coopting directors of state enterprises, presumably thereby obtaining a measure of political control over votes as well as hefty contributions to the party coffers, in return for access to state subsidies, licenses, and less regulation. Second, the regime engaged in limited liberalization but did little to encourage a stable investment climate for businesses—especially foreign investors—expected to make payoffs throughout the central and local state structure. Although the Constitution forbids government ministers from serving on "bodies with commercial purpose" (Article 104), some unquestionably did, the most publicized case being the Văcăroiu government's minister of commerce, Petre Crişan.[24]

Parliamentarians, however, are not expressly forbidden by the constitution from sitting on boards (*consiliile administrative*, or CA) and stockholder assemblies (*adunăriile generale ale acţionarilor*, or AGA). They had to confront precisely such conflicts of economic interest during 1995–96 with a proposed law forbidding parliamentarians' membership on CAs and AGAs in companies with *state* capital (i.e., those at the heart of privatization efforts). Conspicuous through omission, the proposed law said nothing about ownership or decision-making by lawmakers in purely *privately* owned corporations. After all the public posturing against the conflict of interest, the joint session vote on the law was 280 in favor to ten against—with 194 abstentions.[25] That has hardly plugged the demand for other means of access to state resources. Appointments of lawmakers or their clients to various positions in the elephantine bureaucracy of the State Privatization Fund (the agency charged with overseeing the valuation and privatization of state-owned enterprises and other assets, separated into regional jurisdictions) were, and continue to be, highly sought by parliamentarians of all parties, both before and after the 1996 fall of the Iliescu regime.

Regarding the private sector's criminal relationship to the public authorities under Iliescu, a few well-publicized examples will suffice. One was the prevalence of numerous banking scandals under the Iliescu regime, where dubious loan practices led to the disappearance of hundreds of millions, perhaps billions, of dollars. Suspects were either rarely found or subject to suspiciously prolonged, or postponed, investigations and trials. Some, such as Sever Mureşan, the largest shareholder in the "*Dacia Felix*" Bank and reported to be in virtual exile abroad, were frequently photographed by the press while having clandestine meetings with Iliescu and other PDSR luminaries. Similar experiences were recorded in the more "traditional" underworld. Known tobacco, alcohol, and drug smuggling kingpins (e.g., Zaher Iskanderani and Gheorghe "Gigi Kent" Vasile) perennially evaded capture—in some cases, were even granted protection—by corrupt police and customs officials. Columna Bank, reputedly the venture of ex-*Securitate* members, was alleged to be bankrolling the tiny Socialist Party (a splinter from the already small PSM).[26] Lastly, while some of the foregoing criminals are now serving jail sentences, many others are not. George Constantin Păunescu, one of three brothers at the head of a vast financial empire, and considered to be one of the richest men in Romania, eluded investigation and arrest by the post-1996 Romanian authorities by remaining in the U.S.

The fall of Iliescu and the PDSR in November 1996 was largely attributable to structural consequences of patrimonial dynamics. Beginning with the FSN's decision to co-opt xenophobic interests strongly linked to portions of the former *Securitate* and PCR elites, and the ensuing ethnic violence in Tîrgu Mureş in March of 1990, Iliescu and his followers drove the Hungarian Democratic Union (UDMR)—and thereby 7 percent of the electorate—into implacable opposition.[27] Additionally, the split with Petre Roman and the latter's renamed Democratic Party (PD) sent a hefty portion of former Communists into rancorous opposition. Trying to present themselves as the "real" social democrats, they allied themselves with the small, "historical" Social Democratic Party of Sergiu Cunescu (PSDR, which had exited the opposition Democratic Convention of Romania in 1995). Roman's supporters split in the presidential elections in favor of Constantinescu. Hungarians voted for their own presidential candidate in the first round, and overwhelmingly backed Constantinescu in the second. Most decisively, Iliescu and the PDSR—seen increasingly as a corrupt "directocracy" more interested in recruiting famous names and factory directors, while presiding over half-hearted reforms and a catastrophic decline in the standard of living—lost a chunk of their traditional electorate, namely workers and peasants. The PDSR encountered slippage among peasants, but especially among workers, who, while they had heavily backed the FDSN in 1992, switched to the CDR in 1996, voting 32 percent for the latter as opposed to 21 percent for the former. Twenty percent of those who had supported Iliescu in 1992 switched to Roman in the first round of 1996, and fifteen percent backed Constantinescu.[28] However, the 1996 vote was not so much a vote of confidence in the CDR and its vague, often contradictory "Contract for Romania," as a vote against the Iliescu regime.

PATRIMONIALISM AFTER ILIESCU

The change of regime in 1996 marked a momentous step for Romania and a necessary, if insufficient, condition for progress toward democratization. It changed some elements of the patrimonial system, but hardly eliminated it. Opportunism, and the temporary disruption of existing patron–client chains, surfaced with media reports of local "PDSR-ists" applying to join the PNŢCD, the prime mover behind the CDR coalition, and even Roman's PD. More important, Romanian patrimonialism decentralized somewhat, as a dominant party was replaced with a "coalition of coalitions" in government. The effect of this "coalition of coalitions" on institutions since 1996 has been dramatic. President Constantinescu, though a key player capable of significant intervention and pressure, could not dictate to the PNŢCD or the government in the manner of Iliescu and the former PDSR. On the contrary, he was increasingly ridiculed for having promised serious economic reform and a "war on corruption"—a war which he was largely unable to produce, thanks to the blackmail games being played by the parties in his governing coalition.

The power to form governments thus shifted from one to multiple ruling parties. Here, the governing coalition set up an incredibly complicated, extremely office-conscious "algorithm" which governed the partisan distribution of almost every possible post in the government, from the prime minister down to the middle management of every ministry. The blackmail games that combine the dictates of the algorithm with threats to withdraw support in parliament have made Romania almost ungovernable since the CDR-USD-UDMR coalition took over from 1996 to 2000. Corruption and nepotism flourished since the appointed secretary general, Valerian Stan, was sacked in 1997 by then prime minister Victor Ciorbea, after PD threatened to withdraw its parliamentary support if Stan continued with his anti-corruption agenda.[29]

Perhaps the most striking example of patrimonial politics in the post-1996 system was the intra-party warfare that brought down two PNŢCD prime ministers, Victor Ciorbea and Radu Vasile. Indeed, the strongest attacks on prime ministers have come from rival factions in their own party (though other coalition partners are often happy to help). Vasile, taking advantage of

PD's signals that it could not work with a moralistic, unbending Ciorbea (including direct challenges by PD ministers to Ciorbea's authority), undermined the latter—his party's own prime minister—with the help of the faction he led in the PNŢCD. The ambitious Vasile was quickly propelled into Ciorbea's place. The incident underlined how leading political figures in the country are increasingly open targets for the plentiful ranks of hungry office-seekers. It also contrasted with the days of the Văcăroiu government, whose compositional stability ultimately depended on Iliescu's arbitration.

Vasile, however, was hoisted by his own petard. His closeness to the PD, and his arrogant refusals to heed policy directives and warnings from PNŢCD president Ion Diaconescu and the rest of the party leadership, provoked another factional revolt in December 1999, this time led by octogenarian Gabriel Ţepelea and the much younger Remus Opriş. The game of ultimatums eventually resulted in Vasile's resignation, but not before he had humiliated his own party and President Constantinescu by refusing to step down until Constantinescu withdrew his constitutionally dubious announcement that Vasile was fired.[30] His successor as prime minister, Mugur Isărescu, was the former head of the national bank since Iliescu's time, with a strong reputation in foreign financial circles, and was accepted as an independent, presumably to mitigate partisan attacks.

The postscript to the Vasile affair illustrates another key point about patrimonial effects on the party system. Political scientists typically expected that elections and political "learning" would, over time, "winnow out" the explosion of parties and the fragmentation of party systems in new democracies by marrying the (over)supply of parties to the limited "demand" of voters.[31] The fact is that most parties in Romania—and in many other countries in Eastern Europe—are still patron-driven, factional affairs led by charismatic personalities, and they are dealing with volatile electorates. The costs of defections or splits, even after four national elections in the case of Romania, are still quite low. Thus, despite some disappearances, new parties keep forming and old ones keep splintering in Romania, largely in tow behind well-known, ambitious personalities.

Granted, most newly formed parties are small, and so far have been relatively inconsequential affairs, such as former SRI chief Măgureanu's Romanian National Party (PNR). But most of the larger, presumably more entrenched parties have undergone serious, damaging splits.[32] Some of these larger splits were essentially fallout from the electoral loss in 1996 (although it should be noted that individual "leap-frog" defections from party to party are almost a monthly routine in Romania, and heat up when party lists are being drafted in preparation for elections). PUNR underwent a massive split between the camps around Valeriu Tabără (former minister of agriculture) and president Gheorghe Funar (who took his wing into Corneliu Vadim Tudor's PRM). Most notably, Iliescu's PDSR gave birth to the Alliance for Romania (ApR), led by former foreign minister Teodor Meleşcanu and assisted by Iliescu's former campaign manager, Iosif Boda. On the "winners'" side, both outgoing PNŢCD premiers have formed their own parties. Victor Ciorbea created his National Alliance of Christian Democrats (ANCD, largely composed of ex-PNŢCD members) upon exiting the PNŢCD (and reentering after the 2000 election debacle). Likewise, Radu Vasile briefly formed the Popular Party with his faction of followers excluded from PNŢCD, before he and his right-hand man Sorin Lepşa ended up in PD.[33] The future of most factions may seem bleak, but we must remember that many of them are sustained by the presence of parliamentary members and/or other offices at the local and provincial levels. Earlier, such factors helped to nourish small parties, like Victor Surdu's Democratic Agrarian Party (PDAR) and the former National Liberal Party (PNL) faction under Mircea Ionescu-Quintus, during the long political winter between national elections in 1992 and 1996.[34]

CONCLUSION: PROSPECTS OF A PATRIMONIAL FUTURE

Democratization made a major stride in Romania in 1996, but the patrimonial underpinnings of the system remained and remain very much alive. Despite the hopes surrounding the change of regime, the unfortunate reality was that economic reform made only token headway, as parties constantly sought to undercut each others' initiatives, with a smattering of state enterprises having been privatized or closed down. Accusations of nepotism, privatization rigging, kickbacks, and other forms of corruption surrounded almost all ruling parties, but especially PNŢCD, weakened even farther than its predecessor, PDSR, by the conflicts that surround governance and weakened party cohesion. Notions of the rule of law and justice were and are perhaps the greatest casualties of corruption, a phenomenon enhanced because of the somewhat greater transparency to the press. Most disturbingly, inculcation of social attitudes favoring the rule of law was even further impeded by the presence of the algorithm used by the CDR-USD-UDMR coalition. Because so many offices were and are dependent on partisan affiliation, the algorithm effectively took cases of abuse of public office out of the justice ministry and the courts, where they normally belong, and instead moved them behind closed doors to be handled by party leaderships frequently seen as sweeping corruption under the rug.[35]

The politics of the 2000 elections and their aftermath are a continuing case in point despite the protest vote itself. After four years of increasing mismanagement and corruption, particularly in the privatization process where party leaders in PNŢCD were implicated at the highest levels, the CDR, revamped as the CDR 2000 after the departure of PNL earlier that year, failed to cross the increased electoral threshold to enter parliament.[36]

PNŢCD itself spiraled downward for the better part of the next year in an increasingly nasty fight between rival party leaderships for command of the party. PNL, which succeeded in entering the parliament, managed to accomplish the unthinkable—liberal unification—but only by co-opting former party presidents of splinter liberal parties (Dinu Patriciu, Nicolae Manolescu, Niculae Cerveni) as vice-presidents. With the retirement of Mircea Ionescu-Quintus, former first vice-president Valeriu Stoica's leadership and influence has been firm but still, or perhaps as a result, hotly contested by leading figures, some of which, such as former finance minister Decebal Traian Remeş, have departed the party even before the elections owing to rivalries with Stoica. Still, Stoica's PNL also merged on 17 January 2002 with Teodor Meleşcanu's Alliance for Romania (ApR, a splinter from Iliescu's party), again with office rewards for the ApR's top leaders: Meleşcanu became PNL first vice-president, and Viorel Catarамă, who once held that very office in PNL, has returned as a vice-president. Stoica's tenure as president, however, only lasted until 2002, coming under fire as he did from PNL vice-president and businessman Dinu Patriciu (the largest shareholder of Rompetrol, among other firms), with the stalemate resolved only when former premier and presidential candidate Theodor Stolojan agreed to step in and serve as president.

In the spring of 2001, Bucharest mayor and PD heavyweight Traian Băsescu mounted one of the rare successful ouster attempts against PD president Petre Roman, who promptly abandoned his party. Among the radical nationalists, PUNR had been disintegrating into two parts since its 1996 electoral disappointment. When faced with another rare ouster by Valeriu Tabără's wing, the flamboyant PUNR president and mayor of Cluj Gheorghe Funar took his supporters into Corneliu Vadim Tudor's PRM, where Funar himself obtained the post of general secretary, one of the top three positions in the party and which is responsible for cadres. Tabără's wing of PUNR failed dismally in the 2000 elections in an alliance with former SRI chief Virgil Măgureanu's Romanian National Party. PRM, on the other hand, was the major electoral success story of 2000, taking a fifth of the vote and a quarter of the parliamentary seats, and propelling Vadim Tudor into the second-round runoff where he was eventually defeated by PDSR president Ion Iliescu, but only after a significant protest vote in the first round. And, as the icing on the cake, Iliescu's PDSR also accomplished in 2001 what used to be unthinkable throughout the 1990s, merging with Alexandru Athanasiu's tiny Social Democratic Party (PSDR), now that the latter's former president and vehement Iliescu critic Sergiu Cunescu had retired upstairs to an honorary party presidency, and thus creating the renamed Party of Social Democracy (PSD). Institutional obstacles and election defeats, it appears, have produced patrimonial solutions that somewhat simplify Romania's fluid party system, but without changing the basic operating principles.[37]

Patrimonialism should not be seen as a purely static descriptor of Romania or any other post-Communist political system. On the contrary, at least in Romania there appears to be a dynamic shift—at least in the party system—toward what I would call more decentralized patrimonialism, or what could be termed the "baronization" of political parties. In essence, leading party figures, typically parliamentarians with well-entrenched local power bases where they themselves are the undisputed local bosses, appear over the last decade to be gaining at least some limited power vis-à-vis party presidents. Party presidents thus can expect to encounter more resistance to their initiatives, whether in relation to certain economic reforms or simply "cleaning house" within the party itself.

Why is this baronization occurring? I hypothesize that at least two factors are relevant. First, there is increasing turnover in the generation of party presidents who achieved some remarkable longevity in the first post-Communist decade despite occasionally disappointing electoral results.[38] With the impending resignation or retirement of the old "father figure," competition among the second "tier" ensues, deals have to be made, and the new party president, although he still wields tremendous power by statute, nonetheless has informal favors to pay off and is somewhat less immune to challenges than his predecessor. These backroom leadership fights, of course, are more or less normal and are reflected in the literature at least as far back as Duverger, even if patrimonial parties in post-Communist circumstances do not fall neatly into traditional, Western-derived political science categories.[39] Internal party ousters, such as that of Băsescu over Roman, are rare in the attempt and rarer in their success, but they obviously can occur, requiring the same politicking.[40] Iliescu, once the "spiritual father" of the ruling PSD's earlier incarnations, does not appear to retain the veto he once had over PSD appointees to the government; to cite one example, PSD's new president, Adrian Năstase, and parliamentary leader Viorel Hrebenciuc allegedly managed to push through their candidate for the director of the customs agency over Iliescu's "vehement" objections.[41] Indeed, the barons of heaviest weight in the PSD could be seen in the team interviewing prospective prefects for the provinces: Năstase, Hrebenciuc, Miron Mitrea, Octav Cozmâncă, Ion Solcanu, and Doru Ioan Tărăcilă—one of whom, Solcanu, as much as admitted that Iliescu had effectively given up real power in the party to Năstase.[42] But Năstase himself does not have the same authority as his predecessor, having to contend with the entrenched regional party leaders who formally confirmed him as president alongside the rest of the central party leadership on 19 January 2001.[43] Năstase dared to lock horns with Iliescu over early elections, but eventually had to retreat on the question, a clash only partly reminiscent of the earlier Roman-Iliescu struggle.

Second, and more structurally grounded, members of the new business class, whether *nomenklatura* in origin or not, are, not surprisingly, growing in power in direct proportion to their concentrated wealth. This of course is a post-Communist phenomenon hardly limited to Romania. Simply as a case example, there are reports of Romanian businessmen effectively buying either slots on parties' electoral lists for parliament or even parliamentarians themselves. Dan Voiculescu, a media magnate widely suspected of past connections with the former *Securitate* and also the president of a tiny party (Romanian Humanist Party, or PUR) allied to the ruling PSD, announced in 2002 that several unnamed parliamentarians had approached his party, willing to sell their services for the rough equivalent of USD $67,000 each, and that negotiations were underway to see if that figure could be reduced.[44] Campaign finance is generally exceedingly murky such that no party likes to discuss it, let alone adopt or implement laws with teeth on the subject. Business figures appear to be increasingly easing out less-important parliamentarians from the 1990s. That is, new businessmen with party cards possess not just a parliamentary seat or other party function, but also make substantial personal contributions to strengthen their claim to be new party patrons with some force and weight in internal party decision making. Năstase has even gone so far as to hold a meeting where he criticized presidents of the party's county organizations for the perceived image in the press of "local barons" in the PSD and the disservice being done to the party by parliamentarians occupied by office seeking and dubious business undertakings, thereby threatening to put the party in the same bad light as that of 1992–96;[45] whether the PSD president's protests will produce any change in behavior at all remains to be seen.

The obvious implication is that structural economic reforms and legal-institutional reforms that threaten business interests will run into great difficulty where relevant businessmen can control party agendas as well as parliamentary votes. Reform is not impossible, as Adrian Năstase recently demonstrated in helping to force through the 2001 privatization of the enormous and loss-making steel combine SIDEX, but even the prime minister and party leader of the ruling PSD cannot possibly have sufficient resources to do the same for several hundred other large enterprises and simultaneously accomplish a great number of other governing tasks. Moreover, Western pressure, such as that involved with NATO and EU admission, can empower reformist projects over entrenched interest group opposition. However, despite some observers' initial expectations of a supposedly reformed PSD coming to power in 2000 with a stronger commitment to meaningful structural reform, there appears to be very little difference once any patrimonial party gains control of the state. Indeed, clients and even kin of leaders from all parties are frequently found on the managing boards of the regional state agencies responsible for managing privatization, as well as other corporations. Premier Năstase's sister reputedly sits on the board of SIF Muntenia, to which former premier (once from PNŢCD, and now member of PD) Radu Vasile used to belong as well.[46] And the PSD president of the Senate (and former premier) Nicolae Văcăroiu only grudgingly gave up, after repeated front-page press criticism for failing to admit the conflict of interest, his seat as the head of a bank deeply connected both to the regional privatization agencies and also to one Sorin Ovidiu Vântu, the collapse of whose mutual fund continued through 2002 to implicate in public debate political figures across all parties, possibly up to the level of Năstase himself.[47]

Predicting a country's political future is a highly ambivalent undertaking at best, but a worrisome caution is called for. If parties remain responsible for dispensing public justice to politicians and their lieutenants at the helm of the state, the long-term stability of current democratic accomplishments remains open to question. Short of a social explosion or other exogenous shock, however—which in the best case would lead to some kind of progressive movement demanding civil service and other anti-corruption reforms, and in the worst case would mean an authoritarian takeover by the military or radical nationalists—democratic patrimonialism can count on plenty of interests to uphold it. PRM's stunning second-place finish in 2000 is a dramatic reminder of how frustrated the population is with the behavior of its politicians and parties. Romania's roughly 5 percent GDP growth in 2001 and 2002 and PRM's slight dip in interim polls are mildly encouraging, as were Western-prompted moves toward anti-corruption measures and President Iliescu's personal involvement in the process. But should conditions head south, especially if a world recession were to take hold, then the failure of political parties to clean house and restore citizen confidence in institutions will likely boomerang in spades in the next general elections.

NOTES

1. I thank Paul Shoup, Allen Lynch, and Henry F. Carey for their comments and suggestions on earlier drafts, and gladly claim sole responsibility for any errors of fact and interpretation.

2. See John Duncan Powell, "Peasant Society and Clientelist Politics," *American Political Science Review*, vol. 64, no. 2 (June 1970), pp. 411–425. On patrimonial development and parties, see Alex Weingrod, "Patrons, Patronage, and Political Parties," *Comparative Studies in Society and History*, vol. 10, no. 4, (July 1968), pp. 377–400; and Nicos Mouzelis, "On the Concept of Populism: Populist and Clientelist Modes of Incorporation in Semiperipheral Polities," *Politics & Society*, vol. 14, no. 3 (1985), pp. 329–48.

3. Max Weber, *Economy and Society: An Outline of Interpretive Sociology*, vol. 1, edited by Guenther Roth and Claus Wittich (Berkeley: University of California Press, 1978), p. 231.

4. Weber, p. 232. See his comments on patrimonial limitations on capitalist development, pp. 240–41.

5. On sultanism generally, see Part One of H. E. Chehabi and Juan J. Linz, eds., *Sultanistic Regimes* (Baltimore, MD: Johns Hopkins University Press, 1998), pp. 3–81 (chapters by Chehabi and Linz, and by Richard Snyder). On Romanian sultanism and the consequences for the Romanian transition, see Juan J. Linz and Alfred Stepan, "The Effects of Totalitarianism-cum-Sultanism on Democratic Transition: Romania," in Linz and Stepan, *Problems of Democratic Transition and Consolidation* (Baltimore, MD: Johns Hopkins University Press, 1996). For a critique of Linz and Stepan's more "theoretical" framework, see Gerardo L. Munck, "Bringing Post-Communist Societies into Democratization Studies," *Slavic Review*, vol. 56, no. 3 (Fall 1997), pp. 542–50.

6. Linz and Stepan quote Weber on sultanism, but use the word sultanism as both one of five regime types as well as an adjective depicting extreme patrimonialism under totalitarianism. Here, I analyze patrimonialism as a state type. Linz and Stepan, *Problems of Democratic Transition and Consolidation*, pp. 51–56, 358–60, and 362–65.

7. A broader and more in-depth, cross-country treatment of patrimonialism, party systems and regime change in the Balkans is the doctoral dissertation of the author, Frank Sellin, forthcoming in 2002.

8. Michael Shafir, *Romania: Politics, Economics and Society Political Stagnation and Simulated Change* (Boulder: Lynne Rienner Publishers, 1985), pp. 68–73; Dennis Deletant, *Ceauşescu and the Securitate: Coercion and Dissent in Romania, 1965–1989* (Armonk, NY: M. E. Sharpe, 1995), p. 69.

9. Deletant, *Ceauşescu and the Securitate*, p. 72.

10. For details on the rotation principle and centralization, see Trond Gilberg, *Nationalism and Communism in Romania: The Rise and Fall of Ceauşescu's Personal Dictatorship* (Boulder: Westview Press, 1990), pp. 83–89, 93.

11. Matei Călinescu and Vladimir Tismăneanu, "The 1989 Revolution and Romania's Future," and Larry L. Watts, "The Romanian Army in the December Revolution and Beyond," both in Daniel N. Nelson, ed., *Romania after Tyranny* (Boulder: Westview Press, 1992), pp. 22–23 and p. 104, respectively. As Watts shows, Iliescu apparently had been sounding out anti-Ceauşescu sentiment since at least the mid-1980s, the period of his political disgrace. PDSR President Oliviu Gherman asserted that Iliescu was covertly networking in February 1989 (before the famous "Letter of the Six" signed by high-ranking, but out-of-favor, party officials criticizing Ceauşescu's development strategies). Iliescu sounded out Gherman himself on his political and social opinions after ushering him into in an empty room in the state publishing house where Iliescu was director of Editura Tehnică. Author's interview with Gherman (Bucharest, 25 July 1996).

12. On the accommodation of large parts of a fragmented ex-*Securitate* apparatus with the Iliescu regime, see Richard Andrew Hall, "The Uses of Absurdity: The Staged War Theory and the Romanian Revolution of December 1989," *East European Politics and Societies*, vol. 13, No. 3 (Fall 1999), pp. 514–16. On the bargains of the FSN for provincial penetration and recognition of the center by former RCP cadres, in return for pursuit of local nationalist agendas, see Tom Gallagher, *Romania after Ceauşescu: The Politics of Intolerance* (Edinburgh: Edinburgh University Press, 1995), especially pp. 80–81.

13. Gallagher, *Romania after Ceauşescu*, p. 232.

14. Iosif Boda, describing his early work for Iliescu, noted the latter's willingness to conceal material from his own prime minister. Roman proved equally suspicious of Iliescu's staff. *See* Iosif Boda, *Cinci ani la Cotroceni* (Bucharest: Editura Evenimentul Românesc, 1999), pp. 8, 71–73.

15. For the split in the FSN, see Michael Shafir, "War of the Roses in Romania's National Salvation Front," *RFE/RL Research Report* (24 January 1992), pp. 15–22; Shafir, "Romania: Investigation into Government Corruption," *RFE/RL Research Report* (21 February 1992), pp 31–36; Dan Ionescu, "Infighting Shakes Romania's Ruling Party," *RFE/RL Research Report* (3 April 1992), pp 24–28; Ionescu, "Romania's Ruling Party Splits after Congress," *RFE/RL Research Report* (17 April 1992), pp 8–12; and Ionescu, "Another Front for Romania's Salvation," *RFE/RL Research Report* (21 August 1992), pp. 17–23.

16. Ionescu, "Infighting Shakes Romania's Ruling Party," p. 27.

17. Ionescu, "Another Front for Romania's Salvation," p. 19.

18. Starting in 1994, Măgureanu was under sustained attack by PRM's Corneliu Vadim Tudor, who had access to disgruntled SRI officers. In a stunning move, Măgureanu went on state television on 15 January 1996 to complain that the biggest problem facing SRI was information leaks to Tudor by SRI officers. Măgureanu subsequently fired his deputy, Col. Victor Marcu, who had been identified by the SRI press office as Tudor's source. See *Curierul național* (1 April 1996). At least one other SRI officer, Dumitru Cristea was fired along with Marcu; both showed up with Tudor at a press conference which presented another officer, Capt. Constantin Bucur, who played excerpts of taped conversations of politicians and journalists, allegedly made "on orders. " *See Evenimentul zilei*, 15 May 1996. Two other SRI officers were charged with taking out, copying and distributing Măgureanu's *Securitate* dossier (forcing Măgureanu's own publication of a fragment of it). One was the retired head of the SRI branch in Timiș, Col. Petru Pele, and the other, Col. Ion Adamescu, was soon transferred to reserve duty. See *Evenimentul zilei* (23 April 1996). Măgureanu apparently had the greatest problems with the "group" around General Diaconescu [no first name given] and Col. Ilie Merce, judging from the reports of his comments to the parliamentary commission (that allegedly oversees the SRI, if not the reverse) on 19 June, his first ever request to testify before parliament. *See Evenimentul zilei* (20 June 1996, and *22,* 26 June–2 July 1996). *See also* Dennis Deletant, "The Securitate Legacy in Romania: Who Is in Control?" *Problems of Post-Communism,* vol. 42, no. 6 (November/December 1995), p. 26.

19. Măgureanu resigned as SRI director in May 1997. Despite persistent rumors that he would resurface at the head of PUNR, he is the key leader of the tiny Romanian National Party (PNR).

20. The president has the right to appoint prime ministers, fill vacant ministries at the proposal of the prime minister, preside over meetings of the cabinet if he participates, dissolve parliament if it does not honor a request for a vote of confidence in the government in a 60 day period, head councils on national security, call referendums after consultation with parliament, emit decrees (some of which have to be signed by the prime minister) and appoint judges proposed by the Superior Magistrate Council (a body of judges elected by a joint session of parliament). For these and other powers, *see Constituția României* (Bucharest: Regia Autonomă "Monitorul Oficial," 1992). *See also* the reporting and analyses by Michael Shafir, "Romania's New Institutions: The Draft Constitution," *Report on Eastern Europe* (20 September 1991) pp. 22–33, and "Romania: Constitution Approved in Referendum," *RFE/RL Research Report* (10 January 1992) pp. 50–55.

21. Even in the post-Iliescu era, Romanian legal culture seemed to contradict judicial independence. One anecdote recounts how a judge complicated a slander suit against Iliescu for inaccurate testimony, brought by the watchdog group Civic Alliance. The judge refused to provide a copy of the testimony to the Alliance's lawyer, with the excuse: "'I don't want to lose my job; what happens if Iliescu gets angry with me? He might again someday be president!'" *See* Monica Macovei, "Legal Culture in Romania," *East European Constitutional Review* (Winter 1998) p. 79.

The *cause célèbre* of executive meddling in the judiciary was the demotion of the president of the Bucharest municipal court, Corneliu Turianu, for going on record that a hypothetical Iliescu victory in 1996 would be an unconstitutional third term. He was demoted on 15 June 1996 by then minister of justice and Iliescu loyalist, Petre Ninosu. *See* Ion Cristoiu's editorial, "Petre Ninosu şi Tragedia Regelui Lear," *Evenimentul zilei* 9 March 1994, as reprinted in Ion Cristoiu, *Singur împotriva tuturor* (Bucharest: Editura Evenimentul românesc, 1999) pp. 90–91; *see also* Domniţa Ştefănescu, *Cinci ani din istoria României* (Bucharest: Editura Maşina de scris, 1994) p. 324, p. 326.

22. *See* William Crowther and Steven D. Roper, "A Comparative Analysis of Institutional Development in the Romanian and Moldovan Legislatures," in David M. Olson and Philip Norton, (eds.), *The New Parliaments of Central and Eastern Europe* (Portland, OR: Frank Cass, 1996) p. 140. *See also* Elena Stefoi-Sava, "Organizing Legislative Impotence: Romania," *East European Constitutional Review* (Spring 1995), pp. 78–83.

23. The United States has 535 representatives for a population of 260 million, or roughly one representative for every 485,000 people (ignoring bicameral overlap of districts). By comparison, Romania's 471 parliamentarians represent a population of about 23 million, such that one parliamentarian represents roughly every 50,000 people. Part of that is a direct function of districting. Romania has 38 *judeţe* or "counties" and two special regions (Bucharest and Ilfov). It is also a function of improving the supply of patrimonial resources. More districts assist the inflation of parliamentary seats and provincial posts like prefectures, seats in the county legislatures, etc.

Although most Romanian parliamentarians consider the legislature to be "somewhat efficient," as documented by Crowther and Roper in 1992 (Table 13 on p. 154), no one else does. Parliament routinely ranks at the bottom of polls of respect for institutions; only the government ranks lower. A database of such polls can be found at the Soros Foundation for an Open Society, at http://www.sfos. ro/pob/.

24. *Adevărul* (11 December 1995). Crişan claimed that the parliamentary oversight committee had reviewed all his information on commercial functions, and had determined that he had not broken any laws. He made no mention of constitutional Article 104, which reads: "(1)...*Likewise, it [the function of member of the Government] is incompatible with the exercise of a function of professional, paid representation in the body of organizations with commercial purpose* [emphasis added, translation mine]."

25. *Adevărul* (27 June 1996).

26. *See Adevărul* (25 and 29 November, and 11 and 12 December 1996); *see also Curierul naţional* (25, 26, and 27 November 1996), for the fallout in the PS, including allegations of disgruntled party members against Columna Bank.

27. Gallagher, p. 8.

28. The data in the foregoing paragraph are presented in Michael Shafir, "Romania's Road to 'Normalcy,'" *Journal of Democracy*, vol. 8, no. 2 (April 1997), pp. 148, 152, 154.

29. Many of PD's luminaries, including Petre Roman, and including other big names such as Radu Berceanu and Adrian Vilău (the latter resigned after revelations of his collaboration with the former *Securitate*) were named, along with prominent PDSR leaders, in the 1995–96 "Apartment" scandal that threatened to rock parliament, but then was quietly abandoned. The scandal, under increased attention in an electoral year, resulted from press investigations into parliamentarians who live, most likely illegally, in houses nationalized during Communism, still subsidized or owned by the state, and obtained quietly through personal connections.

30. As noted earlier (note 20), the president has the explicit power to *appoint* the prime minister, but nothing in the constitution suggests that the former has the power to *remove* the latter. For a recount of the events surrounding Vasile's dismissal, see *22* (4–10 January 2000).

31. See Jack Bielasiak, "Substance and Process in the Development of Party Systems in East Central Europe," *Communist and Post-Communist Studies*, vol. 30, no. 1 (1997), pp. 23–44, which is also a good review of the literature on Eastern European party systems.

32. Splits have also affected smaller parties such as Tudor Mohora's Socialist Party, and Nicolae Manolescu's Civic Alliance Party (PAC).

33. See *Adevărul* (29 January 2000).

34. For PNL, the support of businessmen such as Viorel Cataramă—also former first vice president of PNL—helped as well, considering that the building that housed PNL's central Bucharest headquarters belonged to Cataramă's furniture firm, Elvila. Cataramă eventually left PNL under pressure, including alleged involvement in the SAFI investment scandal. Although he has consistently denied any connection to the former *Securitate* (a frequent accusation because of his work in the Ministry of Foreign Commerce in the 1980s, and because of his role in complicating CDR tensions and liberal unification), he briefly joined former SRI chief Măgureanu's PNR, and then became a leading figure in Teodor Meleşcanu's Alliance for Romania (a 1997 splinter from Iliescu's PDSR after the 1996 elections).

35. I thank Mark Temple for posing this issue in conversation.

36. By governmental ordinance on 28 June 2000, the electoral threshold to enter parliament was increased to a nominal five percent for a single party, but coalitions faced an additional one percent for each party in the coalition. In the CDR 2000's specific case, that alliance contained five parties (PNŢCD, the Union of Rightist Forces (UFD), the Christian Democrat National Alliance (ANCD, a splinter from the PNŢCD), the Federation of Ecologists (FER), and the Moldavians' Party (PM)). Thus CDR had to cross a 10 percent total threshold, which it failed to do with 5.04 percent of the vote for the House of Deputies and 5.29 percent for the Senate.

37. *Curentul*, 18 January 2002, as reported by www.revistapresei.ro.

38. See the author's forthcoming (2002) doctoral dissertation for more data on party president longevity in Romania.

39. See the chapter on parties and party systems in the author's forthcoming (2002) dissertation.

40. *Ibid.*

41. *Adevărul*, 9 January 2001.

42. *Ibid.* For Solcanu's comments, see *România liberă*, 9 January 2001.

43. For an amusing anecdote of barely disguised and vulgar insults at Năstase's expense by the PDSR leader of Gorj county, Nicolae Mişchie, and the broader power disputes in the relationships between the central government and regional party leaders, see the lead editorial in *Adevărul*, 10 September 2001.

44. *Adevărul*, 25 September 2001. Voiculescu, it should be noted, succeeded in getting a member of his tiny party, Cozmin Guşă, to be nominated and elected PDSR (now PSD) secretary general, that is, Năstase's right hand man in the party. Guşă's appointment came as a total surprise to PDSR leaders. *Cotidianul*, 17 January 2001.

45. *Adevărul*, 21 September 2001.

46. *Adevărul*, 7 September 2001; *România liberă*, 11 September 2001.

47. *Adevărul*, 10 September 2001. For an example of Văcăroiu's previous protests about giving up his private business positions, see *Adevărul*, 10 January 2001, where he insisted his connection to Vântu was normal and unconnected to FNI, and that the conflict of interest was not at all illegal, but only on a "moral plane. " Năstase's alleged connections to Vântu have been a hot topic of debate in January 2002, in events surrounding the arrest of two individuals alleged to have published anonymously on the Internet a report called "Armageddon II" attacking Năstase for corruption and other activities. See *Monitorul*, 17 January 2002, as reported at www.revistapresei.ro, as well as the same site's coverage on 21 January 2002; see also *RFE/RL Newsline*, 16 and 17 January 2002; The Armageddon report itself is unsubstantiated, but some of its details have been previously alleged in other papers such as *Adevărul*.

II

THE STATE AND POLITICS

6

Institutionalizing the Party System

Jóhanna Kristín Birnir

While scholars commonly accept the general characterization of East European parties as personalistic, catch-all parties, the extent of systemic consolidation is still hotly debated. According to Kitchelt, East European party systems show considerable evidence of consolidation. Tóka, however, believes that the high volatility of electoral preferences demonstrate a lack of institutionalization. Others are even more skeptical. Mair argues that the underdeveloped character of civil society, the fractiousness of the political class, and intensity of political competition suggest that there are as yet significant obstacles in the way of East European party system consolidation.[1]

The debate among scholars who study Romania parallels the above. According to Datculescu,[2] politicians are strategic, and voters have not developed significant party loyalties. Furthermore, some argue that Romanian, and more generally Eastern European voters, will not develop stable party identifications for quite some time, but will remain "informed skeptics."[3] Nonetheless, while Crowther and Roper describe the Romanian party system as fluid and fragmented, Crowther[4] also identifies historical cleavages and argues that people are voting along similar politically salient cleavages that formed early during the post-Communist transition in Romania. While this is a plausible argument, Romanian voter alignment is open to further study and debate.

Influential political scientists have concluded that stable political parties are instrumental to the functioning of democracy.[5] Consequently, the debate over consolidation in Romania has important implications. Unfortunately, much of this consolidation, such as the emerging relationships between parties and voters, may only be evaluated over time. Institutional hallmarks of consolidation can, however, be assessed immediately,[6] and are therefore the focal point of this chapter.

First, the chapter discusses the electoral and party laws, which structure the party system. The process of institutionalizing the Romanian party system since 1989 has reduced fragmentation[7] and reinforced the principal existing parties while electoral volatility remains high. Second, the chapter considers the effects of alleged voting irregularities in the first two national elections and the rise of antisystem parties in the second two. Third, the methodological problems which may contribute to the appearance of a highly volatile system are discusses. Finally, the chapter briefly mentions economic and societal factors that contribute to real volatility.

The conclusion of this chapter is that, as the Romanian party system is still developing, it remains quite fluid. However, institutionalization of the party system is progressing as rapidly as one could expect, given the recent redemocratization, the institutional framework selected in 1989, the ensuing reforms, and the alleged voting irregularities. In particular, the chapter emphasizes the effects of an increasing threshold and an increasingly restrictive party registration law. Together these have barred the entrance of small parties and independents, as well as geographically concentrated parties, while allowing for minority representation in parliament.

DEMOCRATIC CONSOLIDATION

As Duverger explains, extension of the suffrage in Western Europe led to the creation of mass parties, which were characterized by strong mass membership, membership fees, and relative organizational decentralization. As Western societies industrialized, the nature of the party systems changed. According to Kirchheimer, the new emerging parties were "catch-all" parties. These parties have a weak membership structure, are hierarchically organized, and their income is, to a greater extent, dependent on the state than on members. Furthermore, whereas ideology had previously been the foundation of the party, it increasingly became a tool used to attract voters.[8] In contemporary East European systems, one can add that "a relatively unimportant role is played by the party membership, and the dominant role [is played] by party leaders."[9] Thus, it appears that East European parties have omitted the mass party stage[10] and developed directly into personalistic, electorally driven, catch-all parties.

While there is some scholarly consensus as to the types of parties in Eastern Europe, the extent of the systemic consolidation is still debated. According to Przeworski, and later Kitschelt, democratic consolidation entails, at a minimum, a procedural consensus about, and compliance with, constitutional rules of conduct. The monopoly of coercion must be under democratic control, and beliefs that there are feasible alternatives to democracy must vanish. Mainwaring and Scully add the condition of stability in the rules and nature of interparty competition, and that the existence of individual parties be fairly stable. Second, major parties must also have somewhat stable roots in society. Third, political actors must accord legitimacy to the electoral process through peaceful transfers of power. Finally, party organizations must acquire value of their own, rather than being subordinated to the wills of their respective leaders.[11]

Since 1989, Romania's military and security apparatus have been under civilian control, and most people have favored democracy. Procedural consensus about constitutional rules has also been apparent. Early on alleged electoral fraud caused concern about compliance with the rules of constitutional conduct, but in the wake of the most recent elections, international election observers consider many of those problems resolved. Furthermore, the short time since re-democratization prevents parties from having established stable strong roots and party autonomy, as these are mainly achieved through a process of signaling between parties and voters. Such signaling processes include, for instance, long-term public appeals, policy positions revealed in legislative votes and executive party coalitions, opinion polls, activities of interest groups and social movements, and elections.[12]

VOLATILITY, FRAGMENTATION, AND INSTITUTIONALIZATION

The last condition for consolidation, stability in the rules and nature of interparty competition and party existence, depends to some extent on the institutional structures of the system. Unlike the more intangible relationship between parties and voters, the institutional effects here are immediately discernible. Electoral law mechanically affects the outcome of elections by, for instance, restricting the number of candidates who may run, determining a minimum amount of votes that a candidate must obtain, or stipulating whether parties or voters are in charge of nominations. Party law may further restrict or increase the power of the party elite, as well as add to the restrictions of what constitutes a party and how that party shall be run.

In Western Europe, and more recently in Eastern Europe, electoral rules have been demonstrated to be closely correlated with party system development both theoretically and empirically.[13] Generally, the more permissive the rules, the greater the fragmentation.[14] A similar correlation has not been established in the literature for electoral volatility, either theoretically or empirically. Notwithstanding this, there is reason to expect that electoral rules may affect electoral volatility, particularly in developing systems such as Romania.

Theoretically, we should be able to observe the same electoral volatility in the most fragmented and the least fragmented system. However, increasingly permissive electoral rules may also promote increased electoral volatility for the following reason: politicians seek reelection.[15] A politician who determines that, due to the electoral rules, her prospects for reelection are better if she runs as a representative of a smaller party, is likely to split off from a larger party, and form a new one between elections. Along the same lines of reasoning, voters seek representation. If the voter determines that the politician better represents his interests after she split off from the larger coalition, he is likely to withdraw his voting support from the larger coalition, and give it to the smaller party between elections. The more permissive the electoral rules, the more likely such splits become, and the higher the electoral volatility. Consequently, any change in electoral rules, whether they make the rules more permissive or more restrictive, is related to electoral volatility.

ELECTORAL AND PARTY LAW

Divergent electoral rules, threshold, and district magnitude most significantly affect party fragmentation. This section first discusses the components of the Romanian electoral law, then the party law, and finally the interaction of these two types of legislation. Table 6.1 demonstrates that fragmentation in parliament has decreased significantly. Compared to the baseline of the 1989/90 party and electoral law, the electoral law of 1992, the party law of 1996, and the electoral amendment of 1999 have contributed to this development. Reduced fragmentation has occurred mainly at the expense of small parties and independent candidates, while reinforcing larger parties and minority representation.

District Magnitude

District magnitude (how many representatives are elected in a district) varies from one in a majoritarian system, to all seats contested in a system of proportional representation. All else being equal, the greater the district magnitude the higher the overall number of parties in parliament. Since the first election in 1990, Romanian deputies have been elected in county constituencies by closed list system or independent candidature, on the principle of proportional representation, the Hare formula.[16] In 1990, the number of elected representatives was 387 and the average district magnitude in the 41 counties was 9.4. An additional nine seats were reserved for national minorities. In 1992, the size of the parliament was reduced to 328 members, in addition to thirteen seats allotted to national minorities. Furthermore, the number of counties was increased to 42. Consequently, the average magnitude was reduced from 9.4 to 7.8.[17] Before the 2000 election two seats were added bringing the total to 345. An average magnitude of 7.8 is relatively high. As a result, it is to be expected that Romania will generally have a higher number of parties in parliament than countries where the magnitude is lower, such as Hungary, where the average magnitude is 1.6.[18]

Table 6.1. Fragmentation in Parliament

1990 *Party*	*1990* *Seats*	*1992* *Party*	*1992* *Seats*	*1996* *Party*	*1996* *Seats*	*2000* *Party*	*2000* *Seats*
FSN[19]	263	FDSN[20]	117	PDSR	91	PSD (2)	155
		PD-FSN[21]	43	USD	53	PD 31	
PSDR[22]	5						
PNL	29	CDR[23]	82	CDR	122	PNL	30
MER	12						
PNT-CD	12						
PER 8							
UDMR	29	UDMR	27	UDMR	25	UDMR	27
AUR[24]	9	PUNR	30	PUNR	18		
PSD (1)	2						
PDAR	9						
GDC	2						
PDM	1						
PLS	1						
PRNR	1						
PTLDR	1						
ULB	1						
NM[25]	11		13		15		18
		PSM 13					
		PRM	16	PRM	19	PRM	84
Seats	396	Seats	341	Seats	343	Seats	345
Parties	16	Parties	7	Parties	6	Parties	5

Sources: Datculescu and Liepelt, eds. (1991), and *Monitorul Official*, various issues.

Threshold

Vote threshold is another important constraint on fragmentation. It refers to the minimum share a party must get in elections before obtaining seats in parliament.[26] No threshold was applied in the 1990 election. Given the high magnitude it is, therefore, not surprising that as many as sixteen political parties and organizations were represented in the parliament.[27] In 1992, a 3 percent national vote threshold was instituted, with an additional 1 percent for each member of a coalition up to 8 percent. Consequently, the number of parties and coalitions represented in parliament after the 1992 election dropped to seven, and subsequently to six in the 1996 election.

On 31 May 1999, the Chamber of deputies raised the electoral hurdle from 3 to 5 percent. Moreover, electoral alliances including two members were required to obtain 8 percent of the vote, 9 percent for those with three members and 10 percent for those with four or more members. This amendment is the result of a compromise reached by the PDSR, which had proposed that an alliance would have to obtain an additional 5 percent for each member. The PDSR and the CDR received 21.5 and 30.1 percent of the vote respectively in the election preceding the adoption of the amendment. The PUNR, which had received 4.3 percent of the vote, opposed the amendment, as did the PRM, which had received 4.4 percent.

Compensatory Seats

Another electoral rule, which influences fragmentation, regulates supplementary seats. The two types of supplementary seats are additional and compensatory seats. The former is basically an additional district, for which the allocation of seats does not take primary district seat allocation into account. In the allocation of compensatory seats, on the other hand, all seats are taken into account. The procedure calculates the seat shares of the parties based on their votes nationwide (or in the regions). It then subtracts the seats already won in the basic districts and compensates the parties for the difference, correcting deviations from proportionality. If fragmentation is expected to increase with increased proportionality, compensatory seats will further increase fragmentation.

In 1990, Romanian electoral law stipulated that compensatory seats were to be allotted on a territorial-administrative basis. The largest parties in each region were allotted additional seats in proportion to the number of unused votes they had received.[28] Following adoption of the new electoral law before the election in 1992, the Romanian upper tier became that of a nationwide, multimember compensatory district. Calculation of representation in that district is done according to D'Hondt.[29] Previously, small parties receiving a sizable share of the vote in a district were compensated with a seat. However, after the change it is likely that, even though sizable, a small party's unused vote share will not suffice to receive an additional seat when competing with the number of unused votes received by large national parties.

PARTY LAW

Just as electoral law affects electoral competition, party law regulates the electoral participation of parties by stipulating, for instance, what type of organization constitutes a party and how many members parties must register and where. All things being equal, the more permissive the party legislation is, the more parties one would expect to see competing in a political system. The party legislation also affects what types of parties will develop. For instance, personalistic, catch-all parties are most likely to prosper where parties are not made to rely on voters through registration requirements or for finances.

The first party legislation passed in Romania after the Revolution was extremely permissive. The only real restrictions were the ban on fascist parties and the requirement that a party have 251 registered members.[30] When one considers that the electoral law imposed no minimum vote threshold on party representation in the legislature, as long as the party had received a sufficient number of votes to be awarded even one seat and independents were allowed to run for office without restrictions, the extreme fragmentation in the first election is not surprising. In all seventy-three different parties, unions, alliances, and independents contested the first election.[31]

CHANGING PARTY AND ELECTORAL LAW

In 1996, half a year before the election, a slightly more restrictive and a much more detailed version of the party law was passed. According to this new legislation, Romanian political parties must now submit a list of 10,000 founding members to the Electoral Tribunal. These founding members must be drawn from at least 15 counties, no less than 300 from each county. While this requirement may appear significant, one should bear in mind that 10,000 members represent only .05 percent of registered voters in Romania.[32]

In order to determine the effect of this new, more restrictive party law, we must again consider its implications in conjunction with the electoral institutions. Given the increased number of founding members, and the geographical restrictions on the location of founding members, these new laws weed out very small parties, as well as geographically concentrated parties. Furthermore, the electoral law stipulates that an independent candidate is only allowed to run if she can demonstrate that she is supported by at least 5 percent of the registered voters in the constituency where she has put up her candidature.

At the same time, however, the electoral law designates that organizations of national minorities participating in the elections shall be considered judicially equivalent to political parties.[33] Consequently, the Hungarian Alliance, which does not define itself as a political party but as an "alliance of associated members,"[34] and which is geographically very concentrated, is nonetheless allowed to contest elections. According to the 1991 Constitution, organizations of citizens belonging to national minorities which fail to obtain 5 percent of the vote have the right to one deputy seat each.[35] In addition, electoral coalitions can only be formed at the national level, preventing regionally concentrated parties from achieving representation through coalitions in regions where they are not popular, while running alone in regions where they are.[36] Increased member and geographical restrictions of the party law are, thus, relaxed by the electoral law when the group is a minority organization. Independent candidates and regionally concentrated parties are, however, restricted by both.

The last piece of the Romanian electoral law that significantly affects the electoral strategies of parties and party system fragmentation is one which appoints parties as the sole nominators of lists. As the party leadership must approve and sign all nomination lists, this provision strengthens the party leadership, as opposed to open nomination processes where politicians rely on voters rather than the party leadership to be placed on a list. The party organizations and leadership are further strengthened by the increased regulation of the finances of parties covered in the new party law, including both acceptable origins and amounts of donations. The law also stipulates that parties, or other groups, which are represented in parliament, shall receive subsidies from the government budget in proportion to their respective mandates. In addition, parties which are not represented, but which received at least 2 percent of the popular vote, shall also receive subsidies. In 1996, a retroactive application of this law, to include parties beginning with the 1992 elections, translated into financial support for fifteen parties and organizations, two of which had not been represented in parliament.[37] While the amounts in question may not suffice to make or break a party, the subsidies indisputably favor established parties. Such allocation of funds to the party as an organization is likely to be managed by the leadership, thereby strengthening its position vis-à-vis the rank and file.

EFFECTS OF VOTING IRREGULARITIES AND ANTISYSTEM PARTIES

Unless accompanied by the compliance of political actors with constitutional rules, institutional consolidation is undermined. Scholars were therefore understandably concerned about intimidation and fraud, which marked the first two sets of Romanian elections. The 1990 election campaign was characterized by the widespread intimidation of parties who opposed the FSN. Foreign observers also witnessed various voting irregularities on polling day, and many more were alleged. For instance, the number of eligible voters was increased from 15.9 million to 17.2 million shortly before the election, and the number of invalid votes, at 7.5 percent, was abnormally high. Likewise, fraud was widely claimed after the 1992 elections, as the number of votes declared invalid rose to 13 percent. An unusually high number of people, constituting 10 percent of the cast ballots, were put on "special lists," which may have circumvented normal registration procedures. Other questionable practices were also observed. Restrictive rules regarding the filing of complaints and the unavailability of electoral data below the county level compounded the problematic lack of accountability.[38]

Scholars agree that the fraud in 1990 and 1992 generally hurt the opposition CDR and the PNL. The opposition, however, won the election in 1996 and, according to international observers procedures in that election, represented a "discernable improvement in election administration." Similarly, international election observers agree that polls in 2000 demonstrated that "democratic elections are firmly entrenched in Romania." Furthermore, despite some minor problems the assessment is that in general Romania's current "legal and administrative framework promote an election process that is accountable, transparent, free, fair, and equal."[39]

Unfortunately, due to the alleged fraud, vote figures from the first two elections have to be taken with a grain of salt. Despite the fraud, however, the FSN would still have gained at least a plurality in the 1990 elections, but in its absence the successor party, FDSN, might have lost the 1992 parliamentary elections.[40] While the political consequences of fraud are serious, scholars are currently more worried about the popularity of antisystem[41] parties, particularly the PRM, which won 19.5 percent of the vote in the 2000 national election. Optimistically, the popularity of the PRM can be interpreted as an economic protest vote while, more pessimistically, one must worry about increasing xenophobia.

This, however, does not change the fact that the institutions discussed above are mechanically reducing fragmentation of the Romanian party system. Furthermore, as the last row in table 6.2 shows, even if we attribute all the invalid votes to the PNT-CD (the principal party in the CDR) and the PNL in the first election, and all 13 percent to the CDR in the second, total volatility increases by only 4 percent while party system fragmentation is reduced greatly.

APPARENT OR REAL VOLATILITY?

While the evidence above indicates that Romanian political parties are institutionalizing, scholars worry that Romanian voters are still unusually volatile in their electoral preferences.[42] The greater the volatility, the more voters switch between parties from one election to the next. The application of the volatility measure is fairly straightforward in Western democracies, where party systems are established, and scholars can simply trace the names of political parties back from one election to the next. In Eastern Europe, however, where parties are merging and splitting, changing names and leaders, the measure has presented certain problems. For instance, one author argues that Romania's volatility between the 1990 and 1992 elections was 63 percent (meaning that 63 percent of those who voted changed their party allegiance). The reason, he posits, is that the FSN won 66 percent in the first parliamentary election, yet it "subsequently split; the remnant of that coalition took only 10 percent of the vote at the second election."[43] However the article does not explain that the "remnant" discussed is Petre Roman's faction, which kept a part of the name in the second election. However, a much larger faction of the original FSN, led by Ion Iliescu, also competed in the second and the third elections. Iliescu's faction won a plurality in the second

Table 6.2. Volatility of Electoral Preferences between Elections

1990		1992			1996			2000		
Party	*Vote %*	*Party*	*Vote %*	*Volatility*	*Party*	*Vote %*	*Volatility*	*Party*	*Vote %*	*Volatility*
FSN	66.31	FDSN	27.7		PDSR	21.5	6.2	PSD	36.6	9.2[44]
		PD-FSN	10.2	28.41[45]	USD	12.9	1.65[46]	PD	7	
PSDR	1.05									
PNL[47]	6.41							PNL	6.9	18.2[48]
		CDR	20	5.67[49]	CDR	30.1	10.1			
MER	2.62									
PNT-CD	2.56									
PER	1.69									
UDMR	7.23	UDMR	7.5	0.27	UDMR	6.6	0.9	UDMR	6.8	0.2
AUR	2.12	PUNR	7.7	5.58	PUNR	4.3	3.4			
PSD	0.53									
PDAR	1.83				1.83					
GDC	0.48			0.48						
PDM	0.38			0.38						
PLS	0.34			0.34						
PRNR	0.31			0.31						
PTLDR	0.31			0.31						
ULB	0.26			0.26						
		PSM	3	3						
		PRM	3.9	3.9	PRM	4.5	0.6	PRM	19.5	10.7[50]
Total Volatility				25.37			11.95			19.5
Volatility accounting for alleged fraud[51]				29.47						

Note: Parties without seats and national minorities got around 4 percent, 20 percent, 19.9 percent, and 18.2 percent of votes in the 1992, 1996, and 2000 election, respectively.

Sources: Datculescu and Liepelt, eds. (1991), and *Monitorul Official,* various issues.

election, and came in second in the third election. All of this is common knowledge in Romania. Consequently, one cannot argue that the PDSR's vote share in the second election is a vote share for a new party. The original FSN voters simply split between Roman's party and Iliescu's party in the second election.

Similarly, we cannot count new coalition votes as votes for new parties. For the sake of party survival and for party patronage, parties in a coalition usually make sure to distinguish themselves within the coalition. Indeed, according to Crowther,[52] continued inter-elite attacks and divisions in Romanian politics can be traced to intra-group competition among ideologically similar parties. He contends that the discord is aimed at distinguishing the parties from one another on dimensions other than issue-related politics, in order to appeal to specific parts of the electorate.

Furthermore, the coalition platform is usually some mixture of the older parties' platforms. Thus, a voter selecting a party according to its platform is likely to vote for the coalition in the absence of her old party. Of course, there can also be some defection of voters who do not like the coalition partners of "their" party. This defection may, however, be offset by voters who did not like any of the coalition parties in previous elections, but who did like the coalition formation enough to vote for it. Thus, the winner of the 1996 parliamentary elections in Romania, the Democratic Convention, was not a new party but a coalition of parties that have competed in every election since 1989. Consequently, the electoral victory of the CDR was not quite as impressive as it might otherwise have appeared, and the electoral volatility not quite as high.

Likewise many of the shifts and changes in the Romanian political spectrum before the 2000 election did not constitute volatility (e.g., the USD coalition split). The PD ran alone while the PSDR joined the PDSR in a new party called the PDS. The vote that the PSDR brought to the PDS as a result of the split and merger is not a new vote and does not constitute volatility. However, any vote that the former opposition parties in the new PDS were able to attract as a result of voters dissatisfaction with the rule of the CDR does constitute volatility.

Similarly, any additional vote that the PRM got in the 2000 election as a result of giving the personalistic PUNR's former leader Funar a leading party position is not volatility.[53] However, the new votes the PRM was able to attract due to voter dissatisfaction with the governing parties does indeed constitute volatility. In short, volatility of electoral preferences does not occur unless the voter changes her vote between elections to another party which previously was not associated with the party for which she originally voted, whether in a coalition, or as a part of a larger party.

ACTUAL VOLATILITY OF ELECTORAL PREFERENCES

In any system where new electoral rules are being implemented, there may be an adjustment period as the public and politicians "learn" to play according to the new rules. As the number of elections increases, the electoral volatility should decrease. This is, in fact, the case in Romania, where actual volatility[54] measured 25.37 percent between the first and second elections. Between the second and third election volatility had dropped to 11.4 percent, and if we account for fraud, to just over 8 percent. Between the third and fourth election, however, volatility of electoral preferences increased again to 19.15 percent.

In the newly formed party systems of Japan, West Germany, and Italy, average volatility during 1948–1959 was over 20 percent, and French volatility during that time was 21 percent. Compared to those party systems, current Romanian electoral volatility is not unusually high. Rather, the level of Romanian volatility is caused by factors that would cause voters to switch parties in any system, such as the economic performance of the incumbent government, length of time since redemocratization, and a change in the institutions that govern elections as discussed previously.

CONCLUSION

The considerable reduction in both the fragmentation and the volatility of the Romanian party system demonstrates that recent changes in electoral legislation, particularly increasing thresholds and the more restrictive party law, have contributed to the solidification of the existing viable parties, as well as minority organizations. Meanwhile, the barriers to the entry of smaller, less viable parties and independent candidates have been augmented. It is therefore safe to say that while the Romanian party system is still quite fluid, it is institutionalizing at a pace consistent with other newly democratizing countries.

Whether the individual parties will continue their development as clientelistic catch-all parties led by charismatic leaders, or become more programmatic with increasingly strong roots in society is, however, still up for debate. Kitschelt argues that with the exception of Albania, Romania is less likely than any of the other East European countries to develop a party system based on programmatic competition. Crowther, on the other hand, disagrees. He posits that, as early as before the 1992 elections, the political forces in Romania had "consolidated into two broad groupings" in terms of attitudes toward economics and minorities. Moreover, he maintains that these key dimensions are "associated with historical divisions located in Romanian social structure, indicating the presence of political cleavages."[55]

As mentioned above the most recent elections were generally considered free and fair, but the lack of permanent electoral authority responsible for general electoral oversight both at the local and the national levels is still considered a problem. The discussion of this reform is accompanied by a lively civil and parliamentary discussion about a possible change of the electoral rules themselves but nothing has been decided yet. Given the effect of electoral institutions on party system development demonstrated in this chapter, all the pending changes provide an exciting topic for further study.

Table 6.3. Romanian Parties Represented in Parliament (excluding smaller national minority groups)

AUR	*Alianţa pentru Unitatea Românilor* (Alliance for Unity of Romanians)
CDR	*Convenţia Democratică Romăna* (Democratic Convention of Romania)
FDSN	*Frontul Democratic al Salvării Naţionale* (Democratic National Salvation Front)
FSN	*Frontul Salvării Naţionale* (National Salvation Front)
GDC	*Gruparea Democratică de Centru* (Democratic Group of the Center)
MER	*Mişcarea Ecologistă din România* (Romanian Ecological Movement)
PD-FSN	*Partidul Democratic—Frontul Salvării Naţionale* (Democratic Party—NSF)
PDAR	*Partidul Democrat Agrar Romănia* (Democratic Agrarian Party of Romania)
PDM	*Partidul Democrat al Muncii* (Democratic Party of Workers)
PDSR	*Partidul Democraţiei Sociale din Romănia* (Social Democratic Party of Romania)
PER	*Partidul Ecologist Român* (Romanian Ecology Party)
PLS	*Partidul Liber Schimbis* (Party of Free Change)
PNL	*Partidul Naţional Liberal* (National Liberal Party)
PNŢCD	*Partidul Naţional Ţăranesc Creştin si Democrat* (National Peasant Christian Democratic Party)
PRM	*Partidul România Mare* (Great Romania Party)
PRNR	*Partidul Reconstrucţiei Naţionale din România* (Party of National Reconstruction in Romania)
PSD (1)	*Partidul Social Democrat Român* (Social Democrat Party)
PSD (2)	*Polul Democrat-Social din România* (Democratic Social Pole of Romania)
PSDR	*Partidul Socialist Democratic Român* (Socialist Democrat Party of Romania)
PSM	*Partidul Socialist al Muncii* (Socialist Party of Labor)
PTLDR	*Partidul Tineretului Liber Democrat din România* (Party of Young Free Democrats of Romania)
PUNR	*Partidul Unităţii Naţionale Române* (Party of Romanian National Unity)
UDMR	*Uniunea Democratică Maghiara din Romănia Magyar* (Democratic Union of Romania)
ULB	*Uniunea Liberală Brătianu* (Liberal Union Bratianu)
USD	*Uniunea Social Democrata* (Social Democratic Union)

NOTES

1. Herbert Kitschelt, *Party Systems in East Central Europe Consolidation or Fluidity* (Glasgow: Centre for the Study of Public Policy, University of Strathclyde, 1995); Gábor Tóka, *Political Parties and Democratic Consolidation in East Central Europe* (Glasgow: Centre for the Study of Public Policy, University of Strathclyde, 1997); and Peter Mair, *What Is Different about Post-Communist Party Systems?* (Glasgow: Centre for the Study of Public Policy, University of Strathclyde, 1996).

2. Petre Datculescu, "How the Voters Respond," in K. Lawson, et al., eds., *Cleavages, Parties and Voters: Studies from Bulgaria, the Czech Republic, Hungary, Poland, and Romania* (Westport, CT: Praeger, 1999).

3. Richard Rose and William Mishler, "Negative and Positive Party Identification in Post-Communist Countries," in *Electoral Studies*, vol. 17, no. 2 (June 1988), pp. 217–34.

4. William Crowther and Steven Roper, "A Comparative Analysis of Institutional Development in the Romanian and Moldovan Legislatures," in D. M. Olson and P. Norton, eds., *The New Parliaments of Central and Eastern Europe* (London: Frank Cass, 1996); and William Crowther, "Romania" in *Handbook of Political Change in Eastern Europe* (forthcoming).

5. Maurice Duverger, *Political Parties: Their Organization and Activity in the Modern State* (New York: Wiley, 1954); Seymour M. Lipset and Stein Rokkan, *Party Systems and Voter Alignments: Cross-National Perspectives* (New York: Free Press, 1967); Samuel P. Huntington, *Political Order in Changing Societies* (New Haven: Yale University Press, 1968); Giovanni Sartori, *Parties and Party Systems: A Framework for Analysis* (New York: Cambridge University Press, 1976); and Stefano Bartolini and Peter Mair, *Identity, Competition, and Electoral Availability: The Stabilisation of European Electorates 1885–1985* (Cambridge: Cambridge University Press, 1990).

6. According to Vladimir Tismăneanu, "a civic commitment to the values and institutions of the emerging democracy" is missing in Romania, despite the establishment of a democratic institutional framework. *Communism and Post-Communism in Romania: Challenges to Democratic Transition* (Washington, DC: National Council For Eurasian and East European Research, 1998), p. 5. The focus of this chapter, however, is the institutionalization of the party system, and it does not address the existence or absence of civic commitment to that system. For a further analysis of Romanian attitudes toward democratic values and practices, see chapter 8 in this volume by Paul Sum and Gabriel Bădescu.

7. The measures of consolidation I use are commonly employed in the literature to gauge institutionalization of the party system. These are fragmentation and volatility. See Rein Taagepera and Matthew S. Shugart, *Seats and Votes: The Effects and Determinants of Electoral Systems* (New Haven, CT: Yale University Press, 1989); Scott Mainwaring and Timothy R. Scully, eds., *Building Democratic Institutions: Party Systems in Latin America* (Stanford: Stanford University Press, 1995); Keith Crawford, *East Central European Politics Today: From Chaos to Stability?* (Manchester: Manchester University Press, 1996); Gary W. Cox, *Making Votes Count: Strategic Coordination in the World's Electoral Systems* (Cambridge: Cambridge University Press, 1997); and Tóka, *Political Parties*. For further discussion of measuring fragmentation,

see Sartori, *Parties and Party Systems*; Bernard Grofman and Arend Lijphart, *Electoral Laws and Their Political Consequences* (New York: Agathon Press, 1986); Markku Laakso and Rein Taagepera, "Effective Number of Parties: A Measure with Application to West Europe," *Comparative Political Studies*, vol. 12, no. 1 (April 1979), pp. 3–27. In this chapter, I count as viable parties only those that have achieved representation in parliament; fragmentation thus refers to fragmentation in parliament. Electoral volatility denotes the percentage of votes gained by any one party and lost by any other party in each election. The standard measure is Adam Przeworski's "Institutionalization of Voting Patterns, or Is Mobilization the Source of Decay?" in *American Political Science Review*, vol. 69, no. 1 (March 1975), pp. 49–67. According to Przeworski, the lower the electoral volatility, the higher the institutionalization of the party system. This measure is also attributed to Mogens Pedersen, "Changing Patterns of Electoral Volatility in European Systems, 1948–1977," in Hans Daalder and Peter Mair, eds., *Western European Party Systems: Continuity and Change* (Thousand Oaks, CA: Sage, 1983). According to Przeworski the formal definition is:

$$\frac{1}{2}\sum_{i=1}^{K}|\Delta Vi(t)|$$

where *t* denotes the election and *K* that all parties that obtained votes in either election are counted.

8. Duverger, *Political Parties*; Otto Kirchheimer, "The Transformation of West European Party Systems," in Joseph LaPalombara and Myron Weiner (eds.), *Political Parties and Political Development* (Princeton, NJ: Princeton University Press, 1966).

9. Petr Kopecky, "Developing Party Organizations in East-Central Europe," *Party Politics*, vol. 1, no. 4 (1995), pp. 515–34.

10. Rein Taagepera, "Book Review of Arter's Parties and Democracy in the Post Soviet Republics," *Party Politics*, vol. 5, no. 2 (1999), pp. 253–54.

11. Adam Przeworski, *Democracy and the Market: Political and Economic Reforms in Eastern Europe and Latin America* (Cambridge: Cambridge University Press, 1991); Kitschelt, *Party Systems*; and Mainwaring and Scully, *Building Democratic Institutions*.

12. Herbert Kitschelt et al., "The Structure of the Vote in Post Communist Party Systems: The Bulgarian Example," *European Journal of Political Research*, vol. 27 (February 1995), pp. 143–60.

13. Duverger, *Political Parties*; Douglas W. Rae, *The Political Consequences of Electoral Laws* (New Haven, CT: Yale University Press, 1971); Russell J. Dalton et al., eds., *Electoral Change in Advanced Industrial Democracies. Realignment or De-alignment?* (Princeton, NJ: Princeton University Press, 1984); Arend Lijphart and Bernard Grofman, *Choosing an Electoral System: Issues and Alternatives* (New York: Praeger, 1984); Grofman and Lijphart, *Electoral Laws*; William H. Riker, "Duverger's Law Revisited," in Lijphart and Grofman, eds., *Electoral Laws and Their Political Consequences*; Taagepera and Shugart, *Seats and Votes*; Matthew S. Shugart and John M. Carey, *Presidents and Assemblies: Constitutional Design and Electoral Dynamics* (Cambridge: Cambridge University Press, 1992); Arend Lijphart, *Electoral Systems and Party Systems: A Study of Twenty-Seven Democracies, 1945–1990* (Oxford: Oxford University Press, 1994); Matthew S. Shugart, *Building the Institutional Framework: Electoral*

Systems, Party Systems, and Presidents (Berkeley: University of California Press, 1994); Crowther and Roper, "A Comparative Analysis"; Cox, *Making Votes Count*; and Olga Shvetsova, "Making Votes Count: Strategic Coordination in the World's Electoral Systems," *Political Science Quarterly*, vol. 113, no. 4 (Winter 1998), pp. 724–25.

14. There are, however, exceptions to this expectation. According to Crowther and Roper ("A Comparative Analysis"), the general concern before the 1992 elections in Romania was that electoral rule changes would increase fragmentation. As I show in this chapter, theoretically, the opposite should have been expected, and empirically, fragmentation actually did decrease. "Permissive and restrictive" refers to the extent to which the electoral parameters resist entry of parties into a system.

15. David R. Mayhew, *Congress: The Electoral Connection* (New Haven, CT: Yale University Press, 1974); and Barbara Geddes, "A Comparative Perspective on the Leninist Legacy in Eastern Europe," *Comparative Political Studies*, vol. 28, no. 2 (July 1995), pp. 239–74.

16. The largest remainder system, which uses Hare quota, divides the total number of valid votes cast by the district magnitude. The parties are given as many seats as they have won quotas, and remaining seats are given to the parties with the largest remainders of votes. According to Lijphart (*Electoral Systems*), the Hare quota is impartial as between large and small parties and tends to yield close to proportional results.

17. Elena Stefoi-Sava, "Electoral Law in Eastern Europe: Romania," *East European Constitutional Review*, vol. 4, no. 2 (Spring 1994); Mihai Constantinescu, et al., *Alegerile Parlamentare Si Prezidentiale—Texte Legale Comentate, Monitorul Oficial*, no. 164 (1992). Current magnitudes per county are 4 in Covasna, Girgiu, Ialomiţa, Sălaj, Tulcea, and the agricultural sector Ilfov; 5 in Bistriţa-Năsăud, Caraş-Severin, Călăraşi, Harghita, and Mehedinţi; 6 in Alba, Brăila, Gorj, Satu Mare, Sibiu, Vîlcea, and Vrancea; 7 in Arad, Botoşani, Buzău, Olt, Teleorman, and Vaslui; 8 in Dîmboviţa, Hunedoara, Maramureş, and Neamţ; 9 in Bihor, Braşov, Galaţi, and Mureş; 10 in Argeş, Suceava, and Timiş; 11 in Bacău, Cluj, Constanţa, and Dolj; 12 in Iasi, and Prahova; and, finally, 29 in Bucureşti. The agricultural sector Ilfov was not considered a separate county in the 1990 elections.

18. Hungary uses a "mixed" (proportional and majoritarian) electoral system and 176 of the primary districts are single member districts. The ADM in the remaining 20 PR districts is 7.6. See Cox, *Making Votes Count*.

19. The FSN split in March 1992, due to a dispute between Iliescu and Roman. For a list of acronyms and full party names in both Romanian and English, see table 6.3.

20. In the 1992 elections, Iliescu's faction ran as FDSN. In the 1996 elections the FDSN changed its name to PDSR. In 2000 PDSR stands for Polul-Democrat Social din România. The coalition includes the merger of the PDSR and the PSDR into Partidul Social Democrat and the PUR.

21. In the 1992 elections, Petre Roman's faction ran as PD-FSN. In the 1996 elections, the PD-FSN joined the USD coalition along with the PSDR. In 2000 the PD ran alone again.

22. In 1992, the PSDR joined the CDR. Before the 1996 election the party split from the CDR, and ran in the USD coalition along with the PD-FSN.

23. In 1992, the CDR included the PSDR, PNL, MER, PNT-CD, and the PER. In 2000 the PNL split from the CDR and ran alone.

24. AUR Changed to PUNR before the 1992 election.

25. FDGR—Forumul Democratic al Germanilor din România and UDRR—Uniunea Democratică al Romilor din România are minority organizations, which in the first elec-

tion obtained one seat each as parties but subsequent elections were allotted a seat as *minoritz organiyations*. The other minority groups which have been allotted seats are CRLR—Comunitatea Rusilor Lipoveni, PR—Partidul Romilor, UAR—Uniunea Armenilor, AMSR—Asociaţia Macedonenilor Slavi, UDSCR—Uniunea Democrată a Sîrbilor si Carasovenilor, UDTR—Uniunea Democratică Turcă, UDSCR—Uniunea Democratică a Slovacilor şi Cehilor, UDTTMR—Uniunea Democrata a Tatarilor Turco-Musulmană, UER—Uniunea Elenă, UPR—Uniunea Polonezilor, UUR—Uniunea Ucrainenilor, FCER—Federatia Comunitatilor Evreiesti, CBBR—Comunitatea 'Bratstvo' a Bulgarilor, UBD—Uniunea Bulgara din Banat, CIRI—Comunitatea Italiana-Socola, Iasi, UCAR—Uniunea Culturala a Albanezilor, LAR—Liga Albanezilor, UCRR—Uniunea Culturala a Rutenilor, UCR—Uniunea Croatilor. *Monitorul*, no. 287; Irina Moroianu-Zlătescu, Ioana Oancea, *The Legislative and Institutional Framework for the National Minorities of Romania* (Bucureşti: Romanian Institute for Human Rights, 1994). Elections in Romania are available at http://www.electionworld.org/.

26. Legal thresholds can apply to all seats or seats allocated at the national level. They can refer to vote share, number of votes, votes as a fraction of quota, or seats won directly, either in districts or nationwide. For a further discussion, see Taagepera and Shugart, *Seats and Votes*.

27. Alexandru I. Bejan, "*Prezentarea şi analiza comparativăa rezultatelor alegerilor de la 20 mai 1990,*" in Petre Datculescu and K. Liepelt, eds., *Alegerile din Romania de la 20 mai 1990: Renasterea Unei Democratii* (Bucureşti: Imprimeria Coresi, 1991).

28. Stefoi-Sava, "Electoral Law."

29. Constantinescu et al., "*Alegerile*" *Monitorul*, no. 164. A highest averages formula, D'Hondt, awards seats sequentially to the parties having the highest average numbers of votes per seats, until all seats are allocated. Each time a party receives seats, its average goes down. D'Hondt systematically favors larger parties. See Lijphart, *Electoral Systems*.

30. *Monitorul*, no. 9.

31. Bejan, "*Prezentarea şi analiza*."

32. *Monitorul*, no. 87.

33. *Monitorul*, no. 164.

34. DAHR, Presidium, ed., Democratic Alliance of Hungarians in Romania (DAHR). *Document 2* (Cluj, 1992).

35. The electoral law stipulates the exact percent. Ioan Muraru, Iancu Gheorghe. *Constitutile Române. Texte. Note. Prezentare Comparativa* (Bucharest: *Regia Autonoma, Monitorul Oficial*, 1995).

36. *Monitorul*, no. 164.

37. *Monitorul*, no. 87. The parties were the PDSR, PNTCD, PER, PD, PUNR, UDMR, PRM, PL'93, PAC, PSM, PSDR, PDAR, PNL-CD, PNL, and MER. *Monitorul*, no. 213.

38. Daniel N. Nelson, "Romania," *Electoral Studies*, vol. 9, no. 4 (December 1990), pp. 355–66; Michael Shafir, "Romania's Elections: Why the Democratic Convention Lost," *RFR/RL Research Report*, vol. 1, no. 35 (1992), pp. 11–18; Henry F. Carey, "Irregularities or Rigging: The 1992 Romanian Parliamentary Elections," *East European Quarterly*, vol. 24, no. 1 (March 1995), pp. 43–66; and Richard Rose, et al., *Elections in Central and Eastern Europe since 1990* (Glasgow: Centre for the Study of Public Policy University of Strathclyde, 1998).

39. See OSCE/ODIHR *Final Reports* 1996 and 2000, available at http://www.osce.org/odihr/documents/reports/election_reports/ro/.

40. The ratio of official votes to seats was proportional in 1990. Even if all of the invalid votes were attributed to fraud and divided between the PNL and the PNT-CD, these parties would still only have received 38 and 23 seats respectively to the FSN's 262 seats. In 1992, the ratio of votes to seats for the three largest parties was around 122 percent. If we assume that all 13 percent of invalid votes were cast for the CDR, the party would have received approximately 140 seats to the FDSN's 115 seats. It is, however, unlikely that the difference is quite that large, as there are generally up to 2 percent of invalid votes in paper-ballot system (according to Carey, "Irregularities or Rigging"), and parties other than the CDR might have been beneficiaries of some of the lost vote. However, it is also unusual that as much as 10 percent of votes are cast on special lists. It is, therefore, possible that some of that vote can be attributed to fraud as well, which might further change the above results.

41. Antisystem parties undermine the legitimacy of the regime, often with serious consequences. Juan J. Linz and Alfred Stepan, eds., *The Breakdown of Democratic Regimes* (Baltimore, MD: Johns Hopkins University Press, 1978), pp. 26–27.

42. Richard Rose, "Mobilizing Demobilized Voters in Post-Communist Societies," *Party Politics*, vol. 1, no. 4 (October 1995).

43. According to Rose, the sum of changes in the vote for parties amounted to 126 percent, out of a maximum of 200 percent. According to Przeworski's index, 126 is divided by half. Rose includes all parties that received over 1 percent as well as "others." My volatility calculations include only parties with seats. Nonetheless, since there was no threshold in the 1990 elections, I include parties that received well below 1 percent of the vote share. My calculations are not biased toward obtaining a lower volatility number when compared to Rose's calculations, because I count as volatility loss of votes from parties that in the second election did not pass the 3 percent threshold or merge with other parties. Rose's count, however, still includes all parties that obtained above 1 percent of the vote. Rose, *Mobilizing*, p. 26.

44. Since the PSDR switched coalitions between elections the volatility of the PSD is the difference between the combined vote of the USD and the PDSR in 1996 and the combined vote of the PSD and PD in 2000.

45. The volatility is a measure of the difference between the vote share of the FSN in 1990, and the combined vote share of the FDSN and PD-FSN in 1992.

46. The volatility for the USD after the 1996 election is the difference between the USD vote in 1996, and the combined vote of the PD-FSN in the previous election, and the vote of the PSDR in the 1990 election because PSDR was a part of the CDR coalition in 1992. The PSDR 1990 share is included so as not to count switching of coalitions as volatility. The vote loss of the CDR is accounted for automatically, either in lost votes or reduced gain of votes. An alternative measure does not account for the 1990 PSDR vote share. This, however, only increases USD's volatility to 2.7, which increases the overall volatility from 11.4 to 11.9.

47. In 1992 and 1996, the PNL ran as a part of the CDR.

48. The volatility of the PNL is the difference between the vote of the CDR in 1996 and the combined vote share of the PNL and the 5 percent that the CDR received in the 2000 election.

49. The volatility is the difference between the CDR vote share in 1992, and the combined vote share of the coalition partners of the PSDR, PNL, MER, PNT-CDM, and PER in 1990.

50. The volatility of the PRM is the difference between the combined vote of the PUNR and the PRM in 1996 and the vote of the PRM in 2000. The reason the PUNR vote gets counted with the PRM vote is that even though the PUNR was not subsumed by the PRM, the PUNR was built around its leader Funar who joined the PRM before the 2000 election.

51. This calculation assumes that 3.25 percent gets added to vote percentage of the PLN and the PNTS-CD in 1990, that 13 percent are added to the vote of the CDR in 1992, and 6.5 percent are added to the vote of the CDR in 1996.

52. Crowther, *Handbook.*

53. On 16 November 1998, Tudor announced plans to merge the PRM and PUNR. Funar was subsequently chosen as the general secretary of the PRM, but the PUNR was never subsumed and ran in the 2000 election in a separate coalition called the Partidul Alianţa Naţionala with the PNR (Romanian National Party) whose leader Magureanu is the former head of the *Securitate.*

54. Calculating volatility, I trace the origin of all the parties and coalitions competing in each election. For parties that split between elections, I measure the aggregate change in the "offspring" vote in the first election after the split compared to the vote for the "mother party" in the previous election. In the second election after a split from a "mother party," I measure the change in the "offspring" vote separately. For parties that joined coalitions, I measure the difference between the aggregate vote for the individual parties in the election before the coalition was formed and the aggregate vote for the coalition. For the second election after the coalition was formed, I measure the change in vote for the coalition between elections.

55. Crowther, *Handbook*, pp. 301–2.

7

Parliamentary Development

Steven D. Roper

Throughout the 1990s, the Romanian parliament was considered a weak and ineffective institution. Public opinion polls showed that the parliament was the least respected state institution. The country adopted a semipresidential, or more specifically, a premier-presidential regime[1] fashioned on the French Fifth Republic in which President Ion Iliescu wielded dominant power and heavily influenced the composition and agenda of the country's first three governments. Parliamentary oversight of the executive was minimal, and while the parliament passed thousands of laws, legislative activity in crucial areas, such as industrial privatization and land reform, was virtually nonexistent.

The 1996 elections finally provided the country with an opportunity to address issues that the parliament, the government, and the president had avoided since 1990. The formation of a parliamentary coalition between the Democratic Convention of Romania (CDR), the Union of Social Democracy (USD), and the Hungarian Democratic Union of Romania (UDMR) was supposed to increase executive and legislative cooperation, and help reassert parliamentary control over the legislative process. However, the promise and optimism of 1996 has faded. Fighting within the parliamentary coalition thwarted necessary reforms. While parliamentary activity has increased, there have been many defections from parliamentary groups, and the institution continues to be held in low repute.

Entering the new millennium, Romania and its parliament face significant obstacles. Parliamentary development during the Communist period was severely limited, and as a consequence, the Romanian parliament confronts the concomitant problem of developing as an institution to meet twenty-first-century challenges while dealing with the political, economic, and social legacies of the Communist past. This chapter examines the factors that have influenced Romanian parliamentary development since 1990. First, I examine the historical antecedents of the current parliament, and observe how the interwar and Communist legacies have had a significant influence on the current process of parliamentary development. Next, I analyze the parliament's institutional structure and the impact of post-Communist institutional choices on policy debates. Finally, I explore the development of the parliament and its relationship with the government, especially in regard to the presidency.

HISTORICAL ANTECEDENTS

Given Romanian parliamentary history over the past 130 years, it is not surprising that the post-Communist parliaments have been so poorly developed, and that they have allowed the president and the government to usurp legislative power. The bicameral structure of the post-Communist parliament is based on the arrangement first adopted in the 1866 constitution. Leading up to World War I, politics were dominated by personalities such as King Carol I and Dimitrie Sturdza. During this period, suffrage was extremely limited, and there was significant cabinet instability. Following World War I and the incorporation of Bessarabia, Bukovina, and Transylvania into "Greater Romania," several necessary political and economic reforms were enacted. Keith Hitchens observed that while there was a belief in the early 1920s that parliamentary democracy would finally be instituted in Romania, the initial promise of democracy soon gave way to authoritarianism.[2] During the interwar period, Romania had only three fair elections (1919, 1928, and 1937), and the parliament increasingly came under the control of King Carol II.[3] The 1938 constitution granted the king considerable power, and less than a month after the adoption of the constitution, he abolished all parties. Furthermore, factionalism, corruption, and scandal racked the parliament. During the interwar period, the parliament never successfully developed autonomy, and this parliamentary culture established a pattern that continues today.

The subordination of the parliament to other political bodies intensified during the Communist period. Unlike other Communist-era parliaments, the Romanian Communist parliament (Grand National Assembly) never developed autonomy from the Central Committee or Politburo.[4] Even after several parliamentary reforms enacted in the mid-1970s, the Central Committee remained the superior body, according to Mary Ellen Fischer. She notes an extremely high turnover rate in the Assembly, which further undermined the parliament's authority.[5]

THE FIRST POST-COMMUNIST PARLIAMENT (1990–1992)

A few critical choices made in late 1989 and early 1990 regarding the National Salvation Front (FSN) and the provisional government strongly influenced the development of the parliament. The provisional government's first decree named Petre Roman prime minister, and its second established the structure and the responsibilities of the FSN Council, with Iliescu as president.[6] From the beginning, Romania adopted a premier-presidential system. Given Romania's affinity for French culture, this decision was not surprising. However, in the case of the Fifth Republic, the constitution provides the president far more influence over the parliament than does the Romanian constitution. Although the French president has few institutional means to directly influence legislation,[7] the flexibility of that system and the fact that voters directly elect the president have had the consequence that France has effectively functioned as a presidential regime for most of the Fifth Republic.[8] With the French experience in mind, it is understandable why Iliescu was also able to influence the legislative process. In the electoral law for the 1990 national elections, the parliament was referred to as a constituent assembly. The primary task of the new parliament was to draft a constitution. Several FSN members of parliament (MPs) used the drafting of the constitution to avoid addressing economic reforms. Even though the parliament was a constituent assembly, it still had to organize itself and behave as a legislative institution.

Structure of the First Post-Communist Parliament

Immediately after the May 1990 national elections, the Assembly of Deputies and the Senate drafted standing orders. In June 1990, the Assembly passed standing orders establishing parliamentary groups as the parliament's working bodies. Both chambers were organized based on these groups, and they were responsible for selecting MPs for assignment to the Permanent Bureau, the permanent commissions, and other leadership positions.[9] Article 2 of the standing orders mandated that a parliamentary group had to consist of at least ten deputies who were on election lists. Of the eighteen parties that won contested seats, only five parties had the number of deputies required to constitute a parliamentary group. Article 2 also stated that MPs who were members of parties or political formulations that did not meet the ten-member requirement could form a parliamentary group or join an already existing group. As a consequence, there were eight parliamentary groups in the first session of the Assembly (see table 7.1) and three in the Senate.

The Permanent Bureau consisted of a chair (who was also the chair of the Assembly of Deputies), four vice chairs, four secretaries, and two quaestors.

Table 7.1. Assembly of Deputies Parliamentary Groups 1990

Agrarian and Socialist Democratic Group
Ecological and Social-Democratic Group
Hungarian Democratic Union of Romania Group
National Salvation Front Group
National Minorities Group
National Liberal Party Group
National Peasants Party-Christian Democratic Group
Romanian National Union Group

Source: Monitorul Oficial al României, no. 89 (1 July 1990), pp. 2–14.

The configuration of the Permanent Bureau reflected the proportional representation of parties. The Assembly allotted a certain number of Permanent Bureau seats to each parliamentary group. The Permanent Bureau was responsible for legislative and organizational matters of the Assembly when it convened ordinary sessions, and received and distributed bills, proposals, and reports from commissions.

Like its U.S. counterpart, the Assembly had permanent, joint, special, inquiry, and mediation commissions. Election to the permanent commissions was to be based on proportional representation. However, this principle has been repeatedly violated. For example, while the FSN held almost 68 percent of the Assembly's seats, FSN MPs held just over 60 percent of the permanent commission seats. The FSN parliamentary group was underrepresented on commissions because it enjoyed an absolute majority in parliament. Therefore, this group offered additional seats to some of the other parliamentary groups with which it was affiliated. The distribution of permanent commission seats indicated the importance that the FSN leadership attached to different legislative issues. While FSN MPs held only 54 percent of the seats on the Commission for the Ecological Equilibrium and Protection of the Environment, they held over 73 percent of the seats on the Commission for Central and Local Administration, Arrangement of Territory, and Town Planning. Unlike in other European parliaments, the Romanian Senate exercised legislative power equivalent to the lower house, though there were differences. For example, the 1990 Senate was one-third the size of the Assembly, with a total of 119 seats. In contrast with the practice in the lower house, no Senate seats were allocated to ethnic minority parties.[10]

Legislative History (1990–1992)

Although there were eight legislative groups in the parliament, the FSN held most of the leadership positions in the two chambers. The presidents of both the Assembly and the Senate were FSN members. Even though the party possessed an absolute majority in the parliament, and held key portfolios in the government, finding consensus on economic matters proved to be difficult. Because the FSN was a catch-all party,[11] its leaders, Roman and Iliescu, held different views on the pace of economic reform. At that time, Roman wanted more reform and privatization than Iliescu.

This is just one of the reasons why the legislative output during the first post-Communist parliament was so low. Table 7.2 shows that during 1990 and 1991, only 124 laws were passed. This was the lowest legislative activity during the entire decade. Not until early 1991 did the parliament began to address privatization and other aspects of economic reform. The privatization law passed in August 1991 became the basis of the first mass privatization program. However, by the time the parliament acted, it was clear that the FSN coalition had fragmented around the issue of economic reform. As the parliament debated economic legislation, MPs became divided over the pace and substance of reform, and two separate factions developed around Iliescu and Roman. The debate was managed and largely kept within the party until the end of 1991.

In September 1991, miners from the Jiu Valley descended on Bucharest to protest their declining living standards. In order to mollify them, Prime Minister Petre Roman offered to reshuffle the cabinet, a move which he evidently felt did not include himself. President Iliescu announced, however, that he had accepted the resignation of the *entire* cabinet and named Finance Minister Theodor Stolojan prime minister. Roman protested that he had not resigned but nevertheless handed in his mandate. The parliament took no action against the president's decision, despite the fact that Iliescu had not consulted the parliament on Roman's resignation and had thereby effectively usurped parliamentary authority. Jonathan Eyal argues that the inherent weakness of first post-Communist parliament provided Iliescu an opportunity to repeatedly subvert parliamentary power.[12] However, it was unnecessary for him to subvert the parliament because it had already delegated

Table 7.2. Number of Parliamentary Laws and Presidential Decrees

Year Decrees	*Parliamentary Laws*	*Presidential Decrees*
1990	42	27
1991	82	80
1992	130	155
1993	95	190
1994	146	287
1995	139	390
1996	142	593
1997	220	572
1998	261	476

Source: Monitorul Oficial al României. Compiled by the author.

much of its responsibilities to the executive.[13] This is one of the reasons why during the 1990–1991 period, Iliescu issued almost as many decrees (107) as pieces of legislation passed by the parliament (see table 7.2).

DRAFTING THE 1991 CONSTITUTION

The membership of the constitution drafting committee reflected the parties' parliamentary strength. The most crucial issue confronting the committee was the distribution of power between the parliament and the executive. Iliescu made it clear to his party that he wanted to continue a strong presidency. FSN members and other MPs overwhelmingly adopted the constitution in November 1991.[14] Significantly, almost all of the members of the National Peasant Christian Democrat Party (PNŢCD) and the UDMR voted against the constitution. They felt that it granted too much power to the executive. However, the Romanian president's constitutional powers are actually rather modest. As in France, the constitution provides emergency powers to the president and the authority to propose referenda, but the president has few legislative powers.

Initially, the parliament maintained the French practice whereby members could not hold government portfolios, but the constitution allowed MPs also to hold government positions. This further undermines the autonomy of the parliament. If individuals can hold seats in the parliament and government portfolios, then the distinction between these institutions is eroded. Following the adoption of the constitution by national referendum on 8 December 1991, the next task for Romania's first post-Communist parliament was to establish a date for new elections.

Between the constitutional referendum in December 1991 and the September 1992 national elections, the tension within the FSN escalated. In March 1992, the FSN held its national convention, which publicly demonstrated the division between the Iliescu and Roman supporters. These factions presented draft platforms at the convention concerning the party's economic policy. At the end of the second day, Roman was reelected party leader. On the third and final day of the convention, the delegates discussed the forthcoming national elections. The victorious Roman wing refused to consider the nomination of a presidential candidate. Iliescu's supporters considered this decision an attempt to embarrass the president and, therefore, most of them left the convention. The next day, several FSN MPs renounced their party membership (most of the FSN MPs were Iliescu supporters) and decided to create a new party. In June, the newly created Democratic National Salvation Front (FDSN) held its first national convention. Although the FDSN held no government portfolios, within three months it held a majority of seats in the Senate and more than fifty seats in the lower house. The FDSN used its support in the parliament to delay the passage of a new electoral law. In the meantime the 1992 national elections, which were initially scheduled for early summer, were postponed until September.

During the pre-electoral period, parliamentary and presidential activity increased. In the months preceding the election, the parliament passed a number of laws reversing whatever economic reform had occurred. In early 1992, Romania was experiencing hyperinflation, and the Stolojan government undertook an export-led growth policy to rebuild the industrial sector.[15] However, the trade deficit and GDP did not improve. The economic failure was attributed to the September national elections, which prevented the government from really pursuing economic reform. For example, in July the parliament passed several amendments to the law governing unemployment benefits thereby providing additional benefits by indexing wages to inflation. This action fueled inflation and increased the budget deficit. Also, during this time, the number of presidential decrees increased. Between January and September 1992, Iliescu issued 118 decrees ranging from appointments to issues dealing with the criminal code, education, and privatization. He issued more decrees in the months before the 1992 national elections than in all 1990–1991.

THE SECOND POST-COMMUNIST PARLIAMENT (1992–1996)

The political environment in September 1992 had changed considerably from the first election. Unlike the 1990 national elections, the 1992 elections saw no clear majority party. The FSN was fragmented while the opposition was a much stronger force. The newly formed CDR was an opposition coalition composed of several parties including the UDMR, the PNŢCD, and the National Liberal Party (PNL).[16] The CDR had done extremely well in the March 1992 local elections, and many polls predicted a CDR victory. However, the FDSN proved far more successful in the elections than the polls had predicted. The party received approximately 28 percent of the popular vote (which translated into 35 percent of the parliamentary seats) while the CDR won just over 20 percent of the popular vote (approximately 25 percent of the parliamentary seats). The FSN received only 10 percent of the parliamentary seats. In the presidential race, Iliescu was reelected with 61 percent of the second-round vote. How was the newly formed FDSN able to consolidate its power so quickly? Undoubtedly, there was electoral fraud in the 1992 national elections, and in addition, Iliescu and the FDSN were able to obtain substantial funding and significant media coverage.[17]

Following the 1992 parliamentary elections, no single party enjoyed an absolute majority; however, the FDSN held a plurality of seats and began discussions regarding the creation of a coalition government. Iliescu appointed

Nicolae Vacariou as the new prime minister. Unlike the first parliament, there was a clear opposition, mainly the CDR, and several extremist parties including the Party of Romanian National Unity (PUNR), the Greater Romania Party (PRM), and the Socialist Labor Party (PSM). Because the FDSN only had a plurality of seats, it unofficially and covertly formed a coalition government with these parties. However, its members held almost all the government portfolios, and FDSN members were chosen to preside over the renamed House of Deputies[18] and the Senate.

Structure of the Second Post-Communist Parliament

Based on a new representational formula adopted for the 1992 national elections, the number of contested seats in the lower house was reduced from 387 to 328. In the second parliament, the percentage of MPs who were reelected in 1992 was quite low. Based on calculations for the House, the percentage of MPs who were returned was only 22 percent. While the number of parties represented in the House decreased after the 1992 national elections, the number of parliamentary groups actually increased from eight to eleven (see table 7.3). In addition, Article 18 of the new standing orders prohibited MPs from switching membership from one parliamentary group to another or from creating new parliamentary groups.[19] This requirement was added to the standing orders so that parties that did not meet the 3 percent electoral threshold (instituted for the 1992 parliamentary elections) could not be represented. Therefore, when the FDSN changed its name to the Party of Social Democracy in Romania (PDSR) in June 1993, it was allowed to keep its status as a parliamentary group. Article 18 was an attempt by the Romanian parliament to prevent the problem of party fragmentation and volatility, which had afflicted many East European parliaments. The new

Table 7.3. House of Deputies Parliamentary Groups, 1992

Civic Alliance Party Group
Democratic Party Group
Greater Romania Party Group
Hungarian Democratic Union of Romania Group
Liberal Group
National Minorities Group
National Peasants Party–Christian Democratic and Romanian Group
Ecological Party Group
Party of Romanian National Unity Group
Party of Social Democracy of Romania Group
Social Democratic Party of Romania Group
Socialist Group

Source: Monitorul Oficial al României, no. 286 (16 November 1992), pp. 2–16.

orders also reflected a shift in the balance of power within the parliament. By limiting the mobility of rank-and-file MPs, the authority of parliamentary leaders was enhanced. However, in May 1994, the Romanian Constitutional Court issued a decision that declared Article 18 unconstitutional because it violated Articles 61 and 66 of the constitution.[20]

Between the first and the second parliaments, there was a high degree of leadership stability in the Permanent Bureaus, and perhaps as a consequence, the new House orders only made minor modifications. The responsibilities and powers of the Permanent Bureau were increased, and in an attempt to increase the professionalization of the parliament, the Permanent Bureau was now required to provide administrative support to parliamentary groups. Article 16 mandated that a specific number of administrative staff be provided to parliamentary groups based on their numeric strength in the parliament. The responsibilities of individual members of the Permanent Bureau were not modified, and the House commission system was not altered. The new orders retained the same number of permanent commissions, and the jurisdiction of these commissions underwent only minor changes. Election to these commissions was still based on the principle of proportional representation, and in fact, this principle was more closely followed in the second parliament than in the first. The proportion of FDSN parliamentary and commission seats was approximately 34 percent. FDSN MPs decided to increase their representation on commissions because their party no longer possessed an absolute majority. While the overall proportion of seats was equal, the principle of proportionality was violated on certain commissions. For example, the FDSN held 44 percent of the seats on the important Commission on Industries and Services and only 27 percent of the seats on the Commission on Human Rights, Religious Denominations, National Minorities and Related Matters. This illustrates the FDSN policy interests.

The new representational formula adopted for the 1992 national elections also significantly changed the number of Senate seats. Unlike in the House, the number of Senate seats increased from 119 to 143. The new standing orders adopted in June 1993 did not substantially change the legislative process of the Senate but did affect parliamentary groups. The new standing orders reduced the number of senators necessary to constitute a parliamentary group from ten to five. Because of this change in the standing orders, and the increase in the size of the Senate, the number of parliamentary groups increased from three to eight (see table 7.4). While the requirement to form a parliamentary group was lowered, Article 14 stated that senators could not move from one parliamentary group to another or create a group that did not run in elections.[21] As in the case of the House, the Constitutional Court ruled that Article 14 violated the constitution. Also similar to the House, the new Senate standing orders allowed senators to hold government positions.

Table 7.4. Senate Parliamentary Groups, 1992

Civic-Liberal Orientation Group
Democratic Party Group
Democratic Agrarian Party of Romania Group
Party of Social Democracy of Romania Group
Hungarian Democratic Union of Romania Group
Party of Romanian National Unity Group
National Party Group
National Peasants Party–Christian Democratic Group

Source: Monitorul Oficial al României, no. 286 (16 November 1992), pp. 2–16.

The new Senate standing orders did not change the composition of the Permanent Bureau, but they did modify its responsibilities and powers. As was the case in the House, the new Senate standing orders mandated that each parliamentary group, depending on its size, receive between one and five experts and a cabinet chief. Even though the new House and Senate standing orders provided for professional staff, John Anelli reports that MPs "tend to see themselves as the experts, and many Members, as a result, see a more substantial professional staff as unnecessary or even threatening."[22] Even with more staff, MPs continued to use outside sources for information. In one survey, 91 percent of the MPs reported using the press as a source of information in their deliberations while only 51 percent stated that they used the parliament's institutional resources.[23]

Legislative History (1992–1996)

Due to U.S. concerns over the validity of the 1990 elections and allegations of parliamentary corruption, no Western government provided foreign assistance during the first post-Communist parliament. However, following the 1992 elections, organizations such as the United States Agency for International Development (USAID), the National Democratic Institute for International Affairs (NDI), and the International Republican Institute (IRI) began to focus on parliamentary training programs.[24] The United States recognized that important economic and social reforms would only occur if the parliament was more professional and active. Organizations such as NDI and IRI conducted training programs, and advised on changes in the standing orders in order to strengthen the committee system and improve legislative work. Interviews conducted by Thomas Carothers indicate that these training programs actually had little to no impact on the professionalization of the second post-Communist parliament. He concludes that the "post-1992 Parliament has not, however, performed well. President Iliescu's party has exercised weak leadership in the Parliament. Relatively few laws of significance have been passed."[25] At the same time, the Constitutional Court was very active in striking down several important pieces of legislation passed by the parliament. For example, the "Law on Social Security," the "Law of Empowering the Government to Issue Orders," and even the "Law Regarding the Status of Deputies and Senators" were ruled unconstitutional.[26]

It is telling that Carothers calls the PDSR "Iliescu's party." This is just one indication that the presidency continued to be a dominant force in parliamentary politics. Part of the problem was that the parliamentary majority was more than happy to delegate legislative authority to the government. For example, during the January 1994 recess, the parliament passed a law which allowed the government to rule by decree in order to continue IMF negotiations. Although the second parliament continued to be deferential to the government and the president, it was a much more active institution. For example, between 1993 and 1995 the parliament passed 380 laws (approximately 127 laws per year). This figure was double the average of the first parliament (see table 7.2).

While the parliament's activity grew, the presidency was unrivalled in the number of decrees it issued. Between 1993 and 1995, President Iliescu issued 867 decrees, or 289 decrees annually. This figure was five times the average number issued during his first term of office. One explanation for this rapid increase has to do with the composition of the parliament. During most of the first parliament, Iliescu's party held an absolute majority of seats, while in the second he had to rely on a parliamentary coalition.

By August 1993, the PUNR leadership was negotiating to officially enter the cabinet.[27] Although the PDSR did not want them included, it needed their support, and so they signed an agreement with the PUNR in January 1994. By August, PUNR was a junior member of the government. After months of further negotiations, the PRM and the PSM also joined the coalition. Once this coalition was formalized, the Vacariou government became much more assertive in defying the parliamentary opposition.

Even though the parliament passed numerous bills, it was still considered largely inactive on several important issues (e.g., economic reform and privatization) allowing the government, and by extension the president, to continue to exercise legislative power. There were attempts to rectify the situation, however, as the CDR and other opposition groups attempted to gain some control. For example, by December 1993, two separate votes of confidence had been taken, and in March 1994 the Vacariou government was reorganized. While the opposition mounted a united front against the president and the government, it soon found itself fragmented over several important legislative issues, especially education. The UDMR and the PNŢCD were often at odds with each other over minority language education in secondary schools and universities. Indeed, Carothers points out that the parliamentary opposition had "engaged in a reflexively negative rather than constructive oppositional mode."[28]

While the parliamentary opposition had a difficult time maintaining its unity, the parliamentary majority also had problems finding consensus on several important issues. Ultimately, it was Iliescu's attempt in 1995 to sign a basic treaty with Hungary that was the catalyst for the ending of the parliamentary majority. The PDSR's coalition partners were the parties most opposed to the treaty, and by October 1995, the PRM had been removed from the government. Later, in March 1996, the PDSR ended its coalition with the PSM; and by September the PUNR was removed from the coalition.

THE THIRD POST-COMMUNIST PARLIAMENT (1996–2000)

By the time of the national elections in October 1996, the Romanian political landscape had changed substantially. First, Iliescu and the PDSR could not control the electronic media as they had done in 1992. The independent and popular television station Pro-TV assured that the opposition would receive equal and fair news coverage. Second, the CDR offered voters a more positive and clear program called the "Contract with Romania." Third, there was a change in the Romanian electorate itself. The new entrepreneurial class distrusted the PDSR's economic policy, and the working class began to change its party allegiance because of the poor economic performance of the Vacariou government and the parliament. The results of the parliamentary and presidential elections indicated a clear rejection of the politics of the past. The CDR received a plurality of seats in both houses (over 30 percent) and formed a coalition government with the USD and the UDMR. The USD was itself a coalition dominated by former Prime Minister Roman and his party the Democratic Party (PD). In addition to its parliamentary victory, CDR presidential candidate Emil Constantinescu defeated Iliescu in the second round.

Structure of the Third Post-Communist Parliament

Even though the parliament was held in low repute, the reelection rate between the second and third parliament actually increased. For the third parliament, the House reelection rate was 34 percent (12 percent higher than for the previous House). The number of parliamentary groups in the third parliament decreased to eight, and, because the orders did not allow deputies to form new groups, over thirty MPs were not affiliated members (see table 7.5). The House orders did not significantly change the structure or functioning of the parliament. However, previous standing orders were incorporated into the new ones. The number of commissions remained the same, but in order to instill some genuine trust between the majority and opposition, six commission chairs were given to the opposition.

Table 7.5. House of Deputies Parliamentary Groups, 1996

Democratic Party Group
Greater Romania Party Group
Hungarian Democratic Union of Romania Group
National Liberal Party Group
National Minorities Group
National Peasants Party–Christian Democratic and Romanian Group
Ecological Party Group
Party of Romanian National Unity Group
Party of Social Democracy of Romania Group

Source: Monitorul Oficial al României. Compiled by the author.

As was the case with the FSN in the first parliament, the CDR was somewhat underrepresented on House commissions. While the CDR held approximately 37 percent of the House seats, it held only 31 percent of commission seats.[29] One factor that can account for this underrepresentation is that the CDR is in a coalition with other parliamentary groups. It has allowed some of its coalition partners to be slightly overrepresented on commissions. Interestingly, while the CDR and its leading party, the PNŢCD, were often associated with economic issues, especially land restitution, the CDR was overrepresented on the Foreign Policy (41 percent) and the Defense, Public Order, and National Security Commissions (38 percent). It was actually underrepresented on the Economics Commission, the Reform and Privatization Commission, and the Budget, Finance and Banking Commission. Because of the importance of NATO and EU expansion in 1996 and 1997, it is not surprising that CDR MPs sought seats in foreign policy-oriented commissions. Like the House, the Senate structure and standing orders did not essentially change between the second and third parliament. The new standing orders require five senators in order to form a parliamentary group, and thus, the number of parliamentary groups was approximately the same (see table 7.6).

Table 7.6. Senate Parliamentary Groups, 1996

Democratic Party Group
Hungarian Democratic Union of Romania Group
National Liberal Party Group
National Peasants Party–Christian Democratic and Romanian Group
Ecological Party Group
Party of Romanian National Unity Group
Party of Social Democracy of Romania Group

Source: Monitorul Oficial al României. Compiled by the author.

Legislative History (1996–2000)

The new parliamentary coalition confirmed the mayor of Bucharest, Victor Ciorbea, as prime minister. Following the electoral success of the CDR, there was a great deal of optimism that necessary economic reforms would finally be enacted by the parliament. The third parliament was much more active than the previous parliaments. Table 7.2 reports that, between 1997 and 1998, the parliament passed 481 laws. This was almost the same number of laws passed during the first five years of the parliament's post-Communist existence. Also, during this period, the opposition was more active in addressing interprellations to the government. In 1997 and 1998, 381 interpellations were addressed to government officials. While the Iliescu-led opposition attempted to assert some control over the government, the Ciorbea administration sent several "emergency rulings" to the parliament for approval. These are omnibus packages that can be voted up or down but cannot be amended. In the first few months following the elections, it looked like necessary legislation was finally going to be passed. However, by the fall of 1997, conflict between the coalition members, particularly the PNŢCD and the PD, made the passage of legislation difficult. Fighting between these members was not surprising. Soon after the formation of the government, Ciorbea and Roman, who was now president of the Senate, clashed over the pace of economic reform. Unlike in 1990 and 1991, Roman was now advocating a more cautious economic reform program. By the summer of 1997, there was open dissension in the coalition.

Beyond economic policy, the reality was that much of the conflict stemmed from a clash of personalities. Roman repeatedly threatened to withdraw his support if the pace of economic reforms continued. The conflict was so severe that to pass the privatization law in December 1997, Ciorbea tied the passage of the law to a confidence vote procedure. Similar to other parliaments,[30] the Romanian parliament's rules provide that unless a no-confidence vote is offered within three days, any law with a confidence vote attached is considered adopted without debate. To maintain their image as a reform party, USD MPs did not table a no-confidence vote. However, this episode finally caused Roman to announce, in January 1998, that all four of his party's ministers would withdraw from the government, and that parliamentary support would be given on a case-by-case basis.

During 1998, there was an anticipation that the Ciorbea government would either resign or fall. The breaking point came when the Senate did not pass a government-sponsored bill on the use of Hungarian in local administrative bodies. Several USD MPs joined the opposition and voted against the bill. This event triggered Ciorbea's resignation on 30 March 1998. After confirming the new government headed by Radu Vasile, the parliament was largely inactive during the spring. There was conflict among the coalition members, as well as strain between the majority and the opposition. The parliamentary majority had initially tried to build trust with the opposition, but by early 1998, the House and the Senate were debating whether to lift the parliamentary immunity of opposition MPs. The Senate majority changed the voting requirement so that the immunity of Corneliu Vadim Tudor (senator and president of the PRM) could be lifted, and the House stripped Gabriel Bivolaru (PDSR MP) of his immunity. Both the PRM and the PDSR boycotted these votes, along with several sessions of parliament.

Ultimately, not even the ruling PNŢCD was immune to conflict. While Constantinescu and House President Ion Diaconescu (also PNŢCD chair) agreed to nominate Vasile as prime minister, conflict eventually arose between Vasile on the one hand, and Constantinescu and the PNŢCD leadership on the other.[31] Vasile resented Constantinescu's attempts to influence cabinet decisions, and he was very open about his intention to replace Diaconescu as head of the PNŢCD. Finally in December 1999, a majority of government ministers resigned, including seven PNŢCD ministers. Ironically, the only ministers who did not resign were PD members (the party that had brought down Ciorbea). The mass resignations were obviously orchestrated by Constantinescu, because immediately after the announcement he issued a presidential decree dismissing Vasile. In the decree, Constantinescu stated that the ministerial resignations made it impossible for Vasile to carry out his duties, and under Article 106 of the constitution, the president in such a case has the right to remove the prime minister. Vasile claimed that Article 106 only applied to the prime minister's health and, therefore, initially refused to recognize the legitimacy of the decree. Most Romanian constitutional scholars agreed that the president's decree was a violation of the constitution, but the Constitutional Court stated that it was powerless to rule, and thus the decree stood. As was the case between Iliescu and Roman in 1991, the president was able to unconstitutionally dismiss the prime minister with parliament's acquiescence.

Until this episode, Constantinescu had far less influence than Iliescu. Although Constantinescu issued over 1,000 decrees during 1997 and 1998, most of these were personnel changes. Because he was so closely associated with the coalition, as the fortunes of the CDR declined, so too did Constantinescu's, along with his ability to influence legislation. As head of state, he also had invested considerable resources on foreign policy issues like NATO and EU entry. With the perceived lack of Western support on economic and foreign policy matters, Constantinescu's popularity diminished; by the summer of 1999, several polls showed a significant decline in his support among the populace. When asked for whom they would vote in the next presidential election, 38 percent of respondents answered Iliescu, while only 20 percent selected Constantinescu.[32] Therefore, many regarded his decree as an attempt to demonstrate his strength, and to eventually to use Vasile as a scapegoat during the 2000 presidential elections.

As previously mentioned, many have described the Fifth Republic as a de facto presidential system for most of its existence. Ezra Suleiman argues that, in the case of the Fifth Republic, the "presidential system derives its strength from the support it receives from a majority party. Without that support in the National Assembly, presidential power is considerably diminished."[33] The argument that Suleiman and others make is that the Fifth Republic is a parliamentary system during periods of cohabitation because the president's party is not the majority party in the parliament. How does this analysis apply to Romania?

During the first parliament, until March 1992, Iliescu's party commanded an absolute majority in the parliament, and, therefore, Iliescu's need to issue presidential decrees was not pressing. Table 7.2 shows that fewer presidential decrees were issued during this period than at any other time in the 1990s. However, during the coalition years 1993–1996, the number of presidential decrees increased every year. Even though Iliescu's party held a plurality of seats, it did not enjoy a majority. Despite the PDSR's need for coalition partners, Iliescu issued more decrees to preserve his party's power. The same logic can also be applied to Constantinescu. The CDR has been in a coalition with the UDMR and the USD since late 1996. Constantinescu's decision to dismiss Vasile demonstrates the coalition's weakness as much as its strength. The coalition could have submitted Vasile to a motion of no confidence and avoided criticism for supporting the president's unconstitutional decree. Instead the president, with the backing of CDR MPs, decided to use his decree power, probably unconstitutionally, to change the government.

THE FOURTH POST-COMMUNIST PARLIAMENT (2000–2004)

The inability of the government to confront serious macroeconomic problems as well as deal with charges of corruption led to a significant loss of voter support by the end of the 1990s. At the time of the 2000 national elections, President Constantinescu announced his decision not to run for reelection and the PDSR and the PRM had supplanted the CDR as the most popular parties. Similar to voting patterns in other post-Communist countries, the 2000 elections marked a return of the former Communist successor

Table 7.7. House of Deputies Parliamentary Groups, 2000

Democratic Party Group
Greater Romania Party Group
Hungarian Democratic Union of Romania Group
National Liberal Party Group
National Minorities Group
Social Democratic and Humanist Group

Source: Monitorul Oficial al României. Compiled by the author.

Table 7.8. Senate Parliamentary Groups, 2000

Democratic Party Group
Greater Romania Party Group
Hungarian Democratic Union of Romania Group
National Liberal Party Group
Social Democratic and Humanist Group

Source: Monitorul Oficial al României. Compiled by the author.

party (e.g., the PDSR). In the 2000 elections, the PDSR received almost an absolute majority of seats (46 percent), and Iliescu was once again elected president in a second round runoff with Tudor.

Structure of the Fourth Communist Parliament

The number of parliamentary groups in the fourth parliament decreased to six (continuing the trend since the 1990 election), and once again, because the orders did not allow deputies to form new groups, four MPs were not affiliated members (see table 7.7). In the Senate, the number of parliamentary groups also decreased to its lowest level (see table 7.8).

CONCLUSION

This chapter has explored the development of the Romanian parliament since 1990. Since its conception, it has been the least trusted and most ridiculed institution in Romania. Charges of corruption and inactivity plagued the first parliament. Coalition instability stymied legislative efforts during the second. The third parliament was supposed to overcome these problems and focus on economic reform, privatization, and other important issues. Unfortunately, the coalition between the CDR, the USD, and the UDMR proved very fragile and volatile. After a flurry of activity in late 1996 and 1997, legislative output dramatically decreased. The resignation of Ciorbea in 1998 and the dismissal of Vasile in 1999 demonstrated a lack of parliamentary coordination. The results from the 2000 elections showed just how unpopular the CDR had become. Since 2000, the parliament has tried to actively involve itself in the Euro-Atlantic integration process with the European Union as well as NATO. The government of Adrian Năstase has proven much more effective than any previous government, and by 2002, the parliament, the government, and the PDSR still commanded significant support among the electorate. In addition, the parliament and the government have been much more assertive vis-à-vis President Iliescu than in the past. Therefore, there is some optimism that after a decade of deferring to the president, the parliament and the government are finally becoming more active participants in the legislative process.

NOTES

1. Matthew Soberg Shugart and John M. Carey developed the concept of a premier-presidential regime as a specific form of semipresidentialism. According to them, the key distinction in semipresidential regimes is whether the president has the power to dismiss cabinet ministers unilaterally that have the confidence of parliament. This is not a power that the Romanian president possesses. See Matthew Soberg Shugart and John M. Carey, *Presidents and Assemblies: Constitutional Design and Electoral Dynamics* (Cambridge: Cambridge University Press, 1992).

2. Keith Hitchens, *Rumania 1866–1947* (Oxford: Clarendon Press, 1994).

3. Authors such as Robert King, Irina Livezeanu, and Martyn Rady argue that the usurpation of power by King Carol II thwarted any attempts at sustained democracy during this period. For a more complete discussion of interwar Romanian politics, see Robert R. King, *History of the Romanian Communist Party* (Stanford, CA: Hoover Institution Press, 1980); Irina Livezeanu, *Cultural Politics in Greater Romania: Regionalism, Nation Building, and Ethnic Struggle, 1918–1930* (Ithaca, NY: Cornell University Press, 1995); and Martyn Rady, *Romania in Turmoil* (London: I. B. Tauris, 1992).

4. For example, Attila Agh argues that by the late 1980s the Hungarian parliament was a more professional organization. See Attila Agh, "Democratic Parliamentarism in Hungary: The First Parliament (1990–1994) and the Entry of the Second Parliament," in David M. Olson and Philip Norton, eds., *The New Parliaments of Central and Eastern Europe* (London: Frank Cass, 1996).

5. One of the reforms enacted during the 1970s introduced multicandidate, single-party elections for some parliamentary seats, though Romania had fewer such elections than other Communist countries. Mary Ellen Fischer, "Participatory Reforms in Romania," in Jan F. Triska and Paul M. Cocks, eds., *Political Development in Eastern Europe* (New York: Praeger, 1977).

6. *Monitorul Oficial al României*, no. 2 (27 December 1989), pp. 2–3.

7. John D. Huber, "Executive Decree Authority in France," in John M. Carey and Matthew Soberg Shugart, eds., *Executive Decree Authority* (Cambridge: Cambridge University Press, 1998).

8. Ezra N. Suleiman, "Presidentialism and Stability in France," in Juan J. Linz and Arturo Valenzuela, eds., *The Failure of Presidential Democracy, Volume 1: Comparative Perspectives* (Baltimore, MD: Johns Hopkins University Press, 1994).

9. Mihai Constantinescu and Ioan Muraru, *Drept parlamentar* (Bucharest: Gramar, 1994).

10. The 1990 electoral law stipulated that ethnic minority parties would receive one seat in the Assembly. Later, this requirement was included in the constitution (Article 59:2).

11. The FSN as a catch-all party is discussed in Steven D. Roper, "The Romanian Political Party System and the Catch-All Party Phenomenon," *East European Quarterly*, vol. 28, no. 4 (January 1995), pp. 519–32.

12. Jonathan Eyal, "Romania," in Stephen Whitefield, ed., *The New Institutional Architecture of Eastern Europe* (New York: St. Martin's Press, 1993).

13. Steven D. Roper and William Crowther, "The Institutionalization of the Romanian Parliament: A Case Study of the State-Building Process in Eastern Europe," *Southeastern Political Review*, vol. 26, no. 2 (June 1998), pp. 401–26.

14. Over 81 percent of MPs voted for the constitution.

15. For a more complete discussion of economic policy during the Stolojan government, see Daniel Daianu, "Dilemmas of the Stabilization Policy in Romania," *Sfera politicii*, vol. 1 (April 1993), pp. 12–13.

16. The PNL withdrew from the coalition shortly before the 1992 national elections.

17. For a thorough analysis of electoral fraud in the 1992 parliamentary elections, see Henry F. Carey, "Irregularities or Rigging: Romania's 1992 Parliamentary Elections," *East European Quarterly*, vol. 29, no. 1 (March 1995), pp. 43–66.

18. The Romanian word for house could also be translated as "chamber."

19. The new standing orders were adopted by the House of Deputies on 24 February 1994 and did not fundamentally change the administrative or the legislative process of the lower house.

20. Because of the Court's decision, Article 18 was modified and the change to the standing orders was adopted in June 1995. The modified article can be found in *Monitorul Oficial al României*, no. 111 (2 June 1995), pp. 4–5.

21. *Monitorul Oficial al României*, no. 178 (27 July 1993), p. 2.

22. John Anelli, "Baseline Appraisal of the Romanian Parliament" (unpublished paper, 1994), p. 7.

23. These data are the result of a 1993 survey of Romanian members conducted by William Crowther in collaboration with Georgeta Muntean and INFORMATIX, AG in Bucharest. There were 357 MPs that responded to the survey.

24. For an excellent account of the development of parliamentary assistance programs in Romania see, Thomas Carothers, *Assessing Democracy Assistance: The Case of Romania* (Washington, DC: Carnegie Endowment Book, 1996).

25. *Ibid*, p. 58.

26. "Constitution Watch: Romania," *East European Constitutional Review*, vol. 4, no. 2 (Summer 1995), p. 22.

27. Michael Shafir, "Ruling Party Formalizes Relations with Extremists," *Transition*, vol. 1, no. 14 (April 1995), pp. 42–46.

28. Carothers, *Assessing Democracy Assistance: The Case of Romania*, p. 58.

29. This figure was the percentage of CDR seats held immediately following the 1996 election. Because of defections, the percentage of seats has changed.

30. An excellent survey of the use of confidence vote procedures in European parliaments can be found in, John D. Huber, "The Vote of Confidence in Parliamentary Democracies," *American Political Science Review*, vol. 90, no. 2 (June 1996), pp. 269–82.

31. The president cannot belong to a party. Once being elected, Constantinescu had to resign as a PNŢCD member; although, he maintained very close relations with the party.

32. See the survey conducted by the Center for the Study of Public Opinion and Market Research during May/June as reported by Mediafax.

33. Suleiman, "Presidentialism and Stability in France," p. 146.

8

An Evaluation of Six Forms of Political Participation

Paul E. Sum and Gabriel Bădescu

Revolution transforms the relationship between citizens and state officials. In 1989, Romania initiated a process of redefining this line of power. Through democratic institutions, Romanian citizens now hold the potential to counterbalance the political power exercised through the state by participating in the political process. The ability to constrain state actions depends, in part, on communication between citizens and state officials. The extent to which Romanians participate politically and the degree to which that participation reflects a plurality of viewpoints reveal aspects of new political relationships under liberal democratic principles.

Romanian democratic institutions establish the basis for a legal framework that maintains individual equality before the law. This enables Romanians equal opportunities for free expression and mass participation. Active citizens, who utilize these institutions to voice diverse preferences, can strengthen democracy and enhance the legitimacy of the political system.[1] Beyond a functional constraint on political power, participation may contribute to individual empowerment and freedom.[2] Therefore, from a liberal standpoint, "[P]articipation is more than a favorable condition of democracy. . . . [I]t is among democracy's most essential results, an end in itself."[3]

Despite its potential value, political participation also poses a challenge to Romanian democratic institutions. Majority rule, through mass mobilization, may erode the principles of liberal democracy by systematically excluding minority viewpoints. Though more than a decade has past since the revolution, Romanian democratic institutions remain fragile, and the potential for tyrannical majority rule is especially acute. Romania continues to face serious economic and social problems, and many individuals perceive policy choices in zero-sum terms. In Romania, as in many post-Communist societies, issues that directly affect the distribution of wealth, such as land reform or privatization, may produce high levels of political demands, which may overburden state institutions and threaten the democratic process.[4]

Volatile political issues are not limited to economic reforms in Romania. Cultural policies aimed at supporting tolerance and ethnic diversity have met with widespread resistance, as citizens respond to what is perceived as a loss for the Romanian majority.[5] Constitutional provisions for minority protection and participation have not been fully implemented, and "so far [have] led to confrontation."[6] The strong electoral showing of the Greater Romania Party in the 2000 national elections suggests that minority cultural rights remain a salient issue for Romanians. Therefore, political participation in and of itself is not enough to sustain liberal democratic institutions.

Alternatively, extremely low levels of political participation suggest that elite-driven interests dominate the political arena and may even begin to erode the democratic process.[7] In Romania, politics have been characterized as possessing a "sultanistic" legacy of personalistic rule.[8] Political participation holds the potential to counter hegemonic social interests and personalistic politics *if* that participation exhibits a broad, pluralistic character which reflects the diversity of interests within society.

Political participation shapes democratic relationships. It is a necessary condition for democracy, but interacts with factors that hold the potential to impede the democratic process. Within this context of changing political relationships, where political activity might assist or hinder democratization, we analyze six forms of participation: voting, electoral campaign activity, contacting media sources, signing petitions, contacting public officials, and joining legal protests. We use Romanian national survey data to answer two fundamental questions: (1) To what extent have Romanians engaged in varying modes of political participation? (2) What are the characteristics among those who participate in the different forms of political activity?

We address the first question through an assessment of Romanian aggregate levels of participation relative to the rates of participation in other political systems. Comparing levels of participation allows us to establish a cross-national range for activities and evaluate whether Romania is an exceptional case. Ceauşescu's attempts to negate Romanian civil society may very well make this a unique case. The national Stalinist legacy may continue to adversely affect political mobilization.[9] Our second question evaluates the attributes which the participants share. Although Romanian democratic institutions are open, we are interested in evaluating the extent to which individuals from advantaged social categories enjoy disproportionate access to the political process. Assessing the breadth of participation illuminates the challenges that Romanian democratic institutions face.

We find that, with the exception of voting, relatively few Romanians involve themselves in political activities. Those who are active demonstrate a higher level of political engagement across several categories. They tend to possess stronger party identification and discuss politics more often. The low general levels of participation appear to accent discrepancies across social categories such as an individual's level of education. Limited organized group activity within Romania contributes to the low aggregate levels of participation. Increased civil society activity would likely increase political participation across social categories.

ROMANIAN VOTER TURNOUT

Voting is perhaps the most fundamental form of political participation in a democratic regime. Along with selecting elective office holders, citizens signal preferences to representatives through elections. The process contributes to a public dialogue concerning political orientations and policies. Elections link individuals to the political system and lend legitimacy to the democratic process. Voting is a uniquely individual act which "requires little initiative or cooperation with others."[10] Although the specificity of the message conveyed through voting is weak, the act aggregates general political orientations and indirectly articulates policy stances. Although groups and associations do mobilize their members, voting is also weak in terms of the actual pressure that it places on public officials relative to other forms of participation such as protest activity.

Romania has held four national elections since its 1989 revolution. The first Romanian general election took place in 1990. The Romanian Central Electoral Bureau reported that 14,825,764 individuals voted of the 17,200,722 eligible voters in the 1990 election. The voter turnout is 86 percent, or even higher if we take into account the possible overestimation of the number of eligible voters[11] International and domestic observers questioned the validity of the 1990 election results due to the registration process and irregularities at the polls.[12]

The 1992 and 1996 general elections met with fewer electoral irregularities, though the lack of a formal voter registration process raises questions about these results.[13] The average voter turnout rate, as reported by the Romanian Central Electoral Bureau, approximates 72 percent for the 1992, 1996, and 2000 parliamentary elections, with the 2000 elections showing a decline to just over 65 percent of the eligible voters participating. The average voter turnout rate for legislative elections in Central-Eastern Europe is roughly 68 percent and just over 78 percent in Western European countries. Average voter turnout rates range from 48 percent in Poland, to over 84 percent in Uzbekistan, Albania, and the Czech Republic.[14]

Voter turnout rates say little about the functioning of democracy or overall patterns of mass political participation. Voter turnout varies among countries due to cultural and institutional differences.[15] However, extremely low turnout rates may signal a crisis of democracy if the democratic institutions offer few other outlets for political participation. Wide fluctuations in turnout rates within a particular country may point to unique and potentially dangerous political circumstances.

Although voting turnout within Romania appears to fall within an average range compared with other democracies, many eligible Romanian voters do not participate. This raises the question of whether individuals who abstain from voting share certain social characteristics. We evaluate Romanian voter turnout using 1996 postelection survey data and correlate individual attributes among voters. The survey asked respondents if they had voted in the second round of the 1996 presidential election.[16]

In Romania, five significant factors correlate with an individual saying that he or she had voted in the 1996 election: party identification, frequency of discussing politics, age, education, and union membership.[17] Table 8.1 shows the percentages among these factors and their relationship to voting behavior. Individuals who identify more strongly with a political party report voting at a rate above the sample average of 77 percent, and those with weak identification fall below the average.[18] Party identification reflects an individual's political engagement. Stronger identification indicates that an individual holds specific preferences concerning electoral outcomes and, presumably, the ideological or policy platform represented by a particular political party. Identification may also indicate that Romanian parties have been successful in eliciting loyalty from voters and linking them more closely to the political system. Thus, it is likely that strong party identification results from at least indirect exposure to the political recruitment efforts of parties. However, no one political party has monopolized strong identification, suggesting that party identification reflects competition of political style and ideas.[19]

The frequency with which individuals say they discuss politics is a second factor that correlates strongly in a linear relationship with voting.[20] Political discussion, like party identification, approximates an individual's general level of engagement with the political system. Overall, 45 percent of the respondents said they discuss politics sometimes or often, and these report having voted at a rate well above the national average. The figures do not comment on the quality of discussions, or the level of political information that individuals possess. However, the finding indicates that public deliberation over politics occurs within Romania, and voters are more likely to be those individuals who have entered into the discussion.

Table 8.1 also suggests that a respondent's age and level of education increase the probability of voting, although these factors appear to hold a curvilinear relationship with turning out to vote.[21] The effect of age came largely from the youngest category of respondents, who were between eighteen and thirty years old. Only 56 percent from this group respond affirmatively to the voting question, compared with over 80 percent in each of the other age categories. Slightly over 20 percent of our sample fell into the eighteen-to-thirty-year-old category. This effect of age is consistent with other studies, which show a positive correlation between age and voting.[22]

Table 8.1. Percentage of Voters According to Significant Factors

Party ID	*Very weak*	*Weak*	*Moderate*	*Strong*	*Very strong*
	70	65	75	85	88
Discuss politics	*Never*	*Rarely*	*Sometimes*	*Frequently*	
	70	75	79	89	
Age	18–30	31–40	41–50	51–60	>60
	56	84	84	84	81
Education	*Primary*	*Agricultural*	*Some HS*	*HS*	*University*
	77	79	75	75	86
	Union	Party	Group		
Member	89	93	86		
Nonmember	74	77	77		

An individual's level of education is positively related to voting in Romania, which is also consistent with studies of voting behavior in other countries.[23] In Romania, the impact of education on voting is limited to those who have pursued higher education. The figures in table 8.1 show that 86 percent of individuals with a university education report having voted. All other categories of education remain close to the sample average of 77 percent. Therefore, the voting preferences of those holding a university education tend to be slightly overrepresented through the electoral process.

Individuals with higher levels of education follow politics more closely, are more informed about issues, and discuss politics more often. Therefore, education interacts with political discussion as a factor associated with voter turnout. Individuals who have attended a university also may attach a stronger sense of civic duty, or political efficacy, to the act of voting, thus increasing their incentive to get to the polls.[24]

Voting does not require high levels of collective action among voters. Nevertheless, organized groups do serve as effective mobilizing agents for their members. In Romania, trade union membership positively correlates with voter turnout. According to table 8.1, union members tend to vote at a higher rate than nonunion members. This result speaks to the influence that such organizations hold over their members in terms of getting out the vote. An individual may be ambivalent toward election outcomes, but the organizations to which they belong are not. Therefore, it appears that unions hold the capacity to mobilize members.

The impact of group membership is not limited to unions. Individuals who belong to political parties or other organized groups, such as housing associations, civic groups, or environmental organizations, also tend to vote at higher rates than individuals who are not active in civil society. Table 8.1 shows that 93 percent of political party members report having voted. Of those individuals who belong to civil society groups other than unions and political parties, 86 percent responded affirmatively when asked if they had voted, though the numbers of participants are small and not statistically significant. These results are consistent with cross-national studies from Western Europe and the United

States, which show that communal activity does stimulate individuals to participate politically, including voting in higher numbers than nonactivists.[25]

The effect of group membership highlights the importance of civil society in articulating preferences through voting. The results in table 8.1 are insufficient to answer the question of whether members of a particular organization may or may not vote as a bloc for a specific candidate, political party, or political orientation. However, the results do indicate that individuals who are active within their communities vote at higher rates.

The absolute numbers of groups is small within Romania, which minimizes their effect on voting turnout. At the end of 1996, there were 11,781 registered nongovernmental organizations (NGOs) in Romania. "About four hundred NGOs are said to comprise the most active core group with nationwide influence, [but] considering the starting point of the associative sector, and the resources available to it, NGOs are on the right track."[26]

To summarize, Romanian voting turnout falls within the range of other European democratic states. Romanian voters tend to identify more strongly with a particular political party, and tend to discuss politics more often, than nonvoters. Individuals under thirty years old tend to vote less than other Romanians, and those who have attended a university vote in rates above the national average. Finally, Romanians who are active within civil society, especially union members, have an increased tendency to vote. However, civil society is weak in terms of the number of groups actively in existence. Therefore, group membership has a relatively small impact on aggregate voting rates.

If we assume that a voting public is a healthy sign of democracy, the picture appears to be positive. Relatively high turnout rates indicate not only an interested public, but also the mobilization capacity of political parties and other groups.[27] Although several social categories, such as age and education, point to a discrepancy in the probability of casting a vote, these differences are consistent with voting behavior in many countries. When we step back for a moment and consider the oppression that Romania suffered under Ceauşescu, the demonstrable change in political relations since 1989, as seen through voting, is impressive.

OTHER FORMS OF POLITICAL PARTICIPATION

Voting is only one form of political participation. Citizens have a wide array of choices beyond voting which can convey their political preferences to elected and appointed officials. We first view Romanian participation comparatively. Using European Values Survey data, table 8.2 presents the frequency with which individuals have engaged. Political activity benefits from social mobilization agents within civil society. Although variance exists, each country began its post-Communist period with limited civil society development. Comparing aggregate participation brings perspective to the levels of political activity in Romania.

The levels of activity for signing petitions, joining boycotts, and participating in unofficial strikes in Romania are lower relative to the average for post-Communist states. For attending lawful demonstrations and occupying buildings, Romania meets the average for other countries in Central and Eastern Europe.

The relative aggregate levels of political activity in Romania are low, but difficult to fully interpret. It is possible that lower levels of participation in activities other than voting indicate that Romanians have had less to contest and are relatively content with the political system. Romanian data from 1996 do not suggest that Romanians are content with democracy or the economy.[28]

Another possible explanation for the relatively low levels of Romanian aggregate participation may be related to the events surrounding the fall of Communism among the various cases. For example, the Czechoslovakian transition relied on a relatively peaceful transfer of power and culminated in the negotiated division of the country into the Czech and Slovak Republics. The process afforded many more opportunities for participation. The breakup of the Soviet Union involved a quite different set of opportunities for citizens to participate.

Activities such as signing petitions or joining a legal demonstration do articulate a more precise message of preferences to political leaders. The question of who participates in these ways takes on greater importance because low levels of participation open the possibility that elite-driven interests may dominate political discourse and interest aggregation, and ultimately begin to undermine the democratic process.

Table 8.2. Frequencies of Participation beyond Voting in Percentages

	Signing a Petition	*Joining Boycotts*	*Attending Lawful Demonstrations*	*Joining Unofficial Strikes*	*Occupying Buildings*
Western Europe	56	13	29	7	5
Eastern Europe	**25**	**5**	**15**	**3**	**1**
Belarus	9	4	16	1	1
Bulgaria	12	4	17	5	2
Croatia	37	8	8	3	1
Czech Rep.	58	9	28	10	1
Estonia	21	3	11	1	0
Hungary	16	3	5	1	1
Latvia	19	4	25	1	0
Lithuania	31	5	14	2	1
Poland	21	4	9	5	3
Romania	**11**	**2**	**15**	1	1
Russia	12	3	24	2	1
Slovakia	60	4	14	2	1
Slovenia	32	8	10	4	2
Ukraine	14	5	18	3	1

Data Source: European Values Survey, 1999.

To assess this question of who in Romania participates in political activities other than voting, we consider five forms of participation derived from the 1996 national survey. These are electoral campaign activity, contacting media sources, signing petitions, contacting public officials, and joining legal protests. Each activity varies according to the amount of resources required, the level of specificity of the message it conveys, and the pressure it generates for officials to respond.[29] For instance, signing a petition requires fewer resources than working on a political campaign. Each activity is more effective through group mobilization, which increases the volume expressed to officials. Compared with voting, each activity requires more resources, produces a clearer message to political leaders, and potentially produces more pressure for leaders to respond.

Estimating profiles of active individuals allows us to assess whether they represent particular social categories that may not reflect broader citizen opinion. For each mode of political participation, only three factors—party identification (excepting contacting officials), political discussion (excepting contacting media sources), and type of locality (urban or rural)—produce statistically significant results for each form of political activity.[30]

In Romania, a respondent's party identification correlates positively with each form of activity except for contacting officials. Party identification approximates the extent to which a respondent is politically engaged. It also suggests that political activists articulate their preferences within the political party system. It is not unexpected that individuals who identify more closely with political parties are also more likely to engage in forms of political activity beyond voting. This result is especially true for campaign work.

Another common characteristic among political activists is that they discuss politics more frequently than other Romanians. Similar to identification, this reflects an individual's engagement in politics, or enthusiasm for political issues. The finding also suggests that despite the low aggregate levels of political participation, public deliberation surrounds political activity in Romania.

Type of locality, either urban or rural, is a significant indicator for each of the five forms of political participation. However, rural residents engage in different forms of activities than urban residents.[31] Rural residents are more likely to work on electoral campaigns and contact public officials than urban residents. Eight percent of rural residents reported having worked on a political campaign compared with less than five percent of urban dwellers. For contacting public officials, 28 percent of rural respondents reported having done so, compared with the national average of 20.7 percent.

Urban residents contact media sources, sign petitions, and join legal protest at a rate above the national average. For contacting media sources, 18 percent of urban dwellers responded positively to having engaged in this activity. Fifteen percent of urban residents reported having signed a petition, and 30 percent acknowledge that they have joined a legal protest since 1990. Therefore, certain forms of activity are associated with a respondent's locality type. This is an important difference since, according to the Romanian 1991 census, approximately 45 percent of Romanians live within rural communities.

Individual motives for participation are complex. Choosing to participate varies according to the resources available to an individual, to attitudes or disposition, and to the exposure an individual has to the political recruitment efforts of mobilization agents. In other words, individuals participate because they can, because they want to, or because they are asked.[32] We can utilize this framework to understand why forms of political participation vary along an urban–rural dimension.

Individuals need different combinations of resources, such as time, skills, and money to engage in each activity. Although individuals may hold more of these resources within urban communities, the logistic regression model does not produce any systematic variance among urban and rural forms of participation, along other factors representing resources, such as education. While levels of education tend to be higher among urban residents, locality type still produces an independent effect when we control for education. Therefore, there is little reason to believe that resources in this sense are the primary factors surrounding the urban–rural difference.

The level of political engagement may produce a more fruitful explanation. Although this term is difficult to define, it generally refers to the amount of enthusiasm an individual has for politics. Political engagement reflects deeper attitudes that an individual holds toward politics and, consequently, shapes political behavior and the decision to act.[33] In Romania, there is reason to believe that individuals in rural communities continue to "emphasize a politics based on the primacy of the household and family" and a subordination of their interests to the state.[34] Therefore, locality type may shape attitudes differently and account for why certain political acts tend to be associated with one type of locality or another. Political engagement also reflects how connected individuals are with the political system. It may be that rural dwellers are less connected than urban dwellers, due to their distance from centers of political power. In the still highly centralized Romanian political system, this is not an unreasonable inference.

We might also account for the variance between urban and rural forms of political participation through political recruitment. Contacting media sources, signing petitions, and joining legal protests are all modes of participation that are maximized through collective action and civil society activity. Active civic groups or trade unions increase the opportunities that individuals have to engage in these activities.[35] Each activity requires an organizational structure that is subject to economies of scale. In other words, as civil society develops, organizations will likely concentrate efforts where they can reach the most people at the lowest cost. Civil society development in Romania is low, especially in rural areas.[36] Therefore, we might explain the variance among participatory activities, in part, through the higher number of opportunities available to urban dwellers for certain activities, such as contacting the media, signing petitions, and protesting.

Limited opportunity for rural residents to participate explains, to a certain extent, why such activities as contacting the media, petitioning, and protesting are more likely to occur within urban areas. However, it does not explain why rural dwellers tend to engage in campaign work and contacting public officials at higher rates than urban residents. In part, the explanation rests with the relative incentives afforded to rural residents for these types of activities.

Political party organizations depend upon their membership to form their bases of campaign workers. According to the data, 65 percent of party members live in urban areas. However, a greater proportion of campaign workers live in rural communities, and party members in rural areas are more likely than their urban counterparts to work on campaigns. Therefore, party membership in rural communities tends to have a larger impact on the propensity to campaign.

The resources available to party organizations may account for the propensity of rural inhabitants to engage in campaign work. Party financial resources are especially important for campaigns in Romania, in offering campaign workers incentives to participate. Political party activists from Cluj-Napoca, in informal interviews, note that it is not uncommon for Romanian parties to pay their campaign workers, even party members, rather than rely on volunteer support. The prospect of employment after a successful campaign may motivate some workers, and it is possible that Romanian political parties rely on this form of political patronage to a certain extent. Although further research is needed, if campaign work does supplement income, it may be more common in rural communities where economic opportunities are more limited.

The parties that are active in rural communities might also account for some of the variance in campaign participation. The development of new political parties has followed a similar pattern to that of other elements of civil society in Romania, with activists focusing their attention on urban areas. However, the Communist legacy in Romania, like elsewhere in post-Communist Europe, left a highly developed infrastructure of political organization that penetrated rural communities under the Communist regime. Relatively speaking, this organizational infrastructure remains more intact in rural areas compared to urban areas due to the lower levels of party competition in the countryside. Former Communist operators control rural political party organizations, though many organizations have changed political banners to include nationalist and liberal variants.[37] Nevertheless, political party organizations face less competition within rural communities than that experienced in urban areas. With fewer opportunities to participate in other ways, political parties play a greater role in the political life of rural residents. Due to fewer, social mobilizing agents other than parties, it is not surprising that rural individuals are more likely to participate in campaign work than urban dwellers.

It is more difficult to explain why rural residents tend to contact public officials more often than urban residents. It may be that the size of a community matters. Individuals within small communities are more likely to know local officials on a personal level, and therefore they would be more likely to approach an official with a problem. The types of problems that rural residents confront also may influence the likelihood of contacting a local official.

It is also reasonable to assume that with fewer alternative avenues to address problems, individuals within rural communities would be more likely to approach local sources of political authority. Finally, it is probable that political party members are more likely to engage in contacting officials, even though they may not involve themselves in campaign activity. This would hold despite relative levels of education or income. Alan Zuckerman and Darrell West argue that political party membership provides access to a social network of contacts. If other political mobilizing agents are absent within the community, social contacting might be the most efficient method for individuals to articulate political needs and preferences. In such situations, the political context may facilitate political patronage and unequal access to political institutions.[38]

Turning to other individual attributes that significantly correlate with forms of political participation beyond voting, we find a mix of effects. For instance, 18 percent of respondents aged 18–30 report having contacted the media. This number decreases with each increase in age bracket. Twenty-two percent of the respondents, ages 18–30, have joined a legal protest, while only 10 percent of all others in the sample respond affirmatively.

Table 8.3 shows that most group activity is strongly associated with political participation. The two exceptions to this tendency both involve union membership. Union members tend not to work on electoral campaigns or contact public officials at a higher level than the national average. These two exceptions also involve the two activities that correspond more closely to rural residency. It is not surprising that union membership does not have an impact on these activities since union members tend to be clustered in urban, industrial areas.

The results in table 8.3 indicate that civil society activity is correlated with higher rates of political participation. Individuals who belong to any association

Table 8.3. Percent of Respondents Who Have Participated in Civil Society Membership

	Campaign	*Media*	*Petition*	*Contact*	*Protest*
Union	8 (17)	21 (46)	19 (42)	20 (37)	30 (66)
Party	28 (19)	23 (16)	22 (15)	45 (29)	25 (17)
Group	25 (15)	33 (20)	30 (18)	43 (26)	33 (20)
Average	6.3	13.0	10.9	20.7	14.8

Note: Data are from the 1996 National Survey. Figures in parentheses are the absolute number of respondents who reported having engaged in the political act.

report that they have engaged in most participatory activities at a rate considerably higher than the national average. Collective action within groups lowers the costs of participation. Therefore, group members articulate their preferences more often through vehicles that lend themselves to conveying specific messages to political leaders. However, table 8.3 also shows that the absolute number of association members is very low, reflecting the general weakness of civil society in Romania.

Overall, aggregate levels of participation beyond voting are low. Differences suggest that disparities extend to viewpoints articulated within the Romanian political dialogue and, perhaps, how government leaders respond to political preferences. The clearest discrepancy occurs between rural and urban residents, and manifests itself through the tendency for rural and urban dwellers to engage in different forms of participation. On one hand, it is encouraging that individuals participate in ways that are readily available to them. On the other hand, the result indicates a bias in the means through which the Romanian national political dialogue transpires. Although there are several explanations for the difference between urban and rural residents, the most compelling is the varying distribution of social mobilization agents or, more generally, the strength of civil society.

Union members tend to engage more often in activities associated with urban settings. Despite the high visibility unions have achieved in Romanian politics through protest activities, the result indicates that union members are underrepresented in campaign work and contacting officials. In other words, they do not utilize these vehicles to articulate their preferences. However, unions are subject to certain economies of scale and gravitate toward larger economic enterprises. Although union membership may include substantial numbers of rural commuters, unions seek advantages through urban forms of participation. Therefore, it is difficult to say whether union members are systematically excluded from political debates.

Other discrepancies among participants include party identification and, to a lesser extent, education, reflecting differences in political engagement and available resources. However, these findings are not inconsistent with patterns found cross-nationally. In other words, we might expect such disparities to exist and to continue.

CONCLUSION

Democracy allows individuals to constrain political power through institutions. The extent of this constraint depends, in part, upon an active public that communicates preferences to elected and appointed officials. Individuals signal preferences to political leaders through political participation, which in turn applies pressure on public officials to respond. In this way, institutions that encourage participation broaden the range of individual viewpoints that enter into the political dialogue of a country. The process creates a more dynamic and open political environment, while also lending legitimacy to the political system. As long as the system can absorb the multiple demands placed upon it, democratic institutions facilitate the process of open political expression.

With the exception of voting, aggregate levels of Romanian political participation tend to be low, and participation rates reflect discrepancies across corresponding social categories. See the multivariate regression results in table 8.4 in the appendix. Certain disparities among available individual resources, such as age and education, are present within all democracies. In Romania, discrepancies extend especially to locality type and group membership. Citizens realize democratic representation partly by articulating political preferences through participation. Assuming that social categories do indicate different preferences, the pattern of participation in Romania suggests that not all viewpoints are voiced equally, a pattern not dissimilar to many democracies.

On another level, low levels of political activism mean that citizens are not in as good of a position to hold state officials accountable and to constrain actions taken by the state. This possibility endangers democracy. Low public interest and participation may result in an increased level of political corruption. Thus, forms of mass participation slowly become less and less effective as public officials become more and more insulated over time.

To a certain extent, strengthening civil society will overcome these discrepancies, especially in rural areas, and constrain public officials. Group activity lowers the costs of participation, refines the message sent to leaders, and increases the volume, and the pressure, of the message. Therefore, strengthening civil society in Romania seems vital to deepening and sustaining democracy.

NOTES

1. Geraint Parry and George Moyser, "More Participation, More Democracy?" in David Beetham, ed., *Defining and Measuring Democracy* (Thousand Oaks, CA: Sage, 1994).

2. John Stuart Mill, *On Liberty* (New York: The Liberal Arts Press, 1956), p. 71.

3. Dietrich Rueschemeyer, Marilyn Rueschemeyer, and Bjorn Wittrock, *Participation and Democracy, East and West: Comparisons and Interpretations* (Armonk, NY: M. E. Sharpe, 1998), p. 6.

4. Adam Przeworski, *Democracy and the Market* (New York: Cambridge University Press, 1991), pp. 159–61.

5. Petru Iluţ, "Rationality and Democracy in Post-Communist Societies: The Romanian Case," in *Studia: Sociologia-Politologia*, 1–2 (Cluj-Napoca: Babeş-Bolyai University Press, 1991), p. 4.

6. Maria Amor Estebanez, "Inter-Ethnic Relations and the Protection of Minorities," in International Institute for Democracy and Electoral Assistance (IDEA), *Democracy in Romania: Assessment Mission Report* (Stockholm: IDEA, 1997), p. 126.

7. Rueschemeyer, Rueschemeyer and Wittrock, *Participation and Democracy*, p. 5.

8. H. E. Chehabi and Juan Linz, "A Theory of Sultanism: A Type of Nondemocratic Rule," in H. E. Chehabi and Juan Linz (eds.), *Sultanistic Regimes* (Baltimore and London: The Johns Hopkins University Press, 1998), p. 20.

9. Tom Gallagher, *Romania after Ceauşescu: The Politics of Intolerance*, (Edinburgh: Edinburgh University Press, 1995), p. 238. See also Daniel N. Nelson, "A Chance for Romania," in Daniel N. Nelson, ed., *Romania after Tyranny*, (Boulder, San Francisco, and Oxford: Westview Press, 1992), pp. 286–87.

10. Russell J. Dalton, *Citizen Politics in Western Democracies*, 2nd ed. (Chatham, NJ: Chatham House Publishers, 1988), p. 36.

11. The 1992 Census found only 16,415,313 people who were 18 or higher, with about 800,000 less than the 1990 estimate for the 18 or more population. Emigration between 1990 and 1992 could also account for a part of difference.

12. International Republican Institute (IRI) and National Democratic Institute for International Affairs (NDIIA), *The May 1990 Elections in Romania* (Washington, DC: IRI/NDIIA Publications, 1990), pp. 59–60.

13. In 1992, there were an inordinate amount of invalidated votes and high numbers of "special list" votes in some counties and precincts indicating systematic fraud. See Henry F. Carey, "Irregularities or Rigging: Romania's 1992 Parliamentary Elections," *East European Quarterly*, vol. 29, no. 1 (Spring 1995), pp. 43–66. Voter registration and the lack of voting cards were a problem in both the 1992 and 1996 elections. See Svante Renstrom, "Electoral Systems and Electoral Organization," in International Institute for Democracy and Electoral Assistance (IDEA), *Democracy in Romania: Assessment Mission Report* (Stockholm: IDEA, 1997), p. 152.

14. International Institute for Democracy and Electoral Assistance (IDEA), *Voter Turnout from 1945-1997: A Global Report on Political Participation* (Stockholm: International IDEA, 1997), pp. 18–21.

15. Dalton, *Citizen Politics in Western Democracies*, pp. 43–46. See also Gary Cox, *Making Votes Count: Strategic Coordination in the World's Electoral Systems* (Cambridge: Cambridge University Press, 1997).

16. The national survey was conducted two weeks after the 1996 Romanian general election. It was generously funded through the Social Science Curriculum Development Program, administered by IREX, and supported by the U.S. Department of State, Bureau of Educational and Cultural Affairs, formerly USIA. The data are available at www.umich.edu/~cses/.

17. The appendix table provides the results from logistic regression.

18. We measure party identification as a five-category scale from weak to strong.

19. The survey also asked respondents to state their support for the major political parties in Romania. Correlations between each party and party identification are low, indicating that no one party monopolizes support among those who report strong identification with a particular party.

20. The survey asked respondents how often they discuss politics: never, rarely, sometimes, or often.

21. We categorize both age and education into five categories.

22. Research in Western Europe supports the conclusion that younger individuals (those roughly in their twenties) tend to vote less often than individuals in other age categories. For example see, Russell J. Dalton, *Citizen Politics in Western Democra-*

cies, 2nd ed. (Chatham, NJ: Chatham House Publishers, 1988), pp. 48–54. See also Herbert Kitschelt, Dimitar Dimitrov, and Assen Kanev, "The Structuring of the Vote in Post-Communist Party Systems: The Bulgarian Example," *European Journal of Political Research*, vol. 27, no. 2 (February 1995), p. 148.

23. Dalton, *Citizen Politics in Western Democracies*, p. 57.

24. Gabriel A. Almond and Sidney Verba, *The Civic Culture: Political Attitudes and Democracy in Five Nations* (Boston: Little, Brown and Company, 1963), p. 133.

25. Hanspeter Kriesi, "Support and Mobilization Potential for New Social Movements: Concepts, Operationalizations and Illustrations from the Netherlands," in Mario Dani and Ron Eyerman, eds., *Studying Collective Action*, (Beverly Hills, CA: Sage, 1992).

26. Christine M. Merkel, "The Development of Civil Society," in The Institute for Democracy and Electoral Assistance (IDEA), *Democracy in Romania: Assessment Mission Report* (Stockholm: International IDEA, 1997), pp. 88–89.

27. Steven J. Rosenstone and John Mark Hansen, *Mobilization, Participation and Democracy in America* (London: Macmillan, 1993), pp. 9–12.

28. According to 1996 Romanian survey, 44 percent of the respondents described themselves as "satisfied with the way democracy works in Romania," and 13 percent felt that the "economy had become better over the last 12 months."

29. Sidney Verba, Kay Lehman Schlozman, and Henry E. Brady, *Voice and Equality: Civic Voluntarism in American Politics* (Cambridge and London: Harvard University Press), pp. 270–71.

30. See appendix.

31. The sign of the urban/rural variable for each activity's coefficient *b* in the appendix table shows the impact of locality type. We coded rural areas as zero and urban areas as one. Therefore, a negative coefficient *b* indicates a higher rate of activity among rural residents.

32. Verba, Schlozman, and Brady, *Voice and Equality*, p. 269.

33. Samuel H. Barnes and Max Kaase, *Political Action: Mass Participation in Five Democracies* (Beverly Hills, CA: Sage, 1979), pp. 61–65.

34. David A. Kideckel, "Peasants and Authority in the New Romania," in Daniel N. Nelson, ed., *Romania after Tyranny* (Boulder, San Francisco, and Oxford: Westview Press, 1992), p. 68.

35. Max Kaase, "Mass Participation," in M. Kent Jennngs, Jan W. van Deth, Samuel H. Barnes, Dieter Fuchs, Felix J. Heunks, Ronald Ingelhart, and Jacques J. A. Thomassen, eds., *Continuities in Political Action: A Longitudinal Study of Political Orientations in Three Western Democracies* (New York: Gruyter, 1990), p. 57.

36. See, David A. Kideckel, "Peasants and Authority in the New Romania," in Daniel N. Nelson (ed.), *Romania after Tyranny*, (Boulder, San Francisco, and Oxford: Westview Press, 1992), pp. 67–81.

37. Kideckel observes that Romanian parties supporting reform have been "largely absent in the villages." David A. Kideckel, "Peasants and Authority in the New Romania," in Daniel N. Nelson, ed., *Romania after Tyranny* (Boulder, San Francisco and Oxford: Westview Press, 1992), p. 76. However, there is no evidence in our data that suggests that a single party dominates others in terms of rural support.

38. Alan S. Zuckerman and Darrell M. West, "The Political Bases of Citizen Contacting: A Cross-National Analysis," *American Political Science Review*, vol. 79, no. 1 (March 1985), pp. 117–31.

Table 8.4. Logistic Regression Model of Romanian Participation

	Vote	*Campaign*	*Media*	*Petition*	*Contact*	*Protest*
Party ID	.14	.30	.17	.22	.06	.18
	1.15	1.34	1.19	1.24	1.06	1.19
	(.07)*	(.13)**	(.08)*	(.09)*	(.07)	(.08)*
Discuss Politics	.32	.86	.14	.27	.41	.39
	1.14	2.37	1.15	1.31	1.50	1.47
	(.11)**	(.19)**	(.12)	(.13)*	(.10)**	(.12)**
Age	.36	.01	−.15	−.09	.06	−.28
	1.44	1.01	.86	.91	1.06	.75
	(.06)**	(.09)	(.06)*	(.07)	(.05)	(.06)**
Education	.26	.16	.15	.29	.21	−.02
	1.30	1.17	1.67	1.33	1.24	.98
	(.16)*	(.20)	(.14)	(.15)*	(.15)	(.14)
Income	−.01	−.10	.17	.05	.02	.13
	.99	.91	1.18	1.05	1.02	1.15
	(.09)	(.13)	(.09)	(.10)	(.08)	(.09)
Gender	−.31	−.51	−.36	.35	−.36	−.34
	.73	.60	.72	1.42	.70	.70
	(.20)	(.32)	(.22)	(.23)	(.18)*	(.21)
Locality	−.23	−1.18	.53	.56	−.89	1.00
	.80	.31	1.70	1.75	.41	2.72
	(.22)	(.34)**	(.26)*	(.28)*	(.20)**	(.25)**
Union	1.04	.04	.33	.35	.04	.52
	2.84	1.03	1.39	1.42	1.04	1.69
	(.29)*8	(.37)	(.23)	(.25)	(.22)	(.22)*
Party	.52	1.08	.12	.09	.49	−.23
	1.68	2.96	1.12	1.09	1.63	.79
	(.51)	(.39)**	(.35)	(.37)	(.33)	(.35)
Groups	.78	1.05	.60	.89	.34	.25
	2.19	2.86	1.82	2.43	1.41	1.28
	(.56)	(.49)**	(.34)	(.35)*	(.51)	(.35)
χ^2	93.65	89.49	62.00	63.92	67.43	113.54
Pseudo R^2	.13	.22	.10	.11	.08	.16
N	735	758	758	753	736	760

* = $p < .05$; ** = $p < .01$

Note: The first number represents coefficient *b*; the second number stands for exp *(b)*; standard errors of *b* are given in parentheses. *Exp(b)* reflects the multiplicative impact on the odds ratio of, for instance, participation (the probability of voting divided by the probability of not voting) for every unit increase in the variable that corresponds to *b* when all other variables are constant. See Alan Agresti, *Categorical Data Analysis* (New York: Wiley-Interscience, 1990).

9

Media in the First Post-Communist Decade

Peter Gross

In the aftermath of Communism's demise, Western media scholars, political scientists, politicians, and pundits assumed that independent, professional media were necessary to help establish democracy in the newly liberated nations. Unfortunately, such media are largely an epiphenomenon of a well-entrenched democratic society and, therefore, are difficult to establish in a transitional society in order to further its transition to democracy. However, the media may still aid the democratization process, unwittingly, indirectly, and in a manner not easily measurable. The Romanian case is one example.

In the first two months following the collapse of Communism, the Romanian media became an experiment in public access media and an avenue of individual and national catharsis.[1] Within three to four years, these media disappeared, giving way to ones that were highly partisan and political, basically divided between newspapers supporting the Iliescu regime and those opposing it, and by the late 1990s to a media-party parallelism.[2] Radio broadcasting, dominated by national Romanian Radio, was quickly faced with competition, particularly on the local and regional level. On the other hand, Romanian Television (RTV) was closely controlled by the president's office and the governments in power from 1989 to 1996; it had no serious domestic competition on the national level until Pro-TV, a joint American-Romanian venture, began to provide it at the end of 1997.

In the simplest formulation, Romanian journalism in the 1989–1996 period was a mixture of polemics, rumor, and half-accurate, incomplete, and biased information.[3] It was a highly politicized and partisan journalism, and the few attempts at neutrality failed. In short, Romanian journalism began its post-Communist era in an amateur state, and by 1996 it had become, at best, pre-professional, a pattern discernible in the majority of post-1989 East European nations.[4]

The yet-to-be completed evolution to a democracy-serving, professional media leaves unclarified the "inestimable" role of the media in the "vast 'Democracy 101' course" in which Eastern Europe is "collectively enrolled."[5] Indirectly and unwittingly, Romanian media are making contributions to the remaking of Romanian politics, political culture, and socioeconomic life; their role, however, is not necessarily central to it. This chapter[6] analyzes the contributions made by the media to the democratic transition in Romania during 1996–2000 and briefly outlines the evolution of Romanian media since November 1996 when the "opposition," led by Emil Constantinescu and the Democratic Convention (CD), ascended to power. In 2000, both were given the boot and Ion Iliescu was returned to the presidency, and the Social Democratic Party (PSD) took the helm of government.

After November 1996, there were four expectations regarding the media:

1. That government/state control over national public television (TVR1) would be lifted—TVR had been manipulated during the Iliescu regime and was guilty of three sins: (a) disinformation and misinformation, (b) discrete manipulation (by the first three post-Communist governments and by the President's office), and (c) a "triumphalist and anesthetic" effect upon its audience.[7]
2. That the 1996 version of the Romanian Penal Code would be reconsidered—it addresses defamation and insults, and provides harsh prison terms for journalists found guilty under the Code, as well as uncalled-for protection for public officials.[8] It was also expected that laws would be enacted guaranteeing access to information and protection for journalists.
3. That media roles would be redefined—a change that would encompass a redefinition of the profession along Western lines, with a consonant and enforceable set of professional standards and code of ethics.
4. That an independent national television station or stations would be introduced to provide competition for RTV, and to provide needed diversity and pluralism in national television broadcasting.

Unfortunately for the media, the Constantinescu/CD era turned out to be a disappointment. It called into question the nature of democratization envisioned by the new leadership and, specifically, its commitment to the establishment of a democratic political culture, a professional working environment for journalists, and a legal foundation that would foster professionalism and freedom for an independent media.

The media showed limited interest in professionalism during the four-year Constantinescu/CD regime, and, for the most part, they mirrored Romanian society, politics, and culture. At a time when a tutorial function in regard to democratization was required, and when media were needed as models in and of themselves, as well as purveyors of unadulterated, accurate, complete, and verifiable information, they largely remained prisoners of old, undemocratic, and even antidemocratic mentalities, and they continued to be expertly manipulated in the interests of owners, directors, editors, and the political and economic elites.

PUBLIC TELEVISION

The major problems that have plagued TVR[9] since its liberation from Communist Party control in December 1989 persisted after 1996. The new TVR leadership appointed after November 1996 was accused of being as self-absorbed, self-serving, politically partisan, and open to manipulation as its predecessor.[10] TVR insiders[11] reported that Stere Gulea, the new post-1996 head of TVR, and Alina Mungiu-Pippidi, the head of the news department, were still directly connected by special telephone to the presidential palace as well as to the prime minister's office. Whether TVR remained co-opted by the President or the prime minister's office is difficult to prove with any degree of certainty. However, there were strong signs indicating that the relationship between TVR's leadership, Controceni (the presidential offices) and *Palatul Victoria* (the Prime Minister's office), continued to be the same as it was during the 1990–96 Iliescu regime.

A scandal in January 1998 reinforced this suspicion. A regularly scheduled program was interrupted in order to broadcast a live press conference from the National Christian Democratic Peasant Party (PNŢCD)—one of the main parties in the CD—in the midst of a political battle between it and its coalition partner, the Democratic Party (PD). The president of the European Christian Democrats, Wim van Welzen, a guest of the PNŢCD, was given the opportunity to comment on Romania's political crisis in a way that made the Democratic Party, in particular, look bad. Whether it really was a case of political manipulation on the part of TVR cannot be ascertained. It did, however, lead to a public uproar among politicians, political parties, and the media. An editorial in the largest circulation national daily, *Adevărul,*[12] concluded that the incident "was more proof that dictatorship and manipulation are at home in the offices of *Palatul Victoria.* The fury in the TVR leadership's communiqués and in Mr. Stere Gulea's declarations attest to the fact that television is under pressure and blackmail."

By fall 1998, TVR again had a new director, Cristian Hadjiculea, as did the news department.[13] The new leadership began its tenure similarly to the old—controversially. Gabriel Liiceanu, a member of the new Administrative Council, fired the first salvo in the new battle surrounding TVR, when he affirmed that "normality cannot make its debut (at TVR) . . . with the inclusion in the Administrative Council of some people like Alexandru Mironov."[14] Mironov was accused of having collaborated with the dreaded *Securitate*, and during the first Iliescu regime he called for Liiceanu and Corneliu Coposu[15] to be dragged into court for supporting the anti-Communist demonstration in *Piata Universitaţii.*

The strong suspicion that TVR's News Department was under the control of outside powers continued to be fueled. The firing of anchor Gabriela Vranceanu-Firea for allegedly being too neutral (as opposed to biased in favor of those holding political power) brought out accusations of political bias on the part of TVR and infringements of press freedom in fall 1999.[16] Such incidents, if we are to believe the allegations, suggest that even if TVR's leadership had a cozy working relationship with the powers that be, others in the institution did not.

Close political ties between TVR journalists and political parties were legion before and after 1996. Former news director Alina Mungiu-Pippidi was a prominent "opposition" journalist who was "rewarded," so the story goes, with the top job in the TVR news department in 1997. TVR's Răzvan Popescu, the man who allegedly interrupted the regularly scheduled program to air the above-mentioned PNŢCD news conference, was subsequently appointed to head the Public Information Department of the Romanian government (controlled by the PNŢCD). Ion Vaciu, the former deputy of the TVR Union, became a personal advisor to Adrian Năstase, a high official of the Romanian Social Democratic Party (PSDR in Romanian).

Aggravating what was already a compromised independence was the fact that TVR's financial situation was precarious at best. State funds were insufficient to sustain its operations and while advertising revenues steadily increased throughout the 1990s, they were still insufficient. One example of revenue shortages: Beginning in June 1999, both Romanian Radio and Romanian Television broadcasts were cut by four hours each day because they had amassed a debt of 19 billion lei (over $2.1 million) to the Society of Radio-Communications.[17] Since the mid-1990s, TVR has been in a losing battle with private television channels, the most successful one being Pro-TV, a joint Romanian-American venture in 1999,[18] which reached 68 percent of the Romanian viewing audience by the end of 1997, around 90 percent by 1999. Other quasi-national television companies in the competitive mixture of private television stations included *Antena1*, *Amerom*, and *Tele7abc*. Local, regional, and even national stations continued to be added to the lineup of the seventy-five television stations that were operational by the end of 1997.[19] Pro-TV produced some slick, American-style news broadcasts that raised standards in the medium, but still fell short of professional journalism. Pro-TV slowly became first in audience ratings in the late 1990s.

Last, but not least, the problematic 1994 law[20] regulating the status of public television was not reconsidered during 1996–2000. Other broadcast laws, however, were changed and brought the Romanian television and radio fields closer to complying with European Union Standards.[21] TVR's journalism remained professionally tenuous, driven by political and personal decisions made by its leadership. A new code of ethics introduced in 1998 could have helped to push its journalism in a more professional direction, but there was little interest and wherewithal to enforce it. Its ambiguous wording did not help; for instance, the new code forbade any "exhibition" of the journalists' political orientation.[22]

THE MEDIA'S LEGAL ENVIRONMENT

The 1996 amendments to the Penal Code,[23] which called for prison sentences for journalists found guilty of defamation and insulting individuals,[24] elicited criticism from Romania's then opposition politicians and journalists, as well as foreign organizations such as the Helsinki Watch and the Paris-based *Reporters Sans Frontiers.*

The criticism by opposition parties and politicians suggested that they would seek to quickly reconsider and rewrite the offending amendments once they were at the helm of the country. No move in that direction was discernible by mid-1999, however, and, in fact, developments in 1997 and 1998 provided a confusing smorgasbord of intentions on the part of the new leaders. First, in September 1997 the new post-Iliescu Minister of Justice, Valeriu Stoica, said that sentencing journalists to prison was not a just punishment, and promised to have prison sentences replaced with community service and additional fines.[25] Four months later, he reiterated his views, adding another alternative penalty: that of prohibiting the convicted journalists from practicing his or her profession.

Then, on 22 January 1998, Stoica proposed an ordinance that would have made it even easier to drag the media into court under the existing definitions of damage to "honor and dignity," and gave the impression that high monetary penalties would be mandatory. The uproar from Romania's media was instantaneous. Ironically, the parties formerly in power, and responsible for the passage of the antimedia Penal Code amendments, also raised a ruckus. On 2 February, Prime Minister Ciorbea stepped in and rescinded the ordinance. Ursu[26] writes that the Stoica ordinance eloquently spoke to the manner in which the "new Power" understands how to treat the "democratic right of freedom of expression."

Journalists continued to be dragged into court, found guilty, and condemned to prison terms and/or penalized with exorbitantly high fines, as illustrated by four cases in 1997–99:

1. In December 1997, Marius Avram, the editor of Cluj's *Stirea*, and a correspondent for Radio Free Europe in Prague, was convicted of defaming the city's mayor, Gheorghe Funar, in one of his editorials. He was fined 6 million lei (approximately $750, roughly the equivalent of 7 months salary).

2. A *România Liberă* reporter, Ada Ştefan, who wrote on a corruption case involving a judge, was found guilty of defamation. At one point in the case's journey through the Romanian court system, a judge who happened to be a close relative of the person who sued Ştefan presided over the trial.
3. Two journalists from Iaşi's *Monitorul*, Ovidiu Scutelnicu and Dragos Stangu, were each sentenced to a one-year prison term and a 100 million lei fine ($8,900) in 1999 for "slandering" a police colonel. The sentence was suspended, but the journalists were put on probation for three years.
4. Also in 1999, Cornel Şabau, editor-in-chief of the private news agency Trans-Press, was sentenced to ten months in prison for libeling a judge. President Emil Constantinescu pardoned him.

The Center for Independent Journalism reported[27] that legal actions taken against journalists were common in 1996–2000, particularly in the countryside, mostly inspired or brought by local authorities. The cases often dragged out for years, and the lack of an independent judiciary only aggravated a situation in which bad laws were applied. There is an additional, potential explanation for some actions taken by the courts: their ineptness in the face of the demands made upon them by a new, slowly democratizing society, one which requires a new type of judiciary, legal thinking, and professional ethic. In broader terms, as Marino[28] accurately assesses Romanian reality, "the notion of a 'nation of laws' is not yet anything more than pallid theoretical-juridical fiction, taken seriously only by the incurably civic-minded."

In all fairness, however, some courts have shown that they do pay attention to the guarantees of freedom of expression in the Romanian Constitution, and they have refused to use the defamation law as a political tool. For example, in March 1998, an appeals court overturned a lower court's conviction of two *Ziua* journalists for seditious libel.[29] It is also fair to mention that the politically partisan and polemical aspects of many articles, in addition to the often inaccurate and unverified information, made for some bona fide defamation cases.

Calls by politicians and government officials for a press law that would, in essence, regulate the work of journalists were rejected throughout the 1990s and relegated to the backburner of parliament.[30] It was difficult to gauge the motives of politicians and government officials for their insistence that a press law be adopted. Was it the concern of responsible leaders for curbing misinformation, or an attempt to craft a legal mechanism to control the media? Ultimately, making the media more responsible and professional is not the job of politicians and government officials. Freedom of the press in a fragile democracy cannot and should not be curbed by the state in the name of strengthening that democracy.

A law drafted with the intention of modifying and completing the Penal Code was finally adopted on 7 May 1998. The original three-month to three-year prison sentence was reduced to a fine, but prison sentences for defamation (two months to one year or a fine)[31] were retained. No matter what changes were made to the Penal Code, however, defamation suits still represent the Sword of Damocles hanging over journalists in a society that does not have an independent judiciary.

Surveying developments in Romania since November 1996, Ursu[32] asserts, "Transparency has become steam, doors are slamming shut one by one, and attempts to shut the journalists' mouths and to snatch the pen from their hands have increased." Throughout the 1990s, each chamber of Romania's bicameral Parliament took turns attempting to restrict journalists' access to its public deliberations; the election of the "democratic" opposition was supposed to have stopped such actions, but it did not. In March 1997, for example, the Senate obliged journalists to be accompanied by "persons from the (Senate's) administration" and to "reflect the activities of the permanent commissions" only on the basis of information offered by the commissions' spokespersons. In other words, journalists were "under guard" and were essentially to function as transmission belts for public relations releases. One year later, on 10 March 1998, the Senate finally reconsidered and modified the rules referring to the press's access to the workings of this legislative institution. The modification specified that the "meetings of the (Senate's) commissions are public, *but not if the individual commissions decide otherwise*."[33]

The next day, 11 March 1998, the education commission of the Chamber of Deputies barred journalists from covering its debate regarding the Education Law, claiming it was a national security issue.[34] In response, the Romanian Press Club reminded the Permanent Bureau of the Chamber of Deputies that any commission barring access to journalists was trampling on the constitution,[35] and it demanded "urgent reevaluation" of the decision.[36] If the Deputies were not forthcoming, the Club warned, it would "institute a total embargo on coverage of the Chamber's work."

This was a strange threat in light of the obligation of the press to inform the public, and, in fact, it played into the hands of the various commissions who obviously did not want press coverage. It was equally strange to have parliamentarians try to control the access of journalists to their deliberations and then complain about the "tendentious" coverage they received from the media.[37] In the late 1990s, parliamentarians were no longer able to control or influence, with any certainty of success, the print or broadcasting media as they did before the disappearance of the party press. Consequently, in late 1998, parliamentarians demanded C-SPAN-like coverage.[38]

Another attempt at keeping the media from covering the work of elected and appointed officials occurred on 22 April 1998. This time, it was the Ministry of Agriculture and Food Supply that was erecting obstacles to media coverage by demanding that journalists be required to have general accreditation to cover government as well as a "special" accreditation. It also demanded a list of the journalists' articles dealing with the Ministry and their curricula vitae.[39] Further aggravating the media's access problems, journalists could no longer put questions to ministers or other officials on the steps of the Victoria Palace, the seat of the Romanian government, as of May 1999. Instead, the government erected a pen-like enclosure in the middle of the palace's courtroom where journalists could question ministers and other officials, but only if they chose to step into the enclosure and submit to questioning.[40]

Two proposed press laws, designed at least in part to strengthen the media's protection and access to information, quickly died in embryo in 1997. One was a proposal emanating from the government and from the *Partidul Alternativa România* (PAR): the "the Law for protection of freedom of expression in the media." A second PAR project, "Law concerning the defense of freedom of expression in all media," was made public in February 1998.

Authoritarianism and confusion appeared to have reigned supreme with most politicians' and political parties' visions of the role of the media in a free society during what was expected to be a more enlightened and democratic Constantinescu/CD rule. Nevertheless, freedom of the press was palpably present during this period, and as Petcu[41] writes, "the moment of absolute press freedom, as it presented itself starting in 1990, only has equivalency in . . . the short period of the 1848 revolution, but the fullness and the forms of its assertion is even greater . . . and . . . is a unique phenomenon in the history of the national press."

JOURNALISM WITHOUT JOURNALISTS AND MEDIA ROLES

The media that had generally described themselves as ones of "opposition" since 1990 quickly changed their moniker to "*presa de tranziţie*" (the press of transition) after the opposition's victory at the polls in Fall 1996. This change in self-assigned function, however, put them in the service of the new powers, rather than having them be independent reporters and analysts. At the other end of the spectrum, the media that had toed the official line before 1996 became the media in "opposition" after November 1996, with the notable exception of TVR, the state television station. In short, the confusion and misunderstanding regarding media roles in a democracy continued, and they affected the very nature of journalism and the effects it had on the democratization process. Alina Mungiu[42] defines the Romanian mass media's role as being

> . . . more in 1990, less so subsequently, but persistently in our day, a substitute for all the absent structures in Romanian society: a substitute of power, and of opposition (to it), a substitute for a political class which has only recently and incompletely been educated, a substitute for justice (system) often weak and inefficient, and for some hesitant investigative organs.

Only a superficial case can be made for the "substitute" role, one that suggests direct media effects. First, the media became highly heterogeneous since 1989, as have their audiences, with each of the audience's subgroups using and interpreting the media in its own idiosyncratic way. Second, the media's role as a "substitute" is effective only if and when the media have high credibility, and the Romanian media could not boast of it during 1998–2000.[43] Also, the audience must have "different news values than those reflected,"[44] and there is nothing to suggest, however, that they do have different news values, other than the circumstantial evidence that there is a disparity between the media's values and those of their audiences. Thus, the press's revolving door (i.e., the death of many publications and the birth of new ones) suggests that audiences are searching for something other than what is offered them.[45] And there was a positive response to new independent, commercial television as well as to the new modes of news presentations offered to the audience.

Additionally, Mungiu's vision of media roles suggests a version of the type of modern media seen as "more powerful, more independent, and more determined to pursue their own interests through a professional culture of their own making," and tending to "take on political functions formerly performed by party and party-controlled media, such as political socialization and providing information to the public about politics and government."[46] There is no indication that Romanian media fully and directly performed that role since 1989 or that they have the required characteristics to do so.

This kind of media role in society depends in large measure, so the argument goes,[47] on their location on a subordination-autonomy continuum. In theory, the greater the autonomy, the more media play the role of major actors, beyond that of "merely . . . channel[s] of communication," particularly in political/campaign coverage, "as [they] select the persons and issues to be covered and as [they] shape its portrayal of leaders."[48] Huntington[49] also argues that weak and controlled media cannot provide the kind of accurate information required for meaningful decision making in a democracy. (The kind of media that are needed in a transition to democracy is briefly addressed in the next section of this chapter).

What developed in Romania after 1989 were media that were extreme representations of the Western European model of a pluralistic, relatively diverse media system of politically, religiously, ethnically, culturally oriented, and market-driven outlets. Thus, the problem in Romania from 1989–2000 was not an absence of pluralist media resulting from "chosen strategies."[50] That may have been true in the television field until the second half of the 1990s when private, commercial national television was expanded; but was not the case in the print media. Romanian media represented the full possible gamut of politics and ideologies, ethnic groupings, religious beliefs, etc. As the first decade of post-Communism came to a close, the media were subordinated to a large number of varied authorities. Still, it is fair to say that they were predominantly, but not exclusively or unalterably, political and commercial. The significant ethnic media, for example, particularly their Hungarian component and, importantly, the Roma media, were more than just political or commercial, as was the case with the religious or religion-affiliated press, they were also sociocultural elements of a multicultural society.

Media ownership was not easy to ascertain during the period under discussion here. Interviewees did not talk about it except in private conversation, and then only on background. Proving a direct connection between the media and political parties, politicians, or state institutions was difficult.[51] Ownership, and the degree of media subordination to other institutions, varied from medium to medium, and they have seen small but important changes in Romania during the first post-Communist decade. In any case, ownership of media is an insufficient gauge of their autonomy or subordination, and the Romanian case proves, once again, that it is the "overall cultural mix . . . that will tend to fix the position of media on this [subordination-autonomy] continuum."[52] However, Romania since 1989 has been in a transition period, and it has been difficult to pinpoint where the media stand on the continuum because the "cultural mix" has been constantly changing, and the legal, conceptual, and structural constraints on media are equally as unsettled, undefined, and unsecured.

Therefore, assessing media autonomy as a test of democratization is, at best, a highly speculative exercise and, in the end, a fruitless one. In the 1970s, Gerbner[53] suggested that independence was less important than "by whom, how, for what purposes and with what consequences are the inevitable controls exercised." In Romania, who controls or influences the media has changed more than once since 1989 and so has the way this control is exercised, the purposes for which it is exercised, and its consequences. In short, while Gerbner's proposition is sound, it cannot be used as a basis for reaching conclusions about transitional media.

Mungiu's description of a "substitute" role also suggests that the media in Romania independently and spontaneously formulated this role for themselves in response to several institutional voids. That may have been true in the 22 December 1989 to 1 February 1990 period, but not after that date.[54] It was not until 1997, when the "press of transition" (formerly the "opposition" press) cut the umbilical cord to the official transition cause, and ended their honeymoon with the former opposition (now the new "establishment"), that they began to selectively and tentatively define their role. At the very least, the press-party relationship thinned out into various strands that selectively connected and disconnected, depending on the issue and the perceived balance of power between the media and the political parties and politicians, as I attempt to show next. This by no means signaled an end to the extreme politicization of journalism, or a change in the even more de-professionalizing partisanships brought about by the various relationships between media and political and economic elites and interests.

Furthermore, the view that Romanian media played a substitute role implies that the journalists were something other than journalists, a full decade after the transition began. It also suggests that Romanian journalists have been something other than journalists as understood in the West, excusing the lack of impartiality, accuracy, completeness, independence, and overall professionalism imposed on them by the demands of their nonjournalistic roles. For instance, many journalists reported on the 1996 presidential and parliamentary campaign while concurrently writing campaign literature, speeches, and commercials for political parties and politicians.[55]

None of the changes in the Romanian media's relationships with other institutions signaled an end to the politicization of journalism and the deprofessionalizing of the media during 1996–2000. A large number of Romanian journalists remained highly opinionated; and they published unverifiable, incomplete, and even fictitious articles, which were often sensationalized, trivialized, and corrupted by personal, political, or financial exigencies. They fashioned themselves to be "analysts" and "experts" in what persisted as a widely recognized practice among journalists of viewing themselves as "different" from the rest of the population and from one another.[56]

Romanian journalism after 1996 remained a dubious blend of advocacy communication and news reporting, mixed with rumor in the guise of "news," all labeled "analytical" journalism. As Harvard Professor Thomas Patterson[57] correctly asserts, increasingly in the United States and almost always in Romania, "the story line get assembled first" and then, selectively, the facts. "That kind of journalism is a swamp in a way that the older [descriptive] style wasn't," he rightly warns.

Nestor Rateş,[58] the director of Radio Free Europe's Romanian department and a close observer of the Romanian scene, admits that, as a journalist, he is often "frightened" at how little most Romanian journalists are preoccupied with verifying information or the quality of their sources, and for the "destiny" of information after it is published. In the final analysis, however, the informational chaos found in Romania cannot be exclusively attributed to the journalists; politicians and government officials are equally guilty.

There have been a string of attempts by various professional organizations to "professionalize" journalism by introducing ethics codes since 1989. None has succeeded because there was no universal acceptance of the codes, no interest in them, and no means to enforce them.[59] The latest attempt was made in February 1998, when the Romanian Press Club, with great fanfare, made public a ten-article-long ethics code.[60] It was quickly forgotten.

There were occasional first-rate investigative stories during the period under scrutiny here, such as the political phone scam on behalf of the incumbent president, Ion Iliescu, and the dominant party, the PDSR, during the 1996 election campaign. Every rule has exceptions, and some articles proved Romanian journalists have the capacity to be professional: articles dealing with economics that were frequently thorough and balanced; coverage of disasters such as the explosion of a military aircraft that killed fifteen people and the floods that ravaged portions of the country in 1997; and the reporting of Romania's responsibility in readying itself for NATO candidacy.

Investigations of the government, the presidency, and the politicians and political parties were another way journalists contributed to political battles and converted journalists into political players. Thus, they elicited contradictory reactions from politicians and political parties themselves: alacrity in using media and their journalists, and fear of them. Politics brought down Prime Minister Victor Ciorbea in April 1998. Nistorescu,[61] who recognizes that politicians spend more time on television and in front of journalists than working "in the real sense of the word," assigns blame for Ciorbea's downfall to the media. The public, he writes, blames the press for the political chaos, and even politicians are worried about the "terror" of the press, and concludes that this "terror" is only "a sign of a freedom wrongly used, coupled with the weakness of politicians."

Put another way, the figurative Dr. Frankenstein (the embodiment of the many political parties and politicians) was being threatened in the late 1990s by the monster that he helped create (i.e., the many media outlets that they had hoped to control, influence, and use). The power of the media has heretofore been derived mostly from politicians and political parties; their relationship with the media was somewhat equalized by the second half of the 1990s. The power of the media in politics grew, and a relative mutual dependency was established. That is, the media remained dependent on political entities and politicians because they were so politicized and partisan; in turn, political parties and politicians have increased their courting of the media, not certain when, and to what extent, they could control or influence them.

Romanian journalism remained an exercise in analysis based on selective reporting. It remained a mixture of Don Quixote and his sidekick Sancho Panza, with a considerable touch of Lenin, Iago, and Machiavelli on one side and Mencken on the other, along with an occasional sprinkling of Woodward and Bernstein, conducting a serendipitous form of politically motivated investigation. It shared with Polish journalism two main enemies, as Adam Michnik[62] correctly describes them: (1) the domination of ideological conviction over informative reliability," and (2) "blindness, which leaves one able to make only trite observations." What was encouraging by 2000 was the creeping infusion of good journalism—the exceptions that from time to time lit up the national skies with the brightness of verifiable facts.

THE MEDIA AND DEMOCRATIZATION

The exact level and extensiveness of Romanian media contributions to resocialization and reeducation during 1996–2000 is simply not known, nor is it measurable with any degree of certainty or accuracy. Can any political, social, cultural, or economic failures identified in this transition period be laid at the doorsteps of the media? Can the media be shown to have engineered whatever successes were accomplished? If we accept Lenart's[63] proposition that media effects should be examined in the context of the climate they create, an argument can be made that Romanian media have positively contributed to the 1989–2000 transition, even when their initial effect was a negative one. First, they contributed to the creation of a public climate of competition, largely missing before 1989, between a range of competitors for political and economic power, as well as cultural predominance. Second, and concurrently, they also contributed to a climate of distrust, chaos, and insecurity, as demonstrated in the varied works on the Romanian media.[64] But this itself may be cause for their audiences, and indeed for the media themselves, to rethink or react to extant values, behavior, and attitudes—a process that has been slowly unfolding in the country.

Romanian media have also managed to inform their audiences. I hasten to add that I see no evidence that they have done so by design but, again, by virtue of their overpoliticization and partisanship, and often in the absence of fact-based journalism. The very overpoliticization and partisanship actually brought to the fore new issues, new parties, new leaders, new ideas and possibilities, new nongovernmental groups, and so on. Furthermore, thanks to the very introduction of political contests, an increasingly wider variety of issues relevant to the audience/citizens were disseminated through news programs, as well as through newly introduced political advertising by politicians and political parties vying for votes. In fact, unlike in the United States, where political contests are reported first and foremost as horse races, and where issue-oriented reporting has increasingly been marginalized, in Romania, the political contests continue to revolve more around both politicians and issues.

The information function was served by the media, thanks to newly established economic and social and cultural competition (e.g., who should get what share of public funds, which ethnic/cultural groups should get certain rights, which definition of "morals" should prevail, etc.). Thus, the media served an information function even when they were meant to serve one of manipulation, propaganda, and mobilization for various partisan causes.

Romanian media were unwitting and indirect agenda setters. The agenda setting process in a society is a combination of the media's agenda, the public's agenda (what the public wants, what it perceives and thinks), and the policy agenda (what is being proposed and carried out by those in power or proposed by those who wish to obtain power). In Romania, the media's agenda was at first identical, and later in the post-1989 decade at least similar, to the policy agenda. The public's agenda was, and still is, represented by the media from their own political point of view. This is in line with major research findings in the Western contexts where a correlation was found between the issues covered or emphasized by the media and those seen as important by the public; but the causal relationship has not been resolved.

For instance, after exhaustive review of research findings, it was concluded that the media have minimal effects, but that they set the voters' political agendas.[65]

In 1987, Iyengar and Kinder[66] demonstrated that the media's agenda setting influences public opinion and attitudes via "priming" (i.e., "calling attention to some matters while ignoring others"), and thus influencing "the standards by which governments, presidents, policies, and candidates for public office are judged." In Romania during 1996–2000, priming was so vastly different from one news outlet to the next that those who chose to expose themselves to the full gamut of matters being discussed gorged themselves on a smorgasbord of information/views. On the other hand, those who chose to avail themselves of a singular news outlet did not gain a full understanding of the events and issues in their communities, countries, continents, or the world. Iyengar[67] outlined a second aspect of agenda setting, "framing," which he described as the contextual cues embedded within a news story, which also influences public opinion and attitudes. Since 1989, this framing function was overdone in Romania. Precisely because of that, journalism does less to influence public opinion and attitudes than to reinforce them, and only if and when the audience finds kinship with, or sympathy for the cues in the journalism offered them.

It is through their pluralism and diversity, and because of their highly politicized and partisan journalism, that Romanian media have attempted to tell their audiences how to think and, *in that context*, what to think about. Romanian journalists, and their editors and news directors, justified this approach by arguing that only in this way can they purposefully guide their audiences in democratization. Yet, considering the varied interpretations of information, the partisan choice of information to be interpreted, and the overabundance of views and polemics, there is some truth in their argument that they are presenting choices to the audience and asking them to choose. It is not an insignificant step in the democratization process considering that the majority was not used to making choices (because they did not have many) prior to 1989. This approach to journalism is the opposite of the trends identified in the United States, at least prior to American journalism's change to a more analytical model, where findings suggest that media tell people less how to think than what to think about.[68] In any case, how successful Romanian media were in this respect remains, in the absence of studies and experiments similar to those carried out in the West, mostly a matter of conjecture.

The Romanian media's contribution to the 1996–2000 phase of democratization rested, first and foremost, on being *symbols* of liberalization and the struggle to continue this process; *examples* of, and conduits for, the availability of political, economic, and cultural options; and *facilitators* of political, market, and cultural competition. It is in this way that the media appeared to contribute to changing political culture in this phase of the transition process away from Communism and toward an as yet undefined future. This was not a situation in which there were "dominant communication agencies," even if certain news outlets had gained ascendancy during 1996–2000, that cultivated "the dominant image patterns."[69] There were no discernable "dominant image patterns" to cultivate in a post-Communist phase in which the battle was raging over which image pattern(s) will dominate. Cultural change may stem "from a change in social relations that makes the old cultural patterns dysfunctional to the new order."[70] Indeed, in post-Communist Romania, those old cultural patterns are now dysfunctional, yet still present.[71] The social relations are still changing and have not yet solidly established new cultural patterns.

CONCLUSION

Since 2000, there has been both progress and regression in Romania's media world. The Parliament passed a Freedom of Access to Information Law in 2001 guaranteeing access to information "of public interest," but not to information deemed important to national security or information on judicial proceedings. The Romanian legislature also approved an ambiguous and restrictive Law on State Secrets.

The European Institute for the Media concluded in 1997 that Romanian journalism was fraught with "certain flaws . . . such as failure to separate between fact and opinion, news and commentary."[72] This journalism continued into the new millennium together with the "Byzantine" journalistic style reflected in verbosity and flowery language, which "creates rumors and is opaquing communication."[73]

Meanwhile, the number of media outlets continued to grow. Three new television stations were introduced in Bucharest in 2001; new radio stations were launched all over the country; new publications were introduced since 2000, however, overall the circulation of print media has decreased; almost 27 percent of households subscribed to cable television; new, web-based media have been multiplying. A major negative development has been the growth of state-controlled media. Rompres, the respected news agency, for example, was placed under the control of the Ministry of Public Information in 2001. Furthermore, the largest, national, commercial television channels have borrowed heavily from state coffers and are now subject to manipulation by government officials.[74]

The basic functions the media are to serve in a society that remains a "work in progress" are yet to be articulated. How could it be otherwise in a transition that is a journey without a well-defined map, often without all the means necessary to make it, and certainly without the guarantee of reaching the articulated designation: a working democracy? The media continue to be expressions and reinforcers of the extant political culture; they are concurrently mechanisms of change by virtue of the new ideas, debates, and opportunities they present to the public. The assumption that only an ideally defined, independent, pluralistic, and professional media could help the process of democratization was a mistaken one. It was partly derived from an equally faulty notion that media are at the core of this democratization when, in fact, they are only adjuncts to it.

NOTES

1. Peter Gross, *Media in Revolution and National Development: The Romanian Laboratory* (Ames: Iowa State University Press, 1996).
2. Colin Seymour-Ure, *The Political Impact of Mass Media* (Beverly Hills, CA: Sage Publications, 1974).
3. Gross, *Media in Revolution.*
4. *Ibid.*
5. Gabor Demszky, "Breaking Censorship—Making Peace," in *Media Studies Journal* (Summer 1995), pp. 79–85.
6. All translations from Romanian and French are the author's.
7. Liviu Antonesei, "Cultura Politica si Terapie Sociala in Romania Post-Comunista," *Revista de Cercetari Sociale* (1994), pp. 118–23.
8. See K. R. Middleton, "Applying Europe's 'First Amendment' to Romanian Libel and Access Law," in Al Hester and K. White, eds., *Creating a Free Press in Eastern Europe* (Athens, GA: James M. Cox Jr., Center for International Mass Communication Training and Research, University of Georgia, 1993), pp. 405–30.
9. TVR is still the only truly national television station. By 1999, Pro-TV and other private, commercial stations were accessible to most Romanians.
10. Dumitru Iuga, the head of the Free Union of RVR, accused the new leadership of again fulfilling a "political mandate." See *Telegrama* (3 June 1997).
11. Author's discussion with TVR personnel in October 1997.
12. *Adevărul* (5 February 1998).
13. Parliament also named a new Administrative Council for TVR in July 1998.
14. *Telegrama* (8 July 1998).
15. Coposu was one of the few legendary figures of the anti-Communist battles; he spent years in prison.
16. "Un Grav Caz de Încălcare a Libertăţi Presei," *Ziua* (10 November 1999).
17. *Telegrama* (17 June 1999).
18. Central European Media Enterprises invested around $20 million in Pro-TV. CEME was bought by Russian media magnate Vladimir Gusinsky in Fall 1999. See "Un rus a cumpărat acţiuni la CME, proprietara Pro TV," *Naţional* (7 October 1999), p. 3.
19. National Audio-Visual Council Bulletin, 1997. By the end of 1997, the NAVC had issued 148 television, 235 radio, and 1,352 cable television licenses.
20. "The Law Concerning the Organization and Functioning of the Romanian Radio Society and of the Romanian Television Society," *Monitorul Oficial*, no. 18 (1994).
21. Post-Communist Media Law and Policy, pcmlp@socio-legal-studies.oxford.ac.uk.

22. *Telegrama* (22 October 1998).

23. Principally but not exclusively Articles 205 and 206 of the Penal Code that call for prison sentences for those convicted.

24. What constitutes an insult is left open to wide interpretation. Furthermore, it places insults on the same level of legal protection as defamation.

25. *Telegrama* (3 September 1997).

26. Adrian Ursu, *Adevărul* (5 February 1998).

27. Fax to author from The Center for Independent Journalism in Bucharest (11 February 1998).

28. Adrian Marino, *Pentru Europa. Integrarea României: Aspecte ideologice şi culturale* (Iaşi: Polirom, 1995), p. 23.

29. Tana Ardeleanu and Sorin Roşca Stănescu were found guilty of seditious libel for an article in 1996 that alleged that then-President Ion Iliescu worked for the Soviet KGB prior to 1989.

30. Gross, *Media in Revolution*, chapter 3.

31. *Telegrama* (8 May 1998).

32. Adrian Ursu, *Adevărul* (5 February 1998).

33. *Telegrama* (11 March 1998).

34. *Telegrama* (12 March 1998).

35. Indeed, Art. 65 of Romania's 1991 Constitution explicitly states "the meetings of both (Parliamentary) chambers are public."

36. *Telegrama* (12 March 1998).

37. *Telegrama* (12 June 1998).

38. *Telegrama* (10 Sept. 1998).

39. *Telegrama* (23 April 1998). Journalists need to be accredited to cover governmental institutions in other Eastern European countries as well, but, in most cases, are not required to present a curriculum vitae or a list of articles written by them about the particular institution to which they seek accreditation.

40. *Telegrama* (19 May 1999).

41. Marian Petcu, "La legislation des medias en Roumanie," *Le Reseau Global*, nos. 9–10 (1998), pp. 117–23.

42. Alina Mungiu, *România Dupa '89: Istoria unei nein͵elegeri* (Bucharest: Humanitas, 1995), p. 254.

43. For example the studies carried out by the US Information Agency from 1990–93; also "Majoritatea popula͵iei României nu are încredere în Televisiune," *România Libera* (3 March 1993), p. 3.

44. E. M. Rogers and J. W. Dearing, "Agenda-Setting Research: Where Has It Been, Where Is It Going?" in Doris A. Graber (ed.), *Media Power in Politics* (Washington, DC: Congressional Quarterly Press), pp. 77–95.

45. There are between 1,500 and 2,000 publications; approximately 150 of them are daily newspapers.

46. D. L. Swanson and P. Mancini, (eds.), *Politics, Media and Modern Democracy* (Westport, CT and London: Praeger, 1996), pp. 15–16.

47. Slavko Splichal, *Media Beyond Socialism* (Boulder, CO: Westview Press, 1994), p. 126.

48. David Butler and Austin Ranney, eds., *Electioneering: A Comparative Study of Continuity and Change* (Oxford: Clarendon Press, 1992), p. 283.

49. Samuel P. Huntington, *The Third Wave: Democratization in the Late Twentieth Century* (Norman: University of Oklahoma Press, 1991), p. 7.

50. Henry F. Carey, "From Big Lie to Small Lies: State Mass Media Dominance in Post-Communist Romania," *East European Politics and Society*, vol. 10, no. 1 (Winter 1996), pp. 16–45.

51. Direct ties between media and politicians or political parties can be established in some cases. For example, *România Libera* was a supporter of the monarchy, of President Emil Constantinescu, and of the Democratic Convention; *Ziua* was run by the Omega Investment Group owned by Dinu Patriciu of the Liberal Party; *România Mare* was the newspaper of the party that bears the same name and the party leader's (Corneliu Vadim Tudor) main mouthpiece.

52. Michael Gurevitch and Jay G. Blumler, "Mass Media and Political Institutions: The Systems Approach," in George Gerbner, ed., *Mass Media Policies in Changing Cultures* (New York: John Wiley and Sons, 1977), pp. 251–68.

53. George Gerbner, "Violence in Television Drama: Trends and Social Functions" in G.A. Comstoke and Eli A. Rubinstein, eds., *Television and Social Behavior*, vol. 1, *Media Content and Control* (Washington, DC: US Government Printing Office, 1972), pp. 28–187.

54. On that day, the National Salvation Front labeled itself a political party, entered the first post-1989 election, and instantly brought politics back into the public domain.

55. Author interviews with editors and journalists in Romanian cities during the 1996 election campaign.

56. Scores of journalists related these practices to the author. Few of them admitted they are culpable of these practices.

57. Thomas Patterson is Bradlee Professor of Government and the Press at Harvard University. Quoted in Judith Sheppard, "Playing in Defense," *American Journalism Review*, vol. 20, no. 7 (September 1998), pp. 48–56.

58. *Dilema* (6–12 February 1998), p. 8.

59. For an outline of the problems, see Kenneth Starck, "Groping Toward Ethics in Transitioning Press Systems: The Case of Romania," *Journal of Mass Media Ethics*, vol. 14, no.1 (1999) pp. 28–41.

60. *Ziua* (20 February 1998).

61. Cornel Nistorescu, *Evenimentul Zilei* (2 April 1998).

62. Adam Michnik, "After Communism, Journalism," *Media Studies Journal*, vol. 12, issue 2/3 (Spring/Summer 1998), pp. 104–13.

63. Silvio Lenart, *Shaping Political Attitudes. The Impact of Interpersonal Communication and Mass Media* (Thousand Oaks, CA: Sage, 1994).

64. Carey, "From Big Lie to Small Lies," and Gross, *Media in Revolution*.

65. Joseph Klapper, *The Effects of Mass Communication* (New York: Free Press, 1960); Maxwell McCombs and Donald Shaw, "The Agenda-Setting Function of the Mass Media," *Public Opinion Quarterly*, vol. 36, no. 2 (Summer 1972), pp. 176–87; and Maxwell McCombs and Donald Shaw, "Structuring the Unseen Environment," *Journal of Communication*, vol. 26, no. 2 (1976), pp. 18–22.

66. S. Iyengar and D. R. Kinder, *News That Matters: Television and American Opinion* (Chicago: University of Chicago Press, 1987).

67. S. Iyengar, *Is Anyone Responsible? How Television Frames Political Issues* (Chicago: University of Chicago Press, 1994).

68. S. Iyengar, Mark D. Peters, and Donald R. Kinder, "Experimental Demonstrations of the 'Not-So-Minimal' Consequences of Television News Programs," *American Political Science Review*, vol. 76, no. 4 (1982), pp. 848–58.

69. George Gerbner, "Comparative Cultural Indicators," in Gerbner, ed., *Mass Media Policies in Changing Cultures* (New York: John Wiley & Sons, 1977), pp. 199–206.

70. *Ibid.*, p. 205.

71. G. M. Tamas, "Capitalism, Socialism, and Modernity," *Journal of Democracy*, vol. 3, no. 3 (July 1992), p. 73.

72. Final Report. Monitoring the media coverage of the 1996 Romanian parliamentary and presidential elections. Dusseldorf, Germany: The European Institute for the Media, March 1997.

73. Mircea Vasilescu, "Media Fair-Play," *Dilema*, September 8–14, 2000, p. 4.

74. Marius Dragomir, "Propping up Propaganda," *Transitions Online*, June 21, 2002, www.tol.cz.

10

Political Culture in Post-Ceauşescu Romania

Richard Andrew Hall

Evidence from the literature on transitions from authoritarian rule generally supports the seemingly counterintuitive claim that democratic political culture usually follows, rather than precedes, the collapse of an authoritarian regime. Indeed, it may even be possible to "consolidate" democracy without the prior institutionalization of a democratic political culture. Nevertheless, nearly fourteen years of post-Communism in Eastern Europe has amply demonstrated that, although a conducive political culture may not be mandatory for the successful institutionalization of democracy and the market, it certainly helps. While new institutions, rules, and incentive structures have the capacity to reshape political culture, political culture also infuses new institutions and relationships with meaning, and helps shape their operation and results. Political culture ensures that the same political and economic institutions found in the West may function differently, and have different outcomes, in Eastern Europe.

This chapter seeks to specify the character of political culture in post-Communist Romania, and to address the issue of how post-Communist political culture is a continuation of Communist political culture. The manner in which I analyze this question—from a societal-wide focus—reflects my frustration with what I find as the tendency, in the literature on post-Communist Romania, to identify differences of political culture with ideological differences. Such an approach neglects those critical features of political culture which are shared by sharply different, and even antagonistic, ideological movements. It is these features of political culture that I find most interesting, and potentially most important, in shaping outcomes; for that reason, I focus upon them here.

COMMUNIST POLITICAL CULTURE

Communist rule bore sufficient similarities across the various countries of Eastern Europe for us to be able to speak, appropriately, of a generic "Communist political culture."[1] This is not to imply, however, that "Communist political culture" was a static property during the entire period of Communist rule in Eastern Europe—the same in 1989 as it had been in 1949. The intensity of fear, repression, enthusiasm, and zealotry that characterized early Communist rule was not the same as the cynicism and corruption which characterized late Communist rule. The political culture evolved with changes in the character of the regime.

Romanian political culture in the 1980s was distinguished by fear, suspicion, *dissimulation* (to borrow a term invoked by Jowitt to describe the disjuncture between public behavior and private beliefs), avoidance, withdrawal, secrecy, rumor-mongering, corruption, dependence on "connections," and a preference for the informal over the formal. These characteristics reflected the more enduring totalitarian features of the Romanian regime (compared to other East European regimes), but they also reflected the overall delegitimation of the ruling ideology (which led to what Jowitt termed the party's "loss of its combat mission") and the lessening of repression which characterized all East European regimes after the 1960s.[2] Specifically, elite political culture reflected the above-mentioned features—with some being more developed (corruption) than others (fear)—and added certain other properties specific to the elite. In the late Communist regime, elite political culture was pedantic, deceitful, corrupt, personalist/clientelist, servile, obsessed with unity (Shafir termed this "factional anxiety"), intolerant of difference and dissent, ideologically barren, nationalistic, xenophobic, and constantly on the lookout for traitors and those suspected of antipatriotic behavior.[3]

Romanian mass political culture reflected the impact of totalitarianism. Although Communist rule was never able to homogenize society to the extent envisioned by ideology or promised by elites, when compared to other regime types, it perhaps came closest to creating a relatively undifferentiated "mass society." Because totalitarian rule simultaneously atomized society and denied its natural propensity toward differentiation, informal networks of *pile, cunoştiinţe, şi relaţii* ("connections, acquaintances, and relatives") filled the void as the primary bases of societal organization, differentiation, and competition in the late Communist era.[4] The result was the paradox of a relatively homogenous but highly fragmented society, where the bases of differentiation were necessarily idiosyncratic and somewhat artificial, but nonetheless potentially very deep and contentious.

POLITICAL CULTURE IN THE POST-COMMUNIST ERA

How much has the political culture of Romania changed since the late Ceauşescu era? It would be foolhardy to contend that it has not changed much at all. Elite political culture in Romania has undergone meaningful change. This applies even to former members of the Communist regime who continue to involve themselves in politics. Despite their criticisms of the post-Communist political and economic systems, their expressions of nostalgia for the totalitarian past, and their attempts to manipulate and evade post-Communist institutions and regulations, they have demonstrated an acceptance of the basic "rules of the game" (pluralistic competition) of the post-Communist system, and have not made any concerted attempt to overturn it. This, as theorists of democratic transitions tell us, is significant.[5] Moreover, it is obvious that the fear, secrecy, servility, and dissimulation (born of fear) which characterized mass political culture during the Communist era have substantially dissipated. The significance of these developments should not be dismissed.

Nevertheless, I maintain that much of the broader features of political culture during the Communist era, both at the elite and mass levels, remains. This is not to suggest that such features are destined to scuttle Romania's democratic experiment, but their impact does at least undermine the democratic content of the contemporary Romanian political system. They compete with the newer, and generally more positive, features of political culture (discussed previously) created by the new institutions and processes of the post-Communist political system. Post-Communism is not a case of either/or: new, more virtuous trends in political culture compete, and mix with, the older, more negative features. Below, I outline some of the more enduring, harmful legacies of Communist-era political culture in contemporary Romania.

THE LINGERING EFFECTS OF MASS SOCIETY

Having been denied the right to ideological differentiation and the ability to articulate real interests, citizens in post-Communist societies continue to bear the marks of the "mass society." They are loath to join with other citizens in order to participate directly in political parties and civil society organizations, and they are leery of making long-term partisan commitments—as is evidenced by the volatility of post-Communist elections. What is left is a relatively nonparticipatory society, which is highly fragmented and floats its support from one political movement to another. Post-Communist citizens have also displayed a tendency to "blame the incumbents" for the non- or underfulfillment of political and economic expectations. This continues the kind of nihilistic, antipolitical tactics—the struggle of the community against "the Power"—which characterized mass publics during late Communist rule.

The comparatively greater totalitarian legacy of the Ceaușescu regime, and the authoritarian reflexes of those who came to power in the immediate aftermath of December 1989, initially retarded the evolution of political diversification and electoral volatility in post-Communist Romania. Nevertheless, more than fourteen years after the collapse of Communist rule, Romania looks strikingly similar to the rest of Eastern Europe with its electoral volatility, "blame the incumbents" popular mentality, absence of fixed cleavages, and nomadic electorate. The electoral decline of the Iliescu regime, which began in provincial urban centers in local elections in the spring of 1992, eventually resulted in the transfer of power to opposition forces at the national level in the fall of 1996. Public opinion polling data in advance of the 2000 parliamentary and presidential elections suggests that the Romanian Democratic Convention has suffered the same price of incumbency that the late Iliescu regime did, and that the electorate has reserved the right to float its support to different political movements as it sees fit. Contrary to the image of elite power that was associated with Romania early in the 1990s, this suggests that the legacy of the mass society contributes to elite weakness—not only in terms of the inability of elites to craft winning and *enduring* constituencies for elections, but in their inability to build such coalitions for successful policy implementation. Post-Communist elites continue to have a difficult time mobilizing citizens. This is, in part, a consequence of the legacy of the "mass society."

ELITE FRAGMENTATION, POLITICAL POLEMICS, POWER STRUGGLES, AND PERSONALITY POLITIC

The absence of well-defined economic interests and ideological cleavages among the public has contributed to elite fragmentation.[6] So too has the comparative lack of importance attached to ideology in post-Communist society, as well as the absence of ideological consensus among the elites themselves. Elite fragmentation is often more derivative of personality clashes, personal ambitions, and position/role-dependent differences in responsibilities and interests than of ideological differences. Hence, fragmentation occurs within particular ideological movements as much as between them (the Liberal movement has been a caricature of this phenomenon in the post-Communist era for many Romanians). The political analyst Dorel Șandor captures this in his description of Romania as "a nation of weak, fuzzy institutions and coffeehouse politics, where, despite the names of the political parties, there are no ideas, only personal vanity and intrigue."[7] The philosopher H. R. Patapievici maintains that "our politics is all intrigue," something he attributes to the "Orthodox habit of communicating traditions orally rather than through written texts, which makes everything forever negotiable."[8]

Personal ambitions, generational differences, and the constitutional/institutional dispersion of power, as much as (and probably more than) ideological differences, propelled the implosion of the National Salvation Front (NSF) between 1990 and 1992. The split within the ranks of the NSF left Prime Minister and party president Petre Roman and Deputy Prime Minister and director of the (in)famous "Interior Ministry unit 0215" Gelu Voican Voiculescu on one side, and President Ion Iliescu and Romanian Intelligence Service (SRI) chief Virgil Măgureanu on the other. This situation has perhaps been replicated in the post-1996 period in the struggle between the prime minister and the leadership of his party (the PNŢCD), with former Prime Ministers Victor Ciorbea and Radu Vasile alternating their previous roles. Indeed, this elite fragmentation, competition, and contention—whether within the former Front or within the ruling Romanian Democratic Convention—has undoubtedly contributed to political instability and the policy paralysis of those in power. This has been particularly evident in the struggles in the post-1996 cabinets among members of the National Peasant, Liberal, and Democratic parties.[9]

Ironically, the personalism and clientelism which dominates many political parties—regardless of their ideological orientation—is perhaps a consequence of disunity and an attempt to overcome it. Moreover, the accentuated ideological rhetoric of these politicians is less a reflection of consensus than an effort to manufacture it. As in the case of the lingering effects of the "mass society," the new institutional framework chosen by post-Communist elites—a system of representation which stresses proportionality and which has (until changes were adopted in 1999) maintained a low threshold for representation—has merely reinforced the tendency toward fragmentation already present in elite political culture.

A PREFERENCE FOR INFORMAL PROCESSES AND INSTITUTIONS OVER FORMAL ONES

In the post-Communist era, Romanians, like many East Europeans, have continued to exhibit a preference for informal personal networks over formal institutions. This appears to be a product of both deeply embedded historical habits and the uncertainty and turbulence which have characterized formal institutions in the post-Communist era.

The experience of repressive and exploitative rule engenders a preference for informal over formal processes. Formal institutions appear wholly for the benefit of those who rule, at the expense of those who do not. The attempt to build unauthorized formal institutions usually meets with the swift response of those who hold power: The unauthorized formal institutions are slated for elimination, crushed, and expunged. By contrast, informal forms of organization and communication are less visible and hence less detectable. They have the capacity to survive longer than formal institutions and even to penetrate formal institutions. The choice of informal networks seems a strategic one, as they are likely to have greater endurance, and can withstand the collapse of formal institutional orders.

In the post-Communist era, the preference for the informal over the formal manifests itself in a number of ways. Although the credibility and validity of statements made by politicians and journalists have increased since the Communist era, popular trust in such statements remains low, and the population remains remarkably cynical and suspicious. The result is an almost magical faith in rumor and a preference for it over official forms of spoken and written communication.[10] Rumor is perceived as more personal and controllable, and hence, credible. It builds community in an uncertain environment, where information is partial, confusing, contradictory, and of questionable motivation, by sharing the dissemination and consumption of "the secret." Indeed, such informal means of information gathering penetrate the new formal institutions of the putatively open society of post-Communist Romania. As the noted Romanian literary critic Nicolae Manolescu observed: "Unfortunately, the Romanian journalist cannot escape . . . the negative effects of rumor-mongering . . . [he] is not educated in the spirit of the profession he is practicing."[11]

The ultimate expression of the enduring preference for informal arrangements is the continued pervasiveness and significance of informal networks of *pile, cunoştiinţe, şi relaţii* in everyday Romanian life. Natalia Dinello's description of the "Russian F-connection—finance, firms, friends, families, and favorites" explains why this should be so.[12] Not only are such networks well established as a result of the character of "real existing socialism"—and thus offer themselves as readily adaptable to the new political and economic environment—but these are mechanisms (as they were under Communist rule) for reducing uncertainty and insecurity, and for overcoming a situation in which resources, credit, and information are poor, scarce, maldistributed, inefficiently transferred, and intensely valued.

Indeed, as Dinello concludes, because formal institutions such as contracts and trademarks are weak, unenforceable (owing in part to the weakness of the state), or nonexistent, "personal connections are often the *only* means of managing economic transactions."[13] One might add that the power and necessity of such informal networks perpetuates dissimulation with regard to existing formal institutions—even if such dissimulation is now instigated more by pragmatism and the desire to emulate Western forms (at least on the surface) than out of fear of reprisal—and, in fact, undermines the successful legitimation and institutionalization of formal institutions. The result is that Romanian society—like other post-Communist societies—now bears economic similarities to other recent, postauthoritarian societies which have made the transition to the market, such as South Korea, where the informal networks of relations developed during authoritarian rule have given rise to so-called crony capitalism.

A STATUS QUO-ORIENTED, RENT-SEEKING ELITE AND A POLITICIZED STATE

Significantly, the transfer of power from the Iliescu leadership to its critics has not resulted in the kind of reorientation in elite political culture for which many had hoped for. This suggests that many of these traits have less to do with ideology than with the broader political context. Ideological commitments and campaign promises notwithstanding, the political leadership since November 1996 has not constituted a radical break in terms of policy (especially economic policy) from the Iliescu regime. Whereas an inability to engage in far-reaching economic reform, owing to the weakness of the state, may be the primary reason for why the post-1996 leadership has not pressed forward with such reforms (in contrast to the Iliescu leadership, where it was largely the result of reluctance), neither leadership has made bold moves in the economic arena. The result has been strikingly similar: a statist elite with a "don't rock the boat" mentality.

Moreover, if "rent-seeking" behavior among state officials was more widespread, more egregious, and almost tacitly encouraged under the Iliescu regime, it was not noticeably reduced under the Constantinescu administration, in spite of its highly publicized anticorruption drives. Out of weakness or pragmatism, the Constantinescu administration appeared to have grudgingly accepted that this was an unavoidable feature of the post-Communist system; one which could not be reformed without causing the kind of political instability which might lead the regime to collapse.[14]

Nor has the long tradition of the politicization of state institutions disappeared. It is important to point out that this is determined as much by state employees and economic elites as the political leadership itself. Passive attitudes—which lead state employees and economic elites to seek and secure the approval of the political leadership on key matters before proceeding further (even in situations where such approval is not, or should not, be legally or constitutionally necessary)—persist. One Western executive has observed that, in the business world, the situation has not changed much from the Iliescu era: "Doing business here by Western standards is difficult. Everything depends on politics. Without Constantinescu behind you nothing happens. No one here likes decisions."[15] The principal Western analyst of the Romanian media, Peter Gross, maintains that workers at Romanian National Television (TVR) confirmed allegations that the post-1996 TVR leadership, like the leadership before it, believes the station has a "political mandate." Moreover, he contends that "the direct telephone line between the offices of the nation's president and the head of the news department remains in operation and is used regularly."[16]

A CULTURE OF NATIONAL SUSPICION: ALLEGATIONS OF ANTIPATRIOTISM AND TREACHERY

Perhaps because of the comparatively (by European standards) late timing of Romanian statehood, and the country's vulnerable geographic location (surrounded throughout most of history by at least four neighboring states), national security has always been a prominent theme in Romanian politics. Not surprisingly, so too have allegations that one's political opponents are in league with, or are serving the interests of, some outside power. The paranoia and xenophobia of the early Communist regime was thus an accentuation, rather than a break with, historical trends. The Ceauşescu leadership frequently discredited dissenters and potential opponents by alleging or spreading rumors that they were working for Western, Hungarian, or Soviet intelligence organizations.

After December 1989, the Iliescu regime continued this base political tradition in its attempt to subvert Romania's nascent political opposition and civil society. Publications supported by, or at least allied with, Iliescu frequently alleged that this or that critic was secretly working for American, Israeli, or Hungarian intelligence organizations. Many Romanian commentators and foreign analysts have been inclined to see the use of the national security card as the exclusive province of the former Communists, but such a characterization seems slightly partisan and unfair. Allegations of antipatriotism and treachery have been equally prominent components in the rhetoric of critics of the Iliescu regime. Anti-Iliescu politicians, intellectuals, and journalists have routinely insinuated or alleged that Iliescu and his associates have been doing the bidding of the Soviet KGB and its Russian successors.[17] Moreover, they have portrayed the failure of Iliescu and his associates to take a more nationalistic stand with regard to the reincorporation of Moldova into Romania as not merely antipatriotic, but a consequence of their treasonous relations with the former Soviet Union and Russia. Such allegations suggest both that the national security card is a generalized feature of the post-Communist Romanian political spectrum, and that elites believe that this issue has great resonance with the electorate (whether this is actually correct is another matter altogether).

THE INTELLIGENTSIA ESTRANGED FROM SOCIETY AND THE CAPITAL FROM THE COUNTRY

Throughout history, Romania's intelligentsia has had a sharply antagonistic relationship with the broader population. The Westward-looking intellectuals of the interwar period spoke French among themselves and appeared painfully embarrassed to be associated with the uncultivated Romanian peasantry with whom they shared their country.[18] Communism redefined, but hardly eradicated, this divide. The collaboration of intellectuals with the Communist regime, and their failure to speak out against repression, discredited the intelligentsia in the eyes of many ordinary Romanians. On the other hand, those among the intelligentsia who longed for change and bravely risked dissent felt constrained, and even doomed, by what they saw as the docile and backward character of the wider society. Ironically, and tragically, even efforts by intellectuals to undermine the regime—such as through the use of esoteric language—tended to further estrange them from the broader population because such messages were beyond the reach of most ordinary Romanians; their only real audience was fellow intellectuals.

The alienation of the intelligentsia from the broader population has continued in the post-Communist era. While much of the intelligentsia attempted to compensate for its failure (or inability) to oppose the Communists by publicizing and denouncing the duplicity and manipulation of the Iliescu regime, the intensity of their anti-Communism often outpaced the sentiments of the broader population. Moreover, many intellectuals continue to depict the backward *homo sovieticus* features of the broader population as the principal obstacles to meaningful economic reform and the consolidation of democratic rule. Given the continuing deterioration in the standard of living in that country, such rhetoric cannot sit well with the average Romanian.

Compounding the divide between the intelligentsia and the broader population has been a deepening of resentment toward the capital, Bucharest. Home to the majority of Romania's intellectual elite and to the levers of state power, the capital has increasingly become a symbol—for those who live outside the capital—of everything that is wrong with post-Communist Romania. The depth of this resentment was revealed during the miners' march toward Bucharest in January 1999, when sympathetic crowds lining the road in the countryside joined in chants of "Down with Bucharest! Down with Bucharest!"

CONCLUSION

The concept of "political culture" is probably insufficient, by itself, to determine the chances for democracy in a given society. Societies, which seemingly had the requisite traits of virtuous political cultures, have either not seen democracy or have seen democracy fail.[19] Moreover, as both the Communist and post-Communist era have demonstrated, political culture is malleable—even if not to the degree most elites would like. Certainly, in post-Communist Eastern Europe, the new institutional frameworks of political, media, and economic competition have changed behavior, and this has in turn eaten away at the influence and existence of older facets of political culture.

But those older facets of political culture often prove stronger, more flexible, and more adaptable than the prophets of change have predicted. Moreover, they have the capacity to shape the operation and outcomes of these new formal institutions. "Real existing post-socialism," no less than "real existing socialism," deviates substantially from the formal institutional configuration. While the legacies of Communist political culture do not condemn Romania to a new authoritarianism—precisely because they compete side by side with the aforementioned newer (and more positive) features of political culture—they do distort the operation of the post-Communist system. Dinello cautions, however, that we should not automatically assume that the outcomes of these negative political cultural legacies are themselves necessarily all negative: they may actually serve a functional (if not optimally efficient) purpose during the transition and circumscribe the dysfunction of the post-Communist system.[20] For this reason and because in the first years of post-Communist rule it has indeed been possible to institutionalize some elements of what is considered a virtuous political culture, we should not foreclose on Romania's democratic experiment just yet.

NOTES

1. Ken Jowitt has perhaps identified the features of Communist political culture better than anyone else. See Ken Jowitt, *New World Disorder: The Leninist Extinction* (Berkeley: University of California Press, 1992).

2. On dissimulation see *Ibid.*, p. 80; on the party's loss of its combat mission, see *Ibid.*, p. 144.

3. On elite political culture in Communist regimes, see again *Ibid.*, esp. pp. 287–94. For specifics of the Romanian case, see Vladimir Tismăneanu, "The Quasi-Revolution and Its Discontents: Emerging Political Pluralism in Post-Ceauşescu Romania," in *East European Politics and Societies*, vol. 7, no. 2 (Summer 1993), pp. 309–48. On "factional anxiety," see Michael Shafir, *Romania: Politics, Economics, and Society* (London: Pinter, 1985).

4. For a discussion of "real interests," see Jadwiga Staniszkis, *The Dynamics of the Breakthrough in Eastern Europe: The Polish Experience*, trans. Chester A. Kisiel (Berkeley: University of California Press, 1991), pp. 90–99.

5. Juan J. Linz and Alfred Stepan, *Problems of Democratic Transition and Consolidation: Southern Europe, South America, and Post-Communist Europe* (Baltimore, MD: Johns Hopkins University Press, 1996), p. 5.

6. Jowitt discusses elite fragmentation as a legacy of Communist rule in Jowitt, *New World Disorder*, pp. 294–99.

7. Quoted in Robert D. Kaplan, "The Fulcrum of Europe," *The Atlantic Monthly* (September 1998), p. 32.

8. Quoted in *Ibid.*, p. 32.

9. Petre Roman's Democratic Party has become a key player, a kingmaker of sorts, in Romanian politics, perhaps somewhat analogous to the Free Democrats in Germany—a small party which can make or break elections, is likely to be part of whatever coalition is in power, and yet likely to prove divisive as members of the coalition (in this sense, they are probably much more problematic than the German Free Democrats).

10. For the classic treatment of the role of rumor in Communist Romania (and especially Ceaușescu's Romania), see Steven Sampson's fascinating "Rumours in Socialist Romania," *Survey*, vol. 28, no. 4 (Winter 1984), pp. 142–64.

11. Quoted from an August 1997 *Dilema* interview in Peter Gross, "Inching toward Integrity," *Transitions* vol. 5, no. 3 (March 1998), p. 83.

12. See Dinello's excellent piece, "The Russian F-Connection: Finance, Firms, Friends, Families, and Favorites," *Problems of Post-Communism*, vol. 46, no. 1 (January/February 1999), pp. 24–33.

13. *Ibid.*, p. 30. It seems similar claims could be made with regard to the uncertainty and weak institutionalization of the political realm, and how informal networks there also function as "mechanisms of risk management."

14. The highly publicized case of Petre Badea, the millionaire patron of Aedifica Carpați, who appears to have had similar access to state resources under the Iliescu regime and the Constantinescu administration, seems emblematic of this "rent-seeking" behavior. The case was covered in detail in late July/early August 1999 editions of the daily *Ziua*.

15. Quoted in Kaplan, "The Fulcrum of Europe," p. 34.

16. Gross, "Inching toward Integrity," p. 84.

17. Significantly, such allegations are not at all out of touch with practice during the Ceaușescu era: As was previously mentioned, the "Russian card" was an effective tool of the Ceaușescu regime for preventing and crushing dissent—in part because it appealed to the genuinely strong anti-Russian sentiments of the Romanian population.

18. This may be true of all "late-developing" societies, even by East European standards, the Romanian situation seemed exaggerated. See, for example, Joseph Rothschild's characterization of the interwar Romanian intelligentsia in Joseph Rothschild, *East Central Europe Between the Two World Wars* (Seattle: University of Washington Press, 1974).

19. See, for example, Andrew C. Janos' study of the Hungarian case, *The Politics of Backwardness in Hungary: 1825–1945* (Princeton, NJ: Princeton University Press, 1982).

20. The concentration of capital post-Communist states, which results from powerful formal networks of personal connections, is frequently portrayed as a uniformly negative outcome. Yet, as Dinello observes: "The fierce battles for financial supremacy in Russia could have been even more vicious without this vehicle [the "F-connection," personal connections] for reducing competition." See Dinello, "The Russian F-Connection," p. 30.

III

CIVIL SOCIETY AND SOCIAL ISSUES

11

NGOs and the Development of Civil Society

Sandra Pralong[1]

In February 1999, as approximately 10,000[2] striking Jiu miners armed with clubs were marching on the capital, Bucharest residents responded with a silent street protest. The protest organizers wanted to show that civil society was strong and ready to defend the young, democratic institutions targeted by the miners' violence. However, only 4,000[3] people showed up for the protest rally—hardly a demonstration that civility can vanquish violence. Having more than twice as many people attack democracy than defend it is not the show of support one expected from civil society. It was, however, a victory of courage over fear if one considers that among the 4,000 nonviolent protesters were some of the very people—mostly intellectuals—whom these same miners had bludgeoned with clubs in 1990.[4] Surprisingly, only four or five organizations spoke up against the miners' hijacking of Romanian politics—the fifth such occurrence in the last ten years. In a country where the growth of the associative sector is relatively strong, and, over time, an estimated average of 400 new associations, foundations, and nongovernmental organizations (NGOs) are registered *each month*, one wonders why so few of them reacted.[5]

In this chapter, I argue that, contrary to those who see in the Bucharest protest proof that civil society (in its Tocquevillian incarnation) is alive and well in Romania, I see in this same event its very weakness. Beyond the numbers, my claim has deeper, structural reasons. Even though the political prominence of civil society is real, and the statistics tallying the development of the NGO sector show a picture of growth, we need to ask ourselves what this growth represents: the development of grassroots collective action and community cooperation, or the transformation of the associative sector into a source of political capital and/or economic profit?[6] I argue that, nearly fourteen years into the post-Communist transition, Romania's civil society corresponds less to the Tocquevillian model[7] than to the Hegelian one.[8] Tocqueville saw in civil society a sphere of grassroots cooperation, where people get together to resolve issues that they cannot (or choose not to) entrust to the state. According to Tocqueville, in a democracy people are free and equal, and relative social equality makes it natural for them to associate—few can pursue their interest without cooperation from others. Collective action, the stuff of civil society, stems from self-interest rightly understood. For Hegel, on the other hand, civil society is the realm in which individuals become recognized in their particularity and difference; it is where the actualization of individual freedom occurs through property and the competition of interests. In Hegel's civil society, a person's ends remain purely private, not communal, and individuals are given their due as free persons through the market. There is little, if any, collective action in civil society, merely individuation. Eventually people do experience solidarity and collective responsibility; however, this happens in the *state*, not in civil society.

It is my contention in this chapter that the Hegelian view of civil society—closer to the state of nature and focused on the market—is more in tune with Romania's current situation than is Tocqueville's. In a country like Romania, Communist communalism has obliterated people's sense of individuality, while collective ownership and political oppression have negated their freedom. The first order of business then, as old reflexes slowly die away, is to develop an intersubjective sense of recognition and help people "become" individuals again. Only then can they associate and cooperate with each other. Until that moment, as long as identities are not yet firmly established, the development of civil society will remain skewed toward the process of recognition and individuation rather than towards association or cooperation.

In his book *The Idea of Civil Society*, Adam B. Seligman defines civil society as an "ethical ideal of the social order, one which, if not overcomes, at least harmonizes, the conflicting demands of individual interest and social good."[9] Seligman's definition points to the constant social tension between the self and the group, and illustrates why civil society—as a space of reconciliation—helps such tension build, rather than destroy, the social fabric. Individuals, each pursuing his own interests, overcome collective action problems because it is in their interest to do so. Hegel's conception of civil society focuses on one moment: the identification of individual interest. Tocqueville focuses on the other: the realization of the common good through mediating associations. In Hegel's world, one evaluates civil society's development by measuring ownership, estates, and corporations—in other words, the market. In Tocqueville's realm, one might measure the number of informal, voluntary, grassroots associations. The literature on democracy has ignored Hegel's view of civil society and focused on Tocqueville. The density of associative life is considered a reliable measure of democracy and proof of its solidity because Tocqueville's measure seeks to capture the extent to which democracy is based on grassroots support.

I argue that Tocqueville's view is not (yet) an appropriate framework for post-Communist Romania. Romania's voluntary associations belong, in fact, to a sub-segment of the market rather than to the sphere of civil society proper, as defined by Alexis de Tocqueville or Robert Putnam.[10] Formal NGOs (registered as not-for-profit corporations), staffed by salaried workers and engaged in the management of structured programs, form the backbone of Romania's "civil society." These are not the small, informal associations dear to Tocqueville or the choral societies and bird-watching clubs popularized by Putnam; they are organizations closer to Hegel's "estates and corporations." It was transnational flows and international assistance that fueled the initial emergence, and much of the subsequent growth, of the NGO sector—not the urge for local, grassroots social cooperation emphasized by Tocqueville. Closer to Hegel's view, foreign support created a "market" (of funds for democratic assistance) which allowed the emergence of a nongovernmental sector and the mutual recognition of civil society actors, but not yet their cooperative association.

THE POLITICS OF CIVIL SOCIETY FORMATION

Unlike in Poland, the Czech Republic, or Hungary, there was no dissident movement and no organized civil society to speak of in Romania prior to 1989. No independent "civil life"[11] was claimed by the few who dared oppose (albeit mostly in oblique and metaphorical ways, primarily through poetry) the absolute power of Nicolae Ceauşescu. Society was atomized and the people were traumatized. Terrorized by the prevailing surveillance of the secret police, the Romanian people were fearful of getting together and speaking up. With the exception of a handful of state-run associations (Communist Youth, Writers' Union, etc.) and a state-run Labor Union with no independent power, there was practically no associative life.

Within the democratization literature, the Romanian case fits the ideal type of "rupture" rather than that of a pacted transtion.[12] Yet the rupture itself was ambiguous: It was the *incumbent* "soft-liners" who came to power, not the opposition. Those in power co-opted societal support by misrepresenting both their credentials and their intentions. Their pro-Western rhetoric notwithstanding, they were initially largely *opposed* to key democratic and market reforms. Given this feat of political coat turning performed by the former Communists, the new institutions were born lacking whatever credibility was conferred by their role in the Revolution. Since it successfully stood the test of elections in 1990 and 1992, the Iliescu administration was perceived as legitimate; but it was not actually *credible* in its democratic, market-driven intentions.[13]

This particular political configuration—of "democratic" power being held by authoritarian and anti-market-reform forces—left few clear political spaces to be occupied by democratic elites. President Ion Iliescu and his team shrewdly occupied two places at once: They colonized the "democratic" terrain (with its expectations for political and economic reform), yet they also secured the space on the left, the home of the former *nomenklatura*, of which they were a part. Thus, the only remaining spaces on the political spectrum were squeezed on the extremes—left and right. Therefore any nonextremist opposition had to draw its legitimacy by traveling not in political space (left or right) but in political *time* (i.e., in the past)! Thus, the democratic opposition had to draw its ideological roots from the pre-Communist days, which perhaps explains why Romania is the only East European country whose "historical parties" (revived from pre–World War II days) returned after 1989. The center-right National Peasant Party was, up to 2001, led by a generation that had spent up to seventeen years in Communist jails; its top leaders were well past their seventies in 1989. Even though the old Social Democratic party of yore was also revived, its political space was quickly absorbed by the National Salvation Front, which ultimately split in the spring of 1992 into two social democratic parties. This left practically no place for younger generations of non-*nomenklatura* to be recruited in democratic parties of the center right or left. Most intellectuals eschewed the National Peasant Party, debilitating the tasks undertaken by the democratic opposition in political society, leaving civil society to act in weak, isolated fashion, and therefore giving civil society a much stronger *political* mandate than should have been the case.[14] Given that the state could retaliate against undesirable civil society claims by withholding the legal authorization to associate, the most frequent call heard from NGOs in those days was a call for "political distance." This transformed one part of 'civil society' into just another arena for politics and left the other inoculated against any political claim, and essentially powerless.

CIVIL SOCIETY AFTER 1989—SOME OPERATING DISTINCTIONS

The Foundation for the Development of Civil Society (FDSC) estimates that, in 2002, there were approximately 16,000 to 17,000 associations and foundations officially registered with Romanian courts, of which almost 6,000 have been included in an official Catalogue of Romanian NGOs.[15] In absolute terms, the total number seems rather low compared to a country like, for example, Hungary, which already had well over 30,000 NGOs by 1992—almost twice as many as Romania for a country with less than half the population. Yet, in relative terms, the situation is quite encouraging, given that even before 1989 there were already over 8,000 such organizations in Hungary and practically none in Romania.

In a recent article,[16] Thomas Carothers decried what he terms "the fascination with nongovernmental associations," which he saw "at the core of the current enthusiasm about civil society." Indeed, several authors warn about automatically equating the growing universe of NGOs with civil society. They remind us that civil society encompasses far more than the NGO sector; it includes all the organizations and associations that exist outside of the state and the market.[17] In new democracies, where there is no tradition of free association, it is easy to equate NGOs with civil society because NGOs represent the most visible and sometimes the only fully functioning part of the associative sector.

A former advisor to the president for the relation with NGOs says, "There are three kinds of civil society in Romania: the professionals, the enthusiasts, and the profiteers."[18] Indeed, this classification accounts for the distinctions one finds among:

1. The Western-funded professional NGOs active primarily in human rights, democracy promotion, and social services. This group is mostly formed of very young people with limited prior professional experience who were trained by Western NGOs in the early 1990s to be "program officers." Commitment to "civil society" represents a call for public service without being a "civil servant" and having to work for the state. This group is managerially well trained, versatile, and politically neutral. Mobility among NGOs is high.
2. The "enthusiastic," but underfunded, local groups (which best correspond to the Tocquevillian idea of self-organized, voluntary organizations) are to be found mostly in the provinces, where Western support has been slower to reach. To these, one should add the civil society activists, such as those in the Civic Alliance, the Group for Social Dialogue, etc. Even though some of the largest groups of local "enthusiasts" have received Western support, unlike the "professionals" they have not employed Western staff, nor were they trained by Westerners. Their staff is local, and their focus is primarily domestic and politically engaged. There are also some nonpolitical organizations in this category: mostly small, local arts and culture associations that manage to just get by with little funding and few projects. These are primarily associations commemorating the life and work of local cultural or past political icons (the Lucian Blaga Association, the Mihai Viteazu Foundation, etc.).
3. The "profiteers" are those shrewd entrepreneurs who took advantage of tax loopholes benefiting nonprofit organizations to disguise profit-making import-export businesses as NGOs. This disease plaguing Romanian civil society is giving a bad name to the nongovernmental sector in general. It is difficult to estimate exactly how many fraudulent

> NGOs there are, but some statistics are worrisome. In a few rural areas, where economic development is particularly slow, numbers as high as 1,638 NGOs for a small, rural community in the mountains of Northern Moldova are not unusual, and an average of 90 foundations per 1,000 people is the norm—which would mean about 1 foundation per (extended) family. Some locals are said to have as many as 20 NGOs registered in their name. One might assume a correlation between the high poverty index and humanitarian assistance or social cooperation, but there is nothing of the sort. These "foundations," mostly staffed by local government officials, are mere fronts for thriving black-market businesses, such as the market for imported cars, that profitably use the tax loopholes granted to NGOs.[19]

To the group of economic profiteers one should add a subgroup, the "*political* frauds." These are either the shadow organizations created by the Iliescu regime between 1990 and 1996 to undermine the segment of civil society involved in politics, or they are the current stream of civil servants who, taking advantage of the administration's slowness, quickly set up foundations to receive Western funds destined to state-run projects—all this, of course, in the name of managerial "expediency" and efficiency. Indeed, in the early 1990s, faced with vocal political opposition coming from civil society, Iliescu had created, out of thin air, myriad associations and foundations, and named them in ways purposefully reminiscent of those already existing (and which were contesting his politics). His goal was to create confusion and thus take the sting out of the opposition, but also, whenever possible, to siphon off funds destined to the NGO sector and use them for the benefit of his ruling party. Now that Romanian politics are less overtly contentious, the siphoning off of funds is the key motivation in most civil servants' great urge to grow the ranks of foundation or association founders (and owners).

FOR LOVE OR PROFIT? ROMANIA'S CIVIL SOCIETY TO THE TEST

What Tocqueville called "habits of the heart" refers both to the courteous ways in which strangers interact in civil society, as well as to their shared ideals, the realization of which necessitates their association. Since it is a "habit of the *heart*," membership in civil society can be said to be a matter of "love"—love for common projects and for one's fellows. The informality normally associated with such groups only strengthens the power of the bond created by common affections. In a modern state, eventually the bonds of civil society become a matter of contractual, rather than informal, affiliation. By legal status, the groups that actually constitute civil society either are associations, foundations, or, generically speaking NGOs. The initial law that regulated the Romanian associative field dated from 1924 and could hardly respond to contemporary social needs. A new law was adopted in 2000, but neither law, for instance, makes distinctions between the institutions of civil society and the organizations in the *not-for-profit* sector, which introduces considerable methodological confusion. If the operational utility of a notion such as civil society is to distinguish this realm from *both* state and market (in the Tocquevillian definition),[20] then the idea of civil society being equated with nonprofits is misleading. The not-for-profit sector only distinguishes a subset of the *market*—one in which the state may very well be involved—rather than accurately capturing the difference between state and nonstate actors. The fact that the approximately 17,000 NGOs (associations and foundations) now registered in Romania are, in reality, actually not-for-profit organizations (i.e., legally a subsegment of the market) is more than a matter of semantics. Self-definitions help position these organizations and determine the way in which they construe their activities. According to Hegel, since private property makes individuation possible, the pursuit of profit is likely to occur in all realms—the private and the public, and hence in civil society as well. People will only cooperate with each other—as Tocqueville noted—once social roles are identified and they are settled in relative social equality—not before that. For the moment, in Romania "there are not enough financially independent and socially and politically conscious people to fulfill the task of building and running NGOs."[21] Also, large loopholes and unclear and unenforced legal restrictions make it more attractive for businesspeople to conceal profits via NGOs than for involved citizens to set up bona fide operations of service to the community.

In Romania, like in other post-Communist countries, especially in the CIS, the "third sector" (the sector of associative life, as opposed to either the public or the private sectors) has become a market in its own right, especially for labor. For instance, in 1995, the third sector had a *salaried* workforce that was higher than that employed in solidly entrenched branches of the economy. At 37,000, employees in the NGO sector were more numerous than those working in sectors such as: oil and gas extraction and processing (36,000), water utilities (33,000), publishing and printing (22,000), radio and telecommunications (18,000), the tobacco industry (7,000), etc.[22] Actually, less than one-sixth (16 percent) of Romanian NGOs work with *volunteers*, while two-thirds (62 percent) employ salaried workers. The remaining 22 percent are reported as having neither salaried employees nor volunteers, and thus presumably represent (dormant?) membership organizations.[23] All together, the man-hours worked in the NGO sector (both salaried and volunteer work) amount to the equivalent worked by an impressive 84,000 full-time persons. Geographically also, the situation is skewed. Despite the fact that Romania's population is 55 percent rural, only one out of ten organizations is active in the countryside, while 90 percent work in the cities.[24] This has, perhaps, less to do with concern for alleviating urban poverty than with the savvy entrepreneurship of city dwellers, who are closer to potential sources of funding and more politically attuned to the need for "developing civil society," "capacity building," and "institution building" promoted by Western donors. In 1997, the cumulative revenues of Romanian NGOs were hovering at approximately $83 million, while the expenses (program and operating costs) amounted to only $66 million.[25] This means that over 25 percent of the capital raised remained unused, presumably representing amounts ready to be reinvested and savings for future programs. Depending on how one looks at it, this might also represent concealed profits.

Together, these indicators support the assumption of this essay: that Hegel's model of civil society—focused on the market—is more suited to Romania's current situation than Tocqueville's. Many see employment with an NGO akin to working in the service sector. It is much better paid than public administration and requires fewer qualifications than managerial positions in the private sector do. Frequent training trips abroad and a high media profile for NGOs add to the appeal. Actually, one hears many a youth say wistfully, when asked about career plans: "I'd like to be president of an NGO." (The matter of which *ideal* that NGO should serve usually draws quizzical, incredulous, or dismissive looks). In short, a new, distinctive, socioeconomic category is emerging in Romania: the NGO professional as a "*private* civil servant," whose livelihood is directly linked to the amount of international assistance destined to support local civil society. At 1.34 percent of the workforce, Romanian NGOs employ comparable proportions of the workforce as the other countries of the region, making the trend toward rapid "marketization" of the sector prevalent in post-Communism. But is this the same as developing the basis for a robust democracy?

As Rueschemeyer puts it, "Organizational density of civil society as such does not guarantee favorable conditions for democracy";[26] nor is it an expression of the civic ethos or "republican spirit" in search of the common good. In addition, Sherri Berman reminds us with respect to Weimar Germany that the high number of organizations does not, by itself, ensure grassroots participation in political, economic, or social decision making; nor is it a sign of a pluralist polity.[27] Yet, despite its limitations, Romania's third sector makes a key contribution to a strong democratic polity: As the (Hegelian) realm of mutual recognition, of identification of needs, and of differentiation, it helps individuals become autonomous and self-reliant. And that is the first step in building a solid, Tocquevillian civil society. Just as Hegel describes the role of estates and corporations, the third sector is, among other things, a means to achieve membership and social identity, which will eventually help develop a need for cooperation.

WHOSE CIVIL SOCIETY? REPRESENTING WHAT INTERESTS?

When one looks at the preceding numbers, an obvious question springs to mind about motives: Whose interests are represented by the NGO sector in Romania? Who finances it? And for what kinds of projects? After the fall of the Berlin Wall, several billion dollars in international aid for the region were earmarked "for the development of civil society and democratic institutions." One is tempted to assume that civil society in the region is primarily a creation of the West. That would, however, miss a key piece of the puzzle—the fact that domestic support of the NGO sector finally has emerged, but did so only after ten years of post-Communism. This produced a set of relationships between foreign donors, the state, and civil society, which continues to make civil society an arena for individuation, differentiation, and actualization rather than for grassroots cooperation and organizing. Not all NGOs represent grassroots concerns or have been created from the bottom up: the majority actually were not. Yet their very attachment to the West (via both funding and programming) is an asset, for in this way NGOs help engage in "social leapfrogging" and create local awareness of issues that may otherwise have taken years to bring forth. Through involvement in civil society, donors facilitate the actualization and the satisfaction of needs, thus helping speed up social maturation. This, in time, will produce (future) viable partners for cooperation. The main beneficiary of the NGOs' work seems to be not civil society per se, but the state. NGOs help differentiate the arena of competence of state and of society, identifying and separating the roles and untangling what was a confused and overlapping arena under Communism.

In a recent essay on the influence of NGOs in Eastern Europe, Steven Sampson[28] cites several areas where NGOs have been successful: the development of a core of professional organizations (staffed with people who know how to formulate and implement projects), the creation of networks of cooperation among NGOs, incipient collaboration between NGOs and the state (developing a public agenda of human rights, consumer and environmental protection, etc.), the achievement of influence in policy making, and so on. These represent areas in which some NGOs in Romania excelled, too. The FDSC and Centras are among the most prominent. They operate both as NGOs in their own right and as resource centers for other NGOs, providing them with training and other assistance. Also active is Pro-Democracia—besides election monitoring, it deploys programs which keep elected officials accountable and citizens informed of their rights. But despite these successes, one problem remains: the way in which the Romanian NGO sector sprang to life deprives it of much of the legitimacy normally associated with grassroots movements. Since December 1989, foreign donors seeking to finance nongovernmental programs in Romania had to channel funds through local organizations, but there were no such institutions in Ceaușescu's Romania. Most

NGOs have thus been created simply in response to available Western funding. The situation was somewhat similar in the other countries of the region. However, Hungary and Poland, for instance, already had a timid nongovernmental sector even under Communism. This direct correlation between Western funding and the development of civil society means that much of the enthusiasm about the vibrancy of civil society in Eastern Europe should be toned down. It is as if, when speaking about democracy in the United States, one were to use Washington's lobbyists and Beltway subcontractors as vivid examples of a mass participatory culture. At best, they help. At worst, they are a pathology. But they are not *it*.

From almost 95 percent in 1990, only a little more than half (56 percent) of the funds supporting the Romanian NGO sector were foreign in 1996. In 1998, that proportion dropped to only 36 percent. In the same period, Romanian private donations, small to start with, have more than doubled, from 3 percent in 1996 to 8 percent in 1998.[29] Despite this encouraging trend, local NGO executives acknowledge to this day that they design their programs to capture Western funds rather than to address local issues needing to be resolved.[30] One could argue that this merely makes them savvy fund-raisers and astute marketers. This is true. But even when NGO programs are geared toward addressing particular local issues, such process puts priorities upside down: Local NGOs first identify the preferences of the likely *donors*, and only after that do they seek the local need that may be satisfied from such cooperation. In other words, they tailor projects to fit Western concerns, rather than appeal to Western donors to respond to *local* needs. As one executive has succinctly put it, "In Romania, foreign money chases projects rather than projects chase money."[31] Perhaps this explains why so many of the funds earmarked by international donors for Romania have remained unspent. This sequence (first find the funds, then seek the need to be fulfilled) stands contrary to the expected logic of civil society development and representation. Normally, associations derive their power and legitimacy from civil society rather than from Western sponsors. On closer examination, then, it appears that many local NGOs are not representative of *Romanian* civil society, but rather they represent the aspirations of civil society in the *donor* country! Western donors often have their own agendas that are clearly beneficial for social change, but not necessarily reflecting local needs.

Yet, as Sampson notes,[32] this is not all bad. Quite the contrary: Even though such a relation obliterates grassroots representativity, it is nevertheless socially profitable. Some of the most progressive social issues would not have been put on the domestic agenda had it not been for Western involvement through NGOs. Specific women's and children's rights, consumer protection, environmental safety, and many other standards designed to help and protect citizens are slowly becoming part of the public agenda in spite of society lacking the preconditions for putting them forward. One may call this phenomenon "social leapfrogging"—the importation of ideas in a social setting not yet ready for their indigenous development. NGOs are ideal agents of social learning and leapfrogging because they are in contact with progressive ideas from abroad and have the means to implement them domestically. Between 1990 and 1996, for instance, the Soros Foundation has been a key importer of social ideas and a founder of NGOs ready to implement them. In short, the cooperation between foreign donors and local civil society yields mutual recognition and identification of needs, and helps promote social change. This, in Hegelian terms, fosters identity formation of social actors and promotes civil society's freedom. But it does not necessarily follow that it also increases local cooperation among civil society actors.

The other effect of Western assistance occurs precisely in this relationship. It has to do not with the quality of representation provided by local NGOs, but with the kind of relationship established between them and the state. After 1989, the all-powerful socialist state lost much of its ability to respond to society's needs. In the process of transition, NGOs have stepped in to take over the tasks that a weak, deficient state could no longer perform and which the market had no incentive to take over. In short, NGOs stepped in to provide public goods. Once the representatives of civil society came to power, between 1996 and 2000, the state started relying even more directly on NGOs: 9 percent of all Romanian NGOs worked in partnership with agents of the local administration, 13 percent with other public institutions, and 16 percent with the central government. This means that over one-third (38 percent) of the work done by NGOs was performed in partnership with the state. While throughout the years the relationship with the central government remained steady, the partnerships with the local administration seem to have declined, showing additional disconnect between NGOs and efforts to serve local communities.[33] Once again, Hegel's vision of civil society as an arena for individuation offers the proper framework for analysis: an undifferentiated, all-encompassing state first differentiates itself as it "passes the baton" (so to speak) to civil society, helping it, in this process, to identify its role. After that, the state can withdraw, leaving social actors and the market alone to solve collective action problems. Tocqueville's model of social cooperation to the exclusion of the state will become operational only after this first ("Hegelian") phase, after the new social actors have defined their roles and competencies.

The question arises whether Romanian civil society, even though it does not meet Tocquevillian standards (yet), can be sustained from domestic sources in the absence of enough economic growth to free up funds and in the absence of serious political will to promote local giving. The state seems, for now, unable to support the growth of local philanthropy; the tax-exempt status of not-for-profits and the tax abatements on charitable contributions are considered a drain on state revenues rather than a boost to civil society development. In 1999, only three years after the NGO "lobby" had won an important victory by gaining tax-exempt status for philanthropic donations, Parliament rescinded the law and, faced with a shortage of cash, has been now taxing donations as if they were investments. The fact that such a measure was taken by a democratic Parliament brought to power in part by a politically militant civil society is not as surprising as it may seem. After all, the "profiteers" have abused the system, so now everyone pays! The importance of civil society in a democracy still eludes many politicians, most of whom pay lip service to it without truly understanding its mechanisms. After all, the "professional" NGO sector in Romania is not considered a fully bona fide representative of grassroots efforts to organize locally; so elected officials are less concerned about a local backlash.

Financial backing is not the only issue at stake. Romanian civil society functions so often for "profit" rather than "love" not just because of a skewed and imperfect legal framework, but also for other, more fundamental reasons. After all, in a democracy, the legal framework eventually responds to social needs once these are articulated. My claim is that, in Romania, the need *has not yet arisen* for a different legal framework that is more protective of local interests, more focused on enhancing grassroots cooperation, and thus ready to grant a different status to civil society organizations.

ELITISM, LIBERALISM, AND THE REDISCOVERY OF THE INDIVIDUAL

As mentioned earlier, in *The Idea of Civil Society*, Adam B. Seligman beautifully captures the essence of civil society as being an "ethical ideal of the social order, one that, if not overcomes, at least harmonizes, the conflicting demands of individual interest and social good."[34] Seligman's definition focuses on how civil society helps reconcile the social tension between the self and the group. Interaction between individuals, each pursuing his or her own interests, requires them to be mindful of each other's rights and tolerant of each other's opinions. One gets respect if one is ready to grant it to others, and one may claim rights if one also grants them to one's fellows.

From this perspective two conditions are sine qua non for the development of civil society: first, a vision of society as being formed by free and *equal* citizens; and second, a definition of the individual as a *moral agent*. Each is indispensable to forming lasting associations. The Tocquevillian principle at work is that equal moral agents voluntarily agree to cooperate because it is in their best interests to do so. Being relatively equal, and aware of their own limitations, they reckon that they can achieve more in cooperation than either of them would be able to do on his own. The emphasis thus is not on freedom, or not on freedom in a *political* sense—although that, of course, is necessary—as it is on the *equality* of social condition and on the equality of moral agency.

Equality of social condition and of moral agency is anathema to an elitist view of the world. Seen from this perspective, the contrary of democracy is not totalitarianism or authoritarianism (which limits political freedom) but *aristocracy* (which condones inequality). In observing the practice of democracy in America,[35] Tocqueville emphasizes the relationship between the principle of association and that of equality. Aristocracy denies equality of social condition and, implicitly, equality of moral agency, and thus is not conducive to the formation of voluntary associations. "Aristocratic communities always contain, among a multitude of persons who by themselves are powerless, a small number of powerful and wealthy citizens, each of whom can achieve great undertakings single-handed."[36] "Among democratic nations, on the contrary, all the citizens are independent and feeble; they can do hardly anything by themselves, and none of them can oblige his fellow men to lend him their assistance."[37] Ties established in civil society are thus created between relatively equal individuals, each pursuing his or her own interests, with their fundamental equality based on the mutuality of recognition and respect of equal rights. However, for Hegel, individual recognition of rights is realized primarily through property; and for civil society to harmonize the demands of "individual interest," such interests need to be deemed legitimate in the first place.

If property is indeed necessary for the actualization of individual freedom, as well as for the recognition of rights and individual interest, then Romania needs first to resolve important issues of ownership, such as the transfer of state property in individual hands. As it was, privatization was extremely sluggish until 1996, and in the absence of genuine private owners—who may seek to pursue their interests through cooperation—civil society cannot develop properly. Even as late as the year 2000, despite the Constantinescu government's efforts to speed up privatization, there was still strong political opposition to widespread private property. As part of the electoral campaign in 2000, the leftist opposition threatened to repeal the new restitution laws if it were to win the December 2000 election.[38] Luckily, to this date, it has not done so; and now that Romania has been extended an invitation to join NATO it is unlikely that the issue will be raised again. But the Romanian Constitution, adopted in 1991, still deals gingerly with issues of ownership: The right to private property is not actually *guaranteed* by the state, but merely "protected."[39]

In addition to well-established property rights, the need to grant equal *moral* agency to all individuals is another stumbling block in creating a fully functional civil society. Communism has pitted classes against each other, recognizing consciousness to some but not to others. In this respect, Lenin's idea of a "vanguard" is merely a socialist version of the old feudal order. It is still prevalent today, as it was under Communism, though now the "vanguard" is intellectual and financial rather than political or ideological. What happened, then, to the enthusiasm that, in 1989, toppled the dictatorship of Communist elites and sought democracy under the impetus of a revived civil society? In an article about Hungary, Bill Lomax explains the paradox through what he terms the "betrayal of the intellectuals." His explanation is valid for Romania as well: "The majority of the progressive intelligentsia in Hungary are not democrats but liberals, and though formally rejecting the tenets of Marxism-Leninism that many of them once believed in, they continue to adhere to an *elitist* belief in the advanced consciousness of the intellectuals, and a fear of and contempt for the uncultured masses, that represents little more than a resurrection of Leninism in liberal guise."[40] The issue, then, is to combat elitism. But since the genuine part of Romania's civil society (the "enthusiasts") is primarily formed of intellectuals, this can only be achieved *after* property enshrines each individual's claim to equal rights.

CIVIL SOCIETY—FROM "PROFIT" TO "LOVE"?

Tocqueville's observation that the relative equality of social conditions is conducive to collaboration in society makes cooperation difficult in Romania, where social hierarchies loom large. Elitism prevails. Individuals are only now in the process of asserting their equal statuses and separate identities. My contention, then, is the following: In this "primordial soup" of the post-Communist transition, as the legal framework has yet to be settled, as social roles have yet to be distributed, and as individual identities are still in formation, people will use just about any means at their disposal to gain their identities and exercise their newly found freedom. This, Hegel tells us, occurs as a function of property ownership. Then, it should come as no surprise that, in a still elitist, "aristocratic" (or, rather, "feudal") environment, the first incarnation of civil society will be as a tool for private ownership—as the way to actual "individuation." Only later can Tocqueville's "equality of social condition" follow, once self-aware individuals, empowered by their new status as owners, start claiming for themselves the right to be considered equal moral agents. Thus, "civil society" in the traditional, Tocquevillian sense, as the arena of cooperation between individuals pursuing self-interest in an enlightened way, can develop only once self-situated individuals are secure in their ownership and in the legitimacy of their pursuits of profit.

In other words, there seems to be a necessary progression of sorts in the development of civil society, a progression from "profit" to "love." The Romanian case could exemplify this trajectory: Civil society first forms as a way for intellectuals to contest the (Communist) state and assert their status as an elite group. In the process, civil society seeks to extract the resources and the power that the state controls. The transfer of property from the state to society initially bypasses the intellectual elite—which is empowered by, and supported with, funds from the outside. But the increase in domestic giving, small as it may be, shows nonetheless the emergence of a domestic property-owning class that is now ready to invest in collective action. As ownership spreads and the enlightened pursuit of self-interest becomes legitimate, the Tocquevillian idea of civil society can finally develop, and the pursuit of cooperation at the grassroots level becomes necessary for individuals seeking to prosper.

I believe Romania is now on the cusp of this changing world, in which property rights are finally about to be settled, and the energies captive in this arena are being freed for other pursuits. The laws of property restitution were finally promulgated in January 2000. The Liberal Party, on the other hand, is hoping to introduce a constitutional guarantee of property and not just its "protection." Once these institutional changes are implemented, I expect that membership in civil society will cease to be a way to individual ownership, and will become instead a collectively profitable enterprise based on cooperation.

To summarize: In civil society, to Tocqueville's cooperation Hegel responds with the mutuality of recognition and individuation through property and profit. I believe Hegel's ideas provide an important explanation for the Romanian situation. They help clarify the importance of property (as the first abstract right to be actualized in civil society) and allow us to evaluate its impact on the development of the NGO sector. Almost fifteen years after the fall of Communism, Romania is just now starting to witness the first results of a process of individuation, the key to which is private ownership. Several pieces of the puzzle start falling together when civil society is observed from a Hegelian perspective: We find an explanation for elements such as the lack of differentiation between the "third sector" and other businesses, the high incidence of "profiteers" (for-profit NGOs), the persistence of a legal framework that places civil society in the market, and other elements which put civil society on the side of "profit" rather than "love." If these are the byproducts of a society struggling to overcome the legacy of Marxism, then theoretically Hegel is vindicated as well. For, in trying to get rid of the old Communist ideology, if one stands Marx on his head,[41] one falls straight into Hegel's lap, so to speak, though without integrating Tocqueville's vision of civil society. Yet, if Hegel provides a more apt description for Romania's present, change is under way, and the first signs of a Tocquevillian order are already emerging.

NOTES

1. This chapter has benefited from criticism by Ancuţa Vameşu, executive director of the Foundation for the Development of Civil Society (FDSC), and data provided by Carmen Epure and Oana Ţigănescu, researchers at the FDSC.

2. Estimate, Reuters Agency and CNN (14–19 January 1999).

3. *Ibid.*

4. In June 1990, miners came to Bucharest to "restore democracy." They did so by ransacking the democratic opposition parties headquarters and by literally beating up intellectuals in the streets, "identifying" them according to whether or not they wore

glasses or carried newspapers or books. Six people died in the incidents. President Iliescu officially thanked the miners for "their efforts on behalf of consolidating Romania's young democracy."

5. Only the Civic Alliance and a few Human Rights organizations responded to the call.

6. Many of my former colleagues in the NGO world, who read drafts of this manuscript, were unhappy with my use of the term "profit" as a metaphor for the Hegelian model. Their reaction was strengthened by the pejorative connotation that the idea of profit still carries in the former Communist world. I, however, intend no such negative interpretation; I merely wish to emphasize that the logic in which Romanian civil society places itself for now is, in keeping with Hegel, that of the market rather than of the grassroots, voluntary, associative sector.

7. Alexis de Tocqueville, *Democracy in America* (New York: The Modern Library, 1981).

8. G. W. F. Hegel, *Elements of the Philosophy of Right*, trans. by H. B. Nisbet (Cambridge: Cambridge University Press, 1991), pp. 220–274. The choice of Hegel to discuss Romanian civil society stems from the very premise of this chapter: Romania does not yet have a functioning civil society, in the way democratic theory, using the Tocquevillian model, anticipates. Hegel's premise, that it is the market (rather than the associative sector) that matters, best represents the current Romanian situation. Locke similarly regards commerce as favorable for liberty. Recall his dictum that the private appropriation of land increases "the common stock of mankind" (Second Treatise, section 37). Madison also sees the representation of propertied interests in factions as inevitable and desirable, if complemented by factions representing a plurality of views. One may contrast these views with those of Aristotle and Rousseau, who reject commerce as vulgar and slavish.

9. Adam B. Seligman, *The Idea of Civil Society* (New York: The Free Press, 1992).

10. Robert Putnam, *Making Democracy Work: Civic Traditions in Modern Italy* (Princeton, NJ: Princeton University Press, 1993).

11. Bill Lomax, "The Strange Death of 'Civil Society' in Post-Communist Hungary," *Journal of Communist Studies and Transition Politics*, vol. 13, no. 1 (March 1997), pp. 41–63.

12. The archetype is Guillermo O'Donnell, Philip Schmitter, Laurence Whitehead, eds., *Transitions from Authoritarian Rule* (Baltimore, MD: The Johns Hopkins University Press, 1986).

13. The idea of the 1990 and 1992 elections being "legitimate" is contestable. Indeed, there were numerous acts of intimidation and electoral fraud, though international observers present at the time validated the results. For an in-depth analysis of the frauds of 1990 and 1992, see Henry F. Carey, "Irregularities or Rigging: The 1992 Romanian Parliamentary Elections," *East European Quarterly*, vol. 29, no. 1 (March 1995), pp. 43–66. As a consequence, from 1990 to 1996 Romania embarked on what Terry Lynn Karl calls "electoralism," Larry Diamond calls "electoral democracy," and Fareed Zacharia calls "illiberal democracy." See T. L. Karl, "Imposing Consent? Electoralism vs. Democratization in El Salvador," in Paul W. Drake and Eduardo Silva, eds., *Elections and Democratization in Latin America, 1980–1985* (San Diego: Center for Iberian and Latin American Studies, 1986); L. Diamond, "Introduction: In Search of Consolidation," in Diamond, et al., eds., *Consolidating the Third Wave Democracies* (Baltimore, MD:

The Johns Hopkins University Press, 1997), pp. xiv–xvi; and Fareed Zakaria, "The Rise of Illiberal Democracy," *Foreign Affairs*, vol. 76, no. 6 (November/December 1997).

14. On the destructive effects on democratization via mutually exclusive civil and political society, see Juan J. Linz and Alfred Stepan, *Problems of Democratic Transition and Consolidation: Southern Europe, South America, and Post-Communist Europe* (Baltimore, MD: The Johns Hopkins University Press, 1996), pp. 9–10.

15. *Catalogul Organizaciilor Neguvernamentale din România* (The Catalogue of Non-Governmental Organizations), Livia Constantinescu and Ancuţa Vameşu, FDSC, (Bucharest: *Fundacia Pentru Dezvoltarea Societaci Civile*, 1999).

16. Thomas Carothers, "Civil Society," *Foreign Policy*, no. 117 (Winter 1999–2000), pp. 18–29.

17. Carothers, "Civil Society," p. 19.

18. Luminica Petrescu, State Advisor, the Romanian Presidency, author's interview, (Bucharest, July 1998).

19. Dragos Căliţoiu, *O Analiza a Fundaţiilor Umanitare din Judeţul Suceava* (An analysis of humanitarian organizations in Suceava county), *Info ONG, Anul* iii, no. 15 (April–May 1989), p. 26. One should note that with the adoption of the new law, such practices are more difficult, though they have not been completely eliminated.

20. Tocqueville's definition of civil society is that of an intermediary between the state and the market, and does not include the market in the associative sector, as do the definitions given by Hegel or Marx. For a more ample discussion, see chapter 1 in Seligman, *The Idea of Civil Society*, p. 17.

21. Ferencz Miszlevitz, "Participation and Transition: Can the Civil Society Project Survive in Hungary?" *The Journal of Communist Studies and Transition Politics*, vol. 13, no. 1 (March 1997), pp. 27–40.

22. *The Globalization of the Non-Profit Sector—A Revision. Summary*, FDSC, (joint Johns Hopkins' project on the Comparative Analysis of the NGO Sector).

23. FDSC, *Dimensions of the Non-Profit Sector in Romania, a Preliminary report*, (Bucharest: Fundacia Pentru Dezvoltarea Societaci Civile, 1998), figures valid for 1997.

24. *Ibid.*

25. *Ibid.* In terms of revenues, Romania is far behind a country half its size such as Hungary. There, between 1992 and 1993, the aggregate revenues of voluntary associations added up to a whopping $1 billion, or 3.1 percent of GDP! See Ferencz Miszlevitz, "Participation and Transition: Can the Civil Society Project Survive in Hungary?" *The Journal of Communist Studies and Transition Politics*, vol. 13, no. 1 (March 1997), pp. 27–40.

26. Quoted in Miszlievetz, "Participation and Transition." See also Sherri Berman, "Civil Society and the Collapse of the Weimar Republic," *World Politics*, vol. 49, no. 3 (April 1997), pp. 401–29.

27. Berman, "Civil Society and the Collapse of the Weimar Republic," *World Politics*, vol. 49, no. 3 (April 1997).

28. Steven Sampson, "Exporting Democracy through NGOs in Eastern Europe," unpublished manuscript, Conference on "NGOs and the Rule of Law," Georgia State University, Atlanta (4 September 1999).

29. *Defining the Non-Profit Sector in Romania* (Baltimore, MD: The Johns Hopkins University, Center for Civil Society Studies, 1998.)

30. Interview (Bucharest, July 1998.)

31. Interview with Viorel Micescu, Director of CENTRAS (Bucharest, July 1998).

32. Sampson, "Exporting Democracy through NGOs in Eastern Europe."

33. FDSC, *Dimensions of the Non-Profit Sector in Romania.*

34. Adam B. Seligman, *The Idea of Civil Society* (New York: The Free Press, 1992).

35. Tocqueville, *Democracy in America.*

36. Tocqueville, *Democracy in America*, p. 405.

37. Tocqueville, *Democracy in America*, pp. 405–6.

38. Iliescu's opposition party, the PDSR, has been repeatedly on record as rescinding property laws if elected.

39. The Liberal Party is seeking an amendment to the Constitution to change the wording from "property is protected" to "property is *guaranteed*" by the state.

40. Lomax, "The Strange Death of 'Civil Society' in Post-Communist Hungary."

41. As Marx claimed to do with Hegel's theory.

12

Multiculturalism and Ethnic Relations in Transylvania*

Claude Karnoouh

This chapter examines Hungarian-Romanian interethnic relations in the context of the controversy over the proposed independence of the Hungarian University at Cluj, currently a mere department of the larger Romanian University located in this city. Advocates for an independent Hungarian University cite the need for the preservation of Hungarian high culture and ethnicity within Transylvania and other areas of Romania. Opponents, which include a majority of Romanians, advocate its continued incorporation into the Romanian University. Their arguments range from those grounded in nationalist and xenophobic mistrust of the Hungarian minority in Romania to the need for an inclusive "multicultural" policy toward ethnic minorities more in keeping with Western values. This chapter directly addresses the arguments on both sides. Specifically, it examines whether the Western concept of multiculturalism is truly appropriate in the context Romanian interethnic relations.

HISTORICAL BACKGROUND

The Romanian-Hungarian cultural conflict is ancient, dating back to the period of Romanian nationalism in Transylvania at the end of the eighteenth century. It became especially acute after the compromise (Ausgleich) in 1867, which gave birth to the dual monarchy of the Austrian-Hungarian Empire and expanded Hungarian political power in their half of the Empire—at the time included territories which are now part of Romania. This power gave the Hungarian elite the liberty to conduct the politics of forced cultural integration and homogenization, with an inflexibility mixed with French Jacobinism and the Prussian *KulturKampf*.[1] For this reason, until 1919, Romanian higher education in Transylvania was reduced to a mere department of Romanian grammar, incorporated in the Hungarian University of Cluj.

After the fall of the Austro-Hungarian Empire and its dismemberment at the Treaty of Versailles, the fortunes of the Hungarians living in these territories changed dramatically. In Transylvania, which was now part of Romania, Hungarians now felt the effects of *Romanian* attempts at forced cultural integration, giving rise to the same sentiments of frustration experienced previously by the Romanians.[2] However, the Hungarians would be given a brief respite during the period of Hitler's Third Reich in Europe. The Vienna *Diktat* of 1940, which had been forced on the Romanian government by coercive Nazi diplomacy, ceded northern Transylvania, including Cluj, back to Hungary. Whereas in 1919, the *Hungarian* University of Cluj had been forced to move out to the Hungarian town of Szeged, in 1940, the *Romanian* University of Cluj was moved out to southern Transylvania (Sibiu), as the Hungarian University was reestablished. It was only after World War II that some kind of a rapprochement was seen, when the Royal Romanian government, after the recuperation of Northern Transylvania, signed a decree in 1946 which moved the Hungarian University next door to the Romanian University at Cluj (recently returned from exile at Sibiu) and sanctioned the right to an education in one's native language.

However, when the Communists came to power in 1948, they unleashed a ferocious political repression. While it was ostensibly in the name of class warfare and proletarian internationalism, these were mere fronts for the pursuit of the same cultural conflict between the two sides and their leaders. Taking advantage of the Hungarian revolution of 1956, the Romanian authorities, with the backing of the Soviets, closed down[3] the Hungarian University in 1959. The right to an education in one's native language was again rescinded. Once independent Hungarian universities became mere departments of other *Romanian* universities, which they remained until 1996. While they possessed the status of a "joint linguistic group" to the Romanian departments, they were without real administrative and financial autonomy, and without the academic freedom to recruit quality faculty.

The Romanian Communist Party also decided to extensively Romanize the cities of Transylvania through a slow, but inexorable policy of reducing Hungarian cultural identity and autonomy.[4] Faced with the option of having their professional horizon in their own language reduced, the Hungarian scholarly elite, with the tacit approval of the Romanian government, began to emigrate either to Hungary or to the West. This helped create a cultural vacuum of sorts, the effects of which we see today in the shortage of qualified faculty at the Hungarian University of Cluj.[5] This policy of the intentional marginalization of Hungarian culture transformed the Hungarian language into a private or semiprivate language.

In the years following the fall of Ceaușescu, successive Romanian governments, under the political influence of nationalist parties, made painfully slow progress regarding the educational rights of ethnic minorities.[6] To exemplify this point, the law on education signed on 24 July 1995 by President Iliescu stipulated, among other provisions, that neither history nor geography, nor civic education, would be taught in Hungarian in the nominally independent Hungarian institutions. To add to this, the law did not provide for the autonomy of secondary education in the Hungarian theater. Also, the schools of law, economics, and natural sciences were excluded. Although in humanistic disciplines, the law admitted Hungarian linguistic groups, they were without institutional guarantees to assure implementation. This is because the autonomy of the University of Cluj was regarded as a crucial provision of the new legislation, where the stability of the new governmental coalition was at stake. Finally, one of the critical flaws of this law, raised by the UDMR party, was the lack of a guarantee of primary, secondary, or tertiary education in the mother tongue.

The elections of November 1996 had brought hope of a new beginning, as they brought to power an opposition coalition that included the Hungarian Party (the UDMR). For the first time since 1919, Hungarians were present in the Romanian government, enabling them to seriously pursue their political agendas. Particular programs regarding the rebirth of cultural Hungarian institutions, which had been dismantled and seriously damaged during the last twenty years of the Ceauşescu era, were then promoted. Among these were proposals to reestablish the independent Hungarian University at Cluj.

THE CONTEMPORARY DEBATE

However, as of this writing nothing has happened, due in part to the strong opposition by the Romanian faculty in Cluj. Arguments against the reestablishment of an independent Hungarian University have ranged from classic Jacobinism ("we do not form universities on ethnic grounds") to the evident need of meeting prescribed norms for integration with the "West" (i.e., "the separation of the two universities hinders our integration in the Euro-Atlantic institutions and the European Community").[7] Of these arguments, the latter is perhaps the most insidious as, on the surface, it seems the most progressive. In fact, according to most Western observers, the presence of Hungarian linguistics groups in the Romanian departments is depicted as the accomplishment of a successful policy of multiculturalism, rather than a denial of ethnic Hungarian rights. This is unfortunate because in the aftermath of the collapse of Communism Western standards of interethnic relations are fast becoming the yardstick by which the laws and institutions created to protect ethnic rights are evaluated. It is precisely this point that I seek to address. Can we refuse the principle of autonomy of a Hungarian University in the name of a newly proclaimed presence of multiculturalism? Is the Western concept of multiculturalism really applicable in the context of Romanian interethnic relations? And are these concepts based on real situations, or are they just a way of hiding the reality of power games used in the new politics of transitional Romania?

It is important to observe that the concept of "multiculturalism" is itself derived from countries where immigration has founded modern society (after, of course, the socioeconomic marginalization, or physical elimination, of the original inhabitants).[8] The multiculturalism of the United States, and to be more precise, of the American left, covers a phenomenon of an entirely different nature from that which exists in contemporary Romania. American multiculturalism ostensibly bases itself on the antiracist struggle, and the recognition of the cultural and social dignity of the African American community and the various immigrant groups which form, socioeconomically, the lower strata of American society. It was born of the phenomenon of urbanization or, perhaps more accurately, "ghettoization" of the North American megalopolis which grew and intensified with the radicalization of liberal capitalism. Whether this was the overt intention or not, multiculturalism was used as a practical and descriptive instrument to manage the social strains engendered by the liberal capitalist system through a sort of social compromise based on a philosophy of cultural relativism.

One might question whether this concept is applicable to the Eastern European context of "interculturalism," where the societies have not been founded on immigration. It is important to remember that it was in Europe where the concept of the nation-state—a state built on an ethnically cohesive "nation" of people—was first established. Of course, few countries in Europe actually approach this ideal type. The dominant "nation" of people is often awash in a conglomeration of minorities that live within the borders of the state. However, this conglomeration is generally composed of longstanding, historically rooted, distinct, and often insular ethnic minorities with strong feelings of nationality. Thus, in the Central and Eastern European context, relations between ethnic groups is more often marked by "interculturalism" rather than "multiculturalism." The Latin prefix *inter* in this context stands intermittently for separation, space, or reciprocity. In contrast to multiculturalism, it is meant to denote the symbiotic interaction between two cultures which remain, at the same time, separate and distinct.

This concept makes more sense in the Central and Eastern European context, where interethnic relations are often marked by policies which emphasize the separateness of distinct ethnic minorities, and which explicitly recognize their rights as a group. In Hungary, there is a specific law that covers relations between these communities and the state, establishing "historical minorities" with communal rights. It is the same in Romania where Hungarians, Germans, Serbs, Bulgarians, Ukrainians, Lipovenians, Jews, Tartars, and their respective churches are recognized through constitutional rights bestowed upon national minorities. Here is a situation in total contradiction with the democratic multiculturalism of the West, one which reveals the special situation of Central and Eastern Europe.

In contemporary Romania, where the Hungarian minority has lived continuously for hundreds, or even thousands of years, there continues to be a marked sense of separation between those of Hungarian and those of Romanian nationality. The students from the east of Transylvania, where the rural and semiurban population is exclusively Hungarian and strongly traditional, generally do not associate with Romanians or even speak Romanian. On the other hand, the students from the large cities of Transylvania (Cluj, Oradea, Arad, Timişoara, Satu-Mare, Braşov) and the mixed villages are often bilingual, are more familiar with the Romanian culture, and are more inclined to associate with those of Romanian nationality.

However, with the exception of the bureaucratic management of the university, and some rare musical or theatrical meetings, there is not, properly speaking, any cultural interaction between Romanian and Hungarian intellectuals and students. There are few common cultural or civic associations where they would have the chance to meet. While in the common rooms, arranged in alphabetical order and organized largely for the purpose of disciplined study, Hungarian students may occasionally seek arrangements with their Romanian counterparts; most relations are strictly functional (or perfunctory) and occur without any knowledge of the reciprocal culture. Of course, there are exceptions to this rule, but even between friends, neighbors, or couples there are certain taboo subjects that cannot be discussed. Recent debates on the autonomy of the Hungarian University have clearly exposed the strength of these taboos by destroying friendships, undermining neighborly relations, and creating tensions among mixed couples

This sense of separatism between the two ethnic groups is pervasive in contemporary Romanian society, manifested in the almost willful ignorance on the part of many Romanian intellectuals of Hungarian high culture. Contemporary Hungarian humanities and literature are very seldom translated, and are unknown to the majority of Romanian scholars, who generally choose to ignore the original language. While they do not hesitate to pounce on even the lowest quality literature from the West, they almost totally ignore the best Hungarian masterpieces.[9]Also, it is not uncommon to hear private conversations among Romanian intellectuals that support views which would surprise Western observers of post-Communist Romania. Despite the fact that the majority of Romanian intellectuals today denigrate most of the decisions and actions taken by the Communist regime in the Ceauşescu era, a large number of them approve, without reservation, of the anti-Hungarian policies they pursued: "It is good to recognize, one of these days," a distinguished art historian and descendent of a Bourgeois family that suffered at the hands of the Communists in the 1950s once told me, "that the only positive action of Ceauşescu was the demographic transition of the major cities of Transylvania into Romanian cities."

Not entirely by coincidence, this attitude is reflected by the representatives of the ultranationalistic parties, a majority of whom view the Romanian-Hungarian relationship through the framework of the old nation-state paradigm where the national minority plays the role of the fifth column for a neighboring state that wishes to conquer lost territory. This belief naturally leads to their opposition to any legislation that would manifest a reawakening of Hungarian culture within the borders of Romania; their steadfast opposition to the reestablishment of the independent Hungarian University at Cluj is a prime example of this.

Ironically, their opposition is joined by the "Modernists" within the Hungarian ethnic community, who simply want to give more autonomy to the Hungarian linguistics groups that are attached to the Romanian departments. These intellectuals, who are the most open to the modern influences from the West, together with the majority of the Romanian faculty at Cluj, agree on the possibility of a multicultural university and are opposed to separate institutions. What the Hungarian "Modernists" do not understand is that the Western "multiculturalism" to which they have become converts may yet reveal itself to be a mere front for the commercialized monoculturalism of the new "Global village" so touted in the West.

MULTICULTURALISM AND THE END OF EUROPEAN CULTURE

Like every other country of post-Communist Europe, the most pervasive cultural phenomenon of post-Communist Romania has been the avalanche of Western norms, ideas, and values which have come to replace the cultural imperialism of the Soviets. This is true for most academic disciplines, whether one is dealing with historians, psychologists, philosophers, or linguists. As far as the Hungarian and Romanian students are concerned, their long-standing cultural differences do not impede them from attending the same pop rock concerts, eating the same fast foods, and watching the same movies. The old symbols, objects, and signs which once formed the foundations of ethnicity are fast becoming obsolete, lost in a cultural sea of commercialized modernity.

While the publicists and politicians prefer the term "globalization"—a more innocent economic and political term—the use of this concept is only one of the numerous forms taken by the contrived posthumanism of the late modernity to describe the phenomenon of global uniformization that is taking place in the late twentieth century. The rapid urbanization and accelerated uprooting of indigenous peoples has expanded and intensified over the last fifty years, and is now coupled with an ever increasing integration of economic interests, a growing web of communication and capital circulation channels, an increasing standardization of products, and even a increasing uniformity of the social relations between people.

This process of uniformity is the inevitable byproduct of the Western economic system. The essence of capitalism, itself bounded by nothing other than its inherent dynamic for infinite expansion, lets nothing in society escape the ever-expanding domain of merchandise and the ongoing commercialization of culture. In its generality, the West, by capturing cultural phenomenon from culture, effects a transmutation of values that will permit their integration in the world of merchandise. In other words, everything that seems different, but could be integrated into the sphere of merchandise, ultimately loses those its spirit.

Simultaneously on a social plan, the term of multiculturalism sheds itself of any political thought that articulates the cultural diversity of endangered interests exposed by the general and global rationalization of production. The notion of social classes is blurred when we refer to globalization and multiculturalism, due to the apparent neutrality of the economy. In the dictionary, globalization and multiculturalism can simultaneously be interpreted as social or political mutatis mutandis. Multiculturalism partially hides the social and cultural atomization of the individual, and is therefore united to the globalization of the planet under the auspices of an economy more and more concentrated by the centralization of its decision making, and more and more shaken by the decentralization of its production. This fragmentation, under the pretext of differences, illusory at best, leaves people without any mechanism of defense facing the onslaught of global uniformity.

This phenomenon gives even more meaning to the definition of the world endangered by capitalism as formulated by Marx: "The world is an accumulation of merchandise." To this definition, we can add only that at present, "The world is an accumulation of unequal information(s)." In effect, how can we speak of multiculturalism when hundreds of television and radio programs air the same images, dialogues, and sports viewed by hundreds of millions of people, and where the only cultural differences are between people who prefer Coca-Cola and McDonald's, and those who prefer Pepsi-Cola and Kentucky Fried Chicken?

CONCLUSION

The autonomy of the Hungarian University is an attempt to maintain and develop the study, in Hungarian, of the scholarly Hungarian and universal culture in Transylvania, the territory of one of its historic lands. To try to treat it through multiculturalism is, at a minimum, to condemn it to its disappearance. We can marvel at the naïveté of the Hungarian scholars, who freely adopt the American semantic in the name of democratic modernity without realizing the implications of this semantic, which transforms the Hungarians in Transylvania to simple immigrants in a land where they have been living for 1,000 years! They do not see the point that the ideology of the "Global Village" is not based on "Man," or the *Heimat* as the Germans call it, but on the language of that culture. This is why this solution seems to meet the approval of Romanian politicians and intellectuals.[10] These are the people who are simultaneously the more willing and, at the same time, most distrustful of the Hungarians. Even if the multiculturalism orchestrated in Transylvania by the Romanian university authorities (and a part of the "Modernist" Hungarian minority) can hide the cultural homogenization under the auspices of Romanian culture, in the long run it will appear in the West as a fake posthumanism of generally Romanian (which is generally of Romanian and more rarely Hungarian) character.

NOTES

*This chapter was translated from French by Mihnea Ion Năstase with Henry F. Carey, and was shortened with permission by Christopher Eisterhold with Carey.

1. Claude Karnoouh, *The Invention of the People: Romanian Chronicles* (Paris: Arcantère, 1990); see Sorin Mitu Chapin, *The Genesis of National Identity of Romanians in Transylvania* (Bucharest: Humanitas, 1997.)

2. P. J. Thomas, *Are the Romanians Our Allies?* (Paris: Sorlot, 1937); and Irina Livezeanu, *Cultural Politics in Greater Romania, Regionalism, Nation Building and Ethnic Struggle, 1918–1930* (Ithaca, NY: Cornell University Press, 1995.)

3. It is in Romania that the leaders of the 1956 Hungarian revolution were detained before being sent back and executed in Hungary.

4. This massive demographic change in the urban population has occurred due to the large rural Romanian population from the Transylvanian country and also Moldova. This was the result of an economic and urban political policy of intense industrialization and urbanization that has led to the actual configuration of Romanian villages.

5. Claude Karnoouh, "Romanians and Hungarians: How to Live Together?" *Korunk*, no. 4 (Cluj, 1997).

6. See Michael Shafir, "Ethnic Tensions Run High in Romania," *RFE/RL Research Report*, vol. 3, no. 32 (19 August 1994), p. 25; and Michael Shafir, "Controversy over Romanian Education Law," *Transition*, vol. 2, no. 1 (12 January 1996), p. 35.

7. The criteria considered by the United States for the integration of Romania to the OTAN are completely separate from any cultural considerations. These criteria consider only economic factors.

8. See Anne Phillips, "Why Worry about Multiculturalism?" *Dissent*, vol. 44 (Winter 1997), pp. 57–63.

9. Two remarkable examples are sufficient. Since 1990, no important texts of the Hungarian sociological school from the 1970s and 1980s was translated; and simultaneously, any of the works of the two most important Czech contemporaries, the romancer Hrabal and the philosopher Patochka, were not translated or commented in Translyvania.

10. The sociological section of the University of Cluj gave some results that demand attention. The majority of the Hungarian students in the humanistic disciplines have a preference for Hungarian departments that are autonomous in a united university.

13

Romani Marginality and Politics

Zoltan Barany[1]

> Xenophobia has something vulgar in it. I am not a bit xenophobic. . . . But I do hate Gypsies.
>
> —distinguished poet Ştefan Augustin Doinaş

> How could one integrate people who do not send their children to school?
>
> —Romanian intellectual[2]

For about 700 years, the Roma (Gypsies) have been an integral part of the ethnic society of the regions which today constitute modern Romania. Most historians agree that the first wave of Roma migrants reached present-day Romania during the thirteenth or fourteenth centuries.[3] Through time, the Roma have maintained their ethnic identity and have refused to integrate with a society composed mostly of Romanians, Magyars, Germans, and others. This persistent defiance is all the more noteworthy because a variety of rulers and political systems, ranging from Habsburg absolutism, Hungarian authoritarianism, and Romanian Communism have attempted to assimilate them. The Roma, although a part of Romanian society, remain worlds apart from its other ethnic entities.

The purpose of this chapter is to analyze the Romanian Romas' socioeconomic and political conditions after the fall of Communism.[4] The first part examines the socioeconomic conditions and interethnic relations of the Roma in postsocialist Romania. The second part analyzes the process of Romani political mobilization. In the final section, the focus shifts to state policies toward the Roma.

SOCIOECONOMIC CONDITIONS AND INTERETHNIC RELATIONS

Determining the number of Romanian Roma is a troublesome undertaking at best, one which is hampered by several incalculable variables. Researchers often come up with figures that lack supporting evidence, and which are often based on guesswork, second- or third-hand information, and hearsay. Censuses offer no sure guide since a considerable proportion of the Roma have refused to be identified due to the fear of discrimination. Some elude the census workers altogether. According to Roma leaders, at the latest census (1992) in such counties as Harghiţa and Covasna, about 70 percent of the Roma registered as Hungarians.[5] Census takers and other government and state officials have been known to underestimate the size of Romani communities, whereas Romani leaders and human rights activists tend to do the opposite. The most objective data comes from demographers, sociologists, and statisticians. According to a 1993 estimate by Cătălin and Elena Zamfir, which they arrived at in a study supported by a rigorous explanation of their methodology, there were approximately 1,010,000 Roma residing in Romania. Given their high reproduction rate, one may reasonably assume that by the turn of the millennium, that figure will approach approximately 1.2 million. Social scientists believe that approximately one-third of them reside in Transylvania, and the other two-thirds, in the rest of Romania.[6]

If one accepts the figure of 1.2 million, one can calculate that the Roma make up 5.27 percent of Romania's population (according to the 1992 census, Romania's total population was 22,760,000), making them the second largest ethnic minority in the country after the Hungarians. While they make up a proportionately larger share in Slovakia (9.49 percent) and Bulgaria (8.5 percent),[7] the Romani community in Romania is, in absolute numbers, the largest in Eastern Europe.

The Romanian Roma constitute an extremely diverse population. The most important differentiation among them is between the majority, who have been settled for many decades, and the minority, who were nomadic or seminomadic until the settlement policies of the socialist era forced them

Table 13.1. Estimates of Romania's Roma Population[8]

1. Census of 1992	409,723
2. Iena and Cătălin Zamfir	1,500,000
3. Romani leaders	2,300,000
4. Roma Federation	2,500,000
5. Isabel Fonseca	2,500,000
6. Isabel Fonseca	3,500,000
7. Iulian Rădulescu	4,000,000
8. Victoria Clark	6,000,000

to abandon their traditional lifestyle. A small portion of the latter community have returned to their traveling ways for at least part of the year since 1990. The main Romani groups continue to identify themselves through traditional occupational distinctions, such as *rudari* (wood carvers), *aurari* (gold washers), *lingurari* (spoon makers), *caravlabi* (coal miners), *cărămidari* (brick makers), *blidari* (bowl makers), and *căldărari* (boilermakers). These distinctions were loosened, however, by the socialist economy, which had no more use for many of these skills. As a result, the boundaries between certain tribes have become more and more vaporous, and an increasing number of Roma have come to identify themselves primarily with those living in the same household. This phenomenon has slowed the emergence of pan-Roma consciousness.

Some Roma speak only Romanian, some speak Hungarian, and some speak Romani; some all three, or any two, of these languages. Their religious identity is likewise diverse: among them there are Catholics, Protestants, and especially Orthodox. Such diversity has frustrated the attempts of Roma leaders who want their people to behave like a coherent group. Since the fall of socialism, the Romani society has become increasingly stratified, with a small number of wealthy Roma, a tiny middle stratum of intellectuals and professionals, and a large impoverished Romani underclass. So far, rich Roma have displayed only limited active solidarity with their needy brethren.

The high reproduction rate of the Romani community has been a source of tension in interethnic relations. Although an extensive survey by Elena Zamfir revealed that 74.2 percent of Romani families desire no children, the birthrate among the Roma is considerably higher (4.35 children per woman) than in Hungarian and Romanian communities (1.79). This gap between desires and outcomes stems from the fact that nearly 90 percent of Romani women of childbearing age use no birth control devices whatsoever. The average Romani woman gets married at age 17 (22.2 for the entire population) and bears the first child by age 18.5.[9] Romani children have been the primary victims of this apparent absence of family planning. They make up 75–80 percent of the 104,000 Romanian children who were reported to be in the care of state-run orphanages in 1995.[10]

In postsocialist Romania—as in the rest of Eastern Europe—the Romas' socioeconomic conditions have considerably deteriorated. Although socialism accelerated the marginalization of ancestral Romani occupations and consequently many elements of traditional Romani life, it also improved the educational, housing, health, and living standards of most Roma. Thousands of Romani families received council flats and houses, many left behind by emigrating Germans and Jews.[11] The majority of their children participated in the education system, and most Roma (especially men) held steady jobs. Many Romanians believe that one of the elements of Nicolae Ceauşescu's minority policy was to extend preferential treatment to the Roma in order "to provoke other ethnic groups, including Romanians, and to divert attention away from Ceaușescu's other policies."[12]

Since the December 1989 Revolution, whatever headway the Roma had made under the socialist period has largely evaporated. Romani attendance at educational institutions from preschool to postsecondary levels has declined sharply. Reasons include the indirect costs of education, discrimination in schools against Romani children by their peers and teachers alike, and, most important, the fact that many of these families do not encourage, let alone insist, on their children's schooling. In the socialist period, school attendance levels were often kept high by social workers and teachers, who picked up truant Romani (and other) children and took them to school. In the post-socialist era, there are seldom any state resources for such services. In 1993, only 51.3 percent of ten-year-old Romani children went to school regularly while 33.1 percent did not attend at all.[13] The virtual unavailability of education in the Romani language is a controversial issue, even though about one-third of them speak no Romani at all. Most of their activists hold that children should acquire the Romani language within the family but should be formally educated in Romanian. In 1994, a total of fifty-five Romanian pupils had the opportunity to study the Romani language for three hours per week (in Bucharest, Bacău, and Tîrgu Mureš). This was, however, without the assistance of a textbook.[14] The fact that there are no postsecondary level courses of the Romani language in Romania precludes the training of future Romani teachers. Some activists admit, however, that the single most important reason for the educational deprivation of their people is their traditional lack of interest in schooling.[15] Even Romani magazines feature reports on the (East) European school systems' "constant battle against the apathy of the [Romani] parents against education."[16] Many Roma contend that, under socialism, unskilled workers often earned more money than some college-educated people (like teachers), so there is no sense in spend-

Table 13.2. What Is Most Important in Life to Succeed? (Romani respondents over age sixteen)

Money	28.5%
Working hard	23.9%
Luck	14.0%
Skill/qualifications	8.0%
Health	7.3%
School/education	4.1%
Job	3.2%
Help from family	2.8%
Relationships	0.8%
Something else (unspecified)	2.3%
No response	5.1%

ing time at school. They often see no need for institutional education at all, preferring their children to go to work, beg, or steal rather than go to school.[17]

In Romania, as elsewhere in Eastern Europe, the employment opportunities of the Roma in the mainstream economy have dwindled in the last decade. This phenomenon is only partially explained by anti-Roma discrimination and the loss of traditional skills during the socialist period. At present, most Roma simply do not possess any marketable skills. According to an independent sociological survey, 50.4 percent of Romani women and 41.2 percent of men could read either with difficulty or not at all, 95.4 percent of the Roma had less than high school education, and 74 percent of adults had neither traditional nor modern occupational skills.[18] The postsocialist land distribution schemes almost totally overlooked the Roma, many of whom had worked in the agricultural sector. This strategy was justified by the notion that the Roma did not own any land prior to the Communist takeover and, therefore, could not have any legal claim on returned land. The fact that tens of thousands of Roma had labored on the collective and state farms for decades appears to have made no significant difference. The loss of agricultural employment has had an especially negative impact on the living standards, social status, and interethnic relations of Roma in rural areas, where about two-thirds of the Romani population resides.

Thousands of Roma were squeezed out of their villages following the breakup of agricultural cooperatives. With their only source of employment gone, many had to resort to subsistence theft. During the Communist period, theft from collective farms was not considered socially unacceptable, and members of all ethnic groups routinely engaged in it. However, stealing from private farms in the post-Communist era is not tolerated, as many Roma have found out the hard way. Many Roma who left their villages established squatter settlements close to the town limits of many Romanian cities. Thousands work in garbage dumps and live in unspeakable conditions.[19] In 1994, nearly 52 percent of the Romanian Roma were unemployed, however, only 2.8 percent received any unemployment benefits. Although some Roma who are registered as unemployed actually do earn money from semi-legal and illegal activities, a May 1992 report stated that 42.6 percent had no source of income at all.[20]

Not surprisingly, the Romas' general economic well-being has plummeted since 1989. Their living standards have decreased to the extent that in 1994, at a time when 16 percent of Romania's overall population lived below the government established subsistence level, 64 percent of the Roma lived under such conditions.[21] The Roma have fared considerably worse in all socioeconomic indicators (life expectancy and health standards, housing, possession of durable goods, etc.) than members of other nationalities residing in Romania. For instance, 73.9 percent of Romani dwellings in rural areas had mud floors (23.3 percent of all Romanians), 8.1 percent had full bathrooms (53.7 percent), and 9 percent had indoor toilet facilities (16.7 percent).[22]

Romani impoverishment has contributed to the growing incidence of crime among them. According to police officials, in the first nine months of 1990, Roma committed 8.8 percent of all crimes in Romania.[23] Since then, the frequency of Romani crimes has increased, although it is still primarily non-violent (for instance, murders among Roma are quite rare). In 1992, more than 2.1 percent of the entire Romani population over age sixteen were in prison.[24] The mainstream media is full of lively reports describing the ostentatious wealth of some Roma, often with the accompanying contention or implication that their riches are ill-gotten. The "Gypsy mafia" and the "Gypsy-Arab crime syndicates" must make good copy, for they are frequent features of Romanian newspapers.[25] The press releases of police organizations do not divulge the ethnic background of arrested individuals except in cases involving the Roma. For example, a report of the General Police Inspectorate in May 1997 stated that among the 21,825 people who had been apprehended, "2,232 are minors, 8,638 are youth, 331 are foreigners, 1,983 are Roma."[26] These figures soon find their way into Romanian newspapers and ultimately serve to increase interethnic tensions.

Romanian media tend to reinforce already widespread anti-Roma prejudices. Although the Roma have their own newspapers and there are a few hours of television and radio broadcast for and about the Roma, their media presence cannot challenge, let alone reverse, the bigotry oozing out of the mainstream media. The central government is practically the only source of support available for the Romani media; however, state resources are limited and, in any event, only few Roma read their own newspapers and hardly any *gadje* (non-Roma) do so. Many educated and integrated Roma distance themselves from their less educated brethren rather than trying to assist them. Therefore, the opportunity to forge role models is usually lost. The mainstream media could be influential in combating intolerance against the Roma and other ethnic groups, but they have yet to rise to the challenge. There is hardly any media discussion of Romani culture, history, and accomplishments, and nearly every media portrayal of them is a negative one.[27] In June 1999, the Council of National Minorities publicly warned against propagating "xenophobic, personal, and collective aggression against members of ethnic minorities" which, according to the Council, were "proliferating every week" and "greatly harming democracy in Romania."[28]

Interethnic tensions between Roma on the one hand, and Hungarians and Romanians on the other, are considerable. One of the few areas in which there is consensus between Transylvania's Romanian and Hungarian communities is in their shared prejudices and discriminatory behavior toward the Roma. During the past decade, this intolerance has surfaced on a number of occasions in the form of attacks on the Roma, the torching of their dwellings, and more generally, in all types of discrimination in a wide variety of social situations. In September 1993, the village of Hădăreni was the scene of the most serious assault to date on the Transylvanian Roma by a mob of Hungarians and Romanians. The casualties included three Roma and one Romanian, and damage to Romani property was extensive (thirteen houses destroyed by fire and another twenty-five partially damaged).[29] The attacks had been ignited by the resentment of the general population to the ostentatious wealth of a small number of Romani businessmen, Romani crimes or provocation, or racist attitudes.[30]

In many cases, the Roma have been used as scapegoats by individuals frustrated by the trauma of the post-Communist transition. According to Nicolae Gheorghe, Romania's most prominent Romani activist, "in earlier days the Jews were blamed for all evil, now it is us."[31] According to a recent opinion poll, 100 percent of ethnic Germans, 77 percent of Romanians, 50 percent of Hungarians, and 24 percent of Roma themselves regard the Roma in a negative way.[32] No other ethnic group is viewed so disapprovingly in Romania. Although some antidiscrimination laws have been passed by the legislature, few people abide by them.[33] The fact that most Roma are unaware of their rights makes their situation even more difficult.

It is noteworthy that ethnic Hungarians seem to harbor the least virulent anti-Roma sentiments in Transylvania. Some Hungarians view the Roma as a marginalized ethnic group just as they are, a factor that may mitigate their overt anti-Romani actions. The fact that Roma actively supported the Hungarians in the March 1990 disturbances in Tîrgu Mureš has no doubt served to moderate anti-Roma prejudices among them.[34] Still, the most typical behavioral norm between Hungarians and Roma is social and residential segregation. Intermarriage (which occurs extremely rarely) is widely considered the most egregious violation of this rule.[35] In village societies, a significant proportion of the Romani elite has tried to integrate with the majority Romanian or Hungarian society. Many of these Roma speak no Romani and have adopted *gadje* lifestyles, but most of their neighbors still consider them merely as "upstart" Roma.[36]

The overwhelmingly negative social attitudes toward the Roma pose a major obstacle to the resolution of their complex social, educational, and economic problems.[37] Many Roma activists and *gadje* experts agree that the Romani communities' socioeconomic integration holds the only promise of long-term resolution to their predicament. After the forceful integrative and assimilative policies of the socialist period, many Romanian Roma are now learning, once again, to adapt to a life of increasing socioeconomic marginality.

POLITICAL MOBILIZATION

Although the postsocialist transition has aggravated the Romanian Romas' socioeconomic marginality, it has brought about a positive change in their political situation. Since 1990, there have been no institutional obstacles in the way of Romani political mobilization. Although Romani leaders have not fully utilized the potential of political participation for improving their overall socioeconomic position, they have carved out a presence in the Romanian political scene, and have been able to pressure the state into devoting more attention to their situation.

The previous Communist regime did not permit the Roma to have any independent associations, or pursue any formal political activities. They were active participants in the Revolution, however, and according to Franz Remmel, the very first victim of the hostilities in Timisoara was a Rom.[38] The Romani population was quick to start forming political and social groups both during and after the 1989 Revolution. During the Revolution, Victor Tănăse reestablished the interwar "General Association of Roma from Romania" in Craiova. The first new group, the "Social and Cultural Federation of the Timiş County Roma," was founded on 25 December 1989. On the next day, actor Ion Caramitru read on national television a long text detailing the destiny and predicament of the Roma, and listing their demands for human, civil, and minority rights.

Although there are dozens of Romani organizations in the country, they continue to be strongly dominated by their leaders, particularly because their memberships are generally very small. The leadership of the Romani community is primarily divided, not by their different political approaches (their programs and demands are very similar), but rather by the fault between those with more traditional nomadic lifestyles and those from more settled backgrounds. Traditional leaders generally have little formal schooling, while Romani activists, hailing from more modern environments, are usually highly educated.

The best-known examples of the traditional Romani leaders in postsocialist Romania are the Cioabă and Rădulescu families in Sibiu. They symbolize the idea that a strong personality is necessary to lead the Romani community. Although prior to the fall of socialism Ion Cioabă was no more than a *bulibasha*, or a local chieftain, in 1992, he had crowned himself "King of all Gypsies Everywhere."[39] As a result, Iulian Rădulescu, Cioabă's nephew and a convicted criminal living not far from the "King," quickly proclaimed himself the "Emperor of All Gypsies Everywhere." Cioabă—an illiterate Kalderash Rom with a "doctorate" from "Texas America University" on his office wall—was often dismissed as a buffoon whose antics and ostentatious lifestyle embarrassed the Roma. Although he lobbied hard for Romani causes (he demanded that Germany stop the repatriation of Romanian Roma and pay reparation to the thousands of Roma victims of the Holocaust), he was rarely effective. Since his death in 1997, his son and "successor," Florin, has continued the feud with Rădulescu, which has centered on the primacy of the emperor versus the king.

In March 1999, Florin was the organizer of a so-called European Roma Conference, during which the 300 participants conducted a symbolic trial of

Adolf Hitler. The hearing culminated in a death sentence which was quickly commuted to a more damning punishment: "His soul should burn forever in hell while all his victims should line up in front of him so he could apologize to them." Still, the high point of the gathering was the tour of the royal palace, complete with throne room, treasury, and stables (which house nine automobiles including four limousines—three Mercedes-Benz and one Lincoln) conducted by the king himself.[40] In reality, the authority of traditional leaders like Cioabă and Rădulescu is rarely recognized beyond their extended families and the people who are keen to do business with them. Whatever prominence they have achieved is due to the momentary spectacle they create and to their long-term supporter, Ion Iliescu's Party of Social Democracy, which has used Cioabă and Rădulescu as puppets to garner the Romani vote.

"We need to prepare for the twenty-first century, not the sixteenth," said Mădălin Voicu, the lone Rom delegate in the Bucharest legislature, when asked to comment on the Romas' traditional leaders.[41] Modern, better-educated leaders are considerably less colorful. Their ranks include Gheorghe Răducanu, an economist with a second degree in social work, who was Voicu's predecessor in the Romanian parliament, and the aforementioned Nicolae Gheorghe, a sophisticated multilingual sociologist with a doctorate in sociology. These and dozens of other committed and well-prepared Roma have been the engines of Romani political mobilization throughout the last decade.

Parties, nonparty political associations, and sociocultural organizations have been the primary institutional locus of Romani mobilization. There are dozens of regional organizations in addition to a few national associations maintaining branch organizations in the region. The largest Romani organization in the country, *Partida Romilor*, was established in March 1990 and has offices in nearly every county. Some of the major Romani organizations include the *Uniunea Democrată a Romilo*r (Roma Democratic Union), the *Asociaţia Natională a Romilor din România* (National Association of Romanian Roma), and the *Partidul Alianţa Democraticăa Romilor din România* (the Democratic Alliance Party of Romanian Roma).

One reason for the existence of so many organizations is the diversity of the Romani population itself. An equally serious problem is the division between, and within, Romani organizations: a phenomenon that seems to have subsided somewhat in the second half of the 1990s. Such divisions are caused and deepened by the competition for the resources offered by the political environment. The main source of financial support for Romani groups are state subsidies, as well as grants from national and international institutions and foundations. The government extends funds to Romani organizations for office rental and equipment, publications, and, in some cases, even campaign funds.[42] Increasingly, some wealthy Roma finance their own campaigns from private resources.

More important are the incidents of active cooperation between Romani groups because they demonstrate the progress in Romani political behavior. Prior to the elections in 1990, 1992, and 1996, some Romani associations and parties formed electoral alliances and umbrella organizations in order to prevent the squandering of the Roma vote. The Romas' various cultural and social associations have also cooperated in a number of projects, from the commemoration of Holocaust victims to the rebuilding of destroyed houses. A fine example of interethnic cooperation is the Association for Interethnic Dialogue, which was founded in Cluj in 1994 with the participation of German, Hungarian, Romanian, and Romani civic organizations.

The programs and demands of Romani political organizations are similar. They seek strict enforcement of antidiscrimination laws, affirmative action programs, better educational and employment opportunities, more positive portrayals of the Roma in the mainstream media, increased television and radio broadcast time, more effective social welfare policies, improved Romani access to state jobs, and the like. The Roma have ardently protested policies damaging to their communities such as police passivity during anti-Roma attacks, the discriminatory procedures of the judicial system, the repatriation of Roma migrants from Germany, the lack of Romani-language instruction, and the government's reluctance to return gold confiscated from the Roma during the Communist period. One of the few tangible triumphs of these protests was the government's withdrawal from the announced official name change for the Roma (from "Roma" to *Ţigani,* or Gypsies, which many Roma consider derogatory) ostensibly introduced to prevent confusion between "Romanian" and "Roma" in May 1995.[43] More recently, in August 1998, the Convention of Cooperation of Romani Associations and the Roma Party (PR) called for an investigation of Senator Corneliu Vadim Tudor, leader of the extremist Greater Romania Party, who said that Roma who were reluctant to integrate should be "interned in settlements."[44] The well-known fact that Madalin Voicu, the single Rom in the Bucharest legislature and one of the PR's leaders, is a personal friend of Tudor hardly does him and his party credit among the Roma and the general population. Indeed, when I asked Nicu Paun and Ivan Gheorghe, the PR's two top leaders, about the Voicu-Tudor relationship, they preferred not to comment on it.[45]

The Romanian Constitution requires registered political parties to maintain branch offices in at least one-half of all the counties in the country, thus ensuring that they have a national political presence prior to entering national elections. The electoral law allows minorities to participate with nonparty organizations in addition to conventional political parties because it is mindful of the fact that some minorities are concentrated in certain counties or regions. Taking advantage of this legislation, the Roma have established a handful of registered parties (such as the Roma Party).

Although Romani political mobilization has not been without success, it has thus far failed to achieve representation for the Roma commensurate with their proportion in the population. This is not surprising given that Romani organizations have few electoral resources such as political tradition and experience, a cohesive leadership, a sound financial base, a dues paying membership, or supportive political allies. Traditionally, the Romani interest in politics has been minimal, particularly since their political participation was forbidden or discouraged by their political environment. Even in the postsocialist period, activists documented cases in Romania when the *bulibasha* went to vote for the entire Romani community.[46] Romani leaders often complain of the difficulty they face in persuading Roma to cast their ballots since most of them have no confidence in the electoral system. They estimate that Romani electoral participation is less than 15 percent.[47] There were also many instances when the Romas' votes were invalid because they voted for all, rather than for one, of the Romani organizations on the ballot. Some Romani organizations, such as the Cluj-based Wassdas Foundation, have been working on teaching Romani communities how to vote properly.[48] The vast majority of Romani organizations have few active members, and most do not even maintain membership lists. The Roma are the best organized in Bucharest; outside of the capital, many Roma are oblivious to any mobilizational activity at all. Still, a modest but clear advancement is observable in Romani interest in politics, which is largely due to the work of dozens of indefatigable Roma and *gadje* activists.

Notwithstanding such disadvantages, it is remarkable that the Roma were able to elect a fair number of local representatives. On the national level, they have not been successful, and have had to contend with an electoral law that allows one parliamentary representative for every national minority regardless of electoral performance (It should be noted that the Romanian Constitution is without peer in the region in this respect because no other East European basic laws allow for such minority representation). In 1992, for instance, when a party needed only 3 percent of the vote to gain parliamentary presence (since then the threshold has been raised to 5 percent), the five different Roma parties received 120,000 votes altogether, which would have been sufficient to secure four seats in the legislature. However, no individual party garnered 3 percent of the vote; therefore, the Roma ended up with no seat other than the constitutionally guaranteed one. In the February 1992 local elections, the Roma succeeded in electing two deputy mayors and 104 councilors.[49] In the 1996 national and local elections, the Roma were able to elect 132 local officials, although they were unsuccessful in the national competition, where the largest vote recipient, the Roma Party, received approximately 80,000 votes.[50]

At its October 1999 national congress, the PR, preparing for the 2000 national elections, concluded an agreement with Ion Iliescu's Party of Democratic Socialism of Romania (PDSR).[51] According to the PDSR-PR concord, the PR would support the PDSR's campaign and encourage Roma to vote for Iliescu's party. In return, the PDSR offered to extend social help to the Roma and involve some of its members in policy making. Participants told me that the ambience at the congress was similar to Ceausescu-era functions: lots of thunderous applause during Iliescu's speech at the end of which the Roma chanted "I-li-es-cu, I-li-es-cu" for minutes. Critics of the "PDSR-PR protocol," like Dan Pavel, the Bucharest director of the U.S.-based Project on Ethnic Relations, are quick to point out that the Romas' conditions under Iliescu's six-year reign were worse than they have been since 1996. Moreover, if the Roma want to support a social democratic party, they should not have chosen the PDSR, which has not even been recognized by the Socialist international.[52]

In contrast, PR president Nicu Paun says that the PDSR-PR protocol is beneficial for the Roma for three reasons. First, for the first time in their history, an important political party was willing to engage the Romanian Roma in substantive discussions and to sign a policy agreement with them. Second, the PDSR committed itself to try to solve the Romas' social problems through a national strategy to be elaborated by the PR. Finally, the PDSR agreed to co-opt the PR into the governing process and promised two important places in the government: a state councilor at the President's Office for Roma affairs and a governmental minister responsible for dealing with the Roma.[53]

The work of the dozens of social, economic, and cultural Romani groups has yielded far more tangible results in alleviating the socioeconomic problems of their communities and enhancing their identity formation than have the political organizations. Although the best organized and most successful groups, such as Costel Vasile's *Societatea Tînăra Generaţie a Romilor* (Young Generation Society of the Roma, YGSR) and Nicolae Gheorghe's *Centrul Romilor Pentru Intervenţie Socială şi Studii* (Roma Center for Social Intervention and Studies, CRISS) are based in Bucharest, their programs have extended to all regions of Romania. The YGSR was established in 1991, and has conducted some national cultural events, Roma advocacy projects, and programs encouraging children to stay in school.[54] By far the most important group, however, is CRISS, which has done a wide variety of practical work ranging from preparing Roma children for school, vaccination campaigns, violence prevention seminars, income generation projects, and training programs for Romani activists.[55]

In sum, the Romanian Romas' political marginality has substantially decreased since 1990. Although they have a long way to go before their political representation approximates their share of the population, they have succeeded, to some extent, in organizing and mobilizing their communities. However, fragmentation and infighting among the Roma is a constant problem plaguing their organizational efforts. Of course, an ethnic group as diverse as the Roma can hardly be expected to create, much less maintain, a unified organization without a great deal of difficulty. The damage is done, not by the existence of a large number of associations, but by the fact that they have not been able to form more effective electoral coalitions, which would have enabled them to enhance their representation on a national level. One significant benefit of their organizational activity, however, has been that it has provided an institutional framework in which hundreds of Romani activists and politicians could mature.

STATE POLICIES AND INTERNATIONAL MIGRATION

Romania, like other East European states, has received much domestic and international criticism for its alleged indifference to the Romas' deteriorating conditions. Undoubtedly, the government could have done more, but it is also vital to understand the reasons why the Roma have not been at the top of its political agenda.[56] First, although Romania is home to the world's largest Romani community, their proportion of the population is well below 10 percent. Second, the Romas' economic resources are inconsequential, and their political power, while growing, remains insignificant. Moreover, unlike other ethnic minorities (i.e., Hungarians, Germans, etc.) the Roma have no "mother state" that protects their interests or speaks out on their behalf. Third, the Roma have been traditionally viewed with a general lack of sympathy in Romania and elsewhere. Fourth, the post-Communist transition and consolidation process has presented a large cluster of complex political, economic, and social problems to Romanian politicians of which the "Gypsy Question" was only one of relatively small concern. Finally, given the economic imperatives of the transition, and the modest financial endowments of the state, the Romanian government has had very few resources for relieving the Romas' social ills.

Although former Romanian President Ion Iliescu (1990–1996) had often been criticized for his insensitivity regarding the Roma, he repeatedly expressed his desire for the Romas' enhanced integration into Romanian society and actively supported international meetings on human rights issues.[57] No doubt, Iliescu's actions, and for that matter, the actions of other East European politicians, had been at least partly motivated by increasing international criticism and accelerating Romania's European integration. Especially in the last couple of years of his tenure, Iliescu was more willing to speak out against racial discrimination. Still, Romani activists and politicians were right to castigate Iliescu for his reluctance to clearly and publicly reproach the perpetrators of ethnic violence. Especially in Romania, where presidential authority is much stronger than in primarily parliamentary states, such as the Czech Republic or Hungary, the president could have played an important role in upholding minority rights. Some of his East European colleagues endowed with far less political power (Václav Havel of the Czech Republic,

Arpad Goncz of Hungary, Kiro Gligorov of Macedonia, and Zhelyu Zhelev of Bulgaria) became active supporters of Romani rights. In December 1996, seven years after the Revolution, Romanians finally elected a president and a government which was publicly committed to substantive democratization. President Emil Constantinescu has displayed considerably more empathy toward the Roma than his predecessor has, although there have been no notable changes in their conditions.

Similar to the president, the Romanian government has not yet responded to ethnic violence decisively. Although by the mid-1990s government representatives had started to condemn anti-Roma attacks, they rarely failed to offer excuses for the perpetrators. At the same time, the government has allocated some funds for crisis prevention and for the payment, at least in part, of damages caused by anti-Roma extremists. Indeed, the lion's share of the operating budgets of Romani organizations, newspapers, as well as that of the newly created Romani theater in Timişoara, come from state coffers.[58] The government has recognized the critical importance of education in its assistance programs. In April 1998, Minister of Education Andrei Marga announced that the government was about to introduce a "mechanism of positive discrimination favoring Roma in state education institutions." According to Marga, his Ministry would set aside places in professional schools and postsecondary institutions specifically for the Roma.[59] There can be no doubt that since the interethnic violence in Hadareni, which received a great deal of international publicity, Romanian governments have shown more sensitivity to, and more concern for, the Romas' situation.

To appreciate the changes in Romania's treatment of the Roma, it is important to evaluate its record in evolutionary rather than in static terms. In the 1950s, the authorities confiscated the Romas' wagons and horses in order to reduce their mobility. During much of the Ceauşescu-era (1965–1989) the Roma were basically ignored in accord with the Bucharest government's declaration that the country's ethnic problems were "solved."[60] Since 1989, several fundamental changes have occurred in the Romas' conditions. They now possess the same "national minority" status as do other ethnic minorities. Although social attitudes toward the Roma have scarcely improved in Romania, the state's treatment of them has certainly taken a step forward. After 1993, the Romanian authorities' approach to human rights abuses and, more generally, to the Romani minority, has shown a modest but unmistakable change. Before 1989, the authorities scarcely acknowledged the Romas' existence. Since then the government has clearly become more aware of the Romas' intensifying problems, although the lack of financial resources has meant that only minimal substantive changes could occur in the Romas' condition. Romanian politicians have come to recognize that one of the many conditions of successful European integration is improved state-minority relations.

In the last few years, there have been several cases that, while ignored in the West in general and by human rights organizations in particular, clearly demonstrated the evolution of the policies of the Romanian government. For instance, in May 1994 in the village of Racşa (in Satu Mare county), ten Romani dwellings were burned by ethnic Romanians. Local authorities, directed by their superiors in Bucharest, put pressure on those who set the fires to rebuild the houses. That signaled not only the authorities' refusal to ignore such incidents but also that they would now force perpetrators to pay for their actions. Other similar changes do not indicate a drastic turnabout in Bucharest's policies, but they do suggest a shift in the state's treatment of the Roma.

In 1993 Romania established an institutional structure for the representation of ethnic minority interests that is considerably more sophisticated than that of some of the other states in the region (e.g., Bulgaria): the Council of National Minorities. Dependent on, and supervised by, the government, the Council is composed of representatives of Romania's eighteen ethnic minorities and of the twelve ministries which have special responsibilities for minority affairs (education, labor, etc.). The Council maintains six working committees (culture, mass media, education and science, defense, finance, and administration). Its main objectives are to take account of the problems of minorities, and to prepare a variety of programs to address them. The Council has tried to unify, or at least mediate between, the various Romani organizations, but so far without much success. In September 1994, for instance, it held a meeting with nearly 200 Romani leaders representing dozens of organizations, but they could not reach an agreement on substantive issues. The Council has proposed several programs, from the training of police personnel regarding minorities to the discussion of the role of minorities in national defense.

Another important political body that represents ethnic minority interests is the Minority Parliamentary Group in the Romanian legislature. This group is composed of the representatives of ten ethnic minorities and includes Mădălin Voicu, a Romani legislator. In 1997 Victor Ciorbea's government established a Department of National Minorities under the Office of the Prime Minister. Its director possesses the governmental rank of a minister without portfolio. The new Department has demonstrated its sensitivity to the needs of the Romani community and has proposed some practical social and economic programs.

Since 1989, a number of Romani experts have been employed in various ministries. For instance, in the Ministry of Education, a special department deals with minority affairs, including those of the Roma. The department has worked on curricula, textbooks, and various educational programs aimed at improving the educational level of the Romani community. The first post-1989 government under Petre Roman made several ambitious plans to solve or at least reduce Romani unemployment. The government promised to set aside fifty-eight positions for Roma experts in key ministries (education, labor, interior), although eventually only thirteen Roma were hired.[61] The Roma have suffered discrimination from all political institutions and the most injurious has been the treatment by local authorities.[62] Local bureaucrats, aid administrators, policemen, and social workers often share the prejudices of the larger society. Some local officials are genuinely concerned with improving the conditions of the Romani community in their jurisdictions, but praiseworthy original intentions are often overlooked in their daily routines, which are usually characterized by poor working conditions, inadequate resources, and low material rewards. A 1998 Amnesty International report contended that incidents of racist violence against the Roma have not ceased in Romania and "a change in the mentality of those representing the state, so that they would consider the protection of fundamental rights of individuals as the ultimate state interest, is yet to take place."[63]

Since 1989, some Romanian local administrators and mayors have publicly called on the Roma to emigrate.[64] As if to heed their advice, since 1990, tens of thousands of Romanian Roma have taken advantage of the relatively free borders and travelled to Western Europe and beyond.[65] In the first six months of 1997 alone, nearly 500 Roma left Romania for Ireland.[66] However, even the Romani activist and politician Gheorghe Răducanu admitted that the great majority of the Roma left for economic rather than for political reasons.[67] In September 1992, the German government signed a repatriation agreement with Bucharest helping the readjustment of some 20,000 Romanians (reportedly 70 percent of them Roma) with DM 30 million. Roma leaders repeatedly complained that they had no control over the funds, only a small proportion of which was being spent on assistance to the Roma.[68] In 1994, Roma in the Bihor county city of Oradea took legal action against Bishop Laszlo Tőkés, accusing him of not handing out the DM 15,000 of German aid allocated to the Free and Democratic Community of Gypsies there.[69] Tőkés said that Germany had asked for payment to be halted because Roma leaders misused funds for purposes different from what had been intended.

CONCLUSION

The situation of the Romanian Roma has been extremely difficult situation since 1989. Indeed, their socioeconomic conditions have deteriorated in nearly all respects since the state-socialist period. Notwithstanding the specific nature of their predicament, the experience of the Romanian Roma is typical of all East European Roma. The two main reasons why they are worse off in Romania than in some other states of the region, such as in Hungary or Macedonia, is that Romania's economic situation has been very difficult, while the social integration of Romanian Roma has been even slower. The one area in which the Romanian Romas' situation has measurably improved is politics. Even so, given the multifaceted divisions within the Romani population, unifying the Roma for political or other purposes remains a formidable task, which makes their own situation and the work of those intending to assist them, particularly trying.

As elsewhere in the region, the Romas' educational level is vastly inferior to the rest of the population, their rates of unemployment and criminal activities are much higher, and they face widespread exclusion from other ethnic groups. In addition, local authorities still routinely discriminate against them, despite antidiscrimination legislation and directives. At the same time, it is important to recognize that, partly as a result of international pressure, Romanian policies toward the Roma have improved in the last several years. Also, there is an institutional structure in place in the country that may well hold the promise of positive developments in future interethnic relations.

Clearly, the most lamentable development in the postsocialist period has been the Romas' declining educational attainment. The only way for them to lessen their marginality is through integration. This could be accomplished primarily through education. Education will generate better job opportunities, it will reduce socioeconomic problems and interethnic tensions, and it will accelerate the creation of a Roma middle class, which, in turn, may be expected to spawn a more effective political elite. Changing traditional Romani attitudes which hold institutionalized education in such low regard is a prerequisite to any substantial long-term improvement in the Romas' conditions. Quite simply, education is the key to their salvation.

NOTES

1. I am indebted to the Ford Foundation and IREX for their financial support of my work. I am also grateful to Larry Watts for facilitating my field research in Romania throughout the last decade. This chapter uses the terminology "Rom, Roma, Romani," which most, though certainly not all, Romanian Gypsies/Roma prefer. The singular noun is Rom, the plural noun is Roma, and the adjective is Romani.

2. Both of these quotes are cited by Dan Ionescu, "The Gypsies Organize," *Report on Eastern Europe*, vol. 1, no. 26 (29 June 1990), p. 40.

3. Gerard Chaliand and Jean-Pierre Rageau, *The Penguin Atlas of Diasporas* (New York: Penguin Books, 1997), p. 96.

4. For studies dealing with earlier periods, see George Potra, *Contribuţiuni la istoricul ţiganilor din România*, (Contributions to the History of the Gypsies in Romania) (Bucharest: Fundatia Regele Carol I, 1939); and Ion Chelcea, *Ţiganii din România: Monografia etnografică* (The Gypsies of Romania: An Ethnographic Monograph), (Bucharest: Editura Institutului Central de Statistica, 1944); Trond Gilberg, "Ethnic Minorities in Romania under Socialism," *East European Quarterly*, vol. 7, no. 4 (January 1974), pp. 435–64; and David M. Crowe, *A History of the Gypsies in Eastern Europe and Russia* (London: I.B. Tauris, Ltd., or New York: St. Martin's Press, 1995), pp. 107–50.

5. Rompres (22 May 1992).

6. Dorel Abraham, Ilie Bădescu, and Septimiu Chelcea, *Interethnic Relations in Romania: Sociological Diagnosis and Evaluation of Tendencies* (Cluj-Napoca: Editura Carpatică, 1995), p. 409.

7. Zoltan Barany, *The East European Gypsies: Regime Change, Marginality, and Ethnopolitics* (New York: Cambridge University Press, 2002), chapter 5, table 1.

8. Sources for these population estimates: (1) The Legislative and Institutional Framework, p. 7; (2) Author's interview with Cătălin Zamfir and Elena Zamfir (Bucharest, 3 November 1999). Their prior estimate was 1,010,000, from Elena Zamfir and Cătălin Zamfir, *Ţigani: între ignorare şi îngrijorare* (Bucharest: Editura Alternative, 1993), p. 206; (3) *Scorpion*, (25 March 1990), as cited by Dan Ionescu, "The Gypsies Organize," p. 40; (4) Smaranda Enache, "*Die Minderheit der Roma in Rumanien,*" *Glaube in der 2. Welt*, vol. 20, no. 4 (1992), p. 20; (5) Isabel Fonseca, *Bury Me Standing* (New York: Alfred A. Knopf, 1995), pp. 146, 179, and 278; (6) Radulescu quoted in Reuters (Bucharest, 12 May 1995); (7) Victoria Clark, "Gypsies Caught in Spell of Hate," *The London Observer* (29 July 1990), as cited in Ian Hancock, "Gypsy History in Germany and Neighboring Lands", in David Crowe and John Kolsti, eds., *The Gypsies of Eastern Europe* (Armonk, NY: M. E. Sharpe, 1991), p. 24.

9. Cătălin Zamfir, Marius Augustin Pop, and Elena Zamfir, *Romania '89–'93: Dynamics of Welfare and Social Protection* (Bucharest: UNICEF, 1994), pp. 68–69; and Elena Zamfir, ed., *The Situation of Child and Family in Romania* (Bucharest: National Committee for Child Protection and UNICEF, 1996), p. 105.

10. Fredrik Folkeryd and Ingvar Svanberg, *Gypsies (Roma) in the Post-Totalitarian State* (Stockholm: Olaf Palme International Center, 1995), p. 61; and *New York Times* (15 December 1996.)

11. Fonseca, *Bury Me Standing*, p. 167.

12. *Destroying Ethnic Identity: The Persecution of Gypsies in Romania* (New York: Human Rights Watch, 1991), p. 32.

13. Elena Zamfir and Cătălin Zamfir, *The Romany Population* (Bucharest: Centre of Economic Information and Documentation), p. 20.

14. The Council for National Minorities, *The Legislative and Institutional Framework for the National Minorities of Romania* (Bucharest: Romanian Institute for Human Rights, 1994), p. 29.

15. Interview with Andrzej Mirga (Krakow, 14 June 1994).

16. *O Drom: Magazine for and about Roma and Sinti in Europe* (Amsterdam, September 1994), p. 12.

17. *Miami Herald* (4 May 1993); and *New York Times* (17 November 1993).

18. Zamfir, Pop, and Zamfir, *Romania '89–'90*, pp. 64–69.

19. Author's interview with Professor Thomas Keil (Bucharest, 2 June 1996).

20. Zamfir, Pop, and Zamfir, *Romania '89–'90*, p. 13.

21. *Ibid.*, p. 65.

22. Abraham, Bădescu, and Chelcea, *Interethnic Relations in Romania*, p. 411.

23. Franz Remmel, *Die Roma Rumaniens: Volk ohne Hinterland* (Vienna: Picus, 1993), p. 105.

24. Zamfir, Pop, and Zamfir, *Romania '89–'90* , p. 65.

25. See *Adevărul*, (12, 23 May 1995); *Libertatea*, (24 May 1995); *22 plus*, no. 15 (7 June 1995); and *Adevărul*, (7 October 1996).

26. *Images and Issues: Coverage of the Roma in the Mass Media in Romania* (Princeton, NJ: Project on Ethnic Relations, 1997), p. 11.

27. *The Media and the Roma in Contemporary Europe: Facts and Fictions* (Princeton, NJ: Project on Ethnic Relations, 1997).

28. Mediafax (Bucharest, 23 June 1999), as reported by Radio Free Europe/Radio Liberty *Newsline*, part II, vol. 3, no. 123, (24 June 1999).

29. *Human Rights Watch World Report 1994* (New York: Human Rights Watch, 1993), p. 229. See also *Sudden Rage at Dawn: Violence against Roma in Romania* (Budapest: European Roma Rights Center, 1996), pp. 12–15.

30. Katherine Verdery and Gail Kligman, "Romania after Ceauşescu: Post-Communist Communism?" in Ivo Banac, ed., *Eastern Europe in Revolution* (Ithaca, NY: Cornell University Press, 1993), pp. 134–35.

31. *Der Spiegel* (19 July 1993).

32. *Evenimentul zilei* (19 October 1993).

33. *Frankfurter Rundschau* (31 January 1994).

34. Tom Gallagher, *Romania after Ceauşescu* (Edinburgh: University of Edinburgh Press, 1995), pp. 88, 120; *Der Spiegel* (3 September 1990); and *Reform* (14 September 1990).

35. Sandor Olah, "*Cigany-magyar kapcsolatok*," *Egy mas mellett eles: A magyar-roman, magyar-cigany kapcsolatokrol* (Csikszereda: Pro-Print, 1996), pp. 181–94.

36. Sandor Olah, "*Szimbolikus elhatarolodas egy telepules cigany lakoi kozott*," *Egy masellett eles*, pp. 207–24.

37. David M. Crowe, *A History of the Gypsies of Eastern Europe and Russia* (London: I.B. Tauris, 1995), p. 149.

38. Remmel, *Die Roma Rumaniens*, p. 81.

39. See the obituaries in *New York Times* (27 February 1997) and *Economist* (8 March 1997).

40. Associated Press (Sibiu, 24 February, 1999) and *Magyar Hirlap* (2 March 1999).

41. *The Wall Street Journal* (12 December 1997).

42. Author's interview with Costel Vasile and Nora Costache of the Young Generation Society of the Roma, and Gheorghe Răducanu, MP, of the Roma Party (Bucharest, 14 March 1995).

43. Daily Digest, Open Media Research Institute (Prague, 3 May 1995); Reuters, (Bucharest, 12 May 1995); and *Frankfurter Allgemeine Zeitung* (23 May 1995).

44. Radio Free Europe/Radio Liberty, *Daily Report*, part II, vol. 2, no. 162 (24 August 1998); and *Agence France Press* (Bucharest, 26 August 1998).

45. Interview with Nicu Paun and Ivan Gheorghe, President and Secretary General of Partida Romilor, respectively (Bucharest, 5 November 1999).

46. Author's interview with Nicoleta Bîţu (Bucharest, 23 May 1996).

47. Author's interview with Gheorghe Răducanu (Bucharest, 14 May 1995).

48. Interview with Nicu Paun and Ivan Gheorghe, President and Secretary General of Partida Romilor, respectively (Bucharest, 5 November 1999).

49. *The Legislative and Institutional Framework*, p. 100.

50. Information from Nicoleta Bîţu (15 December 1996). For a description of Gheorghe Răducanu's campaign, see *Adevărul* (7 October 1996.)

51. See "Iliescut tamogatjak a romak," *Szabadsag* (Cluj), 25 October 1999; and the PR's newspaper which published the PDSR-PR protocol's text, *Asul de trefla*, no. 80 (1999), pp. 17–19.

52. Interview with Dan Pavel (Bucharest, 2 November 1999).

53. Interview with Nicu Paun (Bucharest, 5 November 1999).

54. Author's interviews with Costel Vasile and Nora Costache (Bucharest, 14 March 1995 and 23 May 1996).

55. See Romani CRISS, *Presentation of Romani CRISS and Its On-Going Projects* (Bucharest, September 1994, mimeo).

56. Zoltan Barany, "Orphans of Transition: Gypsies in Eastern Europe," *Journal of Democracy*, vol. 9, no. 3 (July 1998), p. 150.

57. Zoltan Barany, "Minorities in Romania: Favorable Trends for Romania's Roma," *Transition*, vol. 1, no. 19 (20 October 1995), pp. 28–31; and Reuters (Bucharest, 23 May 1995).

58. Vlad-Andrei Moga, "Romania and Its Minorities," *Balkan Forum*, vol. 2, no. 4 (December 1994): pp. 243–68; and Crowe, *A History of the Gypsies*, p. 145.

59. Mediafax (Bucharest, 18 April 1998), as cited by the *Austin American-Statesman* (19 April 1998).

60. Gilberg, "Ethnic Minorities in Romania under Socialism," pp. 442–43.

61. Author's interview with Vasile Burţia, a Romani analyst at the Ministry of Labor (Bucharest, 15 March 1995).

62. Zoltan Barany, "Ethnic Mobilization and the State: The East European Roma," *Ethnic and Racial Studies*, vol. 21, no. 2 (March 1998), p. 323.

63. NCA/Stuart Parrott (London, 21 April 1998).

64. Dan Ionescu, "Migration from Romania," *Report on Eastern Europe*, Special Issue, (1 December 1989), p. 19; and *Transitions*, vol. 4, no. 4 (September 1997), pp. 9–10.

65. For an insightful article on the subject, see Georgia A. Rakelman, "*Die Migration osteuropaeischer Zigeuner nach Westeuropa,*" *Ethnos-Nation*, vol. 2, no. 2 (1994), pp. 19–28.

66. FE/RL Daily Report, vol. 1, no. 105 (28 August 1997).

67. *Der Spiegel*, 19 July 1993. See also *The Times* (London, 24 September 1990).

68. Crowe, *A History of the Gypsies*, p. 148.

69. Hungarian Radio (Budapest, 26 March 1994, 11 GMT). For the larger context, see *New York Times* (26 September 1993).

14

Church and State in Romania before and after 1989

Sabrina P. Ramet[1]

The transition from authoritarianism to pluralism, whether of a liberal democratic type, a nonliberal democracy (against which John Stuart Mill warned), or a multiparty ochlocratic type (such as characterized by Poland in the years 1919–1926), involves challenges of adaptation not only at the constitutional-juridical level, but, in fact, at all levels of society. In the case of societies in which a single party, exercising a strict organizational monopoly, imposed its agenda on all sectors of society, nongovernmental institutions suddenly freed of party control and surveillance confront the need to stage a kind of "resurrection," as Romanian theologian Dorin N. Popa has put it. Moreover, whereas politicians endeavoring to establish a democratic state in the wake of the collapse of an authoritarian order have before them the models of successful democratic systems established in sundry Western societies, nongovernmental institutions, such as the Church, endeavoring to chart a "resurrectionist" course since the collapse of Communism have had to chart a course with neither map nor model in hand. While history affords examples of adaptation after the overthrow of foreign and/or repressive rule, as for example in the cases of Romania and Bulgaria after the overthrow of the Ottoman yoke, these earlier examples have little to do with the contemporary situation and can provide no guide as to the present dilemmas and challenges.

Church-state relations in the Communist world may be analyzed on two axes: penetration by the state and attitude toward nationalism. On the first axis, one may distinguish three patterns: *co-optation,* in which the given Church allows itself to be thoroughly penetrated, its clerics to be drawn into the web of surveillance and reportage under the guidance of the secret police, and its newspapers to be written or screened by the secular authorities (the Orthodox Churches of Russia, Bulgaria, and Romania in the Communist era affording the clearest examples of this pattern); "*tolerance*," in which given religious associations were legally recognized but not as thoroughly penetrated as "co-opted" Churches and hence, too, not as favored with privileges such as foreign travel (for example, registered Baptists in the USSR and Jewish congregations in most Communist societies); and *proscription,* which condemned the illegal associations to an underground existence (as in the case of the Greek-Rite Catholic Church in Communist-era Ukraine, Romania, and, until 1968, Czechoslovakia).

The second axis relates to nationalism, and here one may distinguish among four patterns in the Communist era: regime and Church both hostile to nationalism (e.g., the Jehovah's Witnesses in Ukraine); regime hostile to nationalism but Church nationalist (e.g., the Serbian Orthodox Church, the Greek-Rite Catholic Church in Ukraine); regime and Church both co-optive of the national history and heritage (e.g., the Evangelical Church in the GDR after 1978, the Macedonian Orthodox Church after 1967, major Churches in Kádár-era Hungary); and the regime co-optive of nationalism and Church outside the nationalist discourse (e.g., Protestants in Romania).[2]

THE ROMANIAN MODEL

Where the Romanian Orthodox Church is concerned, the relationship in the Ceauşescu era was overtly co-optive, involving regime co-optation of its own (often fanciful or reconstructed) view of the national history and Church cooperation with the regime on that basis. This cooperation extended far beyond mere agreement about the national history, however, involving the direct collaboration of perhaps as many as 80 percent of Orthodox clerics with the *Securitate* secret service, according to Traian Sima, who, until 1989, was a high-ranking intelligence operative in Timişoara.[3] These priests-agents were expected to provide the *Securitate* with information about believers and to counter the allegations made by Jehovah's Witnesses and other independent sources concerning regime infringements of human rights. All (recognized) religious associations were subjected to strict state control. Party authorities set the themes for church sermons, reviewed pastoral letters and ecclesiastical resolutions to make sure of their "progressive spirit," and scheduled meetings of mass organizations on Sundays and holy days of obligation. Party functionaries routinely attended Church conferences in order to keep an eye on *their* flocks.[4] The country's religious leaders were expected to defend the country's human rights record in international forums and were also expected to sing the glories of Romanian President Nicolae Ceauşescu and of Romanian Communism itself. These expressions of complete satisfaction were not intended, in the first place, to flatter Ceauşescu, but rather to cow the prelates into complete submission and to provide useful propaganda for internal and foreign audiences. The Orthodox Church was not alone in being required to express its total contentment with the conditions in which it found itself. The same requirement was also imposed on the other religious associations that enjoyed legal status in Communist Romania.

Needless to say, many of Romania's religious leaders found it necessary to do some backpedaling, or at least explaining, in the months following the collapse of the Ceauşescu regime in December 1989. "We were not collaborators," Patriarch Teoctist intoned in January 1990 in a typical example of clerical self-justification. "We merely protected what was left of religion in Romania."[5] But, as Teoctist continued, apparently oblivious to the self-contradiction entailed in an "everybody-did-it" defense, "In all honesty, there is not a single Romanian adult who has not been affected by some form of collaboration with Communism."[6]

Bishop Nifom Ploieşteanul, assistant to the patriarch and head of the Department of External Relations of the Romanian Orthodox Patriarchate, adopted the same stance as his boss, telling a visiting American scholar in October 1990 that the end justifies the means[7]—that the goal of providing for the Orthodox Church's material welfare and relative prosperity under Communism justified the hierarchs' endorsement of mendacious formulas and their refusal to criticize injustice or to defend the persecuted.[8]

By contrast, Metropolitan Antonie Plămădeală of Transylvania, who, in earlier times, had praised the restrictive 1948 law on religion for having assured "true and perfect religious freedom and rights for all religious beliefs and bodies in Romania," even conceding that the Communist state's restrictions in the religious sphere were understandable and "natural,"[9] and who had defended Ceauşescu's demolition of churches in downtown Bucharest, was by 1990 parading himself as an anti-Communist zealot.

Somewhat more honestly, the head of the World Council of Churches, General-Secretary Emilio Castro, conceded the Council's failure to take a critical stand vis-à-vis the Ceauşescu dictatorship, recalling that the WCC had dropped a discussion of human rights violations in August 1988, when the aforementioned Metropolitan Antonie, the now self-proclaimed anti-Communist zealot, had threatened to walk out of the session if the discussion continued.[10]

THE COMMUNIST LEGACY

As early as 23 March 1945, the coalition government of Petru Groza issued a decree on land reform, eliminating, at a blow, the wealth of the minority Churches of the Germans and Hungarians. Later that year, the government tried to win over Church leaders to the socialist cause. When this overture failed, the authorities turned to more resolute measures, effecting purges among the Orthodox clergy. Authorities issued a decree in May 1947, imposing a mandatory retirement age for clergy; this allowed authorities to pension off recalcitrants among the old guard. Meanwhile, a Union of Democratic Priests, thoroughly infiltrated by the security police, was established.

Under the provisions of the 4 August 1948 Law on Cults, the Communist government recognized only fourteen faiths, in contrast to the sixty religious associations recognized before 1948. "Unrecognized" faiths were considered illegal. Among those considered illegal were Greek-Rite Catholics, Nazarenes, Christian Scientists, Mormons, and Jehovah's Witnesses. The 1948 law empowered the Ministry of Cults to watch over and control the activity of the religious associations, to regulate any proposed changes in diocesan boundaries, to approve the elevation of clerics to leadership posts within the Church, and to keep watch over all Church publications, among other things.[11] Article 32 of the law warned that "ministers of religious cults who express antidemocratic attitudes may be deprived temporarily or permanently of their salary, which is provided by the state."[12] The law institutionalized state control of episcopal elections and packed the Holy Synod with Communist supporters. In exchange for subservience and enthusiastic support for state policies, the Communist government provided salaries and pensions for bishops and priests, and financial subsidies for the publication of Church books, calendars, and theological journals. Those not prepared to be docile servants of the state were punished. Up to 6,000 Orthodox priests were imprisoned between 1946 and 1964, alongside clerics from other faiths.[13] Among Catholic clergy, at least 450 priests were incarcerated in a forced labor camp, where more than 200 priests died, while another 50 or so were executed outright; some were deported. All Catholic newspapers and other publications were suppressed.[14] After this rough introduction, most surviving clergymen decided that caution and docility were advisable. There were two striking exceptions to this record: Hungarian Catholic Bishop Antal Jakab, who earned a permanent place in history through his consistent refusal to make the usual embarrassing statements praising Ceauşescu;[15] and Fr. Georghe Calciu-Dumitreăsa, who was forced to leave Romania in June 1985 after he had issued an open letter criticizing the regime's violations of human rights and demanding an end to such transgressions.

Jakab and Calciu gained in moral authority as a result of the publicity given to their courage, especially in the West. Lesser-known pastors often proved more vulnerable than either Jakab or Calciu to regime reprisals. For example, Baptist pastors Ioan Ştef and Beniamin Cocar were brought to trial in the mid-1980s for having failed to register with the authorities. Dorel Cataramă, a Seventh Day Adventist, was likewise arrested and put on trial. Constantin Sfatcu, a Baptist pastor from Iaşi, was sentenced to seven and a half years in prison (in July 1985) after being convicted on fabricated charges of attempted murder of a police officer. Yet another Baptist pastor, Rev. Petre Dugulescu of the Hateg Baptist Church, was threatened by security police in August 1985 with a car "accident" unless he stopped preaching; declining to follow this advice, Dugulescu suffered multiple fractures the following month when an unlicensed and unmarked bus collided with his car in Timişoara.[16] Two other clergymen, Baptist pastors Nicolae Gheorghita and Paul Negrut, were stripped of their sacerdotal licenses. There could be no doubt of the state's determination to reward its supporters and to punish its detractors. Not surprisingly, no Orthodox bishop protested any of these violations of human rights.

The Romanian Orthodox Church also maintained a not-so-dignified silence when the regime demolished Bucharest's historic Holy Synod Church on Palm Sunday in 1987, as it did in April 1988, when the regime announced its plans to bulldoze half of the nation's 13,000 villages (including, rather obviously, their churches, some of which were considered to be of historical importance[17]) in order to clear the ground for the erection of concrete high-rise apartment buildings and the construction of new rural factories. One of the Orthodox Church's few victories was to have thwarted a plan on Ceauşescu's part to pull down the Orthodox basilica in Bucharest.[18]

One of the means whereby the Communist state bound the Orthodox Church's fortunes with its own was to turn over to Orthodox Church ownership some 2,500 church buildings hitherto owned by the Greek-Rite Catholic Church. This latter Church, suppressed in 1948 (when it commanded the loyalty of some 1.57 million adherents), continued to function clandestinely, thanks to the loyalty of a half a dozen bishops, roughly 600 priests and monks, as well as several hundred nuns.[19] On the other hand, some 430 Greek-Rite Catholic priests (out of a total of 1,800 in 1948) were reported to have signed a formulary approving of the suppression of their Church (though some of them protested that their signatures had been forged without their consent).[20]

In 1950, the regime of Gheorghe Gheorghiu-Dej broke off relations with the Vatican and ordered the Papal Nuncio out of the country. Conditions for Roman Catholics and Greek Catholics alike continued to deteriorate. Roman Catholics were made to feel the pinch of discrimination, too; they were required, unlike Orthodox believers, to pay a 17 percent tax on the salaries of all persons employed by the Church.[21]

Both the Orthodox and Catholic Churches were subject to infiltration and surveillance. In the most notorious case, Monsignor Luigi Vitoria Blasutti, a Romanian Catholic of Italian descent, is alleged to have used his access in Rome to spy on Vatican officials for some thirty years. According to secret police dossiers unearthed in 1996, Blasutti ". . . was paid by the Securitate to influence the Vatican's East European appointments, to discredit dissidents and opponents of the Ceauşescu regime, and to mislead the Vatican about Romania's true intentions towards its Catholic communities."[22]

The Orthodox Church literally constructed a new ecclesiology to fit the times, justifying its subservience to the state in terms of supposed theological precepts. Justinian Marina, who served as patriarch from 1948 to 1977, developed what he called the theory of the "Social Apostolate," which declared that the Church owed its allegiance to the secular government and should be of service to that government.[23] Similar in concept to the Theology of Diakonia propagated by the Lutheran and Reformed Churches in Communist Hungary,[24] the "Social Apostolate" inflamed opposition from the political right wing of the Church hierarchy; Party General Secretary Gheorghe Gheorghiu-Dej (d. 1965) saw to it that these elements were purged from leadership positions in the Church. The "Social Apostolate" called on Orthodox clerics to become active in the new People's Republic, and, in this way, laid the foundation for the Church's submission to and collaboration with the state.[25] Fr. Vasilescu, an Orthodox priest, tried to ground the "Social Apostolate" in the Christian tradition, by endeavoring to ground it in the writings of St. Augustine, St. John Chrysostome, St. Maxim the Confessor, Origen, and Tertullian. Based on this alleged tradition, Fr. Vasilescu concluded that Christians owed submission to their rulers because it was God's will.[26] With recalcitrants removed from office, those Orthodox bishops who remained in office adopted a servile attitude, endorsing the Ceauşescu regime's concept of nation, supporting the regime's policies, and even applauding Ceauşescu's "ideas about peace."[27]

Of the remaining legally recognized faiths in Romania, two—the Jewish community and the Lutheran Church—were shrinking so rapidly that the Communists scarcely concerned themselves about them (though this is not to deny the ferocity of occasional anti-Semitic campaigns such as that of the early 1950s, during which Ana Pauker, Foreign Minister and Politburo member, was stripped of her offices). The anti-Semitic campaigns notwithstanding, the Communist regime allowed the Jewish community to establish religious schools in Romania and gave a green light to Jewish emigration—both concessions extended in appreciation of the collaborative attitude adopted by Chief Rabbi Moses Rosen (d. 1994) toward the Ceauşescu regime.[28] Of the two aforementioned religious communities, the Jewish recorded the more drastic decline. Having counted some 756,930 adherents in 1930, the Romanian Jewish community calculated that only some 355,972 remained in 1945, after the years of the holocaust.[29] As a result of postwar emigration, the number of Jews remaining in Romania dropped steadily, dwindling to 144,198 in 1956, 30,000 in 1982, 14,000 in 1995, and barely 10,000 in 1999.[30]

The decline in the number of Lutherans living in Transylvania has been slower, but ultimately no less dramatic. Their decline was driven, above all, by the dynamics of nationalities relations: the Lutherans of Transylvania were principally German Saxons (alongside what was, until recently, a much smaller community of ethnic-Hungarian Lutherans). Of the 250,000 Lutheran

Saxons living in Transylvania at the beginning of World War Two, some 40,000 served in the German army, some of them dying on the field. About 35,000 were deported to the USSR. Another 40,000 were evacuated to Austria and Germany in 1944 by retreating German troops. After the war, some of these returned to Romania. Thereafter, the population stabilized for the first two and a half decades. But between 1969 and 1989, thousands of German-speaking Lutherans emigrated to Germany, with Ceauşescu cashing in on Bonn's willingness to pay a ransom for each German released. In 1981, there were still 148,205 Lutheran Saxons in Transylvania,[31] but by 1989, only 105,000 German-speaking Lutherans remained in the country.[32] But it was only after the collapse of the Ceauşescu regime in December 1989 that an avalanche of applications to emigrate sent the number of German-speaking Lutherans in Transylvania plummeting to a mere 30,000 believers.[33] Thus, as a result of emigration, the number of Saxon Lutherans had actually dropped beneath the modest level recorded for ethnic Hungarian Lutherans (35,000 in 1990).

Mention should also be made of the small Islamic community, which enjoyed legal status throughout the Communist era. There were an estimated 38,000 Muslims living in Romania in 1977.[34] Despite its small contingent, Romania's Islamic community played a role in that country's relations with Islamic states, and foreign visits by Romania's Mufti were, accordingly, accorded notice in the Romanian press.

The Jewish, Lutheran, and Muslim communities pale in size, however, before the large Christian Churches. The largest religious associations in Romania are the Romanian Orthodox Church (18.9 million adherents in 1997), the Catholic Church (2.8 million in its Roman and Greek rites combined, 1997), and the (Hungarian) Reformed Church (900,000 adherents in 1990). The fastest growing religious associations in Communist times were the Baptist and Pentecostal communities (recorded at 325,000 and 300,000, respectively, in 1990).[35] Other Protestant and evangelical groups showing resilience included the Unitarians (85,000 adherents in 1990), the Seventh Day Adventists (75,000), the Plymouth Brethren (65,000), and the Jehovah's Witnesses (50,000).[36] The only other group currently present in Romania to record more than 50,000 members is the Islamic community, which claimed some 56,000 believers in 1995.[37] Despite its ample publications, the Evangelical Church in Romania, whose adherents are German-speakers, numbered only 20,000 adherents in 1997, down from 166,000 in 1978, as a result of a combination of steady emigration and a certain number of conversions to newer Protestant groups.[38]

The continuities between the pre-Communist and Communist eras have sometimes been underestimated. Under Communism, as earlier, the Romanian Orthodox Church enjoyed a privileged position. Under Communism, as earlier, Baptists, Pentecostals, and Seventh Day Adventists were subjected to discriminatory treatment and treated as foreign implants. Indeed, these religious associations were declared illegal by the Antonescu regime, which imprisoned their adherents. They were subsequently re-legalized by the Communists, but in the late 1950s, many Baptists were imprisoned on suspicion of being subversives.[39] Under Communism, as earlier, the large Greek-Rite Catholic Church figured as the only ideological rival of the Orthodox Church. Under Communism, as earlier, the German-speaking Lutherans were accorded special treatment, albeit for different reasons. And under Communism, as earlier, anti-Hungarian prejudice played a role in the formulation of the regime's religious policy. Where Bucharest held up official registration of the Hungarian Reformed Church for some twenty years (1920–40) in the pre-Communist era, the Church's bishops (Gyula Nagy and László Papp) were constrained to acquiesce in the confiscation by Communist authorities of some 10,000 Bibles that had been sent to the Reformed Church by agencies in the West in 1981. The authorities sent the Bibles straight to the pulp mill, but Biblical passages reappeared later on locally manufactured toilet paper.[40] On toilet paper as in religious policy, the patterns of the pre-Communist "past" were imprinted on the Communist "present."

POST-COMMUNIST YEARS

In inspiration, Communism was supposed to be about *the future*. In other words, its (ever uncertain) claims to legitimacy depended upon the believability of its quasi-utopian programs and promises. In the sphere of religious life, the believability of the regime's vision of the future depended on the believability of its claim that people could live happily without placing their trust in a Supreme Deity and in a Church. But, as a 1995 opinion poll showed, some 82 percent of Romanians placed their trust in the Orthodox Church; and that high measure of religious trust did not even count those expressing trust of other religious organizations.[41]

Given this significant reservoir of trust in religion, it comes as no surprise that the collapse of the Communist power monopoly brought in its wake a resurgence of interest in religion and a dramatic proliferation of religious activity. The State Secretariat for Religious Affairs registered nearly 400 further religious associations, in addition to the 14 registered by the Communist regime, between early 1990 and the end of 1996.[42] Most of these newly registered associations have only small memberships, but a few may, in due course, establish themselves as major contenders in the religious arena.

In the first weeks after the execution of the Ceaușescus, chaos reigned in the government and establishment circles. Patriarch Teoctist, under fire from critics within the Orthodox Church, resigned his post on 18 January, only to resume his duties a few months later. Similarly, Iacub Mehmet was ousted from his post as Mufti of the Islamic community about the same time, in what was later described as "a plot mounted by a restricted group of imams."[43] But by 19 June, he too had regained his former position. Rev. László Tőkés, the Reformed pastor whose defiance of the authorities had sparked the turmoil which ultimately catapulted Nicolae Ceauşescu from power and who was subsequently raised to the episcopate, found himself accused, in a bizarre twist, of being a *Securitate* agent! Where the Baptists were concerned, they found that repressive policies continued for a while by sheer force of inertia: When, specifically, the Baptist community opened a new church facility the first week of 1990, having accidentally exceeded the size specified in the permit, the authorities had the building bulldozed.[44] In this context of chaos and uncertainty, Pope John Paul II named 12 new bishops for Romania's 2.8 million Catholics (7 new bishops for the country's 1.2 million Roman Catholics and 5 new bishops for the country's 1.6 million Greek-Rite Catholics).[45] The government would later charge, in the face of Vatican denials, that it had not been informed in advance of the appointments, as prescribed by long tradition; evidence suggests, however, that the appropriate ministers *had* been so informed, but had been embrangled in too much chaos to be able to register the information.[46]

After 1989, the Orthodox hierarchy, maintaining its long-established habit of embracing the party in power, aligned itself with Ion Iliescu. Many Orthodox priests, however, began to display a sympathy for ultranationalist ideology, often subscribing to neo-legionary publications.[47] *Vatra Românească* has exerted a particular attraction for Orthodox priests.[48]

Among the sundry issues arising in the religious sphere in post-Communist Romania, five distinct but interconnected issues stand out: the probity of the Romanian Orthodox Church; demands by the Catholic Church, the Reformed Church, the Jewish community, and other religious associations for the return of properties confiscated from them by Communist authorities; tensions between the Greek-Rite Catholic Church and the Orthodox Church; demands for the revival of religious education, as well as for the satisfaction of other related needs; and the persistence of problems of intolerance. These will be treated *in seriatim*.

Probity of the Romanian Orthodox Church

Less than a month before the collapse of the Ceauşescu regime, Patriarch Teoctist made a final statement lauding Romania's "greatest son." It was the last reaffirmation of nearly forty-five years of subservience and docility, in which Orthodox hierarchs had compromised principles for the sake of state approval and support. A few weeks later, Teoctist would have to execute an about-face.

The Orthodox Church understood intuitively that the best way to overcome its compromised past was to ignore it, redefining itself in accord with the changed political and social context. An early hint of this came on 27 January 1990, when *Tineretul Liber* published the text of an address delivered by Fr. Dumitru Staniloae to the young people of Romania. In this address, Staniloae portrayed his Church as "a martyr Church" adding, pointedly, that the Church should ". . . make its contribution to the rebirth of social and historical man, on the sacred foundations of love, dignity, and freedom."[49]

Belatedly declaring its complete independence of state supervision (on 28 September 1990),[50] the Romanian Orthodox patriarchate began to engage in symbolic politics. The patriarchate required minimal resources for this and stood to reap large gains in terms of public approval. An early move in this spirit came in June 1992, when Patriarch Teoctist canonized thirteen new Romanian saints including Prince Stephen the Great, who had ruled Moldavia from 1457 to 1504. Among the 5,000 persons attending the festive pageant at St. Spiridon's Church in central Bucharest were Prime Minister Theodor Stolojan and sundry cabinet ministers and parliamentarians.[51] Later, local Orthodox priests in Cluj-Napoca identified themselves with Mayor Gheorghe Funar's brand of nationalism, consecrating a memorial plaque unveiled on Funar's initiative, to commemorate the 40,000 Romanians who had died during the Hungarian Revolutionary War of 1848–49.[52] More interesting, in some ways, was a commemorative service conducted jointly by Orthodox Archbishop Bartolomeu of Cluj and by Greek-Rite Catholic Archbishop Gheorge Gutiu of Cluj in early September 1997, in honor of some 150 anti-Communists who were purged and executed in the Communist era.

Later that same month, Dorin N. Popa, a young Orthodox theologian, publicly called for dramatic changes in the Church, including the resignation of the patriarch who, according to Popa, ". . . gets negatively involved in State affairs, pushing against reforms and against European integration, . . . gets in the way of dialogue and makes tensions worse in religious matters, . . . [and] is always late with many of the changes [demanded] in this epoch."[53] Charging that theological studies in Romania had become "corrupted" and urging that the Orthodox Church make peace with the Greek-Rite Catholic Church, Popa outlined a vision of ecclesiastical "resurrection" for the Romanian Orthodox Church. One of the problems obstructing any such renewal or "resurrection" is the legacy of forty years of collaboration between Orthodox clergy and the security apparatus. A leading Romanian daily claimed in November 1997 that at least six members of the Holy Synod, as well as thousands of ordinary priests, had collaborated actively with the *Securitate*, among them Metropolitan Antonie Plămădeală of Transylvania (in office since 1982). The paper also charged that Archbishop Bartholomeu Anania, imprisoned by the Communists at one point as an "enemy of the people," later served Communist authorities.[54] As of October 1997, however, only one hierarch—Nicolae Corneanu, Metropolitan of the Banat—had admitted past collaboration with the Communists. Instead of admitting past wrongdoings, however, the patriarchate shot back by accusing Popa of attacking the Church and insinuating that he was a KGB spy. These charges appeared in the publication, *Ziua* [Day], shortly after Popa's charges were made public.[55]

Allegations about collaboration with the *Securitate*, on the part of the clergy, could of course be cleared up by an opening of the files on collaborators. But the Holy Synod of the Romanian Orthodox Church insisted that files on priests who had collaborated with the secret police in the Communist era remain secret. The Holy Synod admitted that some priests had collaborated but insisted that such collaboration had not extended to the revelation of the content of confessions. How the Holy Synod could be certain of this without having inspected the files is another question.[56] In July 2001, meanwhile, the parliamentary commission entrusted with the oversight of the Romanian Intelligence Service, decided to recommend that the clergy be excluded from the list of those public officials whose past collaboration with the *Securitate* had to be made public.[57] Delays in coming to terms with past ecclesiastical collaboration induced Gabriel Andreescu, a prominent anti-Ceauşescu dissident, to sue the National College for the Study of Securitate Archives (CNSAS) for refusing to make public its records on clerical collaboration.[58]

Even more embarrassing for the Church, however, was the revelation, in the daily newspaper *Monitorul* on 13 January 2001, of a document discovered by historian Dorin Dobrincu, which revealed that Patriarch Teoctist had been a member of the fascistic Iron Guard in his youth and had taken part in the rebellion against Marshal Ion Antonescu in January 1941, as well as in the burning of a Jewish synagogue in Iaşi.[59] Although the patriarch denied the allegation, disputing the authenticity of the document, the charges were repeated in the Catholic daily *Libertatea* subsequently.[60] Moreover, as Lavinia Stan and Lucian Turcescu note, ". . . the information contained in one archive has been confirmed by documents found in other archives. This seems to confirm that, even if one document is a fabrication, the information itself may be true."[61]

More troubling than these allegations concerning Teoctist's sympathies and activities more than half a century earlier, however, was a report in the daily newspaper *Evenimentul zilei* on 3 November 2001 that fifteen Orthodox priests from Bihor County had joined the revived Iron Guard, and that meetings of the fascist movement had been held in several Orthodox monasteries in Transylvania.[62] The newspaper reported that Father Gregorie, head of the Piatra Craiului monastery, had declared himself the leader of the Legionary (Iron Guard) movement in northern Romania and had even tried to transform the Oradea branch of the Association of Romanian Christian Orthodox Students into a branch of the movement.

Meanwhile, the leading Romanian Orthodox prelates were, in a manner of speaking, looking over their shoulders lest Baptists, Pentecostals, and American evangelicals should recruit from among Orthodox ranks.[63] At the same time, the patriarchate was concerned lest its particular desiderata be ignored, postponed, and forgotten. In this regard, the Romanian presidential elections of 1996 provided an ideal opportunity for the Orthodox hierarchy, who had, in any event, unilaterally declared theirs the "National Church,"[64] both to remind Romanians as to which Church had been the most closely identified with Romanian national identity, history, culture, and tradition, and to place its agenda under the spotlight. The Church presented itself as a patriotic institution doing battle against the legacy of totalitarianism (the very totalitarianism which it had so profitably served right up to December 1989); meanwhile, the two leading contenders for the presidency—incumbent Ion Iliescu and liberal challenger Emil Constantinscu—competed for the Church's favor, each endeavoring to appear more religious than the other.[65] Constantinescu made a clear bid for favor among believers when, in the course of a televised speech, he challenged Iliescu: "Do you believe in God?"[66] For its part, the patriarchate was not shy about letting its preferences be known. Later, when Constantinescu won the election, the Church conducted a service in his honor (attended by the president-elect) in the cathedral of Alba Iulia, where Ferdinand I had been crowned "King of All Romanians" in 1922.[67]

It would be both misleading and unfair, however, to allow the impression to take hold that the entire hierarchy consists only of self-seeking opportunists and Iron Guard sympathizers. Metropolitan Daniel Ciobotea, age thirty-eight at the time of his election as metropolitan of Moldavia and Bukovina in 1990, is a striking counterexample. Emphasizing the Church's prophetic mission, he has called on the Church to criticize both socialism and capitalism, to speak out wherever injustices arise, and to offer consolation to those who suffer unjustly.[68] Even more strikingly, Metropolitan Daniel is on record as favoring the complete separation of Church and state.

Restitution of Property

All of Romania's religious associations were affected by the Communist program of nationalization and confiscation of properties. Many of these properties were turned to secular use; but some (particularly Church facilities confiscated from the Greek-Rite Catholic Church in 1948) were handed over to the Orthodox Church. At the same time, the Romanian Orthodox patriarchate demanded (in 1997) the return of some 350 hectares of farm land (a modest request given how much had been confiscated originally), together with sundry forest, pasture, fruit-growing, and vinicultural lands.[69] As already mentioned, the Communist authorities had confiscated properties from all the major religious associations. Altogether, the Communists are said to have confiscated 1,593 churches, schools, and other buildings from the Roman Catholic, Reformed, and Unitarian Churches, while the Greek-Rite Catholic Church may have lost as many as 2,500 churches and other facilities under decree 348 of 1 December 1948 on Church "merger."[70] The Jewish community has also been seeking the return of properties confiscated in the 1940s.[71] A spokesperson for the ethnic Hungarian community claimed in June 1996 that while the Romanian Orthodox Church was being afforded rapid restitution of, or compensation for, properties confiscated earlier, not a single property had been returned to any ethnic Hungarian denomination or parish.[72]

During seven years of leftist government under Ion Iliescu, 1989–1996, serious discussion of property restitution to the Churches was avoided and the issue was postponed from year to year. A law passed in 1991 returned only some small land plots to parishes and monasteries. But in October 1997, as a result of the change in government and in the wake of a fresh call from Pope John Paul II to address the issue, the government promised to complete work on a long-delayed law on religion, in which property restitution would be specified, and, in particular, to help the Greek-Rite Catholics to recover nearly 2,000 church buildings and other confiscated property.[73]

In the course of 1997, as negotiations between the two Churches repeatedly hit dead ends, Patriarch Teoctist appealed to the state to resolve the dispute unilaterally. But when the senate followed up on the patriarch's suggestion and proposed a bill requiring the return of churches to Greek Catholics in municipalities with at least two former Greek Catholic churches and an active Greek Catholic presence,[74] Teoctist denounced the measure as "an inadmissible interference in the national Church's problems."[75]

Moreover, the Orthodox Church prelates and clergy continued to behave as the aggrieved party, in spite of the fact that they were holding onto properties stolen for them by the Communist Party. And hence, even in communities meeting the conditions specified in the new law, Orthodox priests refused to cooperate and declined to vacate any churches.[76] In Cluj, for example, Orthodox priests and seminary students armed themselves with sticks to resist the court-ordered transfer of the Church of the Transfiguration to the Greek Catholic Church. Greek Catholic clerics also mobilized and, as the *Sunday Telegraph* reported, "Rival gangs of seminary students then converged on the altar, shouting abuse, swearing and shoving opponents. A table covered in religious icons was overturned, and fighting broke out."[77] Distrust also colored Reformed-Orthodox relations. In early 2001, however, there was a breakthrough, when the Chamber of Deputies accepted the government's proposal to return all real estate which had been confiscated from the "religious cults" in Romania. The deputies also voted to eliminate any restriction to the number of buildings which religious organizations might claim.[78]

Dispute between the Greek-Rite Catholic and Orthodox Churches

Although Greek-Rite Catholic spokespersons claim that up to 2,500 churches and other facilities were confiscated by the Communist authorities, the Church has been seeking the return of only half of this number.[79] The Orthodox patriarchate was loath, in fact, to surrender properties, and instead of simply returning facilities that had been taken from the Catholics, the patriarchate suggested other remedies, ranging from the establishment of mixed commissions authorized to propose compromises to the holding of referenda at the local level.[80] Greek-Catholic representatives decisively rejected the latter proposal during talks with President Iliescu and Orthodox Church representatives on 24 April 1990. But a decree-law issued in the wake of this meeting tentatively endorsed the referendum concept, citing "the wishes of the people"—a formulation provoking the Greek-Rite Catholic Church to protest strongly.[81]

Catholics began to complain of an "anti-Catholic spirit" in Romania, while parliamentary deputy Petre Turlea added fuel to the fire by accusing the Catholic Church of conducting an "offensive" against the Orthodox Church.[82] Both government and Orthodox Church officials began a campaign of innuendo against the Catholic Church, calling the latter "unpatriotic and foreign," and characterizing it as "a foreign body, forced on the Romanian people against their will."[83] In April 1997, the Council of Europe became involved in the dispute, passing a resolution calling on the Romanian government to take it upon itself to resolve the dispute and to assure the return of an appropriate measure of confiscated properties. But as of mid-August 1997, the Greek Catholics had obtained the return of only 97 of the 2,000–2,500 church buildings which had been confiscated in the late 1940s, and Orthodox Church officials were blocking state action by claiming that any such action would constitute state interference in religious affairs, thus violating the separation of Church and state. The Orthodox Church continued, through 1997, to demand the use of referenda to resolve the dispute.[84]

The lack of resolution on the property dispute between Catholics and Orthodox continued to impact the state's relations with the Holy See by forcing repeated delays in scheduling a papal visit to Romania. Because of the bad blood associated with this dispute, it was only in early July 1998 that the Orthodox Church finally gave its approval to the state's standing invitation to John Paul II to visit Romania. Although the Holy See placed especial emphasis on visiting Catholics in Transylvania, the Orthodox hierarchy was adamantly opposed, insisting that the pope's visit be limited to Bucharest. Finally, in mid-March, the two sides agreed that the pope would come to Bucharest 7–9 May 1999 but not travel elsewhere in the country. In spite of this limitation, the visit was seen by all sides as contributing to an easing of interconfessional tensions in the country. Pomp and circumstance lent the visit simultaneous state and ecclesiastical significance, while Patriarch Teoctist became the first non-Catholic to ride in the famed "Popemobile" next to the pontiff.[85]

Religious Education

Religious instruction was restored to the curriculum at state schools in autumn 1990, albeit on an optional basis. But controversy quickly arose because the new education law did not mention that confessional schools might serve as an alternative to state-run schools. The issue of confessional schools is, moreover, inextricably connected with that of property restitution because many confiscated facilities had been Church-run schools. The issue has been especially sensitive in Hungarian minority regions, where locals want to see history classes taught from the perspective of Transylvania and its history as a Hungarian outpost.[86] Further, Church conservatives were disappointed that the state was not prepared to make religion classes mandatory in the elementary and secondary schools, and they were visibly upset when large numbers of high school students opted to skip the weekly classes. In frustration, the Orthodox Church renewed pressure on conservative MPs to make religion classes mandatory.[87]

Problems of Intolerance

Despite the Ecumenical Association's aforementioned commitment to promote ethnic reconciliation, the Orthodox Church has played its role in fanning the flames of ethnic intolerance,[88] while both Orthodox and evangelicals have contributed to religious intolerance between rival Christian confessions.[89] It scarcely helps matters that the Orthodox Church has long considered all other religions to be the tools of Satan,[90] though how the Church can integrate itself into a democratic system if it considers those with other views "satanic" remains to be seen. The Orthodox Church's success in aborting a planned international convention of Jehovah's Witnesses in July 1996 only confirms that Church's inability to see intolerance in its self-righteous arrogation to itself of a supposed right to veto meetings by "heretical sects."[91] The desecration of certain Jewish graves in the course of summer 1995 also served as a reminder of the endurance of anti-Semitic sentiments in this largely Orthodox country.

The Orthodox Church has also waged a relentless war against sexual tolerance since 1989, excoriating same-sex relationships, trans-sexualism, and abortion alike. The Church has not been above citing supposed popular preferences in its campaign to keep same-sex relations criminalized and to suppress psychiatric and medical treatments for transsexuals, but has been markedly less impressed by documented popular preferences when abortion has been the topic of discussion.[92] Over the objections of the Orthodox hierarchy, an international conference on homosexuality opened in Bucharest in mid-October 1997. Rejecting the attitude prevalent throughout the member-states in the Council of Europe, Archbishop Anania declared, on

PRO-TV (a privately owned channel), "To believe that society should become normal by adopting abnormal things is dangerous to our society."[93]

Meanwhile, in 1996, as a price for membership in the Council of Europe, the Romanian government reluctantly amended Article 200 of its criminal code, which had heretofore prescribed prison terms of up to five years for any homosexual relationships. The revised law would declare same-sex relationships punishable only if "homosexual activities" were performed in public or created a scandal, while banning "propaganda or association or any other act of proselytism" designed to promote homosexuality among Romanians[94]—phraseology that sounds paranoid to most Westerners.

The Orthodox Church fought this bill tooth and nail, backed by the right-wing extremist Party of Romanian National Unity and the chauvinistic Association of Christian Orthodox Students, which waged a campaign of intimidation against MPs favorably disposed toward the bill.[95] Archbishop Anania, like other Orthodox prelates, saw the prospect of liberalization for gays and lesbians not as an occasion for the practice of the supposedly Christian virtues of charity and kindness, still less for ideological modesty and tolerance, but, instead, as a battlefront for moral purity. Lumping together various things he disliked, Anania complained in public that "Europe asks us to accept sex, homosexuality, vices, drugs, abortions, and genetic engineering, including cloning."[96] Quite apart from his ignorant notion that Romania was required to endorse cloning and dangerous drugs as a condition for admission to the Council of Europe, in placing sex in first place as the most pernicious danger to Romanian society, Anania exposed the extent of his phobias.

The debate about the *partial* legalization of same-sex relationships dragged on for years. Finally, in June 2000, the Chamber of Deputies approved the "liberal" amendment, in which same-sex relations were nonetheless characterized as "perverted" and "unnatural."[97] As the bill was forwarded to the Romanian Senate for approval, the Holy Synod of the Romanian Orthodox Church appealed to that body to reject the measure.[98]

The Senate ignored the pressure from the Church and repealed Article 200, which had criminalized homosexuality. In November 2001, Romania's first gay nightclub opened in Bucharest.

CONCLUSION

For nearly half a century, the Communist Party of Romania put history on hold. Old arguments between Catholics and Orthodox were stifled, Orthodox preferences for barring Protestant and evangelical Churches altogether were censored, proselytism was disallowed, and even the telling of history could only be undertaken according to a fixed teleological line, in which the national and the progressive were identified with each other and construed as obtaining their fullest embodiment in the Romanian Communist Party and the personal dictatorship of Nicolae Ceauşescu. According to Marxist teleology (in its twisted Romanian incarnation as elsewhere), history can only be the history of the class struggle—which is to say, where the class struggle is said to have been "resolved," history, as an active process, is effectively banished.

In fact, the Romanian Communists failed to resolve anything, succeeding only in muffling and stifling the open discussion of problems. Hence, the "battle between Orthodoxy and evangelicals" continues, Catholic-Orthodox relations continue to be characterized by "mutual distrust and hostility," and anti-Semitism persists as a problem in Romanian society.[99] But in its own rough way, the Communist Party actually "protected" the fourteen religious associations to which it accorded legal registration, by withholding legal status from other religious associations which might otherwise have eroded the demographic strength of the larger, established Churches. And in this regard, the end of Communism has signified an intensification of interconfessional competition and has opened the doors for new entrants, creating the possibility for tangible changes in the confessional structure of Romanian society over the long run.

NOTES

1. This chapter was previously published in Norwegian translation, under the title, "Kirke og stat i Romania før og etter 1989," *Nordisk Østforum*, vol. 17, no. 3 (2003) and is reprinted here by permission of the author and of the editor of *Nordisk Østforum*. I am grateful to Trond Gilberg, Michael Shafir, and Peter F. Sugar for comments on earlier drafts of this article; to Michael Shafir and Patricia J. Smith for sharing research materials; and to Cristina Baltareţu for translating the French and Romanian materials cited in this article.

2. This discussion builds on an approach I developed in Sabrina Ramet, "Politics and Religion in Eastern Europe and the Soviet Union," in George Moyser, ed., *Politics and Religion in the Modern World* (London and New York: Routledge, 1991), esp. pp. 78–90.

3. *Deutsche Presse Agentur* (Hamburg, 6 October 1997), on RFE/RL telex; also *Frankfurter Allgemeine* (7 October 1997), p. 6.

4. Elemér Illyés, *National Minorities in Romania: Change in Transylvania* (Boulder, CO: East European Monographs, 1982), p. 35.

5. Quoted in *Washington Times* (3 January 1990), p. A7.

6. *Ibid.*

7. This view is known, among students of ethics, as *moral consequentialism,* and is at odds with the *moral universalism* customarily preached by traditional Christian Churches, including the Orthodox Church.

8. Alexander F. C. Webster, "Prophecy and Propaganda in the Romanian Orthodox Patriarchate," in *East European Quarterly*, vol. 25, no. 4 (January 1992), p. 519.

Regarding the Romanian Orthodox Church's relative prosperity under Communism, see Alan Scarfe, "The Romanian Orthodox Church," in Pedro Ramet, ed., *Eastern Christianity and Politics in the Twentieth Century* (Durham, NC: Duke University Press, 1988); and V. Chaplin, "Publishing in the Romanian Church," *Journal of the Moscow Patriarchate* (1988), no. 11, pp. 47–48. The Romanian Orthodox Church's failure to defend the victims of persecution has, however, a long history, as the hierarchs' behavior in the face of persecution of the Romanian Jews during 1940–42 amply demonstrates. On this point, see Jean Ancel, "The 'Christian' Regimes of Romania and the Jews, 1940–1942," in *Holocaust and Genocide Studies*, vol. 7, no. 1 (Spring 1993).

9. Quoted in Webster, "Prophecy and Propaganda," p. 520.

10. *New York Times* (10 February 1990), p. 11.

11. Erich Kendi, *Minderheitenschutz in Rumänien: Die rechtliche Normierung des Schutzes der ethnischen Minderheiten in Rumänien* (Munich: R. Oldenbourg Verlag, 1992), p. 105.

12. Quoted in Dennis Deletant, *Ceauşescu and the Securitate: Coercion and Dissent in Romania, 1965–1989* (Armonk, NY: M. E. Sharpe, 1995), p. 10.

13. Dan Ionescu, "Romanian Orthodox Leaders Play the Nationalist Card," *Transition* (Prague, 5 April 1996), p. 25; and *Reuters News Service* (14 November 1996), on *Lexis-Nexis Academic Universe* (hereafter, LNAU).

14. *Chicago Tribune* (16 May 1990), p. 15; Emil Ciurea, "Religious Life," in Alexandre Cretzianu, ed., *Captive Rumania* (London: Atlantic Press, 1956), esp. p. 190; and Illyés, *National Minorities in Romania,* pp. 221, 226.

15. *The Independent* (London, 18 June 1993), p. 24.

16. Pedro Ramet, *Cross and Commissar: The Politics of Religion in Eastern Europe and the USSR* (Bloomington: Indiana University Press, 1987), p. 161.

17. Deletant, *Ceauşescu and the Securitate*, p. 135.

18. *The Times* (London, 2 January 1990), on LNAU.

19. Janice Broun, "The Catholic Church in Romania," in Pedro Ramet, ed., *Catholicism and Politics in Communist Societies* (Durham, NC: Duke University Press, 1990), p. 230.

20. *Ibid.*, p. 214.

21. *Ibid.*, p. 223.

22. Quoted in *Scotland on Sunday* (Glasgow, 15 December 1996), p. 7; see also *Reuters* (9 January 1992), on LNAU.

23. Olivier Gillet, *Religion et Nationalisme: L'Ideologie de l'Eglise Orthodoxe Roumaine sous le Regime Comuniste* (Bruxelles: Editions d'Universite de Bruxelles, 1997), pp. 18–20.

24. See Joseph Pungur, "Protestantism in Hungary: The Communist Era", in Sabrina Petra Ramet, ed., *Protestantism and Politics in Eastern Europe and Russia: The Communist and Post-Communist Eras* (Durham, NC: Duke University Press, 1992).

25. Gillet, *Religion et Nationalisme,* pp. 20–22.

26. *Ibid.*, pp. 56–58.

27. *Ibid.*, p. 125.

28. Michael Shafir, "Jews and Antisemites in Romania since the Death of Rabbi Rosen," *East European Jewish Affairs,* vol. 24, no. 2 (Winter 1994), p. 147.

29. Sabin Manuila and Wilhelm Filderman, *The Jewish Population in Romania during World War II* (Iaşi: The Romanian Cultural Foundation, 1994), p. 35.

30. 1956 figure in *Ibid.*; 1982 figure in *Neue Zürcher Zeitung* (15–16 August 1982), p. 6; 1995 figure in *Neue Zürcher Zeitung* (24 June 1995), p. 2; 1999 figure in *Rompres* (10 September 1999), in *BBC Summary of World Broadcasts* (13 September 1999), on LNAU.

31. "Aus der Evangelischen Kirche A.B. in der Sozialistischen Republik Rumänien," *Kirche im Osten* (Göttingen), vol. 30 (1987), p. 94.

32. Paul Philippi, "The Lutheran Church in Romania in the Aftermath of Communism," in *Religion, State and Society*, vol. 22 (1994), no. 3, p. 349; and Trond Gilberg, "Religion and Nationalism in Romania," in Pedro Ramet, ed., *Religion and Nationalism in Soviet and East European Politics*, revised and expanded ed. (Durham, NC: Duke University Press, 1989), pp. 348–49.

33. Philippe, "Lutheran Church in Romania," p. 350.

34. Estimate for 1977 provided in Frederick De Jong, "Islam at the Danube: History and Present-Day Conditions of the Muslim Community in Romania," *Religion in Communist Dominated Areas*, vol. 25, no. 3 (Summer 1986), p. 136.

35. Orthodox and Catholic figures in *Reuters* (16 April 1997), on LNAU; Protestant figures as given in Earl A. Pope, "Protestantism in Romania," in Pedro Ramet, ed., *Protestantism and Politics*, p. 207.

36. All other figures from Pope, "Protestantism in Romania," pp. 207–8.

37. "A Resurgent Romanian church," *The Christian Century* (5–12 July 1995), p. 674.

38. *Allgemeine Deutsche Zeitung für Rumänien* (Bucharest, 2 April 1997), p. 8 and Illyés, *National Minorities in Romania*, p. 232.

39. Earl A. Pope, "The Significance of the Evangelical Alliance in Contemporary Romanian Society," *East European Quarterly*, vol. 20, no. 4 (January 1992), pp. 496, 500–1.

40. Ramet, *Cross and Commissar*, p. 162.

41. "A Resurgent Romanian church," p. 674.

42. U.S. Department of State, *Romania Country Report on Human Rights Practices for 1996* (Washington, DC, February 1997), on *Nexis*. The Department of State reported that 385 new faiths were registered after 1989, in addition to the 14 enjoying legal status in 1989. But the fact that these figures add up to almost precisely 400 suggests that the State Department may have obtained a round figure and decided to treat it as an exact number.

43. *Rompres* (19 June 1990), in *BBC Summary of World Broadcasts* (22 June 1990).

44. *Chicago Tribune* (9 January 1990), p. 3.

45. *Reuters* (14 March 1990), on LNAU.

46. *Reuters* (16 March 1990), on LNAU; and *Rompres* (23 March 1990), in *BBC Summary of World Broadcasts* (28 March 1990).

47. Gillet, *Religion et Nationalisme*, p. 136. For an account of a nationalistically inspired Orthodox church service, see *Romania Libera* (Bucharest, 23 September 1997), p. 3. For a discussion of extreme-right currents in post-Communist Romania, see Michael Shafir, "The Mind of Romania's Radical Right," in Sabrina P. Ramet, ed., *The Radical Right in Central and Eastern Europe since 1989* (University Park: The Pennsylvania State University Press, 1999).

48. Deletant, *Ceauşescu and the Securitate*, p. 403.

49. *Tineretul Liber* (Bucharest, 27 January 1990), pp. 1, 2, trans. in FBIS, *Daily Report* (Eastern Europe) (9 March 1990), p. 85.

50. Reported in Alexander F. C. Webster, "Romanian Church Seeks to Cleanse Itself," *The Christian Century* (3 April 1991), p. 357.

51. *The Independent* (22 June 1992), p. 10; and *Reuters* (21 June 1992), on LNAU.

52. Romanian Radio (Bucharest, 15 March 1996), trans. in *BBC Monitoring Service: Eastern Europe* (19 March 1996).

53. *Romania Libera* (30 September 1997), p. 20.

54. *Associated Press* (4 November 1997), on *RFE/RL telex.*

55. *Romania Libera* (7 October 1997), p. 2.

56. *RFE/RL Newsline* (9 July 2001), p.21, at www.rferl.org/newsline [hereafter, RFE/RL-NL]; and RFE/RL, *(Un)Civil Societies*, vol. 2, no. 27 (11 July 2001), p. 4, at www.rferl.org/org/ucs.

57. RFE/RL-NL (3 July 2001), p. 20.

58. RFE/RL, *Media Matters*, vol. 1, no. 3 (23 February 2001), at www.rferl.org/mm.

59. RFE/RL-NL (15 January 2001), p. 5; and RFE/RL, *(Un)Civil Societies*, vol. 2, no. 3 (18 January 2001), p. 6.

60. RFE/RL-NL (26 March 2001), p. 5.

61. Lavinia Stan and Lucian Turcescu, "The Romanian Orthodox Church and Post-Communist Democratization (A)," *RFE/RL, East European Perspectives*, vol. 3, no. 4 (22 February 2001), p. 4, available at www.rferl.org/eepreport/2001/02/4-220201.html.

62. As reported in RFE/RL-NL (5 November 2001), p. 5.

63. Alexander F. C. Webster, "Evangelicals vs. Orthodox in Romania," in *The Christian Century* (30 May–6 June 1990), pp. 560–61.

64. Alina Mungiu-Pippidi, "The Ruler and the Patriarch: The Romanian Eastern Orthodox Church in Transition," *East European Constitutional Review*, vol. 7, no. 2 (Spring 1998), p. 2, available at www.law.nyu.edu/eecr/vol7num2/feature/rulerpatriarch.html.

65. *Reuters* (14 November 1996), on *Nexis*; see also *Rompres* (28 October 1995), in *BBC Monitoring Service: Eastern Europe* (31 October 1995).

66. For further discussion of the election, see Anneli Ute Gabanyi, "Rumänien: Parlaments- und Präsidentschaftswahlen 1996," in *Südost Europa*, vol. 46, nos. 3–4 (March–April 1997), pp. 126–30.

67. *Reuters* (1 December 1996), on LNAU; and *International Herald Tribune* (Paris), 3 December 1996, on LNAU.

68. Webster, "Prophecy and Propaganda," p. 523.

69. *Rompres* (4 June 1997), in *BBC Monitoring Service: Eastern Europe* (6 June 1997).

70. The combined figure for Roman Catholic, Reformed, and Unitarian Churches comes from a prepared statement by László Hámos, president of the Hungarian Human Rights Foundation, before the Subcommittee on International Trade, US Senate Finance Committee, Washington, DC, in *Federal News Service* (4 June 1996), on LNAU. The figure for the Greek-Rite Catholic Church comes from *Reuters* (20 June 1994), on LNAU.

71. *Neue Zürcher Zeitung* (4 April 1997), p. 3.

72. Prepared statement by Hámos. See also Hungarian Radio (Budapest), 11 August 1997, trans. in *BBC Summary of World Broadcasts* (13 August 1997).

73. *Reuters* (27 October 1997), and *Reuters* (31 October 1997)—both on *RFE/RL telex.*

74. Lavinia Stan and Lucian Turcescu, "The Romanian Orthodox Church and Post-Communist Democratization (B)," *RFE/RL, East European Perspectives*, vol. 3, no. 5 (7 March 2001), p. 5, available at www.rferl.org/eepreport/2001/03/5-070301.html.

75. *Evenimentul zilei* (17 June 1997), as quoted in *Ibid.*, p. 6.

76. AP (5 February 1999), on LNAU.

77. *Sunday Telegraph* (London, 3 May 1998), p. 33.

78. "The religious cults can claim all the nationalized real estates," *The Metropolitanate of Moldavia and Bukovina* (3 April 2001), available at www.mmb.ro/en/news.

79. *Agence France Presse* (25 October 1995) refers to demands for the restitution of "more than 1,000 churches."

80. *Rompres* (5 April 1990), in *BBC Summary of World Broadcasts* (7 April 1990); and *Dreptatea* (Bucharest, 30 May 1990), p. 1, trans. in FBIS, *Daily Report* (Eastern Europe), (21 June 1990), p. 56.

81. *Dreptatea* (30 May 1990), p. 1.

82. *Rompres* (12 May 1993), in *BBC Summary of World Broadcasts* (19 May 1993).

83. Quoted in Keleher, "Romanian Greek-Catholic," p. 101.

84. *Glas koncila* (Zagreb, 17 August 1997), p. 4.

85. *Frankfurter Allgemeine* (7 May 1999), p. 5; *Süddeutsche Zeitung* (Munich), 7 May 1999, p. 10; and *Rompres* (7 May 1999), in *BBC Monitoring Europe—Political* (7 May 1999), on LNAU.

86. *Reuters* (14 September 1990), on LNAU; *Reuters* (14 September 1995), on LNAU; Hungarian Radio (11 June 1997), in *BBC Summary of World Broadcasts* (13 June 1997), on LNAU.

87. Stan and Turcescu, "The Romanian Orthodox Church (B)," p. 2.

88. See Tom Gallagher, *Romania after Ceauşescu: The Politics of Intolerance* (Edinburgh: University of Edinburgh Press, 1995).

89. Keleher, "Romanian Greek-Catholics," p. 101 and *passim;* Webster, "Evangelicals vs. Orthodox," pp. 560 61; and Sabrina P. Ramet, *Nihil Obstat: Religion, Politics, and Social Change in East-Central Europe and Russia* (Durham, NC: Duke University Press, 1998), chap. 7. See also *Christianity Today* (11 March 1991), pp. 71, 75.

90. Gillet, *Religion et Nationalisme,* p. 138.

91. *The Independent* (12 July 1996), p. 15.

92. *The Daily Telegraph* (London, 27 December 1994), p. 11; Scott Long, "A cause for scandal," *Index on Censorship*, vol. 24, no. 1 (January/February 1995), pp. 97–98; UPI (14 September 1995), on LNAU; and *Reuters* (18 April 1997), on LNAU. For more detailed discussions of the Romanian Orthodox Church's sexual phobias, see Ramet, *Nihil Obstat,* pp. 197–99.

93. Quoted in *Associated Press* (16 October 1997), on *RFE/RL telex.*

94. Quoted in Stan and Turcescu, "The Romanian Orthodox Church (B)," p. 3.

95. *Ibid.*

96. *Evenimentul zilei* (16 April 1998), as quoted in *Ibid.*, p. 3.

97. RFE/RL-NL (29 June 2000), p. 4.

98. RFE/RL-NL (13 September 2000), p. 4.

99. Scarfe, "Romanian Orthodox Church," p. 209.

15

Post-Totalitarian Pre-Feminism*

Mihaela Miroiu and Liliana Popescu

When one of us, Miroiu, made her debut in writing on feminist subjects, the first thing that came to her mind was the image of a caricature drawing. It represented a female kangaroo looking leniently and puzzled at the male kangaroo speaking to the public from her own *marsupium*: "Women are weak creatures who need protection."

WHO KEEPS THE REMOTE CONTROL?

"We may be expected to change jobs, careers, marriages and geographical venues with the same resignation and optimism as we switch channels."[1] These are the words of Patricia Mann in her book on agency in a post-feminist era. They are a suitable description of the situation of women in a dynamic and open society, fighting energetically against conservatism and opening ways to freedom. They belong to a world which, more than thirty years ago, transformed Betty Friedan's *The Feminine Mystique* into the consciousness of a generation of American women who used to be "daddy's dolls,"[2] and who started to explicitly refuse, more and more, to be dolls. The women to whom Patricia Mann referred asserted themselves in a society in which people can afford to change life projects more or less like switching TV channels. Mature liberal democracies allow people to keep the remote controls of their lives in their own hands.

The "socialist female kangaroo" contemporary with Betty Friedan's famous book was involved neither in a war against the beauty myth nor against Re-

*The following chapter was largely completed in 1999 and mostly analyzes the situation then.

publican "family values." She was not fighting for economic emancipation, because she had the *obligation* to work. She was not even contemplating the bust of the male kangaroo delivering speeches about women's helplessness because these speeches were not about such "trivial" matters, but rather about "grave problems of the entire humanity." The Communist regime could not afford to pay attention to "details," as its ideology was concerned with the "essence." In totalitarian regimes, the state is keeping the remote controls of its citizens.

In the Eastern Europe societies in transition, the remote controls have begun to be distributed by decentralization. The distinction between private-local and state channels has become sharper and sharper. The governments have begun to legitimize themselves by their contributions to the process of genuine citizenship recovery. We are going to talk later about this process of empowering citizens, when approaching the issue of "civic minimalism" in transition societies.[3] Two important questions can be raised in this context: to what extent the citizens themselves are claiming their autonomy, and to what extent they actually get genuine autonomy. In other words, to what extent are they waiting for the state to distribute the remote controls, and to what extent are the remote controls simple boxes they possess, but have no idea how to use?

The citizens of the former socialist countries have started to slowly retrieve their remote controls, or at least they have started to acquire the will to do so. However, the state, as former remote control keeper, is being replaced by other, often unidentifiable, agents. The economic uncertainty generated by the totalitarian state, and the "earthquake" of the disintegration of the planned economy, represent the background of citizens' weakness in retrieving their autonomy. In this context, Romanian women citizens are twice deprived: first, as a result of this "earthquake," and second, as a result of a return to an obsolete form of patriarchy.

The majority of women in Eastern Europe, particularly in Romania, are not "remote control" keepers and cannot step into the post-feminist era as yet. In order to live in a post-feminist era, as has already been achieved in countries with a long democratic tradition, we would need to exhaust several stages of the process of feminist development. Without overestimating the notion of evolution in stages, we must acknowledge that we have not as yet reached the stage of having a meaningful feminist movement in Romania. Moreover, we are far from having achieved the internalization (or awareness, at least) of the notion of gender equality as citizens—a stage already reached by women in the West as a result of second-wave feminism. While there was a budding feminist movement in Romania, and some intellectual figures who were concerned with promoting women's rights in the aftermath of the First World War, there is currently no substantial liberal movement in the framework of which feminism could develop. Socialist feminism lost its prestige because it was connected with the emancipation dictated from above by the Communist authorities. Social-democratic feminism is insular. Ecofeminism is an exception, and its development would require a significant change of perspective, one which would allow citizens to become oriented toward nonhuman beings (and at present there are such grave human problems that other species are almost forgotten). Radical feminism, for its part, does not have the appropriate social preconditions to establish itself. Its development would require a structural reevaluation of Romanian culture and traditions.

BACK TO BASICS

An important feature of present Romanian society is the fact that important goals of the feminist movement have been satisfied without any direct participation of an indigenous feminist movement: the right to vote, the right to work in public (women represented over 47 percent of the total workforce during the Communist regime, and almost 44 percent nowadays), the right to an abortion (between 1945–1965, and from 1990 on), the right to parental leave (1997), and anti-discrimination and domestic violence laws (introduced between 2002–2003). In fact, it is only now that the formal character of the rights given to women during the Communist regime (the right and obligation to work, equal salaries for women, and political representation) has been revealed. While citizens had to accept them, and pretend that they truly believed in their importance during the previous regime, their value was not really acknowledged and internalized, and the attitudes associated with this way of thinking are coming out now. While under the Communist regime nobody was grumbling when a woman was appointed to a political position, the situation has, today, changed radically. Now, their political participation is derided, occasionally by women themselves.[4] The right to an abortion, regained in 1990, seems to be more the right of men to have sex without unpleasant obstructions rather than freedom of choice for women (the extremely high rate of abortions after 1989 is meaningful in this sense). The regulation regarding parental leave passed almost unnoticed by the press and public opinion, and in the few public television programs which dealt collaterally with this issue, only conservative evaluations of the new regulation were aired, peppered with comments like, "This law is ridiculous" or "It is natural for women to take this leave." The explanatory factors for this new situation are to be found in the pre-totalitarian patriarchal inheritance, which survived through a hidden underground ideology consistent with our culture and especially with the Christian religion (the religion of the huge majority of Romanians).

FATHERLESS PATRIARCHY

Romanian society could be described, without exaggeration, as conservative regarding issues of gender. The strength and the persistence of this feature is derived from a double inheritance: the totalitarian one, and the patriarchal pre-totalitarian one, which was revived after 1989. One of the differences between the "socialist female kangaroo" and the "transition female kangaroo" is that, for the latter, the microphones of the *marsupium* were reconnected and the speech about women's weakness can be heard again. The transition society has cancelled the genderless ideology of "the new Communist man" and replaced it with different values found in the pre-Communist past. The combination of pre-Communist nostalgia, the post-Communist reality, and the "new woman" model of the consumer society created good conditions for the perpetuation of the "fatherless patriarchy." The present Romanian patriarchy is very different from other kinds of patriarchy (such as the American Republican patriarchy, for example). It is a continuation of the fatherless patriarchy of the Communist regime, when the income differences between women and men were quasi absent and everybody, regardless of gender, was compelled to work by law. This fatherless patriarchy was accompanied by the underground perpetuation of sexist mentalities, fueled by religion and social customs left over from pre-totalitarian times. The patriarchy of the Communist period was not derived from the notion of the man as the "breadwinner" and "head of the family"—which was, and still is, a purely ideological notion without correspondence in the economic reality of the society.

Women in Romania accept a double paternalism. Research on the confidence of the population in public institutions indicate high percentages for the authoritarian ones (the Church, 89 percent and the Army, 81 percent)[5] and low percentages for democratic ones (the Parliament features rates consistently around 21 percent). We may deduce from these figures the inherent bias of citizens toward accepting the paternalist protection of authoritarian institutions, and their bias towards accepting clear-cut hierarchies, orders, obligations, and constraints rather than asserting their rights and liberties.[6] Women tend to subordinate themselves to this authoritarian model on the one hand, and to the patriarchal model that pervades the civil society on the other.

In fact, Romanian women do not have much choice in selecting models. In our histories and in our literature in general, there are few or no examples of significant protest activities, or even assertive behavior, on the part of Romanian women. As it is taught in school, Romanian history says nothing about the struggle for emancipation among Romanian women. The few women figures about whom we were taught in school during the Communist era seem to disappear, or at least are overshadowed by historical male figures disliked by the Communists (it is significant, for instance, that an important road crossing the city of Bucharest bearing the name of an important female political figure in modern Romania, Ana Ipatescu, was renamed Barbu Catargiu—the name of an important conservative politician). The model of the demanding woman who asserts her wants is rather alien in our cultural space. Such a model, if present at all, is associated more or less with prostitutes and is therefore devalued. Instead, Romanian literature and history focus on the standard myth of the self-sacrificing woman. The development of this myth has been facilitated, in large part, by the micro-politics of survival practiced by most women in Eastern Europe, a form of behavior that they have developed in response to the chronic scarcity of resources which characterizes their condition. These micro-politics have been very well described by Slavenka Drakulić in *How We Survived Communism and Even Laughed*.[7] Whereas the West is "flooded" with an increasing number of requests issued by women, in this country there is a "drought" in this sense. Women seem not to want anything for themselves. In fact, they would feel immoral if they did claim anything, instead of offering.

SURVIVAL SOCIETY, OR WHO PROTECTS WHOM?

Romanian post-Communist society has been described in an important book[8] as a society that perpetuates underdevelopment, and as a survival society. Over 45 percent of the population is living and/or working in rural areas. This population is perpetuating a subsistence economy in their households, where they produce everything from flowers to cattle. These people are peasants, not farmers.[9] Without being able to produce anything more than the reproduction of their own survival, they do not support strategies of development and modernization, but strategies of survival. In such households most people are what statistics specialists call "unpaid family workers," 78.4 percent of whom are women. This is the syndrome of a recovery of the rural patriarchy based on premodern agricultural means and on premodern marginalization. For these women, the problem of human rights is just a city business about which they hear on television.

Another significant syndrome of the survival society is the low amount that services occupy in the total budget of the family: about 15.5 percent, and it is mainly allocated for transport, education, and health. Domestic services are almost absent, and where they do exist, they are inevitably performed by the universal "unpaid family workers" (i.e., the women). Women are in charge of the domestic services, the management of family resources (generally scarce), and the physically exhausting labor of the household, which is generally performed with unsophisticated tools.[10] Their performance is "rewarded" in that they are able to retire, on average, five years earlier than men. After performing their work in the private sphere, they are left with no time for themselves. Without trying to be cynical, we think that the expression which best captures their situation is the German expression which graced the entrance to the Nazi concentration camp at Auschwitz: *Arbeit macht frei*.

The formula that "women perform domestic services and sex in exchange for maintenance and protection" has been functionally obsolete for more than fifty years in Romania. We could speak of women's protection only in a cheap demagogical way, similarly to the content of the male kangaroo's speech from the *marsupium*. There were no laws providing protection from domestic violence, street abuse, sexual harassment at the workplace, date rape, or marital rape until 2002–2003, when anti-discrimination and domestic violence legislation was enacted.[11] Women seldom make public complaints against such acts, and the police do not take them seriously unless the case is very grave.[12] The policemen (the overwhelming majority of whom are men) do not intervene in what they consider to be "intimate conflicts of the couple," and they generally sympathize with the men when the latter are accused. Cases of "light" battery are regarded as tolerable behavior, even normal, by policemen and even some women. However, a number of public campaigns and manifestations against domestic violence occurred in the country in the last few years, which made citizens more aware of the phenomenon—starting with the demonstration triggered by the publication of an article by *Playboy Romania* titled "How to Beat Your Wife without Leaving Marks" (April 2000). Nevertheless, it is practically impossible to charge a man with "date-rape" because the woman is generally considered responsible for the outcome of such an encounter.

The economic protection of women is also lip service. In Romania, as in most countries, poverty significantly affects women more than men. Their income is on average 10.9 percent lower than men's, and the areas in which women employees are dominant offer salaries lower than the average in the national economy.[13] Moreover, the number of single-parent families (generally where the mother has been abandoned and left with one or more children) has increased by 1.5 percent since 1989. All measures of social protection taken by the government (installed after the November 1996 elections) have not improved the position of women at all, and have only mildly improved the situation of their children.[14] There is little protection when it comes to unemployment either. Women are generally the first to be fired, and the chances of finding new employment are particularly low for young women (except for secretarial and striptease jobs). About 23 percent of young women are unemployed.[15] When they get hired, young women are extremely vulnerable to sexual harassment. This is another area in which Romanian laws are silent; and as Hobbes suggests, where laws are silent, freedom is absolute.

Despite (or perhaps because of) their hardships, Romanian women have proven themselves to be very resistant and skillful. It is just that these qualities are used as strategies of survival and not of development and self-assertion. In fact, we are justified in saying that, given the way they live their lives and their toleration of the fatherless patriarchy, women contribute substantially in perpetuating the lack of modernity in the Romanian society. Their tacit, but significant, protest is their refusal of maternity and the concomitant incredible increase of abortions over the last decade. Feeling insecure, economically and socially, and having uneducated mates in domestic matters, young women in Romania are increasingly reluctant to have children. For the most fertile women (aged 20–24), the birth rate has decreased by 38 percent since 1989. They no longer want to raise children in poverty, under conditions of reduced paternal responsibility, having to worrying that their employers would fire them if they got pregnant, and knowing that their problems figure last, if at all, on the agenda of parliament.[16]

WOMEN'S CIVIC MINIMALISM

The road to universal suffrage in Romania was a long and difficult one. "Universal" suffrage (i.e., universal *male* suffrage) was not instituted until 1923, after prolonged talks about extending it to women (an idea which was rejected).[17] In 1939, by which time voting had become a purely symbolic act under the Communists, women were finally enfranchised. However, the first semi-meaningful vote for Romanian women did not take place until the May 1990 elections. Women's present civic minimalism is partly explainable by this late enfranchisement. Their present difficulties in adjusting to full citizenship were also due to Romania's pre-totalitarian history, where public life was almost exclusively a masculine one.

The rejection of women in politics at the local level is mirrored by their absence in politics at the national level. Whereas before the 1989 Revolution, women constituted 34 percent of the Communist rubber-stamp parliament, and 11 percent of the government, *after* the Revolution, when political participation became meaningful, the situation worsened considerably. From 1993 to 1996, the government excluded women almost entirely. Only 3.4 percent of the Parliament consisted of women, and there was only one woman minister in the government. Of the present Parliament (formed after the 1996 elections), only 5.5 percent are women. After the 2000 elections the figure increased to above 9 percent. Whereas during the 1996–2000 legislature one woman was appointed as minister, now there are five women ministers. Only 2.7 percent of mayors, 6.1 percent of local councillors, and 5.5 percent of county councillors were women during the 1996–2000 period.[18] There are just two women rectors (as of 2002) or government country representatives (*prefecti* in Romanian)—not even after the 2000 elections. Even counting only the institutions numerically dominated by women, the balance between women and men leaders is 36 to 100.[19]

There is a lack of coherence and coordination among the activities of the fifty women's NGOs in advancing and protecting women's interests. Various parties also treat women's issues rather formally. Their problems are always listed in party programs in connection with the issues of seniors, children, and people with handicaps—thus implicitly stressing their powerlessness. The public perception is that women are weak, that they need to be protected (by males), and that they are "eternally handicapped creatures." The message of most political programs is that women need social protection, but not more than that: they need no developmental support, no affirmative action, and not even tax reductions for domestic appliances. The liberal parties adopt gender-blind strategies, and the social democrats are talking in general terms about "a deeper involvement of women in public life," while the nationalists and Christian-democrats cannot get over the nostalgia for the traditional family that "frees women from being constrained to work." The few exceptions[20] cannot alter the image of women as second-class citizens.

The civic minimalism[21] of women citizens can be defined by several features: they are confined to the role of a voter who merely legitimates the rule of the governments (eventually blamed for their leftist choice in many cases); they are physically insecure (unprotected from domestic violence, subject to sexual harassment at their workplace); they are the poorest citizens (which contributes to their social marginalization); they lack confidence in the laws and in the way they are implemented (especially due to the lack of laws dealing with domestic violence, marital rape, etc.); they have the complex of hierarchical inferiority; they lack the authority derived from being taxpayers (the civil servants keep on disregarding their demands); and they have the image of a "parthenogenetic mother" (society attributes to them excessive responsibility in rearing children, with the result that women tend to dedicate excessive time to this kind of activity and are left with virtually no time for self-development and public life). Their civic minimalism generates a vicious circle of a lack of public participation, and strengthens a feature noticed by sociologists: women are more conservative than men.

VADE RETRO SATANA![22]

Cherishing the fact that the West is prepared to step into a post-feminist era (even though this is a very controversial issue among feminists) we need to estimate our own position, and realize not only that post-feminism is a remote stage from our present state of cultural development, but that it is even dangerous to talk about it. Various "masters" who have preferential access to the *marsupium* media microphones might be tempted to say: "Slow down with your feminism 'cause it's obsolete and you're ridiculous!" Very few in Romania would disagree with this opinion. For instance, Sorin Alexandrescu writes:

> Behind the present general democratic emancipation the fact lies hidden that the emancipation of specific categories did not even start. Moreover, it is only now that the problem becomes visible. In many people's minds, not only of men but, astonishingly, of women too, it does not even exist . . . not to mention the staggering phallocracy of the political world in present Romania in which women are virtually excluded from the parliament, government and from the

"democratic" parties' leadership. For whom are they democratic? This is the reason why a very theoretical discussion about the traps of feminism seems to me disrespectful at a moment when feminism is stringently, painfully necessary.[23]

In the history of Romanian Communism, we find several powerful women leaders: Ana Pauker (minister of foreign affairs and vice-prime minister in the first Communist government), Elena Ceauşescu (number two in the party and state hierarchy before 1989), and a few women ministers during the Ceauşescu regime (for example, Aneta Spornic, education and Suzana Gadea, culture). Certainly, their number appears to be small when compared with male leaders. Yet, how many of the evils of Communism have been attributed to women anyway? The logic goes as follows: "What were women doing in politics? Their place wasn't there anyway! It's precisely because they got involved that things went wrong." The most famous example is that of Elena Ceauşescu. Given the simple fact that the promotion of women broke the tradition of their public invisibility, their displacement (from private to public) is regarded as a sign of the decay of good old traditional morals. The result of this logic is that any woman who is promoted must have been Communist.

While the post-Communist world is populated with "devils" or "monsters"—with the typical "monster" being Communism—feminism has been regarded by many as a smaller "monster," and women are regarded as bad spirits who should be exorcised from the government.[24] It is a truly fearful event when women get out from their shaded corner, enter the public sphere, and face the reactionary politics of Romanian men.

No important woman public figure during the post-totalitarian period has escaped from being "exorcised" through press articles, whose generic essence can be captured in the expression *Vade retro, Satana!* Three such figures are constantly present in the media: Zoe Petre (renowned historian and counsellor to Romania's president), Ana Blandiana (poet and president of the Civic Alliance—part of the governmental coalition), and Alina Mungiu (social psychologist and director of the news department of the public television station). Apart from being hunted for their mistakes, these mistakes are attributed in the most sexist ways to the fact that they are women. Zoe Petre is accused of having subordinated her own son (who is also a part of the president's entourage), who thus becomes "a man who accepts being hired by his mom [and who, therefore] cannot be a real man, and is thus less influential in foreign policy making in Romania."[25] Ana Blandiana, who is an influential person because of the Civic Alliance's participation in the governmental coalition, is accused of transforming the male president (of Romania) into a "cardboard doll," and of performing "the unfortunate role played in the history of Romania in the past of running the country without having any open responsibility and hiding herself behind male politicians."[26] She is compared with a "devilish" female character—the lover of the former King of Romania, Carol II. Alina Mungiu, a strong-willed person, is accused of being too "man-like" and of having a castrating influence on the men with whom she deals, transforming them into "awkward husbands." She is "a man from head to toe with a little, perhaps insignificant, exception."[27] She is compared not with king-lovers but with the "devilish" figures of the Communist regime. Around these women, three myths about women in public life have been created: the maternal one (the mother who acts irrationally, being a mother), the sensitive type who acts perversely subtle behind the appearance of sensitivity, and the virile type who acts dictatorial and castrating as a result of her "maleness." What is worrisome is that the journalists who write about them are the most known and influential in our media.

Women who are authoritative in the media do not react against the sexism; they tend to react against misogynists and only in situations in which famous women are attacked, but not when women as a group are concerned. Even the famous women who are subject to "exorcist" practices by the media declare themselves to antifeminists (Ana Blandiana and Nadia Constantinescu—the wife of Romania's president). Only one of them, Zoe Petre, publicly declared that she was a feminist. Many women who are members of political parties adopt gender-bound standpoints, especially those who have a nostalgia for the interwar period tradition. In private conversations, these women complain that they are exploited in electoral campaigns and then not included on party electoral lists, being kept behind closed doors to prepare local reports and coffees for the newly elected representatives.

SUBORDINATED ROLES, CONSERVATIVE MENTALITIES

Kathy Ferguson explained in a very convincing way that women are not powerless because they are feminine, but rather they are feminine because they are powerless.[28] In confirmation of this idea, many Romanian researchers note that the post-totalitarian society of Romania is excessively feminine. Some of these people are fighting against feminism (they are antifeminists without knowing what feminism is), using as an argument the idea of this excessive feminization of society.[29] The excessive "feminization" is a feature of the "survival society." The Communist regime succeeded in educating people into negative "feminine" features: obedience, fear, and an underlying lack of autonomy and assertiveness. People who live in such a world learn, regardless of their genders, the bitter lesson of humiliation, obedience, and constant dependence on others. Such a society is excessively hierarchical. Those at the bottom of the scale acquire feminine roles: they are the servants, the auxiliary rank. They are compelled to play the bureaucrats' game, to understand their "masters'" wishes, and not to be self-assertive. They have a weak self-confidence, low self-esteem, and subordinate roles.[30]

This "feminization" engenders the fear of radical change, an understandable fear when the daily fight for survival leaves little or no room for a self-constructed sense in life. Various books about the transition note that women are, statistically speaking, more conservative than men. They suffer from a "traditionalist syndrome essentially hostile to change."[31] The gender dimension of Romanian conservatism is acknowledged by the women members of various nongovernmental organizations (NGOs), who explain it by the "fear for tomorrow's survival," which is stronger in women than in men, given that they have more concrete responsibilities in this sense.

What the Romanian anti-feminists seem to ignore is that the fundamental cause of "feminization," and of women's conservatism, is precisely the lack of feminist policies—that is, the lack of feminism as ideology and politics. The Romanian "democrats" are undermining the process of social modernization and of democratic consolidation by obstructing gender-aware strategies, and thus perpetuating the civic minimalism and survival strategies.

"FEMINISM MUST BE ABORTED FROM THE BEGINNING"

The dominant discourses on gender topics are either reverential, traditionalist (including here the classical rhetoric about "women's nature" and her "floral sensitivity"), or simply antifeminist. The reverential type of discourse is displayed by both women and men. Whereas the traditional rhetoric is pretty much the same in most cultural spaces, the antifeminist one is rather original. We will discuss two features of this kind of discourse: (1) feminism is dangerous everywhere, and (2) feminism is dangerous, particularly in our society, and must be aborted before its birth:

1. Feminism is dangerous everywhere because the feminists suffer from a "blind revisionist anger." They are extremists, endangering the great monuments of culture from Plato to Kant. They are out to destroy rationality, to castrate men intellectually, to generate a new kind of eugeny, and to establish the absolute barbarism of an irrational, hysterical kind.[32]
2. Feminism is particularly dangerous for our society, because it is unfriendly, vengeful, and negative. It is dangerous because it is socialist and we have already unsuccessfully experimented with socialist ideas. Feminism attacks the classic bases of human rights. So, we cannot risk experimenting with it now at a time when we are trying to implement these classic rights. We live in a society with serious moral problems, and feminism attacks the traditional virtues, undermining the moral order.

The fact that "in the Romanian society, where the imitation of various stupid solutions is the rule, feminism is (almost) absent and has not been copied as yet" is attributable to the feminization of society (a relic of totalitarian times) and to the acute lack of manly virtues in politics (that is to say, to the lack of phallocracy). In a society such as ours, the fact that we do not have feminist and ecological movements is taken as a sign that "our decay is not that dramatic."[33] It is proof of social normality.

"EPPUR SII MUOVE . . ."

Despite the economic difficulties and despite the two categories of inheritance (the pre-totalitarian patriarchal and the "Communist" one) Romania has started to build up democratic institutions, a multiparty system, and a pluralist civil society. Despite the persistent and obvious obstacles, and the difficulties in reviving community and a genuine public life, individuals are slowly retrieving their autonomy. It is a major step forward in a society in which human rights seemed to be, for a long time, "imported goods," and in which any new ideology had been used to generate cognitive dissonance. This civic "*renaissance*" is essentially linked with the reevaluation of the ordinary citizens' experiences as "political centers of our lives."[34] The politics which focused on "grand problems," that is, which focused on abstract and meaningless problems for the ordinary citizens, reached its peak in Communism. The rediscovery of personal interests and people's daily experiences is a process parallel with the rediscovery of democratic politics as such. It is true, however, that in this process, according to some well-established reflexes, women's problems tend to fall outside this newly personalized sphere of politics.

Women's escape from the "totalitarian yard" follows different routes: going back to rural domesticity, accepting the uncertainty of an urban job, and imitating Western models of womanhood. Regarding the latter route, we note an important aspect. Some Western companies tend to take advantage of the lack of modernity in this region to bring in products that are in increasingly less demand in their original market: new cigarette brands, all kind of products with high health risks, and new models of femininity—consumption femininity.[35] Such commodities do not advance women's emancipation, unless women freely choose consumerism as a model.

Television is extremely influential in this country—even more than elsewhere, given the fact that going out for the evening is an exception for most Romanians. Apart from advertisements in which women are presented with many kinds of detergents (seemingly obsessed with bright, clean family clothes) and aside from images of long-legged women at top-model competitions, television offers few programs for women. Only one program seems to be sensitive to the real problems of women today. This program had been initially conceived as a program "of ladies' liking"—that is, presenting new fashions, hairstyles, and cake recipes. However, an opinion poll conducted to test women's preferences indicated that they were more interested in things other than waving their hair and being nice. They were interested in more practical considerations such as the double workday, domestic violence, prostitution, the absence of partnership relations, etc. Accordingly, the program directors changed the substance of their program.

The daily newspapers are the most sexist part of the media. They tend to present serious cases as trash (the best-selling daily *Evenimentul Zilei* used to "cheer up" its readers, some time ago, with sinister front page hot rapes, presenting them in a kind of funny way). They ridicule the incipient women's movement and lump together feminism, homosexuality, and ecology, whenever the opportunity is there, creating and perpetuating prejudices. No daily newspaper has a special column for gender problems, and an analysis of the content reveals that news about women comprises only 1.5 percent of the total.[36]

The highly cultured journals are in a paradoxical situation to the extent that they are open to both feminist and conservative standpoints. As the latter is dominant, this kind of press plays an ambiguous role: on the one hand, it represents a sort of *avantgarde* of the modernization efforts, and hence it serves the cause of women's emancipation; on the other hand, it disseminates the voices of the "Romanian cultural patriarchs." Here we have a few examples. The journal most open to feminist theories and gender analysis is *Observatorul Cultural*.[37] Another culturally prestigious journal, simply called "*22*," publishes such issues from time to time, without having a special policy in this sense. The journal *Contrapunct* (*Counterpoint*) has allocated several columns to cultural feminism and to reviews of feminist books. The more specialized journals *Sfera Politicii* and *Revista de cercetări sociale* are open to feminist approaches and to fair-play polemics. An interesting case is that of a highly respected publication called *Secolul 20* (*The 20th Century*). An entire issue was dedicated to *Women and Feminism*. The issue was typical for the eclecticism of the contemporary Romanian culture. It contained postmodern approaches, as well as discourses of a pre-Wollstonecraft mold (written, nevertheless, at the end of the twentieth century). It contained arguments in favor of the necessity of feminism in Romania as well as alarmist rhetoric about the damage to society's health resulting from feminism, all mixed in a hybrid which illustrates the present state of people's awareness of this problem (the cultural *avantgarde* included here).

There are also women's magazines, but they generally address women's questions in a pre-feminist fashion and, sometimes, even in a conservative-traditionalist fashion. Some of them promote the "Western model" in an attempt to colonize the native mind—an attempt that precludes the emergence of two important aspects: the feminist approach and the real problems of the native women. Some other magazines for women continue the "healthy socialist" line. Their subjects do not include the themes of civic and political emancipation, and the NGOs that focus on gender studies do not have financial support for journals of their own.

Research and education could also support the process of breaking free from the civic minimalism of Romanian women, through the promotion of feminist approaches and gender-aware policies. Unfortunately, women (much less feminists) are not well represented within the payrolls of higher education. University teaching careers show an obvious imbalance at the top. While women represent 31.9 percent of all faculty, they account for only 9 percent of professors, as opposed to 42 percent of tutors and 45 percent of assistants.[38]

However, there is reason to hope that things will improve in the foreseeable future. For one thing, there are the scholarships available from Western countries, which are not as conservative regarding gender. Romanian women graduates have found a space to assert themselves, especially through Western universities (M.A. and Ph.D. level), and have obtained qualifications that not even the autochthonous establishment can contest or ignore any longer. Also, women are increasingly finding themselves in jobs which allow them to incorporate feminist perspectives in mainstream Romanian academia. In March 1997, one of the coauthors of this chapter, Mihaela Miroiu, became the Dean of Political Science Faculty at the National School for Political Studies and Public Administration (NSPSA) in Bucharest.

Miroiu did not have many difficulties in introducing disciplinary courses, modular courses, and even an M.A. on Gender Studies at the NSPSA. Since 1997 she and her colleagues have introduced modular courses on Public Policies for Women: Feminist Political Theories, Gender and Social Institutions, and Gender and Public Policies. The same year she and Popescu introduced a course on feminist political theory at the undergraduate level. While the idea of teaching feminist courses was, at first, received with ironic smiles, they have become more and more popular, and have begun to be taught in other universities other than Bucharest (such as Cluj and Timisoara). There are now also short-term courses in gender studies—most of which are offered by the Society for Feminist Analysis (AnA) in cooperation with PHARE and UNDP.[39]

Moreover, many of their male colleagues have now familiarized themselves with gender approaches, and have introduced them in their own curricula and bibliography: encouraging students to do research into the gender dimension of Romanian political life. They have also encouraged women students to express themselves more openly and frequently in the classroom (usually, men perform better in the seminar discussions and women in written papers). As a member of the National Commission for Evaluation of Academic Education, Miroiu has influenced other professors from the Universities of Cluj and Iaşi to introduce feminist political theories and public policies for women. Her insistence on feminist approaches in academia is directly related to her interest in allowing women to cultivate "minds of their own." Change in social attitudes and government policies which can influence the status of women ultimately depends, in many respects, on the cultivation of a gender-aware perspective. Because of their status as centers of "higher learning," the universities may be highly influential in furthering this end.

WHO CAN MOVE A FEMINIST MOVEMENT?

Out of some 12,000 NGOs worldwide, there are fifty organizations that are directly and explicitly concerned with women's issues.[40] The question is whether participation in these organizations represents, or will lead to, a movement for women's rights. Our hypothesis is that this kind of participation can spark a movement, but cannot represent its substance. That is to say, women's activism in NGOs represents a *primum movens* but not a *movens* as such; it is focused not on gender-aware policies, but rather on family charity and support work. Some of them are focused only on women's rights, protection against violence, and defending professional rights (such as associations for the professional integration of unemployed women, business women's association, etc.).[41] Only two NGOs openly declare their feminist affiliation, being centered on gender studies (AnA: Romanian Society for Feminist Analysis; and GENDER: Center for the Study of Women's Identity). They cooperate with other feminist organizations, which do not openly declare themselves to be so.

These organizations initiated in 1995 the so-called Group 222, which was established with the goal of democratizing Romanian society on the gender dimension. The project included special training sessions for the electoral campaign of women (there was a joint participation of women's associations from various parties). The results of this project were far from what was expected. The local and general elections in 1996 marginalized, rather than strengthened, the role of women in politics. The women's NGOs have their "sins" and contributed to this fiasco: They lack a common agenda, tend to avoid gender-aware language, are rather amateurish, and fear being considered "deviant."[42] We must stress that the NGOs tend to adopt the perspective of *helping* women, but not of *emancipating* them. The causes of the "Group 222" failure are to found, however, somewhere else. Apart from the fact that the "fatherless patriarchy" is still with us, Romanian political life has yet to reach that stage of maturity that would enable it to engender a liberal movement having widespread support. There were many liberal parties, but no liberal movement that would contribute to internalizing the two main values underlying liberal democracies: liberty and equality. Instead, we have had (and still have) conservatism—a left-kind of conservatism, as in all post-Communist societies, with many people's interests still linked to the remains of the old centrally planned economy (including the working class). Our democrats are faced with making corrections to the injustices generated by statism, not by excessive liberalism.

In countries with a democratic tradition important liberal values have been gradually accepted and internalized by citizens in an "organic" process. They represent the implicit background for any social claim. Unfortunately, in Romania, these values are asserted only here and there. It is true, however, that in order to have a society in which individuals assert their human rights and are concerned with respect for individual differences, there are required certain material conditions that allow individuals to feel human in the first place—conditions that have not been met as yet in our transitional society. Beyond this, there is an inertial feature coming from totalitarian times, in which the individual did not matter, and in which the state offered social protection (work, health service, education, even housing) to individuals on a communal basis. Now, this community has vanished and the majority of citizens are disoriented and subjected to the dramatic waves of transition. People have lost a sense of community, and the process of rebuilding other identities is painful. The consciousness of the inferior-superior relationship is deeply rooted and fueled by the new, enormous, economic inequalities generated by the transition. The promotion of mutual respect would sort out many problems in Romanian society—including discrimination on ethnic bases, on sexual orientation, and on gender difference.

Given this background, a feminist movement in this country would not be similar to a Western one because it is deprived of the prerequisite politics of rights assertion and individual valuation. Romanian society has grown more mature through Social-Democratic, right coalitions (Christian-Democratic and Liberals), and now, again, Social-Democratic experiences. However, the liberal dimension is the "great absent" from the landscape. Liberal achievements in Romania are largely the outcome of external pressures (of European integration, etc.) rather than of internal ones. The new laws that express liberal values were imported and were not the result of internal normative pressures.[43] Therefore, we believe that a feminist movement will share the same fate of the liberal movement—at least in the near future.

NOTES

1. Patricia Mann, *Micro Politics* (Minneapolis: University of Minnesota Press, 1994).

2. This is Sommer Brodribb's expression which is shared by other radical feminists; see *Nothing Mat(t)ers,* (Melbourne: Spinifex, 1992).

3. This subject is substantially discussed in Vladimir Paşti, Mihaela Miroiu, and Cornel Codiţa, *Romania: starea de fapt: societatea, Vol.1* (Romania: The State of Facts: The Society) (Bucuresti: Nemira, 1997).

4. Alina Mungiu Pippidi, *Romanii dupa 1989* (Bucuresti: Humanitas, 1995).

5. People's trust in the Church is rather axiomatic; only 11 percent of Romanians are reported as practicing believers. The figures mentioned in the text were valid in 1997. In a recent poll of IMAS (September 2002), people's trust in the Romanian Orthodox Church is even higher (90.6 percent), whereas people's trust in the army has decreased to above 70 percent.

6. People's trust was shifting toward the president during the spring of 1997 and toward the anticorruption commissions of the Home Affairs Ministry, as we can see from the July 1997 reports in the most important newspapers.

7. Slavenka Drakulić, *How We Survived Communism and Even Laughed* (New York: W.W. Norton, 1991).

8. Paşti et al., *Romania: starea de fapt: societatea.*

9. *Ibid.*, pp. 205–6.

10. Liliana Popescu, "*Cenusareasa tranzitie*" (The Transition's Cinderella), *Dilema*, no. 220 (1997).

11. Ever since this chapter was initially written, some changes occurred in the legal framework: The most significant are changes in the Criminal Code (Fall 2001), meant to better protect victims of domestic violence, and the Equal Opportunities Law (voted earlier in 2002). However, the implementation of these legal provisions is rather problematic, due to a lack of appropriate institutions.

12. See Minnesota Advocates for Human Rights, *Lifting the Last Curtain: A Report on Domestic Violence in Romania* (Minneapolis, MN: MAHR, 1995); Monica Macovei, *Protectia egala si drepturile femeilor in legislatia romana* (Equal Protection and Women's Rights in Romanian Law) in the framework of the UNDP project, *Women in Development.*

13. *Ibid.* That is, education, 92.1 percent; commerce, 79 percent; and health, 73 percent of average salaries.

14. The state money contribution for a child is equivalent to $7 per month. This represents the cost of four pounds of meat and a "half pair of shoes."

15. A young journalist from a well-known daily newspaper, *Adevărul* (The Truth), was sharing with the readers her experience of looking for a job during July 1997. Her conclusion was: "In Romania the only secure 'job' for a young woman is prostitution."

16. The regulation regarding the cost increase for having an abortion (1997) has not been preceded by a regulation referring to lowering the prices of contraceptives and to an efficacious plan of contraceptive education.

17. However, the first time when all men could vote was in 1919.

18. According to the National Commission for Statistics (1996).

19. Pasti et al., *Romania: starea de fapt: societatea,* pp. 189–90.

20. Within the Democratic Party of Petre Roman, women elaborate a social-democratic politics of feminist inspiration and seem to be interested in gender dimensions of current politics.

21. Pasti et al., *Romania: starea de fapt: societatea.*

22. "Step back, you Devil!"

23. Sorin Alexandrescu, "*Alunecosul, necesarul feminism*" (The slippery, necessary feminism), *Secolul 20*, no. 7–9 (1996).

24. This aspect has also been noted in *Democracy in Romania: Assessment Mission Report* (Stockholm: IDEA, 1997), p. 25.

25. *Adevărul* (20 December 1996).

26. *Evenimentul zilei* (21 January 1997).

27. *Evenimentul zilei* (13 January 1997).

28. Kathy Ferguson, "Bureaucracy and Public Life: The Feminization of the Policy," in Nancy Tuana and Rosemary Tong, eds., *Feminism and Philosophy* (Boulder, CO: Westview Press, 1995), p. 377.

29. See, for instance, Cristian Preda, "*Feminismul si efeminarea totalitara*" (Feminism and Totalitarian Feminization), *Dilema*, no. 150 (1995).

30. Mihaela Miroiu, "*Hrana conservatorismului: antifeminismul*" (Conservatism's Food: Antifeminism), *Sfera Politicii*, no. 47 (1997).

31. Dumitru Sandu, *Sociologia Tranzitiei* (The Sociology of Transition) (Bucuresti: Editura Staff, 1996), p. 47. See also, Elena Zamfir and Catalin Zamfir, *Social Policies* (Bucuresti: Alternative, 1995); and Catalin Zamfir, *Dimensions of Poverty* (Bucuresti: Expert, 1995).

32. Mihaela Irimia, "*Amazoniada*," *Dilema*, no. 150 (1995).

33. Preda, "*Feminismul si efeminarea totalitara*."

34. Ann Phillips, *Engendering Democracy* (University Park: The Pennsylvania State University Press, 1991), p. 111.

35. Madalina Nicolaescu, "*Cu cat mai artificiala, cu atat mai feminina—impactul idealului de feminitate occidentala*," (The More Artificial the More Feminine—The Impact of Western Model of Femininity), in Madalina Nicolaescu, ed., *Cine suntem noi?* (*Who Are We?*) (Bucuresti: Anima, 1996).

36. Monica Lotreanu, "*Informare sau manipulare: despre imaginea femeilor in presa posttotalitara*," ("Information or Manipulation: About Women's Image in Post-Totalitarian Press"), in Nicolaescu, *Cine suntem noi?*

37. Especially due to the editor-in-chief, Delia Verdes, who is currently writing her Ph.D. dissertation on a feminist, linguistics topic.

38. Ministry of Education's Commission for Statistics, Bucharest (1997–1998).

39. The Soros Foundation and the Central European University provide substantial suppport.

40. Almost certain, more than fifty in 2002 (the fifty figure was valid in 1998 for sure).

41. Laura Grunberg is the author of the most important research on women's NGOs. This research will be published in a forthcoming volume edited by Gail Kligman.

42. Feminism is still not highly regarded. Feminists risk losing their "good reputation." See Adrienne Rich's comments in *Of Women Born* (London: Virago, 1997), pp. 58–59.

43. See, for example, the Law of parental leave adopted in July 1997. It was proposed by the Minister of Labor and Social Protection and promoted by women who were aware of the international legislation. If this law had been publicly debated, it would not have passed.

16

Gay and Lesbian Rights

Mihnea Ion Năstase

Ceauşescu's legacy of the denial of "equality" to those who prefer intimate relationships with others of their own gender has persisted in the first years of post-Communism. Yet, until recently, political discourse around the subject, as well as homosexuals themselves, remained largely out of the public realm. In this chapter, I explore the legal issues surrounding the issue of homosexuality in transitional Romania. Specifically, I focus on the criminalization of homosexual behavior, the efforts of human rights nongovernmental organizations (NGOs) and the European Union to repeal these laws, and the ongoing political debate within Romania concerning the rights of homosexuals.

HISTORIC MILIEU—REPEALS AND REINSTATEMENTS

Romania's Orthodox culture has leaned toward intolerance of homosexuality, but the legal system has vacillated in terms of how to include gay and lesbian activity as a jurisdiction of government, and how to punish those found guilty of such offenses. The Romanian Penal Code of 1864 criminalized all homosexual acts. This code remained in effect for the better part of a century, and while it was intermittently reinforced, it remained essentially in its original form. Then, in 1936, the code limited reference to homosexuality except in cases of rape. A short time later, legislators were still grappling with the issue, and Article 431 was introduced, stating that homosexuality could be illegal if it caused "public scandal," but not otherwise. A repeal of that particular language then appeared in the Penal Code of 1948. By 1968, the basic code was again reconsidered, and the first paragraph of Article 200 read: "Sexual relations between persons of the same sex are punishable by imprisonment of one to five years."[1] At that point, the infraction moved from the public domain and into the private.

In the post-Communist era Romania has come under significant pressure from the European Union (EU) and the Council of Europe to repeal its laws criminalizing homosexuality. In a September 1993 vote to admit Romania to the Council of Europe, the Council's Assembly made clear that admission was conditional upon repeal of Romania's "sodomy laws." In July 1994, paragraph (1) of Article 200 was struck down by Romania's Constitutional Court, effectively decriminalizing homosexual acts between consenting adults. However, the Parliament did not eliminate paragraph (1) at that time. Moreover, paragraph (2), concerning homosexual relations between adults and children, and paragraph (3), on homosexual relations between nonconsenting adults were not struck down. An observer at the debates noted that "[T]he mere mention of the Council of Europe generated booing and cursing in the hall."[2] After finding that the existing language of Article 200 "violated protections for privacy in Article 26 of the Romanian Constitution,"[3] the Constitutional Court ruled that homosexual behavior would only be penalized if the acts were committed in public and led to "public scandal." However, because the definition of a "public scandal" and "outcry" was not clarified, the legislation was not materially altered.

In 1995, another repeal package which intended to further modify Article 200, failed and Minister of Justice Petre Ninosu, in a now infamous quote, quipped that legalizing homosexuality would mean "entering Europe from behind." The revision with the language regarding public scandal was not sufficient to satisfy the requirements of the Council of Europe, where the expectation was for complete repeal of all sodomy laws. Throughout parliamentary discussions, the reactions from Romanian party leaders had been very negative with respect to loosening the laws any further. The defense used by politicians, traditionally inimical to advocating the civil and legal rights of homosexuals, found its voice in concern over threats to the reproductive capability of the Romanian society, over the "sick," "unnatural," or "sinful" lifestyle of homosexuals, and the insidious nature of homosexuality in the manner in which it leads to a "loss of sense," moral decline, and social decay.[4] Parliamentary debates included legislators' obstreperous pronouncements citing the "perversion" of homosexuality which "would be immoral to legalize," and concerns over the apparent lack of breeding capacity of homosexual couples. In June 1997, one prosecutor shouted that "[a]ll sexual relations are not equal. It is absolute craziness to expect there to be the same law for normal people and for *curişti*!" (the most vulgar word to describe homosexuals in the Romanian language),[5] and another member advised that the value to all of society was served by limiting the rights of few: "The interests of society must prevail over the rights of the individual. This is not the moment to accord individual liberty."[6] As 1998 approached, no progress had been made in the protection of basic human rights for gay and lesbian Romanians.

Ironically, most contemporaneous developments in Romania with regard to civil rights in general have otherwise been consistent with the nation's increasing "Westernization" and the Romanian government had been publicly committed to repealing the antigay law. Throughout 1997 and 1998, it had assured its West European neighbors that revocation was imminent, and had implied that the government was already displaying a genuine intent to change the law; assuring the Council of Europe that it was effectively dead, and that "there have been passed no sentences on the basis of Article 200, paragraph 1 since July 1994."[7] Then in 1998, in complete repudiation of previous official declarations, a bill to repeal Article 200 (1) was rejected by Parliament, stunning the Council of Europe. Romania's strict laws prohibiting homosexuality, instead of being repealed, were in fact intensified. The modified proposal, which was reputed to include a full retraction of the objectionable "Paragraph 200," actually increased the scope of the law and the severity of sentences. Whereas the objectionable criminal code that was in place made homosexuality punishable in cases of "public nuisance," the proposed modification would also criminalize not only all homosexual acts, but also gay organizations, materials or related activities—in public or in private. Finally, the Council of Europe gave an ultimatum that by 24 April 1999, Article 200 had to be eliminated. A bill was introduced in 1999, which would decriminalize homosexuality, punishing only forced intercourse with minors. It reached the stage of a second reading, but there were never a quorum to permit a vote to be taken. As of late June 2000, the lower house was considering a version of that 1999 bill which would eliminate Article 200, but would still criminalize "unnatural sexual acts performed in public" (peculiar language typical of this debate, it nevertheless appealed to opponents of the reform).

While long anticipated, Romania was formally invited to apply to the EU in November 1999. Romania has many laws that must be changed to conform to various European and International conventions, chief among them being the EU's *acquis communautaire*. While EU human rights standards are evolving quickly, it has been made clear that Article 200 must be eliminated as part of the necessary legislative revision. As late as 2000, Romania remained the only state seeking entry into the European Union with a law that criminalized consensual gay activity. Of course, these required changes in European human rights law are recent, and do not reflect universal human rights standards currently, as the standard is only a regional one.[8] Amnesty International called it "the worst such law in Europe."[9] The 1999 reversal of earlier promises to repeal the law was "clearly an anti-European attitude that pays no respect to human rights,"[10] according to Romania's Cristian Rădulescu of the Democratic Party, who objected to the proposal on the basis of its inconsistency with the nation's goal of achieving a human rights approach equal to the rest of Europe. Romania then stood alone in this approach to the gay and lesbian issue.

EUROPEAN COMMUNITY REACTION

The intense condemnation of Romania's continued criminalization of homosexuality by human rights NGOs and the Council of Europe threatened Romania's prospects of entering the EU in the next five to ten years. Romania has officially been a member in good standing of the Council, even though the European Court of Human Rights has banned discrimination against gays in cases since 1981. Furthermore, in 1999, the United Kingdom decided to stop excluding homosexuals from serving in its military because of the unanimous European Court of Human Rights decision in September 1999.[11] While European Court decisions and European Council "Recommendations" are technically voluntary, Romania could not enter the EU if it failed to follow these rulings, as the other fifteen EU members have. Continued criticism by the Council created the opportunity to thwart Romania's desire to join the EU, especially since the draft EU Charter on Human Rights, which is expected to bind all EU members in their *domestic* court decisions in a few years, would mandate decriminalization and discrimination against gays in Romania.[12]

Throughout the mid- and late 1990s, the European Community had understood that Romania intended to modify the criminal code punishing homosexuals as criminals at its earliest possible opportunity. The European Parliament announced that it was "shocked" and described its "profound indignation" regarding the 1996 change, which essentially recommended criminalizing any and all private sexual relations between same-sex adults as well as any public expression of homosexuality. While this 1996 vote in the Senate *did not constitute a final decision*, it clearly established a position and intent. In response European Community members increased pressure and spoke out against the declaration, and implored Romanian President Ion Iliescu to "use all his powers" to strike the law down.[13] In addition to concerns over the human rights issues related to the law, the Council of Europe was angered over the shift in stance that this represented: a full elimination of the prejudicial language had been officially pledged.

> The European Parliament . . . expresses its profound indignation at these decisions by the Romanian Parliament and condemns any attempt to criminalize sexual relations between adults of the same sex. . . . Calls upon the Commission, the Council, and the Member States, each within their respective spheres of responsibility, to exert pressure to prevent discriminatory provisions from being adopted.[14]

Romania's admission to the Council of Europe in 1993 had been conditional upon its repealing such statutes in order to be in compliance with the Universal Declaration of Human Rights and the *European Convention for the Protection and Fundamental Freedoms.* The language of this conditional acceptance was precise. It set an expectation that ". . . Romania will shortly change its legislation in such a way that Article 200 of the Penal Code will no longer consider as a criminal offense homosexual acts perpetrated in private between consenting adults. Yet, in September of 1996, the proposed change in the law appeared to fly in the face of international expectations and previous promises. The statements from the Deputies continued to demonstrate their intent to retain the legal position on gays; Christian Democrat Deputy Emil Popescu was quoted as saying, "Even the act of incest is preferable to homosexuality because it gives a chance to procreation."[15]

The Council of Europe's Parliamentary Assembly expressed its outrage as well in a formal resolution (Resolution 1123),[16] which reads:

> Certain provisions of the Penal Code now in force are unacceptable and seriously imperil the exercise of fundamental freedoms, especially Article 200 on homosexual acts. . . . The Assembly therefore earnestly requests that the Romanian authorities amend without delay the provisions of the Penal Code and the Judiciary Act, which are contrary to fundamental freedoms as set forth in the European Convention of Human Rights.

The Romanian government's public response was initially defensive, charging that the immoral and overly permissive society of the West need not dictate its values to the citizens of Romania. Days later, on 21 April 1998, in a sudden switch in the "official" Romanian posture, the newly appointed Romanian Prime Minister Radu Vasile promised to stamp out cases of human rights violations against gays and lesbians. He announced that the further reform of the sodomy law would soon be adopted in keeping with the standards of the European Community.

Just one week after the controversial Senate vote, on 26 September 1996, a committee of the Parliament resolved to modify the law to include those acts committed in public view and/or those, which cause a public scandal. Already, this language had been proposed and rejected by gay and lesbian activists, as it was insufficient to protect acts or relationships maintained in private by consenting adults. Also, while this new proposition would reduce sentences for private acts from 1–5 years in prison to 6 months to 3 years, it retained the 1–5 year sentence for public or "scandalous acts."

This proposed modification would make unlawful any "organizing or associating, or any act of proselytism"[17] related to homosexual acts or information. This effectively meant that any forming of an organization or group, any distribution of a leaflet, or even having a party in one's home would have been considered illegal. Inclusion of the language to prohibit organizing and proselytism directly attacked rights of privacy, freedom of speech, and assembly. The use of the phrase "public scandal" was of particular concern to detractors as it could be interpreted to mean that a complaint by a neighbor or accusation by a worker might result in a charge and sentencing.

The European Parliament immediately called on President Ion Iliescu to oppose the deputies' proposed version. Amnesty International responded by intensifying its activities to pressure Romania, and to bring public attention to "prisoners of conscience" still held under the law. Also, the International Lesbian and Gay Association (IGLA) and the Romanian Action for Gays, Lesbians and Bisexuals, another nongovernment organization, pressed forward with a campaign of faxes and e-mails to the Romanian government. In a letter to the President and to the Romanian Chamber of Deputies, they challenged that "[t]he vote to continue to criminalize homosexuality contradicts Romania's own constitutional guarantees of equal protection (Article 16), the right to privacy (Article 26), freedom of assembly (Article 36), and the constitutionally stated commitment to subordinate national laws to the international human rights treaties and covenants ratified by Romania."[18] The International Gay and Lesbian Human Rights Commission also protested. Regional demonstrations in front of the *Camera di Commercio Italo Rumena* in Milan included Italy's gay and lesbian groups, some trade unions, and members of the Green and Communist parties. Nonetheless, in 1996, the Romanian Parliament passed the new version of the law, which included provisions for the punishment of any act that might cause public scandal, and for the distribution of literature, forming groups, and the like. In the year ending June 1999, 99 adults had been charged with violating Article 200 of the law.

In January 2002, the notorious Article 200 of the Romanian Penal Code, which criminalized same-sex relations, was finally repealed. Romania's criminal law was finally freed from discriminatory legal provisions against lesbian, gay, bisexual, and transgendered (LGBT) people. At the time of repeal, an antidiscrimination law was also adopted, thereby providing additional legal protection against discrimination based on sexual orientation. A law banning discrimination based on gender was adopted as well, but legal interpretation inclusive of transgendered people has yet to be established.

The repeal of Article 200 and the adoption of antidiscrimination legislation finally allowed Romania's LGBT people to obtain dignity vis-à-vis the law. De facto practices will take longer to change. These changes bring Romanian in line with the human rights standards established by the Council of Europe and the EU for both member and accession states. This ratification should help to pave the way for Romanian entrance in the EU.

GAY AND LESBIAN LIFE UNDER THE LAW

It is useful to understand the context for these changes because de facto changes take much longer to implement than even the effort to establish de jure changes. In recent years, official monitoring of gay and lesbian human rights violations has uncovered significant, extensive and systematic violations. ACCEPT, a Romanian gay and lesbian nongovernment organization, and Human Rights Watch (HRW) both published detailed reports documenting human rights abuses which reach well into 1997, when the Council ceased official monitoring, and well beyond the date that the government claims the law became ineffective. These revealed a dimension of abuse of Romanian citizens that was stunning, and quite unexpected in light of Romania's previous public announcements on the subject. It documents cases of interrogation, intimidation, physical assaults, and the practice of illegal searches of the homes of "suspects." Police have demanded explicit sexual details and the names of friends and lovers. The persistent use of vulgar expletives during interviews is commonly reported, as is the practice of employing threats against family members. Gay suicide attempts are identified in ACCEPT reports. Some victims showed physical scars consistent with reports of abuse, and others fear sitting near open windows. Many homosexuals reported that they had also received anonymous threats in the mail or by phone, as well as threats to their parents or children. One victim was told "if you do not cooperate, we can't ensure your protection—a car can hit you, someone can stick a knife in you on a dark street."[19] Once taken into custody, interviewees reported being touched, slapped, and beaten "like punching bags."[20] According to the ACCEPT reports, they were routinely released only after submitting names of others, and locations where gays in the community might be found. Reports of abuse by police have included the deaths of at least two youths who were badly tortured while in custody.

Human rights abuses, imprisonments, beatings, and tactics of humiliation have been all too common in the lives of gay and lesbian Romanians. While deplorable, such practices are not without equal in Romania's treatment of other minorities. Romas, Hungarians, Saxons, Svabs, and others have been persecuted. Women also experience a status problem that precludes them from full and equal protection of the laws and participation in the society. There are "no specific laws that protect them from domestic violence, street abuse, sexual harassment at the workplace, date rape, or marital rape." The lack of public offices held by women speaks to their institutionalized underrepresentation in government. Abortion rights and policies under Ceauşescu were far afield from those of Western Europe, specifically outlawing the termination of any pregnancy for any reason. Gay and lesbian Romanians live within in a system where certain citizens are worthy of a particular level of legal and social treatment not available to "others." The denial of basic human rights, and the ostracism and punishment of targeted subgroups has been, and continues to be, a grim reality of civil life in Romania.

However, some recent reports indicate that times may be changing, at least in Romania's most cosmopolitan of cities. In Bucharest, there are now two gay bars, a homosexual newsletter, and an AIDS hotline to support the community. However, just one day after the governmental repeal of the language of gay criminalization, one of the gay clubs was raided by police, sending a clear message of intolerance by local authorities. Activist groups continue to assert that harassment and persecution are common, although they admit that formal prosecution under Article 200 has been effectively terminated. There is also concern that a false sense of security may exist among gay citizens. ACCEPT, which still operates as a human rights organization not a gay association, cites continual complaints of citizens who experience persistent and violent interactions with local police. Even following the elusive legal revision, true equality is likely to come slowly.

THE CHURCH AS A FACTOR

The Romanian Orthodox Church has politicized the gay rights issue through its widespread influence in Romanian society. Recent surveys report that 99.3 percent of the population count themselves as "religious," with 86.8 percent being Orthodox.[21] The Church's vehement opposition to homosexual rights has done much to fuel the climate of opposition to conformity with European Council expectations. However, the presence of Orthodox religion in and of itself is not sufficient to explain the influence it holds in the political realm of the gay and lesbian issue. Romania's neighbors, Russia and Bulgaria, also count the majority of their populations as members of the Orthodox Church. However, each abolished their antisodomy laws in 1993 and 1998, respectively.

The power and influence of the Romanian Orthodox Church stems from its peculiar association with Romanian politics. This accommodative allegiance has been a traditional posture of the Orthodox leadership regardless of the system of rule. With the advent and flourishing of a national consciousness throughout Eastern Europe, the Church has been "positioning itself for the very definition of "Romanianism," a shared identity supposedly superceding Moldovian, Wallachian and Transylvanian regional allegiances."[22] The Romanian Communist system recognized, unlike its Soviet bloc counterparts, that the Church might prove useful in furthering the Party's aims. Known as the "Romanian solution," the Church would remain an unconditional proponent for the party in exchange for some freedom from Communist interference.[23] The relationship was not always congenial, and imprisonments, church demolitions, and other restrictions came in periodic waves. However, the Church continued to minimize negative perceptions of such behavior and put a positive front on these incidents for the community's consumption. President Ceauşescu's use of the Orthodox Church reached new heights, as he astutely anticipated the utility of the Church in bolstering his plans for industrialization projects and in acquiring Western sympathizers. Other politicians followed suit, and the Church gained in stature and influence, becoming increasingly linked to political leaders.

With the fall of Communism, both the social and political significance of the Church has grown, and the pattern of close association between Church and state has intensified. Present-day political contenders are careful to be seen at Church functions, and in the presence of Church fathers. With its new freedoms, the Romanian Orthodox Church exerts growing power and leadership in the community and in politics. This influence is used as a means to pressure politicians and to publicly promote its antigay policies. HRW and International Gay and Lesbian Human Rights Commission (IGLHRC) are of the opinion that the Church's influence on politicians is strong, offering a quote from an unnamed government source: "Obviously our point of view is guided by the Church in these matters."[24]

The Romanian Orthodox Church is strictly and unconditionally opposed to homosexuality. A bitter campaign of accusation, denouncement, and intimidation has emerged from the Church regarding the gay issue in general, and Article 200 specifically. Any change to Article 200 has been utterly condemned, and those in Parliament that support its repeal have been denounced. In April 1995, the Church Patriarch issued an official protest of any decriminalization of gay laws, which was signed by all Bishops and Archbishops of the official Romanian Orthodox Church as well as by representatives of other Christian groups. It has executed a crusade calling upon citizens and politicians to protect Romanian society from the immorality that such decriminalization would bring. The Church has also made regular televised statements on its position and has officially condemned parliamentary reformers.

Surprisingly however, the Church's aggressive posture is not necessarily representative of the wishes of its patrons. Citizens responded to a 1993 national sociological survey, indicating that they were not particularly in favor of the Patriarch regulating their bedroom activities. Fully 42 percent indicated that the Church should not take an official stance on homosexuality, with an additional 12.3 percent having no opinion. Yet another survey from the same year (Institute for the Quality of Life) found 25 percent were willing to accept gay neighbors, and 30 percent agreed with a statement proposing equal treatment of gays and lesbians. While public opinion regarding gays appears to be mixed, many Romanians prefer that the Church remain mum on the matter.

TRADITION, MODERNITY, AND THE PROBLEM OF EUROPEAN LAW

As a largely rural nation with an exclusively rural tradition, modernization can be predicted to be more difficult for Romania than has been the case in nations with largely urban populations. Tolerance for same-gender relationships can be viewed as a "modern" idea; in Romania, its timing has been consistent with "Westernization," or modernization. Social mobilization theorists suggest that the more rural an area is, the more traditional and the more resistant to modernization it is. Furthermore, there exists a natural pressure toward homogeneity. Given this, and the influence of the Church, the vehement resistance toward civil rights for gay citizens that has marked Romania should not be entirely unexpected.

Political transition, however, is accomplished by the changing human needs that impinge upon the political process. The persistence and intensity of pressure toward government (by its own citizens as well as by outside forces) is the antecedent of political transformation, and the Romanian Parliament is encountering pressure on this issue from virtually every angle. On an issue where tradition and modernity are in direct opposition, and where the stakes are increasingly high on both sides, Romania finds itself in a vexing predicament.

It is unquestionable that Romania has desired to comply with European standards on nearly all issues, and was faced with the problem of this once outstanding exception. It was highly unlikely, given the emotional nature of this civil concern—and the legal precedents that exist—that any reprieve would be given to Romania to ease the dilemma. Article 119 of the Treaty of Rome, sanctioned by the European Court of Justice and all fifteen EU member-states in practice, provides for no exceptions. Recent EU jurisprudence bears this out.

The *Dudgeon* case upheld the rights of a gay Irish man who registered a complaint with the European Commission of Human Rights, which initially reviewed cases for referral to the European Court in that era, concerning the ongoing harassment he received at the hands of police in his community as a result of his being openly gay (*Dudgeon v. United Kingdom, 1981*). In a 15–4 decision in his favor, the European Court set a precedent to protect his right to privacy under Article 8.1.[25] Just a few years later the Norris case reached the European Court (*Norris v. Ireland, 1988*). The issue in the case was clear: the plaintiff's private homosexual practices had been considered a criminal offensive by the local authorities. There was no police brutality or other civil charge other than the fact that Mr. Norris's private sexual practices were legally in question. In a nearly split vote (6–5), Norris prevailed, with majority holding that discrimination against gays violated the protections of privacy in the European Convention for the Protection of Human Rights. In 1993, the case of *Modinos v. Cyprus* again held against sodomy laws. This finding was directly pertinent to the Romanian case because "the court held that even the Cypriot government's 'consistent policy of not bringing criminal proceedings in respect of private homosexual conduct on the basis that the relevant law is a dead letter' was irrelevant to the government's obligation to repeal the law."[26] The European Court's precedent had been set: Homosexual activity is a matter of one's private life, not subject to criminal code.

With these legal standards holding firm, and with today's European Court of Human Rights likely to demonstrate heightened sensitivity on the issue, Romania's gay policy was not likely to find respite. As of 1998, four European Community member-nations—Denmark, the Netherlands, Norway, and Sweden—recognized same-sex partnerships, and eight others barred any discrimination with respect to employment and social services. As a member of the Council of Europe, Romania is held to the Court's rulings on the Convention. In fact, the human rights of gays have not only been upheld, but *expanded* by the other member-states.

Similarly, universal human rights law prohibits discrimination in a manner that prohibits discrimination against gays. Article 2 of the *International Covenant on Civil and Political Rights* (ICCPR), the most important human rights treaty, states:

> Each State Party to the present Covenant undertakes to respect and to ensure to all individuals . . . the rights recognized . . . without distinction of any kind, such as race, colour, sex, language, religion, political or other opinion, national or social origin, birth or other status.

Article 26 of the ICCPR is clear as well, stating that:

> All persons are equal before the law and are entitled without any discrimination to the equal protection of the law . . . and the law shall prohibit any discrimination and guarantee to all persons equal and effective protection against discrimination on any ground such as race, colour, sex, language, religion, political or other opinion, national or social origin, property, birth or other status.[27]

The Human Rights Committee, which takes cases from individuals in states that have ratified its Protocol One, has ruled on the issue. In 1994, the Human Rights Committee (for the International Covenant on Civil and Political Rights) held that Tasmania, Australia's criminalization of gay sex violated the right to privacy in the ICCPR. This is the first effort to universalize gay rights. As a legal matter, this case is more important because it reinforces the legal and especially the more powerful political influence emerging from the European Court of Human Rights and the attendant expectations for EU admission.

THEORETICAL FRAMEWORK AND CONTEXTUAL POSITION

Opposition to the legalization of homosexuality in Romania has often been justified on the basis of its inherent "deviance." Every societal group accepts that there may be "deviants" within it that must be managed appropriately. The people and groups who are offended by the "deviant" perceive their understanding of normal and abnormal to be absolute and undeniable. That behaviors or attributes *themselves* contain some essential, inherent, and completely negative characteristic is the cornerstone of assigning deviance or "lesser than" status for gays. Such a status can be applied to easily identifiable characteristics (e.g., race) or taboo practices (e.g., witchcraft), either of which society may consider threatening in some way. The unquestionable "deviance" of homosexuality is the premise upon which official—and societal—objections are raised.

Howard Becker explores perceptions of deviance as a symbolic postmodern interactionism, and by viewing deviance as a dynamic system of collective action.[28] One element (person) in the system performs the socially deviant act. The other functions to witness or understand the act to *be deviant*, and then to behave in conformity with that belief. In this model, the behavior is only truly "deviant" when judged to be so in the interpretation of some other (nondeviant) individual or group. Critics of symbolic interactionism posit that labels can be affixed to behaviors not in response to any inherent nature of the behavior, but as a function of a given society's *reaction* to that behavior at a given point in time. In any case, it is clear that the viewpoints differ from the perspective of the agent perpetrating the objectionable act as opposed to the perspective of the assessor who stands in judgment of that behavior or attribute. In the case of gays, lesbians, and others of "queer" affiliation, their self-concept is that they act upon natural internal drives, not as some deviant ritual or behavior, or as possessing some unfortunate peculiarity. They assert that ascription of gayness is involuntary and, to them, quite natural. However, Romania's homosexuals found themselves attempting to function in a society where the "official" (and historical) position has been one which judges them as highly deviant, undesirable, and in fact, *criminal.*

In Stoica's work on "Otherness,"[29] a second model is presented which also defines the predicament of the gay (Romanian) "outsider" and how he or she copes within that cultural definition. He presents social interactionism as the interplay between people which forms the perception of "sameness" and "otherness," and helps us to understand the concept of labels as opposed to absolute values. Again, the use of a comparison group to measure and define what is normal versus abnormal is offered up for consideration. Using Goffman's premise that various types of stigma are used to marginalize those who are not "normal," Stoica proposes that a stigma results from a core of societal mores from which a negative appraisal is made. Whether clearly identifiable or inferred by others to be present, the judgment of normalcy is based only on the assessment of a judging party or group. Both the constructs of stigma and symbolic interactionism suggest that identification of one group, as it views and labels another, is the basis for the formation of a concept for "deviant." In other words, one clearly cannot be "other" unless there is a larger concept of "same."

Romania's dichotomous posturing on the issue of gay legitimacy can also be viewed from the perspective of institutional isomorphism[30] as driven by the government's pursuit of acceptance as a member of the European Community. The benefits and liabilities of membership loom like a two-headed serpent: Romania desperately wants—and needs—one head, but has been loath to welcome the second. Membership in the Council of Europe and potential EU membership both require Romania to submit to decriminalization of homosexuality. Romania has responded to the coercive pull from the threat of European-driven sanctions, and even the potential of outright rejection of membership in the body of the European Community. Institutional isomorphism has developed as Romania has been drawn into a complex situation where European integration directly conflicts with national social policies, the dictates of the Church, and dominant cultural ideology. The government has attempted to balance the dissonance between its need to satisfy the demands of European integration and its simultaneous rejection of the "normalcy" (and legal/social acceptance) of gay relations. This manifests itself in the practice of verbally supporting legal reform while perpetrating practical repression of gay and lesbians. It is seen in the rhetoric around modification of the law that is uttered by the very same persons and parties who vote otherwise. It is demonstrated in the practice of issuing promises to the European Community leaders that are clearly in opposition to the discussions and decisions that take place on the parliamentary floor. And ultimately, a passed reform cannot find its way to ratification by Parliament.

The issue of human rights for gays has arrived abruptly in Romania. There has been no "natural" social evolution for homosexuals, nor any gay awareness movement in Romania. Yet the country must face these issues as part of the quest for recognition within Europe. The press for legal, civil, and social equality for homosexuals is being superimposed as a function of coercive isomorphism, which "stems from political influence and the problems of legitimacy"[31] (i.e., Western Europe is "legitimate," while Romania is *not).* Such is the hegemonic pressure from the body of European states that it can impose significant legal and social changes, however unwelcome they may be. Coercive isomorphism manifests itself by way of "both formal and informal pressures exerted on organizations by other organizations upon which they are dependent"[32] and in Romania, such dependency is both economically driven and a matter of national pride: Romanians want very much to be included in the European Community. Romania's resistance to complete homogenization consistent with European expectations results from the very fact that it is externally imposed.

A considerable barrier to Romania moving toward an attitude of gay tolerance is the fact that it has not had a natural social evolution. The process in Romania is inconsistent with the natural development of greater gay and lesbian acceptance in other nations. In the case of the United States, for example, "gay rights" emerged from a context of rising interest, visibility, and support for greater tolerance and freedom for minorities. The civil rights movement, antiwar activities, women's rights, and the development of feminist ideology were part of America's expansive counterculture experience of the 1960s. This spawned an increase in both social and legal tolerance in the U.S. and also in other nations. As noted in *Queer Theory*, the "coalition of radical movements that constituted the New Left provided much of the impetus for gay liberation," and it ploughed a fertile ground for the seeds of sexual openness and gay rights activism. In fact, "gay liberation understood its goals to mesh with those of other social movements and assumed that the different liberationist struggles of the counterculture were connected."[33] The non-heterosexual option began to transform itself from a separatist subculture to a visible movement. The evolution of broader homosexual acceptance in the U.S. (such as it is) was enabled, even catapulted, by social activism.

Similar social movements then occurred in Australia and Britain. France and Germany already showed signs of general social tolerance for gays, and a vibrant homosexual subculture began to thrive in the 1960s and 1970s. This is not to say that human and civil rights for gays came easily. There have been both violent and nonviolent social reactions on both sides, and there have been both organized and sporadic reactions to increased gay openness. However, this visibility and social discourse created the platform for the current views on homosexual rights in the many parts of the world. Romania enjoyed none of these antecedent stages to its own reckoning with gay and lesbian rights.

VACILLATION OR ENTRENCHMENT?

As the Romanian Parliament met to consider the controversial issue in 1996, it was again apparent that change would not come easily. Some of the Deputy's addresses on 5 September of that year spewed contempt for the international community, calling them "organizations of degenerates," and they included accusations of widespread homosexuality in the European Parliament.[34] So raucous were the proceedings that ongoing debate could not be continued. In the end, the law held firm. "One legislator combating the changes called Article 200 'the Gordian knot of the penal code.'"[35] The final law that was passed on 14 November 1996 and held until 2001 remained clearly intolerant toward gays. It penalized any consensual homosexual act that is committed in public or if it causes any public scandal. A new addition to the law broadened the scope of intolerance yet further. It included language criminalizing "any propaganda or association or any other act of proselytism," as well as "enticing or encouraging a person," to homosexual behavior, and any act involving a minor. Of interest is the fact that a "minor" is legally defined here as a man under the age of eighteen. In cases of heterosexual acts involving a minor, the female must *be under fourteen years of age*. Sentences for these infractions ranged from one to ten years imprisonment (cases involving "grave damage to bodily integrity or health" or death carry up to twenty-five years). No corresponding laws regarding heterosexual acts committed in public exist in Romania.

The issue of an act occurring in public or causing a public nuisance was at the very heart of Paragraph 1 of Article 200. A place is considered "public" as defined by any of five expansive categories in the Romanian penal code, which includes any location that could be accessible to another, even if no one else is present, and where "in any way which the perpetrator is aware is likely to come to the knowledge of the public."[36] The issue of "public scandal" was a particularly thorny one:

> Yet a curious numbers game sets the rules for what constitutes a "public." Prosecutor Luha commented: "To 'come to the knowledge of the public,' it is enough to have a few people from the immediate circle in which the persons live comment negatively on the acts." Prosecutor Eugenia Vărvescu of Iaşi said that "a minimum of three persons must express indignation." A police officer pegged the minimum at "two or more." And a prosecutor in Constanţa identified public scandal as "when the act becomes known to someone else, even one single person, who objects." The chief inspector of police in Constanţa agreed: it happens "when anyone finds out, pure and simple."[37]

Throughout 1997 and 1998, public attention to the matter continued to mount. The circumstances of one woman who was serving a three-year sentence for allegedly asking that her roommate have sex with her, and the violent and malicious treatment that she and others had endured was detailed in a joint report by the HRW and IGLA. In "Public Scandals: Sexual Orientation and Criminal Law in Romania," numerous recent cases of detentions, beatings, harassment, and humiliation were recorded throughout 1997. The NGOs also argued that the language that had been added to Article 200 not only criminalized gays and lesbians' intimate acts, but that even "having a public identity as such"[38] was effectively against the law.

The year 1998 was anticipated by the Council of Europe, human rights groups and NGOs to be a banner year, and significant changes were eagerly awaited. On 14 January 1998, HRW and IGLA's Human Rights Council began the year by making specific recommendations to the Romanian government and Inter-Governmental Bodies. These included the elimination of laws permitting discrimination and those infringing on the privacy of homosexuals. They called upon the Romanians not only to "bring an end to beatings, maltreatment and other forms of abuse," but also to, "punish those found responsible for such abuses in the past."[39]

By 27 January 1998, Romanian President Emil Constantinescu assured the IGLHRC and the HRW that he would pardon all prisoners convicted under the sodomy law.[40] He acknowledged the significance of the problem by stating that, "homosexuality is the last remaining human rights problem we have to address in Romania, and we will address it."[41] That March, after facing significant pressure from the international community and human rights groups, he pardoned several prisoners of conscience. The European Community and international human rights groups embraced this act as a positive and significant gesture.[42]

On 6 March 1998, ACCEPT presented to the Ministry of Justice a draft bill, which would have abolished Article 200 and offered amendments to seven other articles that were inconsistent with human rights standards. On 11 May 1998, draft legislation was released by the Romanian government, which, if approved by both chambers of Parliament, would permit punishment of homosexual acts only if it involved a minor or rape. Indications for full repeal of Article 200 were imminent. But by June's end, the Deputies once again officially rejected any consideration of any further reforms. This vote took place just days after the Council of Europe, encouraged by the release of the prisoners of conscience, accepted Romania's promise to repeal the law and officially announced its suspension of human rights monitoring.[43]

In yet another intensely charged session of the Romanian Parliament, charges of "immoral" acts, impassioned speeches about the potential moral downfall of the nation, and sins against humanity were voiced on the floor, along with a clear commitment from many Deputies to protect the law from repeal efforts. Still, Romania's leaders assured Europe to the contrary.[44] When the reform issue was brought to vote in Parliament later in June 1998, it was again defeated. While the majority of legislators had publicly voiced support for it, eighty-one abstentions caused the bill to fall short of the absolute majority needed for approval. "This vote reveals yet again the utter unreliability of the Romanian government's promises,"[45] commented the IGLHRC in a press report.

As it stood, homosexual relations that might offend others, as well as any gesture, affiliation, publication, gathering, or any act that upset another citizen, was officially illegal in Romania. Article 200, which elicited international condemnation, was officially characterized as being a dead law, and it was asserted that no formal legal charges or convictions against homosexuals were being brought as a consequence of it. Here, Romania was walking a tightrope with the Council of Europe on a key human rights issue. By stating that the law, while remaining "formally" on the books, was not actually *enforced*, the government straddled the metaphorical fence. International pressure for repeal could not be quelled, but Romania continued to struggle with the gay issue. In order to become a member of the European Community and NATO, Romania needed to demonstrate its ability to fall in to the ranks of western democracies. After Hungary, Poland, Bulgaria, Russia, and the republics of the former Yugoslavia (except Bosnia and Serbia), Romania is one of the last countries of the region that is considered to be not yet fully democratized. The repeal of the antigay laws would certainly provide a step forward in the process of Romania's integration with Europe, and would effectively demonstrate and sanction democracy as a new way of life for all citizens. The government's final repeal of the law in 2001 marked a significant milestone toward entry into the EU. The European Parliament may now address the government's application to the Council of Europe, a development that could bring with it a range of political, economic, and civil rights consequences for the citizens of Romania.

NOTES

1. Article 200 of the penal code; 1968 version as published in *Buletinul*, no. 79 (21 June 1968).
2. Letter to Scott Long from Mona Nicoara of the Romanian Helsinki Committee (16 October 1994).
3. *Decizia* no. 81, Curtea Constituţională (15 July 1994).
4. Bucharest Acceptance Group, Report on the Symposium "Homosexuality: A Human Right?" (31 May 1995), available at www.raglb.org.uk.
5. Interview by Scott Long and Bogdan Voicu with criminal prosecutor Ioan Ciofu (Iaşi, June 1997). An approximate translation of the term would be "butt-fuckers."
6. Sydney Levy (IGLHRC), "Once Again Romania Says No to Gays!" available at www.fc.net/~zarathus/abroad.
7. Letter from Neils Helveg Petersen, Minister of Foreign Affairs, Denmark to Bjoern Skolander, Campaign for Romanian Lesbian & Gay Human Rights, available at http://raglb.org.uk/arcive/den.
8. At the time international human rights law was developed, beginning with the June 1945 UN Charter, most member states criminalized sex among males, and some, among women too. While the Charter's human rights provisions were prompted in no small measure because of the Nazi Holocaust, which also targeted gays, universal human rights have only begun to cover issues of sexuality, especially in refugee law for victims of sexual orientation discrimination, as well as female genital mutilation. Some scholars advocate rights for "sex workers." Seventeen states in the U.S. and many countries still criminalize same-sex sexual activity. In 1991, Amnesty International included in its definition of political prisoner, those who were imprisoned for engaging in same-sex sexual activity or those with a gay identity. In 1993, gays were present in the landmark 1993 Vienna Conference on Human Rights, but the 1995 Beijing Women's conference tabled any resolutions on gay rights in the Final Platform for Action. In sum, while gay men and lesbians have gained the right to privacy, European human rights law still does not protect the right to family life or the right to equality of sexual orientation. Transsexuals, by contrast, have been unsuccessful in obtaining the right to privacy (e.g., in birth certificates), but have been more successful than gays in obtaining respect for equality and family life. There is no pending treaty on gay rights. Among the pending cases, the Human Rights Committee is expected to rule on same-sex marriage on a case from New Zealand, following that

country's denial of that right. At a regional level, there is a case for conjugal visits among female lovers before the Inter-American Court of Human Rights, following denial in Colombia, even though married heterosexuals have that right. Details from presentation on "Evolving Human Rights Norms around Sexuality," by Chris Walker, Senior Lecturer at the University of Melbourne, panel on "Evolving International Human Rights," International Law Weekend (New York: 5 November 1999). See David M. Donahue, *Lesbian, Gay, Bisexual and Transgender Rights: A Human Rights Perspective* (Minneapolis, MN: Human Rights Resource Center/University of Minnesota Law School, 2000) and Rhoda E. Howard-Hassmann, "The Gay Cousin: Learning to Live with Gay Rights," in the *Journal of Homosexuality*, available at http://www.du.edu/humanrights/workingpapers/papers.htm, as well as Rhoda E. Howard-Hassmann, "Gay Rights and the right to a Family: Conflict between Liberal and Illiberal Belief Systems," *Human Rights Quarterly*, vol. 23, no. 1 (February 2001), pp. 73–95.

9. *The Independent* (12 September 1996), p. 10.

10. The Court unanimously held in favor of four service men and women who had been discharged during the mid-1990s because of their sexual orientation. It held that the UK policy excluding gays from its military, as well as investigations into applicants' private lives and their subsequent dishonorable discharges, violated their human right to privacy, as guaranteed by Article Eight of the European Convention. The Court also held that the UK violated Article Thirteen of the Convention because the applicants had no effective remedy before a national authority to pursue alleged violations of the Convention. The Court did, however, reject the applicant's argument that the UK government's behavior constituted degrading treatment, as set forth in Article Three, taken alone, and in conjunction with Article Fourteen, which guarantees no discrimination on the basis of race, color, national origin, political opinion, etc. The revised British code of military conduct not only eliminated the bans on gays, but issued new rules on social and sexual conduct, regardless of whether homo or heterosexual in nature. It should be noted that the European Court of Justice, ruling on EU law, held in *Grant v. South-West Trans, Ltd.*, that a railroad company could deny travel benefits to a lesbian travel companion, even though such concessions were offered to a heterosexual, unmarried partner. The ECJ, despite the practice 80 percent of the time, did not follow the advice of the EU Advocate General to strike down the discriminatory policy for travel benefits for lesbian partners. *Grant* case C-249/96 (1998), available on LEXIS, Intlaw Library, Ukcas, at p. 3. See also Carol Daugherty Rasnic, "The Latest Pronouncement from the European Court of Justice on Discrimination against Homosexuals: *Grant v. South-West Trains, Ltd.*," *New York International Law Review*, vol. 12, no. 2 (Summer 1999), pp. 79–92; and Martin Bowley, Q.C., *A Pink Platform, New Law Journal*, vol. 147 (1997) p. 1216.

11. The Draft Charter of fundamental rights of the European Union, available at http://db.consilium.eu.int/df/default.asp?lang=en.

12. United Press International (UPI), "Romanian Anti-Gay Law Sparks Criticism," (20 September 1996).

13. www.qrd.org.world/europe/romania/ep.resolution.on.stiffer.penalties (19 September 1996).

14. UPI, "Romanian Anti-Gay Law Sparks Criticism."

15. www.ilga.org/Information/finding_a_place_in_international.

16. Bjoern Skolander, "Romania Buckles on Sex Law Reform," *News Planet* (26 September 1996), p. 2.

17. Kagendo Murungi, "Letter to the President of Romanian Chamber of Deputies" (2 November 1999).

18. Scott Long and Bogdan Voicu, "Police Abuses against Suspected Homosexuals in Baia Mare and Iaşi,Romania," A report on a fact-finding mission conducted by ACCEPT (23–28 September 1996), p. 13.

19. Long and Voicu, "Police Abuses," p. 24.

20. Mihaela Miroiu and Liliana Popescu, "Post-Totalitarian Pre-Feminism," in this volume.

21. January 1992 census report by FBIS-EEU-93-155 (13 August 1993).

22. Lavinia Stan and Lucian Turcescu, "The Romanian Orthodox Church and Post-Communist Democratization," *Europe-Asia Studies*, vol. 52, no. 8 (December 2000).

23. Ronald Robertson, "The Church in Romania," *New Catholic Encyclopedia*, vol. 19, Supplement 1989–1995, (Washington, DC: Catholic University of America Press, 1996), p. 332.

24. Interview by Scott Long and Bogdan Voicu with Chief Prosecutor Vasile Luha, (Alba Iulia, 1997).

25. *Dudgeon v. United Kingdom*, 4 Eur. H. R. Rep. 149 (1981).

26. *Modinos v. Cyprus*, 16 Eur. H. R. Rep. 485 (1985).

27. *Ibid.*

28. Howard Becker, *Outsiders: Studies in the Sociology of Deviance* (New York: Free Press, 1973).

29. Cătălin Augustin Stoica, "An 'Otherness' that Scares: Public Attitudes and Debates on Homosexuality in Romania," in Henry F. Carey, ed., *National Reconciliation in Eastern Europe,* (New York: East European Monographs/Columbia University Press, 2003), citing Goffman's "Notes on the Management of a Spoiled Identity" (1963).

30. Paul DiMaggio and Walter W. Powell, "The Iron Cage Revisited: Institutional Isomorphism and Collective Rationality in Organizational Fields," *American Sociological Review*, vol. 48 (1983), pp. 147–60.

31. *Ibid.*, p. 150.

32. *Ibid.*

33. Annamarie Jagose, *Queer Theory* (Melbourne: Melbourne University Press, 1996), pp. 32–34.

34. United Press International, "Euro-Parliament Condemns Sodomy Law" (20 September 1996).

35. Emil Teodor Popescu, quoted in Lia Bejan and Dragoş Moldovan, "*Presa n-a scăpat de închisoare*," *Adevărul*, (11 September 1996).

36. Interviews by Vera Câmpeanu with Prosecutors Luha and Vărvescu by and by Scott Long with Prosecutor Mariana Vutcovici, and with Colonel Ioan Cîrlic, Constanţa (June 1997).

37. *Ibid.*

38. IGLHRC, "Gays and Lesbians Face State-Condoned Violence and Legalized Abuse in Romania," available at www.hawaii.conterra.com/jsears/overess6.htm.

39. *News Planet* (21 April 1998).

40. *News Planet* (27 January 1998).

41. *Ibid.*

42. Ben Patridge, "Romania: EU Welcome [sic] Moves to Lift Prosecution Threat against Gays," (22 May 1998), at www.rferl.org/nca/features.

43. *News Planet* (17 September 1998).

44. IGLHRC Press Release "Once Again Romania Says No to Gays" (June 1998), available at www.iglhrc.org.

45. *Ibid.*

17

Higher Education and the Post-Communist Generation of Students[1]

Sorin Antohi

Romania is not exactly a hot topic in Western scholarship. The scant body of international literature on Romania generally lies within the Cold War organization of academic curiosity and is rife with the resilient stereotypes of intra-European Orientalism. There seemed to be more interest in Romania when it was perceived as a rogue Soviet satellite, during the various Communist campaigns such as village "systematization," and finally during the bloody coup of 1989 (or revolution? Or, I would suggest, *restolution*, i.e., revolution *and* restoration.). It has triggered a rather ill-fated transition from the "multilaterally developed socialist society" to yet another avatar of the robber capitalist model.

Dracula, Ceauşescu, and other Romanian figures have been expropriated by a hegemonic Orientalist *and* Gothic narrative, haphazardly produced by the Western media, which had been sucked into covering Romania by the mesmerizing images of the charred corpses in Timişoara (which were later revealed to be a piece of ruthless propaganda). While the Gothic part of the story was eventually salvaged, thanks to the roughly 1,000 real casualties of 1989, the Orientalist part has prevailed because the otherwise grisly (and unnecessary, as it eventually turned out) toll was down from a whopping, surreal 60,000 (a mathematical shrinking that infuriated the very Western journalists who had disseminated this arbitrary figure, which had been advanced by Ceauşescu's expedient executioners).[2]

In the immediate aftermath of the revolution, journalists of all statures, from network anchors to desperate freelancers in search of their lucky scoops, came to Romania, as did world experts in just about everything, second-rate scholars and rapacious fortune seekers, idealistic or merely opportunistic missionaries of every faith, cynical bureaucrats, and clinically, self-servingly optimistic nongovernmental organization (NGO) professionals. They all came to Romania to transform it into a short-lived icon of, successively, popular heroism, mendacity, corruption, and anomie. They came to rob it or to turn an honest penny while the Western aid lasted. They came to save its vagrant souls and to educate it; to teach it democracy, the free market, and civil society 101; and to quickly narrate it in the refereed journals needed by a booming academic market. Lost among these were a small number of genuine, competent, first-rate people of all professions and allegiances. Some of these specialists had already contributed the best available scholarly work on Romania and were ready to go back to that country, often after unpleasant episodes with Ceaușescu's regime, which had made their return prior to 1989 an impossibility. Between these two groups there have been a variety of locals, from the brazen autochthonists to co[illegible]ated Westernizers,[3] from the shrewd impostors to the consummate gentleman scholars, from clients to partners, and from learners to teachers. A brave new world of Romanian studies was on the rise.

Yet, due to decades of isolation, Romanian scholars writing in and on Romania, are rare in the global academic market, a fact that has led to a curious situation: Romanians are almost exclusively represented, analyzed, and interpreted by their Western betters, and seem to be incapable of effectively speaking on their own. This is not the West's fault, as autochthonists or postcolonial critics would not suggest; it is the responsibility of Romanians themselves, if they are serious about sharing the (inevitably mixed) blessings of globalization. Fortunately, this situation is slowly changing for the better, and there is some hope. Even the more sophisticated recent discourses on the "people without history" have been struggling to include the "native's point of view," or the "native's voice," in forms that range from "thick description" (Clifford Geertz) to joint research projects and coauthorship. Thus, something I have called "The Third Discourse,"[4] a fusion of local and international discourses situated at a critical distance from both autochthonism (with its specific Romanian expression, "protochronism")[5] and Westernization (with its local hybrid, imitation, and its reductio ad absurdum political correctness),[6] is being proposed by an increasing, although still limited number of authors.

In this spirit, I will look at Romania's emerging academics, analyzing their backgrounds, their contexts, and their discursive and institutional trajectories. It is, I believe, one of the most important and one of the most neglected stories in Romania, and it is one which I believe ought to be told.

THE PERSONAL CONTEXT

Among the scarce satisfactions I experienced in the short periods I spent between 1993 and 1997 at the University of Bucharest was meeting a few smart, motivated, and gifted students. In hindsight, and taking into account my teaching experience in the United States, France, Germany, and at the Budapest-based Central European University—an international, English-language graduate school where my students have come from twenty-odd countries—I have found that the best Romanian students compare favorably to their Western colleagues, as the Romanians are frequently more ambitious and hardworking.

The ridiculously low wages in Romania (averaging the equivalent of $100 a month), its Albanian-level infrastructure, and the institutional stagnation are thus somewhat counterbalanced—at least for those who have other sources of income and access to Western academic infrastructures—by the feeling, maybe not just the illusion, of a lively intellectual exchange. This is a typical experience among those who teach in Romanian universities, but it is very seldom discussed openly.[7]

Romanian faculty survive materially and intellectually thanks to alternative, extra-institutional resources. They also teach courses at private universities.[8] They work in the widespread private tutoring system that prepares high school graduates for admission examinations (traditionally very competitive for job-market-oriented universities and faculties).[9] They often have a (parallel) career in politics and government, where the salaries and perks are better, and where rampant corruption opens the possibility for generating considerable amounts of quick money. They work for the media, especially for the private and international electronic media. They also translate, take sojourns abroad (usually thanks to European Union–sponsored international faculty mobility schemes), conduct research, and receive publication subsidies granted locally by foreign organizations, and so forth.[10]

Evidently, the energy, attention, and time spent to identify and use such alternative financial solutions strongly impacts the productivity, quality, service, and group cohesion of all those directly involved in higher education. For those who do not use their university positions corruptly to elicit "secondary gains" (Erving Goffman)—from the bribes offered by (mainly foreign) students in exchange for good grades, to the sad profit of Romania's antiquated, corrupt system of in-service teacher training[11]—only pure scholarly passion, the residual, declining prestige of university titles, and the spirit of self-sacrifice keeps them in the otherwise meager business of higher education. All those who can adjust to the higher mobility rate of a democratic society, even a poor, fledgling one, have another way of beating the system: calling it quits in search of more rewarding jobs, whether domestically or abroad.

ELECTIVE AFFINITIES

While I was teaching mainly theoretical and methodological courses with the history faculty at the University of Bucharest, I had the privilege of working with some of the best graduate and undergraduate students drawn from the fields of history, sociology (the largest and most sophisticated cohort), philosophy, and political science. Over time, I developed a certain perspective on the post-1989 institutionalization of these fields and glanced into the "black box" of the post-1989 university student generation. This heterogeneous group has grown up under circumstances that, while being radically different from those under which their 1945–1989 cohorts have struggled, are still dire. Their everyday lives are frequently hard, bordering on despondency and "quiet desperation."[12] Students attending universities outside their native localities are less and less common, as rents and other living costs have outgrown their or their parents' Spartan budgets. To get by, many have had to take full-time jobs, which has proven detrimental to their academic training. Moreover, libraries are antiquated, make little or no use of computers (for cataloging or access to online databases), and lack acquisition funds, even for Romanian books and periodicals, much less Western ones.[13] With poor career prospects, and mandatory ascetic lifestyles, most students and graduates dream of emigration.

The need for the 2000 generation to specialize early (perhaps prematurely), and the pressure to join the work force before graduation, are serious hindrances for those who stay in, or come back to, Romania. The local professional job market is more developed now than it was in the early 1990s, with multinationals hunting heads, and with an increasing number of job ads that are now posted widely by the public sector (especially in order to avoid, or easily refute, charges of nepotism—the latter being a deeply embedded tradition). CVs and resumes are now replacing party or "cadre" files, letters of recommendation and job interviews increasingly resemble their Western models, and evaluation procedures are slowly being introduced.[14] But the best positions, especially those that need some form of job experience or seniority, are not always available for the best trained (even those coming back to Romania with doctorates from major Western universities), as middle-aged competitors have already filled the higher slots in the food chain, taking advantage of having been around at the critical moment. This situation is not entirely unfair to the young because one could argue that, while Generation 2000 was enjoying unprecedented opportunities to study abroad, those who were between thirty and forty years old in 1989 had to keep the institutions running, and even reform them, frequently at the expense of their own further training or research.

Due to the Stalinist purges and constant counter-selection, Romanian universities have lost much of their scholarly and educational capacities. Several fields have barely managed to recover. Even today, those who choose to follow more sophisticated and transdisciplinary academic agendas have had to fight the constraints of the higher education system. Administrative and legal changes have now made it possible for students to attend two or more programs simultaneously (within the constraints of Newtonian ontology, this is possible thanks to the unusually systematic skipping of classes, by both students and faculty) and to choose their courses more freely.

A peculiar feature of Communism was the widespread need for the bright to teach themselves, or to seek mentoring and supervision outside the institutions of formal learning. Of course, the self-taught have existed everywhere in the world, from Flaubert's characters, Bouvard and Pécuchet, who embarked on an encyclopedic self-teaching spree upon retirement, to those who successfully turn their hobbies into professions. It is, however, alarming that, nearly fourteen years after the revolution, teaching oneself can sometimes be the only choice for university students.[15]

A special discussion is deserved for those who have the chance, or fight for the chance, of studying in the West.[16] If they work hard, pick up thriving specializations (such as computer science, medicine, economics, or business administration), outsmart the Immigration and Naturalization Service (or its equivalent), and have a bit of luck, they might land a good job. Such people experience the usual hardships faced by educated immigrants, but can be successfully integrated and socialized in the medium run.[17]

Serious problems, moreover, appear in the case of those specializing in the social sciences and the humanities, a subgroup for which the identity costs of settling in the West are considerably greater. As they have left their native country too early to have mastered its culture, history, and society, these individuals are subject to double alienation. They are more exposed to value-system clashes and cultural shock than their science and engineering counterparts. For the latter, adjusting to the new country of residence is not necessarily easy. However, the often segregated Western "multicultural" societies allow people with different cultural-ideological-religious allegiances to practice a superficial conformism in the workplace or in unavoidable social situations, while sticking to their original values, beliefs, and lifestyles, both at home and in ethnic neighborhoods of the typical postmodern metropolis. For the former, this double life, based on a sharp distinction between the public and the private, is less possible, as sociologists or literary scholars (to give only two examples) have to internalize the host country's discursive practices in order to succeed professionally. One can imagine a "politically correct" immigrant social scientist, even one that would not have a problem adopting values which go against the grain of much of his native culture or worldview. However, if one cannot adopt the discourse of his host country willingly, but still has to practice those discourses in order to keep an academic job, the split between one's public and private lives becomes toxic, even devastating.

Immigrants traditionally struggle to acquire their host country's *cultural intimacy* (Michael Herzfeld). This is not easy, especially when one wants to be an interpreter or an analyst of the host country on an academic level. As is often the case, one ends up in a situation of "double bind" (Gregory Bateson), becoming doubly socialized, or (worse) suspended between two incompletely internalized cultural intimacies: that of the native country and that of the host country. If such a scholar does not choose a third country as his or her area of field work and expertise (thus learning everything from scratch alongside his or her host country competitors), or if one does not engage in scholarly projects that do not require the cultural intimacy of field work in the native country, it does not always guarantee easy readjustment to the (largely) lost *habitus* (Pierre Bourdieu), especially in countries that undergo, like post-Communist Romania, deep transformations in the symbolic sphere.

If they return to Romania to stay, young scholars in the social sciences and the humanities are not better off either. They will have lived long enough in a different (and better) world to experience a painful nostalgia. As observed from the Carpathians, even the experience of a marginal life abroad (modest lodgings, frugality, low-key social life on a budget, bureaucratic hassle, etc.) begins to acquire pink shades. In North America especially, newcomers attain the smallest common denominator more easily, although they climb to the top social strata with as much difficulty as in Western Europe (with the exception of those who marry well, perform exceptionally well, and/or make money very quickly). For this reason, although North American sojourns alienate newcomers more quickly and deeply—due to the dramatic spatial, cultural, ideological, and lifestyle distances from the native country—they generate less anti-Western resentment than a stay in France, precisely because North America offers immigrants a quicker access to lower-middle-class status. I mention this because many Romanians become quite resentful of the West as a consequence of unpleasant experiences abroad, or simply as a consequence of their own perception of having failed at being "accepted" by their temporary host society.

When they take the plane to Bucharest, Romanians have to comfort themselves with the knowledge that it is a round-trip which will eventually bring them back to the West, albeit after a long time. Finding a good job, improvising a household, and relaunching the dynamics of a professional and social life are all difficult. The return of the prodigal sons and daughters is not exactly a celebration: If one comes back, this means that one has failed (at something that many have never tried, but most would have liked to). One may lose face because it is precisely those who "patriotically" stayed home who know best that patriotism alone does not explain one's reasons for staying in Romania.

One may only return to Romania with pride if one has acquired some wealth. Romania is becoming increasingly more expensive, another sign that the country is headed toward third-world status. People who have returned from abroad often adopt a grandiose manner of spending money, the only way you can affirm your status in an impoverished world. They start leading the life of the "nouveau riche," and are introduced to a new community of "intellectuals," politicians, talk-show hosts, and famous athletes. In short, they are considered VIPs. Those with a moderate temperament will be more discreet and modest, trying to keep close ties with their less fortunate friends.

GENERATIONAL CONTEXT

While youth have found it harder to obtain funding for education from the state in the post-Communist era, they have been resourceful in finding other means of supporting their efforts: through international organizations, such as the Soros Foundation, or through scholarships at foreign institutions (as many Romanian families today rely on foreign aid to survive, the day may soon come when social benefits, like scholarships, will be funded by the West as well). A competitive trend has arisen among youth of common backgrounds. However, promising youth who pursued their vocation at state universities and abroad have found domestic jobs in their fields to be scarce and poorly paid. They must compete for the scant resources in Romania. As a result, in trying to achieve status within the country, these youth have to maintain their mobility to work and travel abroad. Because of the current migrations of Romanian students into Western countries, our hospitals will soon be run by elderly doctors and those who were not allowed to emigrate.

There is still hope that those Romanians who have successfully emigrated and achieved financial and professional stability in the West will one day be nostalgic about their mother country, and attempt to contribute to its well-being by returning and contributing their expertise and professionalism to the betterment of the domestic economy. This has occurred in the long run in countries like Italy, Greece, Ireland, and Sweden. However, while it was the case that during the first few years of democracy, youth had optimistic ambitions to revive the arts and other neglected disciplines and to make a contribution to Romanian society, this phenomenon stagnated during the 1990s, as even the most optimistic of idealists have turned cynical toward their miserable society.

SINTANA REVISITED

Generation 2000 can be distinguished from the previous one by its attempts to specialize in a certain field or subject. Whereas the previous generations have had an all-encompassing, encyclopedic style of writing, the new generation at least attempts to concentrate on a single topic of interest. In the West, specialization can be taken to extremes, leading to the fragmentation of intellectual circles and the disappearance of transdisciplinary studies. In Romania, the most important task of this decade will be the revision of local canons, the adoption of intelligent paradigms and discussions, and the development of global interaction.

Two college anthropology students whom I have taught, one from Bucharest and the other from near the Danube, conducted anthropological studies in the town of Sintana for several months. Several vain and vengeful groups cohabit in this town. The two authors, Liviu Chelce and Puiu Litea, often come across stereotypes and inbred dogmas that cause conflict among these groups. The two students noted a strong resistance to change among the inhabitants, who base their knowledge on folk tales and family history. These people speak of Sintana as a historic place of the "great Romanian experience." This place produced dynamic heterogeneous identities resembling the mentality of provincial life.

In Romania, this strong identity is the root of most tension. Ethnic anxieties and constant minority threats supported by neighboring countries are on the rise. Today's Romanian citizen sees herself or himself as the victim of ethnic minority threats. They fail to realize that they are the victims of an ingrained nationalist pride that has obliterated all ethnic influences. Being part of the Romanian majority meant renouncing all individualistic aspects of life and behavior, and buying into a collective identity. It is sad that the rich traditions and folklore of the heterogeneous, Romanian civil society largely vanished during the Communist era for the "greater good" of a common cultural-ideological identity.

A writer who is published in Romania today often partakes of an indigenous, fragmented, and heterogeneous discourse that has reached the point of stagnation, and has failed to grow and merge with the larger international discourse. It remains confined to a parochial backwater, still retaining its old ethno-nationalist habits and overtones, which have been preserved since Communist times. Yet, at the same time, a new culture of "political theorists" has been identified, who are attempting to bring about a new way of writing and new subjects to be debated. Texts written before 1989 have been brought to light, giving credit to previously unknown authors. Nevertheless, the ideological and cultural disorientation produced by the Ceauşescu era is, as of this writing, still far from being replaced with the more progressive (and coherent) ideas and values of the West. Cultural and educational progress remains retarded, as evidenced from the fact that recently published historical texts in Romania are just as erroneous as they were under Communism. Moreover, the persistence of militant, ethno-nationalist overtones in the political context indicates the persistence of underdevelopment in Romanian political culture. The most important task of this decade, both for academia and the larger Romanian society as a whole, will be the revision of local canons, the adoption of intelligent paradigms and discourses, and the transcendence into global interaction.

NOTES

1. This chapter—more a participant observer's account than a study—draws freely on my "Generaţia 2000: contextul şi promisiunile unui debut," a longer text which was originally published in late 1999 by the Bucharest-based weekly *22* and was

reprinted as a preface to the first book of two of my former students (Liviu Chelcea, Puiu Litea, *România profund ın comunism: dileme identitare, contract social local şi economie secundar la Sintana* [Bucharest: Nemira, 2000]). I wrote both that text and this chapter while I was a Fellow at the Center for Advanced Study in the Behavioral Sciences, Stanford University. I am grateful for the financial support provided by the Andrew W. Mellon Foundation ("Lindzey Fellowship") and the Volkswagen *Stiftung*. I also thank Agatha Vlaic and Henry F. Carey for assistance with the English translation of some sections originally written in Romanian, and for Christopher Eisterhold's painstaking assistance to Carey in editing this chapter.

2. Romania's Orientalist (or, as other authors put it, intra-Orientalist, demi-Orientalist, or nested Orientalist) image can be understood in the context of the Western "invention" of Eastern Europe and of the Balkans. See Larry Wolff, *Inventing Europe: The Map of Civilization on the Mind of the Enlightenment* (Stanford, CA: Stanford University Press, 1994); and Maria Todorova, *Imagining the Balkans* (New York: Oxford University Press, 1997). For a recent discussion along the same lines, see my "Habits of the Mind: Europe's Post-1989 Symbolic Geographies," in Sorin Antohi and Vladimir Tismaneanu, eds., *Between Past and Future: The Revolutions of 1989 and Their Aftermath* (Budapest: Central European University Press, 2000), pp. 61–77; more specifically, on Romania's symbolic geography and the relevant uses of Edward Said's concept, Orientalism, see the last chapter of my *Imaginaire culturel et réalité politique dans la Roumanie moderne. Le stigmate et l'utopie* (translated from Romanian by Claude Karnoouh and Mona Antohi, (Paris, Montréal: L'Harmattan, 1999), pp. 267–97; "Les Roumains pendant les années 90. Géographie symbolique et identité sociale." The Gothic side of the same coin is largely organized around the myth of Dracula, inspired by the medieval ruling prince, Vlad Ţepeş. I would suggest that the Gothic narrative is not a mere subspecies of the Orientalist one because Orientalism assigns to its discursive object a passive negativity, whereas the Gothic negativity is active. Thus, the Gothic narrative could be actually used by the "natives" to subvert the logic of Orientalism; even within the paradigm of postcolonial or subaltern studies, someone could claim that colonizing (the imagination of the) colonizer is no small feat: such could be the emancipatory, cathartic function of the Dracula myth. Instead, Romanians have chosen to defend the historical figure "behind" the myth, a strategy which keeps them within the confines of demi-Orientalism. This activation of the passively negative is similar to that underwent by the concept of "Balkanization." During the recent Balkan wars, some Serbs could see in their devastating negative actions a self-liberating escape from demi-Orientalism. Accordingly, "the Balkanization of the West," the threatening potential of too much interaction with the Balkans, could be construed as the revenge of the repressed. See my "Numai Celălalt poluează: analiza unui incident ecologic," which appeared in *Monitorul* (Iaşi) and *Dilema* (Bucharest).

3. One of the side effects of this intensive Romanian-Western interaction was the new vogue phenomenon of a traditional, non-Western elite, self-stigmatization. Romanian authors writing negatively of the national character and blaming their fellow countrymen for their misfortunes became popular again, with their books becoming bestsellers. To classics of self-stigmatization such as D. Drăghicescu, Ştefan Zeletin, and E. M. Cioran, the brilliant post-1989 cultural revelation of H.-R. Patapievici was added, with the pieces now in his *Politice* (Bucharest: Humanitas, 1996). For a theoretical discussion of ethnic stigma and several examples, see my *Imaginaire culturel et réalité politique*, pp.

177–265, "Cioran et le stigmate roumain. Mécanismes identitaires et défintions radicales de l'ethnicité."

4. I have repeatedly argued in favor of what I called "The Third Discourse," a discourse that is neither the autochtonist rejection of the West (and, more generally, of the Other), nor its mindless imitation. This discourse would ideally combine the local ideas and historical experiences with those of the West, without losing sight of the neighbors (which are typically forgotten by most Romanians, due to what I called "geocultural bovarism"—see my chapter in *Between Past and Future*). The last decade has witnessed in Romania the emergence of increasingly diverse, discursive practices, a far cry from the rather dichotomic relationship between autochtonists and Westernizers, typologically close to the one described by Andrzej Walicki in his seminal book, *The Slavophile Controversy: History of a Conservative Utopia in Nineteenth-Century Russian Thought*, translated by Hilda Andrews-Rusiecka, (Oxford: Oxford University Press, 1975). This new discursive diversity includes, alongside all the nuances between the autochthonist-Westernizing poles, odd hybrids due to cultural-ideological confusion, or, in a few cases, to (rather delirious) syncretic projects. In this sense, Romanian culture has certain traditions, going back at least to Ion Heliade-Rădulescu, an author who was looking in the first half of the nineteenth century for the "equilibrium of the antithese." To give only three examples: (a) Romanian champions of postmodernism in the 1980s imported the trend without its original left-wing ideological backbone, as they were more concerned with its formal consequences and its rhetorical dimension (irony and self-irony, inter-textuality, anti-canonical rebellion); (b) after 1989, a phenomenon which is comparable to what I have called "Orthodoxist dandyism" (e.g., in the 1920s and 1930s, the young Mircea Eliade and E. M. Cioran were both consummate connoisseurs of the Western canon and fervent promoters of autochthonism), which merges Orthodoxy and liberalism; and (c) the religiosity of the educated strata seems to be dominated by a combination of traditional, Orthodox Christian ritual and New Age spirituality, something that seems to illustrate the theory of a mutual contamination of religion, gnosis, science and ideology; see Alain Besançon, *La Confusion des langues. La crise idéologique de l'Église* (Paris: Calmann-Lévy, 1978). The latter combination seems inevitable after several decades of Communist "polytechnization" of the imaginary and "scientific atheism." See Lucian Boia, *La Mythologie scientifique du communisme* (Caen: Paradigme, 1994). This cultural-ideological confusion is not devoid of positive potential, along the lines suggested by Virgil Nemoianu, who speaks of a Romanian inclination towards intellectual-spiritual negotiation and synthesis ("Mihai Şora and the Traditions of Romanian Philosophy," *Review of Metaphysics*, vol. 43 [March 1990], pp. 591–605), and by Mihai Spariosu, who explores the creative side of liminality in a number of books and articles. Whether such cultural-ideological products are fortuitous or not, they thrive in Romania.

5. For the best analysis of "protochronism," the doctrine that claims Romanians were first (and, consequently, are still the best) in most domains and human endeavors, from their having an original language to the invention of the alphabet, insulin, or cybernetics, see Katherine Verdery, *National Ideology Under Socialism: Identity and Cultural Politics in Ceauşescu's Romania* (Berkeley, Los Angeles, Oxford: University of California Press, 1991), especially pp. 167–214.

6. Romanians have mixed reactions to "political correctness," which is, of course, a category experienced first hand by only some of them, but is frequently (ab)used to play out indigenous concerns and polemics. A number of radical Westernizers—including human and minority rights activists, feminists, a new breed of left-wing postmodernists reading cultural and literary studies and ethics—have adopted the most dogmatic tenets of their North-American role models. I tend to see in this uncritical adoption, beyond the genuine cases of conversion, and the "normal" opportunism of those who know that their grant applications to Western funders depend on the use of key words such as "democracy," "market economy," etc. (a duplicity that evokes life under Communism and the various *ketmans* described by Czesaw Milosz in his seminal *The Captive Mind*), an almost desperate attempt to assimilate into the normative Western culture, as they perceive it. Many such converts are uncomfortable with the seemingly endemic backwardness of their country and choose this curious *metanoia* as a (potentially self-stigmatizing) way out of the crisis. Other people sincerely believe that the perfect world they read about in politically correct books and gray literature really exists in the West. Many live somehow the experience of activism, free association, and civil disobedience, which they could not live under the Communist regime, for obvious reasons (besides, some were simply too young). Ironically enough, the rejection of political correctness unites in Romania, as in other former Communist countries, real democrats (who fear the import of this "American Communism," as it was dubbed by the very influential essayist and media figure, H.-R. Patapievici) and dubious nostalgics of national Communism. While the former criticize the "logocratic" (Czeslaw Milosz), "crypto-Communist" features of political correctness, the latter abhor it as a capitalist perversion that is threatening national character and decent, hard-working, law-abiding citizens. A study of the reception of the largely extinct American debate around political correctness in the former Soviet bloc would be a great contribution to the social sciences.

7. Curiously, Romanian academics avoid a serious discussion of their everyday misery. People in difficult material situations should not lament incessantly: maintaining necessary social distances asks for a certain discretion. The sharp decline in living standards is something people in post-Communist countries had to learn how to deal with, after decades during which only the "parasites," the lazy petty-bourgeois and other class enemies were spectacularly poor. Nevertheless, while K–12 teachers have gone very frequently on strike, most dramatically in February 2000, faculty have not joined the vocal trade union movements. What would be in theory the faculty's trade union, *Solidaritatea Universitară*, stubbornly abstains from strikes and other open form of protest. This organization seems to be, instead, a political movement in support of the Constantinescu presidency; many ministers and MPs are university professors. Only in February 2000 have faculty organized protest rallies and gone on Japanese-style strikes in support of the teachers, asking for salary raises and a budget for education equal to 4 percent of GDP. So far, *Solidaritatea Universitară*, more vocal when it comes to supporting the restoration of the monarchy or (simultaneously) supporting President Emil Constantinescu, has published a few candid declarations on the real situation of Romania's education. In the most recent and most radical document, released on 19 February 2000, the organization, fully supportive of the otherwise reformist Minister of Education, Professor Andrei Marga, mentioned the dangers of brain drain, of Romania's drifting toward the Third World, and singles out obvious

details, such as the low salaries and the precarious infrastructure. But the declaration concluded that the announced faculty strike was not a good idea.

8. Private universities have mushroomed in Romania since 1990, when a footnote to a document passed by the provisional quasi Parliament (CPUN) mentioned the possibility of offering private educational and medical services. As the first post-Communist education law was many years in the making (primarily due to controversies over the Hungarian minority's education rights) private universities were initially nonregulated and functioned as rather lucrative forms of free enterprise specializing in symbolic goods. Eventually, a National Commission of Academic Evaluation and Accreditation (CNEAA) was formed, which started formulating and implementing internationally recognized higher education standards. Thus, the number of private "universities" went down from hundreds to scores, as this peer-review organization was processing self-evaluations, conducting on-site visits, and recommending to the Ministry of National Education the appropriate course of action: accreditation or the refusal thereof. The surviving private universities are often at levels comparable to those of typical new state universities built on older teacher training colleges or from scratch: that is, at low levels. Most private universities hire faculty from state universities, and some of the financially challenged academics are in such high demand that they commute endlessly between several universities, both private and state, teaching the equivalent of two full-time jobs. The situation is not completely dissimilar to that of increasing numbers of (disposable) adjunct faculty in the U.S., and some of the institutional patterns are international (such as the reluctance on the part of university bureaucracies to offer tenure-track positions that cost them considerably more than part-time, adjunct appointments).

9. The published admissions figures for 1999 illustrate a clear movement away from most specializations that train for bankrupt state enterprises and for (the miserably paid) teaching careers. More significantly, competition for admission to medical schools dropped dramatically, probably as a result of the continuing pauperization of the medical professionals. Law schools (which in Romania are undergraduate) and business schools are the most sought after. This market-bound shift in the higher education supply and demand mechanism, just like the multiplication of universities, are reactions to two structural challenges: (a) Romanian higher education was artificially organized prior to 1989, in order to feed the (rather imaginary) demands of a command economy. Accordingly, while engineering specializations were dominant, social sciences, the humanities, legal and economic professions were statistically and symbolically marginal; (b) in a party-state that relied heavily on a parallel system of cadre schools to train its *apparat*, most high school graduates were not supposed to attend universities.

10. Other emerging trends are significant in these respects. First, as many faculty have alternative sources of income, their incentive to and likelihood of protesting against low salaries or advocating higher academic standards is limited. Second, Romanian and foreign media (including the Romanian-language services of organizations such as the BBC, Radio Free Europe, Deutsche Welle, a.s.o.) pay quite handsomely: The most successful emerging media personalities recruited from among academics and public intellectuals gross thousands of U.S. dollars per month. Third, translations are usually poorly paid, with the exception of translations of business-related documents and of best-selling books for mass consumption. Fourth, most Ro-

manian academics secure their trips and stays abroad through their universities or through the Ministry of National Education; this makes them support and reproduce the status quo, as access to such resources is critically dependent on institutional discipline and trade-offs. Romanian academic *Gastarbeiter*, who have regular visiting professorships compensated at market levels, are still rare; most Romanians teaching abroad do so through bilateral agreements signed by government-related schemes such as Fulbright, IREX, Tempus, Erasmus, etc.

11. Pre-1989 Romanian universities were typically a cross between teacher training colleges, professional schools, and research universities. To qualify for a 5–12 teaching job (K–4 teachers were trained in special high schools), one had to attend mandatory pedagogy and didactics courses and do a certain amount of shadow teaching and hands-on training in designated schools. The in-service training system included a number of exams, class inspections, and research projects. At various moments, the monopoly over this in-service training, which was called *perfecţionare* (perfectionment), was granted to separate bodies, staffed by second-rate academics, but most of the time regularly appointed faculty played the role quality controllers, especially for the research papers submitted by the teachers seeking a promotion and salary raise. Obviously, most research papers were humble compilations or downright plagiarisms, and some of them were enjoying "recycling" by successive cohorts of teachers. Bribes and "tokens of appreciation" were, and continue to be, frequent in this system. Some assiduous faculty travel extensively to villages and towns to conduct site visits.

12. This rather somber image of Romania's students is contradicted by a surprising survey published by the Ministry of National Education on 16 February 2000. The survey was conducted by INSOMAR and financed with a PHARE grant. Covering a national sample of students attending both state and private universities, the survey indicates that 34 percent of them own a cell phone, 26 percent own a computer, 15 percent have a bank account, 13.3 percent have a car, and 12 percent own their flat. Asked by a major national daily, University of Bucharest Rector Ioan Mihăilescu, a sociologist, explained away the striking data, claiming that Romanian students come from upper middle-class families now, and are well off; *Evenimentul Zilei* (17 February 2000). Access to education, from kindergarten up, is indeed becoming a luxury in Romania; recently, the (Romanian) National Institute of Educational Sciences, the technical support unit-cum-think tank of the Ministry of National Education, (gu)es(s)timated that 800,000 Romanian citizens out of the roughly 22 million are illiterate (66 percent of Roma women). Still, as Romanian average monthly wages stand at roughly $120, this alleged student prosperity is strange. The positive image squares, however, with the triumphant discourse of the Ministry of Education, which announced unrealistically high faculty salaries following the February strikes, although some universities have trouble paying the current lower salaries. More credibly, the above-mentioned survey suggests that 66 percent of Romania's students want to emigrate; 45 percent would like to work for foreign companies, 13 percent for Romanian private companies, and 12 percent in the state sector.

13. Under Communism, most universities and research institutes counted on exchanges of publication with "peer" institutions from the West. For some of the latter, this was really a way of helping their Romanian counterparts. After 1989, such exchanges, originally centralized, became irregular or disappeared. Most publishers do

not send free copies to the national libraries, and the law organizing the legal deposit is not enforced consistently. More intrepid librarians manage to get complimentary copies from foreign publishers, something that they also did before 1989. Some very expensive periodicals would send complimentary copies of their first issues each year, expecting a subscription. But libraries would end up having only the first issue in every volume because they couldn't afford the subscription. I tend to count this phenomenon as a mix of marketing and philanthropy on the part of Western publishers.

14. From among the numerous initiatives to disseminate self-marketing skills, I would single out the recent initiative of the World Bank to finance a periodical, *Un viitor pentru fiecare* ("A Future for Everyone"), and 772 centers of professional orientation and career counseling across Romania. The program started in 1998 with a pilot project located at the Bucharest University Dept. of Economics. Other publications include relevant information on available jobs, career opportunities, and job announcements. Job fairs are also a new development. I do not have the data to support my impression that the impact of such initiatives is still quite limited, but from what I gather from media reports and conversations.

15. From roughly the early 1960s through the end, the Communist system of education had many features of a meritocracy. With the exception of politically sensitive specializations such as law, philosophy, or sociology and journalism (the latter two being only offered through the party cadre academy most of the time), admissions to elite schools and universities was open to all, education was affordable, state grants to both schools and students were relatively significant, and the proverbial system of "Olympiads" (student competitions) created the illusion that excellence mattered. It was after graduation that the poorly connected discovered the tough reality of assigned jobs in the countryside, nepotism, and so on. Dissatisfaction with the education system remained high among those seeking spiritual and intellectual freedom and/or planning to specialize in neglected, if not entirely forbidden or heavily distorted fields. Three books perfectly document the formative tribulations of several generations under Communism: Gabriel Liiceanu, *Jurnalul de la Păltiniş* (Bucharest: Cartea Românească, 1983), republished with additions by Humanitas in the 1990s and translated into French as *Le Journal de Paltinis* (Paris: La Découverte, 1999) and in English as *The Păltiniş Diary* (Budapest: Central European University Press, 2000); Gabriel Liiceanu, ed., *Epistolar* (Bucharest: Cartea Românească, 1988, republished with additions by Humanitas in the 1990s); H.-R. Patapievici, *Zbor în bătaia săgeţii* (Bucharest: Humanitas, 1995), translated into English as *Flying against the Arrow* (Budapest: Central European University Press, 2003). For a discussion of the former two, see Katherine Verdery, *National Ideology under Socialism*, pp. 256–301. For a general assessment of the three, see my introductions to the books by Liiceanu and Patapievici published by Central European University Press. Liiceanu's books tell the story of an elite, informal education centered around a Magister and understood as a form of cultural subversion under a regime with infamous totalitarian aspirations; the underground "school," initiated by philosopher Constantin Noica, reminds one of the Goethean Pedagogic Province, Castalia, from Hermann Hesse's splendid classic, *Das Glasperlenspiel* (1943; recommended English translation: *The Glass Bead Game [Magister Ludi]*), translated by Richard and Clara Winston (New York: Holt, Rinehart and Winston, 1969). Patapievici's book is more about another strategy of intellectual

and moral survival under Communism: a program of self-education and self-realization without the help of a living Magister, but within a supporting family and peer-group, with an insatiable encyclopedic curiosity, and with rigorous, self-imposed moral norms rooted in a certain vision of human existence and of the sacred.

16. Romanian students use a variety of means to go abroad for further studies. Fellowships at Western universities are not really available through Romanian Government agencies, or are debatably distributed. Foreign governments, international organizations (mainly the European Union), and foundations (first and foremost, the Soros-sponsored Open Society Institute and its subsidiaries) have offered, over the last decade, thousands, if not tens of thousands of scholarships, ranging from short research or student exchange trips to full doctoral programs. Unfortunately, as many of these funding agencies reduce or phase out their activities, Romanian students have to look for financial support on their own. Internet-based searches are conducted by those who have access at least to an Internet café. Strong applicants are sometimes admitted to more than one program. The trouble is, they are routinely asked to find matching funds or even pay full tuition at expensive U.S. universities. Those who cannot find enough money to use these admission offers are not supported by the state, although a national strategy in this domain is vitally necessary. Minister Marga's initiatives in this respect are commendable but, as yet, insufficient. As it happened with other burning issues of Romania's protracted transition, education remains marginal on the various political agendas. Brain drain is thus further stimulated.

17. I have met, in Silicon Valley alone, numerous Romanian-born multimillionaires, former "Olympics" (evidence that the system was great, only it had to be supplemented by emigration). Over twenty young multimillionaires live in this thriving high-tech area; of the 200 software specialists who have developed Windows 2000, one of these Romanian American multimillionaires told me that forty came from Romania.

IV

ECONOMICS AND ENVIRONMENT

18

The New Business Elite: From *Nomenklatura* to Oligarchy

Anneli Ute Gabanyi

While it is commonly understood in the West that the revolution of 1989 had toppled the old Communist hierarchy in Romania, the facts would tend to suggest otherwise. I argue that the elites of the old Romanian Communist Party, or at least a sizable number of them, were actually the beneficiaries of the revolution. In fact, one could easily argue that they have taken full advantage of the transition to the "free market," using their inside knowledge, political power, and control of state resources to *privatize* their power over the Romanian economy, transforming, quite legally, the political domination of the old *nomenklatura* into the economic domination of a new oligarchy.[1]

As Staniszkis described it, after the revolutions of 1989, many of the old Communist elites undertook the task of selectively using the "institutional remains of Communism" to establish a system of "oligarchic capitalism" in their respective countries. Or, as Russian civil rights activist Timofejew put it in the context of his own country, the revolution was for "the liquidation of the socialist planned economy in favor of a free market for groups who had already taken control of this market."[2] Polish economist Wojtech Lamentowicz makes a similar argument when he notes that, "by enforcing the economic reform (like in Hungary and Poland), the ruling elite wanted to transform its collective privileges into individual property rights."[3] Thus, the "the wave of revolutions from above"—as Staniszkis describes the 1989 revolutions in Eastern Europe—were not so much for the liberation of the people as they were for the "liberation of the *nomenklatura*." They were revolutions for the "controlled abandonment of communism," aimed at maintaining "the status of the former period," for "the networks of the communist past."[4]

PREREVOLUTIONARY ELITE FORMATION

In discussing the process of the transformation of the elite class in the Communist era it is important to note that many of them were already well established *prior* to the revolutions of 1989. By the end of the Cold War, most East European economies had already become rough amalgamations of state owned enterprises and black market companies, owned and operated by the elite members of the *nomenklatura*, who used their political power to defend their business interests and those of their patrons.

Additionally, as a consequence of the oil crisis and recession of the 1970s, the pseudo state-owned black economies of these countries often entered into half-official, business agreements with Western financial interests. In order to carry out those new credit dealings, camouflage companies of the party and the intelligence services were established in most East European states, which engaged in a range of often obscure foreign exchange dealings. Out of these companies and their networks arose many of the successful and wealthy representatives of the new business elite.

THE STRUGGLE FOR THE INHERITANCE OF THE DICTATOR

The Communist regime that ruled Romania from the postwar period to 1989 was characterized by an unusually high degree of clientilism and patronage; it was, in fact, the closest thing in Eastern Europe to Eisenstadt's ideal concept of the "neo-patrimonial state."[5] With his assumption of the office of the presidency in the year 1974, Ceauşescu had increasingly relied on an informal system of personal ties and rewards to maintain power. The operative power within the state became increasingly concentrated in the hands of the Ceauşescu "clan" who had been recruited, not according to modern selection criteria, but according to patriarchal relationships of kin and loyalty.[6]

In order to keep the representatives of the *nomenklatura* from building their own networks and creating their own areas of power, Ceauşescu instituted a policy of "rotation of the cadres," whereby no party member stayed in a position long enough to cultivate personal connections. As a result the normal circulation of elites *upward* was practically halted. The political influence of the party and state bureaucracies was diminished and the economic privileges of the broader elite were dismantled.[7] Additionally, in the 1980s, Ceauşescu also attacked the party apparatus itself.

The growing dissatisfaction with Ceauşescu united a sizable element of the old *nomenklatura* within Romania. Their dissatisfaction was exacerbated by the effects of Ceauşescu's disastrous autarkic economic policies, which had led to plummeting living standards and widespread resentment amongst the general population, leaving the elite with the fear that it too would be swept away by the fall of Ceauşecu, which was becoming an ever more likely event as the 1980s drew to a close. The fear and the anger within the entire state and party apparatus explains why Ceauşescu did not have much support in December 1989, and why a ready made coalition of former elites was ready to take his place when the time came.[8]

While small, privately owned and operated companies were generally not allowed during the Ceauşescu dictatorship, obscure business dealings, in foreign currencies, and with Western partners, were nevertheless rampant at the elite level, as many in the Romanian leadership attempted to secure their financial positions amid the looming economic and political collapse. In this semilegal black economy of the state, billions of dollars were made by a small group of privileged elites. Perhaps more important, experience was gained about the practices of the market economy, and connections were made which would give them an advantage in the period immediately after the fall of Ceauşescu. Some of the more important enterprises were:

- The Central Bureau of Economics, *Carpaţi*, which was established in the mid-1980s, as part of the party's business enterprise to handle clandestine, foreign exchange dealings and transactions with other Communist parties.
- The foreign trade company of the intelligence service *Securitate*, *ICE Dunărea*, established in October 1982 and dissolved in April 1990. Its wares ranged from arms to artificial diamonds. Payments by foreign governments and intelligence services for arms, migration permits for ethnic Germans (*Aussiedler*), and other goods and services were made to secret foreign accounts.
- Domestic and foreign companies controlled and managed by the Romanian intelligence services. The most important perhaps has been *Crescent*, which an Arab businessman started in 1990 in Piräus, Greece, and later moved to Cyprus.[9]

Together with the political power struggle that ensued after Ceauşescu was deposed on 22 December 1989, went the struggle among the Romanian elite for the former property of the dictator and the Romanian Communist Party. After he and his wife Elena had been executed on 25 December, the Council of the National Salvation Front (FSN) declared itself to be the only holder of state power, with the right to take charge of the property of the state (which included the personal fortune of Ceauşescu)—a right that it exercised soon afterward on 18 January 1990.

At the end of 1989, this state property, as administered by the Central Economic Bureau *Carpaţi*, was worth around 40 billion *lei* (then about $2.23 billion).[10] This figure does not include Ceauşescu's personal mansion, and the valuables and gifts contained therein, including 584 pieces of jewelry, a valuable collection of arms, as well as several luxury cars.[11] While it is well known that a number office buildings, companies, and funds owned by the Communist Party were handed over to various ministries and city administrations (as well as to individual entrepreneurs and politicians), the question of what happened to Nicolae Ceauşescu's secret accounts in Switzerland, which contained an estimated sum of between 400 million and 5 billion German marks, has yet to be answered.

During their show trial, and prior to their execution, Nicolae and Elena Ceauşescu both denied the existence of these accounts. They also refused to grant written permission to transfer them into the hands of the Romanian state (i.e., the leadership of the FSN).[12] They are, unfortunately, no longer available for questioning on this matter. Neither is Nicolae's brother Marin, who ran the foreign accounts for the Ceauşescu clan. He was found hanged in his hotel room on 29 December 1989.

There were clues, however. According to eyewitnesses, a notebook belonging to Elena Ceauşescu, listing several bank addresses and accounts, was found during the attack on the building of the Central Committee of the Romanian Communist Party on 22 December 1989. It was subsequently handed over to Ion Iliescu, the future president.[13] No one has seen it since. A notebook of Nicolae Ceauşescu, which had been found in December 1989, was taken from the parliamentary archives. No one has ever seen it again either.[14]

Moreover, at the end of 1992, the measures that had been initiated by the new rulers to find the secret Ceauşescu accounts were terminated. The work of three commissions produced nothing, although the *foreign* investigators employed by the government in fact found evidence indicating the existence of these secret accounts. A contract with a Canadian investigation agency was cancelled by the Romanian government after it had given its information to the producers of a television movie, partially out of frustration with the Romanians unwillingness to continue the investigation—despite, or rather because of, their initial successes.[15] The Romanian government then attempted to ban the television movie from being aired in October 1991.

Five years later, a parliamentary commission led by Valentin Gabrielescu of the opposition Christian Democratic National Peasant Party established that the Canadian investigators had reached the conclusion that only four Romanian firms—covertly operating foreign trade firms for the Communist Party, the intelligence services, and the army—and the Romanian Bank for Foreign Trade would have been able to deposit and transfer money into the secret accounts for Ceauşescu. The circle of suspects had been narrowed considerably. However, the Romanian government under Prime Minister Teodor Stolojan had refused to give the documents of the respective firms to the investigators, claiming that these were state secrets.[16] To this date, no one can say conclusively what happened to these funds but the common suspicion is that they were absorbed, like most state assets, by the successors to Ceauşescu in the FSN.

"ENRICH YOURSELVES": *NOMENKLATURA* PRIVATIZATION

As in most other transition states in Eastern Europe, the development of parliamentary democracy in Romania became the "smoke curtain" behind which the more relevant transformation of political into economic capital took place. In order to initiate the primitive accumulation of capital in Romania, Prime Minister Petre Roman had issued the motto "enrich yourselves." "We are all of the opinion," Roman stated, "that a people living in a society of economic liberty have the right to enrich themselves."[17]

The representatives of the old political Elite were the first to follow Petre Roman's appeal. Despite the threat of severe punishments, they and their family members had amassed large amounts of black money prior to 1989—money which they invested in quickly formed private firms immediately after Ceauşescu's fall. Some of those firms were established as early as December 1989.[18] According to Romanian press reports in September 1994, 1,000 of 1,540 firms with profits of over 1 billion *lei* were in the hands of members of the former Communist *nomenklatura.*[19] Ion Dincă, a former member of the Political Executive Committee of the Central Committee of the now defunct Romanian Communist Party (RCP), whose sons-in-law held prior to 1989 influential positions in the electronics industry (due to the important position of their father-in-law), possessed after the change the capital and contacts to found private firms in the computer and photocopier sector. They made a fortune in no time. Similarly, Marius Ţărlea, the son-in-law of Nicolae Ceauşescu's brother Ion, founded after the change an export company. With the earnings from that business, Ţărlea founded the Romanian-Swiss *Columna* Bank.

The Romanian commentator Andrei Cornea of the weekly journal *22*, has pointed to the importance of the network of economic, political, and administrative actors that was created after the change, a network he has termed "directocracy."[20] This "class" not only consists of the so-called "red directors and managers" of large state companies, it also contains the owners and managers of private companies which are intrinsically linked with the large state companies, as well as parts of the bureaucracy at the local and national levels.

The profitable parts of the oversized state industry and trade complexes of the pre-1989 era had been set apart for privatization, and the former state managers were able to acquire them in the course of the MEBO-privatization program, or by buying the privatization vouchers.[21] These private companies, sometimes called "tick companies," continue to be supplied with capital and other resources directly or indirectly through the government, to the disadvantage of the state companies, and other, smaller, less politically connected enterprises. In 1997, according to a report, 20,789 such companies caused the Romanian state a loss of over 200 billion German marks. Most of these companies are in the fields of telecommunication (10,350 cases in 1997); trade, tourism, food industry, and state-owned agriculture (6508 cases); and in the construction industry and road transportation (3,931 cases).[22]

The strategy of the members of the new "directocracy" is based on the use of the material, financial, and personal resources of the state-run companies for use by their private companies, which continue to be supported by the state bureaucracy through cheap credits and subsidies. The consequences: the continuing inefficiency of the state companies, growing public deficits, the expansion of a parasitic form of capitalism, and the encouragement of official corruption. That is because this network of "directocrats" is interested in keeping to the *gradualist* strategy of reform. It resists the privatization and restructuring of the economy which would eviscerate many of the advantages which its members currently enjoy.

The transformation of political capital, expert knowledge, and personal contacts into business capital can be demonstrated by looking at the strategies employed by the directors and technocrats from the pre-1989 sphere of foreign trade.[23] These persons were well educated, multilingual, had traveled widely, and were well versed in dealing with Western trade partners. As the Romanian foreign trade companies did not have that much in the way of assets, it was easy for these former managers and experts to acquire them.

Political scientist Silviu Brucan has described the steps by which this circle of persons was able to transfer their monopolistic position in foreign trade into the new period. Four steps were necessary to achieve this goal: first, their own companies had to be privatized; second, they had to convince the directors of the Romanian companies with which they had worked before to export their products through their services; third, they had to contact the buyers in the West with the aim to extend the trade agreements that had been reached before 1989; and finally, they had to get in touch with Romanian and Western banks and convince them to continue their transactions in the export-import business the way they had done prior to that date.

To secure their export businesses, the old-new exporters bought stock in the companies that produced for them and pushed themselves on the supervisory boards of the banks of those companies. Some of the most prominent economic elites of the post-transition period have thus emerged from the foreign trade sphere. One can gather the extent to which economic, financial, and political power have become intertwined in the new Romanian economy with a perusal of a short listing of these elites. They include:

- Petru Crişan, who was director of the company *Romanoexport* prior to 1989, which he privatized in 1990 and secured for himself with a majority of the shares. He then bought two large Romanian supply firms and acquired further shares in over 124 such companies. He later became trade minister under the Văcăroiu government.

- Viorel Cataramă, who worked in the 1980s for the export company Technoforest Export, which held a monopoly position in the profitable sector of furniture exports to the West. From 1984 onward, Cataramă was employed by a Belgian company as export director in charge of Eastern Europe. In 1990, he founded several furniture and textile companies in Romania, with Elvila International being one of the most profitable companies in the entire country. Cataramă also holds a leading position in the National Liberal Party, and in 1992 spent a short term as undersecretary of state in the Ministry of Economics and Foreign Trade.
- General Victor Atanasie Stănculescu, who was the former director of the procurement department of the Romanian army, and who also played a role in the East-West arms deals that were carried out before 1989 by Romanian and other East European representatives via obscure channels.[24] Stănculescu was one of the leaders of the coup d'état against Ceauşescu, and, in the first months after the collapse of the Communist regime, was the acting Minister of Industry and Minister of Defense. After the elections of September 1990, he became the Bucharest representative of the British Bali Company, and founded an export-import firm as well as an insurance company.
- George Constantin Păunescu, who, in the 1980s, was director of the Romanian trade mission in Milan as well as a director in the Ministry of Foreign Trade. He founded two large import-export companies in 1991. Together with his brother Viorel, he is today one of the richest men in Romania, with ownership of the Bucharest luxury hotels, Lido and Inter-Continental, the Melody Bar in Bucharest, and the Hotel Rex in Mamaia. His twenty-four-plane airline, DacAir, has already gone bankrupt.
- Dan Voiculescu, who worked prior to 1989 in the export firms Technoforest and Vitrocim, and who also had a close relationship with the *Securitate*-sponsored, Cypriot company, Crescent. After 1989, Voiculescu founded a firm for precision engineering, which soon made record profits. He is the owner of the newspaper *Jurnalul Naţional* and the TV channel Antena 1.

Additionally, the founders of most of the private banks came from the circle of directors and specialists of the old regime's financial apparatus. Marcel Ivan, the CEO of Credit Bank, was, before the transition, the director of a branch office of the state-run Agricultural Bank. Ion Sima, the CEO of *Dacia-Felix* Bank, was employed in an investment bank in Cluj-Napoca. The director of Bankcoop, Alexandru Dinulescu, was previously the director of the credit bank of the consumer cooperatives.

In addition, several "mafia" groups have hooked themselves, like secondary parasites, onto the new companies of the legal economy; but they are to be found especially within the burgeoning "black" economy. For example, an oil mafia exists which has close relations to the old *Securitate*, and to the new leadership group around President Ion Iliescu. Radu Tinu, one of the richest and most prominent members of the oil mafia, was the former local director of the *Securitate* for the city of Timişoara. He was arrested after the transition and sentenced to two years in prison. After his release, he became rich by smuggling oil to the Federal Republic of Yugoslavia. He is currently the director of a German-Romanian export-import company.[25]

Of course, this incestuous relationship between private enterprise and the Romanian state has led to numerous allegations of dubious financial dealings, including the giving of preferential credits and investments in favor of the executives of banking houses, illegal financial transfers, bribery, and money laundering (i.e., the everyday activities with which the incredible profits of the new elite have been made since the transition).[26] Additionally, some of those profits, it has been alleged, have been used to support political parties.[27] Because of all that, the national economy, including numerous individual private investors, have suffered severely, not to mention all those who lost their money in the approximately 600 financial pyramid schemes which have sprung up in Romania during the transition.[28]

Those who have profited display their wealth ostentatiously. Their status symbol is the cellular phone.[29] They drive big cars and are permitted into the most exclusive nightclubs in Bucharest. The prototype of the nouveau riche is Ilie Alexandru, godchild of Marcel Ivan, the former director of Creditbank, who is himself a member of the supervisory board of that bank. Before 1989, Alexandru was a boxer, personal trainer, petty criminal, and a refugee in Austria. He then returned to Romania and founded a business empire on credits arranged through his godfather. At his peak, he owned a ranch close to the southern Romanian town of Slobozia, his birthplace, where he had a fifty-meter high replica of the Eiffel tower erected. The ranch had a swimming pool, a stable with 170 horses, an ostrich farm, camels, and even one llama.[30]

In this gray zone, a black economy has established itself, causing the state huge losses through tax evasion, customs bribery, corruption, subsidy fraud, smuggling, money laundering, etc. These crimes are fostered by both legal shortcomings and the weakness of the institutions charged with overseeing the banking sector and controlling customs.[31] In 1995, a loss of $2 billion (USD) in state revenues was attributed to the black economy. Tax evasion alone accounted for 60 percent of that loss. The data on the extent of this parallel economy are uneven. For the year 1993, the National Commission for Statistics determined that the black economy accounted for 9–10 percent of GDP. In the same year, the director of the Romanian intelligence service (SRI) set this share at 38 percent.[32] For the year 1997, President Constantinescu stated that the black economy accounted for 35–40 percent of the GDP.[33] It is estimated that the number of workers employed within the black economy rose from 850,000 in 1995 to 2 million in 1998.[34]

THE POLITICS OF OPPOSITION ELITES

Representatives of the radical anti-Communist opposition had pointed out, quite early, the coming transformation of the former *nomenklatura* into the new business class. According to one commentator:

> This class, which continues to rule, is in possession of the economic levers of power and has created its own privileges. . . . As "owners of capital," the representatives of the nomenclature have come to occupy the most favorable positions for the start into the new market economy . . . [thus] the "red aristocracy" has managed to secure its survival.[35]

In the "Timişoara Proclamation," which was adopted on 19 March 1990, opposition groups not only demanded that all former Communist functionaries and intelligence agents abstain from politics; they also demanded that the assets of those groups be registered. The ruling Provisional Council of National Union rejected these demands. At a demonstration to commemorate the first anniversary of the Proclamation, one speaker used some drastic words:

> The judiciary did not concern itself with the privileges of the former rulers. Many of them are today owners of very important private investment projects and tomorrow they will be the magnates of the Romanian economy. With the help of the dirty corruption money from the Ceauşescu era, a new bourgeoisie with invisible epaulettes is developing in front of our eyes. Ceauşescu's toadies of yesterday are going to be tomorrow's noblemen.[36]

Political observers see in these developments not a return of Communism, but a return of the Communists: "We are building capitalism with the former communists," wrote the liberal politician Nicolae Manolescu.[37] The new rulers, it was alleged, were telling fairy tales of the free market to distract the public from the ongoing transformation of the old *nomenklatura* into the new owners of capital. It was under the cover of catchwords such as liberalization, de-bureaucratization, and privatization that the assets of the state were rapidly "raided." Critics, in turn, are silenced by appeals to the free market economy, the constitution, democracy, the rule of law, and the prospect of integration into the European Union.[38]

According to one piece in the Romanian press, the "communists in capitalist clothing" now constitute an "economic and political oligarchy" in Romania.[39] There is another disturbing facet of this phenomenon: that the economic power of the new oligarchy inevitably translates into political power over the Romanian state. Within an oligarchic system, as Liviu Antonesei notes, even democracy has to be oligarchical: "In a democracy of an oligarchic type, everyone minds his own business: the oligarchs take care of trade, industry, and the government, we take care of protests and parables."[40]

Especially troublesome from the point of view of the anti-Communist opposition, but also in the view of European institutions, is the network of relations between the new business magnates and parts of the government, the parliament, public administration, and the judiciary.[41] Early on, the Romanian press pointed out the mafia character of this developing elite: "Since 1948, only one political party has been in power. . . . This political party does not present itself as a political party. It is a community, a mafia, a network, a conspiratorial society that is held together by common interests."[42]

ELITE DIVISIONS

This "new class" of elite is not monolithic, however. Rather significant conflicts of interest between the new and the old business elites have arisen. The influential "red directors" at the helm of the oversized state enterprises and the bureaucrats in the ministries were primarily interested in maintaining the status quo. By contrast, the new business elites from the former foreign trade sector, as well as many engineers and lawyers who have good technical and organizational capabilities, want to speed up the process of economic reforms. The interests of the old bureaucracy within the governing party were represented by the conservative faction of the FSN centered on Ion Iliescu, whereas the technocratic new bourgeoisie rallied around Prime Minister Petre Roman.

The tensions led to the split of the FSN and to the violent fall of the Prime Minister in September 1991. An opposition newspaper had predicted the fall of the government at the hands of the directors of the big enterprises already in November 1990.[43] Later, these directors became "patriarchs" of Ion Iliescu's Party of Social Democracy of Romania (PDSR).[44] Roman and his ministers saw themselves, in retrospect, as victims of a bureaucratic team that had been in place since the old regime. Although the bureaucrats had been in a state of fear after the revolution, they soon turned to passive resistance and finally went into an open revolt "to block and destroy the reform process."[45]

In the Parliamentary elections of November 1992, Ion Iliescu's Party of Social Democracy of Romania, which had split from the FSN, did not gain an absolute majority in Parliament. Confronted with symptoms of an economic crisis and a falling standard of living, the public reacted negatively to the increasing disparities in income and the wealth of the very rich which was being displayed ever more garishly by the new elite. The press uncovered the inbred nature of the government's privatization practices, which had clearly bypassed the ordinary people in favor of insiders.[46] Journalists focused on the theme of the winners of the revolution: on people like George Paunescu, who openly admitted that he had used the chaos in the wake of Ceauşescu's fall, and the mistakes of an "incompetent government" to his own advantage.[47] The Romanian public began to realize that there was more than the free play of market forces at work in the transition of the Romanian economy. Instead, they became increasingly aware of the corruption that existed at the intersection of state-owned property and political monopoly.

As the scandals grew in number, the network of influential mafia groups and the government became ever more apparent, such as the scandal involving agricultural minister Ioan Oancea, who had introduced legal measures for the protection of the Romanian farmers, and who had been subsequently dismissed as a result of the pressures that the influential cartel of wheat importers had brought to bear. One of those importers, Angelo Miculescu, had been agricultural minister before 1989. His son in law, Adrian Năstase, was deputy chairman of the PDSR, which was in power at that time.[48]

OFFICIAL REACTIONS

Ion Iliescu and his party were certainly aware of the danger that the dominant anticorruption attitude within the Romanian public posed to their position of political power. In the election year 1996, they voiced complaints about the estimated 10,000 people who had, since 1996, allegedly become Lei billionaires through illegal means.[49] In order not to be blamed themselves, they charged former Prime Minister Petre Roman, who had been dismissed in 1991, as well as his former ministers, with incompetence and corruption.

In contrast, President Ion Iliescu presented himself as a person of honor, claiming to have paid all his taxes in full and of having disclosed all his income and assets. However, during a TV interview he continued to show respect for people like George Păunescu, saying that they had understood how to use the loopholes in existing laws to make "easy, if not really unlawful" profits.[50] At the same time, Iliescu's PDSR blamed its former colleagues around Petre Roman for all the cases of corruption that had occurred during those first years in which they had been in power together.

The attempt to distract the public failed. In view of the cooptation of several directors into the ranks of the PDSR, voters placed the blame for the escalating corruption in the country largely on the shoulders of Iliescu's party. The opposition, and especially Iliescu's challenger in the Presidential race, Emil Constantinescu of the Democratic Convention, had placed corruption in the center of their election platform. Petre Roman's Democratic Party criticized the "unconstitutional and unpopular law which would shortly lead to a division of society into very poor and very rich people."[51]

In response, Iliescu's party began what it described as a major offensive in the fight against corruption. The leadership of the PDSR promised to see to it that businessmen who held a post in the party leadership would have to choose between their political function and their business position.[52] The Minister of the Interior turned to the police for information about the state of the investigations into the numerous cases of corruption which had not yet gone to trial.[53] The government of Prime Minister Nicolae Văcăroiu introduced in the parliament a draft bill which required of the holders of the highest offices of the state, as well as of the representatives of the directory councils of the still state-owned business sector to disclose their financial circumstances.[54] However, a draft bill, which would have forbidden Romanian parliamentarians from holding positions on the supervisory boards of companies and banks, was rejected by Parliament in 1995.

Despite the parliamentarians' efforts, the PDSR's anticorruption campaign could not prevent the ruling party and its President Ion Iliescu, both of whom had spent six years in power since 1989, from being voted out of office. Given the power the elite possessed over the politics of Romanian society, this outcome seems counterintuitive. However, the opinion was frequently voiced that the oligarchy was actually by this time in favor of, or at least not entirely opposed to, Iliescu's removal from power. As one commentator noted, "After national Communism had furthered the transformation of state-owned into privately owned monopolies, it has itself become in turn a brake on the further development of these privately owned monopolies."[55] Indeed, the vote of the citizenry against the ruling party and its President was decisively influenced by the privately owned electronic mass media in the hands of the new magnates.

THE OPPOSITION'S FIGHT AGAINST CORRUPTION

In the campaign for the Parliamentary elections of November 1996, the opposition Romanian Democratic Convention had given the fight against corruption the highest priority in its election program, entitled the "Contract with Romania." With the revenues that the elimination of the black economy was to produce, the opposition wanted to finance its election promises of an improved social security system.[56] Emil Constantinescu, the opposition presidential candidate, was especially concerned with this theme as contemporary opinion polls showed that escalating corruption had become the main concern of the Romanian people.[57]

Following its election to power the new opposition government began its anticorruption fight in earnest. By January 1997, the entire executive of the Fund for State Property, the key department for privatization, was changed. In June of the same year, the chief officer of the fraud squad (*Garda Financiară*) was replaced. Furthermore, President Constantinescu established the National Action Council against Corruption and Crime (*Consiliul Naţional de Acţiune împotriva Corupţiei şi Criminalităţii*), an advisory body including representatives of the government, high civil servants from the Finance Ministry, and the directors of the intelligence services. The Council has had some success, most recently an exhaustive white paper published in July 1998 that was covered in detail by the press. The white paper contained, among other things, suggestions for improving the fight against crime through cooperation with the West and the Council of Europe.[58]

The President also sought international support for his government's fight against corruption. In January 1997, Nadia Constantinescu, the spouse of the president and a lawyer by profession, introduced to the Council of Europe an outline proposal for a convention on the fight against corruption, which she helped to work out in detail. In March 1997, Romania signed conventions of the Council of Europe on the subjects of money laundering and the confiscation of criminal property.[59] During the Europe-Forum in Berlin in November 1997, President Constantinescu called for a common fight of all European states against crime, terrorism, drug and arms trade, and smuggling.[60] At the Europe conference of the European Union in London in March 1998, he suggested the creation of a European center for crime control in Bucharest.[61]

The international campaign of the Romanian government was successful, at least from the standpoint of public relations. Praise came not only come from the Romanian mission chief of the World Bank, François Ettori, but also from U.S. Congressman Tom Lantos, who stated that businessmen and bankers from the United States would be encouraged to continue investing in Romania because of Constantinescu's anticorruption campaign.[62]

The Romanian press also welcomed the new Romanian leadership's initiative to fight corruption. Yet, at the same time, they also expressed doubts whether the President would be able to gain approval from within his own coalition.[63] The doubts were not totally unfounded; Petre Roman's Democratic Party was also a member of Constatinescu's coalition. Not only did Iliescu's PDSR consider Roman's party to be mainly responsible for the privatization of the *nomenklatura*; this charge was also raised by some representatives of the Romanian Democratic Convention as well.

President Constantinescu expressly tried to protect Petre Roman's Democratic Party from criticism.[64] However, charges of official corruption inevitably caused tension within the coalition. This was especially the case when the controlling department of the government, led by Valerian Stan of the Civic Alliance, took the expropriation of former Communist Party villas by members of Roman's Democratic Party on the anticorruption agenda. This action caused the first serious crisis within the coalition. Protests by the leadership of the Democratic Party led to the dismissal of Valerian Stan.[65]

Leading representatives of the Democratic Party began to speak up ever more openly against the anticorruption fight that President Constantinescu,

Prime Minister Victor Ciorbea, and some other ministers of the National Peasant Party had initiated. In an interview with the daily newspaper *Evenimentul Zilei*, Transportation Minister Traian Băsescu criticized the fact that in the fight against corruption, the President had "spun out of control."[66] Bogdan Niculescu-Duvaz, vice president of the Democratic Party, criticized the control that the Romanian Democratic Convention, in effect the National Peasant Party, exercised over the administrative and economic structures.[67]

The media also began to criticize Constantinescu's anticorruption campaign, accusing the new leadership of purging the administrative and economic structures of the representatives of the former government only to place its own people into these lucrative positions.[68] President Constantinescu was personally accused of filling the most important key positions in the state with people from his own staff.[69]

Thus, in practice, the fight against corruption has proved to be more difficult than expected. Despite the many changes made in government personnel, passive resistance to the anticorruption measures inside the bureaucracy *and within the governing coalition itself* has been pervasive. Also, while several of the most "prominent" business criminals had been placed in custody in the first weeks after the new government had come into office, by August 1997 most of them, with the exception of the "small fry," had been released.[70] A scant year after his election to office President Constantinescu expressed his frustrations with the anti-corruption campaign in a public address, calling it "unbelievable" that, in 1997, only seven big corruption cases had been tried by the courts.[71]

In a spectacular press conference in September 1997, President Constantinescu admitted, "In November 1996 we won the elections but we did not win the power, because a big part of the economic power belonged and still belongs almost exclusively to certain mafia networks that do not have any concern for the national interest."[72] The President became even more explicit in a public address he delivered on account of the open crisis which was to lead two months later to the resignation of Prime Minister Victor Ciorbea:

> It is a fact that there are interest groups in Romania who really do not want any reforms or want reforms only for their own benefit. There are circles who are highly alarmed by the fight against corruption, black economy, and mafia structures. There are circles who are opposed to Romania's interests in international cooperation.[73]

The President expressed his concern about the increasing willingness of these groups to use violence, directly or indirectly, to attain their goals.[74] This violence was soon directed against himself. At the end of April, an explosive smuggling affair was brought to light at Otopeni airport, which, in the view of Constantinescu's chief advisor, Zoe Petre, was aimed at discrediting the President and his security service.[75] Indeed, the affair was disclosed at the precise moment in which the office of the prosecuting attorney had completed investigations into some of the most explosive cases of corruption and was about to submit the files to court.[76]

CONCLUSION

After a decade of transformation in Romania one still does not find a "market economy in the sense of a free market," but rather, a "system of relations, benefits, and mutual dependencies" between the members of a "small group of business leaders, members of government, and high state officials."[77] Almost fourteen years after the revolution the Romanian economy remains hostage to "mixed" property relationships, nationalization and politicization of the economy, and concentration through the connection of finance and industry, all of which is based on networks of personal relations dating from the time of Communism. This is problematic for the prospect of true democratic and economic reform in Romania. As Minister of the Interior, Gavril Dejeu of the Christian Democratic National Peasant Party noted, "One can not build democracy with the same people who built the dictatorship; the free market economy cannot be built with the same people who built the command economy."[78] Before this oligarchy is dealt with, other necessary reforms in Romania—whether they involve the environment, the electoral system, or the economy—will inevitably be obstructed by the incestuous networks of interlocking political and economic interests that characterize the new Romanian elite. Thus, as the political scientist Stelian Tănase has put it: "The liquidation of this mafia is not only a judicial or moral issue, or an issue for the economy in the narrow sense, it is especially a political issue—and therefore of vital importance for the process of democratization of the Romanian society."[79]

NOTES

1. This chapter was translated by Mohammed Muammer, Mihnea Năstase, and Peter Wagner. See Attila Ágh, "From Nomenklatura to Clientura: The Emergence of New Political Elites in East-Central Europe," in Geoffrey Pridham and Paul G. Lewis, eds., *Stabilising Fragile Democracies: Comparing New Party Systems in Southern and Eastern Europe* (London: Routledge, 1996), pp. 44–68; Thomas A. Baylis, "Plus Ça Change? Transformation and Continuity among East European Elites," *Communist and Post-Communist Studies*, vol. 27, no. 3 (1994), pp. 315–28; Heinrich Best and Ulrike Becker: *Elites in Transition. Elite Research in Central and Eastern Europe* (Opladen: Leske U.B. Verlag, 1997); John Higley, Judith Kullberg, and Jan Pakulski, *The Persistence of Postcommunist Elites, Journal of Democracy*, vol. 7, no. 2 (1996), pp. 133–47; H.-H. Schröder, *Russische Wirtschafts und Gesellschaftseliten im Übergang, BIOst [Hg.]: Der Osten Europas im Prozeß der Differenzierung: Fortschritt und Misserfolge des Transformation* (Munich: Hanser Verlag, 1995), pp. 266–77.

2. Werner Raith, *Das neue Mafia-Kartell. Wie die Syndikate den Osten erobern*, (Berlin: Rowohlt TB-Verlag, 1994), p. 167.

3. Wojtech Lamentowicz, *Politische Instabilität in Ost und Mitteleuropa: innenpolitische Gefährdungen der europäischen Integration und Sicherheit, Werner Weidenfeld [Hg.]: Demokratie und Marktwirtschaft in Osteuropa. Strategien für Europa* (Gütersloh: Bertelsmann Verlag, 1995), p. 78.

4. Jadwiga Staniszkis, "Globalisierung und das Ende des Kommunismus," *Internationale Politik* (May 1997), p. 21.

5. Samuel N. Eisenstadt, *Revolution and the Transformation of Societies: A Comparative Study of Civilizations* (New York: Free Press, 1978).

6. Trond Gilberg, *Nationalism and Communism in Romania: The Rise and Fall of Ceauşescu's Personal Dictatorship* (Boulder, CO: Westview Press, 1990), pp. 83–109.

7. Kenneth Jowitt has defined this process as "party familialization," in *The Leninist Response to National Dependency* (Berkeley and Los Angeles: University of California Press, 1978), p. 70.

8. Compare the analysis in Stelian Tănase, *Revoluţia ca eşec. Elite şi societate*, pp. 54–85.

9. For details see: Dan Badea, *Averea Preşedintelui. Conturile lui Ceauşescu* [The Wealth of the President. The Ceauşescu-Accounts] (Bucharest: Nemira, 1998).

10. A.a.O., S. 17.

11. Governmental Decree no. 30 (18 January 1990).

12. Dan Badea, *Averea Preşedintelui. Conturile lui Ceauşescu*, p. 61.

13. *Ibid.*, pp. 25–37.

14. *Adevărul* (3 October 1995).

15. Romeo Neacşu and Daniela Georgescu, "*Întîmplări ciudate pe traseul descoperirii conturilor lui Ceauşescu*" [Strange occurences on the road to the attempted uncovering of Ceauşescu's accounts] *Tineretul liber* (30 October 1991).

16. Prior to 1989, Stolojan had served as Ceauşescu's trusted agent in the Finance Ministry, in charge of the foreign exchange dealings. On 29 December 1989, he was appointed Deputy Minister of Finance in the new provisional government. After the May 20, 1990 elections for the Constitutional Assembly, he became Minister of Finance. In May 1991, he took over the directorate of the national privatization agency. After Petre Roman's fall in September 1991, Stolojan was appointed prime minister. After the September 1992 parliamentary elections, Stolojan, highly regarded in the West as an "apolitical expert" received a leading position at the World Bank. For the parliamentary and presidential elections of November 1996, Stolojan disclosed for the first time his political preference—for former President Ion Iliescu. See Viktor Meier, "*Mehr als Iliescus Aushängeschild?*" *Frankfurter Allgemeine Zeitung* (18 October 1991). At the time of publication (July 2000), Stolojan was actively seeking the nomination of the National Liberal Party as presumptive prime minister.

17. *Echipa de sacrificiu. Din culisele guvernării postrevolutionare. 5 ianuarie 1990–5 februarie 1991* [The sacrificial team: Behind the scenes of the post-revolutionary government], (Bucharest: România Azi, 1992), p. 70.

18. Liana Sega, "*În democraţia de tip nou averea dă puterea*"[In the democracy of the new type, property bestows power], in *Azi* (30 June 1995).

19. *Adevărul* (17 September 1994).

20. Andrei Cornea, *Lichidarea directocrației* [The Liquidation of the Directocracy], *22*, no. 33, (19–25 August 1997).

21. Alexandra Petria, "*Irectorii acaparează întreprinderile prin metoda* MEBO" [The directors acquire the enterprises by the MEBO-method], *Cotidianul* (11 October 1994); Henriette Schröder, *Die Nomenklatura von einst sahnt ab*, *Süddeutsche Zeitung*, (22 December 1994).

22. Adina Croitoru, "*În 1997, au acționat in România 20.789 rețele de firme-căpușă*" [In Romania 20,798 tic-firms were operating in the year 1997], *România liberă* (6 July 1998).

23. Silviu Brucan, *Stîlpii noii puteri in Romania* [The Pillars of the New Power] (Bucharest: Nemiar, 1996), pp. 108–14.

24. S. R. Ica, "*România în caracatița spălării dolarilor. Proiectul Demavand*" [Romania in the claws of the money launderers. The Demavand Project], *România liberă* (22 December 1994).

25. *Transition*, (17 May 1996), p. 26.

26. "*Banken und Kommunikation, Minuspunkte für Rumänien*," *Allgemeine Deutsche Zeitung für Rumänien* (1 February 1997); Florina Stanca, Dan Raveica and Alexandru Dinulescu, "*De la venitul prin șpagă la venitul în Calea Rahovei*" [Alexandru Dinulescu—from income through bribery to being put on trial], *Azi* (21 February 1997).

27. "*Geldwäsche mit staatlicher Genehmigung. Die Columna-Bank soll mit dem Geld ihrer Kunden das linke Parteienbündnis finanziert haben*," *Hermannstädter Zeitung* (8 August 1997).

28. *Adevărul* (6 September 1994).

29. Mircea Kivu, "*Purtătorii de celular*," [The mobile phone carriers], *Dilema*, no. 229 (13–19 June 1997).

30. *Adevărul* (16 January 1997).

31. The annual reports by the police provide detailed information on the many forms of white-collar crime. See *Adevărul* (17 January 1997 and 3 March 1997).

32. Lucian Albu, "*Anatomia economiei subterane*," [Anatomy of the Sub-terranian Economy], *Tribuna Economică*, no. 13 (28 March 1996), p. 63.

33. *Azi* (21 January 1998).

34. Liana Rădulescu, "*Munca la negru—o boală ce tinde să devină epidemie*" [Moonlighting—a sickness that begins to become chronic], *Romanul*, no. 19 (15 May 1995); "*O lovitură pentru amatorii de munca la negru*" [A strike against those who like to moonlight], *Azi* (24 June 1998).

35. Roman Toma, "*Criza morală și viitorul României*" [The moral crisis and the future of Romania], *România literară*, no. 8, (21 February 1991).

36. Interview in *România liberă* (4 October 1994).

37. Interview in *România liberă* (4 October 1994).

38. *Adevărul* (17 September 1994).

39. Liviu Antonesei, "*Comuniștii în blană capitalistă*" [The communists in capitalism], *22*, no. 40 (5–11 October 1994).

40. Tudor Octavian, "*Proclamație către popor*,"*România liberă* (6 April 1995).

41. Cătălin Crețu, "*Jocul de interese din interiorul NATO și integrarea României*," [The play of interests in NATO and the integration of Romania] *Sfera Politicii*, no. 49 (1997), pp. 29–30.

42. Stelian Tănase, "*Cine duce greul*" [Who carries the weight], *Acum*, no. 13 (1991).

43. Anatolie Panis, "*Directorii feseniști doboară guvernul Roman*" [The directors of the National Salvation Front topple the Roman government], *România liberă* (24 November 1990).

44. *Adevărul* (15 September 1996).

45. Adrian Severin, "*Lacrimile dimineții: Slabiciunile Guvernului Roman*" [The morning tears], (Bucharest: Scripta, 1995), p. 22.

46. Ion Cristoiu, "*Adevărul despre privatizare*" [The truth about privatization], *Expres Magazin*, no. 33 (23–30 August 1994.)

47. Bogdan Ficeac, "*Profitorii*" [The Profiteers], *România liberă* (18 November 1995).

48. Interview with Agricultural Minister Ioan Oancea in: *Adevărul*, (6 August 1994); and *Adevărul* (20 August 1994).

49. *Süddeutsche Zeitung* (Munich) (6 March 1996).

50. Interview on television station *Antena 1*, printed in *Adevărul* (1 February 1996).

51. *Azi* (10 March 1995).

52. *Adevărul* (27 July 1996).

53. *Adevărul* (29 June 1996).

54. Mircea Moldovan, *Curierul Romanesc*, no. 7 (1996).

55. Adrian Severin, in an interview in *Azi* (4 January 1996).

56. *Adevărul* (23 September 1996).

57. *Frankfurter Allgemeine Zeitung* (24 July 1996).

58. *Azi* (24 July 1998), pp. 21, 22.

59. *Le Figaro* (19 March 1997).

60. *Allgemeine Deutsche Zeitung für Rumänien* (11 November 1997).

61. *Allgemeine Deutsche Zeitung für Rumänien* (14 March 1998).

62. *Financial Times* (6 April 1997); and *Mediafax* (20 January 1997).

63. *Adevărul*, (10 January 1997).

64. Speech during an internal conference of the Ministry of the Interior, *Azi* (21 January 1998).

65. Annemarie Weber, "Hat die Politik den Rechtsstaat besiegt?" *Hermannstädter Zeitung* (5 September 1997).

66. *Evenimentul Zilei* (29 December 1997).

67. "*Tendința de cederizare sau, mai bine zis, de penetecederizare a structurilor administrative și economice*," On this, see Andrea Munteanu, "*PD acuză penetecederizarea structurilor economice*" [The Democratic Party criticizes the taking over of the economic structures by the Peasant Party], *Azi* (7 August 1998).

68. Malte Schnitzer Kessler, "*Die man sich nicht leisten dürfte*," *Allgemeine Deutsche Zeitung für Rumänien* (9 April 1997); and *Adevărul* (6 July 1998).

69. *Adevărul* (17 July 1998).

70. *Adevărul* (16 August 1997).

71. *Allgemeine Deutsche Zeitung für Rumänien* (3 March 1998).

72. Rodica Palade, "*Am câștigat alegerile, dar nu am cucerit puterea*" [We have won the elections, but not the power], *22*, no. 39, (30 Septermber–6 October 1997). See also *Frankfurter Allgemeine Zeitung* (26 September 1997).

73. *22,* no. 3 (20–26 January 1998).

74. Luminiţa Castall, "Structurile mafiote reacţionează cu violenţă" [The mafiosi structures react with violence], *România liberă* (5 February 1998).

75. *Azi* (6 May 1998). See also, Berthold Kohler, "*Dunkle Geschäfte auf dem Bukarester Flughafen,*" *Frankfurter Allgemeine Zeitung* (8 May 1998).

76. Cătălin Popa, "*O perdea de fum,*" [A smokescreen], *Curentul* (30 April 1998).

77. *Frankfurter Allgemeine Zeitung* (21 July 1997).

78. Interview in: *Evenimentul Zilei* (29 January 1997).

79. Stelian Tănase, "*Ameninţările dezamăgirii*" [The dangers of disappointment], *Sfera Politicii,* no. 47 (1997), p. 3.

19

Economic Reform

Wally Bacon

Romanian "economic reform" since 1989 is not, as some critics might suggest, an oxymoron. To dismiss the notion that reforms have not occurred, as did the respected economist Ilie Şerbănescu, is to identify reforms only with totally positive, macroeconomic results. Much microeconomic progress has occurred, improving the lot of individuals, groups, and institutions. International lending institutions and foreign investors tend to overemphasize macroeconomic indicators, while Romanian politicians and consumers have vastly different perspectives on the reform process, as well as conflicting policy preferences.

In this chapter, I evaluate how much economic reform has occurred, as well as the political and economic structures impeding further efforts. While reform processes have been confusing, the politics chaotic, and the results relatively disappointing, significant marketization of property relations, prices, and the state's role in the economy has occurred.

HISTORICAL IMPEDIMENTS

Despite the differing perceptions, almost all observers agree that Romania began post-Communism with more structural handicaps than other East Central European countries. While early Communist economic strategies differed little from country to country, most of the other, maturing socialist economies of the region flirted with decentralization, plan flexibility, partial price rationalization, and consumer oriented budget adjustments. By contrast, Romania, in the last decade of Communism, *strengthened* central planning with more rigid plan-targets, and continued to subsidize failing industries.

Despite statistical inaccuracies, it is generally conceded that between 1950 and 1975, the Romanian economy grew at one of the fastest rates in the world.[1] Large investments in heavy industry (34.1 percent of GDP in the 1971–1975 five-year plan), rather than for consumption,[2] created a *facade* of economic growth. The reality of Ceauşescu's Stalinist policies produced growing structural imbalances in his development strategy.[3] Flagship industries, such as petrochemicals and steel, received too much investment and produced more than both the domestic and foreign markets demanded of their poor quality goods, resulting in later input shortages and underused capacity. Additionally, the Stalinist inclination toward "gigantism" combined differentially sustainable production units, with the lagging and overly depreciated parts dragging down the marginally productive ones. The reliance on material plan fulfillment, rather than profitability, as the measure of success encouraged the falsification of statistics, the buildup of unproductive inventories, and the spread of systemic corruption.

The Ceauşescu regime's ability to perpetuate the illusion of economic success during the last half of the 1970s lasted only as long as the West was willing to finance it through technology imported on credit. Such Western support, based as much on political considerations as on economic ones, waned with the decade's oil price shocks, rising interest rates, and the overall burgeoning of southern debt. As a result, Romania was burdened with hard currency debts, which its structurally imbalanced economy was incapable of repaying.[4]

In late 1981, Romania was obliged to request International Monetary Fund (IMF) lines of credit to order to meet its debt obligations. The IMF's structural adjustment conditions, which included the reduction of trade and current account deficits, and the implementation of long-term managerial and financial reform, would have ordinarily triggered policy changes reducing the imbalances in the Romanian economy.[5] Instead, the Ceauşescu regime embarked on a centralized program of austerity which kept intact its nationalist priorities under the guise of "reform" in the "New Economic and Financial Mechanism." Targets of self-financing and self-managing decentralization never took hold. Detailed and inflexible plan fulfillment remained more important than profit. What energy resources remained for domestic consumption in the aftermath of the austerity measures were funneled into inefficient industries or petrochemical exports; individual consumption was reduced to the point where cities were left in a gloomy semidarkness made worse by the choking pollution caused by the burning of cheap high sulfur coal. By the time of the revolution, the economy was in ruins. As the IMF gloomily summarized the prospects for reform:

> Ceauşescu's legacy was an economy plagued by inefficient industrial structures and an almost obsolete capital stock, a completely disorganized system of production and distribution, a collectivized agricultural sector, a decaying infrastructure, and a population whose living standards had been forced

steadily down to a level where even basic necessities—food heating, electricity, and medical attention—were hard to come by. There is little doubt that the initial obstacles to reform in Romania were far worse than those faced by other reforming East European countries.[6]

INITIAL REFORM EFFORTS OF THE FSN/FDSN/PDSR

In the months following the events of December 1989, Romanian political life was dominated by the National Salvation Front (FSN), an organization largely controlled by dissident Communists, military officers, and former members of the *nomenklatura*. The legitimacy of the Front lay, not in its commitment to democratic political reforms and market oriented economic changes, but rather in its centrality in ridding the country of the Ceauşescu tyranny. Most soon suspected that the Front's leadership had conspired to overthrow Ceauşescu for some time and had manipulated—some would say kidnapped—a genuine popular uprising.

While the FSN's initial communiqué, issued hours after Ceauşescu's flight from Bucharest, made vague declarations of its intention to restructure the economy along the lines of "profitability and efficiency," it contained no explicit promises of an immediate change either in the state's ownership of the means of production or in the central planning system.[7] A few days later, FSN leader Ion Iliescu indicated that the "shock therapy" approach to economic transition was not on the Front's agenda. "We do not intend to demolish the present central organs," Iliescu explained, "as we must rely on the existing structures."[8] The FSN's "Draft Strategy of the Transition," which was released in April 1990,[9] paradoxically called for "a gradual transition effected in a short period of time," and envisioned the initial establishment of an institutional and legal framework for economic reform, to be followed by the reform itself.[10]

This cautious and populist approach to economic change appealed to the FSN's core constituencies, who were the most likely to be hurt by radical economic reforms: former Communist Party bureaucrats, peasants, state employees, and industrial workers.[11] During the initial stages of the reform process, the FSN gave in to worker demands for higher wages and shorter working hours, and aside from a law allowing for the establishment of small scale private companies, it did little to encourage private enterprise and market pricing.

It was only when Petre Roman, the newly designated prime minister, presented his government and its program to the Romanian Parliament on 28 June 1990 that market-oriented reforms were explicitly promised. However, these reforms were neither as bold nor as radical as claimed. Despite the passage of Law 15/1990, which transformed state enterprises into commercial companies and *regies autonomes*, real structural reforms involving price liberalization, *leu* devaluation, and a revitalized banking system had yet to be realized.

By October 1990, the economic situation in Romania had deteriorated significantly. In its first nine months, the post-Communist regime had presided over a 27.7 percent decline in net industrial production and a 22.8 percent decline in worker productivity, the latter having been largely brought about by the government's caving in to worker demands for higher wages (salaries rose by 26.1 percent) and a shortening of the workweek (–16.7 percent). In December, Finance Minister Theodor Stolojan predicted a $1.2 billion trade deficit for 1990.[12]

Roman acknowledged that there was an economic crisis and that reform had to be accelerated despite the attendant social costs.[13] Partial price liberalization and a 67 percent devaluation of the *leu* were implemented on 1 November. The unfreezing of most other prices in February, April, and September 1991, uncompensated by equal wage increases, resulted in a drop of real income of 18.3 percent while nominal net salaries rose 120.6 percent. By the end of 1991, the annual inflation rate was 222.8 percent.[14]

Roman's failure to explain adequately both the purposes and the consequences of genuine liberalization and stabilization fueled the resentment of precisely those constituencies to whom the FSN owed its May 1990 electoral victory.[15] Disrupting labor unrest spread throughout the country.[16] In late September 1991, a fourth *mineriada* was launched to oust Roman, whom the miners and many other Romanians held responsible for the declines in living standards.[17]

However, the new prime minister, Teodor Stolojan, who had resigned as Minister of Finance in March because reforms had not been progressing fast enough, actually turned out to be an even more ardent reformer than Roman.[18] Stolojan, who benefited politically from his image as a nonpartisan technocrat, lived up to his reformist reputation after only a month in office, starting with the painful imposition of the internal convertibility of the *leu*.[19] He supported National Bank Governor Murgur Isărescu's tightening of the money supply, which imposed financial discipline on enterprises. While the Privatization Law 58/1991 left virtually all industrial assets under control of the state, it provided a legal framework for MEBOs, direct purchases of state assets, and a voucher mass privatization scheme. While the implementation of some reform provisions was constrained by FSN political considerations, Stolojan diligently applied those elements of the Roman program which had cost Roman his job.[20] However, economic reforms would continue to be highly dependent on the vicissitudes of Romanian electoral politics.

From November 1992 until November 1996, Romania was governed by the Iliescu wing of the FSN, which had been renamed the Party of Social Democracy of Romania (PDSR) in 1993. Iliescu's ambivalence about economic reform and his party's trumpeted concern about its social costs led to the unexpected choice of Nicolae Văcăroiu, an economist who had served on Romania's negotiating team with the IMF and the World Bank, for prime minister. While not renouncing the achievements of Roman and Stolojan, Văcăroiu advocated a stronger role for the state in the reform process, promising both a halt to the decline in industrial production and a softening of the social costs of reform.[21] In his negotiations with the international financial institutions (IFIs), such as the World Bank and the IMF, he refused to cede to their demand to close down loss-making state enterprises, preferring to continue to subsidize the potentially viable ones while they restructured and recapitalized.[22]

The macroeconomic data for 1993 and 1994 would seem to suggest an unanticipated level of success for Văcăroiu's policies. The decline in GDP was reversed (with 1.5 and 3.9 percent gains, respectively), and industrial production increased (with increases of 1.3 and 3.3 percent, and with overall industrial productivity jumping 9 and 14.7 percent, respectively). However, due to high inflation and further price liberalizations, real wages fell by 16.7 percent in 1993 (with a marginal +0.4 percent recovery in 1994). Moreover, the Văcăroiu government's decision to continue subsidies to state enterprises increased the budget deficit to 4.4 percent of GDP in 1994; and despite the National Bank's reluctance, the money supply was increased by 500 percent during these two years,[23] resulting in inflation of 295.5 and 61.7 percent respectively, for 1993 and 1994.

Critics asserted that while temporary improvement in some areas had been reported, it was largely at the expense of, rather than due to, genuine economic reforms.[24] The 1993 Organization for Economic Cooperation and Development (OECD) *Economic Assessment* had recommended more thorough liberalization, a stricter fiscal and monetary policy, and accelerated privatization and restructuring. However, five years later the OECD could find few indications that the Văcăroiu government had taken the recommendations to heart.[25] The World Bank's comparative analyses of transitional economies (1995) found Romanian liberalization and private sector development near the bottom of Group 2 (which, in addition to Romania, included Bulgaria, Albania, the Baltic countries, and Mongolia).[26]

Then why did the macroeconomic data reflect so dramatic a recovery? The data on the state budget's deficit as a proportion of GDP are enlightening. While the deficit was 2.6 percent of GDP in 1993, the transitional year, it had risen to 4.2 percent in 1994.[27] Despite the attempts by the National Bank to institute a tight monetary policy, the government, out of the political considerations of its dominant constituents, continued to pursue a policy of "soft credit"—heavily subsidizing indebted and inefficient state economic units, directing the state's fledgling commercial banks to provide negative (1993) and low-interest (1994) loans to loss-making enterprises and state farms, and turning a blind eye to the burgeoning problem of inter-enterprise arrears.[28]

Such inter-enterprise arrears, which are a pervasive phenomena among post-socialist economies, are a sort of "temporary quasi-inside money"[29] that accumulate as enterprises fail to pay each other for contracted services. As these grow, the government may impose discipline on the enterprises by restructuring them, or by closing them down and liquidating their assets. More often, it permits them to continue with the hope that the enterprises will "grow" out of debt with an improvement in the general economy. Politically, in the short run, the last of these three options is the least risky. This strategy, in turn, leads to a systemic conspiracy not to demand liquidation in order to prevent the whole illusion of solvency and economic success from collapsing.

In any event, arrears do not appear as part of the budgetary deficit. If they did, the reported ratio of deficit to GDP would be immensely greater. When coupled with easy credit, toleration of arrears distorts markets and adds to inflationary pressures. They act as a disincentive for enterprise autonomy and market responsiveness.[30] They contribute to the lack of budget transparency at both the national and enterprise levels. Finally, inter-enterprise arrears exacerbate economic "blockage," wherein not enough money is circulating to generate supply responses to market forces.

The Văcăroiu government's reluctance to make hard long-term decisions about arrears was politically astute because it kept the PDSR's primary constituencies—manual workers, enterprise technocrats, and state bureaucrats—happy.[31] In the course of his evaluation of economic progress during 1993–1994, Văcăroiu obliquely acknowledged the problem of arrears by promising to impose stricter enterprise and state budget discipline and to push ahead with privatization, all within the (hoped for) context of strong economic growth.[32]

With the promulgation of easy credit, it is not surprising that macroeconomic results in 1995 were even more favorable. GDP grew 7.1 percent, and industrial output grew by 9.4 percent, while inflation fell to 27.8 percent. Real income, electorally the most fungible indicator, rose 12.5 percent. However, the budget deficit remained at an unacceptably high 4.1 percent of GDP.[33] The expansion of the GDP, which should have enabled the economy to "grow" out of indebtedness, had been realized. However, genuine reform within the framework of the "Washington consensus" remained inconsistent. Yet, the second mass privatization law (No. 55/1995), which called for a second voucher distribution, showed that the government had concluded that only privatization could affect enterprise discipline.

The IMF was so dissatisfied with the pace and substance of the agreed-upon stabilization program that it withheld two tranches of credit to Romania. Furthermore, the flood of money into the market as well as the inability of Romanian producers to escape systemic blockage caused current account deficits to more than double to $1.2 billion.[34] The overheating of the economy and the government's inability or unwillingness to follow through with genuine reforms presaged structural imbalances which could only lead to even more difficult decisions in the years to come.

Moreover, if the loose credit policy, the postponing of structural reforms, and the artificial stabilization of the *leu* were tactics adopted by the PDSR to retain the support of its core constituencies for the 1996 general elections their positive effects peaked far too soon. An unexpected energy crisis began a year of discontent for Romania. After some procrastination, the government was obliged in May 1996 to raise prices for basic consumer goods, including energy, after a sharp devaluation of the *leu* forced its hand.[35] The annual inflation rate, projected by the government to be 20 percent for the year 1996, soared to nearly 60 percent by year's end.[36] To add to the uncertainty, two Romanian banks, Credit Bank and Dacia Felix, became illiquid due to massively nonperforming loan portfolios, incompetent management, endemic cronyism, and corruption. The National Bank, already overextended by a looming increase in foreign and domestic debt, had to bail out the banks, all the while trying to counter the government's spendthrift ways.[37]

REFORM UNDER THE DEMOCRATIC CONVENTION

Unlike in the elections of 1992, the opposition ran a coherent campaign leading up to the elections of November 1996. Emil Constantinescu, the Democratic Convention's (CD) candidate for president, and the center-left Union of Social Democrats (UDS), headed by Petre Roman, emphasized economic reform in their platforms. They criticized the government for the falling standard of living in Romania, which had so recently been propped up by the PDSR's easy credit policy.[38] When the CD-UDS coalition came to power in November 1996, IFIs, investors, and various domestic actors anticipated accelerated and deepened economic reform.

The new prime minister, Victor Ciorbea, set about implementing a modified "shock therapy" for the economy. The economic program had four primary goals: strengthening economic discipline (including a reduction of inter-enterprise arrears, estimated at 36 percent of GDP at the end of 1996) by liquidating the worst loss-making units; reforming the agricultural sector through increased price liberalization and reduction of subsidies; making Romania more attractive to foreign investors; and accelerating and enlarging the privatization program.[39] Among the early effects of the program were substantial consumer price increases,[40] a rapprochement with the IFIs (including heeding their advice on *leu* devaluation, budget transparency, and discipline),[41] and the designation of a number of large loss-making enterprises for imminent liquidation.[42]

The Ciorbea reform program achieved a few of the expected results. A group of companies which accounted for 75 percent of the 1996 losses were targeted for elimination or radical restructuring. A number of unprofitable coal pits were closed, cutting the workforce by 44 percent (75,600 miners).

At the same time, productivity in the coal *regies autonomes* rose.[43] Both the IMF and the World Bank demonstrated their initial support for the Ciorbea program by granting nearly $1 billion in restructuring loans for 1997–1998.[44]

By autumn, however, the momentum toward rapid reform had slowed. Union demonstrations in opposition to further reforms returned to the streets in November. The political pressures of domestic constituents soon forced the government to acknowledge the need for fairly generous severance packages for those left unemployed by enterprise liquidation and restructuring reforms. Such additions to the state social fund's liabilities clearly would lead to larger than predicted budget deficits. The renewed inflation in October, as well as the increasingly apparent legislative lacunae, prompted the IMF to press for tougher fiscal restraints. The year-end macroeconomic results were largely a disappointment.[45] Under pressure from both ends, the hapless Ciorbea was forced to resign on 30 March 1998.

Ciorbea's successor as prime minister was Radu Vasile, an economist and member of the same PNT-CD. The differences between his reform program and Cirobea's were minor, as Vasile stressed achieving those goals that had eluded the Ciorbea government.[46] His cabinet reflected a more deferential posture toward Roman's Democratic Party (PD) and its leader's impatience with the pace of reform. Among the government's early objectives was to win back the confidence of the IFIs.[47] To do this, a speedup of privatizations had to take place. However, like its predecessor, the Vasile government would find itself unable to live up to its promises.[48]

Overall, 1998 was another disappointing year for Romania. While a handful of potentially profitable large firms were partially sold to foreign investors (e.g., Romtelecom to the Greek OTE and the Romanian Development Bank to France's Société Générale),[49] only 1,010 of a projected 2,600 state firms were privatized. Restructuring of state enterprises, particularly of RENEL, the state electricity generating and distribution company, were complicated and did not produce the productivity improvements anticipated.[50] Furthermore, the economy continued to worsen. GDP declined 7.3 percent, unemployment rose to 10.3 percent, and labor productivity dropped 6.2 percent. While the rate of inflation improved somewhat, it was still at an unacceptably high level of 59.1 percent. Curiously, real wages rose 6.8 percent, a signal that imbalances still existed in the Romanian economy.[51]

Worse still for the long term, both the IMF and the World Bank, fed up with the government's inability or unwillingness to carry out its promises on stabilization, budgetary discipline, and privatization, stopped disbursements to Romania. The loss of IFI support was particularly critical since external loan service was projected to amount to $3 billion in 1999, far exceeding reserves and anticipated revenues.[52]

Cynicism about the prospects for reform abounded. A public opinion poll in December 1998 found that a majority of Romanians blamed their government for the country's economic decline, and believed they had been better off materially under Ceauşescu.[53] As a result of the abysmal performance of the Romanian economy, Vasile, like many of the prime ministers before him, was sacked in December 1999.

STRUCTURAL IMPEDIMENTS

While few doubt the commitments of these various coalitions to the goal of reform, their efforts have been constantly compromised by the government's caving in to union demands for wage increases and other considerations, such as not shutting down loss-making state enterprises. If Romania possessed a strong state and a strong government, facing down street demonstrators and entrenched bureaucratic interests might be possible; but unfortunately it is not. The fragmented coalitions which have governed Romania since 1989 generally cannot reach a consensus on reform measures. Their parliamentary majorities are usually so slim that the compromises necessary for the preservation of the coalition generally supplant reform objectives as priorities.

One major result of this has been the relatively slow progress of privatization and enterprise restructuring. The privatization process is cumbersome, and the many opportunities for bureaucratic rent seeking are exploited within the Romanian political milieu. The central bureaucratic entity controlling the process of privatization is the State Ownership Fund (FPS), which by law was to temporarily retain 70 percent of the shares in state enterprises until they were privatized. Law 58/1991 had envisioned that every year the FPS would sell off 10 percent of the original asset pool and would thus go out of business in seven years.

As one might imagine, progress toward this goal was slow under the Văcăroiu governments. In the five years from 1992 to 1996, during which the FPS should have sold 4,493 of its original portfolio of 6,291 commercial enterprises, only 2,871 were actually sold; and the overwhelming majority of these were privatized through MEBOs, which tended to profit the PDSR's core constituency of former Communists and to facilitate corruption.[54] Of those 2,871 privatized firms, 2,158 of an original 3,124 were small firms with less than 500 employees, 618 of an original 2,459 were medium-sized enterprises, and only 95 of 708 were large enterprises.[55]

Unfortunately, the larger enterprises were the ones responsible for the majority of inter-enterprise arrears and unpaid taxes. These Ceauşescu era industrial complexes were, and continue to be, difficult to privatize because of their size, their lack of profit potential, and the almost complete depreciation of their production assets. However, because they employ so many tens of thousands of workers, neither the Văcăroiu governments, nor their successors, have dared liquidate most of them for fear of social unrest. Until genuine restructuring or privatization occurs, the financial burden of maintaining of these "strategic" firms will continue to frustrate all aspects of reform.

Epitomizing this dilemma is the Sidex steel works in Galaţi, which is a city unto itself with more than 30,000 employees, and whose products account for 11 percent of Romania's exports and 5 percent of its GDP.[56] As of 31 December 1998, Sidex was owed nearly 1.1 trillion *lei* by 625 clients,[57] but had accumulated debts totaling 6 trillion *lei*, including debts to suppliers, tax funds, and unpaid dividends.

However, each year as its technology becomes more antiquated,[58] it is less able to compete its way out of debt. Foreign investors are sought, but the debt to potential earnings ratio is so high that few with the $1.5 billion the FPS expects to get for Galaţi would be willing to take on the task. If the FPS were to close down even part of the complex, tens of thousands of workers in industries dependent on Sidex steel would become unemployed. On the other hand, if the government continues to allow the growth of Sidex debt and to support the complex with direct and indirect subsidies it will be unable to meet the IMF's demands on budgetary discipline.

The effects of the inter-enterprise arrears of behemoths like Sidex reverberate and are magnified throughout the larger economy. For example, at the end of 1999, Sidex owed nearly a trillion *lei* to CONEL, the *regie autonome*[59] successor to the mammoth state-owned electric monopoly RENEL. Owed 10 trillion *lei*, CONEL itself owes trillions to its coal and natural gas providers. Yet, it recently rejected the National Authority of Regulation for Electric Power's and the Competition Council's recommendations of 18 and 14 percent rate increases, respectively, and insisted on burdening the already overburdened population with 30 percent increases.[60]

Rate increases will not resolve CONEL's problems however. Neither will economic competition. There are virtually no incentives for CONEL to become more efficient because it is a monopoly. Also, disconnecting enterprises in arrears, an experiment briefly tried with relatively unimportant units in 1998, would only worsen an already catastrophic macroeconomic situation by shutting down production and throwing tens of thousands of workers onto the unemployment rolls. Both Sidex and CONEL are major parts in the continuing financial blockage, amounting to some $8 billion, or just under 20 percent of the GDP at the end of 1999.[61] Without firmly addressing the problem, Romania will remain mired in economic stagnation.

These problems, in turn, affect the banking structure. Once bankers become aware of bad enterprise debt, they become members of the same conspiracy that encourages inter-enterprise arrears; if the banks were to call in enterprise loans, the extent of their nonperforming portfolios would itself be exposed.[62] While privatization of these ailing banks and the transfer of bad debts to resolution agencies such as the Agency for Bank Asset Recovery (AVAB) allow banks to recapitalize and to become more attractive for investors, the banks merely pass the indebtedness on to ordinary citizens whose taxes ultimately pay for the government paper.

Also, if the state offers more attractive rates of return on short-term notes than the rate at which banks loan to businesses, there is less bank capital available, and at higher interest rates, for entrepreneurs. Currently, the returns on the Romanian capital markets the Bucharest Stock Market (BVB), reestablished in 1995, and the over-the-counter market (RASDAQ), founded in 1996, cannot compare with the return on government bonds. Without an alternative to direct loans, corporations have no access to alternative debt markets that would more efficiently correspond to risks. This has further retarded economic growth.

Moreover, the assumption of debt by the state, or the forgiving of debts to the state (e.g., overdue social fund taxes) increases the budget deficit, which again troubles the IFIs. During 1998, international rating agencies downgraded Romanian debt, reflecting foreign market pessimism about Romania's ability to pay its debt and to carry out much need banking reforms.[63]

Banking reform in Romania remains problematic. In late 1998, two of the state's seven commercial banks, the Romanian Development Bank and Bankpost, were partially acquired by foreign strategic investors, Société Générale and GE Capital/Banco Portugues de Investimento, respectively. However, both of these banks were profitable, and combined had only 10 percent of the total banking capital in Romania.[64] The remaining five state banks, which control between 65 and 70 percent of total banking capital, have yet to be privatized. Two of them, Bancorex and the Agicultural Bank (Banca Agricolą), were particularly burdened by large portfolios of nonperforming loans, which comprised roughly 60 percent of their respective total loan portfolios (the legacy of the Văcăroiu government's requiring them to make unrecoverable loans to loss-making state enterprises and state farms).[65]

Bancorex, which was responsible for half of the nonperforming loans, was singled out by the World Bank and the IMF as needing rapid and complete restructuring, or liquidation, if Romania were to receive desperately needed IFI support in 1999.[66] On 30 July, the government merged the ailing bank with the Romanian Commercial Bank, itself scheduled for privatization that year.[67] In the process more than $600 million in debts were rearranged, forgiven, or traded for government paper.[68] While the ordered restructuring of the two banks would address imbalances in operating expenses, yet another clumsy state bureaucracy, the AVAB, was given the task of recovering as much of the defaulted loans as possible.[69] Not only did large state-owned banks suffer from the consequences of poor risk management, two private banks, the Albina Bank and Bankoop, failed during 1999–2000.[70]

Commitments to reform the banking sector were among the articulated priorities of "Romania's Memorandum on Economic Policies"—a renewed promise to strengthen and accelerate the reform process made to the IMF in return for an eight-month stand-by credit of $547 million finalized in August 1999.[71]

It is a vicious circle. The privatization of banks becomes problematic due to the high ratio of nonperforming loans in their portfolios. These, in turn, are the result of the failure of privatization programs and the growth of inter-enterprise arrears in business which, due to the political considerations of the ruling coalition, cannot be liquidated. This gridlock is often broken only by the occasional intervention of the World Bank and the IMF, which periodically withholds the loan and credit tranches on which the Romanian economy is dependent, or refuses to negotiate until the Romanian government takes corrective, usually temporary, action. Then, inertia sets back in until the IFIs again crack the whip, or the government falls due to the politically unpopular reform efforts it has been forced to carry out.

RECENT EVENTS

An October 1999 CURS poll revealed that Romanians were disillusioned with market reforms. Eighty-two percent of those polled thought the privatization process was dishonest.[72] Significantly, majorities also endorsed state control of prices and wages, in addition to state ownership of public utilities. Perhaps in response to the general disillusionment, faltering reforms, IFI misgivings, and continuing coalitional infighting, President Constantinescu replaced Prime Minister Radu Vasile in mid-December 1999.[73] His unexpected replacement was Mugur Isărescu, Governor of the National Bank of Romania, who had resisted several governments' attempts since 1990 to increase the money supply in order to cover up economic decline.

Isŗarescu declared economic reform to be his government's foremost objective.[74] In February 2000, his government planned privatization by the end of 2003, a modernization and diversification of the capital markets; making the business climate more hospitable by dismantling bureaucratic roadblocks and fighting corruption; support for small and medium-sized businesses; and better agricultural marketization.[75] Isărescu's task was formidable but, unlike his PDSR and PNŢCD predecessors, his reform priorities were informed by economic necessities rather than by political obligations. His initial record on budgeting responsibility was been a mixed one, though he managed to halt the three-year slide in most economic indicators, a fate only Romania suffered in the region. After GDP decreases of 6.1, 4.8, and 1.2 percent in 1997, 1998, and 1999, it increased by 1.8 percent in 2000.

Since taking power in early 2001, the PSD (initially PDSR) government led by Adrian Nąstase has had some successes, especially compared with the overall decline under the Constantinescu presidency. Inflation declined to

24.4 percent April 2002, from over 50 percent under Constantinescu. GDP rose by 5.3 percent in 2001 and 4.5 percent in 202. The fiscal deficit was 3.3 percent of GDP in 2001, a slight drop from 3.6 percent in 2000. Unemployment dropped to 10.5 percent in 2000 and to 8.6 percent in 2001, only to rise again to 9.0 percent in 2002. Romania finally got privatization of large firms moving ahead with the sale of the huge steel mill, Sidex, to the Anglo-Indian concern LMN Ispat in September 2001. The BCR Bank, one of Romania's largest, was to have been sold in the second half of 2002, as well.

Yet, the IMF and World Bank were cautious, with the former postponing a loan tranche in May 2002 due to concerns over public management and energy sector liberalization. The IFIs were impressed by the Nąstase government's fiscal policy, marketization of energy prices, austere monetary policy, and reduction in trade account deficits, which resulted from the highest GDP and export growth in the region. Reform of the value added tax and corporate profits tax in 2002 reduced the perverse and increased capital formation incentives. High payroll taxes were also reduced by 8 percent by January 2003. Subsidies to state enterprises have been reduced somewhat, though the lack of accountability maintains this devastating practice. Romania still needs to continue privatizing large state enterprises, especially in the energy sector where subsidies have been greatest, as well as to reduce inflation. Negotiations for entry into the European Union will also lead to greater fiscal and monetary austerity, though the governing PSD will feel pressure to its commitment to a working class voter base, especially in industrial zones like Braşov. More effective retraining programs and incentives for small and medium-sized business needs to be improved. Moreover, the lack of rule of law harms the economy, where property and bankruptcy need to be institutionalized, as well as to assure transparent banking supervision and curtail money laundering funding organized crime, trafficking, and terrorism.

CONCLUSION

How, then, is one to assess the progress of Romanian economic reform? If one bases the evaluation purely on the macroeconomic indicators, then reform programs have not yet led to the economic bottoming out that transition theorists assert must precede recovery. Romania has not yet recovered its 1989 GDP, production, and real salary levels. As of the end of 2000, the percentage of the economy in the state sector was only about 25 percent, compared with 66 percent in 1993 and much higher under Communism. The percentage of the population working agriculture has not markedly decreased since Communism.

Foreign investors stay away from Romania in droves, though that trend has been reversing since 2000. They still fear the ever-present possibility of the retroactive loss of incentives, as occurred in 1999, inconsistent tax policies, bureaucratic corruption and organized crime, and legislative complexity and confusion.[76] Local oligarchic interests also make foreign investors feel as though they are unwelcome competitors to their claims to market share.

However, to dismiss reforms as not having taken place, as did the respected economist Ilie Şerbănescu,[77] is to confuse all reforms with completely positive macroeconomic results. What about the establishment of the framework and the institutions of a market economy, however fragile? What about economic "de-statization" of Romania, with well over 50 percent of GDP currently produced by the private sector?[78] What about the hundreds of thousands of private small businesses which have sprung up (even if ephemeral and treated poorly by the government) and which dominate the trade and service sectors? Progress may not have been impressive, but it has occurred. When evaluated by other criteria Romania has made impressive economic changes over the last ten years. Fully 61.5 percent of the GDP is currently derived from the private sector, with only the industrial sector lagging behind (31.7 percent). More than half of all investment is derived from the private sector, and the service sector continues to grow as a proportion of GDP (43.5 percent).[79]

These numbers, however, mean very little for the man on the street. Inflation since the beginning of 1990 is estimated at more than 84,000 percent.[80] Most Romanians have to make do with a buying power that provides only the barest of necessities, which is nominally only two-thirds of what they had in 1989. Seventy percent of the population earns $2 a day or less, while one-third of all Romanians earn $1 a day or less; officially, they are classified as living in poverty.[81] For most of these people macroeconomic stabilization, privatization, and the reduction of government deficits are not the main issue in reform of the Romanian economy. For them, the issue is one of simple survival.

NOTES

1. Andreas C. Tsantis and Roy Pepper, *Romania: The Industrialization of an Agrarian Economy under Socialist Planning* (Washington, DC: The World Bank, 1979), p. 5.
2. *Ibid.*, pp. 6–7.
3. François Fejtö, "*Socialisme et nationalisme dans les democraties populaires* (1971–1978)," *Défense Nationale*, XXXIV (August–September 1978), pp. 25–26.
4. William E. Crowther, *The Political Economy of Romanian Socialism* (New York: Praeger, 1988), pp. 137–42.
5. Marvin R. Jackson, "Romania's Debt Crisis: Its Causes and Consequences," in *East European Economies: Slow Growth in the 1980's*, Vol. 3, *Country Studies on Eastern Europe and Yugoslavia. Selected Papers Submitted to the Joint Economic Committee, Congress of the United States* (Washington, DC: Government Printing Office, 1986), pp. 503–4.

6. D. G. Denekas and M. S. Khan, *The Romanian Economic Reform Programme* (Washington, DC: The International Monetary Fund, 1991), p. 30, as cited in Derek H. Aldcroft and Steven Morewood, *Economic Change in Eastern Europe Since 1918* (Aldershot: Edward Elgar, 1995), p. 215.

7. Radio Bucharest report of 22 December 1989, as translated and reported in *Foreign Broadcast Information Service, Eastern Europe Daily Report* (hereafter cited as *FBIS*) (26 December 1989), p. 66.

8. AGERPRES dispatch (27 December 1989), as translated and reported in *FBIS* (27 December 1989), pp. 59–60. For an interesting commentary on the first, often confusing FSN pronouncements, see Cristian Bocaneca, *La Roumanie du communisme au post-communisme* (Montreal and Paris: L'Harmattan, 1998), pp. 98–106.

9. Ion Iliescu, *Revoluţie şi reformă* (Bucharest: Editura enciclopedică, 1994), pp. 210–11.

10. *Ibid.*, pp. 212–13; and Nicolae Văcăroiu, *România, jocuri de interese. Carte interviu de Gheorghe Smeoreanu* (Bucharest: Editura Intact, 1998), pp. 40–41.

11. Katherine Verdery and Gail Kligman, "Romania after Ceauşescu: Post-Communist Communism?" in Ivo Banac, ed., *Eastern Europe in Revolution* (Ithaca, NY: Cornell University Press, 1992), p. 124.

12. Michael Shafir, "Romania: Promises and Reality," *RFE/RL Research Institute Report on Eastern Europe*, vol. 2, no. 1 (4 January 1991), p. 33.

13. Bucharest Radio, Domestic Service broadcasts (18 October 1990) and a ROMPRES dispatch (18 October 1990), both translated and reported by *FBIS* (19 October 1990), pp. 36–44.

14. *Banca Naţională a României, Rapoartele anuale 1991–1995* (Bucharest: *Banca Naţională a României*, 1997), statistical section p. 9, hereafter cited as p. 9. It is a significant demonstration of the difficulty of reform that the 1991–1995 annual reports of the central bank were not published until 1997.

15. Michael Shafir, "Romania's Tortuous Road to Reform," *RFE/RL Research Report*, vol. 1 (3 January 1992), pp. 96–97.

16. Dan Ionescu, "Labor Unrest Escalates," *RFE/RL Report on Eastern Europe*, vol. 2. no. 28 (12 July 1991), pp. 19–23.

17. Dan Ionescu, "Riots Topple Petre Roman's Cabinet," *RFE/RL Report on Eastern Europe*, vol. 2, no. 42 (18 October 1991), pp. 18–22.

18. Dan Ionescu, "The New Government," *RFE/RL Report on Eastern Europe*, vol. 2, no. 45 (8 November 1991).

19. Shafir, "Tortuous Road to Reform," p. 97.

20. Based upon my conversations with Theodor Stolojan in Washington, DC, in 1994.

21. Văcăroiu, *Jocuri de interese*, pp. 94–95.

22. *Ibid.*, pp. 96–103.

23. National Bank of Romania, *Annual Report 1997* (Bucharest: National Bank of Romania, 1998), pp. 9–14.

24. Michael Shafir and Dan Ionescu, "Romania: A Crucially Uneventful Year," *RFE/RL Research Report*, vol. 3, no. 1 (7 January 1994), p. 124; and "Romania: The Tangled Path toward Democracy," *Transition*, vol. 1, no. 11 (30 January 1995), pp. 51–52.

25. Organization for Economic Cooperation and Development, *OECD Economic Surveys, 1997–1998: Romania* (Paris: OECD, 1998), pp. 22–23.

26. *From Plan to Market*, pp. 14–15.

27. National Bank of Romania, *Annual Report 1997*, p. 11.

28. Gabor Hunya, "The Romanian Economy in 1993/1994: From Stagnation with Inflation to Stagnation with Stabilization," *Südosteuropa*, vol. 43, no. 11–12 (1994), pp. 629, 636.

29. Dăianu, *Transformation of Economy as a Real Process*, p. 195.

30. *Ibid.*, pp. 196–201; and Yves Van Frausum, Ulrich Gehmann, and Jurgen Gross, "Market Economy and Economic Reform in Romania: Macroeconomic and Microeconomic Perspectives," *Europe-Asia Studies*, vol. 46, no. 5 (1994), p. 742.

31. Pasti, *Challenge of Transition*, pp. 294–307 and 327–39.

32. *BBC* (12 January 1995 and 30 November 1994).

33. National Bank of Romania, *Annual Report 1997*, pp. 9–11.

34. Michael Wyzan, "Economies Continue to Strengthen in Building Democracy," *The OMRI Annual Survey of Eastern Europe and the Former Soviet Union, 1995* (Armonk, NY and London: M. E. Sharpe, 1996), p. 185.

35. Michael Shafir and Dan Ionescu, "Radical Political Change in Romania," *Transition*, vol. 3, no. 2 (7 February 1997), pp. 53–54. From September 1995 to September 1996, the *leu* lost one-third of its value relative to the dollar. National Bank of Romania, *Annual Report 1997*, p. 14.

36. *Ibid.*, p. 9; Michael Wyzan and Ben Slay, "Central, Eastern and Southeastern Europe's Year of Recovery," *Transition*, vol. 3, no. 2 (7 February 1997), p. 60; and *Financial Times* (9 July 1996), p. 2: from *Lexis-Nexis Academic Universe*, hereafter, LNAU.

37. *Eastern Europe, the Fortnightly Political Briefing*, vol. 10, no. 7 (27 March 1996), pp. 4–5; and *Banca Naţională a României, Raport Annual 1996* (Bucharest: *Banca Nationala a Romaniei*, 1997), pp. 109–11.

38. *International Herald Tribune* (2 November 1996), on LNAU; and *Contract cu România*, available at http://info.fx.ro/emil/contract.html.

39. OECD, *Economic Surveys 1997–1998 Romania* (Paris: OECD), pp. 25–26.

40. *Eastern Europe, the Fortnightly Political Briefing*, vol. 11, no. 2 (30 January 1997), p. 5.

41. *Ibid.*, vol. 11, no. 4 (27 February 1997), pp. 5–6. The monthly average *leu* exchange went from 3,333/US$ in January 1997, to 7,960/US$ in December 1997, National Bank of Romania, *Annual Report 1997*, p. 34.

42. Tom Gallagher, "Romania's Desire to Be Normal," *Contemporary Politics*, vol. 4, no. 2 (1998), p. 118; Gabor Hunya, "Romania 1990–2002: Stop-Go Transformation," *Communist Economies and Economic Transformation*, vol. 10, no. 2 (1998), pp. 251–52; and *Eastern Europe, the Fortnightly Political Briefing*, vol. 11, no. 4 (27 February 1997), p. 4.

43. National Bank of Romania, *Annual Report 1997*, pp. 48–50; and Adi Cusin, "The 'Black Holes' of the National Economy," *Romanian Panorama*, vol. 75–76 (1997), pp. 18–20.

44. Hunya, "Stop-Go Transformation," p. 248; IMF Press Release vol. 97, no. 20 (23 April 1997); available at http://www.imf.org/external/np/sec/pr/1997/PR9720.HTM.

45. DPA, (29 December 1997), on LNAU; *The Wall Street Journal Europe's Central European Economic Review*, vol. 4, no.2 (March 1998), pp. 18–21; European Union, *Economic Reform Monitor*, no. 1 (March 1998), p. 2, available at http://europa.eu.int/comm/economy_finance/document/eesupport/1998_1/rom.html.

46. *România liberă* (8 April 1998), p. 8, with a point-by-point comparison of both programs.

47. *Financial Times* (5 May 1998), p. 5 (for the IMF) and translated in *BBC Monitoring Europe Economic* (18 May 1998); citing a ROMPRES dispatch of 15 May 1998 (for the World Bank), both on LNAU.

48. *Financial Times* (18 September 1998), p.2; *Hilfe Country Report*, (September 1998), both on LNAU.

49. *BBC Summary of World Broadcasts* (31 December 1998), EE/WO569/WB, on LNAU.

50. National Bank of Romania, *Annual Report 1998* (Bucharest: National Bank of Romania, 1999), p. 39.

51. *Ibid.*, pp. 9–11; *Comisia națională de statistică, Indicatorii macroeconomici anuali (1998)*, available at www.cns.ro/Indicatori/Ean/Rom/Indicatori_economici_anuali.htm.

52. "Romania," *East European Constitutional Review*, vol. 8, no. 1–2 (Winter/Spring 1999), p. 30 and vol. 8, no. 3 (Summer 1999), pp. 25–26.

53. Quest Economics Data, *Europe Review World of Information: "Romania: Review 1999,"* (11 November 1999), on LNAU.

54. See Liliana Popescu-Bîrlan, "Privatisation and Corruption in Romania," *Crime, Law and Social Change*, vol. 21 (June 1994), pp. 375–79.

55. Patrick Turdy, "Romania," in Ira W. Lieberman, Stilpon S. Nestor, and Raj M. Desai, eds., *Between State and Market: Mass Privatization in Transition Economies* (Washington, DC: The World Bank and the OECD, 1997), pp. 223–24; and John Earle and Almos Telegdy, "*Rezultatele Programului de Privatizare in Masă*," *Sfera Politicii*, no. 59 (April 1998), at www.dntb.ro/sfera/nrcrt/htm.

56. Alina Comşa-Durbacă, "*Radu Sîrbu vrea 1,5 miliarde de dolari pentru Sidex*," *Evenimentul zilei* (15 December 1999), at www.express.ro.

57. Dora Vulcan, "*Un combinat cît un oraş: SIDEX—Titanul în genunchi*," *România liberă* (30 October 1999), at www.romanialibera.com/5FPT/30s5fsid.htm.

58. Ioan Romulus, "Modernisation of the Romanian Steel Industry," *Steel Times*, vol. 227, no. 10 (October 1999), pp. 374–76.

59. *România liberă* (3 March 2000), available at www.romanialibera.com.

60. *Romanian Economic Daily*, vol. 323 (1 March 2000), available at www.romanian-daily.ro.

61. George Stoica, "Remedies for Transition Sickness," *Invest Romania*, no. 14 (Winter 1999–2000), at www.investromania.ro. The percentage of GDP extrapolated from *Business Central Europe, HEC MBA Program*, available at www.bcemag.com/_bcedb/history.ide.

62. Lavigne, *Economics of Transition*, p. 188.

63. E.g., *AFP* (22 May 1998) on Standard and Poor's downgrading and the *Financial Times*, (16 September 1998), p. 46, on Moody's.

64. Colin Jones, "On the Road to Reform," *The Banker*, vol. 149, no. 880 (June 1999), pp. 48–49.

65. *Financial Times* (29 September 1998), Survey-Romania, p. 3.

66. *Euromoney*, no. 360 (April 1999), Wilson Web; *Business Recorder*, 7 March 1999.

67. *Romanian Economic Daily* (30 July–1 August 1999), no. 176; Luminiţa Holban, "Countdown Begins for Giant State Bank," *Bucharest Business Week*, vol. 3, no. 35 (4 October 1999), available at www.bbw.ro.

68. *Evenimentul zilei* (1 August 1999).

69. Jones, "Road to Reform," pp. 47, 49.

70. *Central Europe Online, Romania Today*, (9 February 2000), available at www.centraleurope.com/romaniatoday/business.

71. *IMF Press Release*, vol. 99, no. 38 (5 August 1999). For the banking sector commitments, see Section IIB of the "Memorandum of the Government of Romania on Economic Policies" (26 July 1999).

72. *Adevărul* (8 October 1999), p. 5.

73. *Associated Press* (14 December 1999); *Schweizerische Depeschenagentur* (14 December 1999); AFP (14 December 1999); and *Wirtschaftsblatt* (15 December 1999), all on LNAU.

74. *BBC Summary of World Broadcasts* (23 December 1999), EE/D3725/B; and *The Economist* (25 December 1999), both on LNAU.

75. Camelia Popa, "*PROGRAM: Proiectul guvernamental al strategiei economice pe termen mediu*," *România liberă* (28 February 2000), available at www.romanialibera.com.

76. Mark Meyer, "Crisis of Confidence," *Invest Romania*, vol. 13 (Autumn 1999), available at www.investromania.ro.

77. Ilie Şerbănescu, "The Point of No Return (II)," *Romanian Economic Daily* (23 December 1999).

78. Viorel Salagean, "*Evaluări privind 10 ani de tranziţie în România*," *Adevărul economic*, vol. 404, no. 50 (1999), available at http://adevarul.kappa.ro/eco404.html.

79. *Comisia NaţionalaPentru Statistică*, *Comunicat de presă*, no. 10/2000, available at www.cns.ro.

80. *Ibid.*

81. Herzfeld and Rubin, "Ten Years Later," *The Romanian Digest*, vol. 4, no. 12 (December 1999), available at www.hr.ro.

20

Fiscal and Monetary Policies

Daniel Dăianu

Romania started its transition to a market economy at a serious disadvantage, with significantly worse initial conditions than those prevailing in the leading reform countries.[1] Romanian policy makers have had less room to maneuver[2] in taking the painful political steps necessary to liberalize Romania's formerly Stalinist economic system, and they have yet to find a clear path to a well-functioning market economy and sustainable growth. Some analysts have attributed the current state of economic disequilibria to the breakdown of the political process and rent-seeking activities by old elites.[3] While I agree that such analyses do yield important insights, the approach I adopt in this chapter emphasizes the sheer magnitude of the resource reallocation that would be required in any successful transition to a market economy, and the political and economic friction that this generates, which often undermines credible attempts to achieve durable stabilization. I suggest that the success of the leading transition economies is due primarily to their ability to deal with the magnitude of required resource reallocation (*strain*) and friction while not being "captured" by vested interests.

What lies behind this ability is a big analytical issue itself. Together with this *strain,* institutional fragility helps to explain the phenomenon of stop-go policies (*boom and bust cycles*), as well as many of the setbacks and inconsistencies in the transition process. Consider the lack of transparency which characterizes the realm of Romanian public finance. For example, banks were frequently the vehicle for granting subsidies. Primitive banking systems, which are "captives" of entrenched structures, are likely to perpetuate much of the old pattern of resource allocation (or misallocation) inherent in the old system, and engage in significant quasi-fiscal operations, with the latter manifesting as in high rates of inflation or of bank failures.

Romania's experience is a highly relevant example of how *strain* and institutional fragility condition macroeconomic stabilization. In the following analysis of economic developments in Romania from 1990–2002, I suggest that stop-go policies, resurgent inflation, bank failures, and overall macrodisequilibria have been an inevitable outcome of insufficient restructuring and fragile institutions. I submit that large inflows of foreign direct investment (FDI) and the creation of appropriate institutions are essential so that the economy escape from the grip of entrenched structures. The role of the European Union (EU) in providing *The Big Push* for modernization is also examined.

INITIAL CONDITIONS

In comparative analyses of transition economies, insufficient attention has been paid to the initial conditions prevailing when the transformation process got under way.[4] Communist Romania, particularly in the 1970s and 1980s, provides an interesting and instructive case of *immiserizing growth* that was caused by the logic of the system, in particular, the rush to speed up industrial growth and to increase ties with market economies on a very weak functional basis (by totally ignoring market mechanisms). In the literature, this phenomenon is explained by the existence of various price distortions which harm resource allocation, worsen the terms of trade, and lower welfare.[5] But it can also be argued that it was the way the economy functioned as a whole (including the genesis of wrong industrial choices) which constituted *the* distortion that led to *immiserizing growth*. It was shown that the inner dynamics of the system—its incapacity to cope with increasing complexity, and its inability to assimilate and generate technological progress—led to a "softening" of output, characterized by expansion, but with a strong bias toward low value-added industrial goods, which led to a steady deterioration of the terms of trade.[6]

Since *immiserizing growth* limited the potential to increase exports, the targeted trade surpluses of the 1980s—required to pay back the external debt—were achieved through very large cuts in hard currency imports. Apart from the reduced level of investment, growth possibilities were also impaired by a sharp reduction in imports of machinery and equipment from the West. The heavy overtaxation of domestic consumption, which took place during this period in order to meet external debt obligations, resulted in lower growth rates of production, reduced welfare (consumption), and bigger domestic imbalances (both visible and hidden). The immiserizing nature of "growth" in Communist Romania is well illustrated by its income per capita (which has remained one of the lowest in Europe) and the very high energy intensity of its gross domestic product (GDP).[7] Another telling fact is that whereas the GDP (allegedly) grew by almost 28 percent during the 1980s, exports over the same period actually decreased.

The structure of Romanian industry revealed a strong bias toward the creation of gigantic units, with almost no regard for the small and medium-sized enterprises, which are important sources of flexibility in an economy. Prior to the revolution in 1989, 1,075 enterprises of more than 1,000 employees each accounted for, in total, more than 51 percent of all industrial enterprise in Romania. They provided jobs for 87 percent of all industrial workers and supplied almost 85 percent of all industrial output. Enterprises with over 3,000 workers (which accounted for about 16 percent of the total) supplied over 50 percent of total industrial output and provided jobs for 53 percent of all employees in industry. At the same time, the small and medium-sized enterprises (with less than 500 employees) accounted for 4 percent of all workers and 6 percent of total industrial output. The forced reduction of the external debt in the 1980s (a sui generis shock therapy) accentuated the decline in the competitiveness of the economy, exacerbated imbalances among sectors, increased shortages, and generally lowered the welfare of the people.

THE FIRST TRANSFORMATIONAL RECESSION[8]

The early years of post-Communism in Romania were marred by a very large fall in economic output (see table 20.1 at the end of this chapter), an institutional interregnum,[9] and "systematic" policy incoherence. By institutional interregnum, we refer to the melting down of much of the old institutional structure without a concomitant rapid buildup of market-based institutions (this hiatus explains the implosion of public revenues as well). This, obviously, contributed to increasing uncertainty and volatility in the national economic environment. As the inherited structures were in the process of breaking up, the quantity of friction in the system went up considerably, and important energies (resources) were consumed in order to accommodate change. Much boils down not only to a change of the organizational behavior of actors, but to the buildup of new organizational capital. In this phase, market coordination failures combined with an "abandoned child" feeling of many enterprises, which were no longer able to rely on central allocation of resources and customers.[10] For these enterprises, information and transaction costs skyrocketed.[11]

Despite its tortuous path, some institutional change did take place during those years—through spontaneous processes, such as massive land privatization, the emergence of a private sector (which preceded Law 54 of 1990 on the setting up of private enterprises),[12] and measures "from above" initiated by the government. Among the latter was the establishment of the two-tiered banking system (in 1990), the commercialization of state-owned enterprises (Law 15 of 1990), and the privatization Law 58 of 1991, which aimed at giving 30 percent of the equity of commercial companies to Romanian citizens.[13] What happened with the privatization law is symptomatic of the vacillations and inconsistencies of reform policies during that period; Law 58 of 1991 created much confusion regarding the actual structure of property rights and the need for better management of assets.

Overall, and in a formal sense, it can be said that policy makers practiced a sort of "institutional mimicking" by trying to adopt, although in a highly inconsistent way, institutions found in the Western world. A problem with institutional mimicking, however, is that it cannot deal with the fine print of reforms, and it frequently lacks substance because the real functioning of institutions is driven by vested interests.

After December 1989, there was tremendous *pressure from below*, resulting from the years of severe deprivation in the 1980s, to consume tradeables, to reduce exports, and to boost imports of both consumer and intermediate goods. The switch in favor of tradeables was almost instantaneous and virtually unstoppable; it was also strengthened by a "shunning of domestic goods" syndrome. In 1990, the boost in consumption was financed primarily by "dis-saving" (the depletion of foreign exchange reserves).

However, there is another side of the story that needs to be highlighted: policy makers complicated the state of the economy both by commission and omission. By commission, we mean that they faltered in the face of pressures from below and were influenced by the prospect of elections in May 1990. This resulted in the concession of large wage rises[14] and the introduction of the five-day workweek, despite the fact that output was plummeting. Together with the maintenance of wide-ranging price controls, a greatly overvalued exchange rate, and the overall mismanagement of foreign exchange reserves, this action contributed significantly to the resulting disequilibria in the Romanian economy. By omission, we mean that there were no serious attempts to deal with macroeconomic imbalances before November 1990. Events during that year revealed a fundamental flaw in the transformation process: the considerable decision-making power of enterprises when they do not face hard-budget constraints.

Confronted with a rapid deterioration of the economy and unable to contain the growing disequilibria (unsustainable trade deficits, rising prices, and vanishing investment), the Romanian government introduced a stabilization plan supported by the International Monetary Fund (IMF) at the start of 1991.[15] The middle-of-the-road, gradual stabilization program that took shape included a tightening of fiscal and monetary policy (although real interest rates remained highly negative), a tax-based incomes policy, a new devaluation of the currency, and the introduction of a two-tier exchange rate system. The program failed to stop inflation, however. Political factors, linked with the coming elections of September 1992, also weakened the determination of the government to pursue a consistent policy.

1993-1994: "THE INTEREST RATE SHOCK"

Rising inflation and the persistence of a large trade imbalance eventually forced a reconsideration of policies. A breakthrough occurred in the last quarter of 1993 when several key decisions were made in order to contain and reverse the dynamics of inflationary expectations, to start the remonetization of the economy, and to create a transparent, functioning foreign exchange market. An omission in the strategy, however, was the lack of a more clear definition of property rights (privatization), which could have had a major influence on the size of capital inflows, and on the scope and intensity of restructuring.

The main decision, a dramatic rise in nominal interest rates, led to positive real interest rates. This measure had two major consequences. First, it stemmed the flight from the *leu* and started a rapid rate of remonetization. Second, it greatly helped the formation of a transparent foreign exchange market, and thereby strengthened the potential for an export drive. The scale of remonetization explains why the policy shock of 1994 did not lead to a decline of output as had been the case in 1997 (when the economy was subject to a credit crunch). Another key decision was the substantial devaluation (in several stages) of the official, interbank market exchange rate, lowering it, more or less, to the rate prevailing on the grey market. This also increased the transparency of the foreign exchange market, which, in turn, reduced considerably the entry costs for those in need of foreign exchange. The third measure involved a stricter control of base money, and consequently, a reduced rate of money creation. Finally, the fiscal policy was tightened in order to achieve a lower budget deficit (when corrected for the removal of some explicit and implicit subsidies).[16]

Overall, the economy absorbed the policy shock quite well. The ensuing export drive played a major role in the recovery, but it cannot explain why so many enterprises in the weak sectors also did well in 1993, especially as arrears did not "appear" to be rising sharply in 1994.[17] Several explanations can be suggested. One is the existence of important market imperfections, such as monopolies that can extract rents and can operate in the less efficient sectors. Another is that there are huge amounts of "X-inefficiency" in the system. This means that potential micro-efficiency gains are ubiquitous and that, when under pressure, even firms in the backward sectors can realize some of them and cope with the situation. But accepting this explanation requires an evaluation of the resilience of *organizational routines* in the system. An implication of the X-inefficiency explanation is that the pressure for fundamental restructuring begins to bite only when most of the efficiency reserves are exhausted. A third explanation is that there was more reliance on self-financing, although many companies were in fact plagued by a lack of working capital. Last, but not least, unwarranted bank lending (rollover of loans) may have played a significant role in supporting the weaker enterprises.

1995–1996: RELAPSE INTO INFLATION

Romania experienced rapid growth in GDP in 1995: 7.1 percent as compared with just under 4 percent in 1994 and under 2 percent in 1993. At the same time, the inflation rate at the end of 1995 was about 28 percent. The remonetization of the economy continued, as indicated by the expansion of the money supply (71 percent), which far exceeded the rate of inflation (see table 20.1). While exports continued to grow rapidly (by over 20 percent), imports increased by more than 30 percent, causing the trade imbalance to increase again to more than $1.2 billion, and putting pressure on the foreign exchange (interbank) market. What caused the trade imbalance to deteriorate again? Without wishing to dismiss other factors, I would suggest that the higher growth rate of the economy, driven by highly import-dependent branches, led to overheating and the rapid growth of imports.

There was a clear link between inflation and the way the budget deficit was financed in 1996. Whereas the target for the consolidated budget deficit was 2.2 percent, it turned out to be more like 5.7 percent on an accrual basis. More significant than the actual amount of the deficit was the fact that its financing was inflationary. Its effects were compounded by the large infusions of base money that were made to cover a quasi-fiscal deficit which had arisen due to losses in agriculture and the *regies autonomes*. Together, the fiscal imbalance reached 8.4 percent (on an accrual basis) in 1996.

Remonetization had supported the efforts to subdue inflation in 1994 and 1995. Regarding remonetization, several aspects should be emphasized: (a) it involved the expansion of base money through the increase of net domestic assets and not through the accumulation of net foreign assets; (b) it facilitated the subsidization of various sectors of the economy (agriculture, energy) out of the Central Bank's resources, allowing it to simultaneously pursue the goal of reducing inflation; (c) it "helped" put off dealing resolutely with failed banks; and (d) it slowed down the development of monetary policy instruments, namely open market operations. This is because the Central Bank did not face the pressure to cope with a surge of liquidity as would have been the case with substantial capital inflows.

By the end of 1996, several worrisome tendencies had emerged: a very sharp rise in the monthly inflation rate (which was in double digits in the last quarter of the year); the sharp rise in trade and current account deficits (although the growth rate of GDP was lower than in 1995—3.9 percent as compared with 7.1 percent); and still greater distortions in relative prices, due in particular to the delay in adjusting energy prices and to the administrative control of the exchange rate. As the remonetization process came to a halt in the latter half of 1996, maintaining subsidies without igniting inflation was to prove an impossible endeavor. The inflation rate at the end of the year had reached 57 percent. Furthermore, despite heavy borrowing (over $1.5 billion) on the international capital markets,[18] by the end of 1996, the foreign exchange reserves of the National Bank stood at only $700 million.

Moreover, the Romanian external debt was rising rapidly—with peak payments looming in the coming years—while the policies of the Government (multiple exchange rates, price controls, subsidies, etc.) were making it increasingly unlikely that a new arrangement could be reached with the IMF. Such developments were clearly leading to a dead end, making it self-evident that a change of policy was urgently required. The events of 1995 and 1996 underscored both the importance of privatization as well as the danger of "populist macroeconomics."[19]

1997: THE SECOND "TRANSFORMATIONAL RECESSION"

The elections of November 1996 brought new political forces into power: the former opposition, with a platform that was more oriented toward privatization and market-oriented reforms. The first step of the new government was to liberalize the foreign exchange market and other prices which were still regulated by the state. Paradoxically, in a year when renewed efforts were made to achieve macroeconomic stabilization, the expected annual inflation rate, at 90 percent, was much higher than a year earlier in 1996, when it stood at 57 percent. The explanation lies in the sheer magnitude of the effect that the liberalizing of prices and the anticipated devaluation of the *leu* had on the Romanian economy.[20]

The new policy did have some positive results, however: the foreign exchange market finally began to function adequately. The consolidated budget deficit (including formerly quasi-fiscal operations) was reduced to 3.7 percent of GDP;[21] the current account deficit shrank from 7.2 percent to 6.6 percent of GDP; and the Central Bank's foreign exchange reserves soared to about \$2.6 billion.[22] The size of the fiscal adjustment should also be seen against the backdrop of the sharp fall in output, which reduced the tax base considerably. But there was a dark side of the story: The actual inflation rate turned out to be an astonishing 151 percent for 1997, while the GDP fell much more than expected (-6.1 percent compared with -2 percent). Both policy-induced demand and supply shocks lie behind the plunge of the economy; they explain the start of the second "transformational recession."

Another deleterious consequence of the new program was its severe impact on the emerging private sector. The contraction of real credit considerably lowered the prospects of many small and medium-sized companies, and was a major factor in the fall of output. Total real credit (in domestic and foreign currency) declined by 52.5 percent in 1997, and its nongovernment component by as much as 61.3 percent. This development was the reason behind the growing chorus of demands in the private sector for fiscal relaxation; these demands became very intense during 1998. Ironically, a program which had been designed to advance the process of reform in Romania actually wound up hurting the emerging entrepreneurial class and, due to the degree of austerity involved, encouraged the expansion of the underground economy

The delay in the restructuring of major "producers" of arrears—a key element in the reform process—was due to the inherent problems of such an operation when the economy was in steep decline: On the one hand, the overall measures aimed at restructuring implied the need for layoffs, but on the other hand, the troubles confronting the small and medium-sized enterprises in the private sector, a direct consequence of the austerity measures, were discouraging the creation of new job opportunities. Privatization of large enterprises dragged, as did measures for bank privatization. Such a situation provided little incentive for foreign direct investment, exacerbating the shortage of hard currency and further exacerbating the inflationary effects on the Romanian economy. It was clear was that, owing to the very tight credit conditions, a continuation of growth was hardly possible for the year, and this is why the program anticipated a 2 percent decline in GDP.

One might question the decision to undertake a nominal reduction of base money in the first quarter of 1997 instead of, for instance, keeping the money supply fixed for a while. Also, one might question the decision to float the exchange rate concurrent to this. The floating of the exchange rate could have followed the correction of the inflationary surge that had been set off by the excessively rapid expansion of base money in late 1996. I also submit that if Romania had benefited from a stabilization fund (as Poland had in 1991), the *leu* overshooting in the first quarter of 1997 would have been much smaller. Arguably, it would have reduced the rate of inflation and possibly mitigated the fall in output. There might also have been a closer and more critical look at the size of tariff reductions proposed for agriculture. I would conclude that policy makers had underestimated the scale and extent of supply rigidities in the economy when they undertook these decisions, which had some very unwelcome consequences for the Romanian economy.

In 1998, the GDP continued its decline (by -4.8 percent). At year's end, unemployment stood at 10.3 percent (as opposed to 6.6 percent only two years earlier). Inflation fell to 40.6 percent, and the consolidated budget deficit (including privatization revenues) amounted to 3.3 percent. The latter should be seen against the background of a further reduction of the tax base (because of the fall in output) and the implications for government spending on the rescue package put together for the two state-owned banks. Actually, the budget deficit was kept under control by a very severe cut in public expenditures which had been undertaken in August.

Based on consumer prices, the exchange rate appreciated in real terms by about 30 percent from mid-1997 (after the sharp devaluation at the start of that year), which helps to explain the rising trade and current account deficits in 1998. The foreign exchange reserves of the National Bank declined to less than $1.9 billion at the end of the year, a result of its interventions to stem the fall of the *leu*. Excessively lax income policy also helps to explain the size of domestic absorption in a year when there was a further contraction of output. Real wages actually grew by about 6 percent (see table 20.1).

The fallout from the financial crisis in Russia led to the postponement of new external bond issues and cast doubt on the possibility of rolling over a portion of the external debt in 1999. Because of the size of payments due in 1999 (about $2.9 billion), there was threat of a financial crisis and default. This threat explains the considerable efforts to conclude privatisation deals at the end of 1998 (*Romtelecom*, Romanian Development Bank, etc.) and the attempt to deal more firmly with large, loss-making companies.

1999: AVERTING A MAJOR FINANCIAL CRISIS

The year 1999 highlighted three major interlinked threats and policy challenges: the risk of external payment default;[23] the danger of a banking crisis due to the scale of bad loans and the reduction of the foreign exchange reserves of the central bank (which were less than base money and insufficient to stem a run on banks);[24] and a possible financial crisis, as a result of persistently high real interest rates and the bailouts in the banking system. This threat was reinforced by the IMF's new philosophy of burden sharing with private investors, introduced in the context of their withdrawal from emerging markets. Romania's sovereign risk was downgraded to B- (B3) by the leading rating agencies. That move was quite ironic because Romania was not a heavily indebted country; the external debt was below 30 percent of GDP, but the bulging service payments (against the background of the deteriorating international environment) were prefacing a very serious liquidity crisis.

Practically denied access to international private capital markets—due to exorbitant spreads—Romania was able to avert a default through an exceptional balance of payments adjustment. The latter involved substantial expenditure switching and cutting, which almost halved the current account deficit from 7.2 percent in 1998 to 3.8 percent of GDP in 1999. The national currency (*leu*) depreciated considerably in real terms, and the budget deficit was brought to 2.2 percent (when privatization revenues are excluded). But this depreciation caused inflation to climb again, to about 55 percent in 1999.

CAN THE CURRENT ECONOMIC RECOVERY LAST?

Following the pains of 1999, the year 2000 revealed signs of economic recovery. The drop in economic activity was reversed, inflation started to come down again, and an export boom occurred. The surge of exports was enhanced by a much more favorable taxation policy for export-oriented activities (a 5 percent profit tax, compared with the norm of 25 percent). It should be said that the IMF is nudging the Romanian government to end this favorable fiscal treatment of exports. The GDP rose by 1.6 percent in 2000 and inflation came down to 40.7 percent.

Significantly, too, although Romania had some trouble in its financial markets during 2000, the banking system withstood the pressure and continued its convalescence (after the failures of two major state-owned banks, Bancorex and Banca Agricola). As a matter of fact, a massive cleanup of the banking system has taken place in the last few years. At the same time, the share of the private sector in the banking system has increased considerably.

Elections were held in late 2000 and the center-left Social Democratic Party (PSD—formerly PDSR) gained overwhelmingly, which allowed it to form a government on its own, albeit it used the tacit support of the Hungarian Party (UDMR) in order to pass through significant legislation. Actually, the PSD got back in power after a lapse of four years (1997–2000), when the country was ruled by a coalition made up of the Democratic Convention (CDR), the Democratic Party (PD), and the Hungarian Party (UDMR).

Economic recovery speeded up in 2001, with a 5.3 percent rise in GDP. And disinflation has been well under way: from 40.7 percent (December to December) in 2000, inflation dropped to 30.3 percent in 2001. The cleanup of the banking system took another step forward in the sale of Banca Agricola to a foreign consortium led by Reiffeisen. The privatization of the big steel plant, Sidex, was probably the biggest economic event of 2001. This deal would likely save the jobs of thousands of workers and help unburden the public budget of the giant steel conglomerate, which used to cost the budget about 200 USD yearly.

Staying the course of recovery, improving financial discipline and tax collection, implementing prudent wage policy and continuing privatization dominated the economic policy agenda in 2002. Due to the worldwide economic slowdown, and in order to improve financial discipline in the economy and to control the current account deficit, the increase of the GDP is likely to slow to 4.5 percent in 2002, while the current account deficit is expected to remain in the range of 5.5–6 percent of GDP. The budget deficit is programmed to shrink to about 3 percent of GDP, which should help fight inflation and control the external accounts. It will not be easy for the government to reduce inflation to a single-digit level in the next few years. Inflation has become chronic; many enterprises "need" inflation in order to deal with arrears (reduce them in real terms and even get implicit subsidies), and inflationary expectations are quite powerful. But the results of disinflation went beyond expectations, with inflation likely to come around 18 percent in 2002. Clearly, further disinflation hinges heavily on containing arrears so that the economy does not face bottlenecks and policy credibility is not damaged. The upgrading of Romania's sovereign risk, to B+, by S&P and Moody's during 2002, was also good news.

Where does foreign direct investment (FDI) come into the picture? Romania has not been able to attract sufficient foreign direct investment considering the size of its economy, the magnitude of required industrial restructuring and the needs of building up the infrastructure. At the end of 2001, total FDI stood at 7.8 bn USD, far below the volumes registered in Poland, Hungary, and the Czech Republic. The top countries, by investment, as of 30 September 2001 were the Netherlands (14.5 percent), Germany (10.2 percent), France (9.2 percent), the U.S. (8.1 percent), Italy (7 percent), and Austria (7 percent).

Attracting more FDI is a major concern, as it is sorely needed to restructure and modernize the energy production and distribution sector. Clearly, the government needs to foster privatization in the energy sector as a way to bring in capital and impose hard budget constraints. But privatization is not enough. In order to achieve good economic performance in the energy sector, privatization should be accompanied by good corporate governance and an effectively implemented regulatory framework that can deal with monopoly behavior, secure fair prices for consumers, and avoid external overindebtedness.

Romania now has a chance to overcome the familiar boom and bust cycle that characterized its economic evolution over the past decade. The chance must be taken, for this cycle has meant a heavy social cost on the country. For policy makers, this means a tremendous challenge in the years to come—the challenge to battle social fatigue and frustration with policies fostering growth while protecting social cohesion. However, for long-term success the country must continue structural reforms: implementing financial discipline and effective structures of corporate governance, attracting more foreign capital inflows (including foreign direct investment), and developing the financial and banking systems.

CASE STUDY: THE TURNAROUND OF SIDEX: CAN OTHERS FOLLOW?

The privatization of Sidex—the largest steel maker in southeastern Europe—in the second half of 2001 was arguably a milestone of structural transformation in the Romanian economy. Sidex was regarded as one of the largest "black holes" of the economy, becoming an ever-growing burden for the state budget. The lack of a resolute approach on Sidex had been thought to illustrate the insufficient advance of the reform process in Romania; social constraints, underperforming management, and industry-specific problems added to the problem. The new owner of Sidex, LNM ISPAT, a global player in the steel industry, faced the difficult task of turning Sidex performances around. The year 2002 witnessed history in the making; Sidex financial results appear encouraging, while the feared social bomb has not blown off.

The seller's eagerness to sell is a major ingredient in the LNM Group's success. Governments in emerging economies, or in more conservative states, want to escape social pressures and fiscal burdening; at least in the Eastern countries, some international financial institutions give a willing hand as well: EBRD granted a $100 million loan for the LNM's investments in Sidex, and a $450 million loan for the LNM's investments in Karmet. The scandal that burst out in Britain, stressing a contribution from Mittal to Tony Blair's campaign, followed by a letter signed by Blair and addressed to the Romanian Prime Minister in support of the privatization of Sidex, fueled allegations of external political endorsement, not to say pressures, in favor of the Sidex deal. It is noteworthy that the privatization of Sidex marked high on the agenda of IMF and World Bank programs in Romania, and the privatization of Nova Hut came only weeks before general elections were held in the Czech Republic.

Coincidentally or not, another factor that might have influenced LNM's decision to invest in Romania is that the country, considered to belong to the group of developing economies, is therefore exempted from the 30 percent surcharge on steel imports imposed by the U.S. only a few months after the acquisition of Sidex. The LNM Group avoids this barrier through its affiliates in Trinidad and Tobago, Romania, and Algeria, not to mention that it is the only global competitor to run plants in each of the three NAFTA countries. It should be noted that, given the industry turmoil, Sidex's difficult financial position, and other competitors' lack of interest for Eastern European mills, LNM was probably the only potential investor with a global exposure willing to take over the operations of Sidex.

THE SIDEX SALE

LNM's acquisition practice indicates a tendency for paying low amounts for the controlling stake (seeking for market power inducements wherever possible), and committing to invest more in restructuring and technological and environmental upgrading. The Sidex case, quite similar to that of Karmet, made no exception from this approach, as a result of LNM's strong bargaining power and, correspondingly, the low bargaining power of the Romanian state.

The final deal, as set out in the Emergency Ordinance 119 of September 2001—which came to be known as the "Sidex ordinance"—provides LNM with a wide range of incentives and facilities: (1) a debt-equity swap, as all receivables owned by state institutions, companies, and authorities over Sidex were converted into shares, at the nominal rate of 25,000 lei/share. Subsequently, these resulting shares were sold to LNM at a rate of 3,300 lei/share. Existing minority shareholders at that time, two SIFs included, were not permitted to contribute to the corresponding increase in social capital; (2) five years of exemption from customs duties and VAT for imports of equipment, raw materials, and other products related to technological and environmental upgrading; (3) five years VAT exemption on domestic market acquisitions related to technological and environmental upgrading; (4) three years postponement of VAT payable for all other types of transactions; (5) three years postponement of social contributions; (6) five years profit tax exemption; (7) a series of employees' rights are to be provided by the state in case of individual leaves.

The debt equity swap is a common practice in the acquisition of heavily indebted companies. It erases overdue debts (at a discount premium) and it gives the buyer the opportunity to start the operations without historic debts. The LNM itself obtained a similar deal on the acquisition of Nova Hut, all debts to the state being canceled and a large banking loan being rescheduled. However, this should not make us disregard the fact that such global hunters, LNM included, end up paying almost nothing for the assets of the companies they bought. The Mexican company bought by Ispat is a very modern one, built up by the Mexican government in the 1980s for over $2.2 billion; Ispat bought it for an aggregate sum of just above $200 million.

Sidex total assets amounted to over $1.1 billion at the time of acquisition; yet, it is unclear how much LNM actually paid for the business as such (if one leaves debts aside). One might be tempted to submit that the total sum paid by LNM for Sidex only covers for the equity derived from the debt-equity swap. LNM paid $70 million to the Romanian state in exchange for around 90 percent of Sidex, including a 70 percent stake hold by APAPS and an almost 20 percent stake resulted from the debt-equity swap. Sidex financial statements recorded, at the end of December 2001, an increase in social capital, in the form of subscribed unpaid capital, of an amount slightly above $70 million. This subscribed capital was then paid, according to Sidex financial statements as of first semester 2002. Sidex liabilities diminished by around $770 million between end of first semester and end of year 2001 (in this time interval, the "Sidex ordinance" came into force). If we transform this difference in liabilities, at a rate of 9 cents per dollar—as is suggested to us by the discount rate applied in the debt-equity swap—it results in a sum exceeding $69 million. Another striking feature of the postprivatization episode, allegedly not comprised in the privatization deal is that the Romanian government, using RICOP resources as well, is supporting the Ispat and Sidex plans of job reductions (7,400 employees voluntarily left jobs to take advantage of various compensatory schemes); monthly payments add to about $1.3 million and are expected to last until end of 2004.

These controversial aspects asides, one must admit that the new owner of Sidex is doing well to cut costs, improve efficiency, and even increase production. The key elements of the restructuring program implemented by

LNM representatives at Sidex include: top local management was replaced by LNM Group senior executives; an end to the barter system; long-term supply contracts were negotiated; and a system of authorized dealers was implemented. These moves, among other restructuring efforts, led to improved financial indicators shortly after the acquisition. It is remarkable that turnover increased while the number of employees shrank by almost one-quarter. These results should, nevertheless, be treated with precaution, as the financial records of such a global corporation like LNM is a complex web of financial links; one should not overlook the fact that affiliate profitability is influenced by the thrive to achieve overall profitability, and that profits are sometimes recorded on purpose in those countries with a more favorable fiscal environment. In Romania, LNM benefits from numerous fiscal incentives, as described previously.

Is Sidex a Model to be Replicated?

The first thing to emphasize in the Sidex case is the specificity of the industry. Steel is a commodity, hence steel products[15] made in Romania are, at least in theory, competing with steel products elsewhere. From this perspective, the steel industry is comparable to the cement industry. Cement is one of the success stories of the privatization process in Romania; foreign capital has become predominant in this industry since 1998 (following the Lafarge–Romcim deal), and all the major five cement producers in Romania are now owned by foreign companies. Most privatization deals on this market were the result of direct sales, as was the case for Sidex as well. On the other hand, post-privatization competition in the cement industry proved limited, as a former oligopoly industry has changed to a sum of regional monopolies (allocation of market shares between competitors).

Another feature of Sidex is that it already had a large domestic market. Sidex products, despite alleged low quality, had numerous domestic buyers, given their price and accessibility. In this respect, Sidex can be compared to the carmaker Dacia. Dacia had a large domestic market, despite an allegedly low quality product. Although carma king is a global industry, the competing products are different in terms of quality and brand awareness; the product is not a commodity. Renault announced plans for a new car produced at the Dacia plant that would be competitive in foreign markets; however, four years after privatization, Dacia's focus is still in the domestic market. Better management techniques were certainly introduced by Renault, yet the results could not had been as spectacular as in the Sidex case. Steel does not need to be reinvented to make it profitable and competitive in world markets; cars do sometimes, and Dacia is an example. The domestic market is a buffer for Renault's Dacia, until technological upgrading makes the car competitive abroad. Such a buffer does not exist, unfortunately, for other poorly performing industries and firms in Romania. The truck-maker Roman, for example, does not have a sufficient domestic market. The turnover/employee ratio, as of December 2001, was around $4,300, as compared to the Sidex pre-restructuring turnover/employee ratio (also on December 2001), which was $28,300. Roman loses almost $1 for each $2 sold. Roman has constantly lost domestic market in favor of imported trucks. ARO and ROCAR have also constantly lost domestic market in favor of imported vehicles, making them unattractive for a potential buyer in quest for a competitive product. In their cases, technological upgrading is probably more expensive than the cost of greenfield investment, not to mention that, in a restructuring, sensitive job cuts need to be taken. Good examples in this regard are Landini-Laverda in the tractor making and INA-FAG in roll-bear industry. These two foreign investors decided not to buy Tractorul, respectively Rulmentul Braşov, but to set up new production facilities (in Buzau and, ironically, Braşov).

To replicate the Sidex story for another company, we need not only a similar commodity or type of industry and an existing market potential for a company's products, but also, and maybe foremost, another LNM-type of investor. This is to say a global player in the respective industry, aiming at creating competitive advantage over global competitors by taking over emerging markets. In Romania, LNM obtained numerous fiscal facilities, debt swaps at discount rates, and a global advantage by avoiding the U.S. surcharge on imported steel.

Can another foreign investor obtain similar market power inducements? They actually did, but failed in most cases to make a more competitive product and to increase overall welfare. OTE–Romtelecom and Noble Ventures–CS Reşita deals are noteworthy. Both investors obtained numerous facilities and incentives, but the final result was disappointing; CS Reşita is now back under state's administration, while OTE scored rising operational losses and was even fined by the Competition Council for monopolist behavior. An explanation why these deals underperformed might be that these foreign investors had no global reach. They were, at best, regional or niche players; their managerial experience in reviving distressed companies was limited, and their international network was not sufficiently expanded. Therefore, the incentives and facilities obtained in Romania offered them a local competitive advantage, but not a global competitive advantage. This does not rule out the possibility that companies without a global exposure could engage in taking over troublemaking industries or firms. Such cases are, however, the exception rather than the rule, and case-by-case explanations can be found. Take the local investor MYO-O, who bought Semanatoarea a few years ago (after the global investor New Holland abandoned acquisition plans) and is now close to finalizing negotiations for Tractorul Braşov. MYO-O actually used to be a dealer for Semanatoarea and Tractorul products and their market knowledge probably lies behind their acquisitions.

The Sidex case should not be regarded as a benchmark for other large loss-making companies, unless a mix of conditions is met: a commodity-type of industry, or at least an industry with an appetite for consolidation; an existing demand for a company's products; and a global reach investor with focus on emerging markets. This is not to say that other stories (it is too early yet to call them success stories) could not occur, but not necessarily following the Sidex example. The improved financial indicators of Sidex should be treated with caution, given the complex web of financial relations within such a transnational corporation as the LNM Group. Moreover, a precedent has recently been set within the LNM Group regarding disinvestment. LNM closed its Irish mills in mid-2001, only a few years after acquiring them and few months before buying Sidex. It is worth mentioning that, of all countries with LNM operations, Ireland was probably the one with the fastest pace of real convergence with the EU, in terms of wage differentials and environmental norms. The expected time of Romania's admission in the EU, 2007, coincides with the moment LNM's fiscal incentives at Sidex come to an end.

THE OUTLOOK IN MID-2003

Economic recovery has continued after years of massive decline of overall production and a drastic balance of payments adjustment in the late 1990s. The rise in the GDP has been quite rapid in the last couple of years, which matches an evolution one encounters in other accession countries as well. The increase of the GDP in the first quarter of 2003 was estimated by the National Institute of Statistics at 4.4 percent, albeit a question mark arises in this respect in view of the slowed-down pace of industrial production and services during that quarter (these sectors have grown by 2.5 and 3.6 percent, respectively, in the same period).

Disinflation has been well underway, and the economy is moving toward the single digit frontier, which would mark a major achievement against the past decade. Arguably, the U.S. dollar depreciation (vis-à-vis the Euro) in 2002 played a significant role in mitigating inflationary expectations and a quasi-exchange rate based stabilization program operated last year.

Romania has been running relatively small current account (cca) deficits in recent years—below 4 percent in 2002. These deficits have bolstered the country's credentials to get improved ratings and to more cheaply access foreign capital markets. In fact, Romania received better ratings from the main agencies in 2002 (BB-), but is still several notches below an investment grade. Budget deficits of around 3 percent were registered in the last few years, which meet the benchmark set by the Maastricht criteria for EU accession; in 2002, the budget deficit was -2.67 percent. The economy has a low external indebtedness, of cca 30 percent of GDP, and a small part of it is short-term; this fact helps to access foreign capital markets. There has been a large expansion of trade in recent years, but low value-added products continue to hold a major share. Likewise, domestic credit has grown quite rapidly in the same period of time, which supported the growth of the nongovernmental sector and of the economy in general. Capital account liberalization is programmed to be completed, in the main, by 2004. However, two restrictions are put in place; one regards transactions in the Romanian money markets by nonresidents and purchases of land by nonresidents.

The macroeconomic premises underlined above need to be judged against the background of a series of structural features of the Romanian economy that condition its future dynamics:

- whereas the private sector accounts for more than 66 percent of GDP, financial indiscipline continues to be quite high—arrears afflict the energy sector in particular (the losses in this sector amounted to cca 2 percent of GDP in 2002, according to some estimates);
- there is an ongoing crisis of social security, which is due primarily to the stark imbalance between the active and retired population and its aging;
- while the banking sector is much cleaner currently (as evidenced by the small share of nonperforming loans) than in the late 1990s, there is heavy dollarization of the economy (60 percent of deposits are hard currency denominated);
- monetization is low (M2 is only 25 percent of GDP), which exposes the economy to the impact of large swings of capital flows and implies high costs of sterilization for the Central Bank; the low monetization reveals some pitfalls of a too-fast liberalization of the capital account;
- the low current account deficits of recent years have been enhanced by rising remittances from abroad (over $1.5 billion in 2002)—Romania has become a significant exporter of both skilled and unskilled labor.

MACROECONOMIC POLICIES IN 2002 AND 2003

In order to continue disinflation simultaneously with economic growth, macroeconomic policy has relied on a special complexion of its mix. The main traits of this policy mix have been: (a) keeping the budget deficits low and relaxing the tight monetary policy, so that the latter supports economic recovery; (b) a real exchange-rate appreciation as against a currency basket, in order to help disinflation; and (c) declining lending interest rates in ROL (the domestic currency) in order to enhance domestic credit, at a time when hard currency denominated credit grew, arguably in excess. There are several domestic and international developments that have provided the context of implementation and conditioned the efficacy of the aforementioned policy:

- a sharp appreciation of the Euro versus the U.S. dollar, which has complicated the exchange-rate policy and, probably, imparted an inflationary bias to this (the still-high inflation rate in Romania and an exchange-rate appreciation policy as against the currency basket makes it such that, when the Euro appreciates too sharply against the U.S. dollar the implied ROL's depreciation against the single currency creates some inflationary pressure);
- the ongoing recession in the EU, which cuts from the stimulus to Romanian exports (which have been driving economic recovery in 2001 and 2002);
- the great uncertainty in the world economy and the high risk aversion of investors, which makes them highly discriminatory among emerging markets; consequently, there has been more reliance on domestic demand for growth in 2003 (than in 2002);
- a growing current account deficit in 2003, which is not surprising in view of the economic recovery and bigger imports related to domestic investment;
- considerable arrears in a period of disinflation, which perpetuate substantial quasi-fiscal deficits and may imperil future public budgets;
- a nervous domestic foreign exchange market due to capital outflows, and, probably, less capital inflows (errors and omissions turned negative in 2002, to -$776 million, and reached $654 million in the first quarter of 2003).

The goals of macroeconomic policy in conjunction with the developments highlighted above create a set of policy challenges for the second half of this year and 2004.

What Can Slow Down Economic Growth?

The rise in the GDP was estimated at about 4.4 percent in the first quarter of 2003 year by the Institute of National Statistics. More than this number in itself (which includes household and underground output, with these components evincing the most rapid expansion) the figures concerning industrial production and services—which, together, account for over 75 percent of GDP—give some pause for thought. If the dynamic of these sectors does not speed up, on average, in the other three quarters, the official GDP target for 2003 would be hard to attain. In addition, the very likely poor agricultural output would make this outcome more probable.

The bottom line is: the dynamic of the GDP needs to be examined in the context of the overall macroeconomic performance; what matters for Romania, essentially, is to have sustainable growth together with disinflation and easily financed current account deficits. A possible cause of an inflationary slippage could be a continuing sharp appreciation of the Euro (against the U.S. dollar) in keeping with the exchange rate policy practiced by the NBR in the last couple of years. Some argue that this appreciation is not threatening since the U.S. dollar would still shape inflationary expectations in Romania and a large portion of imports is dollar denominated. I find this argument insufficiently convincing for several reasons: already, many transactions and prices are related to the Euro once the single currency became, officially, the reference currency on last March 1; moreover, basic excises (especially for gasoline) are calculated in the Euro, whose nominal and real appreciation vis-à-vis the ROL has been quite high in the first five months of this year. In the first five months of this year the ROL depreciated versus the Euro by cca 8 percent in nominal terms and by more than 2 percent in real terms. At the same time the ROL appreciated both nominally and really versus the U.S. dollar. This is why it makes sense to think about how a possible negative influence can be counteracted.

There are two basic scenarios in this respect. One scenario bets on a U.S. dollar recovery, which would provide an enormous bonus to disinflation in Romania by reproducing the circumstances of last year. In addition, a decline of the Euro would relieve the pressure of the rise in various excises. But this scenario, although with a reasonable likelihood to occur in view of the growth differentials between the United States and the EU, is not a policy contingency plan per se. The other scenario regards a further appreciation of the Euro during 2003, however implausible it may seem to some. But policymaking has to consider such a situation. Should it happen and should the Central Bank not resort to an excessive appreciation of the ROL (as a means to combat the inflationary pressure), a tighter monetary policy may have to be implemented. But a tightening of monetary policy would raise, or slow the decline of the cost of borrowing, which would impact growth negatively. On the other hand, higher interest rates would relieve the strain in the forex market (a negative effect would be, however, a further stimulus to demand for hard currency denominated borrowing). Consequently, the National Bank of Romania would have to calibrate very cautiously its instruments so that it balances the simultaneous goals of sustained growth and disinflation; a good calibration would avert a too-visible trade-off.

The second half of 2002 and the first five months of 2003 witnessed a rapid decline of interest rates. Aside from the need to bolster economic growth the decline of lending rates for ROL-denominated credits was seen as a tool to mitigate the risks of excessive hard currency denominated borrowing. But passive interest rates declined, arguably, too rapidly and this has showed up in a drop of ROL-denominated deposits in the second quarter of 2003. Moreover, the fall in domestic interest rates may have increased the propensity of some capital to flow out of the country, against the backdrop of capital account liberalization. The lesson is: there is need for caution with the speed of lowering interest rates so that bank deposits (ROL) be not harmed and the balance of payments not strained exceedingly.

While the expansion of domestic credit (by more than 25 percent in real terms in 2002) was widely hailed early on, some alarm was expressed by NBR officials lately with regard to the rapid increase of hard currency denominated lending. The concerns revolve around exchange rate risk in view of the wild gyrations on currency markets and the lack of routine of Romanian companies to use hedging for forex risk protection. Some commercial bankers have contended that the NBR's stance in this regard is overcautious since—they assert—most lending is done out of deposits made by residents. However, they seem to overlook that the distinction between domestic credit based on foreign borrowing versus that based on deposits made by residents is fundamentally dented when the capital account is liberalized—which is the case with the current program of KAL in Romania.

The first five months of 2003 showed a significant rise in imports, which have grown to over $8.7 billion, while the trade deficit went beyond $2 billion. If this trend continues the current account deficit may approach 5 percent by the end of 2003. This level of the deficit should not be of concern were the biggest portion of additional imports made up of capital goods and their financing were done easily. What is surprising, however, is that imports have increased so much while the pace of growth of industrial output and services (which make up most of the GDP) was not impressive in the first quarter of 2003. It may be that this pace accelerated in the second quarter.

Financial indiscipline continues to plague the Romanian economy and it shows up in substantial arrears. For instance, the losses in the energy sector amounted to about 2 percent of GDP in 2002 (according to some estimates). Arrears do create quasi-fiscal deficits, which may imperil future public budgets unless addressed in due time. Data for this year are quite scarce, so that an adequate judgment is hard to make in this regard. It is clear, nonetheless, that disinflation strains the balance sheet of inefficient companies, for the latter (and not only) used inflation as a weapon to cut their liabilities in real terms. The evolution of arrears needs to be watched carefully by policymakers.

Areas of possible concern in 2004 include the danger of excessive populist macroeconomics in the 2004 election year. Populism may take also the form of imprudent wage policy (unjustified pay rises in the public sector); dangerously declining interest rates, which may fuel again inflation; leniency toward tax offenders, which may worsen financial indiscipline, and so forth. The Ministry of Finance has aired the idea of a larger budget deficit in 2004 (of cca 3.5 percent), in order to finance additional infrastructure projects. Can Romania afford a higher budget deficit? The IMF would likely oppose such a move in view of the disinflation effort and the need to reduce crowding in the economy. The Maastricht criteria would also point against such a rise. However, there may be leeway for the government to increase the budget deficit assuming that: financial discipline improves in the economy and quasi-fiscal deficits go down; most of the rise in the budget deficit is financed externally and, thereby, crowding out is limited; and last, but not least, the rise in the budget deficit is used exclusively for the purpose of infrastructure work. All this said, the government would have to realize that increasing the budget deficit, unless it is accompanied by remarkably disciplined policy making, poses significant risks—especially in an election year. And major slippage, of any sort, would undermine credibility in a critical period for improving Romania's credentials to join the EU and bring her rating nearer to an investment grade.

Another area of concern is the fragility of the nonbank financial sector, which asks for resolute action and a strengthening of supervision activity. Should capital outflows go on at an excessive pace a reassessment of the current program of capital account liberalization would be needed. As a matter of principle, policymakers should have at the very top of their agenda Romania's not losing contact with other EU accession countries in terms of economic performance. 2004 is the year of EU entry for seven central European countries and Romania needs to do much better economically so that 2007 becomes a realistic admission date.

ROMANIA AND THE EUROPEAN UNION

More than most other European candidate countries, Romania sees in the relationship with the EU a historic chance to overcome the trap of backwardness. Why? Because sustained rapid economic growth and development, or what is called *catching-up* in current economics parlance, is a very rare phenomenon. In the last century, there were only a few cases of rapid and sustained development and convergence that reduced important economic gaps. In Western Europe, Ireland is the most interesting case. Spain and Portugal saw positive, though less spectacular, developments after the end of the Franco and Salazar dictatorships. In my opinion, the so-called miracle economies of some Southeast and East Asian countries should be considered exceptions that confirm the rule.

In general, the experience of economic development demonstrates that the formula, the "catechism" of transformation—privatization, liberalization, and stabilization—is sufficient neither to explain nor ensure rapid sustained growth. So what could become the driving force for Romania, in the spirit of what Paul Rosenstein-Rodan theorized, many decades ago, under the name *The Big Push*? Interestingly, Rosenstein-Rodan introduced this concept through the example of economic backwardness in Southeastern Europe.[25]

Transformation and development could be easily solved if policy makers and private entrepreneurs could simply plant adequate, progressive institutions in unfavorable environments, changing social and organizational networks and infrastructures almost overnight. But institutions cannot be "purchased," nor can they be assimilated instantaneously. They are actually a local sociohistorical outcome. The lesson for Romania is the following: In the absence of adequate institutions and responsible public policy, it will be practically impossible to realize the necessary rapid development. And without this, it will be more and more difficult to join the prosperous EU "Club."

It should be noted that Romania has income per capita that is roughly 25–27 percent of the average in the EU, while the population (22.4 million) is large as compared with the average in Central and Eastern Europe. Various estimates point out that even if Romania achieves an average rate of economic growth of 5 percent over the longer run, while the EU average rate of economic growth is 2 percent, Romania would need twenty years to reach half the average income per capita in the EU.

Sustained economic progress would necessitate much higher savings and investment ratios in Romania (over 30 percent of the GDP). This is why foreign capital inflows, public policy geared toward development of human capital and infrastructure, and increasing use of new developments in information technology (IT) are so important. (Interestingly, Romania is a leader among transition countries when it comes to IT use.) But such improvements depend, in turn, on the functioning of institutions: a competent, uncorrupt, and innovative (central and local) public administration; a solid financial and banking system; good structures of corporate governance (oriented toward higher economic performances); an education system offering equal chances to children and adults; and finally, laws that enjoy social acceptance and create a favorable social ethos.

For Romania, it is not easy to find the key to collective and individual wisdom that would open the doors to progress. Mere openness to a vast global economy where asymmetries, agglomeration effects, and volatile (unstable) financial markets are still present is certainly not enough to ensure positive economic development. In today's world, amazing success stories can coexist with astonishing failures which can become national, collective tragedies. As Dani Rodrik, the Harvard economist, remarked astutely, integration in the world economy cannot be a substitute for an economic development strategy.

If one takes for granted the hypothesis that not just any integration brings about benefits, it makes sense to evaluate joining the EU as a possible solution to the secular desire for modernization in Romania. This type of integration would likely shelter Romania from the instability and troubles of the rest of the world. Romania's relationship with the EU and the invitation (in December 1999, in Helsinki) to start accession negotiations could be *The Big Push* Romania needs.

CONCLUSION

Where resource reallocation cannot take place quickly enough, and without friction, the freeing of prices, and the overall opening of the economy put it under tremendous *strain*,[26] a *strain* that is augmented by congenital in-

Table 20.1. Macroeconomic Indicators, 1990–2002

	1990	*1991*	*1992*	*1993*	*1994*	*1995*	*1996*	*1997*	*1998*	*1999*	*2000*	*2001*	*2002*[+]
GDP	−5.6	−12.9	−8.8	1.5	3.9	7.1	3.9	−6.1	−4.8	−2.3	1.6	5.3	4.5
Unemployment	—	3.0	8.2	10.4	10.9	9.5	6.6	8.8	10.3	11.5	10.5	8.6	9.0
Inflation avg.	5.1	170	210	256	137	32	39	154	59	46	46	30	18
M2 growth rate	22	101	80	141	138	71	66	105	49	45	38	46	30
Depreciation avg.	50	241	303	147	118	23	52	133	24	—	—	—	—
Budget deficit/GDP*	1.0	3.2	−4.6	−0.4	−1.9	−2.6	−3.9	−3.4	−3.0	−4.0	−1.9	−3.7	−3.0
Current acc./GDP	−8.4	−3.5	−8	−4.5	−1.4	−5	−7.3	−6.1	−7.1	−4.2	−3.7	−5.8	−4.8
Real wage index	5.1	−18	−13	−17	0.4	2.6	9.5	−22	6.0	—	—	4.5	—

*Consolidated budget. [+] *Estimates*. Exchange rate variation deflated by the ratio between Romanian PPI and USA PPI. *Source:* National Bank of Romania.

stitutional fragility. The magnitude of the required resource reallocation (*strain*) in economic reform efforts, combined with institutional *disorganization,* can seriously undermine the attempt to pursue a low inflation rate in the short run, particularly if the lack of capital markets, the presence of large and growing budget deficits, low savings rates, and meager foreign capital inflows are taken into account. In a system subject to substantial strain, there are strong pressures to generate inflation as a way of diffusing tension by spreading out, or putting off, the costs of adjustment. Another effect of strain is the massive inter-enterprise arrears, an unintended financial innovation which creates a structural trap for stabilization policy.

Analysts have frequently highlighted the better financial discipline in countries such as Hungary, Poland, and the Czech Republic, as compared with other transition countries including Romania. It is suggested here that an explanation is provided by looking at the *structure* of the former economies[27]—by looking at their geography, their size, their economic policies, and their ability to export to western markets and to attract foreign investment. Furthermore, their *structure* is influenced by whether or not there was a history of partial reforms prior to the revolutions of 1989 (that, in some cases, brought about several of the ingredients of a market environment). It is also influenced by the degree of concentration of industry and the prior existence of a private sector.[28]

Policy credibility can be singled out as a major explanatory factor, but credibility itself depends on how much structural adjustment can be brought about over a stated period; and the *capacity to adjust* is influenced by the initial *structure* and the scale of *resource misallocation* that it contains. If it is accepted that the roots of financial (in)discipline and economic performance are to be sought in *structure,* however multifaceted, and the *strain* to which the economy is subjected, the obvious conclusion is that both *structure* and *strain* have to be targeted by policy. Dealing with *structure* includes a focus on both property rights and corporate *governance.* Attention must also be paid to the development of appropriate and effective market institutions, to finding ways of eroding the existing economic power structure, and to changing enterprise behavior. *Strain,* which reflects the scale of the required resource reallocation, should be approached by starting with the simple truth that structural adjustment is always difficult, even in an advanced market-based economy, and even in cases when reform is credible.[29]

Where policy is inconsistent, privatization is slow, and foreign direct investment is insignificant, high strain persists, undermining macroeconomic stabilization and preserving the *flow problem* of the banking industry. Here, a dangerous vicious circle is at work between macroeconomic policy and the state of the banking system. Unless there is deep restructuring of the economy, both tight and loose monetary policies can equally deleterious (albeit in different ways) as to their impact on banks. Expansion of credit can be accompanied by poor lending and unsustainable trade imbalances (as happened in the second half of 1995 and in 1996), whereas high real interest rates (as during 1997–1999) can damage the payment capacity of banks and enterprises, and unleash mounting pressure for forgiveness of loans (default).

Unless authorities can create and maintain a momentum of policy steadiness, the feeling of overall uncertainty and volatility is unlikely to be mitigated. Although stop and go measures can hardly be avoided under the circumstances, large policy fluctuations are detrimental to the economy. They entail large income transfers among economic sectors and population groups, and unnerve expectations instead of stabilizing them.

Institutions ultimately determine economic performance. Institutions, understood as socially accepted rules and procedures, determine the quality of economic policy and of its choices as well. However, institutions cannot be created by "hocus-pocus economics." Loosening the historical grip of the old *structure* and getting the new institutional arrangements to function properly takes time and patience. In this context, one can evaluate the role of the EU in providing a *Big Push* to Romania's quest for modernization.

Looking at the Romania's EU accession profile, one notices some particular features of the economy: the unusually high percentage of rural population and share of farming in overall economic activity; the costs of upgrading the energy sector and of environmental protection; the costs of overhauling the social security system; and so on. Additionally, Romania needs to bring inflation down to single-digit level and achieve an adequate degree of nominal convergence (according to the Maastricht criteria), supported by continuous real convergence. All these tasks require effective public policy, which, in turn, depends on good public administration. But, as Romania's transition indicates quite clearly, public administration itself is in need of deep reform. Hopefully, the EU can assist Romania in this area as well.

Romania needs the EU more than the other way round. It is proper and sensible to accept this reality. On the other hand, the Union would benefit from Romania's membership if, at the time of accession, Romania can present the EU with valuable, noteworthy institutional and economic features. Owing to the country's size, large population, and geographic position—close to a restless area—Romania can be a significant member of the Union.

NOTES

1. Romania Stalinism continued until the very end of the Communist regime. Initial conditions can be related to the magnitude of resource misallocation, the institutional ingredients of a market environment, the existence of a private sector, to a certain industrial culture, etc.

2. See also Saul Estrin, Michail Dimitrov, and Xavier Richet, "State Enterprise Restructuring in Bulgaria, Albania and Romania," *Economic Analysis*, vol. 1, no. 3 (1998), pp. 239–55. The authors conclude that "when one looks at differences in terms of progress of restructuring, it seems likely that these can best be explained by preconditions than current progress in reforms," pp. 250.

3. The competition among rent seekers, and its impact on output, is stressed by Andrei Shleifer and Robert Vishny in "Corruption," *Quarterly Journal of Economics*, vol. 108, no. 3 (August 1986), pp. 461–88. See also Peter Boone and Joachim Hoerder, "Inflation: Causes, Consequences, and Cures," in Peter Boone, Stanislaw Gomulka, and Richard Layard, eds., *Emerging from Communism: Lessons from Russia, China and Eastern Europe* (Cambridge, MA: MIT Press, 1988), pp. 42–72.

4. An IMF report from 1997 acknowledges that "Romania emerged from communism with an economy that was suffering from considerably more deep-seated structural problems than most former Communist countries in the region." See "Romania—Recent Economic Developments," *IMF Staff Country Reports*, no. 97/46 (Washington, DC: IMF, 1997), p. 7.

5. Jagdish Bhagwati, "Immiserizing Growth: A Geometrical Note," *Review of Economic Studies*, vol. 25, no. 3 (June 1958), pp. 201–5. Harry Johnson, "The Possibility of Income Losses from Increased Efficiency of Factor Accumulation in the Presence of Tariffs," *Economic Journal*, vol. 77, nos. 3–5 (March 1967), pp. 151–54.

6. Daniel Dăianu, "A Case of Immiserising Growth," *Revista Economica*, no. 20 (1985).

7. The energy consumption per unit of GDP is in Romania twice as high as in Hungary and more than 4 times larger than the OECD average. EBRD, *Transition Report* (London: 1995), p. 77.

8. This term was introduced by Janos Kornai.

9. See also Richard Kozul-Wright and Paul Rayment, "The institutional hiatus in economies in transition and its policy consequences," *Cambridge Journal of Economics*, vol. 21, no. 5, (September 1997), pp. 641–61.

10. External shocks (like the collapse of Eastern markets) played a major role. Guillermo Calvo and Fabrizio Coricelli use the notion of "trade implosion" in this respect.

11. Daniel Dăianu, "The Changing Mix of Disequilibria during Transition. A Romanian Background," *IMF Working Paper*, vol. 94/73 (1994); see also Saul Estrin, Michail Dimitrov, and Xavier Richet, "State Enterprise Restructuring in Bulgaria, Albania and Romania," *Economic Analysis*, vol. 1, no. 3 (1998), pp. 239–55; and Olivier Blanchard, *The Economics of Post-Communist Transition* (Oxford: Clarendon Press, 1997).

12. In 1991, the number of private companies rose quickly to 72,277; they operated mainly in trade and services. By the end of 1995, the number had risen to almost half a million. It should be recalled that, in contrast with Hungary or Poland, the Communist regime in Romania did not allow any form of private property.

13. It should be said that commercial companies represented only 60 percent of state assets; the rest belonged to the *regies autonomes*, which were created according to the French model.

14. This development should be seen in the context of the elections in May 1990. Measured real wages rose by 11 percent between December 1989 and October 1990, while output continued to fall. The removal of price controls began in November of that year.

15. See Dimitrie Demekas and Mohsin Khan, "The Romanian Economic Reform Program," *IMF Occasional Paper*, no. 89 (1991).

16. The budget deficit was actually higher in 1994 (4.3 percent) than in 1993 (1.7 percent), but many implicit and explicit subsidies had been removed, which was a key objective.

17. Caution is required with the numbers since arrears can be obscured by inefficient activities being kept afloat by bank lending (via rollovers). Ultimately, these "hidden" arrears will show up in a deterioration in the portfolios of the banks. This is what appears to have happened in 1996 and thereafter.

18. During 1995, Romania was rated BB– by the principal western rating agencies (and BB+ by JCRA), which helped the raising of money on the international capital markets. These accommodating capital inflows fended off a major balance of payments crisis in 1996.

19. The elections of 1996 clearly had an impact on macroeconomic policy and, subsequently, on the performance of the economy.

20. From some 4,000 *lei*/$1 at the end of December 1996, the rate rose sharply to about 9,000 lei/$1 in late February 1997, after which a nominal appreciation took place and the rate stabilized at around 7,000 *lei*/$1.

21. This is an overstatement to the extent arrears stood at a high level. The bailout of *Banca Agricola* and *Bancorex* in 1997 indicated how serious the problem of arrears was and how they can obscure quasi-fiscal deficits.

22. Significant amounts of portfolio capital entered the country, which tested the ability of the Central Bank to sterilize them when base money represented no more then 4.6–4.7 percent of GDP.

23. Despite its moderate level (of about 25 percent of GDP), the external debt has nevertheless been increasing rapidly.

24. At the start of 1998, the $500 limit to the purchase of hard currency by individuals was lifted. This measure can enhance a run on the banking system. However, the lack of a collective experience of a banking system collapse can act as a cushion against such a run.

25. Paul Rosenstein-Rodan, "Problems of Industrialization of Eastern and South Eastern Europe," *Economic Journal*, vol. 53 (June–September 1943), pp. 202–11.

26. For the concept of *strain*, see Daniel Dăianu, "Strain: Explaining Shocks in Post-Command Economies," in Juergen Backhaus, ed., *Issues in Transformation Theory* (Marburg, Germany: Metropol, 1997).

27. A World Bank study shows the median number of employees in a sample of firms in Romania to be 1,327, whereas in other countries it was very low: Slovenia, 213; Poland, 820; Hungary, 241; Bulgaria, 291.

28. Eduardo Borensztein et al. emphasize the role of structural reforms in explaining the speed of economic recovery in various transition countries in "The Evolution of Output in Transition Economies: Explaining the Differences," in the *Fifth Nobel Symposium in Economics* (10–12 September 1999, Stockholm). But one could claim that the quality of institutions (ability of undertaking structural reforms) is rooted in the history of partial reforms, in initial conditions.

29. Michael Bruno, "Stabilization and Reform in Eastern Europe: A Preliminary Evaluation," *IMF Staff Papers*, vol. 39, no. 4 (December 1992), p. 753.

21

Trade Unions and Labor Relations

Larry S. Bush

A *mineriada*[1]—what Romanians call the eruption of violence periodically visited upon Bucharest by the coal miners of the Jiu Valley—is the only thing that most people in the outside world know about Romanian trade union activity. This is unfortunate. These outbursts present a distorted image of a complex labor movement that has played a largely constructive role in shaping the economy and society of post-Communist Romania. Although the dominant events of the decade since 1989 have been confrontations, there is another side to the story. A uniquely Romanian form of "corporatism"[2]—mechanisms for continuous tripartite negotiations among the government, major trade unions, and employer organizations—is being created. Notwithstanding support from Western governments and trade unions, however, as well as nominal support from successive Romanian governments and the trade union confederations, this corporatism remains only weakly embedded in the culture. The formal mechanisms for tripartite decision making adopted in the late 1990s will have difficulty evolving into stable cooperative relationships, especially between the trade unions and the private sector enterprises.

ORIGINS AND DEVELOPMENT OF THE POST-COMMUNIST TRADE UNIONS

Before the Fall: Pre-1989 Conditions

Trade unions have existed in Romania since the late nineteenth century. The period before World War II saw the growth of a modern labor movement, as well as the passage of a series of labor laws, initially liberal, then increasingly restrictive, culminating in Marshal Antonescu's outlawing of trade unions in 1940. After World War II, the outlawed trade unions were in the grasp of the Communist Party, and for the next forty-five years there would be no independent trade unions in Romania. By 1958, an entity known as *Uniunea Generală a Sindicatelor din România* (UGSR, the General Union of Romanian Trade Unions) sat atop a national pyramid composed of branch (industry) federations and, below them, enterprise trade unions. The primary function of the trade unions, according to the Labor Code, was to "mobilize the masses for accomplishing the program of the Romanian Communist Party."[3]

There were a few attempts to found independent trade unions under the Communist regime[4] and only isolated incidents of worker protests against the government. In 1977, 35,000 Jiu Valley coal miners went on strike, and in 1987, spontaneous protests against pay cuts led to huge street demonstrations in Braşov. Neither of these efforts succeeded, however, and their leaders were severely punished or executed.[5]

Trade Union Building: 1989–1999

The absence of a dissident tradition was no impediment to the rapid development of trade unions when Ceauşescu's iron hand was removed. Whether founding new organizations or attempting to restructure the institutions of the old regime, Romania's industrialized workers embraced the idea of "free, independent, and democratic" trade unions. In the chaos of late December 1989, organizations sprang up overnight. In fact, according to one former official of the UGSR, on 22 December 1989, while the street fighting raged outside their Bucharest office, he and fellow UGSR aparatchiks formed the *Comitetul Naţional Provizoriu de Organizare* (the National Provisional Committee of Organization) and the *Sindicatele Libere din România* (the Free Trade Unions of Romania, the forerunner of the country's largest modern confederation).[6] This provisional committee had the blessings of the self-appointed leaders of the National Salvation Front, who had seized power following Ceauşescu's flight. The public learned of the Provisional Committee five days later, when the official Romanian Press Agency announced that it would "replace the [UGSR]."[7] The Committee's leaders treated the vast assets of the UGSR as theirs. They threw their support behind the National Salvation Front's program and offered money and vacation facilities for victims of the former regime and the recent fighting.

Within a few months the Provisional Committee evolved into the *Confederaţia Naţionala a Sindicatelor Libere din România* (CNSLR, the National Confederation of Free Trade Unions of Romania). CNSLR held a national Congress in June 1990, and adopted a constitution, making former UGSR activists ineligible to hold confederation leadership positions. Victor Ciorbea, president of the Free Trade Union in Education, and a former judge and law professor, was elected president of the CNSLR. By 1992, the CNSLR claimed 2.5 million members in 4,300 local trade unions, organized in 19 industrial sector federations and 41 territorial unions.

Rival trade union leaders and many international observers insisted that the CNSLR was simply a neo-Communist successor of UGSR. The CNSLR did build directly on the organizational base of the Communist trade unions, and its original leaders came from them. Nevertheless, a democratizing process of renewal took place within its constituent trade unions, following the June 1990 congress. In fact, CNSLR's leader, Victor Ciorbea—who was regularly maligned in the early 1990s as a front for the Communists—became the protégé of Corneliu Coposu, one of Romania's most respected opposition politicians. As a member of the National Peasant Christian Democratic Party, Ciorbea was appointed prime minister after the 1996 elections.

In early 1990, workers quickly created new trade unions in an explosion of pluralist sentiment. While inertia kept many organizations within the ready-made structure offered by the CNSLR, many leaders refused to affiliate with it and formed their own alliances. The first of these to arise as a challenger to the CNSLR was *Frăţia*, a confederation created in January 1990 by the drivers' trade union and three large Bucharest factory trade unions. *Frăţia* leaders presented themselves as the opposition to the Provisional Committee. As early as February 1990, *Frăţia* attacked the latter as simply a new version of the Communist trade unions. Their fight really was, as much as anything, one for the assets of the UGSR. The president of *Frăţia*, Miron Mitrea, also the leader of the drivers' trade union, impressed Western governments and trade unions and won membership for *Frăţia* in the International Confederation of Free Trade Unions in September 1991. At the time, *Frăţia* claimed a membership of 850,000, organized into 19 federations and 30 territorial branches.

In June 1990, a third large confederation, *Cartel Alfa*, came into being, founded by seven federations representing mainly workers in metal fabrication, steel, electronics, petrochemicals, and paper. By 1991, it claimed 1.3 million members. *Cartel Alfa* was, in some sense, an offshoot of the CNSLR. In early 1990, its president, Bogdan Hossu, received financial support from the Provisional Council to establish something called "Solidarity '90," and it was from this organization that *Cartel Alfa* evolved.[8]

The last of the original "big four" confederations was *Blocul Naţional Sindical* (BNS, the National Trade Union Bloc), which was founded in June 1991. Its constituent federations came from the fields of power production, printing, post and telecommunications, machine building, and electronics. The BNS's claimed membership has been in the range of 650,000–850,000.

Many other Romanian trade union organizations did not affiliate with any of the four large confederations. Smaller confederations abounded. Under Romanian law, an enterprise trade union can be founded with fifteen members.

Two enterprise trade unions in the same branch can found a federation. In turn, a confederation can be composed of a minimum of two federations from different branches. Theoretically, under Romanian law a confederation could exist with as few as sixty members.[9] Independent federations also proliferated, as did completely unaffiliated enterprise trade unions.

Thus, from the beginning, the new Romanian trade union movement was marked by vigorous pluralism. Whereas in Western Europe, trade union pluralism typically reflects ideological groupings (Communist, Christian, socialist), in Romania this is not the case. Instead, fragmentation of the labor movement occurred because of distrust of higher authority, personal ambition, and the unwillingness of leaders to reduce or eliminate their power by merging with larger organizations. As a result, Romania's trade unions are plagued by "atomization." As of 1997, Romanian commentators estimated that there were over 14,000 enterprise trade union organizations, 150 federations, and 18 confederations in the country. These represented between 50 and 70 percent of the workforce, depending upon whether one chose the dues-paying membership figures provided by the trade unions or the total membership figures they supplied.[10]

A closer look at trade unions at the enterprise level shows this "atomization" more clearly. The law neither requires, nor does practice support, the creation of only one trade union organization per enterprise. Instead, it is extremely common, especially in the large industrial enterprises, for there to be multiple organizations. Sometimes, these rival trade unions affiliate with competing federations, while at others, they remain independent. It is widely reported that enterprise managers often create company-dominated trade unions (in Romania they are called "yellow" or "house" trade unions), specifically to limit the effectiveness of the independent trade unions in the enterprise.[11]

The situation at the federation level is similar. In theory, since a federation is intended to function at the level of an entire industry (or "branch"), it might make sense that there be only a single federation for each industrial sector or, at least, one such federation within any given national confederation. This, however, is not the case. For example, within the BNS confederation alone, there are seven different federations in the metal processing unions and nine in transportation.

Recognizing that such extreme forms of pluralism are a source of division and weakness in economic and political struggles, trade union leaders have periodically attempted to coordinate their activities and, more ambitiously, to merge rival organizations. To date, there has been only limited progress, however. In 1991, an alliance of CNSLR, *Frăţia*, and *Cartel Alfa* created *Consiliul Naţional Consultativ* (CNC, the National Consultative Council). Under its auspices, the three confederations reached agreements about the management and distribution of the "patrimony" of the UGSR (its money, holiday hotels, etc.), interacted with the government, and negotiated the first national-level collective bargaining agreement with employers' representatives in early 1992. The CNC was ultimately abandoned, however, as mutual distrust and divergent interests predominated.

The first (and only) major consolidation in the trade union movement came in June 1993 when CNSLR and *Frăţia*, which had previously acted like mortal enemies, merged as CNSLR- *Frăţia*. It was an uneasy arrangement, as reflected in the curious leadership structure the new confederation adopted. The heads of the two older organizations—Miron Mitrea of *Frăţia* and Victor Ciorbea of CNSLR—were given roughly equal top-level positions. A power struggle was inevitable. In August 1994, Ciorbea took his teachers' federation, together with a few other affiliates, and created a new confederation, *Confederaţia Sindicatilor Democratice din România* (CSDR, the Confederation of Democratic Trade Unions of Romania).

There is a growing sense in Romanian trade union circles that a profound reconfiguration could occur in the next few years, as a reaction to the anticipated revamping of the economic structure.[12] Indeed, a greater willingness to cooperate already exists among the leaders of the four large confederations. Since the winter and spring of 1999, they frequently have come together in a campaign of pressure, coordinating tactics and policy objectives. In addition, changes in labor law should encourage consolidation. The right to participate in collective contract negotiations is now limited to trade union organizations which have proven that they are "representative"—a status that, for confederations and federations, requires a high minimum number of members and affiliates, as well as a membership spread across most of the country.[13] As a result of this new requirement, only six of the approximately eighteen confederations in Romania qualified as partners for negotiating national-level contracts after 1997.[14] The new "representativity" standards have also been incorporated into two tripartite agencies—the Economic and Social Council[15] and the National Agency for Occupations and Professional Training[16]—both of which have the potential for exerting real influence.

RELATIONS WITH THE GOVERNMENT, POLITICAL PARTIES, AND EMPLOYERS

Initial Challenges and Confrontations: December 1990–October 1992

The first few months of the new National Salvation Front government were marked by widespread, but localized, labor strife.[17] Strikes, protests, and rallies typically were concerned with improving enterprise conditions and, often, with removing the Communist-era enterprise managers. Some of these local affairs were serious matters, attracting the direct participation of President Iliescu and Prime Minister Roman.

The typical pattern of disputes was established early in 1990 and could still be seen as recently as the *mineriada* of 1999. First, the workers would launch a major work stoppage and demand negotiations with the president or the prime minister. The latter would publicly declare that it was not appropriate for them to participate, and insist that the workers deal with the local enterprise management or lower level bureaucrats. Then, if the work stoppage threatened valuable production or public services (or public safety in the case of the miners), the politicians would cave in and, in an air of great crisis, meet with the trade union leaders and grant most of their demands (although the only agreements that typically were kept were those regarding salary increases; promises to effect structural changes usually were not honored by the government). Thus, the leaders of the emerging trade unions learned very early that to achieve economic goals, they had to succeed in political struggles with the government, notwithstanding the politicians' efforts to devolve responsibility onto the local state enterprise managers when it suited their purposes.

Prior to the 20 May 1990 national elections, the trade unions were active in partisan politics only in one significant respect. The National Salvation Front leaders had promised the country that they were a transitional government and that they would not contest the election. However, they quickly reneged on that promise, registering the Front as a political party in February 1990 and scheduling elections for that May. Their platform was vague, without a commitment to privatization, and advocated a "liberalized, decentralized and diversified system based on market mechanisms."[18] In response, many Romanians—writers, journalists, students, and intellectuals—held rallies in support of the "Timişoara Proclamation," which called for free enterprise and banning all former Communist Party officials from political office. Many trade unions— *Frăţia* and labor organizations in Timişoara in particular—participated in some of these demonstrations.

The National Salvation Front's election victory in May was soon followed by the disastrous *mineriada* of the Jiu Valley coal miners, in June 1990. It is important to note that the vast majority of trade unions and workers did not heed President Iliescu's call to arms against the "enemies of the regime." Many trade union leaders risked retaliation by actively discouraging their members from participating. In fact, President Iliescu publicly castigated them in a speech given in the midst of the chaos, a speech in which he also praised the miners.[19]

Following the *mineriada*, the newly elected government took office. Petre Roman remained as prime minister. His policy program envisioned much more rapid economic change than the Front's election campaign had led voters to expect. Roman proposed eventual privatization of state enterprises and the promotion of a market economy. Rather than immediate privatization, however, Roman intended first to restructure the state enterprises, to make them more autonomous, and to require them to be economically accountable. In the meantime, artificial price supports would be removed gradually ("price liberalization"), so that market forces would, in theory, control the operation of these enterprises even while they remained in the state's hands.[20]

An integral part of Roman's program was his proposal for a six-month trade union moratorium on pay and working condition demands, in return for the government's pledge to eventually compensate the workers for those aspects of the reform that affected them negatively. The major confederations grudgingly gave their consents to this proposal, albeit on the condition that the government meet various demands (e.g., a role in promulgating labor legislation). The government agreed to set up joint government-trade union commissions to focus on issues of concern to the labor movement.

Harmonious relations were short-lived, however. Workers in important industries resorted to industrial actions to protest their working and living conditions. While condemning them as illegal (in light of the moratorium), Prime Minister Roman was forced to go to at least one worksite (the *Tractorul* factory in Braşov) to negotiate a settlement. In the meantime, the Constanţa harbor workers walked off the job, and sailors struck the Romanian fleet. The latter, in a decidedly political move, asked Ion Raţiu, a recently defeated opposition candidate for the presidency (and successful shipping magnate based in Britain), to take charge of the fleet (he declined).

The government's first phase of price liberalization took place on 1 November 1990. Subsidies were ended on the prices of most items except food, power, heating, fuel, and rent. A second round of price liberalization was scheduled for 1 January 1991. The trade unions opposed this "shock therapy," in which prices rose but wages did not. Talks between the big confederations and the government broke down and large street demonstrations, spearheaded by *Cartel Alfa*, took place in major cities.

In an atmosphere of crisis, the drivers union and its confederation, *Frăţia* (both headed by Miron Mitrea), launched a nationwide strike in December 1990. Its stated objective was baldly political—replacement of the Roman government with a national coalition including the opposition. The strike, which proved to be one of the most significant labor events of the post-Communist period, went forward even though the government postponed the January price increases. Six other confederations supported the drivers, including *Cartel Alfa* and the usually nonmilitant CNSLR. The strikers blockaded Bucharest, denying access to everything except essential medical and security services. Faced with its gravest threat since coming to power, the government made major concessions both on wages and on trade union participation in framing legislation. Satisfied, the drivers ended their strike.

In the meantime, the atmosphere around the strike had become highly charged politically, as opposition groups seized on it as a way to topple the government. The drivers' (and *Frăţia's*) willingness to forego their broader political demands and halt the general strike temporarily saved the Roman government, and sparked allegations of a sellout by opposition politicians.[21]

Early in 1991, labor legislation was passed to establish legal standards for collective bargaining[22] and labor disputes.[23] Strikes with political objectives were outlawed and their use for other purposes was severely limited, both in terms of what could be lawful objects (for instance, it was illegal to strike in order to force a change in management) and in terms of what procedures had to be complied with before a strike would be legal. This legislation did not stop the wave of strikes, but it raised the prospect of legal sanctions against strikers. Partly as a result, the threat posed to the government by industrial action eased somewhat. A rally by *Cartel Alfa* in June 1991 was expected to draw 30,000 people. However only 3,000 showed up and a general strike, set for the next day, never took place.

Notwithstanding the new laws and the failure of mainstream confederations to mount serious challenges, the government soon fell victim to the blatantly illegal acts of its old friends, the Jiu Valley miners, who became fed up when Roman did not deliver on the economic promises he had made during their 1990 visit to Bucharest. In September 1991, an estimated 10,000 miners descended on the capital and four days of rioting ensued. The miners, joined by some Bucharest residents, attacked government buildings, held mass rallies, and generally took the city and government hostage. Faced with chaos, Prime Minister Roman and his cabinet "submitted their mandate" to President Iliescu, who promptly accepted their "resignation" and appointed a new coalition government, headed by Teodor Stolojan, a respected non-politician economist.[24] It was widely believed that, although the miners had become antigovernment, they nevertheless remained loyal to President Iliescu and helped rid him of Roman, his rival for power within the party.

The leaders of the major trade union confederations did not support this *mineriada,* though many of them did not shed tears at Roman's fall either. Their relations with the Stolojan government—which stayed in office until the national elections during October–November 1992—were, comparatively speaking, productive and lacking in acrimony.

Genuine tripartite negotiations were not a feature of industrial relations during the Stolojan era. Significant employer associations independent of the government did not exist. Thus, even when so-called tripartite negotiations took place, trade unions and the government were the only autonomous actors. Second, the trade unions themselves were too distrustful of one another, distracted by acrimonious struggles for legitimacy, affiliates, and resources. Finally, there were no trusted institutions in which tripartite negotiations could be conducted.

Paradoxically, a kind of bilateral corporatism—involving only trade unions and employers—was created during this period. The collective labor contracts statute, Law 13/1991, mandated national and branch level collective agreements between trade union confederations and federations on the one side, and employer representatives (named by the Romanian Chamber of Commerce and Industry) on the other. The resulting contracts would, in theory, be legally binding upon all employers and employees within the geographical or industrial scope of the contracts. According to one informed observer at the time—Alexandru Athanasiu, a labor law professor who later became Minister of Labor and Social Protection after the 1996 elections—this format for creating "labor law" by private contract was indispensable during this period because the Romanian government and parliament could not be counted on to revise the Communist-era labor code.[25] The first national-level collective bargaining contracts were negotiated under this system in early 1992. Ironically, there were three competing "national" contracts during that first year, due to the inability of the competing confederations to work together. In fact, during this period, the fragmented labor movement caused both bilateral contract negotiations and tripartite discussions to take the form of separate, parallel proceedings with competing confederations, rather than in an all-inclusive setting—a situation that the government was often accused of manipulating for its own advantage.

Political and Economic Militancy: The Văcăroiu Government, 1992–1996

Elections were scheduled for the fall of 1992. *Cartel Alfa*, *Frăţia*, and CNSLR founded a new party, the Social Solidarity Convention. It failed, however, to obtain a single seat in parliament, and the experiment has not been repeated. The BNS confederation, on the other hand, signed protocols with the opposition Democratic Convention, pledging electoral support in return for the Convention's promise of labor-friendly legislation and greater trade union influence in government.

President Iliescu and his party won reelection in autumn 1992, and a government headed by Prime Minister Nicolae Văcăroiu was installed. It quickly came to be viewed as not serious about economic reform and also as being vulnerable to collapse. Thus, trade union activism entered its most partisan political phase to date from 1993 to 1996, in a fruitless effort to force the Văcăroiu government out of power. At the same time, worsening economic conditions drove many trade unions to launch acrimonious work stoppages in vital industries.

By the end of 1992, wages and pensions had lost 15 percent of their value from 1990, and unemployment had reached almost 10 percent. The Văcăroiu government was not a major threat to further job losses, however, because it dragged its feet on restructuring and privatization. The demands of the unionists, therefore, focused on raising the minimum wage and indexing salary levels to deal with rising prices. By March 1993, further unrest loomed in reaction to the coming round of price liberalizations, scheduled for 1 May. This time, the affected products were basic necessities such as food, water, utilities, and public transportation. When the subsidy cuts were carried out, prices skyrocketed. The cost of bread increased 450 percent. A general strike, nominally supported by the six largest confederations, began on 5 May. The following day five of the confederations (the BNS opted to continue its actions for a time) signed an agreement with the government calling for, among other things, a 70 percent rise in the monthly minimum wage (to the then-equivalent of $49) and promises to link future pay raises equal to 80 percent of price rises. Some observers considered the attempted general strike a failure, however, citing the general absence of worker participation.[26]

August 1993 saw another miners' strike and, more important, the resumption of a general strike by the locomotive drivers of the national railroad that had begun earlier that spring. Their action threatened to cripple the economy, and the government reacted punitively. On 13 August, the Supreme Court decreed an eighty-day suspension of the strike, under a clause in the collective labor disputes statute giving it such power when strikes affected "major interests of the national economy or interests of a humanitarian nature."[27] In response, the locomotive drivers converted the action from a "general strike," conducted in an effort to comply with the law (which required them to continue operating one-third of the railroad's schedule), into a "total strike," effectively halting all operations. Three days later, in the midst of a mounting national crisis, President Iliescu met with the strike leaders to discuss their demands, in what had become, by now, a familiar pattern of response. At the same time, however, government ministers simultaneously pursued a harsher course. The Minister of Justice threatened criminal prosecutions of the strike leaders, and the government instructed the railroad to terminate all workers who refused to report to work by 17 August. Strikers' communication lines were cut and an appeal went out to retired workers to replace the strikers. The strike was effectively broken. Subsequently, the railroad terminated sixty-four trade unionists. The following year, the locomotive drivers and their parent confederation, the BNS, filed a complaint with the International Labor Organization (ILO). The ILO found in favor of the trade unions with regard to most of their contentions, and requested that the Romanian government reinstate the discharged workers and reform labor laws to conform to ILO standards.[28] The state railroad rehired some of the discharged strikers, but the Văcăroiu government never amended the laws in question. Partial reforms did finally come in November 1999, however, as discussed next.

Fitful protests related to wage indexation continued throughout 1994, but the biggest event that year was the schism in CNSLR-*Frăţia*. On 8 August, Miron Mitrea, the former head of *Frăţia* (and executive president of the merged confederation), resigned his position and entered politics as the head of the Social Solidarity Party. A little over a week later, Victor Ciorbea, the former head of the CNSLR (and president of the merged confederation), announced the creation of the Confederation of Democratic Trade Unions of Romania (CSDR). Ciorbea alleged that the split was motivated by politics: Elements within CNSLR-*Frăţia* were allied to the Văcăroiu government, whereas his new confederation would ally itself with the opposition Democratic Convention. This it did, along with the BNS, on 18 August.

In January 1995, the government, faced with chronic high inflation, capped the pay of state sector employees and tied future raises to increases in productivity. Predictably, this did not sit well with the trade unions, and much of 1995 was devoted to strikes and protests against the effects of this decree. State enterprises still accounted for over 90 percent of industrial production at this time, including the crucial energy production sector. Thus, when 37,000 workers at RENEL, the state electrical energy body, resigned en masse in early June 1995 ("resignations" were used because under the collective labor disputes law, it was illegal for workers in this industry to strike), affecting 33 out of 37 power plants, the government responded in much the same fashion it had done two years earlier in the locomotive drivers' strike. It announced that workers who did not return to work would lose their positions. The threat succeeded; within three days most of the workers who had "resigned" returned to work.

Notwithstanding the acrimonious nature of the trade unions' dealings with the Văcăroiu government, incremental progress was made toward institutionalizing social dialogue. The European Union (EU) increasingly made it clear to Romania that social dialogue was part of the *acquis communautaire* (the rights and obligations arising from EU law which aspiring member-states were required to institutionalize before admission). Through its PHARE aid program beginning in 1993, the EU devoted significant resources toward encouraging tripartite and bipartite relations.[29] The Romanian government, in turn, created the Tripartite Secretariat for Social Dialogue in July 1994, charged with developing the framework for an economic and social council that would succeed it.

Employer associations began to emerge during this time, although the slow privatization meant that many represented state enterprises rather than private ones. Their development was also hindered by the fact that no law existed to regulate their creation and operation—a sine qua non in a legal system that begins with the premise that the only rights possessed by organizations (and individuals, for that matter) are those contained in positive laws. Furthermore, the employer associations suffered at least as much as the trade unions from fragmentation. By the end of this period, three of the most important employer associations were: Confederaţia Patronal din Industria României (CONPIROM, Employer Confederation of

Romanian Industry, representing state sector employers), Confederaţia Naţională a Patronatului Român (CNPR, National Confederation of the Romanian Employer, primarily representing state enterprises), and Consiliul Naţional al Întreprinderilor Private Mici şi Mijlocii din România (CNÎPMMR, National Council of Small and Medium-Sized Private Enterprises of Romania—representing private enterprise).

In 1994, the major confederations proposed a legislative package to modernize the labor laws passed in 1991, as well as to create an employers' association statute and an economic and social council. Although progress was made on each of these reforms between 1994 and 1996, the only initiative that made it through the legislative process during the Văcăroiu government was a statute revising the 1991 collective labor contracts law. This statute continued, and rationalized, the format instituted under the old law, by introducing the concept of "representativity" as a requirement for participating in collective negotiations. The trade union organizations and employer associations accorded this status were to be allowed to continue to create rules for the entire nation via these nominally bipartite negotiations, a process arguably contrary to established international standards regarding voluntary negotiations.[30]

Hope and Frustration: November 1996–May 1999

By 1996, it was clear that the Văcăroiu government would survive the trade unions' attacks, as well as those of the opposition parties, and finish its term. The trade unions did not attempt to field a labor party in the elections that autumn; they threw their support to existing parties instead. By the time of the November presidential runoff election, many of the trade unions supported the challenger Emil Constantinescu, the candidate of the Democratic Convention, over the PDSR incumbent, Ion Iliescu (Petre Roman's candidacy not having survived the first round). Partly due to their support, Constantinescu and the Democratic Convention won.

With parties committed to the free market in power for the first time, the trade unions appeared to have achieved one of their primary objectives—a government that would be serious about "real" reform—even though it obviously could mean layoffs of its members by bottom-line oriented firms. Furthermore, the new government was to be led by one of their own, Victor Ciorbea. He was not a universally popular choice among the ranks of trade union leaders, however. His former colleagues at CNSLR-*Frăţia* viewed him with suspicion, as did BNS officials. Nonetheless, most leaders were willing to go along with at least a short-term moratorium on pushing their demands in order to give the new government a chance to develop its program. Even the leader of CNSLR-*Frăţia*, Pavel Todoran, publicly affirmed that his confederation would not resist factory closures. By late January 1997, this cooperation paid off in agreements to modify the collective labor contracts law passed at the end of the Văcăroiu government, as well as, in principle at least, an agreement to take measures for social protection. These included reducing payroll taxes, increasing the national minimum wage, indexing wages and pensions, and increasing child allowances and unemployment benefits.[31]

The honeymoon did not last long, however. By February 1997, CNSLR-*Frăţia* was in talks with the PDSR, now the opposition party of former President Iliescu. BNS and *Cartel Alfa* were grumbling about the government's failure to implement the January agreement. Trade union leaders began to criticize the method of selecting the state enterprises slated for privatization. Talks between the government and the confederations continued through the summer, with complaints, especially by CNSLR-*Frăţia* and the BNS, that Prime Minister Ciorbea was not living up to his earlier promises and was not negotiating seriously. By August 1997, workers in units scheduled for liquidation protested and conducted civil disobedience. The Ministry of the Interior pledged to react forcefully if protests blocked roads or railroads, or turned violent.[32]

After its first year in office, the Ciorbea government had achieved some of the reforms demanded by the International Monetary Fund (IMF), the World Bank, and the European International Bank for Reconstruction and Development. It had liberalized foreign exchange, stabilized the currency, and made headway in fighting inflation. Restructuring and privatizing state enterprises stalled, however. By spring 1998, trade union demands that Ciorbea resign echoed those of the opposition in parliament, as well as those of an erstwhile partner in the government, the Democratic Party led by Roman. In March, they got their wish: Ciorbea resigned and was replaced by Radu Vasile, an economist and experienced politician from another wing of the National Peasant Party.

The Vasile government could not achieve peace with the trade unions either. Under constant pressure from the international lending agencies to cut state expenditures, it had little margin to accommodate labor's economic demands. Disillusioned by the new, post-1996 governments, the trade unionists began talking about "the political class" as the source of their problems, lumping together all the political parties for their scorn. Although at first receptive to an initiative from Prime Minister Vasile for a six-month moratorium on industrial unrest, broached in December 1998, the confederations soon rejected his overtures and began coordinating their policy positions and protest actions to an unprecedented degree.[33]

BNS, *Cartel Alfa*, CNSLR-*Frăţia*, and CSDR escalated industrial action, which began on 24 March 1999 with the largest street demonstrations in at least seven years; 80,000–100,000 people marched in Bucharest alone.[34] These demonstrations were to be followed in April by a two-hour warning strike, which was itself to be followed by a general strike. The warning strike went forward, but the confederations reached a tentative accord with the government and postponed the general strike, pending discussion of their demands, rescheduling it for 24 May. Although the discussions progressed,[35] the twenty-four-hour general strike went ahead as planned. Participation, however, was far below trade union predictions, continuing the pattern of weak worker support for general strikes.[36] Nonetheless, the confederations held out the prospect of yet another general strike, "of an unlimited duration," if their demands were not resolved by the end of July 1999.[37]

No strike took place. Trade unions, especially CNSLR-*Frăţia*, continued to call for the government's resignation, but major demonstrations called for November 1999 fizzled. Meanwhile, Prime Minister Vasile lost his job in mid-December 1999, an apparent casualty, not of union unrest, but of dissent inside his own party, PNŢCD, and of disfavor with President Constantinescu. Mugur Isărescu, the governor of Romania's central bank, was confirmed as the new prime minister.

Alexandru Athanasiu, minister of Labor and Social Protection since the 1996 elections, left office in the cabinet reshuffle that followed Isarescu's appointment. During his tenure, Athanasiu achieved a number of legal reforms. He modified the collective labor contracts law and created a National Agency for Occupations and Professional Training, a National Council for Adult Professional Training and a Labor Inspectorate—institutions needed to comply with Romania's treaty obligations and to satisfy EU entry conditions. In late November 1999, a new collective labor dispute law that he had promoted, Law 168/1999, was approved and a draft labor code was unveiled. The labor code project was the most ambitious attempt to date to rewrite Romania's labor laws, replacing the Communist-era code and incorporating ILO and EU standards. The work was not undertaken in cooperation with either the trade union confederations or employer associations, however, and its prospects for passage are uncertain now that Athanasiu is no longer in office. In addition to the draft labor code, Athanasiu initiated two other important reforms that have yet to be enacted—labor courts and a new pension system, modeled in part on Chile's private pension scheme.

One crucial component of the institutional framework for corporatist relationships was effected in 1997, early in Athanasiu's term of office—the creation of the Economic and Social Council (*Consiliul Economic şi Social*, or CES). It is responsible for making proposals concerning restructuring and national economic development, privatization, labor relations, salary policy, social protection and health, education, and research. In fulfilling this consultative role, the CES is required to give its advice on draft decrees, ordinances and statutes, inform the government about the need for new laws, and mediate industrial disputes at the national or branch level. The CES is a tripartite institution; the government, the nationally representative trade union confederations, and their national employer association counterparts have nine members each in its governing board.

In practice, the CES has fallen short of its promise. It faces unrealistically short statutory deadlines for providing its assessment of proposed laws—twenty days for "organic" laws (concerning government structures) and ten days for all others. The government often ignores the CES advice or refuses to offer the CES a role within its purported ambit. Finally, the trade unions have followed their customary practice of naming their top-ranking officials to CES, thus ensuring that matters before that body do not receive the attention of specialists.

The Final *Mineriada*?

Completing the story of trade union activities in the 1990s requires one last look at the Jiu Valley coal miners. In January and February 1999, they had what should prove to be their "last hurrah." The miners began a strike to protest government plans to close a large number of the mines (most of which were not economically viable). Encouraged by their charismatic leader, Miron Cozma, they once again set out on a *mineriada* to Bucharest, intending to force the government to change its policy. On 20 January 1999, 10,000 coal miners began a slow advance on the capital, battling police, smashing roadblocks, and plunging the country once more into chaos.[38] The interior minister resigned after police failed to halt the miners' caravan in a bloody, tear-gas-choked encounter west of Bucharest. Faced with the prospect of a capital in ruins, on 22 January Prime Minister Vasile reversed his refusal to negotiate personally with the miners, met with Cozma at a monastery, and agreed to his demands—said to include raising pay by 30 percent, reopening two mines previously closed, freezing layoffs, and spending hundreds of millions of dollars of EU development funds on projects in the Jiu Valley.[39] The agreement ended the emergency and avoided a possibly deadly clash with the army, which awaited the miners on the road to Bucharest. The labor dispute had threatened to ignite a social crisis of immense proportions. It was widely feared that disaffected workers in other industries, who were also facing elimination of their jobs, might erupt as well.

Cozma returned to the Jiu Valley as a hero, but within a month he was in prison. This dramatic turn of events came as a result of a Romanian Supreme Court decision. Cozma previously had been convicted and sentenced to three years imprisonment for his involvement in the 1991 *mineriada*. After serving eighteen months, he was released in 1998, whereupon he had returned to the leadership of the Jiu Valley coal miners. Following his apparent victory over the Vasile government on 22 January 1999, he had continued to press his position, announcing a new strike to protest delays by the National Pitcoal Company in negotiating a collective contract that would incorporate the earlier deal with the government. The strike was set for 15 February.[40] On that day, the Supreme Court handed down its decision, increasing Cozma's sentence to eighteen years for "undermining state power" during the 1991 *mineriada*, as well as for illegal possession of a firearm; the court ordered his immediate arrest the following day.[41]

Cozma denounced the sentence and dared the authorities to try to arrest him. The miners vowed to march on Bucharest yet again, this time to bring down the government in retaliation for what they saw as a politically inspired court decision. A convoy of several thousand miners was stopped in a bloody encounter with the police in a village about 100 miles west of the capital. Cozma and over 500 miners were arrested.[42] Several weeks later, Cozma, now imprisoned, was convicted on two unrelated charges of violence—a 1994 assault on a journalist and a 1996 attack on a bar owner.[43]

Cozma's imprisonment may have ended a bloody chapter of Romanian labor relations. Under his influence, the miners rampaged at will several times in the 1990s—first as shock troops for an embattled regime in 1990, then in 1991, to stage a violent coup d'état against the prime minister, who had negotiated pay and benefits the previous year, and finally in 1999, seeking to prevent elimination of most of their jobs. Cozma's removal, combined with an the aggressive government program of coal pit closures (plans had long since been announced to shut down 140 mines across the country) and regional redevelopment efforts intended to foster new, nonmining jobs (heavily subsidized with international support), may consign the Jiu Valley coal miners and their *mineriada* to history.[44]

Labor Relations Following the 2000 Elections

The final years of President Constantinescu's term and of the center-right coalition that governed Romania through 2000 were marked by more acrimonious protests by trade union confederations and individual enterprise organizations, sparked by the chronic poor wage and living conditions of employees of state enterprises (by mid-2000, average wages were said to be as low as 50 percent of 1990 wages), but increasingly ignited by the government's privatization plans for those enterprises. There were major political realignments within the trade union movement as well. Whereas many major trade union confederations had supported Constantinescu and his allies in 1996, by early 2000, both CNSLR-*Frăţia* and BNS had reached formal political accords with the PDSR, under which the political party agreed to accept trade union proposals regarding economic and social legislation. In the elections, seven CNSLR-*Frăţia* members were elected to parliament and two were given places in the new cabinet.

Ion Iliescu and the PDSR's victory in the 2000 election ushered in a period of relative labor peace. Notwithstanding the new government's active continuation of the privatization process (for example, the steel factory Sidex *Galaţi*, the largest state enterprise, was sold to foreign interests), it was able to purchase labor peace, in the form of a tripartite "social pact" signed in February 2001 by the government, the major confederations, and representatives of employer groups. The government was then able to preside over a year in which Romania enjoyed stable government, an economy that grew at the fastest rate since 1995, and hopeful movement toward European integration, with the EU lifting visa restrictions for Romanians. *Adevărul*, one of Romania's major newspapers, editorialized that "the massive infusion of trade union leaders in the administration, politics and civil society, and the signing of the first social Accord between the employers' organizations, the Government and the trade unions were the major social events of the year 2001."[45]

The (renamed) PSD-led government worked closely with the trade unions through 2002, reaching agreement on a new Labor Code—widely perceived to be more favorable to labor's interests than to private enterprise, which was to be presented to Parliament in 2003. Nonetheless, difficult economic days remain for Romania, which was excluded from the ranks of Central and Eastern European nations to be considered for EU membership in 2004. Compliance with the International Monetary Fund's (IMF) fiscal austerity and privatization requirements will assure trade union resistance (BNS sued the IMF in Romanian courts in 2002). Plus, there have been several ugly labor disputes in recent years involving foreign ownership of privatized state enterprises that had distinct xenophobic overtones.

CONCLUSION

Romanian trade unions have affected the course of every government since 1989. The labor movement has used its influence—buttressed by its ability to mobilize workers for street demonstrations and the willingness of trade unions in key industries to strike in support of their demands (though rarely for general strikes)—as a counterweight against reform policies with which its leaders disagreed. Advocates of rapid privatization for most of the time since 1989 (despite the concomitant layoffs), these leaders now must respond to the increasing concerns of their members, who face job losses as large state enterprises are liquidated or sold. This social factor and the accompanying inevitable loss of membership for trade unions as employment continues to shift into the private sector (where employers generally resist unionization) will be one of the key challenges to the Romanian labor movement in the second decade of post-Communist development. Only time will tell whether Romania's trade unions will follow the pattern of many of their Western counterparts and remain strong only in the public sector, or whether they will develop the capacity to unionize workplaces in the private sector.

At the national and industry level, tripartite structures and relationships should continue, if not flourish, in the near future. Every government to date has been committed to this approach, and entry into the EU will require it. The currently governing party, the PSD, as a nominal, social democratic party, should be so committed. A successful corporatism will require more than formal structures, however, and the culture and expertise necessary to support genuine tripartite relations, especially in the private sector, has yet to mature.

NOTES

1. By June 1990, when the Jiu Valley miners invaded Bucharest for the third time in six months, the people of the city had coined the term "mineriada" as a sarcastic play on words, likening them to lavish sporting events that Ceauşescu had sponsored, which he called "daciada."

2. Hans Slomp, *Between Bargaining and Politics: An Introduction to European Labor Relations* (Westport, CT: Praeger, 1996), pp. 1–9.

3. Art. 165(1), Labor Code of 1972.

4. Vlad Georgescu, *The Romanians: A History*, trans. from Romanian by Alexandra Bley-Vroman (Columbus: Ohio University Press, 1991), p. 264; "Romania: A Whiff of Trouble to Come," *The Economist* (24 October 1981), p. 37; and the *Washington Post* (18 June 1985), p. A1.

5. Miron Cozma, a participant in the 1977 strike and the leader of the Jiu Valley miners' trade union for most of the 1990s, in a 1992 interview with the author, corroborated conventional views of many of the 1977 strike's events, including the "disappearance" of the strike leaders. Interview with Miron Cozma, president of the League of Jiu Valley Miners (10 February 1992).

6. Interview with Gavrilâ Henter (Bucharest, 23 March 1999). Henter is currently a retired advisor to the Blocul Naţional Sindical.

7. Programme for Free Trade Union, *BBC Summary of World Broadcasts (Romanian Press Agency in English)* (27 December 1989).

8. Henter interview.

9. Law 54/1991, Arts. 2(1), 42(2), (3). For a discussion of the history and current status of Romanian trade union and collective labor contract law, see Larry S. Bush, "Romanian Regulation of Trade Unions and Collective Bargaining," *Cornell International Law Journal*, vol. 32, no. 2 (Spring 1999), p. 319. On Romanian collective labor dispute law (prior to December 1999) and a relatively detailed treatment of the period 1990–1992, see Larry S. Bush, "Collective Labor Disputes in Post-Ceauşescu Romania," *Cornell International Law Journal*, vol. 26, no. 2 (Spring 1993), p. 373.

10. Sanda Ghimpu and Alexandru Ţiclea, *Dreptul Muncii*, 3rd ed. (Bucureşti: *Casa de Editură şi Presă* "ANSA," (1997), p. 87. The authors, and others familiar with Romanian labor relations, treat these figures regarding trade union density with caution, as there are no reliable databases. It is difficult for confederations to obtain accurate information from their own affiliates, whose interest can be to inflate the numbers.

11. Richard Croucher, *Economic Development and Trade Unions in a Transitional Context: The Romanian Case* (Labour and Society International Discussion Paper, no. 4), (London and Chicago: Pluto Press, 1998), p. 29.

12. Petru Sorin Dandea, "*Mişcarea Sindicală în Cadrul Sistemului de Relaţii Industriale dezvoltat în România după 1989*," in *Ghidul pentru Dialog Social şi Parteneriat din România* (Programul PHARE Pentru Dialog Social; Bucureşti: Valahia, 1998), pp. 201–3. In March 2000, CNSLR-*Fraţia* and BNS were said to be near a merger, but this had not occurred as of early 2003.

13. Law 130/1996, as amended.

14. For a discussion of the strengths and weaknesses of the new approach, as well as some of the inconsistencies with prevailing international labor rights norms, see Bush, "Romanian Regulation of Trade Unions and Collective Bargaining."

15. This council, *Consiliul Economic şi Social*, was created by Law 109/1997.

16. *Agenţia Naţională pentru Ocupare şi Formare Profesională* created by Law 145/1998.

17. Bush, "Collective Labor Disputes in Post-Ceauşescu Romania," pp. 387–90.

18. *România liberă* (7 February 1990).

19. "Iliescu Addresses Victory Square Meeting on Unrest," *BBC Summary of World Broadcasts* (Bucharest Home Service, 14 June 1990).

20. Bucharest Home Service (30 June 1990), trans. in *BBC Summary of World Broadcasts*.

21. Some unpublished accounts credit the settlement to a personal relationship established during this time between Miron Mitrea, on the one hand, and President Iliescu and his advisors, on the other. There may be some truth to this; Miron Mitrea subsequently left the trade union movement and entered politics, eventually rising to the rank of vice-president of Iliescu's political party.

22. Law 13/1991.

23. Law 15/1991.

24. *New York Times* (27 September 1991), p. A3; and *Los Angeles Times* (2 October 1991), p. A4.

25. Bush, "Romanian Regulation of Trade Unions and Collective Bargaining," p. 355.

26. Romanian Press Agency in English (8 May 1993), in *BBC Summary of World Broadcasts*. It should be noted, however, that the objectivity of ROMPRES reports at this time might be called into question.

27. Law 15/1991, Art. 30.

28. Complaint against the Government of Romania presented by the National Trade Union Bloc (BNS) and the Free and Independent Trade Union Federation of Train Drivers of Romania (FSLIMLR), ILO Official Bulletin, Vol. LXXVIII (1995), Series B, no. 297 (Case No. 1788).

29. Renate Langewiesche, *Romania and Bulgaria: In Quest of Development and Integration* (Brussels: European Trade Union Institute, 1999), p. 125.

30. Bush, "Romanian Regulation of Trade Unions and Collective Bargaining," pp. 359–62.

31. "Government and Unions Agree Tax Cuts and Pay Rises Package," *BBC Summary of World Broadcasts, Rompres*, in English (25 January 1997).

32. Romanian Radio (Bucharest) (11 August 1997), trans. in *BBC Summary of World Broadcasts*.

33. "*Sindicatele sper să aibă un dialog mai lung cu Guvernul*," *Cronica Româna* (22 March 1999), p. 4.

34. *România liberă* (25 March 1999), p.1; and *Adevărul* (25 March 1999), p. 1.

35. "Three-thirds [sic] of Government's Labor Commitments Kept," *Romanian Economic Daily*, no. 130 (27 May 1999), p. 9.

36. "Very Low Participation in General Strike," *Romanian Economic Daily*, no. 128 (25 May 1999), p. 3; and Mediafax News Agency (Bucharest) (25 May 1999), trans. in *BBC Monitoring Europe-Political.*

37. Romanian Radio (21 May 1999), trans. in *BBC Monitoring Europe-Political.*

38. *Financial Times* (20 January 1999), p. 3; and *Agence France Presse* (21 January 1999).

39. *Financial Times* (23 January 1999), p. 3; and *The Christian Science Monitor* (25 January 1999), p. 6.

40. Romania Radio (11 February 1999), trans. in *BBC Summary of World Broadcasts.*

41. *Agence France Press* (15 February 1999); *Financial Times* (16 February 1999), p. 2; and Romania Radio (17 February 1999), trans. in *BBC Summary of World Broadcasts.*

42. Jean-Luc Porte, "Romanian Pitmen Routed, Firebrand Leader Captured," *Agence France Presse* (17 February 1999).

43. *Agence France Presse* (4 March 1999).

44. *Financial Times* (12 March 1999), p. 3.

45. *BBC Worldwide Monitoring* (Rompres in English, 3 January 2002).

22

The Environment in Transition

Clifford F. Zinnes[1]

As in other countries throughout Eastern Europe and the Soviet Union during the Communist period, Romania's stress on ideological, and political over economic, considerations led to reduced economic growth and a squandering of its environmental resources. Environmental offenders are generally little affected by the negative impact of their own actions; thus, the need for accountability requires the intervention of a higher authority. However, under the Communists, the Romanian government—which has generally been a poor regulator of itself—did not recognize the severe economic costs of weak environmental management. Without the oversight of an environmental authority, the ubiquitous state-owned enterprises polluted without restrictions. Because of the diffuse nature of environmental impacts, the corresponding input, energy, and motivation for changing environmental policy require not only the central government's regulatory authorities, but also local government institutions and, perhaps most important, the active participation of civil society. The latter may be the most difficult to achieve, as over four decades of Communist rule in Romania centralized authority, bypassing the accountability of individuals in the process and, thereby, effectively smothering individual motivation. After the fall of Communism, the government, often under international donor pressure, developed environmental legislation and follow-up regulation without much, if any, public participation. To make matters worse, an imploding civil service and the underfunding of regulatory enforcement have encouraged noncompliance by enterprises, which, already under financial strain from transition restructuring, have strong incentives to shirk environmental standards in order to minimize costs.

For these reasons, the steps toward protecting (and repairing) Romania's environment have been difficult and sometimes meandering. Old attitudes must be overcome as environmental policies and institutions adjust. Slowly though, environmental law and institutions are taking shape, along with citizen interest and enterprise responses (the latter helped by privatization). These changes may offer the opportunity for environmentally sustainable economic growth, as the environment moves from the arena of "common property" (no ownership) to government stewardship (public ownership). In this chapter, we examine the quality and progress of Romania's environment through the first decade of its transition. The obstacles encountered reflect the moral, political, and economic legacy of Communism, and the continuing lack of accountability, personal initiative, and recognition of the need for quality, as well as quantity, of public services. As such, we find the environment in Romania provides a window into the resurgence and health of its civil society.

ROMANIA'S NATURAL ENDOWMENT[2]

In addition to its population of some 24 million, which is the second largest in Eastern Europe, Romania is endowed with a rich array of natural resources. It has a prodigious quantity of mineral and nonmineral resources. The former includes abundant deposits of ferrous and nonferrous metals and phosphates, while the latter includes coal, oil, and natural gas. These have formed the basis of large mining and quarrying, smelting, metallurgy, fertilizer, petrochemical, and energy sectors. Moreover, the country encompasses eleven[3] mid-sized river basins, totaling almost 22,000 kilometers in length; they are tributaries of the Danube River, which forms the southern border of Romania. Moreover, on its eastern border adjoining the Black Sea, Romania boasts 591,000 hectares of the total 650,000-hectare Danube Delta, the largest wetland—and ecological treasure—in Europe. Twelve national parks cover a further 397,000 hectares of Romania, leaving over 4 percent of the country as designated "protected areas." Of the country's total land area of almost 24 million hectares, 39 percent are arable, 14 percent are pastures, and 26 percent are forested. In fact, Romania boasts the largest remaining "old growth" forests in Europe. These natural assets have allowed the creation of wood processing, pulp, and paper sectors (and, until recently due to pollution, a fisheries industry). Another major national, geographic feature is the Carpathian Mountains, which run through the country as a backward "L," from the north of the country, through the center, and out to the west. These provide ample opportunities for hiking, skiing, hunting, and other outdoor recreational activities. In fact, if environmental degradation can be arrested, land and asset privatization completed, and the service sector strengthened through market competition, these could be the basis for a bright future in the tourist sector.

ROMANIA'S TROUBLED ENVIRONMENT

Clearly, the natural endowment of Romania, if used and managed economically, should be the source of considerable wealth once the trials of the transition period have passed. However, this natural-resource-based economic potential has been, from an environmental standpoint, a mixed blessing. Ironically, countries relatively rich in natural resources tend to experience *lower* long-run economic growth than those less well endowed.[4] At one level, this may be due to the tendency to squander what appears to be abundant. At another level, it reflects a situation in which it was more profitable to use the *political* system to battle over resource "rents" than to use the *economic* system to engage in more productive competition. In any case, a look at some of the more spectacular environmental problems in Romania reveals the effects of the absence of environmental accountability during the decades of Communism, as well as problems and solutions emerging in the economy as it privatizes.

SOURCES OF ENVIRONMENTAL DEGRADATION

Anyone with even a casual familiarity with Eastern Europe may cringe when the words "Romania" and "environment" are placed together in the same sentence. Certain industries in particular have contributed to Romania's tragic reputation on the environment.[5] Nonferrous metals smelting—especially of lead, zinc, and copper—is a major source of heavy metal pollution. Baia Mare, Copşa Mică, Zlatna, and even a suburb of Bucharest are well known for these activities. Major emissions comprise lead, arsenic, and SO_2 into the air, Mn (Manganese) and zinc into the water, and lead, cadmium, zinc, and copper into the soils. The result has been an acidification of soils and water bodies, which have led to the reduction of forestry and fisheries yields, the extinction of fauna, lead poisoning and lowered IQs in children, increased heart disease, loss of tourism, livestock intoxication, and reduced life expectancy in neighboring zones, among others effects.

Fertilizer (e.g., in Valea Calugărescă, Măgurele, Năvodari, and Bacău), chlorine-alkaline (e.g., in Borzeşti, Rîmnicu Vîlcea, Turda, and Ocna-Mureş), and carbon black (e.g., in Copşa Mică) production are the major polluters of the chemicals industry. The emissions from this industry (fluorine, NOX, SO_2, chlorine, and carbon black particulates into the air; sulfates, ammonia, and salts into water bodies; and phospho-gypsum, calcium chloride, and carbon black onto the soils) have had far-reaching consequences. Health effects include increased birth defects and higher child mortality, stomach disease, child blood disease, skin disease, and respiratory disease. Economic costs include the loss of large areas of arable land from contamination, vineyard destruction, livestock intoxication, and higher costs of water treatment for industry and agriculture, to mention but a few.

While the petrochemical industry is strategic, it is also a major polluter: discharging large amounts of oil into underground water aquifers, and volatile organic compounds as well as SO_2, CO_2, and CO into the air. The industry is mostly located in Brazi, Piteşti, Oneşti, Teleajen, and Moineşti. Its pollution has destroyed tens of thousands of hectares of forest and agricultural land, and has left drinking water and irrigation supplies hopelessly contaminated. Additionally, fishing is impossible in the affected areas, and the pollution it emits into the air also destroys the ozone layer. The energy sector—and the high-sulfur, coal-fired power plants in particular—reinforces these effects through particulate, SO_2, CO_2, and NOX emissions, which degrade agriculture and forest yields, ruin soil fertility, and raise mortality rates above the country's average, especially from cancer, tuberculosis, and respiratory diseases.

Given how much rebuilding will be required during the transition, it is unfortunate that the building materials sector, and cement in particular (much of it containing asbestos), is another major source of pollution. Cement powders, which are associated with higher rates of respiratory disease and anemia in children, cover almost 4 percent of all forest areas in Romania. Even animal husbandry, in the form of cattle, pig, and poultry farms, is a major polluter. It is an especially noxious polluter of water, where it causes eutrophication, killing fish life and poisoning water used for drinking and irrigation. Major locations of this industry are Timiş, Bacău, Prahova, Dîmboviţa, and Iaşi. Untreated municipal wastewater discharges in urban areas in particular are also a major source of problems. The release of pathogens, ammonia, and organic compounds are a danger to animal and human health. They eutrophy water bodies, reduce fish yields, and increase the cost of water treatment for industry and agriculture.

Though Romania is rich in minerals, poor mining practices mean that ore extraction (particularly for coal and non-ferrous ores) has been a serious source of pollution. The most affected areas are Gorj, Dolj, Tg. Jiu, Baia-Mare, and Zlatna, among others. Of major concern are the untreated mining waters and gangue that is stored above ground. In addition to ruining the landscape, it has literally killed some rivers biologically, taken soils out of the agricultural circuit, and harmed animal health. The pulp and paper industry has had similar effects.

Vehicle emissions resulting in lead, particulate, SO_2, and volatile organic compounds (VOC) pollution cause anemia, loss of child IQ, cardiopulmonary disease, eye ailments, and increased mortality, as well as deplete the ozone layer and produce greenhouse gasses. During the transition period, the number of vehicles has grown astronomically, and their emissions are posing an ever-greater threat to population health in urban areas.

Three principal sources of soil degradation are industrial activities, household waste, and erosion, but the first is the main source of hazardous waste. Of the approximately 165,000 hectares of known sites throughout the country (almost 1 percent of Romania), the most common source of contamination is from the metallurgical sector. The main pollutants are heavy metals, inorganic compounds, aromatic hydrocarbons, and pesticides. The main counties containing these sites correspond to those involved in the associated activities, namely, Maramureş, Bacău, Sibiu, Alba, and Gorj. Industrial waste deposits, which comprise almost 6 percent of contaminated land, also cause industrial contamination. Such sites are at their most serious in Ilfov, Teleorman, Bihor, Arad, and Dolj, where they represent from two-thirds to practically all of the site contamination by area.

The causes of soil erosion ultimately revolve around land use issues. Rainfall is highly concentrated in brief periods of the year, causing massive runoff into surface water bodies. Historically, forest cover helped to absorb and slow the flow. However, animal grazing and timber cutting have helped destroy this natural protection, and are generally considered the culprits for what is, practically, an annual flood which inundates parts of the country. The runoff not only depletes topsoil, but also clogs hydro-dams and flood-control works.

Romania's Water

The economic values under Communism harmed water resources. The *over*investment in waterworks contrasts drastically with the underinvestment in wastewater treatment. The expense of building wastewater treatment facilities, lack of funding for regulatory authorities, and the vague understanding of the extent and consequences of waste-water pollution—and water quality in general—resulted in a significant lack of attention to water quality by government and industry alike. Water *quantity* on the other hand, which is easily measured and (sometimes) paid for by beneficiaries, received great investment in the form of waterworks.

Sources of Water Degradation

Several problems contribute to water quality degradation. These include damage to ground water aquifers from petroleum and rural household wastewater, nonpoint runoff sources, wastewater treatment, and industrial accidents. In counties where there is an active petroleum sector, such as Prahova, oil drilling and petroleum refining have contributed to large amounts of groundwater contamination. The Allied bombing during World War II created crude oil "lakes." This problem was exacerbated by constant spillage from oil drilling and refining facilities, as well as from their feeder and distribution pipelines.

Another source of water degradation in rural areas relates to the release of nitrogenous compounds from untreated human waste in proximity to water wells that are used for animal and human consumption. A 1992 World Bank report indicated that pollution in over 90 percent of the wells in the country exceeded safe levels. Most of the problem regarding wastewater stems from mammoth underinvestment over the years in wastewater treatment. For example, at the end of 1993, there were only 2,770 wastewater treatment units for industry and municipal use combined nationwide.[6] Of these, 300 were out of service, and at least 535 were officially reported to be defective. Some cities, such as Bucharest, did not even have one.

Finally, due to poor management, inadequately trained and motivated staff, and obsolete equipment resulting from state ownership of enterprises, a host of pollution accidents occur annually. For example, in 1993, *reported* accidents released into rivers such toxic substances as chlorine, a variety of petroleum products, cyanide, hexavalent chromium, sulfuric acid, ammonia compounds, organic residual from slaughterhouses, oil drilling residual, household waste from commercial shipping, several types of detergents, and phenols. This, unfortunately, is only a partial list.[7] One of the most devastating and recent accidents occurred from January to March 2000 as three spills occurred in the Tisza River in the mining region of northern Romania.[8] From there, the polluted water flowed west into the Tisza in Hungary and then into the Danube and Yugoslavia. The first and most serious spill contained a cyanide solution used to separate gold ore from the surrounding slag. A spill two months later involved the accidental dumping of 20,000 tons of lead.[9] The spills, said to be the worst environmental accident in Europe since the 1986 Chernobyl nuclear plant explosion, allegedly killed everything in the Tisza river, including 75 tons of fish, and will cost an estimated $5 billion to clean up region-wide. The incidents, which strained diplomatic relations between Hungary and Romania, brought into stark reality the continued hazards posed by Romania's Communist industrialization, as well as the continued, ineffectual enforcement capacity of the environmental protection agencies. They also illustrate the continued control of information by the state: Romanians found out about the cyanide spill from the Hungarian press, not from their own government or media.

Trends in Water Quality

Over the decade, however, the water quality of surface rivers has been slowly improving. Class III rivers (which are used for irrigation, hydropower, cooling systems, and washing, and which constitute 12 percent of Romania's rivers) and class III+ rivers (which are regarded as a threat to public health, and which constitute 7 percent of Romania's rivers) have been upgraded to class II rivers (which are regarded as suitable for fishing and recreation, and which constitute 27 percent of Romania's rivers). Class II rivers, in turn, have been upgraded to class I rivers (which are considered suitable for municipal drinking water and for use in food processing, and which constitute 54 percent of Romania's rivers). This improvement is the partial result of the slowdown in industrial activity, as state-owned enterprises have been shut down or privatized.

The quality of drinking water in municipalities varies. Some localities are "improving," such as Bacău, Tulcea, and Baia-Mare. In the case of Bacău and Baia-Mare, it is due to a combination of intensive technical assistance to the environmental and water authorities, as well as the closure of the most polluting industrial parts in operation. Tulcea has received much attention, being situated at the entrance to the delicate Danube Delta. On the minus side, we have localities that are "worsening," such as Slatina, Alexandria, Oradea[10] and Suceava, which are deteriorating from a lack of funding for maintenance of water infrastructure. Finally, there are localities that have maintained a "constant" compliance profile over the period, such as Galaţi. Here, we have the "benefits" of decreased industrial production more or less offsetting the effects of deteriorating infrastructure.

ENVIRONMENTAL IMPACT[11]

The impact of environmental quality in any country can range from subtle to dramatic. The effects are far from only environmental; in most cases, there are economic and health impacts. In Romania, losses due to environmental degradation in agriculture and fisheries yields may be reaching over $480 million annually, with the related figure for forest wood mass being $160 million. Pollution to water bodies may be costing the country over $200 million annually in the reduced quality and quantity of water, including the increased costs of water pretreatment, flood control, destabilized water tables, and other pollution-avoidance measures. Another major source of economic damage is corrosion from acidic air emissions (such as SO_2 and NOX). This affects buildings, equipment, and even vehicles. The estimate for this category of damage is over $600 million annually. Also implicit in this calculation is the enormous waste of raw materials from inefficient use (as is seen from the high-energy intensity of output), production methods (materials literally disappearing up a smokestack), transport (e.g., pipeline leakage, particulate pollution from rail transport of coal). These costs are estimated at $160 million per year. Last and not least is the cost of deterioration in human and animal health, which may exceed $370 million. While all these figures, when added up, are equivalent to almost 9 percent of gross domestic product (GDP), they are still do not reflect the true overall costs of environmental degradation, which may be much higher. First, they miss the loss of economic output from the environmental health impact on lower worker productivity and absenteeism, as well as from the increased stress on limited health infrastructure. Second, they do not reflect the negative "value" of pain and suffering which results from living in a polluted environment.

The forestry sector provides a final, poignant illustration of the costs of poor environmental management. On average, of the over 400,000 hectares of damaged forest areas that were recorded in Romania during the decade, fully one-third were directly caused by pollution, with power plant emissions being the main culprit. This shows how production externalities from some sectors (e.g., power and cement) stymie the development of others (fisheries and tourism).

Obsolete technology and poor maintenance of plant and equipment share some of the blame for pollution discharges. However, the economic restructuring process of transition has already begun to address this problem. Market competition and the profit motive should provide a strong incentive to improve efficiency and reduce waste. Firms that survive will be those that have modernized because modern equipment better protects the environment. These trends will be strengthened as legislation becomes better enforced and as firms implement environmental management systems.

THE EVOLUTION OF ENVIRONMENTAL INSTITUTIONS AND POLICIES

We have seen that the degradation of Romania's environment has a wide variety of sources: industry, vehicle use, household waste, and farming, among others. However, we have only mentioned the physical sources. The environmental troubles in Romania also have deeper, less obvious roots in political and cultural stances developed under decades of Communism. The lack of institutional accountability, and a weak civil society unable to voice its concerns and hold the politicians accountable for the failure of their regulators, has also contributed to the current state of the environment in Romania. The development of environmental institutions and policies tracks the steps taken by civil society through the political process toward greater—and necessary—participation in environmental protection.

The modern institutional history of the environment in Romania may be divided into three periods: the Communist period, the initial transition period, and the recently begun institutional reorganization period. Over these periods, we see the difficulties involved in shifting environmental responsibility from the central government to local authorities and the emerging private sector. In the first period from 1974 to 1990, the National Waters Council and a National Council for Environmental Protection had environmental responsibility under the Environmental Protection Law no. 9/1973. Though the law was intellectually ahead of its time, it was never seriously implemented, and remains a legal curiosity. The law placed the National Council directly under the Council of Ministers and assigned it to be the "central specialized body" for environmental protection. Because of the tradition of water management and the emphasis on industrialization at any (environmental) cost, the focus was primarily on water. During this same period, the country created a mammoth, complex system of canals and waterworks. Enforcement of environmental quality was seen as subservient to the country's priority on industrial and agricultural development. The National Council's role was reduced to that of producing only documents requested by various international bodies.

In the second period, which dates from roughly 1990 to 1998, the government created a network of environmental protection agencies (APMs, or *Agenţia pentru Protectia Mediului* in Romanian), including the Ministry of Water, Forests, and Environmental Protection (MAPPM) in 1992. While the APMs originally were given regulatory authority over air pollution, solid and hazardous waste, and water pollution, water quality regulation was soon returned to the public utility managing waterworks and sales, ostensibly due to its greater experience in the field. The MAPPM received large amounts of technical assistance, first from the European Union's (EU) "PHARE" program and then from USAID, and had several legislative breakthroughs. However, over this period it slowly but continuously disintegrated into a moribund and dysfunctional (dis)organization. Also, in a time of declining budgetary resources, Romanian civil society, itself confused on what the best institutional structure should be for environmental protection, sent mixed signals to the politicians. The attitudes of most Romanian policy makers in the 1990s, as in the US in earlier phases of environmentalism during the 1960s and 1970s, were still stuck on command-and-control regulation over modern market-based solutions. Finally, the central authorities still blocked the newly promulgated, public participation mechanisms.

The third and current period, which dates from about 1998, is still nascent, but portends radical change. The MAPPM has taken a tentative step in its reorganization in the direction of recommendations made by international experts.[12] Though not yet fully implemented, these include a reduction in the number of river basin units, the start of a departmental reorganization based on function rather than media, and the development of a sustainable financing mechanism for the APMs. It is hoped that the latter will impose greater accountability on beneficiaries as they begin to pay directly for regulatory services.

Water

The Water Department of the central ministry is responsible for drafting water legislation, setting policy, and for overseeing the water utilities. Water management in Romania is divided into two spheres: "big water," which comprises the river, lake, and flood control infrastructure, and "little water," which comprises municipal water supply and distribution. The MAPPM regulates (in theory) *Apele Române*, which administers "big water" and is responsible for the management and selling of "raw" water nationally, while the Ministry of Local Public Works regulates "little water."

Though the "big water" system was inefficiently run—*Apele Române* had a staff of over 15,000[13]—in many ways the functional system reflected a long tradition in Romania of professionalism in the water sector. The main problem was economic. *Apele Române* sold water to industry and the municipalities at below cost. Worse, with the onset of transition and the decay of the police state, the level of nonpayment has risen dramatically, and with it there has been a decline in *Apele Române's* ability to finance the operations and maintenance of the system. Subsequent declines in service quality have only completed this vicious circle.

Perhaps more than in the "environment" sphere, discussed next, water policy has fit squarely into the three stages mentioned earlier. During the second stage, the MAPPM developed a body of water law based around Water Law no. 107/1996. This law made the state the owner of water, river basins the unit of administration, and *Apele Române* the manager of this resource. The law also explicitly created the rudiments of a financial system for water operations and maintenance, including a "water fund" for capital stock replacement. More interestingly, it introduced the notion of river basin committees (modeled on the French system and the US Delaware River Basin Authority) with the authority to set basin-level water policy, including discretionary pricing, (stricter-than-national) standards, and investment. Public participation was also given prominence through the committees.

Unfortunately, several factors impeded implementation. First, households and firms continued to use their weak financial health as an excuse for not paying water tariffs. This made it difficult to raise tariffs to the levels (legally) required for economically necessary, full cost recovery. Moreover, confusion in public finance law and other "reforms" under way at the Ministry of Finance made the operation of the Water Fund essentially impossible. More important, however, there was an ever-growing awareness that *Apele Române*, far from being the solution to water problems, was actually one of its principal causes. Romania simply did not need twelve river basin management authorities presided over by a top-heavy administration. Likewise, a conflict of interest existed because *Apele Române* was both the guardian of water quality (cum regulator) and the exploiter (cum seller) of water as a resource. As a result, the MAPPM postponed further implementation of the river basin committee concept until the issue of *Apele Române's* reorganization could be resolved. An active role for civil society was, therefore, again thwarted.

As of early 2000, responsibility for regulation of water quality was passed to the APMs. The number of river basins is being reduced, perhaps to six, and *Apele Române* has been converted into a joint stock company with the government holding all the shares. Each basin will have become an independent water company, ultimately managed by a concession contract. Whether this will achieve the results envisioned, only time will tell.

Forests

Forests have followed the pattern of water. A department in the ministry promulgates regulations, which are implemented by a regulated a public utility, ROMSILVA, which, in turn, manages forests and auctions standing timber through its network of forty-one county branches. ROMSILVA has depended on such timber sales for the revenues needed to manage the forests. However, poorly run auctions and price controls have prevented ROMSILVA, and therefore the state, from receiving fair market value for its timber.[14] In addition, harvesters tended to pay ROMSILVA at the very end of the year, making it impossible for ROMSILVA to spend funds before they are due to the state treasury. Equally frustrating has been the accounting problems caused by a public finance law that does not recognize depreciation as a deduction. This has prevented the public utilities from retaining the funds from tariff revenues to replace their capital stocks in a predictable way. The subsequent lack of revenues for ROMSILVA has placed forestry management on a shoestring. Predictably, morale has been falling over the transition period.

ENVIRONMENTAL POLICY IN THE TRANSITION DECADE OF THE 1990S

Policy in the 1990s reflected the challenges of creating regulatory structures in a country unaccustomed to seizing local or personal authority and accountability. After five years of bitter struggle, an environmental framework law was enacted, Law no. 137/1995, which was rather modern and ambitious—perhaps too much so. It mandated the meager environmental department to develop too much regulation and to increase its activities far beyond what its budget and expertise would allow. Over the next five years, with the help of extensive foreign assistance, a body of environmental regulation through permits was developed. Depending on a project's newness and economic type, either an environmental impact assessment or an environmental audit is mandated. To obtain a permit (theoretically), public participation through notices and hearings are required. Thus, the law has regulated the vast majority of large, polluting, and unpermitted enterprises currently restructured or privatized. For the first time, regulations mandate compliance schedules.

A number of factors have led to the system's somewhat checkered success. First, the regulations were released sequentially so that during the period, no complete and consistent set of regulations ever existed. Second, there was neither the quantity nor the quality of environmental experts and certified laboratories necessary for countrywide compliance. Third, regulation had always been centralized; however, simultaneous with the introduction of the new permits, the government was decentralizing regulatory authority out to the local APMs. The local APMs had never been responsible for decisions, and this created confusion in regulatory activities. To compound this there was little, serious training of local APMs as the new regulations were introduced. Finally, at the same time as their responsibilities were rising, real budgets—and salaries—were falling. The APMs had to do more with less.

Over this period, several attempts were made to introduce "economic instruments"[15] into public policy. However, only the World Bank-sponsored, differential pricing scheme to phaseout lead in gasoline has been implemented. Resistance again surfaced. The ministries involved saw these modern policy tools only as "taxes" and felt the environment should be "free." They had not learned the lesson of Communism: that what is free is squandered.

With foreign technical assistance, a set of environmental procedures for privatization was developed and, after a heated political ordeal, was enacted. Unfortunately, the same obstacles that thwarted its implementation also thwarted privatization, this despite a concerted effort to bring together and train the county authorities associated with the State Ownership Fund and the MAPPM. Too much novelty, in too short a period, with too many simultaneous objectives prevented success—especially given the level of suspicion shown by many in government, and in the donor agencies themselves, toward the environmental procedures for privatization.

OBSTACLES TO POLICY AND INSTITUTIONAL CHANGE

Romania's institutions and policies are having varying degrees of success as they strive for environmental sustainability in a changing political climate. We have already mentioned some of the difficulties in this process, including a civil society stifled by Communism and unused to wielding political power, the decentralization of authority, the complexities of implementing governance mechanisms, and the slowly emerging demand for quality as well as quantity of public services. In this section, we look at their effects of other more specific obstacles in the path of change.

Finding a Constituency for Good Policy

On one level, the legislative situation in Romania looks quite healthy. A reasonably good environmental law[16] exists, as does a water law and forestry law. Many modern policy concepts are slowly being implemented, including public participation, the "polluter pays" principle, and the "beneficiary pays" principle. Environmental auditing and environmental impact assessments are now required. Privatization procedures currently must take environmental liability into account. Great progress has also been made in recognizing the importance of transboundary and climate-change issues. The water utility has been incorporated. The APMs are moving toward self-financing. Nevertheless, a closer look still reveals gaping holes in the legislative picture, and more profoundly, a ubiquitous lack of adequate enforcement. Let us look at some examples.

As of early 2000, there is still no law on atmospheric protection, waste, or hazardous substances and their handling.[17] There is still no implemented legislation for the certification of environmental experts, or for reference laboratories, both critical for the issuance of permits and privatization. Nor is there a comprehensive law on environmental liability, which is regulated in a confusing and needlessly complex manner, by two provisions in the Environmental Framework law,[18] by the Land laws' articles on agricultural remediation, and by a procedure in the privatization regulations for allocating liabilities related to assets that have caused or have environmental damage. A coherent law on environmental liability would improve the functioning of capital and land markets—attracting foreign direct investors—as well as stimulate the reuse of "brownfield"[19] sites in urban areas, and the containment of sources of aquifer pollution.

Though Eastern Europe, Romania included, produces exceptional engineers, politics have divorced decision making from technological and economic considerations. Along with inexperience in drafting laws that are feasibly enforceable, this politicization has led the Environmental Department to insist that *every* economic activity be permitted, regardless how small or environmentally insignificant. The result, of course, was the creation of a huge backlog in permit requests, as well as an often shoddy analysis. The lack of a permit induces APM officials to engage in corrupt, rent-seeking activities.

Though Law no. 137/1995 authorizes economic instruments to be used in environmental regulation (articles 3d and 4d), implementation has been modest. Nor has Romania emulated other East European countries by instituting an environmental fund. Despite intense lobbying,[20] the chapters constituting an environmental fund were deleted from the Environmental Framework Law no. 137/1995. Even after the opposition won the 1996 election, and drafts were again circulated, no government commitment was attained, even though an environmental fund was part of its electoral platform. Only at the end of 1999 was a disappointing version of an environmental fund law been adopted by parliament.

Romania also lags behind the other countries in Eastern Europe in developing a national environmental action plan. Despite a series of efforts, no plan has emerged in the five years since the regional action began. The MAPPM had neither the internal capacity nor sufficiently strong political influence over other ministries. Environmental NGOs and others in civil society have not effectively lobbied the legislature effectively.

The Need for Institutional Change

As in any transition, a number of obstacles stem from the shift from a central planning system to a market economy. First, over the Communist period, Romania had become accustomed to highly centralized decision making, with most decisions made only by top management. This delays and complicates implementation by rendering many personnel incapable of taking the initiative. Despite years of central planning, inexperience and lack of knowledge on how to set priorities has hindered effective allocation of limited budgetary resources.

Another obstacle has been that low salaries have led to a gradual depletion of talent from the APMs and ministries, which in turn has led to lower prestige among the EPM staff.[21] There have been no economists or lawyers on the staff of the Environmental Department, nor on any of the APMs, impeding policy analysis. Enforcement will remain difficult, as the private sector hires better lawyers, especially given the regulatory loopholes. The excessive overinvestment in water infrastructure has made the construction of new waterworks very unlikely for another twenty-five years. Unfortunately, the same cannot be said of air and soil monitoring, which continues to suffer from a chronic lack of equipment. Without good and timely data on emissions, industrial pollution "accidents" are more likely to occur. Finally, enforcement is undermined by the loss of status of the MAPPM in the government, the debilitating disorganization and mismanagement of the ministry, general political instability, and the habituated lack of respect for the authorities and the law amongst the Romanian public.

Substantive obstacles include the lack of integrated media management, which can lead to intermedia substitution of pollution streams. This can occur, for example, when a firm takes its solid waste (which leads to soil and water pollution) and burns it, converting it into air pollution. Often, firms have a limited budget for environmentally related compliance investment. A lack of a media-inclusive compliance schedule can mean that one regulator can see itself in a zero-sum game against other regulators for the firm's fixed resources. It can also lead to overlapping investments in compliance by the firm.

These overlaps are endemic and have led to high-cost regulation by the government and high-cost compliance by polluters. Forty-one APMs, each with its own administrative structure and director, are too many for a country the size of Romania. Moreover, each one has its own laboratory (none of which are certified), as does *Apele Române,* which is run by the same ministry. A similar problem that has existed in the water sector is now being addressed in early reorganization efforts.

Probably one of the least recognized areas for institutional reform concerns the sustainable financing of the regulatory agencies themselves. Compare *Apele Române* and ROMSILVA with the APMs. The former are both technically self-financing, with their operating and maintenance budgets supported entirely from the sale of water and forestry products respectively. The APMs, on the other hand, are financed directly by the state budget. The result is that regardless of the measure used for comparison (i.e., manpower, quality of staff, or the amount of equipment) the APMs rank a distant third in performance. Fortunately, based on proposals of the author, the parliament promulgated in July 1999 an amendment to the 1995 *Environmental Framework Law*, which authorizes the APMs both to charge and *retain* fees for operating the environmental permitting system, which comprises issuance, monitoring, and inspection.[22] There is reason to hope that the worst of the EPM's financing problems may soon be over.

THE MIXED BLESSING OF DONOR ASSISTANCE

While the results of foreign assistance, especially at the national level, have been spotty, there is no doubt that it has influenced the tenor of the debate on environmental policy. Without the constant pressure provided by the EU regarding Romania's accession commitments, the MAPPM would not have been able to persuade the government to carry out the institutional reforms recently achieved. On the policy front, all the "achievements" described in this chapter were either conceived and/or designed with foreign technical assistance. As mentioned previously, the results, while encouraging, have been quite mixed. On the one hand, foreign assistance has introduced modern policy instruments, the concept of sustainable development, and the need to integrate environmental policy into the larger economic reform agenda. On the other hand, it has highlighted the need for stronger and more accountable government institutions.

A secondary, and quite interesting, effect of donor assistance has been on certain attitudes taken by nongovernmental organizations (NGOs). Many of the larger ones have benefited from donor training and institutional support. Nevertheless, two dangers have been associated with foreign aid to environmental NGOs. The first is the "fear of activism" syndrome. Environmental NGOs, in order to be effective, need to be activist, taking industry *and* government to task regarding the enforcement of law. Donors, on the other hand, wish to maintain good relations with the host government. They cannot be seen as being too aggressive in their support of the NGOs that are taking the government to court. This has led to the paradox that, while the number of NGOs and their activities have increased enormously, the number of legal battles with the government has not.

Another problem with donor assistance is the phenomena of "donor addiction." While the donors have had as a central goal the creation of a sustainable NGO movement, what they have really created among the survivors are organizations that are good at tapping the donors themselves. The existence of the donors actually prevents the NGOs from developing the skills and contacts outside the donor community to become sustainable in the long run.

WHERE CAN ROMANIA GO FROM HERE?

We have presented a litany of weaknesses that have led to a tepid response to environmental issues. Our underlying theme, that economic incentives are distorted by political and cultural roots, underscores the need to accelerate and cement the tentative but encouraging steps recently taken toward reforming environmental institutions. A number of basic attitudes need to be modified, however, before this can be accomplished. Most important, Romania must correct the assumption that environmental protection is a luxury that must wait until *after* transition, when the country is wealthier. This could not be further from the truth. First, many of the *new* sources of economic growth (e.g., agriculture and tourism) will occur in sectors currently held back by industrial pollution. Second, privatization and enterprise restructuring are occurring now and the resulting investment will determine Romania's environmental performance in the future. It is not economically efficient to apply the environmental regulatory "screws" once the investments are already made. Another misconception is that the environment and its services, like water and waste assimilation, should be free. A more sophisticated, but equally erroneous, version of this is that the government should pay for them. The experience of Communism illustrates that, in order to ensure the supply of anything of value, the direct beneficiaries should pay, wherever possible, the cost of its provision. Otherwise, the item of value will be squandered or even depleted.

We may consider that the first decade of transition ended in November 2000 when Romania voted back into power its first president, Ion Iliescu who, it may be recalled, was also part of the inner circle of dictator Ceausescu. This election, together with the objective of EU accession by 1 January 2007—further stimulated by Romania's acceptance into NATO in November 2002, seems to have accelerated government efforts from the point of view of legislative harmonization in the process of transposition of Romania's environmental *acquis* with the EU. Among these include regulations on environmental impact assessment, volatile organic compounds, vehicle emissions, waste management, and water quality on abstraction of drinking water. Romania has also largely completed the transposition of the EU Directives regarding nuclear safety and radiation protection in its energy sector. Finally, Romania has ratified the Kyoto protocol and the government has adopted an emergency ordinance[23] on industrial pollution prevention, reduction, and risk control. As in the past, however, in each of these instances there was little stakeholder consultation and little thought given to increasing and improving the associated administrative capacities required to implement—and hence make effective—these new laws. For example, in 2002, Romania created the National Environmental Guard but this has been nothing more than transferring the enforcement staff from the local environmental agencies without augmenting them or increasing their budgetary resources. The National Environmental Fund has most of its implementing legislation in place, but is still not operational. Moreover, integration of the environment into other policies is hardly progressing. Opportunities for self-financing of regulatory mandates remain unexplored and organizational rationalization, with the exception of moving the forestry department into the Ministry of Agriculture (a step backward in this author's view), are, at best, cosmetic.[24]

From the environmental perspective, Romania is at a crossroads. Though privatized firms, in seeking profits, could have abused the weak regulatory environment, new evidence[25] suggests that cost minimization and waste reduction incentives have had a dominating effect, and that these firms have proven themselves to be more environmentally friendly than the state enterprises which preceded them. Moreover, as the industrial sector modernizes, it will invest in newer technologies, which are actually far more environmentally friendly. Institutionally, there is hope to believe that the MAPPM has reached a nadir in its institutional capacity.

Most important, cultural attitudes formed during the Communist period are slowly changing along with the politics. The younger political class has shown signs of being more likely to seize personal initiative. Also, the reorganization of Romania's environmental institutions will hopefully reflect a higher level of trust and competence in local government authority. Finally, the accountability avoided for so long by the central government is now being demanded by new legislation, as civil society contributes its voice more and more to the dialogue on environmental protection.

The Cassandras forecasting the impossibility of Eastern Europe ever returning to a healthy environment were clearly wrong. Pollution loads have stabilized and have even started to fall. Nevertheless, much work is still required to ensure that when the economy firmly turns around, the regulatory framework, institutional capacity, and modern technologies are in place to close the door on the polluting past once and for all.

NOTES

1. The author expresses his gratitude to Martha Thompson for her extensive editing of an earlier, longer draft of this chapter.

2. This section draws upon data from the National Commission for Statistics (NCS), *Romanian Statistical Yearbook, 1996* (Bucharest: National Commission for Statistics, 1997). For some recent, indicative articles on the environment in Eastern Europe, see Douglas R. Weiner, "Environmental Issues in Eastern Europe and Eurasia: A Look at Recent Scholarship," *Newsnet: The Newsletter for the AAASS*, vol. 40, no. 4 (September 2000), pp. 1–8; and Mark Hertsgaard, "Russia's Environmental Crisis," *The Nation*, vol. 18, no. 25 (September 2000), pp. 22–24.

3. If we count the "Banat Zone" (the Bega, Caraş, Barzava, Timiş, Cerna, and Nera rivers), there are twelve.

4. A. Warner and J. Sachs, "Natural resource abundance and economic growth," Development Discussion Paper no. 517 (Cambridge, MA: Harvard Institute for International Development, 1995).

5. This section draws heavily upon G. Manea and C. Zinnes, "Summary of the most polluted sectors in Romania," *C4EP/Romania Policy Brief*, Harvard Institute for International Development (October 1994), mimeo.

6. Ministry of Water, Forests, and Environmental Protection, *Raport privind Starea Factorilor de Mediu din România in Anul 1994* (Bucharest: Ministry of Water, Forests, and Environmental Protection, 1994).

7. The list runs several pages in MAPPM (1994). Given the record of poor enforcement and monitoring, one can be certain that this is only the tip of the iceberg.

8. BBC, "Newshour" (29 March 2000).

9. Associated Press, "Pollution from Romania Mine Spill Spreads" (12 March 2000), p. 14.

10. Surprisingly, Oradea has been the focus of much international assistance in the water sector due to its proximity to the Danube and Hungary.

11. U.S. dollar estimates in this section are based on the author's unpublished research done while an advisor to the Government of Romania in the mid-1990s.

12. For example, see Clifford Zinnes, "Strategy for a Sustainable Romania 2000," Harvard Institute for International Development policy brief to Minister Frunzăverde (10 December 1997), mimeo; and D. Phillips et al., "Final Report of the 'ROM101' Project on MAPPM Reorganization" (Brussels: European Commission DG XVII, 1998), mimeo.

13. Compare this to England and Wales with a staff of 7,000.

14. J. Vincent, N. Marecico, C. Tarhoacă, M. Dragoi, and C. Zinnes, "An analysis of timber auctions in Suceava, Romania," Environmental Discussion Paper (Cambridge, MA: Harvard Institute for International Development, 1996).

15. These use prices, taxes, and other financial incentives to stimulate polluters to find cost-effective economic solutions instead of having the regulatory authority dictate rigid pollution levels and technologies.

16. Parliament of Romania, *Law on the Environmental Protection* [sic], Romanian Legislation volume 19 (Bucharest: Official Gazette, 1996).

17. Two exceptions are asbestos and PCB compounds, which will soon be issued into law as a result of international assistance efforts that were, until recently, led by the author.

18. Article 14 on the allocation of liability under changes of ownership and Article 80, calling for strict, joint and severable liabilities.

19. "Brownfield" refers to a site, generally abandoned, that has been contaminated by previous industrial activity.

20. Including parliamentary testimony by the author.

21. Legally, there are now 269 positions in the whole central MAPPM and a bit over 2,000 for the 42 APMs. The number filled is much lower. Either way, the figures are too low given the legal mandate of the APMs.

22. The law is based on a draft conceived and written by M. Pătraşcu and the author over the period 1996–1998.

23. While this is important legislation, emergency ordinances are often used by the executive branch as devices to evade the normal parliamentary process.

24. An additional improvement with institutional implications is that the environmental permitting system is evolving toward simplification. The 1995 framework law was uniform for all companies without regard to size or economic sector. Recent modifications reduce the number of companies required to obtain environmental permits by introducing three categories: null impact, low impact and significant impact. See D. Ghimici, V. Platon, A Ruff, and C. Zinnes, "Assessment of the Environmental Regulatory Compliance Burden on SMEs in Romania," IRIS Discussion Paper (University of Maryland, 2002).

25. See C. Zinnes, C. Tărhoacă, and M. Popovici, "The Impact of Privatization on Enterprise Environmental Performance in Romania," in T. Sterner, ed., *The Market and the Environment* (London: Edward Elgar Press, 2000).

V

SECURITY

23

Romanian Security

Daniel N. Nelson

Invited to commence accession talks with NATO at the November 2002 Prague summit, with membership certain in May 2004, Romanians celebrated in the streets of Bucharest. Their celebration was neither contrived nor premature. But why did it take more than a dozen years for such inclusion, while others were extended the West's hand far earlier?

Romanians see themselves as part of the West and want post–Cold War security guarantees from NATO and the United States. Even *after* being denied a first tranche invitation at NATO's July 1997 Madrid summit, eight in ten Romanians supported their country's candidacy.[1] During NATO's spring 1999 attack on Serbia, support for joining NATO fell substantially from the peak of 89 percent in December 1998; yet it remained higher (52 percent) than in some countries, such as Hungary and the Czech Republic, at the time they had actually been invited to join NATO.[2] More than most of Europe's post-Communist nations, Romanians saw themselves, during the 1990s, as threatened from a variety of internal and external sources.[3] For most of the decade, various Romanian governments tried hard to obtain security guarantees. Until 2001, they were not very successful.

Obstacles that have stood in the path of Romania's Western movement deserve scrutiny—primarily because larger questions are then implicit. First, can small capacity-poor states in threat-rich environments be "secure?" Particularly in a volatile region where peoples and borders are intermingled, can governmental policies generate "security" comparable in scope and duration to that experienced by other countries? Or, is a kind of perpetual state of lesser security "preordained" for some political systems and peoples? And, if true, is the pursuit of the same kind of security that others enjoy—via membership in certain institutions such as NATO—politically quixotic?[4] Will

NATO membership for Romania mean, inherently, less that the same Washington Treaty means for Spain?

A second vexing question has to do with the metamorphosis of the post-Westphalian state system. For several centuries, as every student knows, the notion of a state held sway, by and large, as it arose from the 1648 Treaty of Westphalia—spreading a European notion of political systems, albeit incompletely, around the world. Ideology and national identity did not enter the calculus of a state's security until much later. In the seventeenth and eighteenth centuries sovereignty remained vested in a monarch, and the state was only as secure as its sovereign. Security policies, such as they were, were a product of the interplay among the royal court, nobility, and landed aristocracy.

With the French and American revolutions, and the coming of mass mobilization, popular enfranchisement, and "self-determination," states were compelled to serve wider security needs. Increasingly these security requirements were defined by ideology and national identity. Hence, the twentieth-century Soviet state intervened where no Moscow-based Russian empire would have committed resources—Cuba, Ethiopia, Angola, Nicaragua, and, finally, Afghanistan—because of a global, ideologically driven competition facilitated by twentieth-century technology.

To the extent that party ideology and national taboos guide a country's pursuit of security, its policy makers are denied pragmatic flexibility. Made to protect a particular leadership and its policies, security becomes more illusory, less stable, and far less assured. To the extent that a belief system or national identity becomes a state's purpose, shoving aside any plural, pragmatic viewpoint, the chance for balancing threats and capacities—the core condition of security—is reduced, and the likelihood that such a state will pose an unacceptable threat within the international system is heightened.[5]

In the early twenty-first century, nonideological, de-nationalized foreign and security policies are unmet ideals. Absent robust, collective security organizations with which to abate threats, reliance on the capacities of states and their alliances remains the primary method of ensuring security. Enlargement of both invariably will be sought by states in an insecure world.[6] The balance between threats and capacities, which lies at the core of our meaning of security, will be pursued on behalf of ruling parties or cliques, or their ideological identities.

Romania fits decisively and poignantly into this larger context. Post-Communist Romania has tried to dispense with the ideology of Communist beliefs, while avoiding a slide back into nationalist-driven policies that have no place in the "new Europe." Neither Communist ideology nor Romania's nationalism, separately or in combination, whether favoring security autarky or balancing/bandwagoning with hegemony, has brought security guarantees to Romania. In its first decade of post-Communism after forty years of one-party rule and a prior decade of authoritarianism under royal and then Iron Guard dictatorship, Romania's elites struggled to construct a new basis for the country's international relations.

Post-Communist Romania's goal, by emotional consensus and pragmatic urgency, is Western integration—joining, participating, and contributing. Romania wants "in," but was unquestionably consigned to the antechamber, gray zone, or periphery of Euro-Atlantic security for the first decade of post-Communism. Now invited "in," it remains to be seen how far in such an "in" will be. Were the entry to be perceived as partial, with added responsibilities more prevalent than benefits, the memory of life on the periphery will return.

To make Romanian foreign policy and security a hostage to one party or clique, or to its belief system, would be both counter-democratic and would offer no path toward this larger integrative goal. Likewise, "Romanian-ness," were it to become a dominant theme in the country's early twenty-first century foreign and security policy, would evince parochialism and ensure ostracism. Of course, small states with many minorities, in a conflict-prone region, can hardly be expected to totally expunge such powerful sentiments from public discourse. How to minimize their effect on policy and the conduct of "statecraft" is another matter.

THE SETTING AND CONTEXT OF ROMANIAN FOREIGN/SECURITY POLICY

From the birth of the modern Romanian state at Alba Iulia in 1859 (when the principalities of Moldavia and Wallachia were unified under the leadership of Alexandru Ioan Cuza), Romania's international "place" was divided and troubled. Into an Ottoman and Russian geopolitical milieu, the Romanians brought a German-born monarchy (in 1866, Carol of Hohenzollern became the first monarch) to rule in a country with a Romance language and a Francophile culture. Even when the Treaty of Berlin acknowledged its complete independence in 1878, Romania was a multiethnic state, ruled by a monarch of German origin and with irredentist thoughts about most of the contiguous areas. Or, as one elderly Romanian politician said, regarding his country's future upon returning to Bucharest in 1990 after years in exile, "We Romanians are born to admire Germans, love the French, fear the Russians—and save our hate for most others."[7]

Romania appeared to benefit greatly from the denouement of World War I. From the dismemberment of the Austro-Hungarian Empire, all of Transylvania was awarded to Bucharest in the Treaty of Trianon. In addition to this, other settlements regarding Bucovina, the Banat, and Bassarabia doubled Romania's size and population. Yet, such gains also ensured a perpetuation of conflict with its neighbors and a continuing dependency on great powers for its security. Hungarian and German interests coincided insofar as postwar settlements were fuel for reactionary politics. Romania sought French guarantees through the *petit entente*. However, absent evidence that the French or British would constrain Hitler, Romania fell increasingly under a royal, and then later an Antonescu, dictatorship, and, ultimately, into an alliance with Germany. The alliance with Berlin was not so much the result of "pro" German sentiment in Romania, as it was driven by fear of Russia, a desire to regain Bassarabia (taken by Moscow in the Molotov-Ribbentrop pact), and by the recognition that no other power would guarantee the Romanian state.[8]

While the international behavior of pre-Communist Bucharest will continue to be debated, Romanian diplomats and scholars have exhibited consensus since the time of Nicolae Titulescu, Romania's interwar foreign minister,[9] on some fundamental principles that have guided the formulation of Romanian security policy. They are as follows:

1. Avoid isolation because it means vulnerability, and strive for Romania's inclusion as a European nation with full responsibilities.
2. Avoid one-power domination of Southeastern Europe, regardless of what that power might be. Instead, seek multilayer guarantees at bilateral, regional, and multilateral levels.
3. Protect the unitary integrity of the Romanian state against autonomy, self-determination, or other steps toward fragmentation.

During four and a half decades of Communist rule, these principles remained in place—although the regime itself, save for transient popular support during 1968–1969 in the face of a potential Soviet invasion, could not pursue such goals effectively because of its own lack of legitimacy. Nevertheless, both the Gheorghiu-Dej (who brought Sovietization to a halt, obtained a Soviet troop withdrawal, and presided over the 1964 Party declaration of Romania's separate path) and Ceauşescu leaderships sought to limit Moscow's presence in southeastern Europe, to ingratiate themselves with other powers, and to disrupt any movement that could have provided any autonomy to the sizeable Hungarian minority in Romania.

In its foreign policy, the Ceauşescu regime portrayed itself as independent within the Warsaw Pact, as a "developing socialist state" tied to the nations of Africa and Asia, and as a bridge between East and West. This strategy of cultivating worldwide contacts, and of maintaining a high international profile from a position of uniqueness within the Warsaw Pact, was successful for a decade and a half. At least through the 1970s, Ceauşescu was seen as an important actor in East-West affairs, arranging diplomatic initiatives in the Middle East and helping to inaugurate some of the initial U.S.-Chinese meetings in the Nixon Administration. During the 1970s, both President Nixon and President Ford visited Bucharest in recognition of the perceived independent role that Ceauşescu had established for himself in world politics. Western governments opened their domestic markets to Romanian goods, while Western banks made relatively easy credit available.

The United States, for example, granted "most favored nation" (MFN) status to Bucharest, and repeatedly extended it despite mounting reports of human rights abuses. American efforts to support differentiation within Eastern Europe took the form of visits in the mid-1980s by top officials, including then-Vice President George Bush, Secretary of State George Shultz, and many Congressional delegations. However, Romania's international role had become more limited by 1980–81, to such an extent that in a 1981 assessment of the country's prognosis for the rest of the decade I concluded that:

> the 1980s will see more internal and external constraints. The latitude available for military and foreign policy deviation, already limited, will decline as will Romania's ability to pursue economic plans independent from world markets and energy supplies. . . . Romania's ability to "go it alone" will decline.[10]

Ceauşescu's star began to fade in part because of high levels of debt. When total debt reached more than $10 billion in 1981, and Bucharest was forced to renegotiate its outstanding loans with a consortium of Western banks, it became clear that Romania was an investment fraught with considerable risk. Ceausescu, to make matters worse, provided little information on Romania's economy to the International Monetary Fund (IMF). Continued Romanian obstinacy with the international financial community was evident in a December 1987 decision by Ceauşescu to end payments to the World Bank. Western governments and institutions were further encouraged to dissociate themselves from this bad risk because Ceauşescu's "value," in terms of contacts in important capitals or regions, was less and less unique by the 1980s. In the Middle East, in Beijing, and elsewhere, the West and the United States established other lines of communications.

And, of course, Mikhail Gorbachev had enabled the United States, Germany, and other countries to establish far more direct relations with Moscow—thus obviating the "need" for Ceauşescu's intermediary role. At the same time, Gorbachev's leadership led to a geometric expansion of Romania's political distance from Moscow. Ceauşescu's regime was detrimental to Gorbachev's efforts to reinvigorate Communist Party states through economic and political reform, and he challenged Gorbachev's notions of *perestroika* and *demokratizatsiya*. The Romanian leader made it abundantly clear, only eight months after Gorbachev took office, that Bucharest would stay on the course of state socialism. Gorbachev's visit to Romania in 1987 underscored these deep-seated differences. By the spring of 1988, Ceauşescu was speaking of "rightist deviation" as the "principal danger" to socialism.

Ceauşescu's human rights abuses and the regime's espionage activities abroad also heightened Western indifference to, or suspicion of, Romania from the late 1970s through 1989. In the former arena, evidence accumulated of systematic intimidation, incarceration, and torture of persons suspected of advocating alternative political views (i.e., those critical of Ceauşescu). Even among Communist regimes Romania's human rights record became scandalous. Hungary, faced with a mounting refugee flow as ethnic Hungarians left Transylvania, supported Western condemnation of the Romanian government's human rights record at both the 1988 Conference on Security and Cooperation in Europe (CSCE) follow-up meeting in Vienna and again at the 1989 Paris CSCE session.

Ceauşescu also alienated the Romanian Army during the 1970s–1980s by insisting on a national defense strategy euphemistically called the "struggle of the entire people" (*lupta întregului popor*). As it emphasized mass mobilization and popular resistance, it weakened the Army's hold on resources. Further, the Army's manpower and equipment were increasingly utilized to build Ceauşescu's gigantic construction projects, ranging from canals to the massive "House of the People" in central Bucharest.[11]

Ceauşescu's bizarre and costly tyranny led Romania further from Europe, and alienated the country as never before from virtually all significant states, multilateral institutions, and other international actors. Romania was, by 1989, in the midst of a political, economic, and cultural catastrophe—all of which fed a sense of threat.[12] Highly insecure, Romanians were susceptible to the appeals of politicians who promised to constrain change and limit domestic turmoil. That choice, which brought Ion Iliescu and his party to power in the elections of both 1990 and 1992, made Romania's reentry into global commerce and Western institutions more difficult.

ROMANIA IN THE GRAY ZONE?

At the crux of Romanian foreign policy lie the interwoven goals of avoiding isolation, avoiding any single power's domination over the region, and of protecting a unitary state while ensuring the country's cultural and political integration with Western Europe. However, in the post-Communist era Romania's success in these goals has been partial.

Influential Romanian political figures, analysts, and commentators are well aware that Bucharest, notwithstanding two quite different governments during the 1990s (President Ion Iliescu, 1990–1996, from the left and President Emil Constantinescu, 1996–2000, from the center-right), were unable to gain more than partial, limited acceptance by principal Western institutions. The first Iliescu presidency received no credit for avoiding conflict with neighbors or for maintaining a semblance of social peace. At the same time, Iliescu and his advisors were upbraided for being former Communists who allegedly "stole" the revolution.

That said there was no chance for Romania to quickly climb the steep wall to respectability. Added to such a biased image were the predilections of Iliescu and his party to question privatization, especially when imposed by international financial institutions. It is not surprising, as the European Bank for Reconstruction and Development (EBRD) reported in 1995, that more than 50 percent of all income in Hungary was from privately owned enterprises or businesses, while less than one-third of Romanian income was derived from the then-private sector.[13]

The influential daily *Adevărul* editorialized in August 1998 that, despite the "long road that [Romania] has traveled in the past two years . . . one can notice that Romania has not managed to cross the finishing line in any of its major foreign policy objectives such as NATO, the European Union or the free travel of Romanians in Europe."[14]

The Constantinescu presidency, and Prime Ministers Ciorbea and Vasile, were unable to restart structural reforms for which the principal international financial institutions were waiting.[15] Constantinescu's own popularity, once very high, plummeted after only two years in office. By October 1998, the President received only a 25 percent approval rating, down from 38 percent in June 1998, and almost 60 percent in mid-1997. In a poll published in September 1999, only 10 percent of Romanians surveyed identified Constantinescu as the political personality whom they trusted most, while Ion Iliescu led political figures with 22 percent.[16]

President Constantinescu's support slipped further still after the fifth *mineriada*—that is, the fifth time that miners had staged a large scale revolt since the late 1970s, this time an abortive march by tens of thousands from the Petroşani mining area toward Bucharest in February 1999. Initially, and for some time thereafter, Constantinescu and his then-Prime Minister, Radu Vasile, were perceived as having given in to most of the miners' demands, whose leader, Cozma, was seen as a self-proclaimed regional strongman.[17] That the Interior Ministry had performed abysmally—its forces being routed by the miners at one road block, and hundreds taken prisoner by the miners—forced the Army to ominously suggest that it might have to use force. However, the Army itself saw this as a disastrous outcome of a political process for which the Constantinescu-Vasile government should take the blame. In a scathing indictment of the government generally, and of the Interior Ministry specifically, the Chief of the General Staff singled out the "grave tactical and leadership errors" that had contributed to this perilous episode for Romania's nascent democracy.[18]

As a consequence, the sense of being relegated to a "gray zone"—neither in nor out, not part of the Euro-Atlantic Community and without any viable alternative—became palpable by the late 1990s.[19] In addition to public statements or diplomatic language, less guarded views saw it more bleakly:

> In the early 90's, we saw a dim light at the end of a tunnel. We did exactly as we were told, behaved well, and were told to keep going. We got closer and closer, and we could just about make out figures, faces, and things recognizable. We thought we had almost made it. Then, some invisible hand pulled us back—way back. Suddenly we no longer see any light and we're not even sure we're in the tunnel. But it is very dark, and there are strange, frightening noises all around.[20]

Promises made by President Clinton and other U.S. emissaries in the aftermath of the NATO Madrid Summit regarding a "strategic partnership" between Washington and Bucharest were, likewise, met with doubt by astute Romanian observers—doubt that deepened during 1998–1999.[21]

Yet, the "gray zone" metaphor, popularized by many Balkan, Baltic, and Ukraine observers, has been misleading, and the underlying concept is too simplistic. It assumes that there is still black and white bipolarity, and that there is a political "Sargasso Sea" in the realm of international relations in which the country could be caught forever. Such a post-Cold War, discomfiting state of non-belonging ignores that European countries are increasingly at various stages of belonging, and are not permanently outside the reach of European institutions. It would be far more accurate, and psychologically more attractive, to see European integration as occurring on multiple planes—political, economic, military, cultural—and that, in each plane, movement up or down, forward or back, can vary with particular governments, leaders, and policies. The more such a peripheral status is felt, however, the more one may be confined to such a role; such fears have the potential to be self-fulfilling.

Even as Romanian policy makers *denied* that a gray zone exists, they acknowledged NATO's unwillingness "to involve itself in a new strategic set of challenges" concerning Central and Southeastern Europe. President Constantinescu's principal advisor on foreign policy, Zoe Petre, asserted the indivisibility of European security but, in the same breath, acknowledged "Romania's main and not very comfortable characteristic was to be the very border of different, even divergent, civilization areas." To simultaneously reject the divisibility of the continent's security while buying into thoughts that parallel, if not replicate, Samuel Huntington's "clash of civilizations" thesis is a tough fence to sit astride. Yet, Petre insisted on trying. As she noted: "Situated on both sides of these rifts of civilizations, Romania was, too often, the victim of its status of a 'multiple border.'"[22]

Romania is thus dealt a blow by geopolitics—its status almost taking on the qualities of "fate" or "nature," condemned to the periphery of Europe.

Romanians imply that their Latin nation, sandwiched between Slavs, Turks, and Germans, has been neither accepted nor appreciated. With Romanian policy makers seeing European and global forces with such suspicion, gray tones quickly form the backdrop to images that others form about the country.

The degree to which Romania is truly part of a common European socio-economic, political, and cultural identity is also at issue. For intellectual Romanians, "European-ness" is unquestioned and the country's rightful place in European and Euro-Atlantic institutions is seen as natural.[23] The rejection of the "Balkan" designation, not readily accepted by anyone it seems, was begun in the first Iliescu government adopted by the Constantinescu presidency, and is now part of early twenty-first century Romanian mantra; the preferred term describing Romania's location is "Central Europe."

Romanian intellectuals, wrestling with the dichotomy between what they think they are vis-à-vis how the world perceives Romania, often lament their country's weak government and "chaotic democracy." Their analysis just as often tends to emphasize Romania's "historic handicap"—the bad hand dealt to Romania's democrats and reformers, which from the start (December 1989) meant that the country's efforts and potential would be hindered and slowed.[24]

However, as a Croatian political scientist perceptively observed, the rebirth of national identity in post-Communist Europe underscores a fundamental difference between the eastern and western halves of the continent: The denial of national interest during the Communist era was a form of deprivation for Eastern Europe, and the recovery of the national interest in the post-Communist era has been a form of emancipation. While liberty for the older nations, such as France and Britain, translated into pluralism, tolerance, and mediated conflict of democracy, East European liberty represents release from oppressive foreign rule, assertion of identity, and the establishment of the nation-state.[25] Such an emphasis on national identity in post-Communist Europe stands in contrast to the broader European vision of submerging nations within larger institutions that reduce sovereign prerogatives. Romania's willingness to peel away layers of hard-won independence and sovereignty is uncertain at best.

That Romania, Bulgaria, and others were kept at arm's length for more than a dozen post–Cold War years is sometimes explained as a consequence of these countries' poverty and still heavily "statist economies." Tardy efforts to privatize principal economic sectors, inadequate banking reform, and the lack of other fundamental aspects of a market economy are often cited as problems delaying the assimilation of Romania into the Western "club." Yet, Greece and Ireland were extremely poor when the European Union (EU) accepted their applications and very low Portuguese, Greek, or Turkish living standards did not preclude joining the NATO family.

Other factors must be more powerful explanations for Romania's tardy integration and lesser reputation. One does not hear from Romania a general acknowledgment that post-Cold War membership criteria legitimately may differ from, and be "higher" in terms of democratic behaviors, than expectations in 1949 or the early 1950s. Instead, Romanians suspect that the most powerful explanations rest in the realm of an erroneous judgment about Romania, in inadequate information, or sometimes, a darker conspiracy against their country. Romanian journalists and analysts note with considerable irony any occasion where Romania's needs are ignored or slighted.[26]

Romanians' earnest desire to avoid isolation is shared by all social strata, and corresponds with a strong positive sentiment about the United States, France, Britain, and Germany—although opinion about the latter is clouded by uncertainty about long-term intentions.[27] These mass feelings have not been manufactured by an elite campaign. Rather, such views are steady, resilient, and considered. Romanians want to "join," to be a member of "the club," and to be appreciated as a valued part of the Euro-Atlantic community. That Romania has something to offer the West—as a contributor to peacekeeping operations such as Angola and Albania in the 1990s and a coalition member in Afghanistan and Iraq in the early 2000s, or as an example of a stable multinational state in the Balkans—is a widely shared opinion. NATO's initial decision to enlarge without including Romania—announced at Madrid in July 1997, and implemented at the Washington Summit in April 1999—hurt. Romania had pushed hard, very hard, during 1996–1997 for inclusion in the initial round of NATO expansion. The arguments used to develop Romania's case were numerous, and were presented through diplomatic visits, media, and publications.[28]

Even those Romanian officials who, in both the first Iliescu and Constantinescu presidencies, had been engaged deeply in pressing Romania's case for entry were unsettled by the implications of rejection for their country. For example, today's Defense Minister who had been the Deputy Defense Minister in 1993–96, Ioan Mircea Pascu, wrote in 1997 that it had become painfully clear that Romania had been placed in the company of other states such that "its accession to NATO . . . [was put off] into the distant future."[29] Other well-known Romanian commentators on international politics likewise warned that Romania's inability to make its case with NATO might risk turning optimistic and patient Romanians into impatient pessimists.[30]

NATO's 1999 decision to exclude other applicants for the foreseeable future also brought to the surface fears of Hungarian membership, and of "marginalization" in general.[31] When, in early February 1999, Prime Minister Radu Vasile visited Budapest, one important Bucharest daily—not known as particularly nationalist in tone—wrote that "Radu Vasile Enters the Den of the Young Wolf Viktor Orban" (Hungarian Prime Minister), while noting that the Hungarian press abstained from comments on the visit.[32]

Creeping Russian encroachments in Southeastern Europe were also a concern, and the stuff for speculation in Bucharest. Potential Russian efforts to reassert control in Moldova from Russia's foothold in Transnistria (a Russian populated sliver that broke off from Moldova in a violent mini-war during 1992) are thought to be simmering. Further, a dispute over the speck of land in the Black Sea called Serpent's Island, located between Ukraine and Russia, is important because of potential oil resources in the vicinity. Moscow's behind-the-scenes role is suspect in Bucharest. Senior Russian officials are probed at almost every occasion about such matters, with a subtext of suspicion not far from the surface.[33]

During early and mid-1998, when the Russian firm Lukoil brought controlling interest in the Romanian company oil Petrotel, amidst sharp Russian statements against NATO enlargement, the Russian ambassador in Bucharest was often the focus of attention and some innuendo.[34] When the fifth *mineriada* occurred in January 1999, public speculation by a variety of politicians and journalists about Russian involvement—allegedly to create a crisis in Romania and thereby divert Western attention from Serbia—gained currency. Fortunately, cooler heads pointed to the foolishness of such phobia.[35] Such concerns, although exaggerating Russian capabilities and interest in Romania today, nevertheless reflect Moscow's past record, going back to the Molotov Ribbentrop Pact that allowed the Soviets to absorb Bessarabia at the beginning of World War II, and to threats of Soviet invasion in 1968, when Ceauşescu had opposed the Warsaw Pact's intervention in Czechoslovakia. Even in late 2002, a delayed Russian-Romanian treaty continued to be explained in Bucharest by reference to Moscow's agenda for control.

For public and political consumption, the Constantinescu government redoubled its efforts after Madrid, frequently and vigorously reiterating its intention to ensure Romania's entry via a "second tranche." Asserting that its 1998–1999 arguments would be "strong and well presented, unlike we did in 1997," Foreign Minister Andrei Pleşu and others tried to reinvigorate Romania's NATO campaign in spring 1998.[36] To visiting U.S. Deputy Secretary of State Strobe Talbott, Pleşu said that "Romania's request to be admitted to NATO is not . . . local vanity or a rhetorical ornament, but rather a matter of objective necessity."[37] Yet, even Pleşu admitted to doubts about his county's long-term success at entering NATO: "In order to not remain isolated, on the outskirts of all empires, we need a 'beneficial' invasion."[38]

Many of the same arguments from 1996 and early 1997 continued to be recycled prior to the Washington summit of April 1999—that Romania has a "strategic position of interest for NATO," with an infrastructure vital for the Alliance's southern flank, a large military potential, and many other strengths.[39] External efforts that promoted Romania's interests, such as the Romanian-American Action Commission, housed in and directed by the Center for Strategic and International Studies in Washington, D.C., likewise sought to promote its "strategic value."[40] Among Romania's putative assets were invariably mentioned its "strategic location" (i.e., at the intersection of several critical zones including Central Europe, Southeast Europe, the Black Sea, and the so-called Caspian-Atlantic corridor), the Romanian government's "strategic commitment" (i.e., to reform), and the country's "strategic contribution" (i.e., to peacekeeping and other likely NATO needs).[41] An undercurrent in discussions with France and Italy was Romania's culturally Latinate ancestry.

As with most other NATO aspirants, the sheer frequency of the word "strategic" was indicative of miscalculation. Unfortunately, those who made such "strategic" arguments forgot that domestic accomplishments, which would stabilize the democratic transition, would foster an appropriate image for NATO (or EU) membership far more quickly than the drumbeat of strategic value. Only a cataclysmic event could have altered the criteria for Western inclusion; and, that event was September 11, 2001.

A DIFFERENT CALCULUS

Until the September 11, 2001 attacks on the United States, and the clear threat of global terrorism to democratic societies, post-Communist countries such as Romania were judged by different standards. Those standards—never explicit, but always political—affected Romanian domestic politics even as Western countries based judgments about including Romania on internal conditions. During the 1990s, and until late 2001, Romanians focused on NATO, while being propelled by the unmistakable sense that NATO's arrival had been delayed, if not obviated.

Post–Cold War Romania's unrequited "NATO-ist" foreign and defense policies began to fray in the aftermath of a Washington summit that provided no timetable or precise roadmap for entry. The "Madrid plus" formula, by which the April 1999 summit's script was written, offered nothing more than further tutorials and paternalistic hand-holding to Romania and other NATO suitors. The Military Action Plans (MAPs) that each aspirant was to produce evoked little enthusiasm in Bucharest, where responding to NATO's solicitations for documents, diagrams, and details consumed immense personnel time and scant resources.

Because of the war against Serbia, NATO's Washington summit offered some rhetorical security guarantees to "frontline" states such as Romania, Bulgaria, Macedonia, and Albania. Influential Romanian observers called this NATO offer "Article 4:45" (*"cinci fără un sfert"*), in an ironic reference to the article of the 1949 Washington Treaty—applied fully to members only—that an attack on one would be considered an attack against all. Senior Romanian military and political leaders had made clear through every channel their hope that NATO would do more—a clear step-by-step roadmap with signposts, and a precise timetable. Western diplomats, hearing Bucharests' frequent and plaintive message, began to offer summaries in caricature—"Please promise us something for the summit to make us feel better."

Even if the Washington Treaty's intricacies were unknown, any government in Bucharest, having been denied what Romanians most viscerally want, was bound to feel negative political consequences from Romania's failure to gain entry into NATO in 1999. Constantinescu, whose popularity fell substantially from 1996–1999, had more rough water ahead as NATO's door remained barely ajar. Had the issue of NATO membership not been fundamentally changed, his successor would have had to recalibrate pro-NATO views.

One early casualty of NATO's rejection of Romania's candidacy at Madrid was Romania's enthusiasm for an adapted Conventional Forces in Europe (CFE) treaty. Negotiations to adapt the 1990 CFE treaty, which had been placed into force when there were still two opposing Cold War military alliances, commenced in earnest in 1997. From the outset, Bucharest expressed unease with its designation as a "flank" state, which grouped Romania alongside much of the former Soviet Union. Although such flank status meant little in practical terms, the exclusionary sound of the designation was disliked strongly in Bucharest. Moreover, the original 1990 treaty, and the subsequent amendments regarding military equipment allowed in "flank" areas, meant that Romania was allocated considerably fewer tanks (and other large conventional equipment) than, for example, Bulgaria—which has only 40 percent of Romania's population. In the eyes of the Romanians, the CFE smacked of "unfairness."[42]

A broader questioning also began to be raised. No one spoke, even guardedly, about giving up on NATO. However, ample discussion was generated in Bucharest, and among Romanian analysts and policy makers speaking abroad, concerning a "NATO-friendly, not NATO-dependent" strategy. At the same time, Romanian efforts to stay in NATO's sights and good graces, waiting for the day when a second tranche came about, became not a public relations campaign *talking* about Romania's "strategic" value. Instead, emphasis was placed on *doing* things—especially programs useful to Romanian security.[43] Such a proactive effort, accelerated greatly by the second Iliescu presidency, and by Foreign Minister Mircea Geonea and Defense Minister Ioan Mircea Paşcu, placed Romania in a far better position to respond as a future ally after September 11.

Yet, just after the Washington summit, no turnaround seemed feasible. One prominent editor, writing just after that NATO meeting on 27 April 1999 expressed this view rather succinctly:

> The NATO summit is over, but Romania is left with its problems and anxieties. This moment should mark the end of illusions and a return to reality. It is good that we still have the attention of the NATO countries. . . . However, neither NATO nor the EU will fill in the black holes in the Romanian economy . . . for now. [The government] will have to demonstrate its commitment to western values by what it does to make Romania prepared for Euro-Atlantic integration.[44]

Romania's guarded foreign and defense policies were evident in the 1990s. During the 1991–1995 wars in the former Yugoslavia, Bucharest enforced a UN embargo against Serbia and other combatants, losing perhaps $7 billion in revenues and sales. Yet, Romania exhibited reluctance during those years to distance itself from Belgrade, or to create an irrevocable rupture in relations. During the Serb-Croat and Serb-Bosnian wars, Romania delivered oil to Belgrade through the Romanian firm Solventul in Timişoara,[45] despite a UN embargo, and was reported to have negotiated deals to transship Russian and Ukrainian arms to Croatia.[46]

In 1998, as Kosovo slid into full-scale war, caution about backing NATO threats of air strikes against the Serbs was echoed from the opposition and the government in Bucharest.[47] Several days before NATO air attacks commenced, President Emil Constantinescu did issue an endorsement of unspecified "NATO intervention," yet he made no mention of force, and emphasized the Romanian desire for the success of the Rambouillet Agreement.[48] Romanian military and diplomatic channels did make American authorities aware of the availability of Romanian air space if the need arose and the Parliament eventually voted to endorse such an offer. However, Romania had not sought or encouraged the use of force, and studiously avoided the most severe condemnations of Serbia or its government.

The consequences of this latest Balkan war were not those from which Romania could take much comfort. With the Danube effectively closed to commercial traffic, both because of NATO's destruction of bridges and Serb desire to "repay" Romania and Bulgaria for their cooperation with NATO, substantial economic losses were incurred. Totals were imprecise, but net losses to the Romanian economy were certainly in the hundreds of millions of dollars.

However, far more damaging to Romanians' sense of their own interests is the use of NATO power to ensure de facto independence for Kosovo, heretofore a province of Serbia. While most Western decision makers remain convinced that such force was necessary—to preserve standards of international behavior as well as to maintain NATO itself—Kosovo is seen as an unhealthy precedent by Romanian politicians. Regardless of party affiliation, Romanians prominent in their country's foreign policymaking regard NATO's apparent military success with uncertainty and even with an ominous tinge. Sure that they have not seen the last of the wars of Yugoslav succession, Romanians are also afraid, justifiably or not, that other minorities might get the same idea—pushing violently for more than cultural autonomy, sensing that NATO will come to their side if a unitary state tries to reassert itself.

When Polish, Ukrainian, and Romanian foreign ministers met in late November 1997, there was also a hint of thinking in Bucharest about where NATO's enlargement was headed. Then-Foreign Minister Adrian Severin noted at that meeting that NATO was "not only in the process of expanding, but . . . should increasingly become a system of collective security."[49] A consensus existed across parties and ideologies that the OSCE would never suffice as a substitute for NATO. For example, Oliviu Gherman, the *Senat* leader when Ion Iliescu's party, the PDSR, governed prior to the November 1996 election, made clear the inadequacies of the OSCE for Romanian security.[50] Nevertheless, any notion that NATO itself will metamorphose into a collective security entity, although heard in Western capitals as well, departs from "mainstream" thinking within NATO, which envisions the Alliance as retaining its core military function while developing new cooperative security roles.

In the same period, Romania's principal arms manufacturers, such as Aerofina and Romtechnica, attracted the attention of U.S. and NATO military analysts and intelligence circles for its dealings with governments and institutions, which are not necessarily the best friends of the West. In some cases, it shipped arms in violation of UN embargoes. Between 1994 and 1996, *Aerofina* (which manufactures missile components and guidance, among other products) negotiated with Iraqi emissaries, and actually signed an agreement with Iraq in 1995, which was forbidden by UN sanctions. Deliveries may have been prevented by coordinated intelligence agency sting operations, but the episode spoke poorly about control of Romania's military industry.[51] Moreover, it appears that Romania shipped large amounts of small arms in early 1997 to Rwanda via Yemen (to conceal the final destination), despite the UN embargo to that country.[52] Other private discussions with Romanian officials have raised additional concerns about contacts regarding arms sales to questionable foreign governments.

Efforts to link Romania's considerable airframe and aircraft engine manufacturing capacity to NATO via licensed production agreements have been troubled. IAR (Întreprinderea Aeronautică Română) and Turbomechanica are both large firms that carry over from the Communist era. In 1998, Bell-Textron thought, after discussions which some sources date from 1994, a deal had been finalized to build ninety-six advanced AH-1 Super Cobra attack helicopters using the airframe and engines built by the two firms, with assembly in Romania. However, IMF objections and severe doubts within Romania that the country could afford to produce such a large fleet of advanced helicopters, in a questionable external market, led Finance Minister Daniel Daianu to resign in mid-1998. Although the project's final death is still uncertain, the budgetary consequences would affect Romania's ability to direct resources to other pressing needs. Requiring a Romanian investment of $1.5 billion or more, as compared with a defense budget of never much more than $1 billion per year, suggests a large additional deficit even if such a project were stretched over many years. For many Romanians who have led the drive to integrate with Western security institutions, such spending is a price the country must pay.

In these and other respects, Romania's actions suggest recognition that, no matter how integrated Romania will become within NATO after its spring 2004 accession, complete dependence on the Atlantic alliance may be ill advised. NATO-related countries, such as Israel, have become close partners of Romania in modernizing Mig-21 and other aircraft, while vigorous exploration of markets for Romanian arms exports and technology have continued. At the very least, some aspects of Romanian security require a different calculus.

The search for *additional* (not other) anchors with which to maintain Romanian security in the turbulent waters of the post-Communist era has also meant creating or strengthening ties with neighboring states. A concerted effort in this regard, which had the added benefit of underscoring the "strategic" importance of Bucharest's diplomacy, was the "Romania at the Crossroads" project launched by the Constantinescu presidency and the Ministry of Foreign Affairs. Multiple bilateral and trilateral summits and ministerial meetings became more numerous in the Constantinescu years, and the second Iliescu presidency continued this pattern, designed to cement cooperative structures in Central and Southeastern Europe.

France and Italy, Romania's "Latinate" NATO advocates, remained in favor of the Alliance's extension to include Bucharest and Slovenia during the 1999–2000 period. Romanian diplomacy consistently cultivated these ties.[53] But such four-way (including Slovenia) cooperation also evoked memories of the entente between the wars, or of a "southern approach" to NATO's open door, neither of which seem to discerning Romanian policy makers to be a strong hand in the game of international security. That transnational terrorism generated a far different scenario for NATO enlargement after September 11, 2001 obviated the need for such stratagems.

RETURN TO NATION AND IDEOLOGY?

Romania's invitation to join NATO, issue at the Prague summit in November 2002, changes Romania's security environment; but the transformation is neither immediate nor complete. Even with full accession to the Alliance in May 2004, the ties will have weak links.

Romania's military is not modern, its democracy remains rough around the edges, and its socio-economic conditions will require heavy and prolonged investment. More important, there is a danger that, under duress, people who have experienced the "comfort" of authoritarian rule will long for the assurances which authoritarianism brings, rather than worry about the absence of freedom which it implies. The threshold at which such a tradeoff would be made is likely to be high (i.e., ample research has demonstrated that socioeconomic pain and other threats would have to be extremely severe before a dramatic shift from democratic values would occur).[54] Yet, civil society can hemorrhage and ebb quickly once that threshold is crossed.[55] In 1999, near the tenth anniversary of rebellion against Nicolae Ceauşescu, most (51 percent) Romanians believed that life was better under Ceauşescu, and 64 percent thought that Romania was "headed in the wrong direction."[56] At the same time, the extensive and prolonged NATO air war against Yugoslavia sent ripples of discomfort and fear through the Romanian population during the spring and summer of 1999.

There is a danger that the precarious sovereignty of small, poor states will confront increasingly strong challenges to territorial integrity, policy autonomy, and control over economic development.[57] While a post–Cold War environment has implied greater "freedom of action," the relative capacities of small states—particularly those without substantial wealth in a continent of great wealth and proximate powers—are mismatched with this new latitude. Put another way, there is more "freedom" than they can use to their advantage, and such incapacity in the face of opportunity heightens national frustration as perhaps nothing else could.

For Romania, the "new world order" has been no picnic. Bucharest's policy makers have been peripatetic but ineffective, free to roam but without a place to land. Even a few years after 1989, it was abundantly clear that Romania confronted "numerous intractable problems that [made] the country less secure than most of the other formerly Communist states of Eastern Europe" and that Romania had "neither the military nor the economic capacity to confront such threats."[58] If that was true in the early 1990s, it had become far more poignant by the new millennium.

By mid-1998, Romanian views had become much more blunt. Cătălin Harnagea, then chief of Romania's Foreign Intelligence Service (SIE), spoke publicly about the palpable dangers of Mafia-like groups taking over instruments of power in a given country using economic force and violence; and that Romania, specifically, was endangered by large-scale organized crime.[59] As Romanians looked at a NATO enlargement from which they were excluded in 1997–1998, they wondered about Hungarian intentions, and listened, perhaps much too closely, to each conspiracy. Reflecting on Romanians' hope to enter NATO with a European strategy (given American disinterest until after September 11, 2001), the venerable ex-Communist intellectual, Silviu Brucan, wryly noted that Romania would have improved its chances of getting into NATO with a Middle East strategy—by renewing old ties with the Middle East, thereby generating both new trade and heightening Bucharest's value for the alliance.[60] Still Europe-focused, but reading the tea leaves very accurately, Bogdan Chirieac wrote in early February 1999 "Adio NATO–Europe, the Only Hope." Led by German Chancellor Schroeder, but endorsed by other Alliance leaders at a critical meeting in Munich, it was flatly stated that NATO would not be inviting anyone else soon.

Accordingly, bilateral ties with principal European countries, not the United States, became the country's security focus until 2001.[61]

In this milieu, humble, obedient Romanian diplomacy was nearing an end. Having seemingly fallen off the NATO bandwagon, many Romanians might have not wanted to climb on again. This became, during 1997–2001, an audible subtext to elite discussion on this issue. Even former Romanian Foreign Minister Pleşu, while insisting that Romania had no alternative to NATO membership, pointed out "one cannot rely on metaphorical pronouncements with an indefinite time scale."[62] Had that become a popular consensus, the national and ideological components of Romania's international policy would have become much more prominent. Several of the trends—moving away from NATO dependence, and focusing on real or perceived internal dangers with foreign components–sent troubling signals for domestic tolerance and civil society.

After a more than a decade of post-Communism, it appeared circa 2000 that Romanians had only post-Communism. That this was so was the "fault" neither of Romanians and their governing elites, nor of a callous or prejudiced West.[63] However, the failures of both created a potential for at least partial re-nationalization of Romanian foreign and defense policy. Had Romanian political figures to increasingly emphasize heightened threats and a need for their country to rely on its own capacities, rather than on integration with, and security guarantees from, the West, a troublesome corner would have been turned.

Terrorist attacks on the United States in September 2001 created an unexpected opening for stronger ties to Washington. A concerted and obvious effort was mounted by the government of President Ion Iliescu and Prime Minister Adrian Nastase to position Bucharest as close as possible to George W. Bush's global war on terrorism. Such a strategy was orchestrated by Defense Minister Ioan Mircea Paşcu and Foreign Minister Mircea Geoana, with behind-the-scenes efforts by Ioan Talpeş (Presidential National Security Advisor).

Romanians did everything feasible to make their country visibly allied with American policy. Romanians sent a battalion of troops to Afghanistan, cooperated closely on intelligence matters, and eagerly agreed with Washington's views as war with Iraq loomed. After the war led to an American occupation of Iraq, Romania did not criticize officially, but rather evinced support and understanding of the U.S. view. For good measure, on issues as diverse as missile defense and the International Criminal Court (ICC), Romanians jumped quickly to endorse the U.S. government's positions even when they risked damage to links with the EU. These steps changed minds in the Bush administration and encouraged, by early 2002, a favorable view toward Romania's inclusion in the second tranche of enlargement. These steps did not, however, endear Bucharest in the minds of policy makers in Berlin, Paris, or elsewhere in continental Europe.

As the metamorphoses of states and European institutions continue, however, the message to small or poor states on the periphery may be unwelcome. Their needs are palpable and their preferences evident. Deferring such needs and preferences until the interests of a uniquely global power are at stake may generate reconsideration about a different calculus by which to ensure security. In the Romanian case, NATO's delay risked generating a national consensus that pursuing NATO alone was counterproductive. September 11, 2001 changed that calculus, and opened the door more widely.

Romania's experience suggests that Western policy makers ought to listen closely and rethink the relationship between security and democracy. In the Romanian case, a radical change in international circumstances in late 2001 shifted U.S. and NATO thinking about enlargement and precluded any further erosion of Bucharest's pro-Alliance policy. But, as documented here, elite and popular sentiments sensed that their country was condemned wrongly to a gray zone or periphery from whence there was no escape. Where such views become conventional wisdom, it is not far to revisionism and democratic setbacks.

NOTES

An earlier version of this chapter appeared in *Brassey's Central and East European Security Yearbook, 2002 Edition*, edited by Daniel N. Nelson and Ustina Markus (Washington, D.C.: Brassey's, 2002).

1. United States Information Agency, "Romanians Prepared to Continue to Push for NATO Membership," *Opinion Research Memorandum* (6 October 1997).

2. These data were reported by the United States Information Agency, *Opinion Research Memorandum* (28 April 1999), p. 6, from a CURS survey conducted in Romania during early to mid-April of that year. Details about the sample were not reported.

3. See, for example, a study using public opinion data for the early and mid-1990s by Claire Wallace and Christian Haepfer, "Changes in Attitudes Toward Internal and External Security in Post-Communist Europe," unpublished manuscript, 1998. The authors found Romanians to perceive more threat than Hungarians or Poles (ranking four among ten for which data were available).

4. Many of these general issues have been raised perceptively by Efraim Inbar and Gabriel Sheffer, eds., *The National Security of Small States in a Changing World* (London: Frank Cass, 1997), especially the "Introduction" (pp. 1–8) and Gabriel Scheffer, "The Security of Small Ethnic States," pp. 9–40.

5. That a state which marshals resources to enhance security, driven by the ideology of a certain party or clique or by a sense of national destiny, can connote a threat to others is reflected in the large mass of literature about a "security dilemma." Although mentioned by countless authors, John Herz in the 1950s and Robert Jervis in the 1970s and 1980s probably contributed more than others to the discussion and definitions. See John Herz, *Political Realism and Political Idealism: A Study in Theories and Realities* (Chicago: University of Chicago Press, 1951) and Robert Jervis, "Cooperation under the

Security Dilemma," *World Politics*, vol. 30, no. 1 (October 1978), pp. 167–214. A recent work focused particularly on the concept's applicability to the superpower confrontation and post–Cold War world is Alan Collins, *The Security Dilemma and the End of the Cold War* (Edinburgh: Keele University Press, 1997).

6. Daniel N. Nelson, "America and Collective Security in Europe," *Journal of Strategic Studies*, vol. 17, no. 4 (December 1994), pp. 105–24.

7. Personal communication with the author (Bucharest, February 1990).

8. This controversial argument is made, with substantial documentation, by Larry Watts. See his volume *Incompatible Allies* (Umea, Sweden: Umea University Press, 1999), p. 294: "The immediate goal of [Finland and] Romania and their principal motivation for their alliance with Germany was the removal of the Soviet threat." Watts's earlier, thorough research examined General Antonescu's regime in wartime Romania.

9. Titulescu assumed that Romanian capabilities alone were insufficient to ensure the country's security and, instead, focused on bilateral, regional, and global guarantees with which ". . . to compensate for national deficiencies." See Walter M. Bacon Jr., "Security as Seen From Bucharest," in Daniel N. Nelson, ed., *Romania after Tyranny* (Boulder, CO: Westview Press, 1992), p. 191.

10. "Conclusion" in Daniel N. Nelson, ed., *Romania in the 1980s* (Boulder, CO: Westview Press, 1981).

11. More detail is provided in Daniel N. Nelson, "Ceauşescu and the Romanian Army," *International Defense Review*, vol. 22, no. 6 (January 1989), pp. 737–42.

12. For details about the Ceauşescu catastrophe, see Daniel N. Nelson, "Romania: Economic, Social and Political Disasters," in Zoltan Barany and Ivan Volgyes, eds., *The Legacies of Communism in Eastern Europe* (Baltimore, MD: The Johns Hopkins University Press, 1996), pp. 198–226.

13. European Bank for Reconstruction and Development (EBRD), *Transition Report, 1995* (London: EBRD, 1995), p. 28.

14. *Adevărul* (8 August 1998), p. 1.

15. Center for Strategic and International Studies (CSIS), "*U.S.-Romania: A Strategic Partnership*" (Bucharest: CSIS, 1998), pp. 3–4.

16. Metro Media Transilvania, *Barometrul Politic* (September 1999), p. 17.

17. *Adevărul* (4 February 1999), p. 1.

18. General Degeraţu provided copies of his report on the January 1999 miners' protests to the author on a private basis in the first days of February. The report was apparently leaked, however, and appeared in most Bucharest dailies on Saturday, 6 February 1999. See, for example, *Adevărul* (6 February 1999), p. 1.

19. *Jurnalul Naţional* (14 March 1998), p. 17.

20. A senior diplomat at the Romanian Ministry of Foreign Affairs in a conversation with author in early February 1999.

21. An early sign of such doubt about the Clinton administration's promises was Liviu Mureşan, "*Un parteneriat strategic prea indepărtat?*" *Lumea* (October 1997), p. 9. By late March 1998, the so-called partnership was being compared to "wishful thinking." See Emil Hurezeanu, "*Un Parteneriat Numit Dorinţă*," *Curentul* (23 March 1998).

22. Zoe Petre, untitled essay in response to CSIS draft document on Romania's strategic importance (October 1998), pp. 1–2.

23. Teodor Meleşcanu, "The Accession to the European Union: The Fundamental Option of Romania's Foreign Policy," *Romanian Journal of International Affairs*, vol. 2, no. 4 (1996), p. 27.

24. See, for example, the rather ponderous study of Dorel Şandor, *Ambivalenţa factorilor politici in susţinerea politicilor reformei in România,"* (25 October 1999).

25. Branko Caratan, "The New States and Nationalism in Eastern Europe," *International Politics*, vol. 34, no. 3 (September 1997), p. 286.

26. For example, considerable bitterness was expressed on just one small bit of news: World Bank agricultural investments had been $500 million for Poland and zero for Romania. See, for example, *Adevărul* (4 February 1999), p. 1.

27. Many measurements of public opinion in Romania all point to the same pervasive support for NATO, the United States, and other Western countries, as well as integration with the West in general. The U.S. Information Agency, for example, commissioned a number of national samples in Romania (and other countries of the former Warsaw Pact) about security perceptions, and found Romanians to be among the most positive regarding entering NATO and also vis-à-vis specific countries such as the United States. See, *The New European Security Architecture, II* (Washington, DC: USIA Office of Research and Media Reaction, September 1996).

28. A compendium of these arguments is presented in the Ministry of Foreign Affair's *White Book on Romania and NATO* (Bucharest: MFA, 1997).

29. Ion Mircea Paşcu, "Security Through NATO Enlargement and the Partnership for Peace: The Experience and Expectation of Romania," unpublished manuscript (August 1997), p. 12.

30. Liviu Mureşan, "*NATO şi 'generalul Iarna,'*" *Lumea Magazin* (September 1997), p. 30.

31. For example, President Iliescu was quoted as having said, while on a trip to Bonn in late June 1996, that "Romania and Hungary should be admitted simultaneously in NATO if the Alliance wishes to avoid the production of tensions in Eastern Europe." See *Ziua* (26 June 1996), p. 2. Iliescu's last defense minister, Gheorghe Tincă, was quoted about the same time as having warned that "If we do not enter NATO . . . [with Poland, Hungary, the Czech Republic] . . . Romania will be marginalized." See *Jurnalul Naţional* (21 June 1996), p. 1.

32. "Radu Vasile intră în bărlogul 'lupului tînar' Viktor Orban," *Cotidianul*, vol. 9, no. 229 (8 February 1999), p. 1.

33. See, for example, the interview with Vasily Lipitski, President Boris Yeltsin's senior advisor on constitutional matters, by Marcela Feraru in *Cotdianul* (6–7 February 1999), p. 5.

34. *Interviu: Valeri Fiodorovici Keneaikin, Ambasadorul Federaţiei Ruse*: "*Rusia este pregătită să ofere orice garanţii de securitate oricărui stat european,*" *Jurnalul Naţional* (6 March 1998), p. 16–17. A wider interpretation of Russian strategic goals that threaten Romania was Bogdan Chirieac's editorial in *Adevărul* (9 March 1998).

35. Valerian Stan, "*Rusofobia: un snobism păgubos,*" *Cotidianul*, vol. 9, no. 229 (8 February 1999), p. 1.

36. "Bucharest Reiterates Commitment to NATO Entry," Rompres dispatch (5 March 1998), in *Daily Report*, FBIS-EEU-98-064 (6 March 1998).

37. "Pleşu to Convince Talbott of 'Necessity' of NATO Entry," Radio Romania (17 March 1998), *Daily Report*, FBIS-EEU-98-076 (17 March 1998).

38. Andrei Pleşu, "The Indivisibility of Security," *Central European Issues*, vol. 4, no. 2 (1998), p. 26.

39. "Defense Minister Lists Arguments for Romania's NATO Entry," Rompres Dispatch (20 August 1998), *Daily Report*, FBIS-EEU-98-232 (24 August 1998).

40. See, for example, "Policy Paper: Key Elements of Romania's Security Strategy," U.S-Romania Action Commission, Security and Foreign Policy Working Group (Washington, DC: Center for Strategic & International Studies, October 1998).

41. *Ibid.*

42. Author's discussions with senior military and defense officials in Bucharest in February and August 1998.

43. Such an emphasis became apparent in 1998 with, for example, the submission of a twenty-one page document to NATO proposing three regional NATO-AFP training centers in Romania—a center for defense resource management, a peacekeeping training center, and a simulation training center. That NATO was almost certain to avoid concentrating such centers in one country did not obviate the Romanian Ministry of Defense attempt to draw resources for purposes critical to modernizing the Romanian military.

44. Dumitru Tinu, Editorial, *Adevărul* (27 April 1999), p. 1.

45. AFP Dispatch, "UN Gave Nod To Embargo Breach by Romania," (9 March 1998).

46. *Buletin de Ştiri Telegrama*, No. 524 (8 April 1996), Part II.

47. Lucia Dumăchiţă, "PDSR Vice Preşedinte Ioan Mircea Pascu: Despre Kosovo," *Azi* (19 June 1998), p. 2.

48. Statement by Mr. Emil Constantinescu, President of Romania (19 March 1999), in English, as distributed by the Romanian Embassy, Washington, DC.

49. As quoted in an AFP Dispatch, "Polish, Romanian, Ukrainian Heads Meet for Regional Stability" (26 November 1997), as cited at C-afp@clari.net (26 November 1997).

50. Ovidiu Gherman as quoted in *Buletin de Ştiri*, no.549 (15 May 1996).

51. See, for example, Associated Press, Agence France Presse, and other sources on the report, originally aired on the Cable News Network (3 December 1998).

52. The Bucharest daily *Evenimentul Zilei* first reported this shipment (24 October 1997).

53. Dozens of ministerial and sub-ministerial meetings took place in 1998, for example, involving diplomats or representatives of Italy or France, or both, and their Romanian counterparts. The second formal session of the "four-way cooperation" took place in Paris on 26 February 1998, at which Romania was represented by Deputy Foreign Minister Lazăr Comănescu. See *Rompres* dispatch (26 February 1998).

54. Raymond M. Duch, "Economic Chaos and the Fragility of Democratic Transition in Former Communist Regimes," *Journal of Politics*, vol. 57, no. 1 (February 1995), pp. 121–58. At the same time, punishing incumbents is likely, and other findings indicate substantial skepticism underlying most public attitudes about politics. See, for instance, William Mishler and Richard Rose, "Trust, Distrust and Skepticism: Popular Evaluations of Civil and Political Institutions in Post-Communist Societies," *Journal of Politics*, vol. 59, no. 2 (May 1997), pp. 418–51.

55. Daniel N. Nelson, "Civil Society Endangered," *Social Research*, vol. 63, no. 2 (Summer 1996), pp. 345–68.

56. Radio Free Europe *News Report* (30 November 1998) cited an Open Society Foundation (a Soros-funded think tank in Bucharest) poll.

57. Inbar and Sheffer, eds., *Ibid.*, p. 4.

58. Daniel N. Nelson, "Post-Communist Romania's Search for Security," in F. Stephen Larrabee, ed., *The Volatile Powerderkeg* (Washington, DC: The American University Press, 1994), p. 85.

59. Mugurel Ghiţă in *Adevărul* (10 July 1998), p. 16.

60. Silviu Brucan, interview on ProTV (5 February 1999).

61. *Adevărul* (8 February 1999), p. 1.

62. Andrei Pleşu, "From the Madrid Summit to Washington and Beyond," text in English as distributed by the Ministry of Foreign Affairs (15 February 1999).

63. A good feel for American media's extreme bias toward Southeastern and Eastern Europe (all of the regions excluded from EU or NATO enlargement) is presented by Katia McClain, "The Politics of Discourse in US Media Coverage of Eastern Europe," *International Politics*, vol. 36, no. 2 (May 1999).

24

Romanian Bilateral Relations with Russia and Hungary: 1989–2002

Robert Weiner

The guiding factor in Romanian foreign policy in the post-Communist era has been the pursuit of its national interest, based on a realism designed to end its isolation from the world community and to resolve its security dilemma. Romania's concept of its national interest is based on the traditional notion of the preservation of the physical security, territorial integrity, and independence of the country.[1] An important Romanian foreign policy goal within that context has been the full normalization of its bilateral relations with its neighbors, Russia and Hungary, which are both former enemies. Therefore, since 1989, Romania has concentrated on the long-range foreign policy goal of constructing a juridical framework for the promotion of bilateral relations with these two states, through the negotiation of basic treaties of friendship and cooperation, as well as the development of economic and political relations. However, since 1989, Romania's efforts to normalize its relations with its two neighbors has evolved along different trajectories, as its foreign policy orientation has focused more on a "return to Europe" through its integration into European and Euro-Atlantic institutions.

ROMANIAN-RUSSIAN RELATIONS

The Romanians believe that they have just as much to fear from a weak Russia as from a strong one. The general perception is that Russia is weak and unstable at the present time. Because of former Russian President Boris Yeltsin's past history of erratic leadership, the high turnover of prime ministers during his administration (which was associated with the difficulties of democratization and the transition to a market economy), and the internal unrest as amply illustrated by the wars in Chechnya, this perception would seem to be well founded. The difficult transition to democracy in Russia has resulted not only in the rise to power of a corrupt financial oligarchy which wields an inordinate amount of power, but also in negative social and economic consequences for the country, which have been accompanied by a resurgence of nationalism and the perpetuation of the influence of the Communists in the Russian Duma.[2] However, Bucharest maintains the hope that, at some point in the future, it will be possible to develop an equal partnership with a democratic and stable Russia. However, the situation in Russia stabilized somewhat since the assumption of Vladimir Putin to the presidency, although he has displayed some distinct authoritarian tendencies. In the meantime, a weakened Russia has engaged in a series of actions which have been interpreted by some as threatening to the national security and interests of Romania. These include the adoption of a Resolution by the Russian Duma in 1995 calling for the reconstitution of the Soviet Union, the designation by the Russian Parliament of the Transnistria as an area of strategic interest, and the union of Belarus and Russia, which threatens the security of Ukraine, a state which shares a border with Romania.[3] Romania has also watched the improvement in Russian-Moldovan relations in 2001 with concern. Bucharest has also followed Russia's involvement in international peacekeeping operations in the Balkans, as well as the ongoing wars in Chechnya, which Moscow considers to be an internal affair of the Russian Federation.[4]

The 1991 Romanian-Soviet Friendship Treaty

In the early years following the 1989 revolution, Romania's foreign policy orientation had yet to completely extricate itself from the Soviet sphere of influence. This was illustrated by a rather controversial bilateral treaty, which the Iliescu administration signed with the Soviet Union on 5 April 1991. Romania committed itself in the treaty not to join any offensive (as opposed to defensive) alliance considered to be directed against Moscow's vital interests. This obviously referred to Romanian membership in NATO. The treaty was never ratified by the Romanian parliament, however, Petre Roman, who was the Prime Minister in 1991, would later take credit for the fact that the treaty was not ratified.[5] The 1991 Romanian-Soviet treaty was supposed to serve as a model for similar agreements between the former members of the Warsaw Pact and Moscow. However, unlike Romania, Poland, Hungary, and Czechoslovakia all refused to conclude such a pact with the Soviet Union.[6] Critics of the treaty, inside and outside of Romania, viewed it as an infringement of the independence and national sovereignty of the country, which if implemented, could have resulted in its "Finlandization." Furthermore, the democratic opposition at the time also lambasted the treaty because it recognized the Soviet-Romanian frontiers as given, effectively legitimizing the Molotov-Ribbentrop Pact of 1939, which had resulted in the loss to Russia of such territories as Bessarabia and Northern Bukovina. Also, because it appeared to accept the territorial consequences of the Molotov-Ribbentrop Pact, it was castigated as a betrayal of Moldova. The Iliescu administration attempted to defend the treaty by arguing that it was not substantively different from similar treaties that it had negotiated with other countries—a specious argument at best. Romanian diplomats also tried to justify it by emphasizing, in an unusually frank manner, the economic dependency of Romania on the Soviet Union for critical raw materials, such as energy.[7] Whatever the scenario surrounding its rejection, the issue of a treaty became moot when the Soviet Union disintegrated in 1991.

A New Romanian-Russian Basic Treaty

Since the collapse of the Soviet Union in 1991, Romania has yet to conclude a new basic treaty with Russia. Earlier, the Russians had claimed that the treaty concluded between Romania and the Soviet Union in 1970, which came on the heels of Romanian opposition to the 1968 Soviet invasion of Czechoslovkia, was still in force.[8] However, most Romanians wanted to establish a new relationship with Russia, the successor state to the USSR, in the post-Communist era. Shortly thereafter, Moscow and Bucharest reached a verbal accord which stipulated that the 1970 Friendship Treaty was no longer viable, and that the matter was therefore closed, even though there was actually no formal legal agreement to that effect.[9]

Inconclusive negotiations for a new basic treaty have been conducted for a number of years, at the level of experts, foreign ministers, and prime ministers, all to no avail. The two sides appeared close to signing a treaty in 1994, but there was a hiatus in negotiations between 1994 and 1996. Russian-Romanian relations at this time had become frayed due to the conflict in Moldova between Chişinău and the separatists in Transnistria. Romania had delivered arms to the Moldovans, and had accused the Russians of helping the secessionist forces in Transnistria.[10] Another point of contention between Russia and Romania revolved around the imprisonment of Ilie Ilaşcu by the separatist authorities in Tiraspol. Ilie Ilaşcu, an opponent of the separatist regime there, was considered in Bucharest to be a patriot, and something of a martyr as well. However, this point of contention was removed when he was subsequently released from prison.

Unfortunately, this lack of a basic treaty then contributed to the delay in Romania's admission into NATO. One of the conditions for NATO membership has been for aspiring candidate states to conclude treaties with neighboring states to resolve any outstanding differences which may exist between them. Although Bucharest has claimed that it wants to negotiate a basic treaty with Moscow, its conclusion was not a government priority, as its post-Communist foreign policy continued its Western orientation, even though the United States favored such a treaty. Romania considered concluding basic treaties with Hungary and Ukraine to be more important than a one with Russia.[11] On the other hand, then Romanian Foreign Minister Andrei Pleşu stressed that a basic treaty with Russia would be "useful" because it could induce a lasting rapprochement between the two countries.[12]

Still, Romania believed that it would be possible to conduct normal relations with Russia in the absence of such a treaty. The Russians, for their part, have continued to stress that they are interested in concluding a basic treaty with Romania, especially in the economic sector, as trade relations between the two countries have plummeted within the past several years. For example, when Ion Diaconescu, the chairman of the National Peasant-Christian Democratic Party visited Moscow in September 1997, Russian Foreign Minister Evgenii Primakov complained about Romania's neglect of the Russian market and stressed the need for the two countries to improve their trade relations.[13] By 2002, the trade between the two countries was still out of balance, as Romania suffered from a negative balance of trade with Russia. Romanian Prime Minister Adrian Nastase visited Moscow on 21–22 February 2002 and met with Russian Prime Minister Mikhail Kasyanov, in an effort to improve trade relations between the two countries.

The United States had been pressuring Romania to negotiate a basic treaty with Russia, to increase Bucharest's prospects for NATO admission in the second wave of enlargement. Washington considers a basic treaty between Romania and Russia to be a factor which can contribute to the stability of the region. However, Russia might have wanted to delay a basic treaty to block Romanian NATO membership. Clearly, Moscow has not wanted the Western military alliance closer to its borders, especially in the Black Sea area, which has historically served as an invasion route to Russia.[14] Speaking at the Nobel Institute in Oslo in 1998, then-Romanian Foreign Minister Andrei Pleşu speculated that Romania had not been admitted in the first wave of NATO enlargement for fear of alienating Russia.[15]

The finalization of a treaty has also been delayed because the Romanian side is well aware of the fact that it would have to be approved by its parliament. Some of the major stumbling blocks in the parliament have revolved around the insistence that it contain a denunciation of the Molotov-Ribbentrop Pact of 1939 and that the issue of the Romanian treasure, which had been spirited to Russia for "safekeeping" during the First World War, be addressed as well.

A Russian diplomat expressed the fear in 1995 that any reference to the Molotov-Ribbentrop Pact within the framework of a Romanian-Russian treaty would have destructive consequences for both parties, because such a step would encourage extremists in each country.[16] However, the Romanians considered the nullification of the Molotov-Ribbentrop Pact as critical to the "re-establishment of a historic truth."[17] The more nationalistic Russian Duma later declared the dissolution of the Soviet Union to be illegal, an action which, in a sense, re-legitimized the territorial changes that had been brought about by the Pact.[18] The Russians have argued that the declaration in 1990 by the People's Congress of Deputies, which declared the pact null and void, put the matter to rest.[19] Furthermore, a resolution calling for the reconstitution of the Soviet Union was adopted by the Duma on 5 April 1996; this also effectively recognized the annexation of Romanian territory under the Pact.

The Romanians and the Russians have tried to devise different formulae over the years to solve this problem, as Bucharest sought to base its relations with Moscow on the principles of "equality, active partnership, and reciprocal advantage."[20] A Romanian delegation led by Prime Minister Nicolae Văcăroiu, which visited Moscow in the fall of 1993, hoped that an agreement could be reached to denounce the Molotov-Ribbentrop Pact in the preamble to the basic treaty. Although there was no resolution of the differences concerning the Pact, Prime Minister Nicolae Văcăroiu met with President Boris Yeltsin and, in a press conference, stated that the meeting had marked an important step on the way to the development of bilateral relations, especially in dealing with such commercial matters as the delivery of natural gas.[21] A Romanian-Russian commission was set up to discuss the treaty, as well as other questions such as economic cooperation and the delivery of natural gas. However, in 1995, Evgenii Ostrovenko, the Russian Ambassador to Romania, rejected the idea of including in the preamble a paragraph referring to the Pact.[22] According to the Russian Ambassador it was unnecessary because the Pact had lost its viability when the Germans had invaded the Soviet Union in 1941.[23] Another formula suggested was that a declaration could be issued by Russia at the time a basic treaty was signed, claiming moral responsibility for the pact. However, according to the Romanian side, such a declaration would have no legal ramifications.

Bucharest also experienced some difficulties in finding a solution to the problem of the return of the Romanian treasure stolen by Russia during World War I, which reportedly consisted of some ninety tons of gold from the Romanian Central Bank, as well as some of the royal family's jewelry, in addition to rare coins and archives, among other things.[24] However, the Russians have been especially reluctant to engage in negotiations over this issue, and no real progress has been made on it over the last thirteen years.

Boris Yeltsin never visited Romania while he was President, although he met with Ion Iliescu in 1994 in Budapest at an Organization for Security and Cooperation for Europe (OSCE) conference, where there was a discussion of the possibility of a meeting at the highest level to deal with the problem of the basic treaty.[25] However, such a meeting never materialized.

Following Nicolae Văcăroiu's visit to Moscow, the next visit of a Romanian prime minister did not take place until 1999, a hiatus of six years, underscoring the stagnation of relations between the two states. Romanian Prime Minister Radu Vasile finally paid a working visit to Moscow on 25 November 1999, at the invitation of then Russian Prime Minister Vladimir Putin, in an effort to re-launch Romanian-Russian relations, especially in the economy. It resulted in an agreement between the Romanian company Romgaz and its Russian counterpart, Gazprom, which provided for the allocation of credit to Bucharest to construct a pipeline that would carry energy across Romania to Turkey. The pipeline deal embodied Russia and Romania's functional approach to bilateral relations without a basic treaty. The Romanians and the Russians have also been able to work together through mixed commissions in order to deal with such issues as curbing drug trafficking and organized crime, as well as cooperating in such fields as atomic energy, educational, and consular issues.[26] Radu Vasile also signed a Romanian-Russian convention when he was in Moscow, which deals with economic and technical cooperation in nutrition and agriculture, an agreement on the equivalence of diplomas, and one on cooperation between their ministers of youth and sports.[27]

Radu Vasile's visit was followed by a mission to Moscow in December 1999 by then-Romanian Defense Minister Victor Babiuc, who met with then-Prime Minister Vladimir Putin, as well as with the Russian defense minister. They reportedly discussed military cooperation between the states of Eastern Europe and presumably Romania's membership in NATO.[28] Prior to this, there were periodic meetings between the Romanian and Russian defense ministers, where NATO expansion had been discussed. Russia opposed NATO expansion eastward in principle, but not specific country membership. In 1999, the two sides also discussed the payment to Romania of a $90 million Russian debt through the provision of military equipment to Bucharest. (It is worth noting that the visit of the Romanian defense minister took place at the same time the Russians were launching a ferocious assault on the Chechen capital of Grozny.) In any event, it appears that the Romanians have calculated that their national interests are best promoted by continuing to maintain military, economic, scientific, and cultural relations with Russia in the absence of a basic treaty.

However, the terrorist attack on the United States on September 11, 2001, resulted in a renewed effort by the Romanians to finalize negotiations for the basic treaty with Moscow. The Romanians calculated that the Russian decision to support the United States in the war against terrorism had resulted in a change of heart, which provided Bucharest with an opportunity to move its policy toward the East forward and normalize its relations with Russia, especially in economic and commercial areas. The finalization of the basic treaty, if completed on time, might also have improved Romania's chances of being included within the next wave of NATO enlargement in 2002. Romanian Foreign Minister, Mircea Geoana, also functioning in his capacity as chairman-in-office of the OSCE, met with Russian Foreign Minister Igor Ivanov in Moscow on 23 October 2001, as a new round of negotiations were initiated. The Romanian side reportedly wanted the treaty to include within it, reference to the right of Bucharest to join any security alliance system which it preferred, since this apparently still was a contentious issue which had contributed to the failure of negotiations in 1996. The Romanians also displayed a new pragmatism in their position by not insisting that the Molotov-Ribbentrop Pact be renounced or that the "Romanian treasure" be addressed. At the same time, the Romanian government insisted that its national interest would not be sacrificed in any agreement that would be reached. On 8 November 2001, President Iliescu stated that the issue of the Molotov-Ribbentrop Pact was no longer relevant, and that the issue of the treasure could be dealt with in an annex to the treaty. However, both *Romania Mare* and the National Liberal Party were very critical of the above-mentioned compromises. Nevertheless, on 9 November 2001, the Chamber of Deputies rejected a proposal by *Romania Mare* that it debate the basic treaty while negotiations were still under way, although ultimately the treaty would still have to be submitted to Parliament for approval. Finally, there were plans for President Iliescu to visit Moscow in 2002, and it was hoped that the basic treaty could be signed in the presence of the two Presidents. As the NATO Prague summit of 21 November 2002, approached, the Basic Treaty had not yet been signed. After 11 September 2001, Russia was still stalling on the negotiations. Romania was invited to join the process of NATO entry by 2004 at the Prague Summit. Nonetheless, President Iliescu expressed hope that Moscow and Bucharest could resume negotiations on the Basic Treaty after the Prague Summit.

The Balkans

As consummate realists, the Romanians are also aware that treaties and juridical instruments alone are not sufficient to protect the national interests of their country. They realize that participation in an alliance system, preferably NATO, is necessary in order to guarantee its security from a resurgent Russia in the Balkans. Full normalization of relations between Russia and Romania is inhibited by Moscow's wishes to be considered an active player in the "great game" in the Balkans and still seems to consider that the region falls within its traditional sphere of influence. In this connection, the Russians consider Romania a transit corridor to the center of the Balkans. As a semi-landlocked state, Russia has traditionally sought direct access to warm-water ports in the south, a geopolitical fact of life. Romanian principalities were in the past reduced to Russian protectorates. During the Russo-Turkish War of

1877, Moscow demanded passage for its troops through Romanian territory.[29] The Russians have historically sought to create a string of satellite states in the Balkans to gain better access to the Danube, the Dardanelles, the Black Sea, and the Mediterranean. Control of the Dardanelles was especially important because "Russia wanted to dominate the Straits either directly or indirectly in order to protect its commerce and as a sign of great power status."[30] The great powers tended to view Romania as a weak state, whose territory could be traded between one another to maintain the balance of power in the region. As NATO has extended its power into the Balkans, Moscow preferred that Romania be confined to an intermediate zone between the Commonwealth of Independent States and the Western military alliance.

Consequently, Bucharest may have grounds for fearing that Russia, as weak as it is, is taking advantage of the turmoil in the Balkans to promote its long-term historic interests in the area. Romania has expressed concern over Russian participation in the NATO-led Implementation and Stabilization Forces (IFOR and SFOR), which had been sent into Bosnia following the conclusion of the Dayton Peace Accords in November 1995. Romania was also concerned over the Russian force dispatched to Kosovo in June 1999 (even though it supported Russian mediation to end the conflict, which it preferred to marginalizing and demonizing Russia).[31] Romanian Foreign Minister Andrei Pleşu stressed that "We cannot accept that history should move backward and that Southeastern Europe should be subordinated to a power which comes from the East."[32] The suspicion that the conflicts in the Balkans were seen as providing the Russians with an opportunity to reestablish themselves in the Balkans[33] appears to be confirmed by several recent incidents. For example, Russian troops raced ahead of NATO forces in June 1999 to seize control of the airport in Priština, the capital of Kosovo. On 27 June 1999, Russian aircraft flew over Romanian territory, violating an agreement, which Romanians maintained required two days separating Russian flights.[34] Turmoil continued in this region in 2001 as the Albanian minority clashed with Slavic Macedonians in the Former Yugoslav Republic of Macedonia, although by 2002, the situation had calmed down there somewhat. Nonetheless, the future of peace and stability in the Western Balkans still seemed problematical, given the uncertainty surrounding the future status of Kosovo.

The Caucasus and Chechnya

There is also the fear that Russia is interested in reincorporating Romania into its sphere of influence because of the latter's important geopolitical position relative to Caspian oil transportation routes. Post-Communist Romania has become more interested in increasing its activity in the Caucasus and

Central Asia, as its foreign ministry opened new diplomatic missions in the Caspian basin states. For example, Romania has pursued improved relations with Georgia and has probably viewed the establishment of Russian military bases there[35] as a threat to their national interests, especially because Georgia lies just across the Black Sea from Romania.[36] From Romania's view, it may appear that Russia is bent upon reducing not only Georgia to the status of a satellite, but also Armenia and Azerbaijan as well. Moscow could then maintain control of the flow of Caspian oil. This scenario threatens Romania's desire to be a major transit point (especially the port of Constanţa on the Black Sea) for the export of Caspian oil to the West. Romania thus hoped not only to benefit economically, but also to strengthen its NATO candidacy.

Bucharest has also carefully followed the wars waged by Russia in Chechnya. In 1999, the Romanian media generally focused on Russia's ruthless, illegal use of force against civilians, especially in Grozny.[37] Romania has stressed the need to find a peaceful resolution to the latest conflict there. As Romanian Foreign Minister Petre Roman stated in connection with the war in Chechnya in January 2000, "We are of the view that a political solution has been and remains much better than a military conflict."[38] However, given that Romania assumed the OSCE presidency in 2001, it prefers a somewhat neutral position, especially as the OSCE attempts to mediate. Russia did not oppose Romania's assumption of the OSCE presidency, just as it has not opposed Romanian EU membership, given their cool relations. Bucharest has also been concerned that the international community could not persuade Moscow to cease its military operations in Chechnya 1999. At the November 1999 OSCE summit in Istanbul, Russia asserted that the conflict was an internal matter outside the OSCE purview, and Russia managed to avoid a harsh condemnation.[39] After 9/11, Russia has contended that the war in Chechnya should be seen in the context of the war against terror. Nonetheless, Romania expressed its concern about Russian threats to undertake extensive military action in Georgia, unless the government there rooted out the Chechen bands of rebels who had taken sanctuary in the country.

At the OSCE meeting, Bucharest noted that Beijing had offered moral support to Russian efforts to crush the rebellion in Chechnya, drawing a parallel between Chechnya and Taiwan. China considers both to be domestic matters. Moscow claimed that its military operations were a legal suppression of secession to preserve its territorial integrity.[40] To Bucharest, it may appear that Russia has attempted to improve its relations with China to counterbalance NATO expansion and U.S. hegemony.[41] Russia attempted, without palpable success, to develop a strategic partnership with its former enemy China—and Vladimir Putin's accession to the presidency is likely to stifle such effort. However, the two countries did resolve a dispute about several islands on their common border.[42] Romania also followed Russian efforts to construct a strategic triangle allying with India as well as China, which were depicted as a multipolar diffusion of power in the post–Cold War international system, as well as to counter U.S. hegemony. While underscoring Romania's efforts to enter NATO, then Foreign Minister Andrei Pleşu on 22 December 1998 unwisely encouraged regional destabilization and anti-U.S. sentiments by wishing Russia success: "Each country has the right to engage in its own network of alliances and structures of security and cooperation. We respect this right and expect the Russians to respect our right."

ROMANIAN-HUNGARIAN RELATIONS

Unlike its relations with Russia, Romania's relations with Hungary have improved over the past fourteen years, until the controversy surrounding the implementation of the Hungarian Status law emerged. Since the denunciation of the Hungarian-Romanian Treaty of Friendship by Budapest on 21 December 1989, the desire of both countries to join NATO and the EU has motivated them to resolve their differences and to cooperate. The centerpiece of the rapprochement has been the 1996 Basic Treaty of Mutual Understanding, Good Neighborliness, and Cooperation, which was concluded after five years of intense negotiations. The Treaty had been preceded in 1995 by an *Aide-Memoire* signed by the Romanian and Hungarian foreign ministers, a step toward normalizing relations.[43] The Basic Treaty, which is supposed to last ten years, resulted from the two countries' desire to join NATO, which mandated establishing normal relations between these historic enemies. Then-U.S. Ambassador Alfred Moses predicted at the Treaty's signing that it would smooth the way for the two states' integration into Europe.[44] The Iliescu presidency had calculated that the negotiations were worth risking destabilizing the red-brown alliance formed in Romania after the 1992 parliamentary elections. (Instead, Romania was not admitted to NATO; the parliamentary coalition collapsed; and Iliescu and his party were defeated at the 1996 polls. Nevertheless, as then Romanian Foreign Minister Theodor Meleşcanu pointed out at the time, the Treaty fits with the "national interest of both Romania and Hungary, particularly with the fundamental interest of our joint integration into the European and Euro-Atlantic structures."[45])

The Treaty has also increased security and reduced threats to both countries, as both promised each other not to threaten or use force against the territorial integrity of the other[46] and renounced any territorial ambitions against the other. In 1995, the year before the conclusion of the Treaty, Hungarian Prime Minister Gyula Horn stated that Budapest had no territorial pretensions,[47] and that any revision of the Treaty of Trianon of 1920, which would restore some of the two-thirds of its territory it had then lost, would gravely injure Hungarian interests.[48]

The Rights of National Minorities

In the negotiations leading up to the finalization of the Basic Treaty, there was a considerable amount of discussion whether or not Recommendation 1201 of the Council of Europe, requiring minority rights protection through limited autonomy or real federalism, should be included explicitly. Tons of ink were spilled in the Romanian media discussing this question, as all Romanian parties except the Hungarian Democratic Union of Romania (UDMR) opposed even limited autonomy. Romania has, despite its constitution, no functional federalism, as all taxation is centralized and local elected officials share power with and are sometimes overshadowed by centrally appointed prefects. Bucharest was afraid that if 1201 were included, ethnic Hungarians might assert collective, as opposed to just individual rights and obtain limited autonomy in Covasna and Hargovita. Ethnic Hungarians number between 1.6 to 2 million. Given the past history of Transylvania, even limited autonomy is perceived as a stepping-stone to the secession of Transylvania, despite Hungary's explicit renunciation of such ambitions.[49] Furthermore, Romania had accepted Recommendation 1201 by joining the Council of Europe. Bucharest contended that it had not accepted it, yet still followed "European standards" in its treatment of the Hungarian minority.[50] The Council has been willing to accept this double-talk because many member states, particularly France, offer no limited ethnic autonomy and do not want to be forced to do so. A compromise solution resulted in a reference to 1201 in a Treaty Annex, which contained references to several other relevant international instruments protecting minority rights. The UDMR opposed the compromise, as did ethnocratic Romanian parties like Greater Romania and the Party of Romanian National Unity.

Article 15 of the Basic Treaty identified limited group rights protecting Hungarian and Romanian national minorities. Article 15, section 2 stipulates that states parties must protect and promote the ethnic, linguistic, and religious identity of the Romanian minority in Hungary and the Hungarian minority in Romania.[51] Minorities, either as individuals or group members, are to freely maintain and develop their ethnic, cultural, and linguistic identities[52] and the right to maintain their own cultural and religious institutions and organizations, as well as to be educated in their own languages.[53] Furthermore, the Basic Treaty guaranteed that national minorities had the right to maintain contacts with their kith and kin across national borders.[54] Compared to the violent ethnic clashes in March 1990 in Târgu Mureş, ethnic Hungarian-Romanian relations have been mostly nonviolent since then, though Cluj Mayor Gheorghe Funar has engaged in ethnic hate speech and discriminatory policies since his 1992 election. From 1996 to 2000, the UDMR was included in a coalition government for the first time, enabling ethnic Hungarians to be included as a group and not just as individuals.

Implementation of the Treaty

The Basic Treaty has yet to be fully implemented, but has been relatively successful, until the passage of the Hungarian Status Law in 2001. A mixed governmental commission, cochaired by the foreign ministers of both countries, was set up to oversee the implementation[55] of the Basic Treaty. A very important symbolic step was the reopening of the Hungarian consulate in Cluj in 1997.[56] This was later followed by the opening of an honorary Hungarian consulate in Constanţa.[57] Furthermore, relations between Hungary and Romania are now viewed by Bucharest as a strategic partnership and as a model for good-neighborliness in the region, as underscored by then Romanian Foreign Minister Adrian Severin when he visited Hungary to exchange the instruments of ratification.[58] A dense network of bilateral relations has resulted from a dozen working commissions on topics ranging from history to agriculture. Discussions have focused on opening more border crossings, as called for in the Basic Treaty. Romania's membership in the EU-sponsored, Southeast European Stability Pact should provide the financial assistance needed to make this possible. The two sides have also worked together to finance cultural centers and Romanian schools in Hungary, and to resolve religious disputes like the status of the Romanian Orthodox Church in Hungary. In addition, Hungarian President Arpad Goncz paid his first official visit to Romania in 1997.

Romanian-Hungarian military relations have been excellent. They have already engaged in joint military maneuvers,[59] in addition to the "Open Skies" agreement concluded as a confidence-building measure between the two countries as early as 1991.[60] A military cooperation treaty has also been concluded. When Romanian Defense Minister Gheorghe Tincă visited Hungary in the summer of 1994, he proposed that the two sides cooperate in the production of military equipment, reciprocal scholarships for officers, and periodic consultations at the level of defense minister.[61] A Romanian-Hungarian agreement creating a mixed peacekeeping battalion was signed on 20 March 1998.[62] Furthermore, during the seventy-eight-day war for Kosovo in 1999, Romania allowed Hungarian troops to cross its territory. The Romanian Defense Ministry has believed that the good track record of military cooperation between the two states has reinforced the rapprochement since the Basic Treaty.

However, despite Romanian hopes and the great strides, only Hungary was included of the two countries in the first wave of NATO enlargement in March 1999. There was concern that Hungary would be able to veto future Romanian NATO membership. However, Hungary had repeatedly stressed that it supported Romanian membership in NATO in the next wave of enlargement.[63]

Since the conclusion of the Basic Treaty, Romanian-Hungarian relations have been characterized by some difficulties, ranging from environmental problems to the delicate issue of setting up a Hungarian-language university in Romania. Article 10 of the Basic Treaty called for cooperation between the two countries in ecological protection. Both are supposed to inform each other immediately after an environmental accident.[64] Romania's relations with Hungary were set back in February 2000, when the largest environmental catastrophe in Europe since Chernobyl in 1986 occurred at an Australian-owned gold mine in the Tisza River in Romania. A large amount of cyanide fed into the network of rivers leading into the Danube near the two countries and Yugoslavia.[65] Despite Romanian denials of responsibility for containing the damage (as well as denials by the Australian firm Esmeralda), thousands of fish died in Hungarian waters. The two sides traded charges and countercharges, with the Hungarian government threatening to sue Romania for the damages that it had suffered. The resulting controversy over Romania's ability to meet European standards of environmental management could not have come at a worse possible time, as Romania prepared to engage in accession negotiations with the EU.

The delay in establishing a Hungarian-language university in Romania, which is required by the Basic Treaty, resulted in periodic UDMR threats to withdraw from the ruling coalition. The Hungarian minority in Romania is not entirely satisfied with the multicultural, bilingual approach to instruction used at the Babeş-Bolyai University in Cluj. Victor Orban, who had led a center-right coalition to victory in Hungary in 1998, adopted a more activist approach toward the protection of the rights of the Hungarian minority, even suggesting that the Basic Treaty should be revised.[66] As prime minister, he was more interested than his predecessor, Gyula Horn, in looking after the interests of Hungarians living "beyond the borders." Orban visited Romania in July 1999 and met with UDMR leaders and expressed his support for the idea suggested by the honorary president of the Hungarian Democratic Forum of Romania, László Tökés, that the Hungarian Churches in Romania set up a Hungarian-language university by themselves.[67] This issue has yet to be resolved. The official Romanian position is that relations between Budapest and Bucharest should not be affected by what happens internally in Romania, contradicting the treaty.

However, Romanian-Hungarian relations suffered a setback when the Hungarian parliament adopted the Hungarian Status Law on 19 June 2001, which was originally designed to take effect on 1 January 2002. The law extended special rights to ethnic Hungarians living in neighboring states (Romania, Slovakia, Ukraine, the Federal Republic of Yugoslavia, and Slovenia, while Austria was subsequently excluded) by issuing to them so-called "certificates of nationality," which were, in effect, national identity cards. The idea on the part of the "kin" state (Hungary), was not only to preserve the cultural and linguistic identity of Hungarians living abroad, but also to extend to them special economic and social rights (such as the right to work for three months in Hungary, medical benefits, pensions, etc.), which could be exercised only in Hungary. Bucharest objected to what it characterized as the extraterritorial nature of the law, and was opposed to its implementation in Romania, unless it was amended with input from the neighboring countries which were affected. Bucharest also consulted with Slovenia and the Federal Republic of Yugoslavia to discuss the problem. Bucharest also took the position that it did not object to the provisions of the Hungarian Status Law that were designed to preserve the cultural and ethnic identity of the Hungarian minority living in Romania, but rather to the economic and social aspects of the law. The law was viewed by Romania as a form of colonialism that was designed to exploit the labor of the Hungarian minority living in neighboring states. Moreover, Bucharest believed that the protection of the rights of the Hungarian minority living in Romania could be negotiated bilaterally within the framework of existing treaties and mechanisms that had been established for that purpose, according to the international legal principle of *pacta sunt servanda*. The Romanians also argued that the Hungarian Status Law did not conform to European standards of international law, and furthermore that the law was discriminatory against Romanians who wanted to work in Hungary. Therefore, on 21 June 2001, Romanian Prime Minister Adrian Nastase requested that the Venice Commission of the Council of Europe issue an opinion on the matter. Romanian Foreign Minister Mircea Geoana argued the Romanian case before the Venice Commission on 19 October 2001, focusing on the virtues of the Romanian notion of a civic definition of citizenship as opposed to the ethnic definition of citizenship that was embodied in the Hungarian Status Law. A careful reading of the nonbinding opinion, which was issued by the Venice Commission on 22 October 2001, clearly shows support for the Romanian position. For example, the Venice Commission observed that NGOs (nongovernmental organizations) in Romania, designated by Hungary, could not issue documents such as "certificates of citizenship" that had a quasi-official status, but rather this function had to be performed by consulates. Furthermore, the Venice Commission pointed out that Hungary had adopted a law which undermined good-neighborly relations between the two states in the region. Moreover, the Hungarian Status Law, which affected the state authority of Romania on its own sovereign territory, had also been adopted without adequate consultations with the Romanian government On 22 December 2001, the Romanian and Hungarian governments were able to work out an agreement which provided ethnic Romanians with the opportunity to work in Hungary three months out of the year. However, the new Socialist regime that assumed power in Hungary in 2002, opposed the agreement and sought to revise the Hungarian Status Law by the end of 2002. Negotiations on this matter continued within the framework of the mechanisms that had been created by the Basic Treaty to deal with the national minority question, as Bucharest sought to do nothing that would jeopardize its chances of being invited to join NATO in 2002. In conclusion, it is difficult to predict the extent to which the Hungarian Status Law, if implemented, will damage relations between Bucharest and Budapest, but experience indicates that laws of this nature invariably lead to an exacerbation of ethnic tension.

The Balkan Conflicts

Despite the above-mentioned differences, it is clear that relations between the two sides have generally been calm, especially in comparison to the ethnic conflict elsewhere in the Balkans. Nonetheless, the eleven-week, 1999 war over Kosovo might have harmed Romanian-Hungarian relations. NATO's willingness to intervene unilaterally in Yugoslavia without UN Security Council authorization, as mandated by UN Charter Article 53, to protect the Kosovar Albanians from Serb atrocities and ethnic cleansing, nominally violated Yugoslav sovereignty. NATO thus offered a politically unsettling model for resolution of any potential conflict in Transylvania, unlikely as that seems. Romania reaffirmed NATO's official position that that any peace settlement over Yugoslavia should not redraw state boundaries in Southeastern Europe, especially which could affect Transylvania.[68] The position of the nearby Hungarian minority in the Serbian province of Vojvodina could affect ethnic Hungarian demands in Transylvania, but the ethnic Hungarians in Yugoslavia were relatively quiescent, though between 50,000 and 100,000 ethnic Hungarians were driven from Vojvodina between 1991 and 1999. The Hungarian government supports the restoration of political autonomy in Vojvodina, which has about 16 to 17 percent ethnic Hungarians.

Regional and Subregional Cooperation

Despite their differences, Romania and Hungary have shared a common concern in containing and resolving the conflicts in Yugoslavia, and generally, in promoting stability in the region. In an effort to do so, they have cooperated with each other within the framework of a number of regional and subregional organizations under Article 7 of the Basic Treaty. To integrate itself into European and Euro-Atlantic organizations, Romania will need to behave consistently with its self-image as a Central and Southeast European state. Fortunately, Romania has a useful framework for cooperating with Hungary, such as the NATO Partnership for Peace, as well as the Romanian-Hungarian-Austrian Trilateral, which also encompasses military cooperation.[69] Hungary supported Romania's full membership in the Central European Free Trade Association,[70] which Romania finally joined in 1997, although Romania has complained about the adverse balance of trade with Hungary. By November 1998, the total commercial trade between Romania and Hungary was about $704.5 million, actually larger than Romania's trade with Russia.[71] Bilateral trade had reached about $900 million by 2002, and it was hoped that this figure would grow to about $1 billion in 2003.

CONCLUSION

Romania has opted for a realist approach in its relations with Russia and Hungary. After the fall of Communism, Romania sought its identity with the West and not the East, especially after 1991. Romania's bilateral relations with these former enemies appear to have been based on rational calculations about its national interests. The long-range goal of Romanian foreign policy was a return to Europe and its admission to NATO and the EU, the former presumably achieved in 2002 by a 2004 formal entry, and the latter presumably to occur in 2007. Romania's efforts to bring about full normalization of its relations with Russia and Hungary are meant to serve those goals. In the final analysis, Bucharest fears a resurgent Russia attempting to regain its sphere of influence in the Balkans. On the other hand, Romania considers that good relations with Hungary are required but not sufficient to integrate into Euro-Atlantic structures. Furthermore, in the post–Cold War structure of power, Romanian realism appears to be based on the sensible assumption of a shift from a bipolar to a multipolar world. Bucharest assumes that order and security can be best pursued by alliances in its national interest. Of course, should the global correlation of forces change, then Romania might change its choice of alliances. For now, foreign policy realism is pointing Romania Westward with no impulse immediately foreseeable to impel it to look back East.

NOTES

1. *Adevărul* (20 August 1998), p. 3.

2. *Adevărul* (20 December 1995), p. 7; for Romanian comments on the results of the Russian parliamentary elections in 1995 and the Presidential elections in 1996, see *Adevărul* (3 July 1996), p. 7.

3. *România liberă* (9 December 1999), p. 4.

4. *Adevărul* (20 January 1994), p. 8; *România liberă* (23 May 1995), p. 8.

5. "Roman Refutes Russian Objections to NATO Expansion," *Foreign Broadcast Information Service*, hereinafter cited as *FBIS*, EEU-96-102 (24 May 1996), p. 46.

6. Mark Kramer, "NATO, Russia, and East European Security," in Uri Ra'anan and Kate Martin, eds., *Russia: A Return to Imperialism* (New York: St. Martin's Press, 1995), p. 116.

7. For a discussion of Romania's continuing dependency on Russia for natural gas, see *România liberă* (25 September 1993), p. 9; according to the Romanian media, 80 percent of Romania's imports from Russia in 1999 consisted of oil and natural gas. See *Adevărul* (25 November 1999), p. 1.

8. *Adevărul* (3 November 1994), p. 3.

9. *România liberă* (9 November 1994), p. 3.

10. *România liberă* (6 April 1994), p. 8.

11. *Libertatea* (4 July 1995), p.3.

12. "*Principalele Repere Ale Actualei Diplomaţii Române*," (4 October 1998), available at http://domino.kappa.ro/...2f005.Open Document.

13. Radio Free Europe/Radio Liberty, (19 September 1997), available at www.rferl.org/.

14. *Adevărul* (20 February 1998), p. 11.

15. Address by Andrei Pleşu at the Nobel Institute, Oslo, Norway (12 January 1998).

16. *Libertatea* (4 July 1995), p. 3.

17. *Dosar Aldine* (21 August 1999), p. 3.

18. *Adevărul* (20 March 1996), p. 11.

19. *România liberă* (9 November 1994), p. 3.

20. *Central Europe Online* (26 November 1999).

21. *Tineretul liber* (30 September 1993), p. 1.

22. *Adevărul* (24 January 1995), p. 7.

23. *Ibid.*

24. For a discussion of what the treasure supposedly contained, see *România liberă* (12 December 1995), p. 20; for a Russian explanation of what happened to part of the treasure, see *Adevărul* (3 February 1998), p. 11.

25. *România liberă* (8 December 1999), p. 3.

26. *Adevărul* (26 November 1999), p. 16.

27. *România liberă* (25 November 1999), p. 3.

28. *Rador* (28 December 1999), available at http://indis.ici.ro/romania/news/.

29. For a discussion of the period in which the Romanian Principalities were Russian protectorates, see Keith Hitchins, *The Romanians, 1774–1866* (Oxford: Clarendon Press, 1996).

30. Nicholas Constantinesco, *Romania on the European Stage: 1875–1880* (Boulder, CO and New York: East European Monographs/Columbia University Press, 1998), p. 54.

31. Interview by Andrei Pleşu, with the Swiss newspaper *Neue Zürcher Zeitung* (12 July 1999), available at http://domino.kappa.ro/mae/presa/inf/articole/Q.

32. *Ibid.*

33. *România liberă* (14 June 1999), p. 1.

34. "Russian Federation Request to Fly Over," (27 June 1999), available at http://domino.kappa.ro/9e3156f?Open Document.

35. *Adevărul* (12 February 1998), p. 11.

36. *România liberă* (20 February 1998), p. 5.

37. *România liberă* (16 December 1998), p. 4.

38. "*Conferinţe De Presă ale Ministrului*," 19 January 2000 available at http://domino.kappa.ro...6c0038ea3?Open Document.

39. *Adevărul* (17 November 1999), p. 11.

40. *Adevărul* (10 December 1999), p. 9.

41. *România liberă* (8 December 1999), p. 4.

42. *România liberă* (10 December 1999), p. 4.

43. *România liberă* (8 March 1995), p. 1.

44. *România liberă* (17 September 1996), p. 3.

45. "Meleşcanu: Hungarian Treaty in National Interest," *FBIS-EEU-96-167* (26 August 1996), p. 57; opposition leaders Emil Constantinescu and Petre Roman also stated that they believed that the Treaty was in Romania's national interest. See *România liberă*, (17 September 1996), p. 3.

46. See Article 2 of the Treaty, *România liberă* (29 August 1996), p. 10.

47. *Tineretul liber* (25 May 1995), p. 1.

48. Richard Holbrooke, who was the American Assistant Secretary of State for Europe and Canada in 1995, stressed that the Treaty of Trianon should only be discussed in history books. See *Adevărul* (27–28 May 1995), p. 1. It should also be pointed out that in 1994, Hungarian Prime Minister László Kovacs had stated that it would be possible to modify frontiers through peaceful means, especially if the original conditions in which the Treaty had been concluded had changed. See *Adevărul* (23 September 1994), p. 1.

49. "Dinu Welcomes Finalization of Treaty with Hungary," *FBIS-EEU-96-165* (23 August 1996), p. 4.

50. "Presidency Spokesman Rejects Hungarian-Slovak Treaty," *FBIS-EEU-96-103* (28 May 1996), p. 75.

51. *România liberă* (29 August 1996), p. 10.

52. *Ibid.*

53. *Ibid.*

54. *Ibid.*

55. *România liberă* (30 December 1996), p. 4.

56. *România liberă* (21 April 1997), p. 3.

57. This took place on 6 April 1999.

58. *Adevărul* (4 January 1997), p. 5.

59. *Tineretul liber* (5 October 1995), p. 7a.

60. Howard E. Frost, "Eastern Europe's Search for Security," *Orbis* vol. 37, no. 1 (Winter 1993), p. 53.

61. *Tineretul liber* (August 1994), p. 3a.

62. "*Relaţii Bilaterale: Republica Ungară*," available at http://domino.kappa.ro/… f0003f115d?Open Document.

63. *România liberă* (20 February 1998), p. 4.

64. *România liberă* (29 August 1996), p. 10.

65. *Central Europe Online* (18 February 2000), available at http://www.centraleurope.com/news.php3?id=135853.

66. *Adevărul* (10 June 1998), p. 11.

67. *RFE/RL* (28 August 1998), available at http://www.referl.org/newsline/w999/0813-cee/cee-050899.html.

68. *Adevărul* (14 June 1999), p. 1.

69. *România liberă* (23 December 1997), p. 3.

70. *Adevărul* (28 November 1994), p. 5.

71. *Adevărul* (11 April 1998), p. 7. Bucharest has complained about the adverse balance of trade that has emerged with Hungary since Romania joined the Central European Free Trade Association.

25

The Security Services since 1989: Turning over a New Leaf

Dennis Deletant

The clearest test of Romania's commitment to break with its Communist past has, arguably, been the introduction of democratic accountability to the Romanian security services, and the "purification" of Ceauşescu-era personnel involved in the crimes of that regime.[1] This chapter examines the extent to which that purification has been carried out; it charts the composition and structure of the security services which have succeeded the Department of State Security (the DSS, better known as the *Securitate*); and it assesses the degree of accountability introduced to those services.

RESTRUCTURING THE *SECURITATE*

Under Decree no. 4 signed on 26 December 1989 by Ion Iliescu, then de facto head of the Council of the National Salvation Front (CFSN), the DSS was removed from the control of the Ministry of the Interior and placed under the Ministry of National Defense. On 29 December 1989, Iliescu promulgated CFSN Decree no. 33, which abolished the DSS (*Securitate*) and placed its directorate chiefs under arrest or in the reserve. This move has been largely suspected of being "window dressing" rather than substantive reform. Iliescu tasked the deputy prime minister in the provisional government, Gelu Voican Voiculescu, with the responsibility for assembling a new security structure. On the very same evening that the decree disbanding the DSS had been issued, Voiculescu convened an extraordinary meeting of all the heads of *Securitate* units who had not been arrested. He assured them that while the new government planned to dismember the former, Communist police structures, it would not take action against individual *Securitate* officers.[2]

In effect, the *Securitate* was integrated into the system and legitimized, thus enabling its officers to organize the release of all their colleagues held on suspicion of firing on demonstrators during the revolution. The unreliability of witnesses, bureaucratic inertia, and the desire to protect vested interests—such as Iliescu's bodyguard organization, the Presidential Protection and Guard Service (SPP) (which contained officers from the former Fifth Directorate of the *Securitate,* which had protected Ceauşescu) and the antiterrorist brigade of the Romanian Information Service (SRI) (which included members of the *Securitate* antiterrorist unit, USLA)—explains why the investigations into the deaths of the officially recognized 1,000 or so victims of the revolution have not been completed, and why relatively few charges have been brought.

Nevertheless, some senior *Securitate* officers were prosecuted. The first was Iulian Vlad, the last DSS head, who was arrested on 28 December 1989 on the absurd charge of complicity to genocide, which carried a maximum penalty of life imprisonment.[3] The charge was later reduced by a military court to "favouring genocide," and his sentence was subsequently reduced to nine years, which was to run concurrently with two other lesser terms. The first was for three and a half years, which Vlad received in March 1991 for illegally detaining the number two man in the National Salvation Front (FSN), Dumitru Mazilu, in December 1989. The second was for four years, which he received in May 1991 for the "abusive detention" of more than 1,000 demonstrators in late December 1989. On 4 January 1994, Vlad was released on parole, after having served a three and a half year term.

Other high *Securitate* officers were sentenced in May 1991 to terms of two to five years of imprisonment each for "illegally detaining" and "abusively interrogating" an unspecified number of protesters during the revolution. On 10 May, Major General Gianu Bucurescu received a prison term of four years, while Lieutenant General Gheorghe Dănescu received a term of three and a half years. Colonel Marin Bărbulescu, head of the Bucharest militia, received a term of five years. Lieutenant General Gheorghe Vasile, the military counter-intelligence chief, and Colonel Gheorghe Goran, head of the Bucharest DSS, were both acquitted of these charges.[4] In a separate trial, Major General Marin Neagoe, head of the Fifth Directorate of the *Securitate,* was sentenced on 28 May 1991 to seven years in prison for "abusing his office."[5] General Aristotel Stamatoiu, head of the Foreign Intelligence Service, and General Morţoiu were also sent to prison, but were released in November 1992. Nicolae Andruţa Ceauşescu, the commandant of the Ministry of the Interior military academy, was sentenced in June 1990 to fifteen years imprisonment for leading some 2,000 officer cadets in the shooting of demonstrators in University Square on 21 December 1989. He died in the hospital of cancer on 14 December 2000. The former Minister of the Interior, Tudor Postelnicu, was also tried on the charge of genocide at the end of January

1990, and was sentenced on 2 February to life imprisonment. He was released on medical grounds on 4 February 1994.

Of the abuses committed by the *Securitate* before the revolution, only a handful have been addressed. Postelnicu's most notorious predecessor, Alexandru Drăghici, fled the country with his Hungarian wife Martha shortly after the revolution, and joined his daughter Alexandra in her Budapest flat to which she had moved in 1988. A request for his extradition was made to the Hungarian Ministry of Justice by the Romanian procurator general on 19 August 1992, but was turned down on the grounds that the statute of limitations had expired. However, the Hungarian Ministry of Justice made it clear that this was not their final word on the matter, and requested further information on the case. On 29 December 1992, the Romanian authorities renewed their extradition request, arguing that the statute of limitations had been suspended after the December revolution, a dubious legal move. Again, the Hungarians refused to hand Draghici over, and, therefore, on 23 May 1993, the trial of Draghici and other *Securitate* officers for "incitement to murder" began in his absence. Accused alongside the former Minister of the Interior were Colonel General Nicolae Briceag, former head of the Sibiu district of the *Securitate*, Colonel Ilie Munteanu and Colonel Nicolae Luţenco.[6] Drăghici's death, announced on Romanian radio on 13 December 1993, robbed his victims of any remaining chance of justice.

Replying in February 1990 to public disquiet about the position of the former DSS General Victor Stănculescu, the Minister of Defense listed the names of the *Securitate* generals arrested, and reported that 611 of the 1,073 officers in the Fourth Directorate in charge of military counterespionage, and that all 436 officers of the Fifth Directorate had been placed in the reserve. Stănculescu also claimed that the eavesdropping systems used by the *Securitate* had been dismantled on 22 December 1989, and that all listening centers and devices had been sealed off and placed under army guard. Furthermore, he invited public inspection of the former bugging and listening centers. Stănculescu also announced the institutionalization of a new security structure which was to be nonpolitical, with the leading positions in them filled "only with officers of the Romanian army who have shown, through their abilities and deeds, loyalty to the country, the people, and the revolution, and who do not belong to any political party or movement."[7]

However, his assurances that "no telephone conversation will be intercepted or listened to now, or in the future," and that "no citizen, regardless of nationality, political affiliation, or religious convictions" would be the target of this new security structure was received with disbelief by the public, coming as it did from an officer who had been a deputy Minister of Defense under Ceauşescu. That disbelief was justified by the discovery, in late May 1991, of hundreds of files on opposition figures compiled by the newly organized SRI, and by allegations in the Romanian press that Stănculescu had been directly involved in the sale of Romanian arms through the agency of the Foreign Trade Company Dunărea.[8]

Also, Stănculescu's "frankness" about the elimination of former *Securitate* personnel from the new security structure did not extend to the fate of the 595 officers in the First, Second, Third, and Sixth Directorates, who were passed over in silence: This gave rise to suspicions that they had been integrated into the new security regime, which had been established by decree on 26 March 1990. The director of the new service, Virgil Măgureanu, admitted as much in a report to the joint session of the Romanian parliament on 22 November 1990, which he submitted in response to growing public demands for information about the structure and activities of the newly formed SRI, in an attempt to allay suspicions that the new organization was nothing more than a revamped *Securitate.* The very act of reporting was an indication that the SRI was, unlike its predecessor, at least formally accountable to parliament, and Măgureanu did not hesitate to make this point at the beginning of his report.[9]

THE CREATION OF THE NEW SECURITY SERVICES: SRI, UM 0215, AND SPP

Nine Romanian security and intelligence services have been set up since the disbandment of the *Securitate* and may be characterized as follows:

1. *Serviciul Roman de Informaţii* (SRI), the Romanian Security Service.[10]
2. *Serviciul de Pază si Protecţie* (SPP), the Presidential Protection and Guard Service.
3. *Serviciul de Informaţii Externe* (SIE), the Foreign Intelligence Service.[11]
4. *Direcţia Informaţiilor Militare* (DIM), the Directorate of Military Intelligence, subordinated to the Ministry of Defense.
5. *Direcţia de Contraspionaj a Ministerului Apărării Naţionale* (DCS), the Directorate of Counter Espionage of the Ministry of Defense.
6. *Serviciul de Informaţii al Ministerului de Interne* (UM 0215), the Intelligence and Security Service of the Ministry of the Interior. This was rechristened, in June 1998, as the *Direcţia Generală de Informaţii şi de Protecţie Internă* (UM 0962), the General Directorate of Information and Internal Protection.
7. *Direcţia de Supraveghere Operativă si Investigaţii a Inspectoratului General al Poliţiei* (DSOI), the Directorate of Surveillance and Investigation of the Ministry of the Interior. This has been merged with UM 0962.
8. *Serviciul de Informaţii al Direcţiei Generale a Penitenciarelor* (UM 0400), also known as *Serviciul Operativ Independent* (SOI), the Intelli-

gence Service of the General Directorate of Prisons, subordinated to the Ministry of Justice. This became *Serviciul Independent de Protecţie şi Anticorupţie* (SIPA), the Independent Service of Protection and Anti-corruption, of the Ministry of Justice.

9. *Serviciul de Telecomunicaţii Speciale* (STS), the Special Telecommunications Service.

Interestingly, each of these services was formed around the nucleus of a former *Securitate* directorate or unit. The SRI initially drew its personnel from the directorate of internal security; the SPP drew from the directorate responsible for the protection of Ceauşescu (Directorate 5); the SIE took over the activities of the CIE (the Foreign Intelligence Service of the *Securitate*); the DCS inherited the role of Directorate 4; and the UM 0215 recruited from the Bucharest office of the *Securitate*.

This multiplicity of services has done little to allay Romanians' suspicions that they continue to be the subject of close scrutiny by the successor organizations to the *Securitate*; it also raises questions of overlap and even duplication of tasking by these services. Such questions are particularly relevant to the activity of the SRI, which is subject to parliamentary oversight, and to that of UM 0962, which is not. Any chance both services had of gaining the public's confidence was undermined by their involvement in several acts of political violence in the early 1990s.

The most notorious incident involved the miners' invasion of Bucharest in June 1990. The failure of the police to disperse the rioting crowds in University Square—who attacked the police headquarters, the offices of Romanian television, as well as the Foreign Ministry—prompted President Ion Iliescu to appeal to miners from the Jiu valley to defend the government. Special trains brought 10,000 miners, armed with wooden staves and iron bars, to Bucharest at dawn on 14 June. They were joined by vigilantes who were later credibly identified as former officers of the *Securitate*. For two days, the miners (aided and abetted by the former *Securitate* members) terrorized the population of the capital, attacking anyone they suspected of opposition to the government.

Despite the government's presentation of the findings of a parliamentary inquiry, this event raised a number of questions concerning the new security regime to which satisfactory answers have yet to be given. It was not until November 1997 that the police files on the miners' incursion were sent to the prosecutor's office. In the meantime, most of the 760 complaints against the miners and the police had already reached the effective statute of limitations, and, thus, the possibility of prosecution had been obviated.

However, the serious damage which this episode did to Romania's image abroad prompted members of parliament to raise the question of the SRI's accountability. While its powers had been codified in the National Security

Law, passed on 26 July 1991, an effective mechanism to supervise them had not been put into place at the time. The authority to break the law in the interests of national security was given to the SRI in article 13, with certification of this national security interest to be provided by warrants of six months duration issued by "prosecutors especially designated by the Attorney General of Romania." However, the law did not specify what standing these prosecutors should have, and there was no credible mechanism for the investigation of complaints. Thus, a credible system of judicial or legislative supervision of, and checks on, the exercise of this potentially abusive authority was lacking in the law.

While the safeguards were wanting, authorization to break the law in the interest of national security was not. Articles 6, 8, and 9 of the National Security Law stipulated that the SRI, the SIE, the SPP, the Ministry of National Defense, the Ministry of the Interior, and the Ministry of Justice were *all* empowered to defend national security. This overlapping of functions has caused Romanian security operations to become duplicated, confused, and unaccountable. The only coordinating power rested with the Supreme Defense Council (*Consiliul Suprem de Apărăre a Ţării*), a collective body of security organizations chaired by the President. It was set up before the promulgation of the first written Constitution under law 39 of March 1990. The Council's duties are, among others, to analyze reports and information regarding the application of the National Security Law (article 4), and to approve the structure, organizations and administration of the SRI, the SIE, and the SPP (Article 5). However, the Council has no constitutional link with Parliament. The pernicious lack of independent supervision of the state security agencies was demonstrated during a second binge of organized violence—the miners' invasion of Bucharest in September 1991.

In testimony before the parliament, the SRI director, Virgil Măgureanu, revealed that he advised President Iliescu to use the event to force Prime Minister Roman's resignation. Parliamentary clamor for control over Măgureanu and his agency became pronounced, resulting in the institution, on 23 June 1993, of the Joint Standing Committee of the Chamber of Deputies and Senate for Control and Supervision of the SRI (*Comisia de Control Comună a Senatului şi a Camerei Deputaţilor asupra activităţii SRI*). The membership consisted of nine members of parliament who were to be nominated by their respective parties and then elected in a joint session of the Chamber of Deputies and Senate. They were then required to take an oath of secrecy before the two chambers. One of the members serves as president, a second as vice president, and a third as secretary. The holders of these three posts must be drawn from different political parties to ensure a nonpartisan supervision of the SRI. While this act did set up what was at least a formal system of supervision for the SRI, parliamentary oversight was not extended to two other security services: UM 0215 and SPP.

UM 0215

At the beginning of January 1990, General Nicolae Militaru, minister of defense, gave orders that the entire DSS Directorate for Bucharest (566 officers), and the majority of men in the Fourth Directorate (responsible for counterespionage in the army) be placed on the reserve. Voiculescu, who had been appointed by Iliescu to organize the new state security structure, took this opportunity to obtain Iliescu's agreement to recruit these officers for a new intelligence organization. It was set up on 1 February, given the title UM 0215, and placed under the nominal control of the Ministry of the Interior. Its first head was said to be a former *Securitate* officer, Ion Moldoveanu, a man who had allegedly been in charge of surveillance in the late 1970s of the dissident writer Paul Goma. He held the position for only one week, when he was replaced by Vice-Admiral Cico Dumitrescu. However, real control over the organization remained in the hands of Voiculescu.

After the departure of Admiral Dumitrescu in March 1990, Voiculescu installed two associates to the top positions in 0215: Colonel Florin Calapod (alias Cristescu) and Colonel Harasa. In these initial months, officers of 0215 were given several false identities and acted largely at their own discretion. On 18 February 1990, they were believed to have been responsible for a Watergate-style break-in into a government office in an attempt to compromise the opposition parties. At the same time, officers from 0215 were involved in the printing of anti-Semitic leaflets in Bacau and Bucharest.

On 22 March 1990, Petre Roman approved a request from the Minister of Internal Affairs, General Mihai Chiţac, to create 174 new posts in the new state security structure, with the majority of them in UM 0215. During the premiership of Petre Roman (a man with whom Voiculescu, the de facto head of UM 0215, was on close personal terms) was allowed to double its strength to around 1,000 officers. Măgureanu (who headed of the SRI and who had a deep personal dislike for the prime minister) saw this development as a threat to his own service and warned President Iliescu of 0215's potential use as a personal intelligence service by Roman. In December 1990, acting with Iliescu's approval, Măgureanu forced Voiculescu from his position with UM 0215.

It is against the background of this dispute that the allegations made by Măgureanu and the SRI against UM 0125 should be seen. In March 1992, after his removal from the organization Voiculescu addressed these accusations. He dismissed as fabrications SRI claims that UM 0215 had infiltrated the opposition rally of 18 February 1990, that it had selectively released *Securitate* files in the run-up to the May 1990 elections in an effort to compromise opposition leaders, and that it had participated in the attacks by miners on bystanders in Bucharest in June 1990. He did, however, admit that he had supported the use of *Securitate* files in the election campaign. Nevertheless, in February 1994 a Bucharest court found two 0215 officers, Colonel Ion

Nicolae and warrant officer Corneliu Dumitrescu, guilty of ransacking the house of Ion Raţiu, a leading figure in the National Peasant Christian Democratic Party, during the miners' incursion, and stealing $100,000. They were sentenced to four and three years, respectively.

Immediately after he took over the post of Minister of the Interior in June 1990, Doru Viorel Ursu attempted to put UM 0215 on a more legitimate basis. The use of false identity papers was, at least officially, abandoned. There was also a change in leadership. Colonel Jenic Iosif was appointed director and Colonel Ion Condoiu, formerly of the SRI, his deputy. In the spring of 1991, Colonel Stoian Rusu took over as head of UM 0215. However, in February 1993, the minister of the interior, General Ioan Dănescu, replaced him with Colonel Dan Gheorghe, who had been sacked from his post as head of the SRI anti-terrorist brigade by Măgureanu.[12]

Judging from the details contained in operational manuals of UM 0215—which had somehow found their way into the offices of a Bucharest daily in March 1994—it would seem that the agency had resumed the practices of the former *Securitate* under the new regime. They included the gathering of information about Romanians living, working, or studying abroad, about employees of foreign firms in Romania, and about foreign residents. These manuals also demonstrated that UM 0215 was monitoring the movements of political personalities, journalists, and trade unionists, with all sensitive information to be entered into the SRI's computer system. These revelations led to the summoning of Interior Minister Doru Ioan Tărăcilă and UM 0215 head Dan Gheorge to explain themselves. While they conceded that some officers might have exceeded their authority in conducting surveillance operations and other activities they contended that, overall, the agency was acting in accordance with the National Security Law, and that those under surveillance were suspected of terrorist or criminal links. Both denied that UM 0215 sought to influence political developments. These arguments were accepted without demur by Roman, to the surprise of many who remembered his previous criticism of the SRI, and its alleged part in facilitating the miners' entry into Bucharest in September 1991 (which prompted Roman's resignation as prime minister). *România liberă* tried to explain Roman's change of mind by reminding its readers of his part in setting up UM 0215, but Roman denied that he was vulnerable to political blackmail.[13] Thus, strong doubts remain about the political accountability of UM 0215, whose members are drawn largely from the ranks of the Bucharest DSS. In March 1994, Major General Ion Pitulescu, chief of the General Police Inspectorate, told the Senate that he was unable to limit the tasks performed by UM 0215, and urged that a new secret service be created that would be fully responsible to the Ministry of the Interior. UM 0215 was widely suspected of trying to take over some of the intelligence gathering activities of the SRI, and Măgureanu complained of interference by the agency in a letter to the Defense Committee of the Senate in December 1995.[14]

Concern expressed by the Romanian media and Western security advisors about the lack of parliamentary control of UM 0215, and its duplication of many of the activities of the SRI, culminated in a decision of the Supreme Defense Council, taken on 22 May 1998, to restructure the organization. Gavril Dejeu, the minister of the Interior, gave the official reason for this decision as, "the image and perception which public opinion has about 0215. It was set up for a specific purpose, which has probably been achieved since 1990."[15] The government approved the restructuring proposals on 4 June 1998. UM 0215 was to be divided into two bodies. One would remain under the direct control of the minister of the Interior and would be charged with the task of rooting out corruption in the Ministry. The other was to be placed under the authority of the head of the General Inspectorate of Police and would have crime prevention responsibilities. Dejeu announced that UM 0215's complement of 1,440 officers would be reduced by roughly 150 personnel. This reduction would be achieved by the compulsory retirement of staff over the age of fifty-two. The remaining staff would be screened by a special comission under the command of Lieutenant General Teodor Zaharia, first deputy minister of the Interior. The commission would examine the past record of every officer and determine which of the two bodies to which they would be assigned. Defending this move in a press statement, Minister Dejeu concluded:

> In any case the Ministry of the Interior should not be at a disadvantage in the work that it does because of the disbandment of 0215. What is clear is that the Supreme Defense Council (CSAT in Romanian) discovered that this military unit was formed largely from former *Securitate* officers, a fact confirmed by Gelu Voiculescu Voican.[16]

There was much comment in the press as to whether 0215 had been abolished or simply restructured. The title of a piece in *România liberă* on 5 June, "0215 is dead! Long live 0215!" was indicative of the skepticism with which the CSAT's decision was greeted in some quarters. The reaction in political circles was mixed. Senator Alexandru Nicolae, president of the parliamentary Defense Commission, considered the decision justified, arguing that 0215 had exceeded its mandate and was interfering in the activity of the SRI. Senator Radu Timoftei, vice president of the same committee, held an opposite view. He maintained that the CSAT's action was illegal and represented a danger to the constitutional nature of the Romanian state. He claimed that UM 0215 had been abolished precisely because the CSAT was not in proper control of the relevant activities in the Ministry of the Interior and in the Ministry of Defense. He further contended that under President Constantinescu, the CSAT had become a "superpower," placing itself above parliament, the government, and the law.[17]

It is the contention of this author that UM 0215 does in fact continue to exist, headed by General Virgil Ardelean (since August 1999), under the name of General Directorate of Intelligence and Internal Protection (*Direcţia Generală de Informaţii si de Protectie Internă*), and the number 0962 (it dropped its military call-sign UM on 24 August 2002 as part of the drive to demilitarize the Ministry of the Interior). Like its predecessor the new organization has a confused mandate, which includes internal affairs (taking anti-corruption measures against Ministry of Interior staff) and the gathering of intelligence concerning external threats to the Ministry of the Interior. The nature of this mandate is questionable because the GDIIP has no infrastructure to allow these activities to be pursued with robustness. Ideally, internal affairs should be separated from the other activity of intelligence gathering. That said, the GDIIP has no constitutional mandate to gather intelligence, yet despite this its numbers are believed to have expanded to 2,200 staff. Not only does the GDIIP duplicate the work of the SRI, there is, to complicate matters further, little coordination between the two agencies.

SPP

Similar doubts about accountability concern the SPP, the service which is primarily responsible for the protection of the President, Romanian party leaders, and foreign diplomats. The SPP was developed from the *Unitatea Specială de Paza şi Control* (USPC), an organization which was set up to protect the President of the Provisional Government on 7 May 1990, under decree No. 204 of the Provisional Council of National Unity. On 15 November 1991, the USPC became the SPP under law No. 51. According to details given by former head Major General Dumitru Iliescu, during the SPPs first-ever press conference on 4 April 1995, the organization has approximately 1,500 personnel, most of whom were recruited from the army. It is divided into three sections, which deal with security of buildings, VIPs, and intelligence.

The intelligence and surveillance role of the SPP came to light in March 1995 over the case of Horia-Roman Patapievici. A thirty-eight-year-old physicist who was one of the anti-Ceauşescu protesters arrested in Bucharest on 21 December 1989, Patapievici had made a name for himself as a political analyst for the weekly *22*, the publication of the independent Group for Social Dialogue, where he intensely criticized what he called the "Iliescu regime" as well as the activities of the SPP. While Patapievici was in Germany in February 1995, his wife was told by a neighbor that a man, claiming to be a police officer named Captain Soare, was making inquiries about Patapievici's political beliefs. A GDS press conference exposed this incident, and the case was quickly taken up by opposition newspapers.

The SRI disclaimed any interest in Patapievici's political ideas and argued that the media was trying to "stir unrest by hounding Romania's main intelligence service."[18] The minister of the Interior, Doru Ioan Tărăcilă declared that "the type of officer like 'Soare' disappeared with the revolution. It is amazing that someone can believe that political police methods are still being practiced."[19] Taracila's reply revealed just the kind of obtuseness which characterized many who were responsible for security matters in Romania, particularly before 1997. The chairman of the senate Commission for Defense, Public Order, and National Security, Radu Timofte, made the startling suggestion that "Soare" might belong to "an illegal intelligence structure," thereby giving credence to SRI Director Virgil Măgureanu's allegations of interference from rival intelligence agencies in Romania. Just a few days after Justice Minister Iosif Chiuzbaian's declaration of his own ministry's innocence,[20] "Soare's" identity was revealed. He was a Captain Marius Lucian of the SPP. The Soare case demonstrated how deeply the old *Securitate* mentality was inculcated in the structures of the security services, how embarrassingly archaic that mentality was, and how incongruous its claims were that the security services had been democratized. Additionally, Soare's identity was acknowledged only days after another case of harassment, this time perpetrated by an SRI officer, came to light.

Mihai Răzvan Ungureanu, a young history lecturer at the University of Iaşi, sent a complaint in March to the Parliamentary Commission for Oversight of the SRI, in which he alleged that he had been harassed by an SRI officer, Major Ioan Chirilă, that his friends had been questioned by this officer, and that the officer had tampered with his correspondence. In its defense, the SRI argued that contact had been made with Ungureanu in his own interest, namely to alert him to the fact that he might be drawn into anti-Romanian activities by a foreign power. Yet, the SRI admitted that Chirilă had been overzealous in insisting on additional meetings with Ungureanu when the latter had made it quite clear that he wished to be left in peace.[21] However, in this instance, and in contrast to the Minister of the Interior, the SRI reacted rapidly by announcing on 16 March the dismissal of Chirilă. This was the first time that the SRI had admitted that one of its officers had acted improperly.

REFORM OF THE SECURITY SERVICES

In a demonstration of his commitment to the Romanian electorate and to the West to make the security services more accountable, newly elected president Constantinescu announced on 13 January 1997 that both the SIE and UM 0215 would come under parliamentary control. (Interestingly, the move to place SIE under parliamentary control was partly driven by accusations from SRI that SIE officers were encroaching upon their territory).[22] The commission of the Senate and Chamber for public order would investigate claims that the telephones of public figures and journalists had been tapped by UM

0215. Furthermore, pressure mounted in the independent press for SRI Director Virgil Măgureanu's dismissal. In an incisive piece in the influential weekly *22*, Serban Orescu accused the new government of "cohabitation" with the SRI director for failing to dismiss him:

> If the new administration wants to wipe the slate clean of the SRI's director's loaded past, there are doubts among those who elected it, and in foreign governments, that it is willing to do so. The manner in which the post of SRI director is filled has major importance in establishing the internal and international credibility of the new regime.[23]

However, an obvious choice for the successor to Măgureanu did not present itself. Constantinescu refused to act hastily. The first indication of significant change in the leadership of the security services was the removal of General Dan Gheorghe as head of UM 0215, on 28 February, by the Minister of the Interior Gavril Dejeu.[24] This was followed by the announcement, on 14 March, that Mircea Gheordunescu, a former member of the National Peasant Christian Democratic Party, had been appointed first deputy director of the SRI. Măgureanu saw the writing on the wall. Recognizing a lack of confidence in his role from the new government, he tendered his resignation to the President on 25 April 1997, which was immediately accepted.

President Constantinescu nominated Costin Georgescu, a Deputy in the National Liberal Party, as Măgureanu's successor. Georgescu's appointment was approved in a joint session of the two chambers of parliament on 26 May. Despite the clean sweep which the president had brought to the SRI leadership, the public was soon reminded of the continued presence of former *Securitate* officers in the SRI's senior ranks. The announcement, in July 1997, of the appointment of Colonel Gheorghe Atudoroaie as head of the Western command of the SRI met with strong criticism in the pro-government press. Atudoroaie had been deputy head of the *Securitate* in Timişoara at the time of the anti-Ceauşescu protests in mid-December 1989, and had allegedly ordered the cremation of the bodies of demonstrators. He was tried and acquitted of murder after the revolution, but the stigma of his service to Ceauşescu remained and led to President Constantinescu's intervention after Atudoroaie's appointment was announced. After being called to the presidential palace on 21 July 1997, Georgescu' appointment was revoked.

The case of Atudoroaie should not be allowed to obscure the fact that the SRI has put much distance between itself and the former *Securitate* over the course of the last decade. Currently, only 18 percent of SRI staff are former *Securitate* officers. There has also been an emphasis on the professionalization of the service. The SRI now has its own college, Academia SRI, with an annual intake of some 80–100 students, who follow a four-year course of study. While university graduates are also eligible to apply to join the SRI, before being accepted they must undergo a course of eight months training at the SRI Academy. This training has been modeled on its counterparts in the West and assisted by Western security agencies, such as the FBI.

FILES AND SCANDALS

The most damaging scandal involving security and intelligence erupted in autumn 1997. On 22 September 1997, the Foreign Minister Adrian Severin claimed in an interview given to the daily *Azi* that he had seen "incontrovertible proof showing that two or three directors of mass circulation newspapers were agents of foreign intelligence services" and that "two famous and respected party leaders are also foreign agents who receive considerable sums from abroad." President Constantinescu declared, "If the accusations are completely unfounded, the Foreign Minister will have to resign." Constantinescu ordered the SRI and the SIE to look into Severin's claims, and their reports were considered by the Supreme Defense Council in a meeting held on 22 December 1997.

The Council's conclusions were made public in a statement issued immediately after its meeting. While accepting Severin's complaints that there had been some "actions which had compromised the Romanian parliament and government" the Council found that "in the documents handed over to the SRI and SIE by Mr. Adrian Severin, nothing could be found to support the charge that the public figures mentioned were tools of foreign secret services." This being the case, the Council asked Severin "to assume political responsibility for the situation which had been created."[25]

Severin did so by resigning on the following day. In his place, the Democratic Party (PD), which held the foreign ministry portfolio in the government coalition, nominated Andrei Pleşu to take his place. The scandal had made the necessity of a law regulating access to the files of the *Securitate* painfully obvious. The government had announced earlier in the year, on 15 February 1997, that it was to introduce a law allowing every citizen access to his or her own *Securitate* file, and that it intended to publish the files of those in public positions. At the end of the year it adopted a private bill with similar provisions, which had been introduced earlier by Senator Constantin (Ticu) Dumitrescu.

The need for a law regulating the release of, and access to, the *Securitate* files became obvious yet again when two scandals rocked the government of Radu Vasile in June 1998. The first concerned the newly appointed chairman of the parliamentary Comission of Control of the SIE (*Comisia specială pentru controlul activităţii Serviciului de Informaţii Externe*), which had been set up on 3 June 1998. The chairman of the commission, PD deputy Vilau, was rung up by an anonymous person on the very day he had submitted the Commission's rules of procedure to the Parliament. The caller informed Vilau that he had his *Securitate* file, which showed clearly that he had been an informer, and that it would be a good idea if they met on the following Monday; otherwise, the caller threatened, the file would be published. Vilau told the caller to go ahead and publish the file, in its entirety, in any newspaper he desired. The caller did so, and details of Vilau's undertaking to act as a *Securitate* informer appeared in the press on 15 June.

Vilau spoke to Traian Basescu, the PD Minister of Transport, and PD Leader Petre Roman about the matter. Roman told him that he should have made his association with the *Securitate* public before putting his name forward as chairman of the SIE Commission. In an interview on 15 June, Vilau admitted that he signed an undertaking in February 1984 to become an informer while a member of the law faculty of Cluj University, and provided information about three colleagues who were alleged by the Securitate to be threats to national security. When contacted later, in 1987, with a request for further assistance by a captain Marian Manăila, responsible in the Cluj *Securitate* for the area of culture and the law profession, Vilau refused.[26] Vilau claimed that was the end of his association.

Nevertheless, the PD withdrew its support for Vilau, and on 29 June he resigned as President of the Commission. Vilau claimed that the accusations were politically motivated, and that his file had been removed from the *Securitate* archive in 1992, after he had called for the resignation of Virgil Măgureanu, then director of the SRI. Măgureanu, he alleged, was now using it "in a political war against him."[27]

Another leak of Securitate files, this time of a page from the file of Francisc Baranyi, the minister of Agriculture and a member of the Hungarian UDMR party, was allegedly traced to an SRI officer, Captain Constantin Alexe.[28] The page was a signed undertaking to provide the *Securitate* with information. Baranyi admitted on 17 June that he had signed such a document, but claimed that the agreement was coerced ("They were threatening me with a pistol," he claimed.), and that it was made under false pretenses (the Securitate officers had presented themselves as members of the frontier police). Baranyi contended that he did not consider himself guilty.[29] Nevertheless, he offered his resignation to Prime Minister Radu Vasile.

The UDMR Council accepted Baranyi's resignation, but made clear in a communiqué its opinion that there were extenuating circumstances surrounding his collaboration with the *Securitate*. There was one good thing to emerge from the scandal: For the first time, a minister resigned from office simply because he had not disclosed his relations with the *Securitate*. Baranyi took an honorable course of action, offering a welcome corrective to the widely held view that politicians do not regard a background in the Securitate as a source of shame. Something appeared to be changing in the Romanian political mentality.

Both the Baranyi and Vilau cases highlighted the lack of precision in the use of the term "informer" in the Romanian media. Its indiscriminate application to anyone who entered into a written agreement to pass information to the *Securitate*, irrespective of the type of information conveyed, has betrayed a lack of sensitivity in treating the somewhat more nuanced, and morally ambiguous, nature of the former *Securitate's* relationship with the Romanian public. Few Romanians would have considered it wrong to alert the authorities to external threats to the state frontiers or to help monitor the activities of Romanian-based, Middle Eastern citizens who were thought to have links with terrorist groups from outside the country. While it is quite another matter, of course, to have reported on one's friends and colleagues, many would have regarded the former examples as a patriotic duty.

Called to give information in June 1998 during the debate in the Senate on Dumitrescu's bill regarding access to the *Securitate* files, Mircea Gheordunescu, deputy director of the SRI, said that some 270,000 files of deceased informers had been destroyed on Ceauşescu's orders during the 1970s, and that a further 1,870 informers' files had been destroyed between 22 December 1989 and 30 March 1990.[30] Nevertheless, a substantial body of *Securitate* files still exists. The scandal involving Vilau and Baranyi persuaded parliament of the urgent need to codify access to, and the release of, these files. Without such controls, selective leaks of personal dossiers, designed to embarrass the government and to discredit certain politicians, could continue to occur at any time. It did not escape the notice of political commentators that no members of the opposition had been targeted by the recent leaks; it was a pattern which seemed to confirm a political agenda behind them.

The "Ticu bill," Dumitrescu's bill on access to the *Securitate* files, was finally passed in the Senate on 25 June 1998 by an overwhelming margin of 106 votes to 7. The bill gives individuals the right to consult any files held by the former *Securitate* on them. It also allows members of a newly established National Council for the Study of the Archives of the former *Securitate* (*Colegiul Consiliului National pentru Studierea Arhivelor fostei Securitati*, or CNSAS), composed of eleven members of parliament drawn from the various political parties, unfettered access to *Securitate* documents (save those relating to national security). The Council is also empowered to verify, upon request from any Romanian citizen, whether a candidate or incumbent of a public office has been a member or informer of the *Securitate*.

However, in its passage through the Senate the bill suffered a number of amendments, the most controversial of which concerned an article which originally provided for the transfer of the *Securitate* files to the new National Council. The adoption of an amendment rescinded this provision, thereby leaving the files under the control of the SRI. As a consequence, "Ticu" Dumitrescu publicly disowned his own bill, arguing that it had been mutilated and that he had been betrayed and misunderstood by those who ought to have stood beside him. The bill, including the new amendment, was adopted in a joint session of both chambers on 20 October. Whether this new law will be applied is open to question. Supporting legislation providing the necessary financing for the National Council was eventually enacted. The new Council was in existence during the 2000 elections and provided lists of those candidates who did not voluntarily declare the past associations with the security services, about several dozen in total. The Council, in response to criticism that its lists were in complete, noted that it did the best it could given its limited resources.

The CNSAS ran into major problems in Autumn 2002. A majority of its Council—six of the eleven members—frustrated at the failure of the SRI to provide them with files detailing the suspected *Securitate* membership or collaboration of dozens of political and business figures, tried to convene a meeting of the Council on 28 October 2002 to force the issue. The other five members, sponsored by the ruling Social Democratic Party (PSD) and the ultra-right Greater Romania Party, failed to attend. And, Gheorghe Onisoru, though delegated by the National Liberal Party, acts as if he is a member of the PSD, which he may well implicitly be. *Inquorate*, the meeting was adjourned. The Council has not met since, for the same reason. It is widely believed that the government would suffer great embarrassment should the requested files be released and has therefore instructed its members on the Council to block proceedings. To remove this impasse the government appears to be considering the passage of a new law which would led to the election of a Council reflective of the new political complexion of parliament, thereby making it obedient to the Social Democratic party and removing the recalcitrant members—the present Council members were elected for a term of six years in the previous parliament.

In September 2002, a majority of CNSAS members submitted a list to the SRI to verify whether fifty-four individuals had been members of the *Securitate* political police. In October, the SRI responded with the names of three of those on the list who were retired from the *Securitate* in January 1990. No verification had been provided at the time of writing of those who had been political police. By the beginning of November 2002, only 9,300 files had been handed over to CNSAS, even though the *Securitate* archives are an estimated twelve kilometers in length.

The political sensitivity of the CNSAS's activity and of "purification" had been highlighted in February 2001 when the PSD deputy Ristea Priboi swore an oath on his appointment as head of the Parliamentary Control Commission of the SIE (Foreign Intelligence Service), as required to do so by law, that he had "not collaborated with the structures of the former political police." When it was revealed in the press that Priboi had been an officer in the foreign intelligence directorate of the *Securitate*, Priboi offered the specious defence that he had "not collaborated with the *Securitate*" but had been "an employee of the *Securitate*." On 19 April 2001, the rising clamour in the media forced his resignation,[31] but the episode came back to haunt him in December 2002 when a Romanian poet, Ion Gheorghe, discovered in the file the *Securitate* kept on him—provided legally by the CNSAS—that Priboi had allegedly been involved in "political police activities." Such activities were a bar to candidacy for parliament and it was on those grounds that the Liberal Party senator, Radu F. Alexandru, alerted the prosecutor-general (attorney general) to Priboi's alleged infringement of the law.[32]

CONCLUSION

Ultimately, the most efficient watchdog of the new state security service structure has been the mass media. The tabloid press has been extremely vigilant in highlighting SRI and 0215 abuses. Public interest in the activities of the Romanian intelligence and security services is mirrored by the fact that every major daily has a correspondent devoted to security matters. There are also pressures generated to reform the security services in order to make Romania a fitter member of NATO, to which she received on invitation to join at the Prague summit on 21 November 2002. Additionally, the evolving system of parliamentary controls means that the use of the SRI to the advantage of one political faction over another will become increasingly problematic. Under the leadership of Costin Georgescu and Mircea Gheordunescu, the SRI ostensibly moved away from a secret service driven by domestic political interests and factionalism, and toward becoming a public institution dealing with the "objective" problems of state security. That trend has continued under the directorship of Radu Timofte.

The period of President Constantinescu's mandate (November 1996–November 2000) witnessed a determined effort on the part of President Constantinescu to complete the revolution and the democratic transition. He promoted to the leadership of the security services figures of a democratic mold, who understood the need for transparency, and who were responsive to the demands of accountability. At the same time, he retired thirty generals from the security services. President Ion Iliescu, returned to office in November 2000, continued the trend, although he also reactivated a number of those retired by his predecessor.[33]

Yet, problems of accountability remain. The constitutionality of the Supreme Defense Council has yet to be addressed. The absence of a constitutional link between the Supreme Defense Council and the parliament has prevented the latter from exercising democratic supervision of the former—a phenomenon which has been exacerbated by the opacity surrounding its deliberations. Until it becomes more accountable, the CSAT lays itself open to the charge that it is above the law and therefore susceptible to abuse. Even more acute is the lack of accountability of the Ministry of the Interior Security Service (0962) which is ultimately responsible to the Prime Minister's office.

While a case can certainly be made for a counterintelligence security service to monitor the staff of the Ministry of the Interior, the tasks assigned to 0962 extend far beyond such a remit. It is charged with monitoring the activity of politicians, a role for which it has no constitutional authority. As such 0962 acts as a political police, outside the law, and its continued existence in its present form threatens the health of Romanian democracy.

It is now up to the Romanian parliament to use the legislation at its disposal to enforce accountability. The question remains: Will it have the political will to do this effectively? Or, will the skeletons in the closet of many of its members make them wary of monitoring effectively these new state security bodies? The form of the law on access to the *Securitate* files suggests that the answer to the first part of the question is no, and to the second, yes.

NOTES

1. Research for this chapter was carried out with the help of a grant from The Nuffield Foundation of Great Britain.

2. Dan Ionescu, "UM 0215: A Controversial Intelligence Service in Romania," *RFE/RL Research Report*, vol. 3, no. 30 (29 July 1994), p. 28. Voiculescu was named head of the *ad interim Securitate* in December 1989 by the Council of the National Salvation Front, but held the position for only three days before being dismissed by General Militaru and replaced by a military officer, Colonel Logofatu.

3. Editor's note: The 1948 Genocide Convention defines genocide as the *intent* to destroy part of a people, defined on racial, religious, or ethnic criteria, not cultural or political. Thus, the December events could not be genocide because the motive and targets were political. Intentional genocide is therefore also tautological.

4. BBC Monitoring Service, *Summary of World Broadcasts* (henceforth, *SWB*). EE/1074 (17 May 1991), p. B7.

5. *SWB*. EE/1086 (31 May 1991), p. B/18.

6. *Evenimentul Zilei* (24 May 1993), p. 1.

7. Dennis Deletant, "The *Securitate* and the Police State in Romania, 1964–1989," in *Intelligence and National Security*, vol. 9, no. 1 (January 1994), p. 36.

8. *România liberă* (21 May 1991), p. 1.

9. *SWB*, EE/0932 (27 November 1990), p. B/10.

10. Its current head, appointed in February 2001, is Radu Timofte.

11. Its current head (2002) is Gheorghe Fulga.

12. Dan Ionescu, "UM 0215: A Controversial Intelligence Service in Romania," *RFE/RL Research Report*, vol. 3, no. 30 (29 July 1994), p. 28.

13. Ibid., p. 30.

14. *Ziua* (9 December 1995), p. 1.

15. *România liberă* (26 May 1998), p. 24.

16. Ibid.

17. *România liberă* (25 May 1998), p. 2.

18. *Curierul Naţional* (10 March 1995), p. 2.

19. *România liberă* (16 March 1995), p. 16.

20. *România liberă* (13 March 1995), p. 3.

21. Among those who advised Ungureanu on what course of action to take against Chirilă were Liviu Antonesei, Nicolae Manolescu, Ştefan Augustin Doinaş, Andrei Pleşu, and Gabriel Liiceanu. See *Monitorul* (16 March 1995), p. 1; and *România liberă* (16 March 1995), p. 16. Ungureanu's first meeting with Chirilă was on 5 September 1994. Chirilă summoned him on the pretext that Ungureanu's name had been found in the papers of a foreigner in Bucharest who was suspected of being a spy. Chirilă used this allegation to bring up the subject of "traitors" and advised Ungureanu to stop writing about minority issues in Romania. In an interview given to a Iaşi newspaper, Ungureanu surmised that he had probably become a target of the SRI because of his actions during the revolution. On 19 December 1989, he left Iaşi for Cluj, and on the morning of 21 December, was given shelter in the flat of Professor David Prodan. He was wounded in the street protests and taken to the hospital. After the revolution, his telephone was tapped and his mail intercepted. See "*Îngerii Securităţii. De la Soare la Chirilă,*" *Gaudeamus* (27 March–8 April 1995), p. 4.

22. *România liberă* (13 January 1997), p. 24.

23. Ş. Orescu, "*Noul regim si d-l Măgureanu,*" *22*, no. 50, (11–17 December 1996), p. 3.

24. Colonel Dan Moise, deputy head of 0215, took over from Gheorghe until 31 March when Colonel Constantin Dângă, former head of the Control Commission of the General Inspectorate of Police, was transferred to lead 0215. (*România liberă*, 1 April 1997, p. 1) General Gheorghe was made head of the frontier police but resigned from this position on 19 August 1997. The current (winter 2002) head of 0215 is General Ardelean.

25. *România liberă* (24 December 1997), p. 3.

26. *România liberă* (16 June 1998), p. 3.

27. *Academia Caţavencu* (30 June–6 July 1998), p. 4.

28. *România liberă* (4 July 1998), p. 2.

29. *România liberă* (18 June 1998), p. 1.

30. Romanian *Acasă* TV report (25 June 1998). If the 1,870 files were simply removed from the *Securitate's* central computer, it would still be possible to reconstitute them from the records held by the resident officer who ran each informer and also from the files of the directorate to whom the resident was attached, assuming that the latter also escaped destruction.

31. *Azi*, 20 April 2001, p. 3.

32. *România liberă*, 11 December 2002, p. 1.

33. Among them was Marian Ureche, appointed head of SIPA, who had been a senior officer in the First Directorate (domestic intelligence) of the *Securitate*, Tudor Tănase, placed in command of STS, who between 1978 and 1989 worked in the communications unit of the *Securitate* charged with intercepting the telephone calls of foreign embassies in Bucharest, and Gioni Popescu, named deputy director of the SRI who had worked in the foreign intelligence directorate of the *Securitate*. For a list of those retired, see *Adevărul*, 5 May 2001, p. 1.

26

Civil-Military Relations: Continuity or Exceptionalism?

Larry L. Watts

The Romanian Army was unique for the degree of its involvement in the fall of the Communist dictatorship during the Revolution of 1989, and for its ability to steer clear of politics during the early stages of its democratic transition. That ability was uncharacteristic, not only of other post-Communist militaries, but also of most of NATO's southern flank members.[1] Since it did not conform to the pattern evident among its *confrères*, the Romanian military was generally excluded from comparative studies of post-Communist civil-military relations.[2] This exclusion was unfortunate, as the reasons for Romania's uniqueness may further our understanding of civil-military relations in transition states.

THE NATURE OF ROMANIAN MILITARY EXCEPTIONALISM

This exceptionalism was a further consequence of the "maverick" autonomous status which Romania had established for itself within the Warsaw Pact during the 1960s.[3] The core elements of this autonomy included independence of the Romanian Army from Soviet military command,[4] the early establishment of a strictly national defense strategy, and a relatively untarnished reputation as national defender rather than an instrument of Communist repression.[5]

The fact that the Romanian military was subordinated neither to Moscow nor to Soviet military planning for over twenty years prior to the 1989 revolution had broad ramifications for civil-military relations and military reform in the post-Communist period.[6] Chief among these was a relationship of trust between the Romanian population and its army. The generally positive role of the military during the December 1989 revolution that brought down Ceauşescu's regime was thus not entirely unexpected.[7] This contrasted sharply with the evident distrust among the populations of Hungary, Czechoslovakia, Bulgaria, and, to a lesser degree, Poland who, because of the continued subordination and presumed loyalty of those armies to a foreign entity, were markedly suspicious of their military establishments.

The preparation of deployments and force restructuring appropriate to Bucharest's independent territorial defense policy also necessitated new modes of civilian-military interaction. The army and civilian leaderships were compelled to establish an effectively cooperative relationship due to fundamental policy choices in the 1960s—placing Romania on an entirely different footing than other former Soviet allies in the process of building a healthy civil-military relationship in the post-Communist period.

Romania's legacy of nonintervention against the domestic population created a situation in which the military was not viewed as a threat to democracy by the general population, by the newly elected governments, or by the new opposition parties. This was not the case with virtually every other former non-Soviet Warsaw Pact state where the opposite held true to a greater or lesser degree, prompting their new civilian authorities to approach their militaries in a fundamentally adversarial fashion.

The 1989–1990 Civil-Military Crises

Romania's advantages notwithstanding, serious civil-military crises were created during the political turbulence which marked the first year of the post-Communist transition. In a misdirected attempt to eliminate the possibility of pro-Ceauşescu holdovers in the army, the initial National Salvation Front (FSN) government named as defense minister an officer known to have been cashiered by Ceauşescu in 1978. The officer, General Nicolae Militaru, then reactivated some thirty reserve officers into senior leadership positions. The move was similar to that employed by the new Czechoslovak leadership, where officers purged in 1969 were reactivated and granted leading roles in the military as a hedge against undue Soviet influence. The Romanian army, however, was already under national control while most of Militaru's appointees were Soviet-trained.

The situation was made worse by the fact that the reactivated officers had been out of active service for at least twenty years, and hence out of touch with the institution and its development. This provoked a backlash within the general staff and service branches, and prompted the creation of the Action Committee for a Democratic Army (CADA) by a group of mostly junior officers.[8] Less than two months later, in mid-February 1990, Militaru was replaced by General Victor Stănculescu.

In an effort to stem further demonstrations the NSF government under Petre Roman precipitously institutionalized CADA as the leading reform instrument within the military.[9] As the effects of delegating de facto authority over senior officers to their erstwhile subordinates began to threaten the command hierarchy, the same government that had institutionalized CADA began cracking down on the organization, creating further tensions.[10]

Consequences stemming from the extremely harsh nature of the Ceauşescu regime and the violent character of the Romanian Revolution further exacerbated the situation. All the institutions of domestic coercion and social order, including those required for the normal functioning of the rule of law (i.e., the militia/police), were popularly regarded as instruments of the former dictator's repression. Despised by the public, those institutions virtually disintegrated with the Revolution. Until they could be reconstructed in a more legitimate form, the new government lacked the basic ability to produce social order on a daily basis, or to deal with legitimate nonmilitary security threats.

This problem was unique to Romania. All the other former Communist dictatorships had been removed from power more or less peacefully. As a result, police and state security functions continued throughout the early transition process. Military refusal to answer calls to act as an internal security force prompted further tension between civilian authorities and military leaders as the issue of civilian control was brought into question. Consequently, Stănculescu's tenure was largely one of avoiding the potential for disaster that lay in these misguided civilian initiatives, while persuading the civilian authorities that the military fully accepted its subordination to their authority.

These crises compelled Romanian military and civilian authorities to focus on what was recognized only later throughout Central and Eastern Europe as the number one challenge to civil-military reform and the establishment of civilian control: the creation of civilian defense management experts. The problem and necessity of creating a viable civilian defense community was first raised at the beginning of 1991 by Presidential Counselor for Military Affairs, Colonel Ioan Talpeş. Immediately thereafter, the Supreme Defense Council (*Consiliul Suprem de Apărare al Ţării*, CSAT) decided on the creation of an educational forum that could provide the necessary expertise to civilians and create linkages between civilian and military authorities.[11] The discussions quickly expanded to include the best methods for instituting stable civil-military relations over the long term and "civilianizing" the defense ministry while maintaining military effectiveness. As a first step, a group of military and civilian educators were charged with the design of an appropriate training facility for civilians.[12] The result of their efforts was the creation of the National Defense College (*Colegiul Naţional de Apărare*, CNA), where civilian politicians would study national security issues alongside senior military officers. Parallel to this effort, Defense Minister Nicolae Spiroiu (who replaced Stănculescu in the spring of 1991) and Chief of Staff Dumitru Cioflină were authorized to begin a reorganization that would permit effective civilian control over the military.[13]

New Crises: 1997–2000

The coalition which took power at the beginning of 1997 did not share the harsh experience of 1989–1990 that had jolted their predecessors, tempering their behavior and paving the way for an improved civil-military relationship. Consequently, they adopted a very different approach to reform. The new team failed to incorporate the useful experience of their predecessors, particularly in opting for unilateral civilian decision making over civil-military consensus-building, and, at times, denying any real progress in military reform or Euro-Atlantic integration prior to 1997 whatsoever.[14]

Compounding the new leaders' inexperience and greater partisanship was their suspicion toward the senior military leadership. This was manifested, for example, in the unexpected replacement of General Dumitru Cioflină, widely considered by NATO as the most impressive chief of staff in Central and Eastern Europe at the time, with the far more junior General Constantin Degeratu. Subsequent tension in civil-military relations accompanied allegations that the Democratic Convention was seeking to fill the MApN with their partisans.

Civil-military relations were further strained by a series of budgetary restrictions during 1998–2000. Budget cuts that threatened basic military restructuring goals and NATO compatibility and interoperability targets drew criticism from both current and former defense ministers and chiefs of staff, as well as from the Parliamentary Defense Committees.[15] The inadequate handling of a series of corruption scandals implicating defense ministry officials, senior officers, and the presidency also caused tension within the officer corps and cynicism among the public at large.[16]

By far the most serious civil-military crisis was generated, as from 1989–1990, by civilian attempts to employ the military as an internal security force and enlist it as an ally in domestic political competition. There are myriad problems associated with assigning police functions to the military, not the least of these is that the army is simply not trained in using gradations of force for nonlethal crowd control. When the army is placed before angry demonstrators it does not take much to provoke massive casualties. The principal difficulty, however, stems from the fact that policing is an inherently politicized and partisan task.[17] By their very nature, police functions politicize the military and have historically led to an expanded domestic political role for the army in transition states.[18] Those states in which the military is given an internal police role typically evince the "worst pattern of civil-military relations."[19]

The former Communist regimes intentionally sought to combine the military and police in a supra-institution of state coercion that hypothetically could be employed against internal threats to the party leadership. Under conditions in which the police had yet to be demilitarized, the Iliescu administration was careful to maintain the separation of personnel and tasks after 1991 in an effort to re-differentiate the two institutions. During the entire period from 1992 through 1996, for example, no officers or civilians from the defense ministry were transferred to the interior ministry (police) or vice versa.

This differentiation of police and military institutional roles suffered under the Constantinescu administration, beginning with the 1997 appointment of a former interior minister as defense minister. During the miners' march of January 1999, the minister, Victor Babiuc, and his deputy, Constantin Dudu Ionescu, publicly stated that the army was available to intervene domestically "with all the means at their disposal."[20] Deputy Defense Minister Ionescu was then transferred to the post of interior minister, bringing three military generals along with him. These transfers, and the subsequent mobilization of the army against the miners, indicated a profound lack of understanding regarding police and military roles and the negative repercussions of employing the military for internal security tasks, on behalf of the Democratic Convention coalition.[21]

Along with gross irregularities in army promotions, particularly among the senior officers where promotion policies ran counter to restructuring needs and actually worsened the problem of the reverse pyramid, politicization of the army also became overt during 1998–2000. In November 1998, improper influence was alleged against Democratic Convention appointees in the defense ministry and on the electoral commission during the Bucharest mayoralty elections, when voting patterns in military sectors diverged widely and consistently from general voting patterns.[22] In November 1999, the presidency issued a circular letter to all military commandants asserting that the main opposition party, the PDSR, was hostile to the military and police.[23] At the beginning of December, the defense ministry spokesperson—a Democratic Convention appointee—issued an official communiqué condemning the PDSR for allegedly offending the military.[24] These were unprecedented actions contravening both the constitution, which mandates the nonpartisanship of the presidency, and the Law on the Status of Military Personnel (no. 80/1995), which prohibits the carrying out of activities in support of (or against) political parties.[25]

The rejection of the civil-military consensus building practiced during 1991–1996, and its replacement with a misapplied civilian supremacy model that emphasized unilateral civilian decision making and military subservience, resulted in the breakdown of MApN-General Staff relations and a decline in overall civil-military relations.[26] In consequence, military reform failed to progress, actual democratic control suffered a setback as communications broke down, and civilian-initiated reforms could not be moved from paper to practice. This was reflected, for example, in the NATO Membership Action Plan (MAP) process. The Romanian government's ability to fulfill only 2 of the 88 partnership goals it assumed during the first MAP cycle in 1999–2000 undermined credibility both at home and abroad.

Problems were particularly evident in (1) promotion and retention policies, where the reverse pyramid of the officer corps had worsened and levels of professionalism had declined; (2) in defense planning and budgeting, where civilian opinion had little actual impact on primarily military planning and budgeting processes; and (3) in parliamentary oversight, where interpellation powers diminished and authority over restructuring had been transferred to the executive. Military reform performance was so poor under the Constantinescu presidency and Democratic Convention governments that Romania fell from being considered the first in line for a new wave of NATO enlargement at Madrid in July 1997 to last place among the MAP states seeking membership by the end of 2000.[27]

2001-2002: Military Reform "Back on Track"

Given the poor state of reform inherited by the new Iliescu administration in December 2000, the rapid progress of military reforms and improvement in democratic civil control over the armed forces in 2001 was impressive. To a large degree, this was due to the upgraded expertise at the top of the defense management chain. The new defense minister, Ioan Mircea Paşcu, previously served as MApN state secretary for defense policy and international relations in 1993–1996, and as the chairman of the defense oversight committee in the lower house in 1997–2000. Paşcu understood not only what was wrong and what had to be done, but also the sort of team that would be required to do it. On his appointment in December 2000, Paşcu placed the creation of a fair and transparent personnel management system, the institution of joint defense planning and budgeting, and increased parliamentary oversight at the top of his list of needed reforms, appointing the very able diplomat George Cristian Maior as state secretary for defense policy to carry them out.[28]

All these goals were achieved within the first ten months of 2001. A new *Military Career Guide* was introduced with the assistance of British military and civil-military advisors that established clear criteria for promotion and retention, including new stipulations limiting promotions to specific jobs rather than awarding them simply for time-in-service, as was the case previously.[29] The *Guide* also provided for independent military selection boards modeled after NATO practice, with the first selection board convening in July.[30] By October, 4,138 senior officers, including 44 generals, 888 colonels, 1,442 lieutenant colonels, and 1,335 majors had been made redundant.[31] A further 2,200 officers were released during 2002, bringing the active service peacetime army down to 93,000 personnel by mid-2002—approximately one-third of its size in December 1989. Further downsizing to 75,000 is projected by 2007.

This was not accomplished without resistance as a number of senior officers sought to influence their job security through informal means, and the achievement of these downsizing targets owes much to the close collaboration established between the minister, state secretary Maior, chief of the general staff General Mihail Popescu, and his deputy for reform, General Constantin Gheorghe. Significant achievements were also registered in "civilianization" of the MApN, with 600 new appointments in the first five months of 2001, 33 of which were in key positions.[32]

Defense planning and budgeting, keys areas of civilian control, were brought from general staff control into a joint process under the MApN.[33] The Planning, Programming, Budgeting, and Evaluations system (PPBES) used by the U.S. Armed Forces was introduced in the MApN in January 2001, and the 2001 defense budget was the first to be program-driven rather than means based—a prerequisite for forward-looking planning. Romania's reform credibility gained considerable ground when all thirteen priority objectives assumed during the second MAP cycle were completed by the cycle's end in September 2001. Similar success was registered in the third MAP cycle.

The re-empowerment of parliamentary oversight was pursued on three levels. First, the parliament was given authority over the approval of flag officers and the appointment of military attaches, and its interpellation powers were enhanced to enable it to hear senior officers without the presence of the civilian defense minister.[34] Second, a legislative reform was introduced designating the committees as the primary working groups of the parliament, and the presence of either the minister or a state secretary was made obligatory on all measures regarding military restructuring and organization.[35] Finally, a new secretary of state for parliamentary liaison and legislative harmonization was established within the MApN, and his office properly resourced.[36]

The effectiveness of the 2001–2002 military reform was most strikingly illustrated after the terrorist attack against the United States on 11 September 2001, when President Iliescu declared Romania a de facto ally of the United States and NATO.[37] By April 2002, Romanian troops were patrolling with British Forces in the International Security Force (ISAF) in Kabul, Afghanistan, having been airlifted by Romanian aircraft. By June, Bucharest had deployed a motorized infantry battalion to Kandahar for the U.S. Operation *Enduring Freedom*, where the battalion earned high marks for their performance.

Aside from maintaining troops in Kabul, Bagram, and Kandahar, Romania maintained a substantial liaison team at U.S. Central Command (USCENTCOM) in Tampa, Florida as part of the war on terrorism. On 21 November 2002, Romania, along with six other states, was invited to join NATO. Romania also has 700-plus men serving with all three divisions—the British, the Americans, and the Polish—in Iraq. It is the only country to participate in all three. Although economic reform progress had also improved markedly during 2001–2002, no one was in doubt that successful military reform, along with ability and willingness to contribute to the alliance, had been the ace card in Romania's NATO bid.

REFORM OF STATE SECURITY AND INTELLIGENCE

After the military, the reform of the state security apparatus is probably the most urgent priority in post-authoritarian states because of its central role in maintaining the former dictatorship in power and the obstacle it presents to democratic consolidation. At the same time, the secrecy that surrounds intelligence work tends to encourage suspicion and worst-case presumption in analyses of intelligence and security services and in evaluations of their reform. This is particularly the case in the aftermath of revolution when, at one and the same time, these services constitute a focal point for conspiracy theories and a principal bulwark against the chaos that accompanies radical transition.[38]

Myth and exaggeration are further fueled by the hyperbole associated with the extremely partisan political competition common to new democracies. For more than a decade after the fall of Communism, domestic opponents questioned the democratic worthiness of incumbent governments by alleging continuity between pre- and post-Communist security institutions.[39] As core intelligence tasks remain the same no matter the political system, all transition states are vulnerable to allegations of security apparatus "continuity" to some degree.[40]

Media and Intelligence

The media have often been less than helpful when treating intelligence issues.[41] The Polish media, for example, were criticized for uncritical propagation of "slander campaigns" and "leaks originating in the services."[42] In Bulgaria, a journal fabricated an al-Qaeda meeting in Sofia to increase circulation, with serious foreign policy consequences.[43] The Romanian press was likewise hobbled by "tendentiousness" and "low reporting standards."[44] A 1999 study of the International Federation of Journalists (IFJ) rated the Romania print media the "least responsible" in comparison with that of Croatia, Bulgaria, and Albania.[45]

Complicating the problem, ex-security apparatus officers and their collaborators were often drawn to the media because of their professional specialization or because publicity was considered an important element in economic empire building.[46] As a result, intra-service rivalries and contests between the services and ex-officers were also played out through the press, where allegations and fabrications were often presented as fact.

For example, after his nomination for the post of director of Romanian security intelligence (*Serviciul Român de Informaţii*, SRI) in early 2001, the press alleged that Radu Timofte was complicit with an ex-*Securitate* businessman, Sorin Ovidiu Vîntu. Paradoxically, Timofte unraveled the skein behind which Vîntu hid his illegal financial dealings.[47] Until the publication of Timofte's report to the Romanian National Bank on the Vîntu case, the media uniformly interpreted his involvement as complicity and cause for dismissal.[48]

Some print media behaved similarly in other areas of security sector reform as well. For example, National Security Advisor Ioan Talpeş, responsible for coordinating Romania's NATO integration effort during 2001–2002, was labeled as "anti-NATO" by the press and portrayed as an obstacle to alliance integration.[49] Talpeş was similarly accused of breaking the Yugoslav embargo in the early 1990s when, in fact, he bore primary responsibility for bringing in U.S. monitoring teams to work with the Romanians in ensuring embargo enforcement.[50]

The most detailed example of media implication in intra-service rivalry is the "Timofte-KGB" affair. The media began reporting a linkage between Radu Timofte and the KGB even before the 2000 elections and again with renewed vigor prior to his appointment as SRI head, demanding his withdrawal from consideration for the post.[51] A career soldier until the mid-1980s, Timofte was harassed by the *Securitate* and forced to leave the army after his sister emigrated to the United States. As a result, he was perceived as a threat by some *ex-Securitate* officers in the SRI beginning in 1990, when he was named chair of the Senate oversight committee for defense, national security, and public order.[52] To combat this threat and discredit Timofte, a dossier alleging a KGB-tie was forged within the SRI during Virgil Măgureanu's tenure.[53]

Timofte served continuously on the oversight committee until assuming the SRI post in 2001, and his vocal criticism of the cover-up surrounding the *Ţigareta II* smuggling affair in 1998 apparently provoked a further elaboration of the dossier during Costin Georgescu's tenure as SRI director.[54] Parliamentary investigation, followed by an internal SRI investigation, into the accuracy and provenance of the dossier uncovered the involvement of seven senior officers including the first deputy director, one division chief, and two regional heads.[55] Throughout the investigation, press coverage was overwhelmingly biased against Timofte.

Placing this in perspective, the ease with which the press was drawn into disinformation campaigns was problematic throughout the region. In the Czech Republic, such tactics were used in an unsuccessful attempt to compromise parliamentary candidates and a former head of the intelligence in

1996 and 1998.[56] Polish intelligence was implicated in the manufacturing of false KGB links with President Aleksander Kwaśniewski and former President Lech Wałęsa before elections in 2000.[57] The same tactic was employed against President Iliescu during 1995–1996, and revivified during 1999–2000, including forged documents and non-existent interviews with fictitious KGB officers.[58] Similarly false allegations were leveled against Iliescu's candidate for the SIE directorship, Gheorghe Fulga, in 2001.

REFORM IN COMPARATIVE PERSPECTIVE

In such a medium, it is difficult to extract fact from fiction unless there are comparative reference points. Intelligence services in democratic states can be usefully broken down into categories according the type of information and their subordination. *National security* or *strategic intelligence* services seek to identify threats and gather information to help policy makers make decisions regarding the security of the state and society. It is the broadest category since "the defense of national security" is the most legitimate rationale for curtailing civil rights and liberties. These services are often constituted as state rather than party-based governmental organs and they are the principal concern of this study. *Criminal intelligence* is aimed at bringing criminals to justice. Undertaken only after a crime has been committed or when the commission of a crime is imminent, it is subject to much tighter legal standards required for the legal prosecution and conviction of perpetrators in courts of law. *Specialty intelligence* targets specific domains such as military preparations and postures.

The division of large "all-purpose" security structures, and their proliferation into smaller and less powerful services subject to both parliamentary and judicial oversight, are common elements of all democratic intelligence reform projects. Traditionally, the democratic reform project requires two basic separations of tasks. Foreign and domestic intelligence are separated because the former is regularly involved in breaking the laws of foreign states whereas the latter is required to function in accordance with the law. Law enforcement functions are separated from national security intelligence gathering because of the much more legally restrictive requirements of the former and the open-ended nature of the latter.

Although the last to throw off Communist dictatorship, Romania was the first post-Communist state to complete this separation when it transferred the Department of State Security (DSS) from the interior ministry to the defense ministry and removed its law enforcement powers in December 1989. Law enforcement powers were excluded from the foreign intelligence and domestic security intelligence services (SIE and SRI) created during January–March 1990. Czechoslovakia accomplished this in February 1990, while Bulgaria completed it during 1991–92. Until mid-2002, Polish intelligence reflected the greatest continuity in terms of structure and combined functions within a single institution: the Office of State Protection (UOP).[59] Even after Poland separated the UOP into foreign and domestic services (AW and ABW) in June 2002, it did not remove their law enforcement authority.[60] Slovakia combined foreign intelligence and domestic security tasks within its intelligence service (BIS) in 1993, when it achieved independence, but did not grant it law enforcement powers.[61]

The number and array of intelligence services is conditioned by state-specific risks and threats and varying degrees of external engagement. Lacking a comparative basis in a field where information is scarce, country-specific studies often judge the number of post-Communist services exaggerated and the intelligence community "bloated," even though it may fall well within average dimensions.[62] France, for instance, has around a dozen structures that undertake covert intelligence activity: four services engaged in national security intelligence and structures within the ministries of interior, justice, foreign affairs, defense, science and technology, transport, trade, and communications.[63] Hungary's dozen structures include security intelligence, foreign intelligence, technical intelligence, and two military intelligence services, along with more than a half-dozen criminal intelligence structures in the police, border guard, tax authority, and finance guard.[64] Aside from the ABW, AW, and military intelligence (WSI), Poland's system of covert intelligence structures includes reconnaissance units of the military, VIP protection, a section within customs, and structures within the border guards, police, military/prison police, and the revenue office.[65]

Romania's intelligence bodies include the principal national security intelligence services—SRI and SIE, the main subjects of this analysis—and the specialty services of the military (*Direcţia Generală de Informaţii şi Apararii*, DGIA) and VIP protection (*Serviciul de Paza şi Protecţia*, SPP). The SPP is entitled to request warrants for surveillance and communications interception but relies on the SRI and SIE to carry out these tasks. The Special Telecommunications Service (STS), often erroneously cited as an intelligence service, has no covert intelligence collection authority.[66]

Criminal intelligence responsibilities have fallen under the government and prime minister rather than state authority since 26 December 1989 and, therefore, are a not a concern of this study. However, the interior ministry's Directorate of Intelligence and Internal Protection (*Drectia Generala de Informatii si Protectie Interne*, DGIPI)—formerly known as UM 0215 and UM 0962—has a history of exceeding its criminal intelligence remit and engaging in unauthorized political intelligence activities. Successive governments have been seduced by the lure of their own intelligence service beyond the purview of parliament without ever really managing to control it. As a result, it has developed an independent set of stakeholder interests unfavorable to democratic oversight and accountability. For example, in March 2001, Prime Minister Adrian Năstase pushed through an emergency ordinance granting broad powers to the DGIPI including national security intelligence collection (article 17) and wiretapping, surveillance, and search and seizure without a warrant from the General Prosecutor's office.[67] Only after the presidency sent it back to the government for reanalysis was the ordinance withdrawn.[68] The DGIPI continues to claim unauthorized national security prerogatives (see www.mi.ro).

Vetting Personnel

Security intelligence services created after the fall of Communism were commonly vetted of officers most directly implicated in political policing and human rights abuses. The timing, degree, and manner of vetting depended primarily on whether the revolution was negotiated or sudden, and whether it was "velvet" or violent. Where the revolution was negotiated, as in Poland and Hungary, security sector institutions maintained greater continuity in both personnel and structures. Where the revolution was sudden, vetting of the services was immediate and extensive. Czechoslovakia, for example, vetted more than 13,000 State Security (StB) members, finding 86 percent of them suitable for further employment, before opting to replace all legacy personnel.[69]

The SRI

By the end of January 1990, more than 10,000 members of Romania's 15,312-strong DSS (*Securitate*)—66 percent of its entire manpower—were excluded from the personnel pool from which the SRI would draw its members. 4,138 vetted personnel—27 percent of the former *Securitate*—were incorporated into the new service. Initially forming 60 percent of the SRI's 6,800 personnel in March 1990, subsequent vetting and turnover reduced their presence to less than 36 percent by 1994, and less than 20 percent by the end of the decade.[70] This percentage further decreased to 15 percent of the SRI's approximately 7,000 personnel during 2001–2002, with more than two-thirds of SRI central and territorial unit chiefs appointed since the spring of 2001.[71]

One of the primary obstacles in fully realizing the benefits of personnel renewal during 1990–1997 was the leadership of the SRI's first director, Virgil Măgureanu. Măgureanu concealed his earlier *Securitate* career from Iliescu when he was named to the post, thereby compromising the effort to fully break with the past and perpetuating the old institutional mentality within the newly restructured organization. The failure to sanction Măgureanu's disingenuous publication of part of his own file in order to stave off further revelations violated Romanian law and demonstrated an unfortunate precedence of expediency over the rule of law. The appointment of party politicians to operational deputy director posts during the Constantinescu administration from 1997–2000 also caused problems. These political appointees were removed in 2001, and a more professional human resource policy introduced.

The SIE

None of the post-Communist states systematically vetted their foreign intelligence services, and the Foreign Intelligence Center (*Centrul de Informaţii Externe*, CIE: January–December 1990) and its SIE successor were no exception. The collection of intelligence abroad was presumed to have distanced foreign intelligence personnel from the tasks of domestic repression. Although broadly true, foreign intelligence was only a section of the Communist security apparatus within which personnel were freely transferred. For example, the first chief of the CIE/SIE, Mihail Caraman, was an agent posted to France when the *Securitate* was still under KGB tutelage. In the 1970s, he was reassigned as head of the Bucharest *Securitate* Inspectorate (ISMB)—an eminently political policing job.[72]

Caraman favored his counterintelligence colleagues, appointing one of them to head personnel and creating a counterintelligence-heavy organization marked by paranoia and self-isolation. This changed only in April 1992, when Caraman was replaced with Ioan Talpeş, the first intelligence director with no previous *Securitate* background. Talpeş reversed personnel priorities to focus on collection and analysis, broke the self-isolation of the SIE by launching the first bilateral service relationships beginning with the CIA, and initiated the first joint training programs with NATO state services. As of 2002, in a service that numbers around 1,700, one-third of the operational personnel and 15 percent of the leadership at the directorial level had trained in joint programs with NATO member services (primarily German, Italian, and American). 18 percent of SIE manpower is currently made up of officers from the pre-1990 DSS.

Despite the general lack of systematic vetting in foreign intelligence, Romania enjoyed an advantage over the other post-Communist states. In Czechoslovakia, for instance, foreign intelligence "operated as the extended arm of the Soviet KGB," and was trained and tasked by Moscow until 1991, thus raising issues of sovereign control and personnel loyalty.[73] The even greater personnel continuity in the states that negotiated their revolutions—Poland and Hungary—caused considerable apprehension in NATO prior to their accession.[74] And the Slovak Intelligence Service continued to send officers to Moscow for training even after the collapse of the Soviet Union and up until July 1996.[75]

In contrast, the Romanian security apparatus gained independence from Soviet control at about the same time as did the Romanian military, in the mid-1960s.[76] A former NATO intelligence service director, responsible for monitoring the activity Central and East European services during the Cold War, notes that Romanian intelligence officers "did not carry out anti-NATO missions," "did not participate in joint operations with the KGB," and did not collaborate with the GRU.[77] According to the former director, Bucharest's creation of "departments specialized in anti-KGB counterespionage" merely underscored this lack of collaboration, which provided the Romanian services with "historical precedents more honorable and more "compatible" with NATO, which entitle them to enjoy, from the very beginning, a superior level of confidence from NATO."[78]

Creating the SRI

The violence of the Romanian revolution and the perceived involvement of the DSS in defending the Communist regime made the control and oversight of intelligence and security services a much more immediate priority in Romania than in those states which experienced peaceful revolutions. In the midst of the revolution, on 22 December 1989, all surveillance and communications interception centers of the DSS were closed down and sealed off—a prohibition that remained in effect until the passage of the National Security Law in July 1991.[79] No other post-Communist state undertook such a radical measure, and few were in a worse position to do so. Coupled with the lack of functioning public order bodies, this critical intelligence gap left the fledgling government vulnerable to the point that its headquarters were stormed on several occasions during January and February 1990.

The 19–20 March 1990 ethnic clashes in Tîrgu Mureş again found central authority unprepared and refocused attention on the immediate creation of a domestic security service that could provide some forewarning.[80] The SRI Decree of 26 March 1990 established parliamentary oversight as an aim of first priority (article 2), stipulating that the SRI was "responsible for all of its activities" before the 20 May 1990 elections to the ad hoc legislative body—the Provisionary Council for National Unity (CPUN), formed in February 1990—and afterward to the Parliament. The director of the SRI was obligated to "submit regular reports regarding the main issues resulting from its specific activity and directly answer questions regarding the service" to the legislature. The decree explicitly authorized the CPUN and future Parliament set up dedicated "committees for the oversight of the SRI's compliance with constitutional principles and norms, and the fundamental rights and liberties of citizens."[81] Only in article 3 did the decree establish presidential control.

EXECUTIVE CONTROL

In order to insulate the service from party struggles and politicization, and render its use against political opponents more unlikely, the team decided not to subordinate the service to party-based government. Instead, the SRI was established as a state organ subordinated to the president.[82] An earlier decree did the same for the SIE, although it was organizationally dependent upon the defense ministry until the formation of the CSAT in December 1990. The CSAT was empowered to organize and coordinate SRI and SIE activities (as well as those of the SPP), and assist in their tasking.[83] CSAT's ten voting members include the president, prime minister, the ministers for industry, defense, interior and foreign affairs, the president's national security advisor, the directors of the SRI and SIE, and the chief of the general staff.[84] The CSAT makes an annual report to parliament.

Although the CSAT is obliged to meet once each trimester, it has met almost monthly over the last eleven years. In comparison, the Czech coordinating council met less than twice a year until the late 1990s, the Slovak Defense Council met very seldom before 2001, and the Polish Commission on Special Services did not meet at all during 1997–2001. While unambiguous central control and coordination shields intelligence services from competing partisan interests in government, its absence is often marked by problems and politicizing tendencies. As one Polish intelligence chief remarked at the end of 2001, "During the last twelve years, there has not been a mechanism created preventing the [Polish] secret services from intervening into political games."[85]

LEGISLATIVE OVERSIGHT

After the May 1990 elections, Committees for Defense, Public Order and National Security were set up in both chambers of Parliament. Competing priorities in the national security domain, particularly the major restructuring of the army and the reconstruction of a police force, coupled with a combined lack of parliamentary experience and intelligence expertise, kept oversight superficial on many levels during 1990–1992. Oversight effectiveness was also conditioned by institutional design choice. One criticism leveled at purely parliamentary systems is that "the same party controls both legislative and executive branches of government," effectively fusing the two and rendering parliamentary oversight less influential.[86] Oversight committees in such systems are often "not very keen" to criticize or control institutions directly tied to the same executive to which their members are subordinated along party lines.[87] Some systems, like the British and German, even allow government members to sit on parliamentary oversight committees; a practice which can have a dampening affect on their independent behavior.[88] In Romania's semi-presidential system, the president has responsibility for national security, internal order, and defense and the prime minister looks to domestic administration and economy especially. Parliament, therefore, has fewer qualms about overseeing intelligence bodies that are subordinate to the presidency. By the same token, whereas the SRI and SIE are credibly overseen and monitored, the sub-ministerial structures of the DGIA and DGIPI receive much less attention in the Defense, Internal Order, and National Security Committees of parliament.

The SRI

Despite competing priorities, public obsession with a possible *Securitate* restoration focused committee members on the problem and the SRI delivered its first report to Parliament in November 1990. The 1991 Romanian Constitution required that both chambers meet in joint session "to appoint on proposal of the President of Romania, the director of the SRI, and to exercise control over the activity of this service."[89] The SRI Law of February 1992 also stipulated "a joint Committee of the two Chambers" for its oversight.[90] Parliament was empowered to name the SRI director based on the report of the joint committee after hearing the president's nomination (article 23), and to control the SRI budget (article 42). Delayed by preparations for the 1992 national elections, the process of defining the structure, functioning, and methods of exercising parliamentary control lasted until mid-June 1993.[91]

To place this in regional perspective, Romania, Czechoslovakia, and Hungary were the only states to establish any level of parliamentary oversight over the security services, no matter how perfunctory, before 1993. Bulgaria created its general defense and security committee in 1993 and Poland's first commission on the special services was not established until 1995. Romania and the Czech Republic opted for single service committees, while Hungary and Poland eventually established one committee to cover most of their principal intelligence and security services. As of the end of 2002, Bulgaria's general committee still bore all responsibility for intelligence oversight.

This level of oversight compares favorably with the rest of Europe. France does not provide for any parliamentary oversight of its intelligence services.[92] And this is the case de facto for all of the southern European NATO states. Spain, Portugal, Italy, Greece, and Turkey limit oversight to overall budget approval and passage of laws, when they deal with the issue at all.[93] Although UK parliamentarians are engaged in intelligence oversight, they are appointed by and report to the prime minister rather than to the parliament.[94]

Nowhere are parliamentarians fully satisfied with their degree of oversight and control, and judgments as to its effectiveness tend to be subjective. However, effectiveness is directly related to the frequency with which oversight bodies meet, the scope of their authority, and the degree to which committee members must divide their attention among other committees. Since its formation, the SRI oversight committee has met at least once a week during the parliamentary schedule and two or three times a week throughout 2001–2003, and its members serve on no other committees. Until 2000, the Czech oversight committee met less than once a month—less than four times a year during 1990–1994. The Slovak committee is described as having "overlooked rather than overseen" the services during 1994–1999, and the work of the Bulgarian oversight committee has been described as "almost nullified" by organizational problems during its infrequent meetings.[95] The SRI Committee is responsible for:

- verifying the Constitutional and legal compliance of SRI activity;
- examining reported breaches and determining measures necessary to restore legality;
- investigating citizens' allegations of civil rights abuses committed in intelligence gathering that are forwarded by either of the committees for defense, public order and national security;
- examining and resolving other complaints regarding legal violations by the SRI;
- holding hearings on the presidential nominee for director and submitting a report to the Parliamentary plenum;
- examining the annual report submitted by the SRI director and submitting its own report on the report to the plenum;
- examining the budget drafts submitted by the SRI and presenting its own proposals and observations regarding budget allocations to the specialized parliamentary committees;
- monitoring the way in which the SRI uses its allotted funds from the budget and from extra-budgetary sources; and for
- verifying the legal compliance of the SRI's autonomous corporation and production companies, as well as health, cultural, and sports institutions.

The Committee is empowered to request reports, informative notes, handwritten accounts, data, and other information from the SRI, except when they involve current operations, the identities of agents and sources, and the specific intelligence means employed. The Committee may summon the SRI director, senior officers, and other witnesses. It may also visit the SRI's central or territorial offices unannounced for inspection and monitoring purposes, and it regularly does so. Its members receive daily reports concerning ongoing activity from the SRI. The SRI is obliged by law to make requested reports, information and data available to the Committee within a reasonable period of time, and to produce for hearings those persons designated by the

Committee who are SRI employees. The SRI must grant the Committee full access when it undertakes field inspections.

During 2001, the Committee carried out seven field inspection in the SRI's central offices and ten in territorial offices. It conducted four special investigations and twenty-three hearings of SRI officials.[96] The Committee also requested and received fifty-five reports, accounts and documents. As a result of these controls, the Committee identified the need to improve the legal framework for countering corruption and organized crime, for protecting civil rights and liberties against abusive incursions by private security agencies—particularly regarding illegal surveillance and wiretapping, and for strengthening the nation's antiterrorist defense system.

The SRI Committee has three administrative staffers and, in December 2002, doubled its expert staff to four, better than the European average.[97] The Committee is composed of nine members, allocated according to the parliamentary representation of their parties. In 2001–2002 there were four members of the ruling party (PSD), two members of the opposition PRM, and one member each of the opposition PD, PNL, and UDMR (with which it had a cooperation protocol).

The SIE

Very few democratic states have established parliamentary oversight or even a statutory basis for their foreign intelligence agencies. The UK first did so in its 1994 Intelligence Services Act. France and most of Europe have not. Among the post Communist states, those with "umbrella laws" (Hungary's Act CXXV of 1995 and Poland's joint intelligence act of 2002) empower the same body to oversee all intelligence agencies. The Bulgarian parliament does not oversee foreign intelligence and Czech foreign intelligence has "never been under parliamentary oversight, and it is unknown how many of its analysts worked for Communist intelligence."[98]

Romania was the first and, as of 2002, the only state in the region to establish a separate parliamentary committee to oversee foreign intelligence based on the SIE Law of December 1997.[99] The organization and procedural rules of the SIE Oversight Committee were completed, and the Committee began work, in June 1998.[100] The SIE Committee is composed of five members, two of which are members of the ruling PSD with one each from the PRM, PD, and UDMR. Although structurally a subcommittee of the Defense, Public Order, and National Security Committee, its members do not serve on other committees and its meetings are scheduled at the same time as those of the parent defense committee. When parliament is in session the SRI Committee meets two to three times a week and it is empowered to:

- verify the Constitutional and legal compliance by the SIE;
- ensure that the orders, instructions, and other regulations issued by SIE are in compliance with the Constitution, the law, the decisions of the CSAT, and those decisions of the government that enforce the decisions of the CSAT;
- examine the draft budget and monitor the use of allotted funds by SIE through inspections made by competent bodies;
- hear the presidential nominee for director and submit a consultative report to the president (The Committee can also submit a report revoking the director.);
- examine cases of Constitutional and legal violations in SIE activity and decide on necessary law enforcement measures;
- investigate and resolve citizens' allegations of civil rights abuses committed in intelligence gathering by the SIE;
- investigate and resolve all other complaints and denunciations that are addressed to it regarding legal violations by the SIE;
- verify the selection and promotion criteria for SIE personnel;
- monitor how the targeting of SIE activities, particularly in assessing, controlling, and eliminating national security risks, promotes Romanian interests;
- monitor the degree of cooperation and interoperability between the SIE and other institutions with national security responsibilities;
- monitor the manner in which cooperation is undertaken with similar foreign institutions;
- endorse draft laws that address the activity of the SIE; and
- fulfill any other responsibility established through Parliamentary decision (article 6).

Except for details concerning current operations and identity of agents and sources, the Committee can demand information and call any persons connected to the issue under discussion from the SIE. The SIE must answer the request "in due time" (articles 7, 8, and 9).

PUBLIC OVERSIGHT AND OUTREACH

Citizens may address complaints to the Committee, or directly to the SRI (by mail, in person, or through the internet via the SRI's website: www.sri.ro). In 2001, the Committee addressed the problems raised in 142 complaints, heard 62 citizens, and conducted 11 investigations based on citizen's complaints.[101] In several cases, SRI personnel were brought to trial. The SRI website contains major press coverage and SRI communiqués as well as information on the SRI, its history and attributions, education system, and career opportunities. A sanitized version of the annual SRI report for 1998–1999 is posted on the website. Reports for 1999–2000 and 2000–2001 will be posted when they are released by Parliament. The website also contains special reports originally prepared for the Committee.[102]

For obvious reasons, the SIE is much less transparency-oriented than the SRI. However, it also maintains an active website (www.sie.ro) with contact information as well as information on its mission, history, guiding legislation, and organization. Keynote addresses by the director and political leaders are posted almost immediately, as are cleared presentations given at various bilateral and international conferences.

The post-2000 leadership of the SRI and SIE identified the broader lack of security expertise related to intelligence and its legitimate functions among civil society as constituting a significant challenge for their effective operation. This problem was akin to the lack of civilian defense expertise that confronted political and military authorities immediately after the 1989 revolution. In order to redress this shortcoming, the SRI and SIE created the Higher National Security College (HNSC) on the model of the National Defense College (CNA). The HNSC provides instruction on security and intelligence issues to public authorities and parliamentarians, other intelligence structures, civic organizations (particularly those with preoccupations in the defense and security sector), journalists, and independent analysts. Opening its doors to students in April 2002, it is the first initiative of its kind in Europe.

Despite the problems confronting the Romanian media, their role in signaling real abuse has often been critical in starting internal SRI and SIE investigations as well as SRI and SIE Committee inquiries. Although they have proven a double-edged sword in terms of increasing public awareness, most Romanians understand how their media operates and are able to sift the wheat from the chaff.

JUDICIAL OVERSIGHT

Judicial oversight is primarily limited to the consideration and issuing of warrants for technical surveillance that infringe on civil rights and liberties. By requiring the approval of judicial authorities—whether judicial commissioners, prosecutors, or judges—a preemptive control is established. However, even in developed democracies these judicial authorities are not known for "high rates of refusal" when warrants are requested and there appears to be little cause for preferring one legal authority over another.[103]

The 1991 National Security Law, which empowered the SRI and the SIE to undertake technical surveillance, also stipulated judicial authorization. Requests for warrants must be approved by the General Prosecutors' office and must contain the same detail required elsewhere in the democratic world. Citizens "who consider themselves unjustly targeted by the activities authorized in the warrant . . . may address a complaint against the designated prosecutor who issued the warrant" directly to his hierarchical superior (article 13)." It is further stipulated that any citizen "who considers that their rights or liberties have been infringed upon through the use of means" employed in obtaining information "may notify either of the permanent commissions for defense and public order of the two chambers of Parliament (article 16)." According to SRI oversight committee Chair Ioan Stan, checking the legality and propriety of warrants and surveillance procedures is one of his committee's most frequent tasks.[104] Judicial oversight over the SIE functions in the same manner as it does for the SRI.

INTERNATIONAL COOPERATION

Intelligence sharing became an essential element of alliance cooperation with the shift of terrain after the Cold War, from interstate military conflict to combating the non-national and cross-border threats of terrorism, organized crime, and trafficking in arms, persons, and narcotics. Multinational intelligence cooperation, extremely rare before 1990, also provides a new realm of oversight. Cooperation, joint training, and joint operations transfer expertise and experience not only in operational domains—the main focus of such cooperation, but in terms of oversight and control expectations as well. The SRI and SIE cooperate regularly and closely with NATO member services, especially since the SRI established a new department for counterterrorism in 2002 and the SIE restructured its organization. The SRI now has bilateral institutional relationships with over sixty states, while the SIE maintains bilateral institutional relationship with over seventy states.

Romania's policy of providing regional security has led it to pioneer a number of intelligence cooperation initiatives. In April 2002, the Romanian presidency, the SRI, and the SIE jointly organized the first conference of NATO member and candidate member (MAP) security and intelligence services with the participation of fourteen states. A second conference, with the participation of services from twenty-one states was held in September 2002 outside of Bucharest. In May 2002, the SIE was a principal organizer of the first meeting of the "Conference of South-East European Intelligence Services," another Romanian initiative, with the participation of services from Albania, Bulgaria, Croatia, Greece, Macedonia, Slovenia, Turkey, and Yugoslavia (Serbia and Montenegro). This was the first meeting that brought together the intelligence services from the successor states of the former Yugoslavia.

CONCLUSIONS

Romanian exceptionalism in its early military independence from the Soviets since the 1960s enabled the first Iliescu administrations to establish a remarkably constructive civil-military relationship throughout 1991–1996, despite a series of crises during 1989–1990. The Constantinescu administration and its governments during 1997–2000 were unable to maintain the relationship as persistent failures to establish a functional civil-military leadership or to reconcile military reform plans with available resources undermined military morale and discipline, and undercut Romania's credibility as a candidate for NATO admission.

The new impetus given the civil-military relationship after the 2000 elections, with the appointment of experienced defense managers and the relaunching of performance-oriented reform, enabled Romania to recover the ground lost in its pursuit of NATO membership and earned it an invitation into the alliance in November 2002. More important, it has brought the Romanian military into much greater conformity with Western armies in terms of organization, structure, and actual democratic and civilian control.

Military and civil-military reform performance during 2001–2002 was a tour de force indicating what Romania can accomplish when political will is united with the necessary expertise, hard-won experience, and assistance from the democratic community of states. With the accelerated pace of military reform projected for 2003 and 2004 in order to meet all the objectives established for NATO accession in the spring of 2004, attention to this domain is unlikely to waiver.

The autonomy of the Romanian security apparatus from Soviet intelligence prior to the December 1989, the suddenness and violence of its revolution, and the perceived role of the *Securitate* during that revolution placed Romania in a favorable position for launching wide-ranging intelligence reform. Since the early 1990s, Romania has been an enthusiastic participant in joint training and joint operations with NATO member states, and, since 11 September 2001, an active contributor to U.S. and NATO efforts in the Global War against Terrorism.

Viewed within the purely European context, the SRI and SIE are sound institutions, and the Romanian legal framework permits an oversight more robust than that which many EU members exercise. Coordination and control by the Supreme Defense Council has proven relatively effective, even if a department within the presidency or the CSAT dedicated to the intelligence community would enable it to deal better with the greater complexity and number of new non-state cross-border threats in the post–Cold War, post–September 11 environment. After numerous difficulties regarding transparency, outreach, and regional cooperation, it is now a leading innovator.

Over the last fourteen years, Romania has made considerable strides in first-generation security sector reform—the building of structures and legal frameworks necessary for institutional effectiveness and for control, coordination, and oversight—and in second-generation reform—instilling those structures and frameworks with real content. For all of its many shortcomings and remaining problems, accomplishments within the realm of defense and security sector reform justifiably constitute a point of pride for Romanians.

NOTES

1. Robert D. Kaplan, "Europe's Fulcrum State," *Atlantic Monthly*, vol. 282, no. 3 (September 1998), p. 35.

2. See Anton A. Bebler, ed., *Civil-Military Relations in Post-Communist States* (Westport, CT: Greenwood Press, 1995); Jeffrey Simon, *NATO Enlargement and Central Europe: A Study in Civil-Military Relations* (Washington, DC: National Defense University Press, 1996).

3. See, e.g., Alexander Alexiev, *Romania and the Warsaw Pact: The Defense Policy of a Reluctant Ally* (Santa Monica, CA: RAND, 1979).

4. One former Soviet officer stated that: "To the Soviet Union, Romania is an opponent. An enemy." Victor Suvorov, *Inside the Soviet Army* (New York: Berkeley Books, 1982), p. 11. A senior Polish officer confirmed that in contrast to Poland, "Romania has remained the sole decision maker with respect to its armed forces and its own defense potential." Interview with Colonel Ryszard J. Kuklinski, "The War against the Nation as Seen from Inside," *Kultura* (Paris, April 1987) vol. 4, no. 475, pp. 3–57.

5. By the late 1970s, the national defender role was part of both popular mythology and party doctrine. Alexander Alexiev, *Party-Military Relations in Romania* (Santa Monica, CA: RAND, 1977).

6. Czechoslovakia, for instance, had sixty-six officers training in the USSR in the summer of 1991 with eight more planned for 1992. Thomas S. Szayna and James Steinberg, *Civil-Military Relations and National Security Thinking in Czechoslovakia* (Santa Monica: RAND, 1992), p. 18.

7. See, e.g., Larry Watts, "Party-Military-Security Relations," paper presented at Uppsala University, Sweden, in December 1982.

8. For a discussion of CADA, see Larry L. Watts, "The Romanian Army in the December Revolution and Beyond," in Daniel N. Nelson, ed., *Romania after Tyranny* (Boulder, CO: Westview Press, 1992), pp. 95–126.

9. *România liberă* (25 July 1990).

10. Sixty-two of CADA's officially registered seventy-six members resumed their military service while eight remained in the Border Guards when it was transferred to the Interior Ministry.

11. The preliminary discussions prior to the CSAT deliberations in 1991 included then Colonel Ioan Talpeş from the Presidency, chief of staff General Dumitru Cioflină, defense minister General Nicolae Spiroiu (appointed in the spring of 1991), and General Lucian Culda. Talpeş was appointed head of the group of counselors in the MApN on 14 February 1990, and was responsible for designing the initial reform of the military and of the intelligence services. In July 1990, Talpeş was named as presidential counselor.

12. The principal civilian educators were Drs. Liviu Mureşan, Ioan Mircea Paşcu, and Vasile Secareş. General Cioflină was preoccupied with education reform within the military since his initial appointment as deputy chief of staff in January 1990. General Spiroiu supported the development of the facility. The principal military educators were Generals Gheorghe Şchiopu and Neculai Bălan.

13. As British analysts noted, "Romania's unique military position within the Warsaw Pact ensured that the military were able to think and take decisions for themselves." See, UK Ministry of Defense, *Review of Parliamentary Oversight of the Romanian Ministry of National Defense and the Democratic Control of its Armed Forces*, DMCS Study no. 43/96, (London: Directorate of Management and Consultancy Services, 1997), p. 30.

14. Szayna and Larrabee, *East European Military Reform*, pp. 25, 41; and Joo, *The Democratic Control of Forces*, p. 57. Since 1993, analysts recommended an "institution such as a national defense academy" to provide civil-military education, without referring to the CNA, which had been operating since 1992. Directorate of Consultancy Services, *Review of Parliamentary Oversight of the Romanian Ministry of National Defense*, pp. 33–34. See also, Donnelly, "Developing a National Strategy for the Transformation of the Defense Establishment," pp. 11–14.

15. See, e.g., Zoe Petre, "The Role of the President in Romania's Approach to NATO Integration," in Kurt W. Treptow and Mihail S. Ionescu, eds., *Romania and Euro-Atlantic Integration* (Iaşi: Center for Romanian Studies, 1999), pp. 92–94, 96.

16. The chief of the financial directorate stated that the budget "could not assure the development of even the minimum necessary activities specific to the military," *Ziua* (22 March 1999).

17. For example, the *ŢIGARETA II* smuggling scandal of April 1998, which implicated the chief of staff of the air force and the presidency, was prominent in most of the national media in mid November 1998 and late February 1999. See, e.g., *Cotidianul* and *Ziua* (21–24 February 1999). The *ELTA-AZUR* arms procurement scandal implicating the defense minister and government broke in November 1999. *Adevărul* (9, 12, and 16 November 1999).

18. See, e.g., David H. Bayley, "Police and Political Development in Europe," in Charles Tilly, ed., *The Formation of National States in Western Europe* (Princeton, NJ: Princeton University Press, 1975), pp. 328–29; and Otwin Marenin, "Police Performance and State Rule: Control and Autonomy in the Exercise of Coercion," *Comparative Politics*, vol. 18, no. 1 (October 1985), pp. 101–22.

19. Larry Diamond and Marc F. Plattner, eds., *Civil-Military Relations and Democracy*, (Baltimore, MD: Johns Hopkins University Press, 1996), see pp. xxix–xxxi, 6, 12–14, 26, 56. The officer commanding that operation, General Mircea Mureşan, was transferred to the interior ministry along with Dudu Ionescu and made a deputy minister of the interior. In 2000, Mureşan was permitted to transfer back to the MApN, adding to general military dissatisfaction.

20. Michael C. Desch, "Threat Environments and Military Missions," in Diamond and Plattner, *Civil-Military Relations and Democracy*, p. 14.

21. See, e.g., *Cronica Română* and *Curierul Naţional* (20–21 January 1999).

22. The former Deputy Defense Minister and Justice Minister supported an amnesty to enable the army's use as an internal security force. *Cronica Română* (26 February 1999).

23. A government press conference criticized the whistleblowers for undermining Romania's image abroad. *Cotidianul* (9 November 1998).

24. *Curierul Național* (1 November 1999); *Cotidianul* (4 November 1999).

25. *Adevărul* (2 December 1999); *Curierul Național* (3 December 1999).

26. Gheorghe Diaconescu, Florea Şerban, and Nicolae Pavel, eds., *Democratic Control over the Army in Romania* (Bucharest: *Editura Enciclopedică*, 1996), pp. 312–14.

27. Larry L. Watts, "The Crisis in Romanian Civil-Military Relations," *Problems of Post-Communism*, vol. 48, no. 4 (July/August 2001), pp. 14–26.

28. Thomas S. Szayna, *NATO Enlargment 2000–2015: Determinants and Implications for Defense Planning and Shaping* (Santa Monica, CA: RAND Corporation, 2001), p. 21.

29. Ioan Mircea Paşcu, *Immediate Defense Priorities* (30 December 2001).

30. Human Resources Management Directorate, *Military Career Guide* (Bucharest: Romanian Ministry of National Defense, 2001). Brigadier General Richard Smith and Ms. Jacqueline Callcut were seconded from the British Defense Ministry to give assistance in these matters already in spring 2000, but were denied access to information and decision makers until Paşcu's appointment. Paşcu instituted an "open door" policy, permitting the British advisors (and the U.S. and German advisors) to sit in on his weekly council meetings, thereby making better use of their expertise.

31. *Military Career Guide*, chapter V, articles 51–53.

32. Human Resources Management Directorate, Romanian Ministry of National Defense, October 15, 2001.

33. This was facilitated after the *Recruiting, Selection, Training, and Career Development of the Civilian Staff Employed in the Romanian Armed Forces*, first prepared in June 1999, was updated to incorporate provisions regarding civil servants in accord with the Law on Public Functionaries.

34. See, e.g., Law no. 389/10.07.2001, which approves Government Ordinance no. 14/2001 on the Organization and Functioning of the Ministry of National Defense. See also, Larry Watts, "Democratic Civil Control of the Military in Romania: An Assessment as of October 2001," in Graeme P. Herd, ed., *Civil Military Relations in Post Cold War Europe* (Camberley, Surrey: Conflict Studies Research Centre, Royal Military Academy Sandhurst, December 2001), pp. 14–42.

35. Paşcu, *Immediate Defense Priorities*, 2001.

36. The reform of parliamentary procedures is outlined in *Regulamentul Senatului [Senate Regulations]* and *Regulamentul Camerei Deputaților [Chamber of Deputies Regulations]* (Bucharest: *Parlamentul Romaniei*, 2001).

37. The secretary of state for parliamentary liaison and legislative harmonization presides over six offices: liaison with Senate, liaison with the Chamber of Deputies, NATO legislative harmonization, EU legislative harmonization, relations with NGOs, and relations with the Media.

38. Larry L. Watts, "Introduction: The Convergence of Reform and Integration," in Watts, ed., *Romanian Military Reform and NATO Integration* (Iasi; Oxford; and Portland, OR: Center for Romanian Studies, 2002), pp. 9–24.

39. Kieran Williams, "Introduction," in Kieran Williams and Dennis Deletant, eds., *Security Intelligence Services in New Democracies: The Czech Republic, Slovakia and Romania* (New York: Palgrave, 2001), p. 1.

40. J. F. Brown, *Hopes and Shadows: Eastern Europe after Communism* (Durham, NC: Duke University Press, 1994), pp. 100–1.

41. This is a central theme, for example, in V. G. Băleanu, *A Clear and Present Danger to Democracy: The New Romanian Security Services Are Still Watching*, (Camberely, Surrey: Conflict Studies Research Centre, 1996), and in Dennis Deletant, "The Successors to the *Securitate*: Old Habits Die Hard," in Williams and Deletant, *Security Intelligence Services in New Democracies*, pp. 211–62. The Czech intelligence director notes on his service's official website that the "dismal" experience of Czechoslovakia's Communist security apparatus "raised, and to be quite frank, still raises fear and suspicion that the new service will once again turn into a secret political police," available at www.fas.org/irp/world/Czech, 27 October 2002.

42. J. F. Brown considers that the media "set a particularly low standard" in Romania and Poland. Brown (1994), p. 101.

43. Andrzej Zybertowicz, "Transformation of the Polish Secret Services: From Authoritarian to Informal Power Networks," Paper presented to the Geneva Centre for Democratic Control of the Armed Forces (DCAF) Workshop on Democratic and Parliamentary Oversight of Intelligence Services (Geneva, 3–5 October 2002), p. 3, www.dcaf.ch. See also, Maria Los and Andrzej Zybertowicz, *Privatizing the Police-State: The Case of Poland* (London: Macmillan, 2000).

44. Nikolai Bozhilov, "Reforming the Intelligence Services in Bulgaria: The Experience from the Last Decade," Paper presented to the DCAF Workshop on Democratic and Parliamentary Oversight of Intelligence Services" (Geneva, 3–5 October 2002), p. 10, available at www.dcaf.ch.

45. Thomas Carothers, *Assessing Democracy Assistance: The Case of Romania* (Washington, DC: Carnegie Endowment for International Peace, 1996), pp. 85.

46. See, e.g., Silviu Achim, "*În presă şi Biserica Ortodoxă se gaseau si urmăriti, şi turnători la Securitate*," *Adevărul* (6 October 2001); "*Emil Constantinescu: Securiştii epuraţi de mine sînt azi patroni de ziare*," *Evenimentul Zilei* (4 October 2002).

47. Timofte's report is cited in "'*Vîntu—instigator, autor, sau complice' la fraudele FNI-BID-BRS-Astra-Gelsor*," *Evenimentul Zilei* (23 May 2002).

48. See, e.g., in *România Liberă*, P. P., "*de la escrocheria FNI la Radu Timofte*," (22 October 2001); George Rădulescu, "*Afacerile lui Sorin Ovidiu Vântu au afectat componenţa economică a siguranţei naţionale*," *Curierul National* (7 February 2002).

49. "*Spionii lui Bebe: Adio NATO/Preşedenţia şi SIE pot compromite definitiv orice şansă de aderare a Romanei*," *Ziua* (30 August 2001).

50. Sorin Rosca Stănescu, "*Lovitura lui Talpeş*," *Ziua* (17 September 2001).

51. See, e.g., Romulus Georgescu, "*Radu Timofte a fost acuzat ieri in plenul Parlamentului că a colaborat cu KGB*," *România Liberă* (8 February 2001).

52. Oana Sima, "*Virgil Măgureanu pune pe tapet o noua problemă: scurgerile de informaţii din cadrul Serviciul Român de Informaţii*," *Curierul Naţional* (26 April 2001).

53. Dan Bucura, "*Scandalul 'Timofte—agent KGB' a fost declanşat din înteriorul SRI*," *Adevărul* (7 May 2001).

54. Emil Berdeli, "*Stafia rosie din conacul SRI*," *Cotidianul* (11 May 2001).

55. Diana Toma and O. C. Hogea, "*Directorul SRI a fost lucrat de şefii contraspionajului*," *Cotidianul* (16 May 2001). See also *Adevarul* (16 May 2001).

56. Williams, "The Czech Republic since 1993," in Kieran Williams and Dennis Deletant, *Security Intelligence Services in New Democracies: The Czech Republic, Slovakia and Romania* (London: Palgrave, 2001), pp. 101–2.

57. David M. Dastych, "No 'Zero Option' but a Shake Up: The Reform of the Polish Secret Services," available at www.fas.org/irp/world/Poland (7 November 2002), p. 4.

58. The entire project was revealed in a court trial that *Ziua* lost in 1996.

59. *Urząd Ochrony Państwa*, UOP.

60. *Agencja Bezpieczeństwa Wewnętrznego*, ABW, and *Agencja Wywiadu*, AW.

61. *Bezpecnostni informacni sluzba*, BIS.

62. This is another central theme of Baleanu, *A Clear and Present Danger to Democracy*; and Băleanu, "The Enemy Within: The Romanian Intelligence Service in Transition" (January 1995), available at www.fas.org/irp/world/Romania.

63. Alain Faupin, "Reform of the French Intelligence Services after the End of the Cold War." Paper presented at DCAF Workshop on "Democratic and Parliamentary Oversight of Intelligence Services" (Geneva, 3–5 October 2002), pp. 6–10.

64. Laszlo Majtenyi, *Reconciliation and Developing Public Trust: Opening State Security Files to the Public*, paper presented at DCAF Workshop "Democratic and Parliamentary Oversight of Intelligence Services," (Geneva, 3–5 October 2002), p. 3.

65. Zybertowicz, "Transformation of the Polish Secret Services" p. 2 and available at www.abw.gov.pl.

66. See Deletant, *Security Intelligence Services in New Democracies*, pp. 218–19; Baleanu, *A Clear and Present Danger to Democracy*, and Manuela Ştefănescu, "Security Services in Romania," "In the Public Interest: Security Services in a Constitutional Democracy" (Warsaw: Helsinki Foundation for Human Rights, 1998), p. 3. Within the DGIA (*Direcţia Generala de Informaţii a Apararii*) are the Directorates for Military Intelligence (*Direcţia Informaţii şi Reprezentare Militara*, DIRM) and Military Security (*Direcţia de Siguranţa Militara*, DSM). Originally, separate directorates that have undergone several name changes since 1990, the two were brought together and formally subordinated under a single Directorate—the DGIA—in 2000. Both subdirectorates were engaged in fundamental restructuring in 2003.

67. George Rădulescu, "*Comisia parlamentară SRI semnalează pericolul apariţiei unei poliţiei politice*," *Curierul Naţional* (22 March 2001).

68. Laura Ciobanu and Lucean Gheorghiu, "*Iliescu îl loveste pe Năstase în 'doi şi-un sfert': Soliticitând reanalizarea ordonanţei prin care UM 0962 a căpătat puteri sporite*," *Cotidianul* (22 March 2001), and "*Talpeş este hotşrât să taie din atribuţiile UM 0962*," *Cotidianul* (27 March 2001).

69. Williams, "Czechoslovakia 1990–2," in *Security Intelligence Services in New Democracies*, p. 61.

70. Press conference of Virgil Măgureanu in *România Liberă* (30 March 1994).

71. Press conference of SRI Director Radu Timofte on occasion of NATO-MAP state conference "Intelligence and Security Services and the Security Agenda of the 21st Century," Sinaia (10–14 April 2002).

72. See, e.g., Romulus Georgescu, "*In 1969, tânărul şi ambiţiosul locotenent Priboi îi supravegbea pe scriitori şi poeţi*," *România Liberă* (6 December 2002).

73. Williams, "Czechoslovakia 1990–2" in Williams and Deletant, *Security Intelligence Services in New Democracies*, p. 64.

74. Jane Perlez, "Touchy Issue of Bigger NATO: Spy Agencies," *The New York Times* (4 January 1998); and "*Spionage bei Freunden*," *Der Spiegel* (6 April 1998).

75. Williams, "Slovakia since 1993" in Williams and Deletant, *Security Intelligence Services in New Democracies*, p. 145.

76. U.S. 98th Congress, Senate, Committee of the Judiciary, *Communist Bloc Intelligence Activities in the United States*, testimony of former Czechoslovak StB officer Josef Frolik (18 November 1975).

77. Interview with Tjeerd Sbbeswijk Visser, former director of Dutch Intelligence and president of the Europe 2000 Association, by Radu Tudor, "*Tradiţia anti-KGB a României poate fi un avantaj in cursa pentru integrare*," *Ziua* (8 June 2002).

78. Interview with Tjeerd Sbbeswijk Visser, *Ziua* (8 June 2002).

79. Communique, Romanian Ministry of National Defense (21 February 1990).

80. The team that designed the framework of the SRI was led by Colonel Ioan Talpeş, and included Mihai Stan, Eugen Donose, and Alexandru Kilm.

81. Decree Regarding the Establishment of the Romanian Intelligence Service, CPUN Decree no. 181 (26 March 1990), article 2.

82. *Ibid*., article 3.

83. Law on the Establishment, Organization, and Functioning of the Supreme Defense Council, no. 39 (13 December 1990), article 1; Law no. 51/1991 on National Security, article 7; and Romanian Constitution, articles 92 and 118.

84. Most coordinating councils have similar membership.

85. Interview of Colonel Marek Dukaczewski by A. Walentek in *Życie Warszawy* (2 December 2001), as cited in Zybertowicz, "Transformation of the Polish Secret Services," p. 1

86. Elizabeth Rindskopf Parker, "The American Experience: One Model for Intelligence Oversight in a Democracy," Harvard University, Cambridge, MA, Project on Justice in Times of Transition (15 October 2001), p. 4; Arend Lijphart and Carlos H. Waisman, "The Design of Markets and Democracies: Generalizing Across Regions," in Lijphart and Waisman, eds., *Institutional Design in New Democracies: Eastern Europe and Latin America* (Boulder, CO: Westview Press, 1996), pp. 238–39.

87. Hans Born, "Parliamentary Oversight of the Intelligence Services," presented at NATO conference on "Intelligence and Security Services in the 21st-Century Security Environment," Sinaia, Romania, 10–14 April 2002, p. 8. Party leaders also commonly exert control over committee appointments, their budget, and their staff.

88. Jeanne Kinney Giraldo, *Legislatures and Defense: The Comparative Experience*, Occasional Paper no. 8, Monterey, California, The Center for Civil-Military Relations Naval Postgraduate School, June 2001, p. 24.

89. Ian Leigh, "The Legal Norms of the Geneva Centre for the Democratic Control of Armed Forces (DCAF) and Security Sector Reform," Oaper presented at 5th International Security Forum, "Setting the 21st-Century Security Agenda" (Kongresshaus, Zurich, 14–16 October 2002), p. 5.

90. Law no. 14 on the Organization and Functioning of the SRI (24 February 1992), article 1.

91. Parliamentary Decision no. 30 on the Organization and Functioning of the Senate and Chamber of Deputies Joint Standing Committee for the Exercise of Parliamentary Control on SRI Activity (16 June 1990).

92. Faupin, "Reform of the French Intelligence Services after the End of the Cold War," p. 2.

93. *Ibid*., Jean-Paul Brodeur, Peter Gill, and Dennis Tollborg, eds., *Democracy, Law and Security: Internal Security Services in Contemporary Europe* (London: Ashgate, 2002).

94. The UK did not have a statutory charter for MI5 until 1989, and for its Secret Intelligence Service and signals intelligence (MI6 and GCHQ) until 1994.

95. Williams, "Slovakia since 1993" in Williams and Deletant, *Security Intelligence Services in New Democracies*, p. 140; and Bozhilov, "Reforming the Intelligence Services in Bulgaria: The Experience from the Last Decade," p. 5.

96. Communication to the author by Ioan Stan, Chairman of the Joint Parliamentary Committee for Oversight and Supervision of the SRI, 18 July 2002.

97. See, e.g., Jeanne Kinney Giraldo, *Legislatures and Defense: The Comparative Experience*, Occasional Paper no. 8 (Monterrey, CA, The Center for Civil-Military Relations, Naval Postgraduate School, June 2001).

98. Williams, "The Czech Republic since 1993," in Williams and Deletant, *Security Intelligence Services in New Democracies*, p. 111.

99. Law on the Organization and Functioning of the Foreign Intelligence no. 1/1998, *Monitorul Oficial* (6 January 1998).

100. Rule no. 44 of 3 June 1998 (subsequently amended in October 1998) on the Setting Up, Organization, and Functioning of the Special Parliamentary Commission for Overseeing the Foreign Intelligence Service, *Monitorul Oficial* (8 June 1998).

101. Communication to author from Ioan Stan (15 July 2002).

102. As of December 2002, there were eighteen special reports on the website.

103. Leigh, "The Legal Norms of the Geneva Centre for the Democratic Control of Armed Forces (DCAF) and Security Sector Reform," p. 11.

104. Communication to the author (15 July 2002).

Conclusion: Ambiguous Democratization?

Henry F. Carey

Romanians abroad have been commenting, "You will be amazed or shocked how much Romania (or Bucharest) has changed." By that, they generally mean for the better. The first thing one notices is the number of restaurants, bars, and stores, especially neighborhood grocery stores that are open in evening hours accessible for working people. For those with the funds, the changes have made urban life much more pleasant. There has also been the loss of kiosks, which brought "stores" to less bourgeois neighborhoods at very affordable prices. Initially, the kiosk owners were forced to pay taxes and health fees, but even that was not acceptable to the mayoralty, which insisted that Bucharest resemble Western cities (which do permit street salespersons who pay for their licenses). Young women particularly are well dressed. Ceauşescu's "children," resulting from the regime promotion of reproduction, are visibly abundant in numbers, creating a youth culture that is exhilarating in its vitality and disturbing in its political alienation and apathy. A variety of bars and discos cater to their whim and fancy, as the vitality of interwar Bucharest revives. High-quality food is abundant and affordable for many, even if utilities alone exceed the monthly pensions for senior citizens and are exorbitant for those with the average monthly salaries of $130 or less.

A few high-quality items are cheap. In August 2003, magnificent tomatoes and watermelons from the neighboring private farms around Bucharest went for 6,000 lei (under 20 cents U.S.) and 15,00 lei (under 5 cents U.S.) per kilo, respectively. Certainly, the large construction and reconstruction in the capital is a sign of development potential, with unskilled construction labor hard to find though largely unregulated except at the largest and most modern building projects—notwithstanding the new labor code, one of the many legal reforms mandated by the European Union (EU).[1] The steady, if gradual emergence of a middle class without Communist-era connections hardly existed until the late 1990s. There are EU-mandated warnings on cigarette advertisements and no beer commercials on televised soccer matches, which include African players on the squads. EU law, which must be incorporated into Romanian law, regulates such advertising in a manner that is no less effective than in the rest of Europe. The old rich of pre-Communist days are sometimes getting their apartments or homes back if they did not live in the neighborhoods of Ceauşescu's Civic Center—the razed wasteland of about three miles diameter with the monstrosity in the middle that passes as a parliament.

Of course, much has not changed or increased in scope. On the solid front, Romanian families remain tight-knit and mutually supportive in old age—unlike many of their Western counterparts. The new rich are the old rich. For example, the Dragomirs affiliated with the rightist Greater Romania Party own most of the restaurants in Herastrau Park and various soccer teams. The marginally employed are very scared of losing their jobs, whether in the state or private sector—particularly as 2007, the presumed year of EU entry, approaches. The cost of apartment expenses, anger at corruption, and potholes remain the three major complaints of urban residents. Many survive by farming small plots on weekends, not unlike in Communist days—though not to the extent of the situation in Russia where estimates are that half the population grows some of its food. The rest dream of emigrating to the West, but relatively few, as before, risk going illegally, other than the highly resented Roma. Prosecutors do not prosecute top politicians, who enjoy homes in various parts of Europe and the West.

After a violent withdrawal from Communism and a delayed and unintended, democratic transition, has Romania turned the corner to where public support for democracy's robust institutions cannot be overturned? By the NATO and EU summits in November and December 2002, the West thought so. A year later, Radio Free Europe came to an end because of this positive Western view. This acceptance will help anchor democratization, though it has been the main basis for the affirmative belief that Romania is no longer an illiberal democracy. One does not have to be a historical determinist, a la Tony Judt,[2] to question claims of robust Romanian democratic and market achievements and prospects. Its ambiguous democratization is epitomized by the paradoxical image of a former Communist Party Secretary becoming the country's leading reformer, as has President Ion Iliescu in the first decade of the new millennium. The country has traveled far from Communism; invited into NATO no later than 2004, looking toward admission to the EU in 2007, after the U.S. deemed the country a functioning marketing economy in March 2003, but still not maintaining illiberal practices that prevent the regime from completing its democratic transition.[3] Optimists[4] and pessimists[5] inside and outside the country alike agree that Romania has been democratizing in some important ways, partly based on a decisive Westward tilt, in spite of a post-totalitarian state, a flattened civil society, a post-national Stalinist political society and economic hardship during the first half of the 1990s. Institutional decay and public disillusionment made it possible for the radical right to become the second largest political force in the 2000 elections of this semi-democratic, partial regime with authoritarian institutions, "rule by law," ethnic intolerance, and feeble checks and balances. The dissident-scarce Communist society produced a political society composed mostly of former Communist Youth leaders, who supplanted the few non-Communist activists. These leaders and much of the morally compromised civil society regard anyone articulating positions of moral principle as unctuous, self-righteous, and out of touch with Romanian (cynical) political culture and the lack of options for advancement other than under Communism. Most intellectuals who experimented in party politics have quit, in some cases because the moral and legal compromises were unethical, leaving the field to the unscrupulous. The more successful parties have adopted forms of sultanism (extreme patrimonial politics, as depicted in Frank Sellin's chapter) with a quasi-democratic face.

The classic critique of flawed transitions, "the procedures, but not the substance of democracy," is too laudatory in Romania. Among the fundamental flaws in procedure have been the failure to hold a single parliamentary election with spoiled-ballot rates less than 6 percent; the failure of political parties and nongovernmental organizations (NGOs) to verify the voters lists or conduct a parallel vote count of the results; the inordinate number of governing decrees; and the tendency of the executive to control the judiciary. The less successful Romanian parties have split into factions while the stronger ones rely on sultans to resolve conflicts over the distribution of patronage and ill-gotten gains.

On the other hand, the first electoral transfers of power since 1937 have occurred twice, in 1996 and again in 2000, meeting some minimal definitions of democracy. Contemporary institutions in historical perspective have never been as democratic. If one had been asked on 22 December 1989 where the country would be in 2004, many would have predicted even more political persecution and/or a democratic breakdown. The only advantage Romania had then was a low foreign debt. Otherwise, it was the most communized and impoverished of the six Soviet satellites. Its prewar political memory was of electoral fraud and then polarization, as well as an enormous gap between urban and rural, as well as between intellectuals and masses. Finally, Romania had continuous fascist traditions dating to the Iron Guard, with no substantial movements for social democracy, democratic socialism, or trade union organizing. Yet, Romania has a chance to become an electoral democracy if the 2004 votes are credible, and could consolidate democracy if the radical right is marginalized in votes while a reasonably strong, moderate alternative to the Social Democrats emerges.

Thus, post-Communism has seen both many authoritarian and post-totalitarian continuities and democratizing efforts. Changing the political culture to independence and autonomy of organization and thought should take another three decades. In Communist Romania, ideas and organizations were completely dependent upon and led by the state. Romania has begun the gradual evolution of independent civil and political societies. Not only will the debris from the sultanistic totalitarian regime not be easily replaced by different sets of elites, but political learning by the same elites will be inordinately influenced by the carrot of NATO and EU integration, rather than primarily from internal evolution. The Communist regime was able to prevent the strengthening of civil society resistance by branding anti-Communism as anti-Romanian. Such trends have been mitigated by the incentives and requirements for national reconciliation[6] and of Euro-Atlantic integration. The temptation to create an ethic-based majority in order to distract it from the democratization project is a cooked-up formula appealing to nationalism to consolidate power. Yet, it is an option that Bulgaria has learned to avoid—even where its ethnic divide involves a clash with a Muslim nationality rather than a Western one.

The ambiguous democratization has alternated not between clear political choices but between two political styles: Iliescu's soft sultanism and Constantinescu's unresolved power plays. The consequent semidemocracy has endowed a cycle of an executive-dominating Ion Iliescu and a rudderless Emil Constantinescu-era parliament: stable authoritarianism and then unstable efforts to establish parliamentary autonomy and civilian superiority over the military. Illiberally, post-Communist Romania has governed more effectively under Iliescu, in terms of democratic results, than with military autonomy and parliamentary subordination. Alas, democratic processes are thereby stultified. Sultans or failed sultans seeking clients within a largely inactive society were a common approach under both presidents. Still unknown is whether the significant, if incomplete, political learning and institution-building under both leaders have been impelled by genuine belief in democratic norms or by the instrumental opportunism necessitated by foreign aid and Euro-Atlantic integration incentives, or both. If what elites really think and do is more important than what they say, then the disturbing pattern of politics by, for, and through patrimonialism and corruption, whether via a sultan or leaderless bickering, inhibits efforts to realize the most idealistic of stated intentions. Worse, ostensibly idealistic words that are just a means to personal wealth and power, more than the radical, but inchoate demagoguery of rightist Corneliu Vadim Tudor, debilitate democratization through organized cynicism and half-hearted governing procedures and institutions.

Romania's pre–World War I elite democracy and its interwar, "mimic-democracy"[7] regimes never completed a democratic transition, let alone institutionalized democracy, though they avoided formal dictatorship and repression until the late 1930s. No more than two or three credible elections were ever held. Governments typically alternated in power via pressured resignations, monarchical dismissals and imputed shifts in public opinion and constitutional gimmicks—the pattern of many transitional, constitutional monarchies like Iraq, Italy, and Belgium. With a democratization process based on cultural and institutional memory of mimic democracy, followed by the polarized democracy after the 1937 election, the country is left with few democratic models, unlike in the *redemocratized* Czech Republic. Though prior to 1989 it had more semi-democratizing experience than Poland, Hungary, or Russia, Romania now requires more sustained democratic learning and institutionalization than those three states, whose civil societies developed during their phases of transitional, authoritarian Communism (or what Stepan and Linz call post-totalitarianism[8]). Like Argentina, where German-inspired military and Nazi-admiring military leaders adopted ineffective military governments, Romania's continuous quasi-fascist sectors laud the anti-Soviet courage of a Marshal Ion Antonescu instead of the democratic courage of a Corneliu Coposu.[9] Members of the Iliescu-led ruling party have frequently alternated between praise and condemnation of both leaders as it suits them, sending ambiguous signals about national ideals. Yet, Argentina, even with the legacy of Juan Perón, has achieved greater democratization than Romania, in part because its truth commissions and prosecutions of top generals, while far from complete, and subsequently reversed in part, have discredited those who committed crimes against humanity.[10]

Romania's founding, post-totalitarian moments of 1989–1992 sent signals internally and abroad that Iliescu could ensure that any alternative to his reformed post-Communists would more likely be the occasionally mobilized, nationalist, armed rejectionists of nonviolent politics than the nonviolent demonstrators for democracy occasionally mobilized from civil society. Opposition and dissident participation in politics from the non-Communist activist sectors would be tolerated but would not initially involve real inclusion and compromise. The party system, initially and artificially dominated by Iliescu's established followers and networks, was protected only by brazen electoral irregularities, fraud, and unaccountability and tolerated by a disinterested, deliberately misinformed, or naïve public. The prevalent politics of prevarication would be practiced by glorifying ignominious eras in the past, not by goring the ox of those in power, while a ruling elite with everything to hide about the Communist system of government would rule in malevolent and deliberate denial of any connection to the crimes of that era. Those who have challenged these Iliescu signals rarely find themselves in the media or are deemed unpatriotic.

As a result of this initial regime trajectory, symptoms of authoritarian consolidation and democratic decay are pervasive. New parties often appear, but are usually led, or backed, by would-be sultanistic oligarchs, their wealth derived from the post-Communist networks depicted in Anneli Ute Gabanyi's chapter. Both within and among these networks, democratic political pacting and compromise are rare, though deals pursuing authoritarian goals are more common. Submission to a domestic or foreign dispenser of patronage, sometimes with a technocrat in charge, can be a common route to legitimation and some democratic reforms. The desire for power by dispensing patronage, however, tends to erode any interparty consensus, as political forces seek to serve new financial sources of power. Public opinion consequently shows some disenchantment with democracy per se, as well as about crime, job security, and the direction of the country. Even if desire for autocracy is limited, casual discussions in informal settings astonishingly reveal palpable nostalgia for the Ceauşescu-era, or at least its financial security. The largest incentive for democratization has not come from within, but anomalously, from without, via the effort to meet NATO and European Union reform criteria again to obtain financial support. Greater interparty cooperation is needed, instead of unilateral decision making, to incorporate broader political participation; reduce cultural resistance to democracy (e.g., to say exactly what one means);[11] alter perceptions of personalist exclusion by rivals; and reduce the extent of party factions, endless power plays, patrimonialism, and cooptation.

The first section of the remainder of this chapter reviews the Iliescu (1990–1996 and 2000 to the present) and Constantinescu (1996–2000) presidencies. The second section considers how and why Romania has nearly, but never quite, completed the democratic transition phase. The third then analyzes three key arenas of the democratic consolidation project: political society, civil society, and the rule of law. The final section assesses Romania's prospects for improving the quality and stability of liberal democratization.

HISTORICAL OVERVIEW

The still unresolved controversy of the "December Events" (of 1989) resembles the conspiracy theories of President Kennedy's assassination, except that the less likely scenario, that Iliescu and his cabal staged combat, is the most widely believed. More convincing is Hall's deconstruction of the counterrevolutionary myths and lies based on ballistics evidence and circumstantial evidence linking former *Securitate* writers to this "staged-war" theory of a coup, followed by combat with terrorists. The original press reports were more accurate in stating that elements in the USLA Anti-Terrorist Forces and the *Securitate* Fifth Directorate together continued resisting after 22 December 1989.[12] This pervasive "coup" theory with staged combat is demonstrated in a survey by the Center for Regional and Urban Sociology, cited in the chapter by Ely and Stoica, which found that 36 percent of Romanians believed that the events constituted a coup in method and 40 percent a revolution in its effects. Similarly, *Ziua* reported from a November 1999 poll that only 11 percent continue to believe in the "tall" tale about the terrorists, confirming the view of that newspaper's editor, a former *Securitate* informer, that there were no *Securitate* terrorists, only Iliescu coup forces. So, *Securitate* may have lost the battle in 1989, but its heirs, its politically marginalized rivals, have won the post-1989 propaganda war by avoiding exposure and prosecution for murder or state terror, despite the pervasive anti-*Securitate* and Iliescu discourses. Nor did former President Constantinescu ever succeed in identifying the USLA terrorists, indicating the effectiveness of this disinformation and armed intimidation.

The use of violence needs underscoring. In contrast to Bulgaria's peaceful politics, whose 1990 street protests led to the voluntary resignation of the neo-Communist president, Iliescu-collaborating, paramilitary coal miners crushed Romania's spring 1990 street protests at University Square in Bucharest of about two months led by anti-Communist students and Bucharest urbanites against the newly elected Iliescu/National Salvation Front government. Some of the protestors included provocateurs working on behalf of rightist forces of both "radical return" and "radical continuity," to use Shafir's phrases. They attacked the police station and its forces during the confusion, in what was probably a "white coup," which succeeded in gaining authoritarian concessions. The consequent 1990 pact with Iliescu was not with the beaten democratic opposition forces in political and civil society, but with the radical right forces, which had been excluded from the National Salvation Front after the demise of Communism in late December 1989.[13] Iliescu halted his persecution of the right-wing forces through selective prosecutions and threats of exposure and invited them to invest in business and establish a literary and journalistic presence.

In September 1991, in another violent visit by marauding miners (part of a total of four or five to Bucharest), the government of Petre Roman was coerced to resign (a coup?). This consolidated the new Iliescu-ex-*Securitate* entente. Iliescu's former foes were welcomed into business, politics, and journalism, with scant regard for their methods, legal or dubious. Over the next year, the marriage of convenience extended to elections and electoral fraud, with former *Securitate* officers involved. The January 1999 mobilization of the miners, though having different motives and targets, again underscored the role of violence in regime direction. Once again, outside of Bucharest, the miners and other figures attacked the police, which failed or chose not to resist. The attack on the Constantinescu presidency was a signal that any fiscal austerity agreements could not be imposed on the mining sector. In 1990, the miners served President Iliescu and Prime Minister Roman against both the civil society demonstrators and perhaps against Iliescu as well by attacking his coercive apparatus. In 1991, the miners attacked Roman for having reneged, in their perception, on economic promises to that sector. By 1999, their new patron was Corneliu Vadim Tudor, who was particularly rewarded in the 2000 polls by economically downtrodden ethnic Romanians in Transylvania, who were attracted to his promises and his populist nationalism.[14]

Usually, even pacted democratic promises are compromises with authoritarian elements and can only become democratizing to the point of democratic consolidation if there is a subsequent rupture, *reforma pactada, reforma ruptura* in Stepan and Linz's concept. Since Romania abandoned Communism through rupture followed by authoritarian pacts, it could not emulate Bulgaria's pacted transition from Communism, which was followed throughout the entire decade with pacted incremental improvements, and occasional ruptures. When the Bulgarian Socialist Party resigned from power nonviolently in 1991, democratic reforms were exchanged in return for the opposition agreeing to call off its protests. Stepan and Linz argue that democratization can accrue if a nonviolent rupture follows a pact with authoritarian traits. Unfortunately, Romania's rupture in the violent December 1989 events occurred before any democratic pacting. However, pacts of the mid-to-late 1990s with the EU have served to reconfigure Romania's institutions and economic policy in ways that would not otherwise have been generated by its initial post-Communist regime path.

This initially disadvantageous trajectory came from Romania's regime transition path of the two least auspicious, nondemocratic ideal-types: sultanism and totalitarianism.[15] Advancement opportunities were reserved for Communist elites, many formed by nepotism. The children of the original Communists, who had been marginalized by Dej's and Ceauşescu's sultanism, have included both President Iliescu and Prime Minister Petre Roman, who represent the maximum opposition tolerated under this regime type. Other "opposition" has come from "reformist" circles such as the "Trocadero Café" (e.g., the House of Deputies leader from 1992 to 1996 and current Prime Minister, Adrian Năstase[16]) and the former Communist Party school (such as Virgil Măgureanu, the leading intelligence official from 1990 to 1997 and a former professor and *Securitate* colonel[17]). These Gorbachev-mold Communists joined the Iliescu regime after the Ceauşesist system had proven its inefficacy, corruption, and brutality. Other opportunists had made their peace with Communism. Among Iliescu opponents, "liberals" like Dinu Patriciu made a fortune in architecture and construction based on Communist connections, while onetime Peasant Party member Emil Constantinescu had been Communist Party leader at Bucharest University. It has been difficult for the proverbial opposition kettle to call the pot black. Most have continued to use their *pile* to make connections for their own advantage.

Among the various difficulties of the opposition, one stands out as remarkable in the failure to acknowledge an ongoing problem that could be rectified simply through organization and vigilance. For all of its attempts to advocate, the opposition to this day has failed to protect itself by documenting electoral irregularities in every national election since Communism. In the 1990 elections, Iliescu collected over one million more votes than the total number of eligible voters, as indicated in the subsequent 1991 census. At the December 1991 and 2003 constitutional plebiscites, turnout was exaggerated above the minimum turnout, as frequently occurs in such ratifications, as in Russia in

1993 and Haiti in 1987. The 1991 constitution seemed not unreasonable, but endowed the new regime with the threat of extraordinary emergency powers, routine decree powers, an established, unitary ethnic Romanian state, an unwieldy bicameral legislature with very few differences between the two houses other than the number of seats, and a semi-presidential system without the presidential prerogatives of the Gaullist constitution. Semi-presidentialism has encouraged either the adoption of sultanistic informal powers over a weak legislature (Iliescu), or cohabitation, but without the robust French-style cooperation necessary for that system to work, where putative allies consistently disagree with a president except when given patronage (Constantinescu).

The initial, turbulent period of 1990–1992 established a transition from totalitarianism to post-totalitarianism, thus improving on the initial regime path, which lacked the phase of post-totalitarianism under Communism, which would tolerate dissent. Unlike the common Romanian refrain of a "stolen revolution," in fact, civil society produced no sustained opposition to the revolution of 1989 led by Iliescu other than the significant spring protests of 1990. Instead, Iliescu stole the state from the prior regime's hardliners and then gradually coopted these elements. The fraudulent May 1990 elections, in which the result was exaggerated rather than altered, however, were primarily to legitimate that revolution with participation of weak new democratic parties that were denied sufficient time and conditions to openly contest for power. Iliescu's strongest, covert opposition from the prior regime had not yet organized into political parties. New opposition emerged after the 1990 elections in a generational split inside Iliescu's coalition. Iliescu again dispatched coal miners to force Prime Minister Roman's resignation in September 1991. Iliescu then appointed a technocrat from abroad, Theodor Stolojan, who lacked any political base to contest his authority.

In the second general elections of September–October 1992, democracy was not inaugurated because of the massive fraud. Another falsely huge lead in 1992 in the first round of presidential elections resulted from dubious "special list votes," supposedly constituting ten percent of the ballots cast. The National Peasant Christian Democratic Party (PNŢCD) sought to protest the fraud in parliament and on the media, but was denied access to complain both that rates of 13 plus percent spoiled ballots and 10 percent of total votes cast on special lists were not remotely credible. Ten out of forty-two counties had special list voting rates over 16 percent. Eighteen out of forty-two counties had nullification rates over 16 percent for both the House and the Senate. Two counties had two to four point differences between the nullification rates for the Senate and the House. The spoiling of ballots, through the falsification of county-based election returns, was not checked against aggregations of precinct-level returns collected by the opposition or independent poll watchers during the early hours of 28 September 1992. With nullifications and special list additions, several extremist parties were able to reach the 3 percent entry threshold to qualify for parliament, while the National Liberal Party consequently fell short of that minimum percent. The 10 percent lead for Iliescu in the first presidential round appeared unbridgeable and induced many opposition voters not to turn up in the second round, during which few foreign observers were present.

The 1992 parliamentary electoral fraud were subtle but hugely significant aftershocks from the more dramatic miners' mobilizations in June 1990 and September 1991. The rigging strengthened and legitimated the radical right while the democratic opposition was repressed with impunity. The rigging was done subtly, changing results on the margins of electoral system rules, while maintaining results not too inconsistent with overall public opinion, and consequently produced a transition from post-totalitarianism to an electoral authoritarian regime.

Examples of Prima Facie, Selective 1992 Parliamentary Fraud (in 15 of the 42 counties, rates in percentages)

Special Lists	*Additions*	*Senate Nullifications*	*Deputy Nullifications*
Botoşani	17.64	22.11	22.92
Brăila	17.02	18.81	17.88
Braşov	17.11	11.33	11.74
Calaraşi	15.86	25.58	22.25
Caraş Severin	20.81	12.27	10.70
Constanţa	22.81	14.50	14.18
Gorj	18.46	19.38	20.07
Hunedora	17.74	8.69	8.14
Iaşi	14.69	24.45	24.16
Mehedinţi	20.32	16.59	16.10
Olt	12.97	28.00	24.16
Vaslvi	18.49	24.88	23.29
Vilcea	17.20	21.67	20.90
Vilcea	17.20	21.67	20.90
SAI	20.31	15.78	15.33

Democratization under authoritarian auspices proceeded based on "ill-defined, but predictable norms," in Juan Linz's formulation. Co-opting non-party technocrats with a Communist pedigree, Iliescu from 1992–1996 gradually liberalized opposition associations as Iliescu's extremist allies that had opposed him in the post-totalitarian period became useful adversaries, which in a "good cop–bad cop" game, made Iliescu appear like a political moderate. Had these extremist parties ever seriously opposed Iliescu, they could have forced a vote of no confidence against the government of Prime Minister Nicolae Văcăroiu. Thus, an elaborate song and dance continued that in almost any other country would have led to the oft-predicted "early elections," which have never occurred in Romanian post-Communism.

Since I published my 1993 analysis of the stealing of the 1992 parliamentary elections,[18] commentators have frequently asked me why the foreign and Romanian observers did not complain more about the fraud.[19] My answer is that the issue was raised in Congress, but not within the administration, which took the position that it would work with whatever party or coalition was deemed victorious so long as the election was not blatantly fraudulent. Six days after the parliamentary vote, I unexpectedly encountered then U.S. Ambassador John R. Davis Jr. and his Chargé des Affaires, Jonathan B. Rickert, who were hosting a reception the House of the Men of Science for a conference on psychiatry and political repression held at Bucharest University. I told them that the election was the least effectively monitored of the several dozen elections that I had observed in Haiti, Nicaragua, El Salvador, Pakistan, and the Philippines. Under such conditions, fraud could be perpetrated with impunity. Ambassador Davis responded, "It is up to the political parties to organize enough observers to be present at all the polling precincts and to show their displeasure at irregularities."[20] As a career ambassador, Davis deferred to the U.S. line that the opposition did not adduce any evidence of fraud. In effect, the U.S. decided that the Iliescu presidency was a fact, and it was already working that very week with NATO representatives in Bucharest to enforce the UN embargo of the former Yugoslavia. Yet, the foreign observers, whether those organized by the U.S. Embassy or the other 500 certified from various organizations, failed to monitor the one phase of elections for which they indeed had adequate numbers, the late-night aggregation of precinct-level returns at the 42 county prefect offices. Aside from the U.S. Embassy, the group influential enough to delegitimate the parliamentary, if not the presidential votes, the combined National Democratic Institute/International Republican Institute (NDI/IRI) delegation, was divided. NDI wanted a fair election to occur after having trained about 5,000 domestic observers from the new NGO, the Pro-Democracy Association (and whose leaders had originated from Iliescu's party.) On the other hand, IRI concluded that the elections were stolen and months later circulated its unofficial report detailing its conclusion—unofficial only because NDI and IRI could not agree on a unified conclusion, that the parliamentary elections were stolen. Romania 1992, like the elections of Pakistan 1990, Philippines 1987, and the Dominican Republic 1994, were all cases where U.S. foreign policy interests trumped harsh criticism of obvious electoral irregularities or fraud discovered by USAID or Congressionally funded observers in those countries. For the U.S. to have reached a more modest conclusion, not that the elections were stolen, but just that they again, as in 1990, failed a democratic test, would have been more reasonable, even if it would have changed little. As in 1946, any U.S. complaints registered in public or private were offset by the ongoing recognition of the de facto "selected" government.

The history of West European party systems shows that the results of the first few elections gave those parties legitimacy and long-term status very similar to those initial results.[21] If the election had not been stolen, the Romanian parties, Greater Romania, Democratic Agrarians, and Socialist Labor, would have, as a result of entering parliament, splintered or gone out of existence, while the Romanian opposition could have governed. Midway through the second Iliescu presidential term, in 1994, the regime halted its alliance with radical parties, who would not cooperate, and began intense democratization in anticipation of much more honest and competitive elections in 1996. Practicing "good government as good politics," Iliescu's Romanian Party of Social Democracy (PDSR until the name change after the 2000 elections) exhibited extensive democratic political learning. Iliescu undertook a number of reforms, especially the dramatic rapprochement with Hungary, gambling that a sincere effort to gain entry into NATO would be rewarded at the polls.[22] In an additional test, Iliescu chose to govern effectively with only a plurality, but avoided a hung parliament by occasionally allying with his opposition. The former satellite parties (Greater Romania, Socialist Workers, and Democratic Agrarians), for whom he had to cheat for in order to gain parliamentary entry, abandoned the PDSR, as Iliescu did not take their demand for an eastward, authoritarian direction. Finally, the electoral process itself was less unreliable as the opposition was better organized to verify electoral fraud, forming partnerships to cover more, but still not all of the polls on election day.

In 1996, the opposition Democratic Convention tried to stop the post-poll rigging by monitoring the prefects' offices, where votes at the county level are aggregated (because Romania still does not have a permanent electoral commission), but were only partly successful. The 1996 legislative elections, which were perceived as credible, were also marred by an excessive, 6 plus percent rate of ballot nullifications in the parliamentary vote and the continued absence of minimum reforms in electoral administration, including a formal voter registration process[23] and mandatory release and publishing of all the results from each precinct. By repeating the inordinate nullifications of votes, the opposition coalition, Democratic Convention's share of seats, now including the National Liberal Party, was reduced. The government lost a stable majority of the legislature, which could have been formed with just the UDMR ethnic Hungarian party. Instead, the Democratic Convention had to ally with the Democratic Party Coalition (USD/PD), which had from 5 to 7.5 percent of the opposition votes and thus 7.5 to 10 percent of the seats (the inordinate nullifications creating the uncertainty). The irregularities, including the 6 percent nullification rates, continued in the 2000 votes, facts virtually ignored by most commentators. In 2000, they could have kept the Peasant Party out of parliament. Even if the exact effects are less clear than in 1992, the irregularities meant that the 1996 and 2000 elections were still not free and fair.

Nullification Rates in Parliamentary Elections (in Percent)

1992		*1996*		*2000*	
Deputies	*Senate*	*Deputies*	*Senate*	*Deputies*	*Senate*
13%	12.3	6.5	6.2	6.3	5.8

Source: Anuarul Statistic al României, Seri de timp time series 1990–2001, CD-ROM, Institutul Naţional de Statistică, 2003.

These practices date to the largely tolerated ballot falsifications of Romania's interwar, "mimic democracy." This culminated in Carol II's rubber-stamp parliament at the start of World War II in 1939, which in turn were followed by such bogus votes as General Ion Antonescu's March 1941 plebiscite and the Soviet-backed November 1946 votes where Stalin's Yalta and Moscow Conference promises of electoral credibility were ignored. Rothschild commented that they "were (predicatably) quite other than free and open, as an old Romanian tradition of ballot falsification was compounded by newer Communist techniques of intimidation."[24]

West European and U.S. toleration of irregularities at least, both by governments and foreign election observers, in several national elections have had disastrous initial consequences for democratization, especially after 1990 and 1992. The elections legitimated the already installed pragmatists from Communist networks, not liberal reformers, and incorporated the radical right and left into the party system. It could be argued that the rigged 1992 elections were not so harmful. First, the Iliescu presidency handed over power in 1996, a very significant step for democratization, and the subsequent Democratic Convention-led coalition proved its ineptitude from 1996–2000 because of each party's distinct interests and goals. Moreover, if Iliescu had handed over power in the much more polarized era of 1992, before his tilt to the West, the result may have resembled the violent polarization that followed the 1937 elections, arguably the first credible election in Romanian history. In both cases, the country did not yet have a consensus on democratic regime norms, power sharing and conflict resolution, but did seem to accept the fragile equilibrium of the semi-democracies of the interwar and immediate post-Communist epochs. Moreover, the comparative stability of the Iliescu-led eras suggests a puzzle why Romanians, perhaps like Russia under Yeltsin and Putin, should enjoy greater levels of public support under mild autocracy than they would under democratic rule.

Still, the electoral fraud certainly comes at a cost, not least that typically democratic rule has produced greater economic growth in the region.[25] Moreover, electoral fraud harms democratization by definition since almost any definition of democracy presumes free elections. Third, the regime consolidated the control of national security and Communist bureaucracies and party systems, instead of establishing more robust democratic forces, which might have established civilian supremacy at an earlier juncture. Finally, the Social Democrats (then FDSN) learned in 1992 that "crime pays," as the ease with which the elections were stolen provided signals of impunity that reinforced the opportunities for corruption that has pervaded Romanian politics ever since.

The results of the 1996 and 2000 votes merit comparison. Constantinescu won the presidency in the second round on 17 November 1996 with 55 percent. The parliamentary campaign of the opposition, itself dominated by the National Peasant Christian Democratic Party (PNŢCD), received much more television coverage on the independent station Pro-TV than it had in the 1992 votes (virtually none occurred in 1990). With a plurality of 30 percent of votes and about 35 percent (122 Deputies and 53 Senators) of seats from the 3 November 1996 parliamentary elections, the Democratic Convention of Romania (CDR) formed a governing coalition with the Union of Social Democracy (USD), dominated by the Democratic Party (PD), as well as the Union of Democratic Hungarians of Romania (UDMR). The Iliescu-led PDSR received 22 percent of the votes (91 Deputies and 41 Senators) and joined the loyal opposition. As in the 1992 local elections, the PDSR had won most rural local elections and the CDR most urban.

The 2000 elections had roughly the same turnout as those in 1996, more than 65 percent (the exact figures varying because of the invalidated votes issue). After four miserable years in office, the former Democratic Convention only received a total of just over 20 percent of the electorate (for the Senate: National Liberals, 7.45 percent; the Union of Democratic Hungarians, 6.89 percent; the Democratic Convention 2000, 5.23 percent; and the National Liberals–Câmpeanu faction, 1.22 percent, the latter two parties failing even to enter parliament). The Democratic Party won also 7.5 percent and 13 Senate seats. While the fault for the lack of intercoalition cooperation lies partly in the self-serving interests and to a lesser extent in ideological differences of the CDR-led coalition, particularly from the Democratic Party, the death of Corneliu Coposu in 1995 left the strongest CDR party, the National Peasants, leaderless.

Without a political visionary, it became divided by Communist-era opportunists and an elder generation, both sides pursuing patronage at all costs. The National Peasants came to resemble the Democratic and National Liberal Parties in lacking coherence in ideology and discipline in morals. The National Liberals, which ran separately from the CDR in 2000 as it had in 1992, articulated the most coherent ideology, but since 2000 was effectively led by a former Justice Minister, Valeriu Stoica, who allegedly steered government business to his family law firm, imposed press censorship (see Peter Gross's chapter), and reassigned or fired judges, contradicting the most important principles of liberalism: freedom of expression, judicial independence, and the rule of law. With so much graft and incoherence, along with economic bleeding, much of its 1996 swing vote opted for the radical Greater Romania Party or returned back to the PDSR of Iliescu. (Duverger's scholarly warning about the susceptibility of swing voters to populist and radical ideals was confirmed in the 2000 elections.) Greater Romania received 21.03 percent of the Senate vote, 37 of 140 seats in the Senate, while Iliescu's PDSR officially received 37.17 percent and over 40 percent, 65 of 140 seats. It began to govern with the surprising support of the UDMR, the ethnic Hungarian party, which saw an opportunity to leverage its majority-creating support for the PDSR government. Despite tensions over issues such as rebuilding statues of Hungarian heroes, the relationship had held through 2003. To its credit, the PDSR was unwilling to enter into a pact with Greater Romania (PRM), which found the relationship with UDMR to be abominable. Greater Romania won about one-quarter of the legislative seats in both houses. Incredibly ominous for both the short and long runs, Greater Romania received 3 million votes from one-third of the voters aged eighteen to thirty-five. This "mass phenomenon" also drew considerable support from one of the most developed regions in Romania: Ardeal. Its leader, Tudor, is waiting next in line to take power, if the Liberal and Democratic Parties cannot become the unified, loyal opposition. Toward that end, PRM continues to mouth words of wickedness like: "Down with the mafia. Up with the country. Liquidate the mafia in forty-eight hours. Confiscate the wealth of the rulers. Introduce a state of siege with legal dictatorship."

In "post-Haider-effect-Europe,"[26] Western tolerance for extremism in Romania may be excessive. The large PRM presence, 84 of 345 Deputies (24 percent) and 37 of 140 Senators (27 percent), as the "loyal opposition" to a minority Nâstase government, has not made Romania an isolated pariah state, as it nearly was from June 1990 to September 1991 following the miners' twice rampaging through Bucharest. The sultanistic-totalitarian institutions, especially the army and the intelligence agencies, have only been partly reformed, admirably or apparently supporting the rapprochement with Hungary, but not punishing or purging their large, anti-Semitic, anti-Hungarian, and pro-Antonescu elements. Though President Iliescu has occasionally condemned the radical nationalists and even hinted at Romania's complicity in helping Hitler to initiate the Holocaust, his government, following its NATO acceptance in mid-2003, insisted that the Holocaust did not occur under Romania's authority from 1940–1945.[27] In addition to the army, nationalist anti-American remnants remain in various intelligence agencies, especially UM 0215, headed by Virgil Ardelean, which contains ex-*Securitate* from abolished cadres who were vetted from the SRI. Sadly, this group is reportedly linked to the supposedly reformist Premier Nâstase, suggesting that Romanian nationalism is also a mainstream virus. Some of its various anti-U.S. manifestations also represent rivalries among different factions within the Iliescu-Nâstase regime. Though a split is difficult to predict, a PSD reelection in 2004 will surely test the ability of a "retired" Iliescu to maintain the unity among factions in his party, where the nationalist card would be used to gain personal advantage or leverage.

In the second round of the 2000 presidential election, some of the first round's protest voters for Tudor either switched to Iliescu or did not turn out to vote—a reassuring development. Officially, Iliescu received 66.83 percent of the votes while Tudor garnered 33.17 percent. Tudor's shocking entry, aptly called the "Zhirinovsky of the Carpathians," into the second round of the 2000 presidential elections, also resulted from public apathy that produced lower than expected voter turnout. However, the nationalism of Tudor is not so strange to Romania. As Irina Livezeanu shows,[28] intolerant nationalism has been part of Romanian "mainstream" parties since the 1920s and, therefore, has deep legitimacy, far more than any leftist tradition. Exit polls showed an astonishing 27 percent of the vote for Constantinescu in 1996 went to Tudor.

During and since the 2000 elections, the watered-down "Ticu" law was hardly enforced. After an eight-year quest to promote accountability, the ostensibly dramatic 1999 legislation (no. 187), which had been initiated by Senator Constantin Dumitrescu, but from which he disassociated himself, created the National Council for the Study of the *Securitate* Archives (CNSAS). It required State Security collaborators to confess their associations prior to running for office, lest they be exposed and disqualified prior to competing.[29] Since few felt they would be exposed, few confessed. In the 2000 local and general elections, only a handful of the former, and less than two dozen of the latter, were thereby disqualified, even though thousands of the 20,000 candidates for the November general elections alone had collaborated with the secret police in one form or another. The CNSAS's excuses for not listing these thousands were: (1) the SRI had not turned over all the files; (2) the sheer number of candidates with a "serious" chance to win parliamentary seats were few; and (3) insufficient staffing.[30] Even among the opposition presidential candidates, the CNSAS made no revelations about Tudor, Stolojan, Isârescu, and Roman—all of whom, except possibly Iliescu,[31] had *Securitate* connections of one sort or another. Nor did any confess. *Securitate*'s progeny have continued to act with impunity.

ADMISSION TO NATO AND THE EU

Had Romania been denied entry into NATO, then foreign sanctions requiring democratic reforms would have lost their potency. With the country into NATO and EU admission very promising, positive sanctions permitting regime monitoring and economic aid and trade, Romania now has about a 75 percent chance of graduating from the current, unconsolidated, corrupted, semidemocracy to completing its democratic transition by the 2004 elections and about a 50 percent chance of consolidating its party and legal systems by 2010.[32] Any coup plotters in the radical fringes have been marginalized where "democracy is the only game in town," Linz's dictum for consolidation. While Romanians understandably resent foreign pressure, criticism, and arrogance, the U.S. and European stipulations for integration have been worth the admission price.[33]

Even though Romania became, in 1993, the first country in NATO's Partnership for Peace, it was rejected for admission to NATO in its first round in early July 1997, when the Czech Republic, Hungary, and Poland began talks toward joining the alliance in 1999. A sense of national catastrophe pervaded the feelings of almost every Romanian. Even in January 2002, NATO Secretary-General Lord Robertson said that NATO membership "was not a gift." However, an invitation to join NATO no later than 2004 was delivered at the Prague Summit of November 2002, with a momentous visit to Bucharest from President Bush immediately thereafter. Romania's decade-long dream was realized. But did it result more from new geopolitical priorities of the U.S. or because of internal reforms? I would suggest more of the former than the latter, though both count.

First, in public opinion polls over recent years, Romanians repeatedly and consistently supported entry into NATO and the EU, at higher rates than the publics in the other former NATO candidate countries (Albania, Bulgaria, Estonia, Latvia, Lithuania, Macedonia, Slovakia, and Slovenia). A 6 June 2002 poll, for example, showed that 80 percent of Romanians supported NATO accession, while 14 percent opposed. The report noted that the poll results mark the first time that the percentage of optimists exceeded the number of skeptics pertaining to the country's chances of admission into NATO: 48 percent to 41 percent.[34]

Second, Romania has participated in over a dozen NATO peacekeeping missions, including in Bosnia, Kosovo, Macedonia, and even a small contingent of thirty in Afghanistan, as well as cooperating in antiterrorism intelligence and military exercises. Romania has made itself a Western strategic asset. The country specifically links Bulgaria and Turkey with Hungary, and more generally East Central Europe with Eastern Europe, as well as Transcaucasia and Central Asia, from which terrorism, drugs, arms, and human trafficking, as well as illegal migrants, have come. It has also been negotiating with Ukraine (its prime minister visited Romania for the first time in a decade in January 2002) and Russia to resolve territorial disputes and normalize foreign relations without the debris of treaties established in the Communist era.[35]

Third, since the November 2000 elections, Romania has made larger progress toward democracy and economic reform than many anticipated. Freedom House, in its annual surveys of civil and political rights from 1997 through 2001, placed Romania (and Bulgaria) in the top tier of free states, with ratings of 2.0 each year (on a scale of 1 to 7, with "1" as the best rating, with Bulgaria receiving a 3 for political rights and a 2 for civil rights). Larry Diamond has depicted Romania (and Bulgaria) as "liberal democracies," instead of the lower rating of "electoral democracy," which he assigned to many Latin American cases.[36] Romania is now a stable regime, albeit not as democratic as both Freedom House and Diamond maintain. They, like so many observers, overrate the state of democracy in Eastern Europe and underrate it in Latin America because Eastern Europe has traveled further in its democratization since Communism than has Latin America, but the latter has institutionalized democratic institutions more to date. Though Romania still is an illiberal polity with corruption a large, intractable problem, NATO's exceptions in the past for dictatorial Greece and Turkey provides precedents for leniency, just as the Organization of American States has overlooked similar Latin American military dictatorships. Moreover, corruption in Greece and Turkey is not categorically less than in Romania, which, in turn, is less than Russia's.

Fourth, Romania's economy from 2000 to 2003 has grown at the fastest rates since 1995, positive facts recognized favorably by the West because the situation had been so dire from 1996 to 2000, if official statistics are to be believed. Romania's average monthly income has risen to an estimated $130 monthly during the third Iliescu presidency, up from about $100 monthly during Constantinescu. Inflation remains high at about 30 percent, with the current account deficit at about 6 percent of the GDP. Corruption remains rampant. Privatization of large state enterprises and large farms has just begun since 2001, but with setbacks.[37] The sale of the largest money-loser, the Sidex steel mill, the third largest in Romania, will reduce losses of hundreds of millions of dollars in subsidies and lost tax revenues, and a $1 billion-plus debt. However, the Reşita Steel Works halted production after its U.S. owners, Noble Ventures, which purchased 95 percent of the company, failed to pay its 3,800 workers after promising to invest $24 million by August 2001 and pay the $45 million in debt in its first year in operation. The company refused because the government did not reschedule the debt, and the steel did not meet quality standards. After the Romanian government had initially taken the company's position, it then decided that Nobel Ventures had breached its contract. This decision has discouraged other investors in proposed companies for privatization. Moderate labor unrest has also continued, particularly at state enterprises, whether or not they were specifically slated for privatization. The most active is the National Trade Union Bloc, which has 750,000 members, especially among postal, auto, and defense workers.

Fifth, and perhaps most important, was the "September 11" effect. Europe's East has, in effect, moved its boundary eastward because Romania has suddenly been perceived as an asset to the West's newfound war against terrorism (actually a much longer-term phenomenon). While Romania may not receive many or even more than a few of the U.S. military bases it hopes to be transferred from Germany, Romanian cooperation with and involvement in Western counterterrorism efforts have mitigated its inferiority complex. This feeling, too often shamelessly expressed, has reflected Western contempt for Eastern culture and Romania's peripheral status. Now, Romania feels pride of place, on the front lines against the threatening Islamic civilization. While geography has become a sudden asset to Romania, the West has also not lost sight of Romania's predicaments.

It was not so long ago in 2000 that Romania was the only EU candidate country that did not appear to able to apply neoclassical economic approaches to its economic predicaments.[38] While Iliescu convinced the West of *his* interest in allying with the West generally and the U.S. in particular, doubts have remained about Romania's reliability, given Western perceptions of deception and internal factions more receptive to the East or internal concerns. These concerns arise, for example, from Romania's past failure to police the trafficking of arms and petroleum across the Danube to Serbia during the Security Council-mandated embargo of the former Yugoslavia from 1992 to 1995. The UN initially condemned the frequent violations, including 210 illegal flights from Timişoara to Belgrade. The U.S. eventually concluded that Romanian cooperation was sufficient.[39] On 7 September 2000, the chief prosecutor of the International Criminal Tribunal for the former Yugoslavia, Carla Del Ponte, accused the Romanian government of failing to arrest indicted Bosnian Serb war criminals Radovan Karadžić and Ratko Mladić both of whom had periodically visited Romania.[40]

Still, the West acknowledges that Romania has avoided Russian-style oligarchy *cum* gangster violence seeking monopoly control. Romanian crony capitalism, currency crises, and resistance to privatization under the auspices of reformist Constantinescu-appointed governments created a malaise of rather desperate proportions, which have vanished. The Iliescu presidency since 2001 has created stability, based on extant Communist era networks and the decision to make the prime minister the formal head of the ruling party for the first time.

The rubrics and rigors of European integration have enjoyed broad support since the new government of 2001 differentiated itself from the radical right. In the end, continuity of policy, even if second best, is preferable if feasible to an incoherent commitment to reform. If sustained, it will ensure Romania's Euro-Atlantic integration and eventual economic and democratic stability. As Arend Lijphart and Samuel Finer have argued, "economic development requires not so much a *strong* hand as a *steady* one."[41] In this regard, the Euro-Atlantic process has been both a target to adapt Romanian political-economy to local circumstances, but also provided some consistency and consensus that Romania's lack of political pacting among its domestic leaders has not and would not have generated without the Euro-Atlantic cooperation *cum* EU and NATO entry requirements for reform.

In addition, the U.S. has tilted toward "New Europe," even as "Old Europe" has extended its hand to its southeast. On 1 August 2002, Romania became the first country in the world to sign an Article 98 bilateral agreement of the statute of the International Criminal Court (ICC) with the U.S.[42] Romania remains one of the few among NATO and EU members and candidate countries that had not opposed the U.S. provision to exempt U.S. soldiers from ICC prosecution (though at the time of writing, Romania [and Bulgaria] still had not ratified the bilateral treaty with the U.S.). The Romanian offer had been an obvious play to enhance its chances for admission to NATO in November 2002 (though Romania denied that this was its motive). Similarly, after its initial NATO rejection, Romania supported NATO's seventy-eight-day aerial attacks on Serbia in 1999, despite wide internal opposition, especially from nationalist-collectivist forces. Different Foreign Ministry spokespersons repeatedly advanced the argument that Romania's support for the humanitarian intervention not only merited second-round entry into NATO, but also qualified Romania for compensation for an estimated $900 million lost in Danube River traffic and elsewhere during the eleven-week war.[43] Romania was not successful on the latter score.

Based on NATO's Membership Action Plan, Romania's military has since continued reforming, with its forces reduced from an estimated 100,000 in 1998 to 45,000 planned for 2004. 5,000 officers were laid off in 2002 alone. Its defense budget for 2002 reached $1 billion for the first time, amounting to 2.5 percent of GDP. Eighty percent were professional soldiers, replacing the Communist system reliance on conscripts. More than half of its soldiers will be "elite troops," preparing for more specialized, mobile missions against terrorism;[44] $14,000 was spent on annual training for each member of the armed forces.[45]

The EU did consider Romania in dire need of significant economic and political improvement to become a viable EU candidate. Shortly after Romania's rejection by NATO for first round entry, on 16 July 1997, the European Union's executive commission recommended that the EU open negotiations to admit five Central and Eastern European countries—the Czech Republic, Estonia, Hungary, Poland, and Slovenia—plus Cyprus. In 1990, the EU regarded Hungary, Poland, and the Czech Republic as the next logical choices for members. This assumption was transformed partially into reality with the inclusion of these three nations in NATO. On 8 November 2000, the EU published "Agenda 2000," ranking EU applicant states. Romania ranked second to last, behind the Baltic states,[46] and last on economic criteria, even though the country had been having a small recovery in 2000. The report also noted that Romania had a "long way to go to gain membership" by 2007, but which the EU called a reasonable target date. The Report noted, "Romania cannot be considered a functioning market economy and is not yet able to respond, in the medium term, to the competitive pressures that exist on the EU market."[47] The report cited Romania's insufficient response, despite several warnings, to respond to the wave of orphaned and institutionalized children. The EU also found its aspiring democratic institutions to be working improperly, including overcentralization and inadequate agriculture reform. In November 2001, the EU, through its Commission, announced that of the twelve candidate states, Romania and peer state Bulgaria were both excluded from the list of likely expansion states tentatively set for 2004. Romania's pace of economic and political reform and anticorruption initiatives were regarded as "too little, too late."

One example of Romanian resistance to European integration was telling. After the late January 2000 spill of about 100,000 cubic meters of cyanide and copper, Romania denied legal and financial responsibility. A joint venture involving a Romanian state enterprise for gold, silver, and other minerals, failed to prevent effluents from entering Romanian rivers. They flowed into the Tisza River in Hungary, where most fish and aquatic life were wiped out. Twelve days later, cyanide arrived at the Danube River at the Serbian border. This accident was called the largest environmental disaster in Europe since the 1986 Chernobyl nuclear explosion in the Ukraine—though arguably worse, nuclear storage facility explosions in Western Siberia have also occurred since the end of Communism. The Romanian government initially denied factual and legal responsibility. Romania was effectively arguing European legal standards should not apply to it, reinforcing perceptions of Romania's lack of EU readiness.[48]

Yet the EU has greatly changed its negative evaluation of Romania since November 2001. EU Enlargement Commissioner Guenter Verheugen promised Romania in mid-December 2001 that he would make some serious efforts to obtain due consideration for Romania in its efforts to be admitted to the EU. This meant that Romania would not be admitted in 2004, but would have an excellent chance in the second wave by 2007.[49]

As with its impressive military reform and cooperation with the West, the Romanian government has begun to assume some, but not all, the required responsibility for the burdens of reform and European legal requirements. EU integration processes represent a pragmatic compromise between neoclassical economics, in setting regional monetary, fiscal, and inflation targets and heterodoxical, institutional adaptation,[50] in facilitating sequenced adaptation. If and when all the *acquis communitaire* are negotiated and legislated, Romania will assume a regionally consistent, liberal regime in intent or purpose. However, both political and economic development will still require the rule of law to protect property, enforce contracts, prevent extortion, fraud, and embezzlement, as well as political and civil rights. For that reason, the largest remaining section in this chapter will address Romania's progress toward the rule of law. While international factors have impelled a more or less general pattern of political-economic development, Romanian characteristics will both frustrate and impel the process in different directions, especially if the rule of law is not consolidated, and if unreliable policing, prosecution, and judicial independence persist. In January 2004 Arie Oostlander, a member of the European Parliament, proposed that Romania's EU-accession negotiations be suspended. One factor was the continuation of international adoptions after the Romanian government had established a moratorium, as well as the suspicious manner in which the October 2003 constitutional referendum was held. Then, in February 2004, Baroness Emma Nicholson, the European Parliament's rapporteur for Romania, said that she still believed that the EU's accession negotiations with Romania should be suspended, but that Romania could still gain entry into the EU by the previously planned date of 2007. Nicholson said that Romania's meeting that timetable would require it to reduce corruption, which is still widespread in political parties and in the judiciary, and to end threats to freedom of the press.

The improved EU attitude results from several developments. First, Romania's initial complaints about the June 2001 Hungarian status law, enacted by Hungary to aid ethnic Hungarians outside of Hungary, subsided after effective diplomatic cooperation. Romania has offered to allow an annual three-month work permit in Hungary for its 1.7 million ethnic Hungarians. In December 2001, Prime Ministers Nâstase (of Romania) and Viktor Orban (of Hungary) agreed to allow all Romanians to apply for such permits. Moreover, the number of foreigners permitted to work temporarily in Hungary was reduced in January 2002 by Hungary to only 81,000, far fewer than the number of expatriate Hungarians. In December 2001, Hungary also pledged not to assist any ethnic Hungarian political organizations in Romania, such as the UDMR. Hungary also agreed to grant identity cards needed for these benefits only on Hungarian territory, thus reducing Romanian claims of Hungarian encroachments on its sovereignty.

Second, on 1 January 2002, Romania became the last of twelve EU candidate countries to gain automatic visa access to all EU countries except the United Kingdom and Ireland and the non-EU states of Norway and Iceland (the Schengen states). This was achieved largely because Romania promised to impose restrictive financial requirements for exit visas. These included credit cards or funds of up to $100 per day, up to a total of $500, plus medical insurance and a return ticket to Romania (though the cost of trips was estimated to be 20 percent less without the visa having to be purchased). The effect was to reduce travel to all but wealthy and/or business people. Romania also had to promise to restrict the entry of Ukrainians, Moldovans, and migrants from other neighboring countries who had formerly entered Romania easily. Visas were introduced in early 2002 for those from these countries. Others are more dubious that continued corruption at the border will prevent migrants from illegally entering and leaving Romania. However, at least one important recipient country has been so convinced. The Czech Republic, in particular, agreed to lift the restriction because the Romanian government had reduced the number of illegal migrants, particularly Roma, who had entered the Czech Republic from Romania. This included the identification of 500 tour operators smuggling illegal Romanian migrants to the Czech Republic.[51] While 500,000 Romanians gained visas in the first five months of 2002 and while 100,000 were denied exit visas, fewer Romanians traveled abroad to the Schengen countries than had traveled to them before the visa requirement was lifted! All the EU and Schengen states lifted the visa requirements on 1 January 2002, but they figured out other ways to prevent implementation, such as by requiring additional funds.

Third, the EU has indicated that Romania will need more than just a few years to establish a credible legal system, but that it also thinks that it can reach the requisite performance level sometime thereafter. What seems particularly needed are functional property protection and contracts to encourage foreign and domestic investment, as well as the prosecution of official corruption and the separation of prosecutors from decisions on continued detentions and on appealing decisions of the highest courts (see analysis of the rule of law below). While the property restitution law resulted in an avalanche of claims in the first eight months of 2001, including from former King Michael to his former summer palace, the effort to return unjustly confiscated property to the original owners seemed to move only haltingly forward. By contrast, President Iliescu announced in June 2002 that Greek Catholic Churches confiscated on behalf of Orthodox Churches would not be returned "unless local congregations favored it." This decision is likely to arouse consternation from EU sources, which favor the return of properties that had been owned by the Greek Catholic Churches before Communism.

Fourth, Romania has taken steps to improve ethnic relations. The UDMR, ethnic Hungarian Party has supported the Năstase government, though without cabinet representation, after it had supported and participated in the cabinets appointed under the Constantinescu presidency before it. A law permitting the use of minority languages in public affairs, where a minority group comprises at least 20 percent of the population, was enacted in 2001. While Cluj Mayor Gheorghe Funar, reelected twice, has continued to flaunt his opposition to this and other measures, the Iliescu presidency has distanced itself enough from the ultranationalist Greater Romania Party, led by Tudor, with Funar as second in command.

Fifth, in January 2002, the notorious Article 200 of the Romanian Penal Code, which had criminalized same-sex relations, was finally repealed. Romania's criminal law was thereby freed from provisions discriminating against lesbian, gay, bisexual, and transgender people. Article 200 had been designed to punish same-sex acts, but in practice it was interpreted to outlaw homosexual identity as such. Article 200 was also used to create a legally sanctioned culture of intimidation, fear, and repression of Romania's sexual minorities. At the time of repeal, an antidiscrimination law was also adopted, thereby providing protection against discrimination based on sexual orientation. It will take longer to change actual behavior and practice. These changes brought Romanian law closer into line with the human rights standards established by the Council of Europe and the EU for both member and accession states. The influential Romanian Orthodox Church, which opposed the repeal of this law through the 1990s, will continue to oppose normalization of treatment and favor reinstating Article 200.

Finally, Romania partially halted international adoptions and has attempted to improve the situation facing street children. While this was criticized by human rights groups, particularly after a judge said the early 2002 decision was illegal, the EU special envoy, Emma Nicholson, in June 2001, had condemned the prevalence of trafficking in adopted babies. The ban was partially lifted in December 2001, but controls over adoptions are designed to prevent this unseemly corruption. The foreign press has been silent about the positive efforts of the Romanian government to help homeless and abandoned children, as only the scandals were covered. Yet, slowly and without much fanfare, various institutional opportunities, especially halfway houses, have been established to address this dire need.

Thus, Romania has met the West about halfway, which is to say, making enormous strides from where it was in 1990, but still far from Western standards. The EU has been more impressed by Romanian actions over the economy and ethnic measures than it has with the legal reform efforts. Still, Romania is no further from Western standards than Greece had been when it applied to the Common Market and has a better chance than Turkey to enter the EU.

Prior to 2007, Romania must enact legislation to meet EU standards before the country becomes directly governed by EU law-proper in 2007. Moreover, Romanians wonder in what areas the country's economy will become competitive when it faces direct, foreign competition. Long has been the talk that electricity, petroleum, tourism, and software development might provide the country with comparative advantages. Can Romania turn them into a reality? Or, will it be swallowed up as a late-developing, dependent, peripheral economy? Will Western standards really be embraced and implemented according to the oligarchic elite's sense of enlightened self-interest, or will it turn to short-term, zero-sum practices that provide the kind of relative advantages that are stultifying under a more open, competitive, globalized economy? Some of these questions can only be answered after long-term efforts at democratization.

COMPLETING THE DEMOCRATIC TRANSITION

In this section, I examine the challenges for completing the democratic transition. The third Iliescu presidency, like its predecessors, has felt both the liberal pull of West European integration and the illiberal tug of populist demagoguery posed by authoritarian forces. Consequently, Romania has only met the narrowest definitions of democracy, parsimoniously in terms of freedom,[52] but has not completed the transition because of its continuing inability to hold minimally honest elections and establish the rule *of* law to replace the rule *by* law. Political parties in the Democratic Convention's 1996–2000 "coalition of coalitions" were unwilling to support common policy reforms, squabbling instead for patronage and ill-gotten gains. Corruption so frustrated Constantinescu that, faced with certain defeat, he decided in summer 2000 not to run for reelection in November 2000. While some interpret this LBJ-type decision as an abandonment of the democratic forces, no incumbent could have credibly competed for office after three straight years of steep economic decline. The Iliescu presidency has still not quite chosen between democratic statecraft and the politics of patrimonial ambiguity. Its regime is a combination of both.

To complete its democratic transition, according to the criteria of Linz and Stepan,[53] Romania must work to assure that (a) the three branches of government can generate new policies, without sharing power with the army and intelligence agencies; (b) the Constitution must be enforced by the courts and not the Justice Ministry, presidency, or intelligence agencies; and (c) electoral administration must become reliable. Romania has come close, but has not quite completed these three tasks. Regarding the first issue, the government de facto does have the authority to generate new policies, though the difficulty is augmented by the five-plus party system, fostered by highly proportional electoral rules as well as its dual-executive, semipresidential constitution. The persistence of autonomous bureaucracies, especially the military, is the largest obstacle. National defense and military policies cannot be enacted without the consultation and presumed veto of the army and intelligence agencies, as the chapters by Deletant and Watts in this volume suggest, though both see signs of improvement. However, the army has supported policies against its own interests so long as it encourages NATO integration prospects. For example, in connection with the defense budget, for which NATO demanded both modernization and force reduction, the parliament has been more willing to generate bipartisan support. From 1992 to 1996, the Iliescu-led PDSR, which had a plurality, maintained party discipline, and enacted his agenda until 1995–1996, when the PDSR's coalition parties stopped supporting the coalition in protest of the rapprochement with Hungary. Subsequently, Constantinescu's inability to obtain coalition support created a vacuum in which bureaucratic interests insisted on perpetuating the status quo.

The second dimension asks whether the executive, legislative, and judicial powers in a new democracy have to share power with other bodies de jure. Most of the de facto power sharing just examined is theoretically unconstitutional, except in national security and intelligence. The National Defense Council includes representatives from the military in policy formulation. The Romanian Information Service legally, but without accountability, conducts business activities, often utilizing its intelligence to make more deals and profits. Both violate this second criterion.

Regarding the third requirement, there has been a lack of interest in the exorbitant nullification rates in all of Romania's parliamentary elections through 2000 and the inordinate special list voting in 1992. Three negative consequences result from huge irregularities in the 1990, 1992, 1996, and 2000 parliamentary votes. First, the results were altered to diminish the strength of the opposition to the Iliescu coalition, as indicated previously. Second, the institutionalization of fraud set precedents for anomalous voting processes, instead of a competent, permanent electoral commission and unimpeachable voter registration, vote counting, and reporting process, all of which Romania still lacks in the twenty-first century. Third, civil society and the opposition have faced a bad choice, as in 1992, among three alternative courses of action: (1) ignore the fraud (what most of the inactive civil society did); (2) complain about the fraud (as did the National Peasant Party's Corneliu Coposu's approach); or (3) deny that it occurred (Civic Alliance Party's Nicolae Manolescu's approach). Coposu got nowhere because the U.S. favored Koštunica as a stable alternative to Serbia's Milošević[54] and because Manolescu would not cooperate with Coposu, who, along with Constantinescu, had not supported Manolescu's candidacy from the Democratic Convention for the presidency.[55]

President Ion Iliescu and Premier Năstase have refused to acknowledge some of their illiberal practices, such as limiting press freedom. For example, they complain about an international NGO, *Reporters sans Frontieres,* which had accurately criticized the country for intimidating the press. The Supreme Council for National Defense debated a document dealing with "counterstrategic options" for combating media reports that harm Romania's image. Moreover, the legislature considered a law requiring that newspapers offer anyone a right of reply to allegations, under criminal penalty if denied. The Defense Minister Ioan Mircea Paşcu actually claimed that "Romania will be more democratic with this law than without it."[56] In addition, the Balkan Stability Pact, which was created by the EU, sent a letter in late 2001 to Information Minister Vasile Dancu to complain of his ministry's takeover of Rompress, the state media agency in 2001. Since then, Prime Minister Nâstase has received at least twenty times as much media attention as all the opposition politicians put together.[57]

We now turn to consider the consolidation phase of democratization, the subsequent and overlapping deepening of democratic institutions and processes. Linz and Stepan proffer five arenas in which the deepening of attitudes, behavior, and constitutional practices (intervening variables) is needed to consolidate democracy.[58] Given limited space for the rest of this chapter, I will confine my analysis to the first three, definitional prerequisites, political society, civil society, and the rule of law.

POLITICAL SOCIETY

Few if any democracies in history have ever thrived without parties developing into effective advocates (articulation function) and compromisers (aggregation function) of interests and ideas. Romanian politicians are more interested in patronage and foreign aid than in building grassroots organizations and serving the public good (as opposed to "the nation"). Symbolically, the Romanian parliament is architecturally designed to avoid deliberation and compromise. Instead of putting government and opposition on opposite sides, Romania's parliament faces the podium from a theater-type audience, ready to be lectured to, rather than deliberating with each other. The parties themselves have often been dominated by a single personality. The sultanistic leader keeps the loyalty of followers, but not through a common ideology—most of the Romanian political class was socialized under Communism and seems to lack genuine convictions. Instead, the parties, whether dominated by a leader or not, are mostly machines for obtaining patronage. Furthermore, illicit corruption is rarely prosecuted, even when it occasionally does become a public scandal. The West expects legitimate political competition, meaning real alternatives based on real choices, rather than pseudo-ideological differences that amount to a cover for patrimonial debts. Historically, party systems began to reflect the composition of the electorate as the latter broadened.[59] Even if Romania had the largest Communist party membership at over four million, there were still three times as many adults who were not party members. Some of them should have emerged by now as party activists.

As most of political society came from the *nomenklatura*, Romania's great disability is the absence of a dissident-oriented party like Bulgaria's UDF and a real left-center or leftist party with ideological views. Compare this to Poland and Hungary where former dissidents and trade unionists formed the initial opposition to Communism. Most of Romania's few "dissidents" stayed out of politics as parties were formed, or chose to ally, with a host of dubious characters with few liberal convictions. More than any former Communist country aside from the former Soviet Union, Romania's politics is dominated by politicians who were socialized by the Commmunist Youth Organization (UTC), where convictions were overshadowed by the desire for personal enrichment and advancement, creating an ideal political culture of patrimonialism, personalism and corruption. Only in a political society of UTC hegemony could liberal octogenarians with distinguished prewar political records, who advocate accountability and monarchy, the constitutional form of government associated with the most stable democracies of Europe, be regarded universally by elites as out of touch. The UTC hegemony has so afflicted the "historical parties" that it has become ludicrous any longer to refer to them as such. The historical liberals were quickly shunted aside by the post-Communist oligarchs like Dinu Patriciu, whose ill-gotten, instant fortunes made the old-time liberals irrelevant only two years into the post-Communist regime.

For the National Peasants, it took longer for the party of Maniu, Mihalache and Coposu to be overcome by ex-Communist opportunists interested in power and patronage. Soon after Coposu's death, they helped destroy the unity behind the principles upon which the previous, "historical" party had stood. It is no wonder that the opposition government under Constantinescu was unable to enact any significant privatization of the large-scale behemoth firms. They had the same self-interest in preventing privatization as the "left-wing" PDSR of Iliescu, seeking employment and contractual patronage, subsidies, and world-class salaries for cronies. The fragmented party system results from the Liberal and Peasant parties being discredited after their economic failures. Paradoxically, the middle class does not support the Liberals, and peasants do not support the Peasants. Historically, these parties have represented elites more than masses, and little has changed in this regard in their post-Communist manifestations.

Oligarchic capitalism has made converts of all the former UTC activists. They found a home under various party label fronts for their economic pursuits. The corruption and lack of accountability is common to the entire Romanian political spectrum because they all joined Communism for reasons of personal advancement alone and treated the state as their own patrimony—and they still do. Who was shocked when the Liberal Party made overtures to the splinter Aliance for Romania party from the PDSR, since both party leaders came from the Communist security or party apparatus? The lack of a real opposition in Romania makes it difficult to meet expectations of democracy. Even the hegemonic party systems of East Asia (Japan, Korea, Taiwan) had oppositions drawing from different social bases and more credible ideological differences.

When Constantinescu came to power in 1997, he was a politician with less Communist socialization, and with inferior credentials, he was unable to assert his authority over the untamable. After he chose not to compete in the 2000 presidential elections out of frustration, the four leading candidates,[60] Iliescu, Mugur Isărescu, Teodor Stolojan, and Corneliu Vadim Tudor, all overshadowed the bases of parties that were nominally in charge of their candidacies. Stolojan and Isărescu were technocrats with impeccable Communist credentials: Stolojan was one of Ceauşescu's budgetary advisers. Isărescu would be considered a failure in many countries, though diplomats speak highly of his record. As Central Bank President, he presided over the monetization of the currency, the insufficient regulation of banking, and watched an average of 87 percent annual inflation between 1990 and 1998. The inflation rate of 48.7 percent in 1998 was the highest of the former Communist countries.[61] Yet, he was promoted to prime minister, decided to run for president, even though the EU and the World Bank had questioned his claim that an economic recovery had finally emerged in 2000. Iliescu and Tudor, both sultans, closely control their respective parties with patrimonial resources and through extant Communist Party connections. Thus, Romania lacks the type of institutions and parties which could transcend its historical lack of democratic leaders, models and structures. This lack of ideology is reinforced by the historical absence of genuine leftist politics. Aside from the brief honeymoon with Communism among certain underclasses in the mid-1940s, which resulted from repression, electoral fraud, and opportunism, Romania has had a "natural" void of political forces emphasizing help to the poor. This is a project notably lacking in the "leftist" discourse of the PDSR, which is more focused on boosting national prestige and in aggrandizing personal power in practice. The underclasses do not expect, for reasons of historical negligence, to be helped, but it does isolate the political class from society.

A few parties keep disappearing and reappearing in new form. Romania was the only East European country where historical parties were all revived after Communism, but the liberals have regenerated many different faces. The Social Democrats and Peasants kept their pre-Communist identity until the older generation started passing from the scene after 1996 and are sadly following the patrimonial, corrupt, and ideology-less greed of their liberal counterparts. Fragmentation, defection, excessive personalism, and massive corruption debilitate the development of an accountable and dynamic political society. Now, however, the party system is paradoxically less stable as cleavages have segmented. The explanation for this atypical pattern is that the parties do not constitute a system based on ideology. State security forces are still active in politics, even after the defeat of the Iliescu forces. Greater Romania, which sometimes favors military rule, has grown in popularity and gained additional leaders (Funar, Cozma, and Ilaşcu). The threat from the radical right constitutes the greatest danger to Romanian democracy,[62] as well as from the pressure from economic stagnation. The parties are not yet distinct ideologically, while electoral competition remains a contest of personalities. Thus, campaign issues involve frequently repeated, but still unsubstantiated, charges, such as allusions to Petre Roman's purported relationship to the miners and the *Securitate* in the paramilitary repressions of 1990. Without much monitoring from an autonomous public opinion or political pacting to establish a consensus on the rules of democracy, the parties routinely ignore the democratic spirit of compromise on which parliamentary politics depend. Rival factions emerge from patronage, not ideology. The Democratic Convention lost the participation of the National Liberal Party, creating a weak coalition for the 2000 elections. The Liberals, in turn, refused an alliance with the Social Democratic party, Alliance for Romania (ApR), but maintained its relationship with the Communist intellectuals associated with the Communist Party school, who were linked to former Prime Minister Teodor Stolojan. Three social democratic parties competed in 2000, but only the PDSR entered parliament. The absence of pacting among allies, as well as between government and opposition, has undermined constitutional clarity and stability while encouraging more party factions and splinter groups. Meanwhile, the lead, FSN/FDSN/PDSR/PDR party of the past decade, while divided between older dinosaurs and younger reformers, remains a power party, more interested in power and patronage and adopting the party line as a modus operandi than in ideology and policy. Deference to Iliescu has kept the party coherent, a short-term strength that augurs conflict whenever the inevitable succession crisis emerges.

The electoral legitimization of the anti-system, Greater Romania Party and its leader Corneliu Vadim Tudor[63] in the 2000 elections has not yet heralded a democratic breakdown, but does reflect erosion and decay. Tudor had already been a Senate Vice President during Iliescu's second presidential term (1993–1994). Now, the position is filled by another bigot, "historian" Gheorge Buzatu. Anti-system parties in France and Italy, once enjoying support from a third of their electorates, were converted to democratic capitalism by the 1980s. The rough equivalent, radical right parties, abound in post-Communist Europe, but in few countries are they so clearly fascist as in Romania, exploiting, rather than rejecting, radical politics and ideological polarization. Without the hope that the Marshall Plan engendered, Romanian moderate parties have less and less time to cooperate and end economic travail and official corruption in order to prevent polarization and rule by a neo-fascist, Greater Romania coalition.

However, two significant hypotheses must be included for a complete explanation: infiltration of parties with agents and rigging of elections. As with electoral rigging, which I have detailed elsewhere in this chapter, the prejudice against conspiracy theories in general should not prejudice the analysis of actual problems that require explanation. These operations to place agents with missions to divide and disrupt parties have been low-key and subtle, but make decisive differences on the margin. The destruction of the National Peasant Party and the Civic Alliance Party had been a political project of particular intelligence agencies from the beginning. New recruits, who arrived with much larger sums of money than any of the "old guard" among the Peasant Party and the intellectuals in the Civic Alliance Party, eventually took over. A student of mine pointed the finger at future Prime Minister Radu Vasile as someone who suspiciously took over his party youth group by 1992. The late Corneliu Coposu complained to me in 1993 that he had to control his party to try to prevent various agents under forty-five years old from infiltrating it. Likewise, Emil Constantinescu blamed the former *Securitate* for the demise of his presidency.[64] The activities of Mircea Ionescu-Quintus in the Liberal Party were actually documented as an intelligence operation. Most of the political activities of agents remain hidden because the *Securitate* past of any covert agent of an intelligence agency remains a legally protected secret, including the nondisclosure of his Communist-era *Securitate* file. Parliamentary opposition to mandatory disclosure of *Securitate* files remains robust. Communist-era activities are an open secret for almost all elected parliamentarians (Constantinescu himself was head of the Communist Party organization at the University of Bucharest). Why non-*Securitate*, Communist activities are considered always blameless is indefensible.

As of January 2004, there were still no formal voter lists to verify or modernize voting systems. The excuse that Romania had limited experience in competitive elections should no longer be valid; yet the political, journalistic, and intellectual communities ignore these aberrations. A few scholars, convinced of Romania's uniqueness, particularly of the underdevelopment of its peasants, who were exploited for centuries (somehow) in worse fashion than neighboring countries, believe they continue to spoil 6 percent of their ballots. Romanian peasants may in fact be demoralized, inactive, and prone to clientalistic incentives, but this culture is hardly unique to the country. Nor do such traits make them, in effect, stupid. Notwithstanding what the peasantry does (dissemble, defer, or cheat),[65] the country does not utilize standard electoral controls. It is a disgrace that the United States, the EU, and Romania itself tolerate the situation. Why should Romania have in the 1996 and 2000 elections more than six times the average rate of nullifications of ballots of most democratic countries, including Bulgaria or

Hungary? Of course, these are unacceptable irregularities if they merely resulted from incompetence on the part of either voters or electoral administrators. The more probable explanation, given that no other EU candidate country has such spoiled ballot rates, is forgery. Romania is no further ahead in electoral administration now than it was in 1989 or than Russia was then or now. NATO and the EU violate their democratic membership requirements for Romania in tolerating electoral fraud, as recently as in the farcical 2003 constitutional referendum. How could the EU *acquis communitaire* accepted for Romania's legal changes tolerate laws that facilitate electoral irregularities and fraud in every election?

While the possibility of a split in the ruling (thrice renamed) Social Democratic Party (PSD) is a topic of constant speculation, most feel it is unlikely. Even if Iliescu partisans were to divide with those of Prime Minister Năstase after the 2004 elections, the PSD domination over politics could continue. The PSD enjoyed a robust 40 percent approval in polls as of August 2003, which even with the vagaries and unpredictability of every general election, suggests the danger of a hegemonic party system. The International Socialista finally in 2003 accepted PSD as a democratic, center-left party, joining the chorus from Europe and the U.S. opting for the stability of the party's influence over unstable competition in Romanian politics. A danger is that Euro-Atlantic forces will greatly reduce their reformist pressures after 2007. On the other hand, these foreign parties retain many carrots and sticks. They may remain quite suspicious of the PSD, should it not face significant political competition in the 2004 elections, the anticipated parliamentary votes four years later and the presidential vote five years later, as approved in the 18–19 October 2003 plebiscite on constitutional amendments. (It just happened to achieve a few points more than the minimum 50 percent turnout. That such crucial and very complex fundamental laws could be changed via another dubious electoral process, even if at the initiative of the EU, as well as motivated by PSD interests, is disturbing. Unlike in past elections, various domestic observers questioned the credibility of this vote, including both the Pro-Democracy Association and the *Caţavencu* monitoring units, among them.) For example, an NGO, Think Tank Romania, concluded that the referendum violated at least five major laws and called for an investigation to see if the positive result should have been voided if these or other allegations enabled the legal requirement for a 50 percent turnout to be achieved.

In the absence of a non-*nomenklatura* party, other than the new businessmen's party that is barely noticeable in polls or on televised mass media, Romania can best hope for a two and a half party system, with competition between a united Democrat and Liberal Party and the ruling PSD. Greater Romania would wait in the wings, ready to enter power should the economy ever falter. One task of the quasi-democratic opposition, currently led by

Stolojan of the National Liberals and Băsescu of the Democrats, would be to capture the center-right of the political spectrum by attempting to pick up the center-right and rightwing voters who supported the National Peasants. If the latter do not revive, as current polls suggest, this would be a plausible scenario—except that ideological differences in Romania are widely understood as superficial and cover for the pursuit of interests.

CIVIL SOCIETY

Romania's relatively inactive, and highly uncivil, civil society has been largely static in political participation, with cultural continuities maintaining elite deference and shrill nationalism. Evaluating the state of Romanian civil society involves recognition of the huge distances from whence it came and must still travel. Romania has in some ways advanced further than any other state in southeast Europe, considering the extent of *Securitate* and Ceaușescu repression, which had flattened civil society. The country has developed a private sector with many for-profit NGOs. Second, Romania's human rights record has advanced enormously, even though there are violations. By 2001, Freedom House actually rated Romania a 2 out of 7 on both political and civil rights (1 is best). Bulgaria, curiously, received a slightly worse 2 and 3. This means that the Romanian press is mostly free, though subject to legal intimidation of journalists and that associations can freely form, though the influence of the Communist networks still remains dominant. The ratings do not account for extremists inside and outside of the state, nor for the lack of economic reform, which postpones a day of reckoning with structural uncompetitiveness. Third, Romania has taken its human rights obligations in a formal and legalistic way more seriously than most countries in its reports to the UN Human Rights Committee in New York and in its efforts to improve ethnic relations to the Council of Europe. As a consequence, there has been some training in nondiscriminatory, multiethnic policing, criminal law reform, and human rights protections. While state-sponsored political violence is now rare, surveillance violating privacy remains subtle. However, if efforts to institutionalize these reforms continues to improve, then civil society associations which are more independent of the state and foreign aid can emerge. Until that time, Romania has the business-oriented civil society of Adam Smith rather than the pluralist models of de Tocqueville or Madison.

While there is a plethora of nominal NGOs, there is a lack of vibrant ones. One study found that only 11 percent of the population were even members of any association.[66] Romanian inferiority complexes stimulate erroneous, heinous, but oft-stated convictions that "Europeans regard us as Gypsies."

Yet, deep societal changes have occurred. Demographically, it has gone from the pro-natalist policy of Ceaușescu to the highest abortion rate, and one of the highest emigration rates, in the world for a country at peace. While this is a regional trend and will not be permanent, Romania's particularly acute emigration to the West and greater economic difficulties mean that reproduction rates will likely remain among the lowest in a very low region.

Intellectuals

Romania suffers from a pathology of self-deceiving or prevaricating elites, whose discourse and thoughts have been: "We all resisted; we all suffered; we are all dissidents." Such a comment could only make sense in a society which had only a handful of dissidents after the first-phase of Communist consolidation because, in part, the sultanistic culture exposed everyone to the risk of arbitrary despotism. In the post-Communist era, the attempts to establish new networks of patrons have been built on the Communist era networks, as in most post-Communist regimes, but this has meant that Romania lacks true anti-Communist networks forming the opposition. Everyone is compromised, and the ex-Communist activists can thus convince themselves that they should not be singled out for "retribution" and should jointly keep quiet about their pasts, except for the occasional attack on someone's KGB or politburo ancestry.

Under Communism, there was almost no tradition of dissidence or *samizdat*. Intellectuals were privileged tools of the state. Describing the situation in Romania in the 1960s, Joseph Rothschild writes, "The Romanian intelligentsia lacks the traditional aura of being deemed the conscience of the nation that is borne by the Polish and Hungarian intelligentsias, and it has remained rather aloof from the grievances of the peasants and workers, and the Churches (again in contrast to Poland) are weak and disorganized."[67] Mihail Sebastian's *Diary*[68] eerily portrays not only the Nazification of the Romanian intelligentsia and society, but also the absence of self-criticism characteristic of Romanian society then and today. In the name of Romanian nationhood and intellectual open-minded relativity, a deconstructed amorality remains in vogue in Romania (and the West), which has prevented the "catharsis," to use Manea's phrase, that Romania desperately needs to come to terms with its past and present. Democratic opposition intellectuals, polarized over Romania's interwar and wartime legacy, instead languish in personalized polemics and ad hominem attacks. George Voicu's cultural explanation of Romanian intellectual denial of anti-Semitism and state and societal crimes committed under the Iron Guard and Antonescul[69] is central to understanding the *current* intellectual and political denial of any guilt on the part of the entire political class for the crimes committed under Communism. That the U.S. South has its Confederate flag and Spain its Franco foundation indicates a common tendency, but is no excuse for glorifying a dictator and creating nostalgia for a shameful period of Romania history, notwithstanding Antonescu's supposedly noble attempt to stop the installation of Communism. Intellectuals hold the political class as guiltless, which has legitimated the political party system, which has excluded anyone over forty and under eighty who was not active in Communist youth recruitment. In other words, mass denial by politicians and intellectuals of any responsibility for and remorse about the crimes of the Communist system has consolidated a political system based on exclusion and prevarication. Only the threat of Vadim Tudor unites the intellectuals against others, but not in favor of a self-analysis, resulting in the pseudo-liberalism that is a cover for corrupt auto-privatization, or a pseudo Christian Democracy which encourages official Orthodoxy and nepotism, or pseudo social-democracy which exploits Communist connections and networks as the basis for decision-making coalitions.

Particularly troubling for democratization is the anti-intellectual, collective amnesia or distorted memory of the events associated with World War II and Communism. Intellectual discourse usually focuses on the loss of territory and not on the affinity for Nazi fascism, which occurs not only among rightist movements but also in civil society. In 2000 a cultural foundation, *Buna Vestire*, named after the most important *Legionari* newspaper, published a dictionary of intellectuals, generals, and leaders who supported the Iron Guard movement, without any corresponding indignation by mainstream intellectuals at the effort of glorification of those who were often imprisoned for murder, not only of their adversaries, but among their fellow travelers, following ideological disputes. The ephemeral and ignominious *Legionari* government existed from September 1940 to January 1941. Throughout the 1990s, there was no acknowledgment of, let alone shame for, the Romanian genocide of the Jews and Roma. Many ethnic Romanians suffered injustices, both during World War II and under Communism, such as deportation, death on the site of the Danube canal construction, or even imprisonment in the *Gulag*. The "*Gulag* vs. Holocaust" question of who suffered more is irrelevant. Romania needs to come to terms with the ignominy of its dictators King Carol II and Marshal Ion Antonescu. Antonescu, in particular, whatever his merits as an anti-Soviet, Romanian nationalist, is not an apt model for a democracy. The Romanian state should not be glorifying his image on mass media and with statues and streets named after him.[70] A first step was President Iliescu's 9 May 2001 belated tribute to King Michael, who ended the Nazi alliance. However, only four months before, on the sixtieth anniversary of the Bucharest pogrom, which killed 120 Jews, President Iliescu had again denied the Romanian role in the Holocaust by claiming that the pogrom was exceptional. While Hungary participated in the Holocaust during the Arrow Cross period, as well as fought with the Nazis, its regime does not glorify the Arrow Cross the way Romania does Antonescu. Antonescu should be remembered both for what he did and failed to do in Romania's genocidal participation in Operation Barbarossa, which helped to start the Holocaust, as well as for what he did to stop deportations to Auschwitz after Stalingrad. Hitler did not require mass murder *because there was not a single recorded case of anyone punished by the Nazis for refusing to commit war crimes or crimes against humanity.* Antonescu was actually less evil than Hitler, Corneliu Codreanu, or Horia Sima in that his evil, as with some of those prosecuted under the Tokyo War Tribunal, was as much from acts of omission as presumed commission. However, Antonescu had command responsibility for the genocide of at least 100,000 Jews and 20,000 Roma and probably more than double that.[71] Of relevance for the twenty-first century as well, Antonescu opposed democracy.

At the core of the ongoing controversies over the legacy of World War II dictator Ion Antonescu is the notion of national values, symbols, mythologies, and vision for the future. Many Romanian intellectuals admire him openly or fail to condemn his errors.[72] Romanian television documentaries, politicians' speeches, and history textbooks have still not blamed him for helping Hitler start the Holocaust in Europe, nor for committing aggression against the Soviet Union east of Bessarabia in a losing military campaign which cost the lives of hundreds of thousands of Romanian troops. Antonescu epitomizes the continuity of fascist, nationalist, anti-Semitic, anti-Western, and anti-legal approaches to politics. The costs of submitting to Hitler's project ultimately exceeded the benefits to Romania.

Though perhaps the simplest of democratic freedoms to establish, by restraining the government from censorship and repression, civil society has enjoyed freedom to criticize and associate. However, even the Constantinescu regime was marked by the arrests of journalists and intelligence agency intimidation of newspapers. Greater openness has included the unfortunate freedom to vilify someone in print or speech based on petty ethnic or political intolerance without the discipline of factual accuracy. As Peter Gross explains, the law on defamation was used extensively in the latter 1990s, based on article 238, as well as 205 and 206 of the Penal Code, along with Article 31, paragraph 4 of the constitution, which requires the media to provide correct information to the public. While much more competition exists in broadcast media, state broadcasts are still dominated by the presidency. As a result, in the first two comparative evaluations of 166 countries by the Paris-based Reporters without Borders, Romania ranked 45th in 2002 and fell to 59th place in 2003. In 2003, three journalists were physically assaulted for investigating corruption in the PSD party. Robert Menard, General Secretary of Reporters without Borders, noted that the ruling party knows exactly who are committing these violent human rights violations, differentiating the situation in many countries with intimidation of journalists, which occur from armed groups outside the regime. Therefore, he concluded, "The situation in Romania is particularly worrying us. I would say that it is the only country (among other EU candidates) in Europe where there are such serious problems with freedom of expression."

Ethnic Relations

The main legal reforms have been President Iliescu's 1991 Declaration on Minority rights and subsequent laws prohibiting hate speech and incitement to violence, according to conventional human rights standards.[73] Romania went forward in de jure terms by banning racial, class-based, or religious hatred in the Law no. 41/17 June 1994 regulating state broadcasting. However, very few, if any, consequences have resulted from this law, as hateful or prejudicial statements and attitudes remain common. The Romanian Constitution also theoretically protects cultural, linguistic, and religious identities and practices, as well as bans discrimination on the basis of race and ethnicity. However, most politicians, parties, newspapers, and even broadcast media who have engaged in illegal "hate speech" have rarely, if ever, been prosecuted—in stark contrast to the rigorous enforcement in the Bonn republic, which first institutionalized hate speech proscriptions. Only a few investigations by the Department for the Protection of National Minorities occurred. Broadcast licenses should be revoked for offending media outlets if civil society hostility is ever to be mitigated. Another threat in the 2004 elections is the proposal to utilize only majoritarian elections with single-member districts. This would end the proportional election system which has provided the ethnic Hungarians with legislative and cabinet representation. Most of the UDMR's elected officials cannot win outside of a few majority, ethnic Hungarian areas. The issue is dangerous.

While the Constantinescu presidency sought to coordinate policies affecting the Roma among the ministries, no special advisor on Roma policies was ever appointed. In its evaluation of Romania, the expert committee of the Convention against Racial Discrimination concluded that Romania's laws still "do not conform to the provisions of Article 2 (1)(d) of the Convention against Racial Discrimination (CERD)," and complained about "persistent xenophobic attitudes" in the country. Racist attitudes toward the Roma, dating to the Romanian provincial slave-owning ideology, is ubiquitous in both Romanian and expatriate media[74] and society. Hopefully, the efforts begun in late 2000 by the Project on Ethnic Relations to encourage an electoral coalition between the UDMR ethnic Hungarian Party and Roma parties in future elections might produce effective pressure.

The creation of Prime Minister Năstase, the National Council to Prevent Discrimination will likely help build a firm norm against unjust discrimination. How it relates to the other government initiatives is somewhat unclear. However, Romania was the first of the ten EU candidate countries to empower such a government agency with sanctions to punish discrimination against seventeen categories of people, including HIV positive individuals, religious minorities, and women. Yet, neither a Hungarian nor a Roma representative was named to the seven-member Council board, which sanctions those who discriminate, even though those two groups represent a fifth of the country's population. In an August 2003 interview, the Council's chair asserted that he did not feel there was any necessary need for representation of either group on his board.

Freedom of Religion

The final act of the Congress of Paris, which ended the Crimean War (1854–1856), guaranteed freedom of religion in Wallachia and Moldavia, then part of the Ottoman Empire. It was not long before the provinces comprised independent Romania. It was perhaps not long enough to institutionalize deep habits of religious tolerance. There are now approximately 18.9 million Orthodox, 2.8 million Catholic, including both Roman and Uniate/Greek rites, 900,000 Hungarian reformists, 325,000 Baptist and Pentecostal adherents and 300,000 members of other faiths alongside 56,000 Muslims.[75] The superficial commitment to liberal democracy by the Church leaders appears more opportunistic than sincere. Most threatening is the Orthodox Church's apparent embrace of nationalist policies, as well as its efforts to prevent legislation permitting freedom of religion for other denominations and ecumenical associations. The Orthodox Church could enjoy a privileged position without encroaching on religious human rights, such as with the established Church of England. For the moment, the line across which the government and that Church manage each others' affairs has not been crossed. Without clear guidelines, the Ministry of Cults (the derogatory word still used since Communism) has discriminated against Jehovah's Witnesses, which is not recognized as a legitimate religious group. The Romanian Orthodox Church has assumed the junior partner status to the government, having grown in importance, as political leaders exploit rising religiosity in the wake of Communism's demise. As in Russia, the efforts to defeat legal reforms on ecumenical tolerance, to provide advantages to the Orthodox Church, and to discriminate against other religions have been consistent and usually successful. Rarely do such efforts generate any publicity or reaction, creating an environment of intolerance that resembles another EU member, Greece.

RULE OF LAW

As students of international relations like to put the Sherlock Holmes question about the three-legged dog and the League of Nations, what is amazing is that rule of law reform can "walk" at all. Given Romania's lack of interest in legal and judicial reform, why has there been so much of it, even though it still falls short of liberal standards? In developing a democratic state, the Iliescu and Constantinescu administrations have focused on changes in laws, institutions, and practices, though they are more superficial than what Western countries want. In return for these "attempted" reforms, they have expected to obtain Western aid and investment, rather than making the legal system function, the sine qua non for economic recovery and democratic consolidation. Romania avoided Russia's fast-track economic reform plans without legal reform; instead, Romania opted for "slow-track" reform. Of the two, Romania may be better off because its piecemeal, incremental approach, if the public is involved, will provide more transparency, accountability, and evolution of its domestic legal process. In international law, Romania has supported peacekeeping activities in the former Yugoslavia and elsewhere, while also violating the UN embargo of Yugoslavia.[76] Romania may culturally have a rule-oriented society, as a rational way of dealing with uncertainty, but it does not have confidence in its dysfunctional judicial institutions. Moreover, deliberate policies have been instituted that undermine the independence, impartiality, and competence of lawyers and judges, which harms constitutional and judicial procedures.

"The scandal is not what is illegal, but what is legal." Legality can be a nebulous concept for a host of acts that are not considered by a civil law system in which judges are not permitted to create law by establishing precedents, and scholars have not yet interpreted these new legal regimes. Hosts of businesses and real property were transferred to *nomenklatura* prior to 1995, when the first reform law on the judiciary was established. Virtually any grand act(s) of theft, embezzlement, extortion, and the like had not been explicitly forbidden and to criminalize past acts would constitute ex post facto laws, under concepts of legal positivism.

The obfuscation of de jure processes with many subsequent emergency ordinances and implementing regulations has made de facto implementation of the rule of law difficult. Judges and lawyers have interpreted the conflicting rules in almost any fashion. The implementing rules, usually promulgated by particular government ministries, are often inconsistent with the original purposes of the newly enacted laws or ordinances. For example, sometimes government agencies hire representatives from regulated special interests to assist in the drafting of implementation rules, which often leads to complex modifications of enacted laws. Lawyers of good faith could come to many different interpretations of such secondary and tertiary rules because they have to sift through about a dozen statutes, promulgated regulations, and implementing rules, adding to the ambiguity, rather than clarification, of existing laws. Such modifications amount to dissimulation by regimes more interested in exploiting than in simplifying the development of rule of law processes.

To the Anglo American, accustomed to neutral judges overseeing adversarial trials based on precedent-binding common law, this activity sounds quite scandalous. To a French person, which also has civil servants acting as judges in a civil law tradition used in inquisitorial trials, where judges act like prosecutors, Romania's system seems less untoward. Indeed, the criteria applied to Romania, de jure would be, indeed is, quite acceptable in France, in the same way that the lack of prosecutorial independence in the U.K. might seem unethical to someone from the U.S. Yet, France and the U.S. have legal cultures where the integrity of judges, prosecutors, and lawyers are, at least comparatively speaking, presumed to be beyond reproach. However, Romania's lack of a credible legal track record, along with ample suspicion of insider deals, especially in important cases, means that structures susceptible to conflicts of interest are presumed to cause them. We begin with an analysis of constitutional issues, followed by the administration of justice.

Constitutional Issues

While accordance with constitutional norms is at the heart of the effort to promote the rule of law, Romania's Constitutional Court does show improving signs of independence along democratic lines. While there is a strong tendency not to strike down many laws, because that would require reversing the initial reviews on constitutionality to which all new laws must be subjected, the court can and does take challenges from court cases all the time to consider the merits of the challenges. In the Romanian system, such challenges come immediately and only in terms of the particular constitutional issue, not the overall case. Thus, the constitutional court is very burdened with many reviews.

In addition, Romania does have some important legal contributions. First, de jure changes may lead to de facto changes in practice, if there is enough pressure to monitor legal practices. Romania's civil society may be weak, but it does have the ability to mobilize attention from the opposition and the international community. The significant U.S. foreign aid, over $300 million since 1990 (not including military assistance), ought to be leveraged so that elected parties remain responsive to improvements in judicial administration and for combating corruption.

Romania's constitution makes all provisions of international law, most significantly the European Convention on Human Rights, as self-executing in Romanian law. (This is a position that is not accepted in U.S. law.) As a result, the European Court of Human Rights has held that Romania must implement that convention and strike down practices inconsistent with that convention. The European Court has ordered Romania to return homes confiscated under Communism, to pay compensation for homes destroyed under Communism, and to empower judges, not prosecutors, with monitoring detention of those arrested after seventy-two hours.

There have been about a dozen constitutional crises, which were always resolved, by Iliescu and Constantinescu alike, by the assertion of presidential power, instead of legal authority asserted by an independent and credible judiciary. These unconstitutional actions include the miners' attacks on civilians and the rightist attacks on the police station during the University Square protests in June 1990; the miners' 1991 attack on civilians and against the Petre Roman government; the bogus 1991 and 2003 constitutional plebiscites; the 1992 stolen parliamentary election; the 1998 forced resignation of Prime Minister Victor Ciorbea; the January 1999 miners' protests attempting to overthrow the Vasile government; and the December 1999 forced resignation of Prime Minister Vasile. The failure to implement rule of law is epitomized by President Constantinescu's inability to prosecute Virgil Măgureanu and other intelligence officials responsible for fraud in the 1990, 1992, and 1996 elections, as well as other forms of massive corruption. Despite his efforts to end impunity, Constantinescu called it "unbelievable" that in 1997 only seven big corruption cases were tried by the courts. Yet in a July 1996 interview, Constantinescu told me he believed the 1992 parliamentary elections were stolen.

More generally, there have been no truth commissions about the Communist period; only a few, selected top Ceauşescu officials have been prosecuted and imprisoned. This was less in pursuit of justice (most were released from prison after a year or two) or even retribution than as a signal to the right that attempts to topple the regime, such as by those who stormed police headquarters in June 1990, would not be tolerated. The lack of such a commission is not unusual in the former Soviet Union and most of the Balkans, but is below standard for East Central Europe and Bulgaria, which have had active lustration laws. While Romania's record on human rights is its strongest achievement, with relatively free speech and association and no political prisoners, both sides still attempt to use the state to constrain the opposition, which in turn is becoming, but is still not yet, loyal to the Constitution. On a formal level, Romania's protection of political and civil rights[77] was ranked sixth in 1999–2000 by Freedom House among post-Communist states.[78]

In terms of separation of powers, Romanian constitutional practices lack clear guidelines demarcating authority between executive and judicial, and executive and legislative authority. The two main sources of ambiguity come from the semipresidential constitution, which creates two leaders of the country and permits the practice of issuing decrees ("ordinances") when the parliament is in recess. Finally, subsequent legislative ratification of both types of ordinances is not necessary where the government decides that the enabling legislation does not mandate such ratification. However, the Constitutional Court did rule that emergency decrees cannot be issued unless a valid emergency has been demonstrated to the court's satisfaction. In his first year, Constantinescu followed Iliescu's pattern of excessive promulgation of decrees by issuing some 500 of his own, followed by more than 200 ordinances in 1998, primarily in economic reform. This supplanting of the policy prerogative of the legislature caused piecemeal reform without large-scale privatization.

Three other anomalous processes have been used by both Iliescu and Constantinescu. The first is based on Article 113 of the Constitution, which permits the government "to take responsibility" for legislation. Whatever it proposes is enacted as law, with the risk that the opposition has three days to file a no-confidence motion, which would force the government to resign if it passes. The second process is the "emergency ruling," which is presented as a package and cannot be modified by parliament, except to accept or reject everything. This approach prevents amendments, which can incorporate the most vital interests of oppositions and minorities. The third approach has been for the president to issue decrees when the legislature is not in session. The claim has been made that no subsequent, authorizing vote by parliament is necessary unless mandated by explicit, prior legislation. When used excessively, these three approaches to legislation are at the margins of democratic norms. Iliescu, through his appointment of prefects, dismissed hundreds of elected officials, including 133 elected mayors.[79] These dismissals, especially where no alleged illegality has occurred, goes further beyond the bounds of democratic administration. Finally, since 2001 Iliescu has persuaded many in the opposition to join the PSD, making a mockery of the collective party responsibility norm of democratic regimes.

Two opposing, normative views exist on civil-military relations. One, orthodox ideal-type, argued by Alfred Stepan, Samuel P. Huntington, and

Morris Janowitz, holds that civilian supremacy is the desired form of control, with the military consulted on strategy, but not making policy. Another view, held by Defense Minister Ioan Mircea Paşcu, Head of the National Security Department Ioan Talpeş, Larry Watts, and Daniel Nelson, argues for greater consultation and implicit military vetoes over policy during a transition when civilians lack sufficient military knowledge.[80] The latter group finds Romanian civil-military relations wanting because of civilian politicization (in attempting to assert civilian control) of the military.[81] Romania's practice of civilian deference to the military accrued stability at the cost of distorting democratization by endowing authoritarian military prerogatives at consultation with and veto over civilians. Thus, the army threatened to mutiny when ordered by Constantinescu to arrest the miners in January 1999.

Among the reforms of intelligence agencies that need to be enacted or controlled legislatively: First, the two parliamentary commissions that supervise the Romanian Information Service (SRI), especially in the lower house, ought to sanction the SRI with budgetary reductions if it refuses to routinely provide information relevant to national security, not just in its annual report. Otherwise, the SRI will still amount to a secret police, albeit one that has for now desisted from extensive abuses. Second, the SRI, as with the FBI or the U.S. Justice Department, should be subordinated to the Justice Minister (as was the interwar, Romania Information Service). Third, the SRI Director and subcabinet ought to be directed by a more prestigious individual shrewdly committed to its civilianization. Finally, the *Securitate* past of all parliamentary and cabinet officials should be revealed by the CNSAS, including the replacement of current intelligence officers from civilian occupations outside of intelligence roles, as normally understood, and not in politics.

Administration of Justice

Justice reform in Romania recently has been an excellent case study of the dynamics of a resistant regime that, against its will, reluctantly attempts some liberalizing changes under foreign pressure. As a result of the requirements for European integration, Romania has undertaken various legislative reforms, which are legally incorporated as *acquis communitaire*, which all EU member states and candidate countries must enact across a range of policy sectors and institutions. These sectors encompass most areas of governance, though the topic where the European Commission had found Romania's reform process most wanting, as of 2002, had been judicial reform. Operationally, the process of European integration theoretically makes EU law self-executing; that is, automatically incorporated into Romanian law, even without enabling legislation. In practice, these EU-based treaties and judicial and administrative decisions have not been self-executing and are only binding after explicit legislation and administrative promulgation of their implementation rules. This delays and impedes the achievement of EU norms in practice. Moreover, since late 2002 it has been perceived that Romania will likely gain entry to the EU in 2007, suggesting that Romania will not be as pressured to continue its reform as the price of EU admission. On the other hand, European monitoring processes are quite intense and amount to a much stronger international regime than is typically the case. Not only is entry into the EU not guaranteed, but many incentives will still exist after EU membership might be earned, including annual budget allocations, EU judicial checks, as well as reputation and prestige within the organization, which would keep the pressure on Romania to abide by EU standards.

Some of the effort on legal reform has been on major amendments to the main civil, criminal, and administrative codes, which unlike most laws, cannot be subsequently altered in any fundamental way through administrative ordinances or promulgated regulations. Some are also particularly frustrated with the lack of progress because of Romania's likely admission to the EU in 2007.[82] They sense that the regime will continue corruption of elections, patronage, and business.

Among the studies of Romanian judicial reform, the Romanian Academic Society (SAR) has concluded that no progress was made in the year 2002–2003, since its last report in August 2003. The causes of the problem remain the same: lack of political will results in secret deals in parliament to change or delay promised reforms to the EU as well as the lack of implementation of laws that have been changed or already existed.[83] A time-series of poll surveys shows that the judicial system has had the lowest levels of confidence of any public institution. For example, the poll by the Center for Urban and Regional Sociology during July 2002 found that only 3.4 percent of the public felt that "justice served the public interest," whereas 29 percent said not at all, 40 percent said "hardly" and 18.5 percent "to some extent."[84] A July 2003 poll found that 40 percent had concluded that corruption had increased since 2000, and that 35 percent found that it had remained the same.[85] According to SAR, the lack of progress is due to the fact that a hegemonic party system has reemerged since 2000. The ruling PSD party installed a few reformers in key positions reporting to the modernizing Prime Minister, Năstase, but these reformers have not had decisive power. Moreover, their Communist socialization also constrains the extent to which they aspire to real reform. Their interest in clientalistic privilege has trumped concerns for enhancing the rule of law.

The Open Society Institute (OSI) shares SAR's frustrations and assigns blame primarily to the Ministry of Justice's control over the activities of judges and prosecutors.[86] One source of difficulty is the Superior Council of Magistrates, which supervises judges and prosecutors but cannot make any decisions to appoint or discipline judges without the permission of the Justice Ministry and the president. Since only Supreme Court judges have renewable terms and Constitutional courts have single terms, all the country's remaining judges are under the supervision of the Superior Council. In addition, only a few judges have been prosecuted. The OSI, SAR, EU, and numerous think tanks have all repeatedly recommended that judges elect some or all of the representatives to the Council. Yet, this action has not yet been undertaken. The proposal had been made by the Constantinescu presidency's Justice Minister Valeriu Stoica, but the legislature ignored it. Another fundamental problem has been that the Council supervises the activities of both judges and prosecutors, when these functions should be separated.

These policy institutes/think tanks, however, are unofficially sympathetic to the opposition or are at least against the ruling PSD party of Iliescu and Năstase. This means that they have not tried to acknowledge any progress, even if unintended by the government. In particular, the role of foreign pressure from the U.S. and especially from the EU accession process has not been acknowledged, even in terms of identifying de jure changes in the law (even if not implemented in practice or if it is too early to determine whether the new laws are being followed). Certainly, Romania has much further to travel in terms of judicial reform than many other EU candidate countries; and so, its tasks are larger. In terms of de facto charges, Romania has major problems, which the think tanks are correct to identify.

Since the question was first asked in June 1998, justice has ranked as the institution with lowest public confidence ratings, even below the parliament. However, unlike the Bonn Republic, which purged a significant portion of Nazi judges and prosecutors, Romania had no formal purges of judges and lawyers. Some important prosecutors and some judges have left to become higher-paid lawyers. Some of these lawyers in some county court systems routinely petition the chief of the county's judges to have the presiding judges replaced. (Prosecutors are never able to petition to have judges replaced.) Then Justice Minister Stoica, under President Constantinescu, placed judges under the Ministry's authority, where it has remained institutionally. This practice has continued under the current Justice Minister, Mihaela Rodica Stanoiu. The latter has shown no interest in limiting the many attempts at PSD interference in the administration of justice, and has resisted the establishment of a really autonomous Superior Council of the Judiciary to supervise judges and prosecutors. The particular prosecution of Judge Andrea Ciucu of Târgu Mureş, because of her independence from political interference, is unbecoming of a prospective EU member state. The action reportedly enraged the EU Directorate for Enlargement during the summer of 2003. However, Euro-Atlantic security concerns depicted previously have trumped this concern, which the EU has insisted is the least developed of all the sectors that the European Commission has been supervising in Bucharest in the past six years.

The trajectory against reform under Constantinescu turned somewhat toward the rule of law under Iliescu. The main reason is that younger Justice Ministry officials have engaged Brussels with the process of negotiating the mandated legal reforms and with training judges and magistrates. The EU is hoping that these generational investments will pay off in the long run. Romania has accepted the EU accession progress generally and is in the process of implementing the transposition of over 400 pieces of European legislation that were transposed. The EC may be "diplomatic" in its written interpolations with the various Romanian government counterparts, but it does assure that Romania's efforts move in the same categorical directions as the other nine EU candidate countries must move. After 2007, Romania will be required to enact laws strictly in accordance with EU legal requirements and to implement them in practice.

Still, corruption goes back at least to the Pharionites—Greeks in Constantinople who bought their positions and then got them back through various schemes, including taxes before and after the harvest. The causes include a lack of resources for judges, who can be bribed, though the extent of this activity is difficult to know or measure, and, more importantly, the lack of political will. Legal corruption, in particular, means that Romanian leaders are almost never prosecuted for corruption except when visible, such as Ion Stoica's Caritas scheme or Sorin Ovidiu Vântul's investment fund. None of the politicians behind these schemes have ever been linked or prosecuted. Since 1989 no lawyer in Romania has been disbarred! No major political leader, whether in the government or the opposition, has been prosecuted for corruption, and only a few "small fish" have. This is despite the obvious lifestyle improvements (e.g., the prime minister and several of his predecessors all having several foreign houses, even though their official salaries are less than that of senior judges, who earn 5,000 Euros/month). Only the one judge mentioned has been investigated for corruption, and she was a political opponent of the 2003 Năstase government. The new anticorruption courts have been ineffectual, in part for lack of political will but also because evidence of corruption is not found in direct evidence, but rather easily inferred from improbable lifestyle enhancements.

Foreign criticism of Romanian corruption has been mounting from Western governments. At a prominent April 2003 conference, U.S. Ambassador Michael Guest, followed the next day by the head of the American-Romanian Chamber of Conference Obie Moore,[87] blasted the Romanian government for its inaction. Several weeks later, anticorruption legislation was enacted, with the major requirement being the revelation from elected officials whether or not their net wealth exceeded 10,000 Euros, not a meaningful indicator of corruption. Such a law should have required disclosures at the beginning and end of one's term to note any increases. Most politicians conceded that they had more than 10,000 Euros and those who claimed less, such as EU Integration Minister Hildegard Puwak, had transferred their assets to other family members (without paying any gift taxes). She subsequently resigned, but was exonerated, initially at least, of any guilt.

As in the former Communist East, large increases in the number of judges, prosecutors, and lawyers have emerged because of the much greater need for them. Under Communism, the state allowed few if any claims against itself or among private citizens. For example, in 1989, Romania had 1,067 judges and 1,440 prosecutors. A decade later, it had triple that number: 3,479 judges and 2,303 prosecutors. Three appellate courts have been established in Bucharest, Iaşi and Târgu Mureş, and they preside over three levels of courts within each *judet*. Together they heard appeals on over 100,000 of the country's approximate 375,000 criminal cases and 375,000 of Romania's 1,360,000 civil cases annually from 2000–2001. Eighty percent of these appeals were resolved! One could question whether the quality and integrity of case procedures are really respected, but delays have not been a problem.

Administratively, defendants in criminal trials are often poorly defended, and discrimination against Roma is enormous. Judges most often write their decisions by hand and file them in their own cabinets without circulating their opinions. Consequently, it is difficult for well-meaning judges to keep abreast of the law, and easy for judges with bad intentions to ignore it.

A large problem is determining what exactly the law is at any given time. A visit to a lawyer's office reveals that Romania has modern databases available to laptop computers listing each legal topic. What one discovers, as I did with a lawyer, is that any legal topic might be governed by about six basic laws, six emergency ordinances, several more administrative promulgations, and several judicial interpretations. As mentioned above, what is most cynical is the practice of hiring outside "experts" to promulgate implementing regulations ("rules of application"), which serve the experts' interests and contradict the enacted provisions of the legislature. Add to this situation the fact that civil law systems do not have binding precedents, and one realizes that legal interpretation is a dubious activity. For example, Law 14/3/96, a typical law, has eight rules of application and six constitutional court challenges, as of August 2003.

The Peoples' Spokesman (Ombudsman Office) is supposed to be an independent office, but its staff, like most official human rights organizations, has lacked independence and supports the government line on human rights controversies (otherwise, its officers would not be appointed), even if they provide some pressure inside the government to educate and protect human rights. Its most serious deficiency, compared with other government human rights organizations of this type, is the lack of ability to prosecute or litigate cases, which it can only refer to prosecutors.

The most important initiative taken to encourage judicial independence by enacting the principle of the nonremovability of judges. Yet, the executive routinely interferes with judicial decisions. Another disturbing trend has been the controls by the Justice Ministry of prosecutors, magistrates, and judges.[88] Ironically, prior to 1991, the prosecution service was independent, but this was a holdover from Communism, when the prosecutors (mostly men) were more dependent on the regime, though they were more powerful than the judges (mostly women) to whom they handed the criminal files. Since then, the Justice Ministry has managed prosecution, on the theory that prosecutorial autonomy inhibited reform, which was probably initially true. Other undemocratic meddling by the Justice Ministry on behalf of the executive in the judicial branch occurs. The Ministry has also prevented appeals that should occur from autonomous processes.[89] The Ministry also has arrogated to itself the authority to extend pretrial detention, withdraw due process safeguards and extend the pretrial detention period of thirty days when its control is supposed to pass to the judicial branch.

Another concern for judicial independence has been the low salaries of judges, compared with what lawyers can earn in the private sector. Judges do earn more than most government officials, sometimes more than three times as much as top officials, and perhaps they do earn enough that bribes should not tempt. However, given the shortage of qualified judges, their salaries should probably be raised, especially if judges not tainted by Communist track records are to be recruited.

Another important development is the country's commitment to provide free legal aid for criminal cases and even for many civil disputes among non-state actors. This assistance takes the form of two programs, one of which is for people who are not poor but can demonstrate the inability to make a defense or claim. This is an important development for a country of limited resources. In another example, the Romanian chapter of Transparency International lobbied, with the support of the U.S. Embassy, for a freedom of information law. While after one year, at the time of writing, it is too soon to assess how effective the law has been in practice. That the U.S. never had such a law until the mid-1960s, and that it has not always been effectively implemented, suggests that there are some modernizing imperatives at work, as well as remarkable civil society pressure, particularly from the Transparency International of Romania.

One of the areas of law that was most criticized by civil society was the outrageous practices of appeals to nullify the decisions of the highest courts in the country. These "nullifications" were very common and universally condemned as a blatant, politically motivated encroachment of the independence of the judiciary. However, in 2003, under intense criticism, the country removed the possibility of nullifying civil cases. Unfortunately, the practice is maintained in criminal trials. This is combined with the practice of opening politically motivated investigations, such as the current one against Democratic Party leader Băsescu of the opposition.[90]

Changes in civil and criminal procedure, which cannot so easily be modified by regulations, were required by the *acquis communitaire*. Institutions do matter, and the EC has several key priorities in which it has been effective. Other provisions, which are also part of the *acquis*, can be more easily ignored in practice, but are still subject to the emerging debates regarding the EU accession process and democratization more generally. The passage of the criminal procedure rules in parliament in the summer of 2003 was a crucial step forward. Most of these changes will be required throughout the country in 2004, and there is not much room for deviating from these norms on legal grounds. Any deviation, if occurred, in the Supreme or Constitutional Courts, could immediately be appealed to Strasbourg and could be overturned. The 3,500 judges and 2,000 prosecutors in Romania, in addition, will look to the text of this new criminal procedure, and not to the many other sources of legal interpretation, in implementing judgments, handling arrests, making criminal appeals, and so forth. It probably will not be long before Romania's constitutional court or the European Court of Human Rights will strike down nullification of criminal judgments.

While prosecutors and judges are still effectively supervised by the Ministry of Justice, reforms are afoot to assure that the Superior Council of Magistrates will retain control. This will allow judges under suspicion of taking bribes or making erroneous legal applications to be supervised without compromising their integrity. Except for the case of Judge Ciuca, there will not likely be any more cases of investigations or prosecutions of judges for allegedly acting too independent of the regime.

To conclude, then, Romania obviously has far to go before reaching legal credibility. However, few countries in my experience have undertaken such a rapid modernization of its legal practices in such a short time with such initial preparation or political will. The direction is very positive and only a radical change in the political environment is likely to alter this relatively optimistic trajectory in an otherwise illiberal regime.

COMPLETING THE LIBERAL PROJECT

Romania's improvements have perhaps been better than what might have been predicted in 1989. The Western requirements for NATO and EU entry of formal democracy and liberal institutions have impelled institutionalization, albeit *far* short of a liberal democracy. This has been a long route, which could have been interrupted, but which also could have been completed had the first three years of post-Communism not focused on consolidating a Gorbachev type of *pereistroika* with a democratic façade. The initial end to Communism, whether it is called a palace coup or revolution, may have prevented sustained Yugoslav or Moldovan-type violence, which reactionary political and military activists were prepared to implement, even as it prolonged and distorted democratization and marketization. One can call Romania (and to a lesser extent Bulgaria) a "third way" model of post-Communist democratization. Unlike the consolidated democracies of East Central Europe, the former Communist elements began an immediate "social-democratization" of their ideology and lost their control of the post-Communist state. Pacting with the anti-Communist parties that initially came to power limited the democratic development of institutions. However, Romania's transition can be contrasted from most in the former Soviet Union, particularly Russia. In those transitions, anti-system parties are so active as disloyal oppositions, and the European Union so remote an influence[91] that the ruling parties have had an easier time avoiding democratic regime norms. With a disloyal opposition ready to come into power, a host of illiberal acts and policies by the ruling parties of Yeltsin and Putin are tolerated by the West and the Russian establishment.

In Romania, anti-system forces have never achieved power because their electoral base is to a large extent a protest vote, not an ideological core. Furthermore, prior to the late 1990s, there was limited democratic political pacting, where the ruling party of Iliescu sought to limit accountability under the cover of democratic forms of election and governance. Pacts brought anti-system parties into politics through electoral fraud, though never deep into his government. His own party was purged of extremists, but not those who were loyal to his project of semidemocracy. However, since the form of electoral fraud was covert and marginal, rather than blatant and open, it became too risky to rely on double-digit rates of ballot nullifications to stay in power. In isolating the radicals, Iliescu by the mid-1990s began achieving a rapprochement with the West. Later in the decade, instead of pacting with extremist forces, with whom his moderate, pragmatic post-Communist policies were incompatible, Iliescu in loyal opposition signaled that he could deliver on pacts with the European Commission of the EU. While Constantinescu had also promised the West he would reform, he never delivered much and presided over interparty bickering. By the late 1990s, Iliescu purged his then opposition party of disloyal democrats, while belatedly reforming politics through his comparatively reformist premier Năstase. The PSD and Iliescu's 2000 elections, never questioned in legitimacy still suffers continued irregularities, the consequences of which indicate the massive extent of post-totalitarian debris in the current electoral authoritarian regime. It will be interesting to observe the advantages and disadvantages of this staged development of what promised to become an electoral democracy, but whose illiberal elements will long delay democratic consolidation.

An important difference from Russia, where both the radical right and left remain prominent anti-system forces, the post-Ceauşesist forces were more pragmatic and capitalist and have opted to exploit the business advantages and political participation, which Iliescu offered them in the early 1990s.

Generational, political, and cultural changes may or may not mitigate their potency, though they persist as a political and dangerous subculture, waiting for an economic downturn to legitimate their power—which presumably would come through elections. Furthermore, Iliescu, Năstase, and the post-2000 ruling PSD party engaged in some democratic political learning while in the opposition from 1996 to 2000. While it continues illiberal practices and hegemonic recruitment of elected officials with patrimonialism, the country's commitment to democracy should and can be proven with not only new laws, of which Romania is never in short supply, but administrative actions to secure the rule of law.

The key decision was Iliescu's decision to integrate into Europe. This was a major—if strategically motivated—decision that has made Romania particularly interdependent on Western norms. The country is now not only European, but also as much a hybrid political culture of Western and Eastern. His move began with the 1993 Partnership for Peace, the 1995 normalization of relations with Hungary, and the support for the U.S. military attacks in Serbia in 1993 and Iraq in 2003 (though as a crafty opposition politician, Iliescu opposed the Kosovo invasion). This is a somewhat ambivalent leader who told the international press community at a breakfast meeting at Cotroceni Palace in spring 2003, "Capitalism is not so great. You should try socialism, which is a pretty good system." Yet, he made the practical choice to bring the country out of the "glamour" of being the West's favored East bloc country until the late 1980s to just another ex-Communist country attempting to integrate with the West. His motive was presumably because the financial resources, even if not a panacea for the country's development, were sufficient to facilitate the enrichment of a *nomenklatura* already attuned under Communism to the benefits of Western business.

The result has been a political-economic success for the "new class" and a tilt away from Eastern political culture. Still, the lack of effective political competition, both in formal elections and in public debates, has produced parties of interests, not meaningful ideological differences. What counts are the personalities and their access to mass media[92] exposure and patronage, which makes the Communist networks function in a post-Communist context. The oligarchy is in power as a political class. The anti-oligarchy opposition died. To a significant extent, voters punished the Democratic Convention in the 2000 elections after its ineffective leadership, natural disruption and squabbling over the spoils of patronage, and inaccessibility to entrenched Communist networks.

Thus, Romania's democratic transition is not as bad off as Tony Judt portrays, or as pessimistic as the 2001 EU assessment. It is closer to the much improved, 2002 EU assessment a year later, as well as the even more robust evaluations out of Washington, both at Foggy Bottom and the IMF, which led to Romania's eighteen-month Stand-By Arrangement of $76 million through

15 October 2003. To say that Romania is not Tony Judt's basket case is also not to deny that ambiguity characterizes Romanian democratization more than optimism or pessimism, but ambiguity reinforces its likely continued ambivalence, skepticism, and rudderless path. It is ambiguous and lacks direction both because it combines authoritarian and democratic elements and because the hybrid institutions produced have resulted form political pacting with the Euro-Atlantic institutions, not other political parties. Having examined Romania's apparently dire situation, why have there not been worse consequences? Political science suggests at least three theories: relative deprivation, moral economy, and rational choice. Using, rather than testing, these frameworks, we can begin with the idea that expectations in, and of, Romania have been low. While Romania had been going downward during the late 1990s, the protest vote for Greater Romania and Vadim Tudor was not necessarily an endorsement of a rightist or leftist agenda in 2000, any more than it was for conservatism in 1996, or social democracy in 1992. Secondly, the political culture of Romanian society has not been overturned: it is an exemplar of limited social change and disruption at the cost of economic decline. Furthermore, while the country has long lost fear for intellectuals to speak out (and be ignored), the average peasant and worker still fears the retribution, mainly economic, from those who protest openly against any corruption or low wages that they find unacceptable. Finally, in terms of rational choice, the costs of state repression are indeed greater than toleration and the state has done little to halt open opposition, except in the dismal arrests under Constantinescu of journalists reporting on corruption. Consequently, the main reformist pressures will remain from the Euro-Atlantic institutions, and not from the body politic.

The modernization hypothesis is unlikely to be true: this hypothesis holds that Romania will emulate either liberal democratic capitalism or some ill-defined convergence between "Eastern and Western democracy." Wagner's claim of a *Sonderweg* in the case of Romania therefore appears to be well-founded.[93] It captures the special status that Romania holds both in transitology and East European Studies. And in so doing, Romania actually synthesizes the structural and the historical (alleged) properties of this special case into one eye-catching formulation. Western forms of democracy, however superficial and largely demanded from abroad, are still significant and have set Romania on a vector, which is still democratic in trajectory though Eastern in intensity and culture. It resembles the distortions of another quasi-Western society, Brazil, where "rule of law, usable state, and a strong political society" are "problematical," where people felt that the judiciary was for those in power, and the police were not trustworthy, because the poor do not get a fair shake in the judicial system, where police executions of blacks (Roma in Romania) attest to the people's mistrust, and change is unlikely due to the financial pressures.[94] Thus, Romania's problems are structural, but also not uncommon to semidemocracies with highly autonomous states. On the other hand, Romania's additional problem of sultanism means that institution building needs to proceed without excessive reliance on individuals at the top.

Romania's transition, therefore, could go either way, as it is just about where one would expect its transition to be, in light of its low political-economic development and sultanistic-totalitarian regime path. Its most likely future is to muddle through as a semi-democracy. In one way, Romania's *Gestalt* appears unusual among the Third Wave democracies.[95] Romania's liberalization is limited by the politicization of the Orthodox Church, continued state control of state broadcast news, and continued intelligence agency eavesdropping. These negative trends could pose serious obstacles to liberalization at a time of more acute ethnic or partisan polarization. However, under the modified polarity of this regime, where opposition is ignored rather than confronted, despised and subverted, and where oppositions are largely sidelined, as opposed to either explicitly loyal or disloyal, illiberality from Church and intelligence agencies is less significant than the continued delay in establishing democratic institutions, rule of law, tolerating gay and women's rights, permitting an open media without secret infiltration, and preventing future electoral fraud.

Most threatening to its democratization have been the (1) absence of consensus between the government and the opposition on the procedures needed for an elected government, producing a horizontal gap between the political parties and forces; (2) governments unable to generate public policies, which are unduly influenced by post-totalitarian institutions in the secret police instead of the legislative majority and an affiliated executive; (3) permitting in some cases, legal power-sharing with intelligence agencies and its affiliated and legal, private corporations; (4) a huge vertical gap between elites and masses; (5) a huge elite-mass gap, with the latter geographically located in towns created for the Communist factory workers; (6) enormous IMF control over economic policies,[96] which, however rational, inhibit domestic consensus on policy-making procedures; and (7) a closed political society comprised of the same elites as produced by the Communist hierarchy, without mass parties from civil society or intellectuals who visit the peasantry and working classes, except via telephone polls, in order to learn what reforms might undermine the prevailing culture of instrumental cynicism and Communist networks of policy formation and implementation.

With Huntington's two-turnover test having been met in the 2000 election, the chances of democratic breakdown is much lower. However, what type of "democracy with adjectives" Romania will become remains undetermined. There is still enormous power concentrated in business oligarchs, for example, decentralizing power from the unitary state, but also offering nontransparent power through covert financial donations from these oligarchs to the parties. Romania must make a choice, as Dan Pavel suggests, between a "mafia state" and democratic consolidation.

To conclude, here are a few parting tasks for Romania's ruling party, opposition, and civil society to conduct in order to consolidate democracy:

- Mitigate rhetoric about "Old" and "New Europe" rather than searching to face one direction or the other, which deepens dependency and polarization and may jeopardize chances for EU admission.
- Fulfill the promises to NATO and the EU of democratization, particularly involving the rule of law rather than of personal relations. Remain realistic about the benefits of NATO and EU membership, which will prove arduous before the benefits become obvious.
- Build memorials to victims, rather than to victors cum tyrants.
- Pact a working consensus—reaffirming leaders within coalitions, among parties, and especially between the prime minister and the president, who put the country's interests and respect for the law above those of individuals.
- Crack down on corruption, particularly organizations inside or linked to intelligence agencies and the army who dominate procurement, exports of excess inventory, smuggling, and official and unofficial subsidies. The opposition should take on democratic tasks instead of forming such unseemly coalitions of PD, PNL, and PRM opposing government reforms on corruption, as in March 2003.
- Establish a permanent electoral commission to provide immediately verifiable, precinct-by-precinct election returns, instead of aggregating them by county in a nontransparent manner.
- Proceed with privatization and end subsidies of large state enterprises, no matter how complicated or difficult. Negotiate a social compact with trade unions to assure that restructuring of the economy can proceed in an effective, consensual, and inexpensive way. Continue economic reforms even in the unlikely event that France seeks revenge and makes good on President Jacques Chirac's threat that Romania will no longer remain on track to get into the EU, as a result of its support for the U.S. campaign against Iraq.
- Liberalize and end bias in private televised news reporting, where the state media is now the better rather than, rather than worse than private stations.
- Use the United States, with its nearly exclusive geopolitical concerns, not as a "terrorism card" to replace the Cold War "USSR card," but as an opportunity to aspire to desirable Western values and practices.
- Focus on modernization of agriculture, which has continued to deteriorate after Communism.

- Establish more explicit commitments toward limited autonomy in Transylvania in return for a Government of Hungary apology for the dual monarchy's repression beginning in the late nineteenth century.
- Allow the CNSAS to really control all the security files and investigate documentation of crimes against humanity.

NOTES

1. On the reform process, see the symposium on "The Next Great Transformation: The EU Eastward Enlargement," *East European Politics and Societies* vol. 17, no. 1 (Winter 2003).

2. Tony Judt, "Romania: Bottom of the Heap," *The New York Review of Books*, vol. 48, issue 17 (1 November 2001 and written on 1 October 2001), pp. 41–45. Most of the widely circulated analysis on post-Communist Romania of Professor Judt, one of the most influential analysts on Europe, concerned Romania's pre-1990 history. Judt deftly depicts that history and its lack of liberal forces. He overlooks that the EU had greatly changed its negative evaluation of Romania in the year since its 2000 report, cited by Judt in this article. He concludes that Romania is worst off in Europe, overlooking Belarus, Ukraine, Moldova, and Russia. Nor did he mention the 5 percent real economic growth that Romania then expected in 2001. For more balanced views, see: Tom Gallagher, *Romania since Communism: Distrusting Democracy* (London: Hurst, 2003); Duncan Light and David Phinnemore, eds., *Post-Communist Romania: Coming to Terms with Transition* (New York: Palgrave, 2001); Vladimir Tismăneanu and Gail Kligman, "Romania's Post-Communist Decade: From Iliescu to Iliescu," *East European Constitutional Review*, vol. 10, no. 1 (Winter 2001), pp. 78–85; and Lavinia Stan, ed., *Romania in Transition* (London: Ashgate, 1997).

3. According to the criteria of Juan J. Linz and Alfred Stepan, who stipulate that officials must be elected honestly and establish their authority over authoritarian institutions, neither of which, despite popular beliefs, has emerged. *Problems of Democratic Transition and Consolidation* (Baltimore, MD: The Johns Hopkins University Press, 1996), ch. 1.

4. Such as Vladimir Tismăneanu, Dan Pavel, Jóhanna Kristín Birnir, and William Crowther.

5. Such as Michael Shafir, Tom Gallagher, Lavinia Stan, and myself.

6. See Henry F. Carey, ed., *National Reconciliation in Eastern Europe* (Boulder: East European Monographs/Columbia University Press, 2003).

7. Mattei Dogan, "Romania 1919–1938," in Myron Weiner and Ergun Őzbudun, eds., *Competitive Elections in Developing Countries* (Durham, NC: Duke University Press, 1987), pp. 369–389.

8. Linz and Stepan, *Problems of Democratic Transition and Consolidation.*

9. See Corneliu Coposu, *Corneliu Coposu Confessions: Dialogues with Doina Alexandru* (Boulder: East European Monographs/Columbia University Press, 1999).

10. Mario Sznajder and Luís Roniger, "The Unsolved Legacy of Human Rights Violations in the Southern Cone," *Human Rights Review* (October–December 1999), vol. 1, no.1, pp. 45–64. On Romania's Communist legacy, see the chapter of Vladimir

Tismăneanu in this book and his *Stalinism for all Seasons: A Political History of Romanian Communism* (Berkeley, CA: University of California Press, 2003); Linz and Stepan, *Problems of Democratic Transition and Consolidation*, "The Effects of Totalitarianism-cum-Sultanism on Democratic Transition: Romania," ch. 18. pp. 344–65; Gail Kligman, *Politics of Duplicity: Controlling Reproduction in Ceaușescu's Romania* (Berkeley, CA: University of California Press, 1998); Zoltan Barany and Ivan Volgyes, eds., *Legacies of Communism in Eastern Europe* (Baltimore, MD: Johns Hopkins University Press, 1995); Patricia Vawter Klein, Arthur W. Helweg, Barbara P. McCrea, and Wendy Hollis, eds., *Struggling with the Communist legacy: Studies of Yugoslavia, Romania, Poland and Czechoslovakia*, (Boulder: East European Monographs/Columbia University Press, 1998); *Democratic Consolidation in Eastern Europe: the Influence of the Communist Legacy in Hungary, the Czech Republic, and Romania* (Boulder: East European Monographs/Columbia University Press, 1999).

11. Tismăneanu refers to the lack of pacting as a crisis lack of communication. Without negotiations, neither hardliners nor softliners on both sides of the table can reach a consensus among each other, as well as the rest of their parties. AAASS Panel on Romania (Denver, Colorado, 10 November 2000).

12. Richard Andrew Hall, "The Uses of Absurdity: The Staged War Theory and the Romanian Revolution of December 1989," *East European Politics and Societies*, vol. 13, no. 3 (Fall 1999), pp. 501–42. This view is also supported less strongly by Dennis Deletant, who gives this USLA explanation on USLA, but ignores everything else. Rady also accepted USLA, but also Fifth Directorate. David Binder of the *New York Times* quotes Liviu Turcu on 23 December 1989 that the terrorists are from the USLA, even though he later changed his story. It should be noted that Western scholars using the term coup or palace coup are not referring to Hall's staged war theory.

13. Henry F. Carey, "Post-Communist Right Radicalism in Romania", in Peter Merkl and Leonard Weinberg, eds., *The Revival of Radical-Right Extremism in the Nineties* (London: Frank Cass, 1997), pp. 149–76; Francisco Veiga, "On the Social Origins of Ultranationalism and Radicalism in Romania, 1989–1993," in Lavinia Stan, ed., *Romania in Transition* (Aldershot: Dartmouth, 1997), pp. 49–66; Z. Ornea, *The Romanian Extreme Right* (Boulder: East European Monographs/Columbia University Press, 1999); Tom Gallagher, "Romania's Greater Romania: Defying Political Categorisation?" Paper presented to the ECPR Conference (Marburg, Germany, 2003); and the many essays (and citations therein) of Michael Shafir, including: "The Mind of Romania's Radical Right," in Sabrina P. Ramet, ed., *The Radical Right in Central and Eastern Europe since 1989* (University Park, PA: Penn State University Press, 1999), pp. 213–32; and, "Radical Continuity in Romania: The Greater Romania Party," *RFE/RL East European Perspectives*, vol. 2, no. 16, Part VIII (A) (16 August 2000).

14. Michael Shafir, "The Greater Romania Party and the 2000 Elections: A Retrospective Analysis," *RFE/RL East European Perspectives*, vol. 3, nos. 14–15, (22 August and 5 September 2001); Monica Ciobanu, "Problems of Democratic Consolidation in Eastern Europe: The Case of Romania in Comparative Perspective," *RFE/RL East European Perspectives*, vol. 5, no. 17 (20 August 2003); Grigore Pop-Elecheș, "Romania's Politics of Dejection," *Journal of Democracy*, vol. 12, no. 3 (July 2001), pp. 156–69; Alina Mungiu-Pippidi and Sorin Ionița, "Interpreting an Electoral Setback," *East Eu-*

ropean Constitutional Review, vol. 10, no. 1 (Winter 2001), pp. 86–91; Alina Mungiu-Pippidi, "Enlightened Participation? Political Learning in a Post-Communist Environment: Lessons from the Fall 200 Romanian Campaign," Working Paper, Romanian Academic Society, at www.sar.org.ro.

15. The other two are authoritarianism and post-totalitarianism. See Linz and Stepan, *Problems of Democratic Transition and Consolidation*, ch. 3.

16. Năstase's self-perception as a reformer is significant, despite his entry as a parliamentary leader via the 1992 electoral fraud and current wealth far exceeding his salary. He has recently found time to direct at least two doctoral dissertations as a Bucharest University professor while serving as Premier and has published. See Adrian Năstase, *Battle for the Future* (Boulder: East European Monographs/Columbia University Press, 2001).

17. According to Martyn Rady, *Romania in Turmoil* (London: I.B. Tauris, 1992), p. 117.

18. In Romania, a short version was published as "The Art of Rigging," *Sfera Politicii*, (October 1993). In the U.S., see my "From Big Lie to Small Lies: State Mass Media Dominance of Post-Communist Romania," *East European Politics and Societies*, vol. 10, no. 1 (Winter 1996), p. 36.

19. Grigore Pop-Elecheş, for example, asks why more foreign observers did not respond to these irregularities, in "Separated at Birth or Separated by Birth? The Communist Successor Parties in Romania and Hungary," *East European Politics and Society*, vol. 13, no. 1 (Winter 1999), p. 136. The author suggests that Western media silence is evidence of no fraud. The West was not interested in finding fraud because of its overtures to Iliescu before the 1992 election, in return for his cooperation on the UN embargo of the former Yugoslavia and because the new Ambassador, John R. Davis Jr., was a recent arrival in the country. Articles on suspicions of fraud did appear in *Cotidianul* and *22* in issues right after the vote. They did not continue because the opposition did not make an argument alleging fraud, because of a disagreement between the PAC's Nicolae Manolescu and the PNŢCD's Corneliu Coposu, who were on bad terms anyway. To be convinced, some readers will need to examine the congeries of circumstantial evidence provided in Henry F. Carey, "Irregularities or Rigging: The 1992 Romanian Parliamentary Elections," *East European Quarterly*, Vol. XXIX, no. 1 (March 1995). Several points are worth noting here: IRSOP and its German polling firm were the only one that predicted such a low voting percentage for the Democratic Convention. They provided the ruling party with the mid-afternoon exit polls, on which others (not IRSOP) calculated the cheating method. In fact, the highest rates of nullifications were in counties that supported Iliescu, where it was easier to cheat in the absence of opposition or neutral poll watchers, especially at the post-poll recounts in the prefects' offices early the following morning. All that was necessary was to reduce the total number of votes needed to meet the 3 percent minimum so that the three satellite parties could join FDSN and PUNR to enter parliament and gain another 15 percent of the total seats. So, the cheating strategy was ingenuous: to reduce the number of votes any party needed to enter the parliament. The nullification rates were higher in Iliescu bailiwicks, where the cheating could be effected centrally without a local challenge. If the nullification rate had been the maximum credible level of 2 percent, then only Greater Romania would have qualified for parliament. If the nullification rate had been the

average for democratic elections, which is under 1 percent, then none of the three parties would have qualified. Many in Romania, then and now, have not understood how the election was stolen. According to Peasant Party figures, it covered about 6,000 polling stations and its partner in the Democratic Convention, the Civic Alliance Party, another 2,000, out of nearly 14,000 polling stations, while the independent poll watchers from the Pro-Democracy Association only covered 5,000 and the latter were not coordinated with the Democratic Convention's observers. Finally, the journalistic opposition was divided, both in the "democratic press" (e.g., Octavian Paler, who was head of Communist Propaganda at one point) and the *Securitate* press (*Europa, România Mare*), both of whom had many former Communists activists who opposed Iliescu, but did not favor Constantinescu because he might open the lid on their past. Iliescu and his party shrewdly never criticized the *Securitate* in the past decade. Two scholars who have politely disagreed in conversations with me about fraud in these elections, Michael Shafir and Alina Mungiu-Pippidi, both argued that the rates of special list voting and nullifications were credible and that the rates of spoiled ballots among votes for the opposition as well. I maintain, first, Romania's large peasant population not that stupid to spoil over 13 percent of their ballots in 1992 (or six percent in 1996 and 2000). They are only not organized to complain. Second, I am not persuaded that they documented this fact. Yet, even if it were true, the incredibly high rates of nullifications were primarily designed to reduce the number of votes needed by any party to reach the 3 percent of total *valid* votes cast in order to qualify for parliament. Any reductions in votes for the Democratic Convention was irrelevant since it was way above 3 percent. Most importantly, both inordinate rates, nullifications, and special list votes, have no precedent in any *credible* election worldwide history. They are only comparable to bogus elections, such as throughout much of the former Soviet Union, like Georgia in 1991 and 1992 and Russia in 1993, 1995, and 1996. On the latter, see Vladimir Brovkin, "Time to Pay the Bills: Presidential Stabilization in Russia," *Problems of Post-Communism*, vol. 44, no. 6 (November–December 1997), pp. 34–42. The EU and NATO were equally mum about all the problems with the October 2003 Constitutional Referendum. The explanation again resulted from the desire of the EU and the United States to include Romania, so long as the desired constitutional reforms were approved. Yet many foreign observers found the process to have been rigged to achieve the minimum 50 percent turnout and approval. See, for example, British Helsinki Human Rights Group, "Romania: Electoral Fraud Up to European Standards" (28 October 2003), which concluded, "The conduct of the Constitutional Referendum of 17–18 October 2003 shocks even Romanian observers." Available at www.bhhrg.org. In January 2004 a Dutch member of the European Parliament issued a report complaining that Romania still had not enacted any basic electoral reforms.

20. The interaction occurred in the calling line at the reception at the House of the Men of Science for the Psychiatry and Human Rights Conference that was held at Bucharest University School of Law (actually one of the best conferences that I have ever attended). I initially made the comment to the Chargé (who is Deputy Chief of Mission), who then repeated it to the Ambassador for comment. I take Ambassador Davis's response to mean, at least, that the U.S. was not going to get involved publicly in this election, no matter what the evidence of fraud available to the U.S. Embassy was from the NDI/IRI observers, the U.S. Embassy's own observer delegation, and other sources.

21. Stein Rokkan, "The Development of West European Party Systems," in Rokkan and Seymour Martin Lipset, eds., *Party Systems and Voter Alignments: Cross-National Perspectives* (New York: Free Press, 1967).

22. Zoltan Barany, *The Future of NATO Expansion: Four Case Studies* (New York: Cambridge University Press, 2003). Laure Paquette, *NATO and Eastern Europe after 2000: Strategic Interactions with Poland, the Czech Republic, Romania and Bulgaria* (Huntington, NY: Nova Science Publishers, 2001).

23. Press reports at the time stated that the nullification rate was 7.5 percent, but official records have it at about 6 percent. On Romania's lack of registration and voter cards in 1992 and 1996 (and remaining true in 2000), see Svante Renstrom, "Electoral Systems and Electoral Organization," in International Institute for Democracy and Electoral Assistance (IDEA), *Democracy in Romania: Assessment Mission Report* (Stockholm: IDEA, 1997), p. 152. Since the 1991 law on elections, all Romanians have been required to present a voter registration card before voting, but these cards have never been distributed because that would have entailed creating a valid voters' list, which would have assured that the distribution of seats represented the electorate's geographic distribution and that no district would have excessive numbers of phantom voters with which to pad the returns. This illegal and fraudulent situation, amazingly, still persisted through the 2000 elections and was unlikely to change before the 2004 general elections.

24. Joseph Rothschild, *Return to Diversity: A Political History of East Central Europe since World War II* (Oxford: Oxford Univeristy Press, 1989), p. 111. In these votes, the opposition only was allotted 66 seats compared with the 348 seats to the Communist coalition. According to Dinu Giurescu, the Communist alliance only received about 8 percent. Lecture in his history course, Bucharest University (8 December 1992).

25. Thomas Carothers, "Western Civil-Society Aid to Eastern Europe and the Former Soviet Union," *East European Constitutional Review*, vol. 8, no. 4 (Fall 1999), pp. 54–62.

26. Vladimir Tismăneanu, "2000 Elections" AAASS Presentation (2000).

27. Henry F. Carey, "Genocide Denial and Antonescu as Democratic Role-Model: 1984 in the Twenty-First Century," *Romanian Journal of Politics and Society*, vol. 1, no. 1, (2001): 33–69.

28. Irina Livezeanu, *Cultural Politics in Greater Romania: Regionalism, Nation Building, and Ethnic Struggle, 1918–1930* (Ithaca, NY: Cornell University Press, 1995); Z. Ornea, *Romanian Extreme Right: The Nineteen Thirties* (Boulder: East European Monographs/Columbia University Press, 1999).

29. See Lavinia Stan, "Acess to Securitate Files," *East European Politics and Societies*, vol. 16, no. 1 (Winter 2002), pp. 145–81 and L. Stan, "Moral Cleansing Romanian Style," *Problems of Post-Communism*, vol. 49, no. 4 (July/August 2002), pp. 52–62.

30. My thanks to Mark Temple for this information.

31. Michael Shafir reported that the CNSAS "rejected the Democratic Convention of Romania 2000's (CDR2000) appeal against an earlier ruling that Ion Iliescu did not collaborate with the Communist secret police." CDR 2000 launched the appeal on the grounds that as a former Communist Party first secretary in Iasi County, Iliescu was in charge of coordinating the activities of the *Securitate* in that region. Committee chairman Gheorghe Onisoru said nobody can be suspected of collaboration with the

Securitate without "proper documentation," proving such was the case. Onisoru added that an inquiry into the activities of the *Securitate* in Iasi County between 1974 and 1979, when Iliescu was first secretary there, would require "a huge effort," RFE/RL's Bucharest bureau reported" (22 November 2000).

32. Unless otherwise indicated in the text, the information in this chapter is valid through September 2003.

33. Many of the French, in turn, resent the British insistence on equating its friendship with the U.S. with the rest of Europe. Romania would be unwise to try to exploit these Euro-Atlantic divisions, as the U.S. is the hegemon. Many Romanian elites resent the negative foreign media impressions of Romania, as essays by Mihai Coman have argued. Such negative stereotypes, which focus on Dracula, Ceauşescu, and the pediatric AIDS epidemic, are part of an embedded, negative Western view of all the post-Ottoman, Balkan states, as British journalist H. N. Brailsford argued in 1908 ("The most miserable corner in Europe"). Edith Dunham in her 1908 tour noted that "All Balkan people are 'savages'" and "are as bad as each other." The Serbophile, Rebecca West, noted in 1937, "All over the Balkans there is an association between highway robbery and revolutionary idealism." Quotes are from Tim Judah, *Kosovo: War and Revenge* (New Haven, CT: Yale University Press, 2000), pp. 11, 295, 100.

34. RFE/RL *NEWSLINE* (7 June 2002). Other polls have placed support as high as 85 percent.

35. Romania's treaty with the USSR was signed in 1991. See chapter 24 by Robert Weiner.

36. Larry Diamond, "Thinking about Hybrid Regimes," *Journal of Democracy*, vol. 13, no. 2 (April 2002), pp. 27–32.

37. On company privatization, see John S. Earle, "The Results of Mass Privatization in Romania: A First Empirical Study," *Economics of Transition*, vol. 6 (1998), pp. 313–32; John S. Earle and Álmos Telegdy, "Privatization Methods and Productivity Effects in Romanian Industrial Enterprises, *Journal of Comparative Economics*, vol. 30, no. 4, pp. 657–82 (December 2002). On land reform, see Rachel Sabates-Wheeler, "Land Reform and Farm Choice in Romania," *Problems of Post-Communism*, vol. 48, no. 4 (July–August 2001), pp. 27–37; Berch Berberoglu, "Transnational Capital and the Impact of Privatization and Market-Oriented Reforms on East European Agriculture: Focus on Romania in Transition, 1989–2000," *Intenational Review of Sociology*, vol. 13, no. 2 (July 2003), pp. 273–303; Sophia Davidova and Kenneth J. Thompson, eds., *Romanian Agriculture and Transition to the EU*, (Lanham, MD: Lexington Books, 2003); Katherine Verdery, *The Vanishing Hectare: Property and Value in Postsocialist Transylvania* (Ithaca, NY: Cornell University Press, 2003).

38. Economic Policy Institute, Sofia, "Bulgaria and Romania: Winners and Losers of EU Integration," in Helen Tang, ed., *Policy Issues for Central and Eastern Europe* (Washington, DC: The World Bank, 2000).

39. *New York Times* (30 July 1995), p. 8. My telephone interview with former Ambassador Alfred Moses (22 July 2000).

40. Del Ponte is the third chief prosecutor since the UN Security Council created the Tribunal in 1993 at The Hague. The BBC Newshour and the BBC Romanian Service both reported, "Del Ponte urged Romania to arrest indicted [Bosnian Serb] leaders whom she said during her news conference in Bucharest had visited the country from time to time" (Quote from BBC Newshour, 7 September 2000).

41. Arend Lijphart, "Constitutional Choices for New Democracies, *Journal of Democracy*, vol. 2, no. 1 (Winter 1991), p. 83.

42. Critics of Article 98 agreements argue that it places the U.S. above the law. The U.S. holds that as a nonstate party to the ICC treaty, its soldiers and officials should not be subject to ICC's jurisdiction.

43. Foreign Ministry spokesman Cristian Diaconescu denied, for example, Romania's motives for the ICC amendment. Similarly, Foreign Ministry Spokesman Mihail Dobrescu claimed that Romania should be compensated for Kosovo war damages, as reported by Radio Free Europe (27 January 2000).

44. Eugen Tomiuc, "Romania/Bulgaria: Balkan Neighbors Press Ahead with NATO Bid, Vow to Tackle Corruption," (7 February 2002), available at www.rferl.org.

45. Eugen Tomiuc, "Romania: Bucharest Steps up NATO Military Reforms, but Political Reforms just as Crucial," (18 January 2002), available at www.rferl.org.

46. Irena Brinar attributes much of Slovenia's economic success to its receipt of large foreign aid, which Romania has not enjoyed. See "Slovenia: From Yugoslavia to the European Union," in Karen Henderson, ed., *Back to Europe: Central and Eastern Europe and the European Union* (London: UCL Press, 1999). Unfortunately, foreign skepticism is reinforced by the pervasive corruption, above all issues. Romania ranked 77th out of 102 countries in Transparency International's 2002 survey.

47. RFE/RL *NEWSLINE* (9 November 2000).

48. The Australian firm Esmeralda built the dam, which failed to stop the water from traveling beyond the accident area. The European Union and the UN Environmental Program have investigated the facts, but not the legal issues. The source of international law includes treaties mandating the good neighbor principle and the principles that the polluter pays for the damages caused and that caution should be exercised under situations of high uncertainty. Also relevant are human rights treaties and norms specifically protecting the means of subsistence of fishermen, as well as the more general and non-derogable right to life, as well as the rights to health and healthy environment of those affected by pollution. The most important international environmental law comes from the International Court of Justice's (ICJ) *Trail Smelter* precedent (involving Canada and the U.S.), which has been recognized in about a dozen court cases, arbitrations, and diplomatic notes over the past half-century that appears to establish clear precedents of financial liability for harm. In another case, the ICJ ordered Albania to compensate the UK for damages from a mining operation. Hungary has accepted ICJ jurisdiction, but Romania has not, though theoretically, Romania could accept ICJ jurisdiction for the particular case to avoid Hungarian jurisdiction and obtain greater impartiality. In the dispute between Hungary and Slovakia, a treaty that permitted Slovakia to submit to ICJ jurisdiction in the particular case was affected. The Tisza River case is more likely to go to Hungarian domestic courts because the ICJ cannot compel Romania's participation and because of Romania's probable liability under regional European customary international law. A West European treaty gives jurisdiction to national courts of the country harmed, most of them civil code systems like Romania and Hungary's. So, no issue of sovereign immunity would arise. That Romania cannot afford its likely share of the potential damages does not mean that Romania should deny obvious factual (as opposed to legal) responsibility, a denial that has already harmed perceptions of Romania's EU readiness. If Romania (and Esmeralda) were to negotiate an affordable settlement with Hungary and Yugoslavia, instead

of arbitration or a suit for damages, foreign assistance to pay the reparations might be obtained. Part of the preceding comes from my notes from the panel, "Environmental Law in Ferment," Annual Meeting of the American Society for International Law (Washington, DC, 7 April 2000).

49. This optimism has been somewhat constrained by the August 2003 revelations, alleged in the Romanian press, such as by Mircea Toma in *Caţavencu* earlier, that the Romanian Minister for European Integration, Hildegard Puwak, had misappropriated 150,000 euros from the EU after she became Minister, violating the spring 2003 anticorruption laws. Earlier, she had even denied, under the requirements of the law, that her net worth exceeded 5,000 Euros, claiming that the family's wealth had been shared among its various members.

50. Marie Lavigne, "The Economics of the Transition Process," *Problems of Post-Communism*, vol. 47, no. 4 (July–August 2000), pp. 16–23.

51. Eugen Tomiuc, "Czech Republic: Government Drops Plan to Introduce Visas for Romanians" (20 December 2001), available at www.rferl.org.

52. John Mueller defines it narrowly as the right to petition one's government in *Quiet Cataclysm* (New York: HarperCollins, 1995).

53. Linz and Stepan, *Problems of Democratic Transition and Consolidation*, p. 3.

54. The U.S. policy repeated the pattern of false support for free elections of the post-war period, when the U.S. never protested the massive electoral fraud in the 1946 elections stolen by the Communists. Joseph Rothschild noted "The American stance, of repeatedly calling for a Romanian government that would be freely elected and truly representative as well as friendly to the Soviet Union, was really a political contradiction, for these two qualifications were simply incompatible. Stalin, in his bluff fashion, was more candid and consistent when he stated, 'A freely elected government in any of these countries would be anti-Soviet, and that we cannot allow.'" Rothschild, *Return to Diversity*, p. 113. Though the U.S. was unwilling to intervene militarily to protest the fraud, it did attempt unsuccessfully to establish networks through front groups in Romania, Albania, Poland, the USSR, and its other satellites to support resistance efforts. Such efforts were to prove far more successful in marginalizing pro-Soviet factions in socialist and Communist parties in France and Italy. See Peter Grose, *Operation Roll-Back: America's Secret War behind the Iron Curtain* (New York: Houghton-Mifflin, 2000).

55. Manolescu did genuinely believe there was no fraud in the 1992 parliamentary election. Manolescu is an exemplar of the personalism that many Romanian politicians have instituted and thus prevented the development of a stable party system. Having quit several parties in his political career, in 2000, he quit the National Liberal Party and supported the independent candidacy for president of Mugur Isărescu, which, putting aside his excellent personal qualifications for office, appeared likely to encourage more personalism and antipolitics and harm party development.

56. RFE/RL *Newsline* (7 June 2002).

57. Eugen Tomiuc, "Romania: Balkan Stability Pact Criticizes Control of News Agency" (9 November 2001), available at www.rferl.org.

58. Linz and Stepan, *Problems of Democratic Transition and Consolidation*, pp. 7–15.

59. Robert A. Dahl, *Polyarchy: Participation and Opposition* (New Haven, CT: Yale University Press, 1971), pp. 20–21.

60. The PDSR released a poll it commissioned from the IRSOP firm. It found the four leading candidates in a poll taken in mid-September to have been Iliescu with 40 percent, Isărescu with 18 percent, and Stolojan and Tudor with 12 percent each. An indication of the poll's possible bias can be seen as well with its results for the parliament in the same poll: PDSR: 45 percent' PD: 8; PRM: 10; UDMR: 7; PNL: 12; CDR-2000: 13; and ApR: 8. Radio Free Europe (3 Oct. 2000).

61. Marie Lavigne, "The Economics of the Transition Process," table 1, p. 22.

62. See Carey, "Post-Communist Right Radicalism in Romania"; and Shafir, "The Mind of Romania's Radical Right."

63. See Carey, "Post-Communist Right Radicalism in Romania"; Francisco Veiga, "On the Social Origins of Ultranationalism and Radicalism in Romania, 1989–1993," in Lavinia Sta, ed., *Romania in Transition* (Aldershot: Dartmouth, 1997), pp. 49–66; and the writings of Michael Shafir, including: "The Mind of Romania's Radical Right," in Sabrina P. Ramet, ed., *The Radical Right in Central and Eastern Europe since 1989* (University Park, PA: Penn State University Press, 1999), pp. 213–232, and especially, "Radical Continuity in Romania: The Greater Romania Party," *RFE/RL East European Perspectives*, vol. 2, no. 16, Part VIII (A) (16 August 2000).

64. For an important discussion of these two *Securitate* hypotheses (as well as a major critique of the Constantinescu presidency, see Dan Pavel and Iulia Huiu, *"Nu putem reuşi decît împreună," O istorie analitică a onvenţiei Democratice, 1989–2000* (Bucharest: Polirom, 2003), esp. pp. 435–55. Lavinia Stan did not consider these two *Securitate* hypotheses to be opposition myths in her analysis, "Democratic Delusions: Ten Myths Accepted by the Romanian Democratic Opposition," *Problems of Past Communism* 50, no. 6 (November–December 2003), pp. 51–60.

65. See, for example, Alina Mungiu-Pippidi, *Politica după comunism. Structură, cultură şi psihologie politică* (Bucharest Humanitas, 2002); also, Alina Mungiu-Pippidi and Gerard Althabe, *Secera şi buldozerul. Scornicesti şi Nucşoara. Mecanisme de aservire ţăranului român* (Bucharest, Polirom).

66. Foundation for the Advancement of Civil Society, "The Associative and Charitable Behavior of the Population" (1998). The question polled for the study was: "Are you a member of a voluntary association?" as cited in Dan Pavel, "Civil Society in Romania," paper delivered to the November 2000 AAASS Congress in Denver, Colorado.

67. Rothschild, *Return to Diversity*, p. 165.

68. The *Diary* (*"Jurnal, 1935–1944"*) was first published in 1996 by Humanitas, with an introduction and notes by Leon Volovici. For excerpts, see: Mihail Sebastian, "Diary: Friends and Fascists," *The New Yorker* (2 October 2000), pp. 106–13.

69. "Reacţia de prestigiu" [A Reaction of Prestige], *Sfera politicii*, vol. 6, no. 63 (October 1998), pp. 57–62. For a French-language translation of this excellent essay, see "L'honeur nationale roumaine en question," *Les Temps Modernes*, vol. 54, no. 606 (November–December 1999), pp. 142–52. I am not referring to Voicu's grouping of intellectuals, but rather his overall argument, which was at first ignored by Romanian intellectuals and then condemned when the essay was published a year later in France: important segments of the Romanian intelligentsia ignore or deny Romanian complicity in the Holocaust. Once this fact is acknowledged, then the intellectual culture of denial of individual and state responsibility can be seen as persistent and perverse.

70. If Antonescu had fought with the Africa Corps, instead of the SS, the Gestapo, and the *Einsatzgruppen*, he might not have helped start the Holocaust. But Antonescu was

no General Rommel, the "Desert Fox," who refused Hitler's orders effectively to commit war crimes or to exterminate the Sphedardic Jews of North Africa. The effort to legally rehabilitate Antonescu by exoneration by President Constantinescu's Prosecutor General Sorin Moisescu, one of the few legal rehabilitations ever attempted in postwar Romania, was suddenly halted after foreign pressure on 22 November 1997.

72. Associated Press, "Romanian-Gypsies Wait for Slave-Labor Payments," *New York Times* (24 July 2000), p. A4. Only 6,000 Roma returned to Romania, as many died of typhoid, starvation, and maltreatment. For additional information, see the research of Michelle Kelso.

73. For what some would consider Holocaust denial, see Gheorghe Buzatu, "Mareşalul Antonescu şi problema evreiască," *Revista de Istorie Militară*, no. 6 (1994), as cited in Victor Eskenasy, "Historiographers against the Antonescu Myth" in Randolph L. Braham, ed., *The Destruction of Romanian and Ukrainian Jews During the Antonescu Era* (Boulder and New York: Social Science Monographs, 1997), pp. 271–302. For an analysis of the political uses of what some consider to be Holocaust denial, see Michael Shafir, "Marshal Antonescu's Post-Communist Rehabilitation: *Cui Bono*?" in Ibid., pp. 349–410. For some who may not, from a historical viewpoint, though not from the legal criterion of command responsibility, hold Antonescu personally responsible for the mass murder of Jews and Roma and/or who use lower estimates on the number of Jews killed, see Majorie Hale, "Ion Antonescu's Role in the Holocaust: A Reconsideration," *Romanian Civilization*, Vol. V, no. 3 (Winter 1996–97), pp. 17–34; Alex Mihai Stoenescu, "*Armata, Maresalului si Evreii,*" ("The Army, The Marshal, and The Jews: The Cases of Dorohoi, Bucharest, Iaşi, and Odessa,") (Bucharest, RAO, 1998), p. 507; and Dinu C. Giurescu's "*Evreii Romani—1939–1944*," *Realitatea Evreiasca*, no.1, (May 1997), pp. 16–31. Though sympathetic to Antonescu from an historical viewpoint, Larry Watts does admit that Antonescu is legally responsible for crimes against humanity, according to the Nuremberg principles. With his permission, I quote his correspondence to me: "I do not think of Antonescu as a democratic role model for anyone today. My point is that, within the context of the time, he was—as the head of the U.S. mission in Bucharest reported on several occasions—a 'moderating' force rather than an extremist one. If he was a model for anything it would be restricted to the military and its administration—anticorruption, correctitude, etc. The military of that time was hardly a place teeming with model democrats, much less liberal democrats. I would like to emphasize that beyond aspects of his character like honesty and correctitude, which are rather singular attributes in any case even if the plague of corruption and betrayal that seems to have infected Romanian politics might benefit from them, his political leanings do not and cannot serve as model for any Romanian in the twenty-first century." See Larry Watts, *Romanian Cassandra: Ion Antonescu and the Struggle for Reform, 1916–1941* (Boulder, CO: East European Monographs, 1993).

74. The U.S. is the only country that has made a reservation to permit hate speech, consistent with the U.S. constitution.

75. On the "Weekend" show of the BBC (12 May 2001), Dimitrina Petrova, director of the European Roma Rights Centre in Budapest, was scandalized by the comment by London-based, BBC correspondent for the Romanian service, Tatiania Niculescu, who said, "When they came last year from Romania in London, they were illegal immigrants. . . . So, they are illegal immigrants because they are Romanians,

and in Romania, we have a democratic government; so, they have no reason to become illegal immigrants and to feel discriminated against in a democratic society. But if they are to be recognized as discriminated against, then they would have to be accepted as legal immigrants." Petrova responded, "I disagree. When some, in fact, very limited numbers of Roma traveled to the United Kingdom escaping racially based persecution in Romania and claiming asylum." Then Niculescu interrupted, saying, "No, they come for money. . . . They used to do it in Ceauşescu's time as well." Niculescu's ignorance of the International Refugee Convention is matched by her misunderstanding that well-founded Roma fears of persecution can not only occur under Communism, but can emerge under democracy as well, just as racial persecution of African Americans can occur routinely in the U.S.

76. See Sabrina P. Ramet's chapter 14 in this book. In percentage terms, the figures have been categorized as 86.8 percent Romanian Orthodox, 5 percent Roman Catholic, 3.5 percent Reformed Protestant, 1 percent Greek Catholic, 1 percent Pentacostal, 0.2 percent Muslim, and 0.2 percent Jewish and others, according to Moldovan, UN Document CCPR/C/SR.1767 (5 August 1999), at p. 9 paragraph 41.

77. *New York Times* (30 July 1995). President Constaninescu charged that between 1994 and 1995, "entire trains" loaded with ammunition and gas were smuggled into Yugoslavia from Romania. The operations were supported by the Romanian Customs Office, the Transportation Ministry, and the police, and were controlled by the Romanian Intelligence Service. According to Constantinescu, the Prosecutor General's Office has finished investigating the case. RFE/RL Newsline (22 November 2000).

78. The other main human rights (economic, social, and cultural) are not ranked by Freedom House. "Freedom in the World: The Annual Survey of Political Rights and Civil Liberties," (New York: Freedom House, 1999), available at www.freedomhouse.org/survey99 as of 22 January 2004.

79. "Constitution Watch: Romania," in *East European Constitutional Review*, vol. 4, no. 2 (1995), p. 22.

80. Larry L. Watts, "The Crisis in Romanian Civil-Military Relations," *Problems of Post-Communism*, vol. 48, no. 4 (July–August 2001), pp. 14–26.

81. Though a student of Romania, Stepan has not written on its civil-military relations. See Daniel N. Nelson and Marybeth P. Ulrich, "Intractable Problems: Armies, National Security and Democratic Transition." Paper presented to the International Studies Association (Los Angeles, March 2000).

82. Unless Corneliu Vadim Tudor were elected president in 2004.

83. Romanian Academic Society, "Bad Politics Prompts Bad Justice," *Early Warning Reports* (July 2002); Romanian Academic Society, Policy Warning Report, no. 2, "Judicial Reform Buried in Scandal" (August 2003).

84. CURS (July 2002).

85. CURS-SAR, Figure 4, "Corruption Since 2000," SAR, "Policy Warning Report," no. 2, (August 2003), Section on "Judicial Reform Buried in Scandal," p. 5.

86. Open Society Institute, "Judicial Capacity in Romania," EU Accession Monitoring Program," (February 2002).

87. At a 3–4 June 1994 Bucharest conference on national reconciliation organized by the author, Moore made similar, unequivocal condemnations of corruption that were surprising to many in the audience. See the book that resulted from that conference: Henry F. Carey, ed., *National Reconciliation in Eastern Europe*.

88. The lack of judicial independence in Romania is not comparable to the French system, on which Romanian courts have been modeled. The French constitution is designed to place some quasi-judicial functions such as judicial review and administrative law in executive tribunals. The Romanian interference has resulted from executive policies not found in the constitution, and these policies are often not legislated either.

89. This is quite different from the French Council of State and the Constitutional Council, both of which have judicial functions, but are constitutionally intended to exist within the executive branch.

90. The case involves an investigation that was conducted in the pre-1996 Iliescu government against the former Transportation Minister. Băsescu was one of the few former ministers willing to give up his parliamentary immunity, and nevertheless, was found not worthy of prosecution. Now that he is the leading challenger to the ruling PSD party, the investigation was reopened without any clear indication of new implicating evidence.

91. The EU has still attempted to establish rules for Russian companies, particularly in natural gas, to export to the EU. So far, Gazprom and other Russian companies have resisted adaptation. Jan S. Adams, "Russia's Gas Diplomacy: Extending Russia's Reach," *Problems of Post-Communism*, vol. 49, no. 3 (May/June 2002), pp. 14–22.

92. See Peter Gross, *Mass Media in Revolution and National Development: The Romanian Laboratory* (Ames: Iowa University Press, 1996); Henry F. Carey, "From Big Lie to Small Lies: State Mass Media Dominance of Post-Communist Romania," *East European Politics and Societies*, vol. 10, no. 1 (Winter 1996), pp. 16–45.

93. Richard Wagner, *Sonderweg Rumänien. Bericht aus einem Entwicklungsland.* (Berlin: Rotbuch, 1991).

94. Stepan and Linz, *Problems of Democratic Transition and* Consolidation, p. 174–77.

95. Samuel P. Huntington, *The Third Wave: Democratization in the Late Twentieth Century* (Norman: Oklahoma University Press, 1991).

96. Robert Weiner, "Romania, the IMF, and Economic Reform since 1996," *Problems of Post-Communism*, vol. 48, no. 1 (January–February 2001), pp. 39–47.

Afterword: Ten Points, Ten Years After

Pavel Câmpeanu

The decade-plus since the revolution of 1989 is too short a period to reach definitive conclusions about the transition to democracy and the free market in Romania and Eastern Europe. The most common feeling, however, is of disappointment, rather than gratification. Yet, as Ortega y Gasset has said, the censuring of phenomena does not always lead to their comprehension. The following observations attempt to provide an objective presentation of the facts surrounding Romania's transition, rather than my subjective reaction to them.

1. Irreversibility

There was a period of significant vulnerability following the revolutions of 1989, in which their gains seemed somewhat tenuous. Yet, they have by now proven themselves to be, for the most part, irreversible. While these revolutions did not entirely overturn the Stalinist social order, they did seal the fate of its previous disintegration, which had, by 1989, already reached its critical limit.

2. Teleology

The transition has not replaced the Stalinist social order through an alternative social order, but through a social disorder that symbolizes a movement toward that alternative order. The transition does not appear as a specific type of social order, but as a historic process that simultaneously annihilates the existing traces of the remaining Stalinist social structures while attempting to develop new ones with superior functional potential.

The necessary passage from a society in transition to one of consolidated social order implies a teleology. While society is aware of the necessity of the goal, it is unaware of exactly what the goal is, or why it is being pursued.

3. The Agent

Two factors condition the teleology: the social agent and the doctrine through which this agent affirms its legitimacy. The agent of transition toward post-Stalinism is qualitatively different from the agent of the anti-Stalinist revolution. The active agent of the anti-Stalinist revolution was society as a whole, homogenized by the overwhelming failure of the Stalinist dictatorship, and committed to the singular goal of the overthrow of the Stalinist state. In contrast, the commitment to the transition has not homogenized society; it has divided it. The differentiated interests of the diverse segments of society are expressed through their differentiated representations of the virtual goal of the transition, and these differences are manifest through political affiliation. Thus, for the time being, political pluralism functions as a pluralism of interests related to the transition. Politicization of interests allows for their variants to be disputed in the electoral process. Ratified through this process, the social agent of the transition can be none other than state power. Yet, over the past ten-plus years, state power has not been held solely by one political party; it has alternated. Yet, the discontinuity of the principal agent of the transition has been accompanied by a discontinuity of the process itself. The progress of the transition does not seem to depend in a decisive manner upon any one principal agent.

4. Substitution

If we judge the transition in terms of the economic market, then its natural agent would be a class of entrepreneurs. Yet, the socioeconomic progress of the transition has been asymmetrical. It has not generated a new entrepreneurial class which would have been its natural agent and which would be responsible for spawning a substitute political class to replace the ranks of the old *nomenklatura*.

5. The Doctrine

The revolutions of the modern era have had a negative premise: the incapacity of the old regime to reproduce itself. At the same time, the preparation of these revolutions simultaneously developed two positive premises: the emergence of a social agent that incorporated the imperative of change and the establishment of the indoctrination of this imperative. The most active agent in preparing the French Revolution was the bourgeoise, inspired by Enlightenment doctrine. The agent of the Russian Revolution of October 1917 was partly the Bolshevik Party, inspired by the doctrine of Marxist-Leninism. The anti-Stalinist revolutions were only affected by the negative premise, while lacking the positive one. The presumed agent did not prepare the revolutions and did not animate the transitions. The transition must form an agent independent of its identity where an indoctrinated legitimacy cannot prevail.

6. Ability to Govern

The lack of a doctrine in the anti-Stalinist revolution also extends to the lack of a doctrine in the transition to post-Stalinism. As a result, the alternation of governments does not translate into a corresponding alternation of doctrine, or the direction in which the transition manifests itself. The different political parties, which seem so far apart in the disputes over their government positions, are congruent in the sense of how they choose to use their government positions. All sectors of society, whether specialized analysts or ordinary citizens, assert the same diagnosis: the country is poorly governed. The unspoken assumption is that the transition is a process that can be governed—an assumption that has been negated by the experience of the past decade.

7. Imitation

As they have lacked a doctrine of their own to guide them, and as they have been unable to define the goals of the transition, the various governments that have ruled Romania since the revolution have simply defaulted on the policy of emulating the West, which has provided a ready-made model for reform. The West, in turn, has not been satisfied with simply providing a model for the East to aspire to—it looks to impose its influence.

One problem still remains: Why would a historic process as specific as de-Stalinization lead to social structures similar to those produced by different secular, historic processes? For now, the mimetic strategy of transition has managed to reproduce certain formal political and judicial institutions. However, it has not succeeded in instituting a functional democratic order, but rather a hybrid regime, which has been named *democradura* by scholars of Latin American transition (Phillipe Schmitter and Guillermo O'Donnell). Despite all its enormous gaps, *democradura* represents substantial progress compared with Stalinist dictatorships. It has led, among other things, to a respect for personal freedom, pluralism, the separation and alternation of powers, the outset of legislative reform and decentralization, freedom of the press and of religion, minority rights, and so forth. Yet, it has also led to social and political dysfunction, such as social injustice, job instability, increased organized crime, and direct or indirect military aggression. Moreover, it led, in the first decade of transition, to a constant overall decline in the standard of living in Romania, manifested in the dramatic impoverishment of large segments of the population.

8. Integration

Having failed to effectively emulate the Western social model, transitional countries have also attempted to integrate with the Western political-military structure established by the Cold War. The rationale behind this modification could be provided by the idea that integration into the political-military structures of the West facilitates the assimilation to the Western social model. Yet, in regard to the strategy of NATO integration, it is important to keep in mind the following. First, it must be conceded that the experience of two World Wars would suggest that the military utility of an ally depends less on its economic prosperity and more on other factors—most important, its geostrategic position. Yet, while it may be true that, after the downfall of the USSR, the West has felt the need to cultivate new allies in Eastern Europe, Western leaders have made it clear that they need strong allies, and not the kind, like Romania, who sink deeper into misery. Those who believe the West will come running to make alliances with weak countries for the altruistic reason of helping them out of their present state of misery are in for a rude awakening. Second, it may very well be the case that the West does not need allies in this region, unless it still considers Russia a serious threat, which it may not. Third, the strategy of integration puts even greater strain on the relations of East European countries with Russia. Fourth, in certain circumstances—such as in the war in Yugoslavia—it feeds domestic, anti-Western opinion, and contributes to xenophobic, nationalist, and culturally chauvinistic thought.

9. Inheritance

At the end of the first decade, it was evident that transition did not spawn similarities, but distinctions among countries. For example, the differences between Romania and the Czech Republic were far more profound in 1999 than they were in 1989. No doubt this is due, in part, to the inequality between the Havel and Iliescu-Constantinescu regimes, as well as to the difference in Western aid to the two countries. Some changes are also due to preexisting conditions. Even before 1989, satellite countries added new characteristics to formal Stalinism, making it distinct in every country. While in most satellite countries control was achieved by outside military force, in Romania the Stalinist model was imposed from within, by the will of the dictator. While in most countries the downfall of Stalinism was caused, in part, by the movement for national independence, in Romania Stalinism lay at the root of national independence, which offered Stalinism a certain legitimacy. So, when the revolution finally did come it did not go down without a fight.

10. The Conflict

As a result of the bloodshed in December 1989, the Romanian transition faces two consequences of its ill-fated inheritance: having to be subject to the lowest rank of Stalinism in the region and having to bear the burden of its bloody downfall. The transition bears the stigma of violence, which leads to two further consequences: one that leads to constant tensions and conflict, and the other, which leads to the breakdown of conflict into violent clashes.

CONCLUSIONS

Fluidity

1. A democratic social order integrates the conflicts it produces by solving them within the confines of the political process. The state of social disorder known as "transition" integrates conflicts by conferring on them its own disorderly character.
2. The defining characteristic of transitional disorder is instability. The main symptom of instability is fluidity. The social actors, the relationships between them, and the values guiding them alter until they lose their identity.
3. The unmediated mechanism of fluidity is substitution, manifesting itself as a permanent redistribution of social roles and actors.
4. Both at the level of society, and at the level of the conflict, the basic substitution is the transformation of structures into conjunctural changes.
5. By permanently reconfiguring its actors, issues, form, character, and dimension, in the course of time the conflict loses its identity. Its duration becomes doubtful: one can say that the conflict in Reşiţa lasted nine days—but also that every day brought about a new conflict.
6. Unlike society, the conflict seems to contain an element of negative order: its fluidity points in a direction that implies a worsening of the situation.

The Main Issue

1. The conflictual energy of a society in transition seems to concentrate around labor—particularly industrial—disputes.
2. The negative energy from the restructuring of the economy concentrates around the point with the utmost force. To a large degree, the restructuring of the economy appears to be coterminous with the destruction of industry
3. The transition reveals the hidden shortcomings of the command economy, but before an alternative structure of economic activity comes into being. One of these shortcomings is its overwhelming redundancy, in terms of both places of work and workers, in all branches of industry.

4. The disclosure of these shortcomings has social and economic effects that are both immediate and devastating: a transition from virtually full employment to large-scale unemployment without prospects for new work; from job security to general insecurity; from the invulnerability of parasitic industrial giants to their rapid disintegration; and from the protection of unskilled labor and the equalization of wages to the drastic shedding of surplus labor and realistic wage differentials.
5. The major historic "achievements" of Stalinist industrialization were the very causes of its breakdown. The transition is an acceptance of this failure, showing what had been concealed for a long time: that industrial relations are not the catalyst of social order, but its most harmful disturbance.
6. The genetic malformation of Stalinist industrial relations is the main reason for the social conflicts that have shaken the societies in transition. The most active generator of these social conflicts is labor disputes in industry.

The Situation of the Industrial Labor Force

1. The economic vulnerability of Stalinist industry during transition becomes the social vulnerability of the industrial labor force.
2. The process of transition cannot avoid perturbations, and it is the Stalinist industry and its labor force that are most profoundly affected. The opposition of the industrial labor force to these perturbations risks degenerating into an opposition to transition as such.
3. The most extreme exposure to perturbations provokes the most extreme resistance, sometimes in the form of social conflict.
4. The conflicts of transition started by industrial labor have a social rather than a class character, and, therefore, cannot be assimilated to the class struggle, for the following reasons:
   a. The bearers of the conflict do not rely on class solidarity, but on that of the family and the neighborhood.
   b. The social agent against whom they act is usually not the class of private industrial employers, but the state.
   c. The content of their demands is not revolutionary, but strongly populist.
   d. Despie its frequency and intensity, conflictual behavior is not based on a conflictual ideology.
   e. The de-institutionalization of industrial conflicts corresponds to their de-ideologization. The industrial labor force has not created operational institutions for the support or guidance of conflictual activities—such as politically significant "class-based" parties—while the trade unions, rather than consolidating, tend to disappear in conflict situations.

The Feeble State

The conflicts of transition do more than reveal the feebleness of the state: they feed its debility and thereby aggravate it. They emphasize, and further stimulate, the negative connection between the weakness of the institutions of the state and the low governability of society.

General Effects of a Local Conflict

1. Even if concessions won by the demonstrators are presumed to be strictly localized, they cannot be ignored by the rest of the labor force. Thus, they generate new pressures at the national level, bringing about changes in the government's transition strategy.
2. Such changes may also represent corrections or simply incoherency in the ongoing process.
3. The socioeconomic changes may be generated either by strategic policies or by social disturbances; by means of conflict, the latter may prevail over the former.
4. Under circumstances of conflict what remains of the old regime can come to have more influence over social evolution than the rational choices of the political actors of the present.
5. Such choices might be more or less rational. Whatever the case may be, the secondary role of these choices in comparison with the Stalinist legacy reveals a tendency of transitional societies to be more sensitive to irrational, rather than to rational, orientations.
6. On the other hand, conflict emphasizes and promotes the vagueness of the usual roles.
7. In our case study, the confusion of the roles is enhanced by the confused behavior of the principal actors, representing both the demonstrators and the public authorities.
8. As a synthesis of all these trends, the legitimate mobility of social relations has a propensity to degenerate into instability or destabilization.

Pavel Câmpeanu
Bucharest

Index

About the Contributors

Sorin Antohi is Professor of History at the Central European University. He is most recently coeditor of *Between Past and Future: The Revolutions of 1989 and Their Aftermath* (2000) and author of *Imaginaire culturel et réalité politique dans la Roumanie moderne: Le stigmate et l'utopie* (1999).

Wally Bacon is Associate Professor of Political Science at the University of Nebraska at Omaha. He is the author of numerous essays on Romanian and Moldovan diplomatic history, civil-military relations, the political economy of transition, and political leadership and is a past President of the Society for Romanian Studies. His most recent book, *Nicolae Titulescu and Romanian Foreign Policy,* based on his doctoral dissertation under Dr. Josef Korbel, was published in Romanian.

Gabriel Bădescu is Associate Professor of Political Science at Babeş-Bolyai University, as well as Director of the Laboratory of Political Analysis there. He is coauthor of *Statistical Methods Applied in Social Sciences* (1999).

Zoltan Barany is the Frank C. Erwin, Jr. Centennial Professor at the University of Texas at Austin. He is author of, most recently, *The Future of NATO Expansion* (2003), *The East European Gypsies: Regime Change, Marginality, and Ethnopolitics* (2001), *Waiting for NATO: Four States Prepare for Membership* (2002), and coeditor of *Russian Politics: Challenges of Democratization* (2001) and *Dilemmas of Transition* (1999).

Jóhanna Kristín Birnir is Assistant Professor of Political Science at SUNY-Buffalo. She specializes in voting behavior and electoral institutions in Eastern

Europe and Latin America. The title of her dissertation is "Party System Stabilization in New Democracies: The Effect of Ethnic Heterogeneity on Volatility of Electoral Preferences," which she wrote at UCLA.

Larry S. Bush is Executive Director of the Clarke Center for International and Comparative Legal Studies at Cornell Law School. Previously, he was Professor of Law at the University of Mississippi. He was a Fulbright Lecturer in the faculty at the University of Bucharest, Romania, during 1991–1992. He has participated in numerous academic and labor conferences in Romania since then. He has been a contributing editor of *The Developing Labor Law* and has authored two articles on modern Romanian labor law.

Pavel Câmpeanu, late, was Executive Director of the Independent Center for Social Studies and a founding member of the Group for Social Dialogue. He was author of a four-volume series on Stalinism and numerous books and articles published in Romania and abroad. He was a Fulbright Senior Scholar affiliated with the New School for Social Research and a Fellow at the Collegium Budapest. His last published book, *Ceauşesu: From the End to the Beginnings* (2003) describes his firsthand experiences of the dictator-to-be in a political prison on Jilava, as well as his rise to power.

Henry F. (Chip) Carey, Associate Professor of Political Science at Georgia State University, has published two dozen essays on East European Politics, international human rights, and democratization. He has edited, most recently, *National Reconciliation in Eastern Europe* (2003), coedited *Mitigating Conflict: The Role of NGOs* (2003) and *NGOs and Institution Building* (2004), and edited the special journal issue of the *Journal of Human Rights* on "NGOs and the Rule of Law."

Daniel Dăianu is Professor of Economics, Academy of Economic Studies, Bucharest, and was Romania's Minister of Finance from December 1997 to September 1998. He is author of *Transformation as a Real Process* (1998) and *Economic Vitality and Viability: A Double Challenge for European Security* (1996).

Dennis Deletant, OBE, is Professor of Romanian Studies and Head of the Department of East European Languages and Culture at the School of Slavonic and East European Studies, University College London. He is author of *Ceauşescu and the Securitate: Coercion and Dissent in Romania, 1965–1989* (1996), *Romania under Communist Rule* (1999), *Communist Terror in Romania: Gheorghiu-Dej and the Police State, 1948–1965* (2000), and coauthor of *Security Intelligence Services in New Democracies: The Czech Republic, Slovakia and Romania* (2000).

Christopher Eisterhold is a Master's candidate in political science at Georgia State University and received his B.A. degree from the University of Oregon.

John F. Ely is an Associate Professor in the Departments of Anthropology and Sociology at Saint Mary's College of California. He was Associate Producer for PBS Frontline/World's "Andrei Codrescu: My Old Haunts" (2002) and coauthored "Right-Minded in Romania: 'Movement for Romania' and Radical, Nationalistic Intellectualism in a Romanian Youth Group" (1994).

Anneli Ute Gabanyi is Area Specialist for Romania and the Republic of Moldova at the Munich *Südost-Institut*, and she was former head of Radio Free Europe's Romanian Research Department. She is the author of *Partei und Literatur in Rumänien seit* (1975), *Die unvollendete Revolution. Rumänien zwischen Diktatur und Demokratie* (1990), *Systemwechsel in Rumänien. Von der Revolution zur Transformation* (1998), and *Revoluţia neterminata* (1999), and coeditor of *Frauen in Südosteuropa* (1998).

Peter Gross is Professor and Gaylord Family Endowed Chair at the Gaylord College of Journalism and Mass Communication, The University of Oklahoma. He is the author of *Mass Media in Revolution and Development: The Romanian Laboratory* (1996) and *Entangled Evolution: Media and Democratization in Eastern Europe* (2001).

Richard Andrew Hall holds a Ph.D. in Political Science from Indiana University, where his dissertation was titled "Rewriting the Revolution: Authoritarian Regime-State Relations and the Triumph of *Securitate* Revisionism in Post-Ceauşescu Romania." He is the author of "The Uses of Absurdity: The Staged War Theory and the Romanian Revolution of December 1989," published in *East European Politics and Society* (Fall 1999).

Claude Karnoouh is Senior Research Fellow at the National Center for Scientific Research and at INALCO in Paris. He is also Permanent Visiting Professor of Philosophy at the Babeş-Bolyai University in Cluj. He is author of *Postcommunism fin de siècle. Essai sur l'Europe du XXIe siècle* (2000).

Norman Manea is Francis Flournoy Professor of European Studies and writer in residence at Bard College. A recipient of MacArthur and Guggenheim fellowships, he is the author of over two dozen books, including *The Hooligan's Return: A Memoir* (2003), *October, Eight O'Clock* (1992), *On Clowns: The Dictator and the Artist* (1992), *Compulsory Happiness* (1993), *The Black Envelope* (1995), and *The Hooligan's Return* (1993).

Mihaela Miroiu is currently Visiting Assistant Professor at Indiana University. Previously, she was Professor and Dean of the political science faculty of the National School of Political Studies and Public Administration in Bucharest. She is author of *Gândul umbrei. Abordări feministe în filosofia contemporană* (1995); *Convenio. Despre natură, femei și morală* (1996); and *România. Starea de fapt* (1997). She is coauthor of *Învățământul românesc azi* (1998).

Mihnea Ion Năstase is a Ph.D. candidate at Georgia State University, from which he earned his B.A. summa cum laude. He is currently on a Fulbright grant for doctoral research for his dissertation on Romanian Communism. From 1985 to 1995, he played professional tennis and was once ranked eighty-fifth in the world.

Daniel N. Nelson is Editor-in-Chief of *International Politics* and Dean of the University of New Haven. He was previously Professor at the George C. Marshall Center for European Security Studies in Leipzig, Germany. He is the author or editor of over a dozen books, including *Democratic Centralization in Romania* (1980), and editor of *Romanian Politics in the Ceaușescu Era* (1988) and *Romania after Tyranny* (1992).

Liliana Popescu is Director of the Romania and Bulgaria Program of the Civic Education Project organization, and teaches at the National School of Political Science and Public Administration in Bucharest. She holds a Ph.D. in political theory (University of Manchester, 1996). She is editor of *Gender and Politics: Romanian Women in Public Life* (1999) and author of *Individual Freedom and Political Manipulation* (2003) and *Democracy and Gender in Contemporary Romania* (forthcoming).

Sandra Pralong teaches political science at the University of Bucharest, is a Ph.D. candidate at Columbia University, and is a consultant to the UN Development Programme. She coedited a volume on Karl Popper, *The Open Society after Fifty Years* (1999). From 1990 to 1993, she was Executive Director of the Soros Foundation-Romania, and from 1999 to 2000 was Advisor to the Romanian President Constantinescu.

Sabrina P. Ramet, the original series editor of this book, is Professor of Political Science at the Norwegian University of Science and Technology (NTNU) in Trondheim, Norway. Her most recent book is *Balkan Babel: The Disintegration of Yugoslavia from the Death of Tito to the War for Kosovo*, 4th ed. (2001). She is the author of six other books and editor or coeditor of a dozen books, mostly about Eastern Europe and Russia.

Steven D. Roper is an Assistant Professor of Political Science at Eastern Illinois University. He is the author of *Romania: The Unfinished Revolution* (2000) and has published articles in the *American Review of Politics, Communist and Post-Communist Studies, East European Quarterly*, and *Nationalities Papers*.

Frank Sellin is Visiting Assistant Professor of Government at Bowdoin College. He received his Ph.D. from the University of Virginia, based on a dissertation on patrimonialism, party systems, and regime change in post-Communist Southeast Europe.

Michael Shafir is Senior Regional Analyst, covering and/or coordinating coverage on central and southeastern Europe in the daily *RFE/RL Newsline*. He also edits *East European Perspectives*, an RFE/RL Internet, bimonthly journal, to which he also contributes. In addition to journalism, his extensive scholarship includes *Romania: Politics, Economics and Society, Political Stagnation and Simulated Change* (1985) and over 200 articles on Communism and post-Communist politics.

Cătălin Augustin Stoica is a Ph.D. candidate in sociology at Stanford University. He is currently researching the contours of inequality in postsocialist societies, and (with John F. Ely) issues of collective memory and the 1989 Romanian Revolution.

Paul E. Sum is Assistant Professor in the Department of Political Science and Public Administration at the University of North Dakota. His doctoral dissertation from Northwestern University was "The Origins of Nationalism: An Inquiry into Emerging Nationalism within Tudor England."

Vladimir Tismăneanu is Professor of Government and Politics at the University of Maryland, College Park. He was the editor of the journal *East European Politics and Societies*, the author of *Stalinism for all Seasons: A Political History of Romanian Communism* (2003) and *Fantasies of Salvation: Democracy, Nationalism, and Myth in Post-Communist Europe* (1998), and the editor of *The Revolutions of 1989* (1999).

F. Peter Wagner is Senior Research Fellow of the German Science Association in the Department of Political Science, University of Giessen, Germany. He received his Ph.D. in political science (political theory) from Rutgers University in 1993. His publications include "*Der Wandel der Lebensverhältnisse in Rumänien nach Ceausescu*" (1996). He is presently finishing a manuscript on *The Romanian Mirror: Political Identity and Post-Communist Transformation in Southeastern Europe*.

Larry L. Watts received his doctorate at Umea University, Sweden. His most recent publications include *Incompatible Allies: Neorealism and Small State Alliance Behavior in Wartime* (1998), and the Romania chapters in *Crisis in the Balkans: Views from the Participants* (1997) and *Eurasian/East European Security Yearbook* (2000).

Robert Weiner is Professor of Political Science at the University of Massachusetts, Boston, and an Associate at the Davis Center for Russian Studies at Harvard University. His books include *Romanian Foreign Policy and the United Nations* (1984) and *Change in Eastern Europe* (1994).

Clifford F. Zinnes has a joint appointment at the Department of Economics (IRIS) and the School of Public Affairs at the University of Maryland, College Park. He has worked in more than twenty countries, currently focusing on transition economies. From 1989 to 2000, he was an Institute Associate at the Harvard Institute for International Development, during which time he spent five years in Romania as a senior policy advisor to the ministers of Reform, Privatization, European Integration, and Environment.

www.ingramcontent.com/pod-product-compliance
Ingram Content Group UK Ltd.
Pitfield, Milton Keynes, MK11 3LW, UK
UKHW020257051026
15470UKWH00020B/359